THE WORKS

OF

JAMES PILKINGTON, B.D.

The Parker Society.

Instituted A.D. M.DCCC.XL.

For the Publication of the Works of the Fathers and Early Writers of the Reformed English Church.

THE WORKS

OF

JAMES PILKINGTON, B.D.,

LORD BISHOP OF DURHAM.

EDITED FOR

The Parker Society,

BY THE

REV. JAMES SCHOLEFIELD, A.M.,

REGIUS PROFESSOR OF GREEK, CAMBRIDGE.

WIPF & STOCK · Eugene, Oregon

Wipf and Stock Publishers
199 W 8th Ave, Suite 3
Eugene, OR 97401

The Works of James Polkington, B.D., Lord Bishop of Durham
By Pilkington, James
ISBN 13: 978-1-60608-433-5
Publication date 1/14/2010
Previously published by Cambridge University Press, 1842

CONTENTS.

	PAGE
BIOGRAPHICAL Notice of Pilkington	i
Exposition upon the Prophet Haggai (1560, 1562)	1
Exposition upon the Prophet Obadiah (1562)	201
Exposition upon certain chapters of Nehemiah (1585)	275
The Burning of St Paul's Church: Confutation of an Addition, (1563)	497
Answers to Popish Questions (1563)	617

MISCELLANEOUS PIECES.

Sermon on Bucer and Phagius (1560)	651
Letter to the Earl of Leicester (1564)	658
Extracts from the Statutes of Rivington School	663
*Tractatus de Prædestinatione	673
*Epistola ad Andream Kingsmill (1564)	679
Notes	683
Index	689

* Now first published.

BIOGRAPHICAL NOTICE

OF

BISHOP PILKINGTON.

JAMES PILKINGTON[1] was born at Rivington in Lancashire in the year 1520, and was the third son of Richard Pilkington Esq. of Rivington Park, a gentleman of an ancient and honourable family, which had early embraced the doctrines of the reformed religion. There is no record to shew where he received the rudiments of his education; but about his sixteenth year he was admitted a member of St John's College[2], Cambridge, where he proceeded to the degree of A.B. in the year 1539, and was elected fellow on the 26th of March in the same year. He afterwards took the degrees of A.M. 1542, and B.D. 1550, but it does not appear that he ever took the higher degree of D.D.; whether out of disregard to it, as Baker intimates, or from the whole course of his pursuits being suddenly interrupted by the troubles consequent on the accession of queen Mary.

[1] It appears from Baker's MSS. that the bishop's brother, Leonard, signed his name Pilkinton on his admission to his fellowship, and on his restitution (having been ejected under queen Mary) Pilkington.

[2] This is doubtful. Mr Whitaker in his memoir of the bishop, prefixed to the "Statutes and Charter of Rivington School," conjectures that he was first admitted at Pembroke Hall, from the circumstance that the fellows of that college, in their congratulatory letter to archbishop Grindal (1576), boast of having had among their *alumni* bishops of Carlisle, Exeter, Winchester, *Durham*, London, and York. But Baker's MS. History of St John's College distinctly asserts that he was admitted of St John's; which however is not incompatible with his having first entered at Pembroke, and afterwards removed. In one of the Registrary's lists of degrees James Pilkington of Pembroke occurs; but it is doubtful whether this can have been the same that was elected fellow of St John's in 1539.

He was zealous in forwarding the Reformation; and while residing on his fellowship, read theological lectures gratuitously on the Acts of the Apostles in the public schools; of the importance of which in that deeply interesting crisis, as well as of the general estimation in which he was held, we may judge not only from the testimony of Bucer, that he "acquitted himself learnedly and piously," but also from the fact of his being subsequently appointed to take a part in the disputation on the popish tenets, held at Cambridge on the 20th and 24th of June, 1549, a record of which is preserved in the second volume of Foxe's *Acts and Monuments*. In December, 1550, he was appointed, by Edward the sixth, to the vicarage of Kendal in Westmoreland, which however he resigned in the following year, probably from his preference of a college residence. We hear nothing more of him until about the year 1554, when, to avoid the Marian persecutions, he, with many other eminent divines, retired to the continent; and lived at Zurich, at Basil, and lastly at Geneva. At Basil he read lectures on Ecclesiastes, both epistles of St Peter, and that of St Paul to the Galatians; but there is no evidence to shew that these lectures were ever printed, and Tanner's statement to that effect may naturally be traced to the mistake of his authority (*Bal.* i. e. *Bale*) confounding the delivery of the lectures, and the conversational discussion of them, with publication[1].

---

[1] "John Bale says, he had expounded both the Epistles of St Peter, and had then Solomon's Ecclesiastes under his hands; but these, I suppose, were never published." Baker's MS. *History of St John's College.* Bale's words are: Quorum Jacobus (sc. Pilkintonus) Salomonis Ecclesiasten, utramque D. Petri epistolam, ac Paulum ad Galatas; Ricardus, &c. * * * nobis qui adhuc Basileæ sumus, piissime ac doctissime exposuerunt. Sed eorum scripta nondum prodierunt in lucem: quod tamen, Deo fortunante, *futurum speramus.* Vivunt hoc anno Domini 1558, quo ista scripsimus. Balei Scriptorum Illustrium M. Brytanniæ posterior pars, p. 113. Basil. 1559.—Strype says the same thing, but he does not any where speak of these expositions as having been

Upon the death of queen Mary, in 1558, the exiles made preparation for returning home. Pilkington was then at Frankfort; and when the letter from the English church at Geneva was received there, exhorting to "unanimity in teaching and practising the knowledge of God's word" upon arriving in their own country, he was the first to sign on behalf of the church at Frankfort, and therefore probably was himself the writer of, the "peaceable letter" sent in reply, which is certainly marked by great wisdom and moderation; the general purport of which was, that the appointment of ceremonies would rest not with themselves, but with persons duly authorised; that they would "submit to such orders as should be established by authority, being not of themselves wicked;" that the reformed churches might differ in ceremonies, so that they agreed in the chief points of religion; and lastly, that in case of the intrusion of any that were offensive, they would "brotherly join to be suitors" for their reformation or abolition[2].

On his return to England, he was associated with Bill, Parker, Grindal, Cox, Guest, Whitehead, and May, as commissioners to revise the Book of Common Prayer; being appointed to that office by a proclamation issued in December, 1558, and the work was completed in April of the following year. In this year, 1559, he was appointed also one of the commissioners for visiting Cambridge, to receive from the heads of houses and others their oath of allegiance to the queen and of her supremacy. By this visitation all ordinary jurisdiction in the university was suspended; and on the 20th of July he was admitted Master of St John's College and Regius Professor of Divinity: whether "by the act," or only "with

---

printed; nor are they mentioned in the Catalogue of English printed books, 1595, by Maunsell, where the expositions of Aggeus, Abdias, and Nehemiah, printed in this collection, are noticed.

[2] See Strype, *Annals*, I. i. p. 263. 8vo.

But in this volume there is only one prayer stated to be Pilkington's, viz. that printed in p. 273 of the present edition.

The "Defence of the English Service," which Watt also adds, is no doubt that defence which is contained in the Answer to popish Questions subjoined to the "Confutation." For Strype (*Annals*, I. i. p. 201.) speaks of it as an answer to "a paper of questions;" and in his account of the answer quotes the substance of what is contained in pp. 626-8. of this edition.

The author himself refers more than once to his Exposition on Ezra; and particularly in p. 367 of this volume he seems to speak of it as if it were in print. If it ever was printed, it seems to be now irrecoverably lost. Probably bishop Pilkington wrote comments on several books of scripture, which have perished in MS.

COMMENTARY

ON

THE PROPHETS

HAGGAI AND OBADIAH.

[PILKINGTON.]

¶ Aggeus and Abdias Prophetes,

the one corrected, the other newly added, and both at large declared.

The earnest loue that I

beare to thy house hath eaten me. Psal. lxix.
Ioan. ii.

Phinees hath tourned

awaye my anger because he was moued with loue of me. Num. xxv.

A PREFACE

TO ALL THAT LOVE THE EARNEST PROMOTING OF GOD'S GLORY IN HIS CHURCH BY TRUE RELIGION.

ALTHOUGH the common usage of dedicating books is to require the defence of some worthy personage of learning or authority for the thing that is written; yet the majesty of the matter in this book is such, that it rather defends than seeks defence; and the example of the Prophet, which writes it not to one, but many, suffers me not to send it to any one sort of men particularly, but generally to all that should unfeignedly promote the increase of God's glory, because all degrees of men do owe a duty to the building of this God's house. And if any offence be taken (as, God knows, none is purposely given) the defence of many is greater than of a few; and that authority or credit, which one man alone cannot bring to pass, all jointly together shall more easily obtain.

The Prophet is sent from God to the prince, the high priest, and the people: so I speak to the rulers, the ministers, and commonalty. The chief intent of his prophecy is to stir all to the speedy building of God's house, which they had so long neglected: my labour is to bring some of every sort (for all is not possible) to an earnest furthering of God's true religion, of late most mercifully restored unto us, which not long ago most cruelly was persecuted, of many yet hated, and of every man almost now too coldly followed and practised. But if this prophecy were read and deeply considered with such a hungry desire of God's glory, as the Prophet spake and wrote it, and I for my part and poor ability have declared it; I doubt not, but the good should be stirred by God's Spirit more earnestly to seek God's glory, and the froward should be afraid of God's plague, and ashamed stubbornly to strive against the truth continually.

The state of religion in these our miserable days is much like to the troublesome time that this prophet lived in: God grant that after many grievous storms it may take like root in us, as it did then in them! After the long captivity of God's people in Babylon, God gave them gracious king Cyrus, which set them at liberty and sent them home to build God's house: so after our long Romish slavery God raised us up good kings, which restored us God's book that long had been buried, and loosed us from the bondage of strange gods, foreign powers, cruel hypocrites, and wicked idols. And as after that short freedom under good Cyrus ensued the cruelty of Haman, for negligently handling God's building; and not long after mild Ester, came bloody Antiochus for their falling from God: so for our talking gospel, and not worthily walking nor following it, under our gracious late Josias, crept out a swarm of Romish wasps, stinging to death all that would not worship their gods, nor believe their doctrine.

God for his mercy's sake grant, that now for our unthankful coldness in God's cause under our mild Ester burst not out again bloody Antiochus with his whelps, justly to avenge our cold slackness in God's religion and insensible dulness. God's word is never offered and given in vain, or to use at our pleasure: but it works either salvation in them that hear, believe and follow it, or else condemnation in them that proudly despise it, sturdily rebel, or forgetfully do hear, and unthankfully receive his mercies. Therefore as after a storm follows a calm, and after winter comes summer; so now, where God hath given a breathing time, (lest our weakness had not been able to have borne his heavy displeasure any longer,) let us earnestly apply our work, while we have time; for the night will come when no man shall be able to work.

If this be true (as it is most true indeed) that every deed of our Saviour Christ is our instruction; and also that what things soever are written, they be written for our learning, as St Paul teacheth; let us call to remembrance, what zeal and earnest love our Saviour Christ especially shewed in building his Father's house, and restoring the true understanding of the scriptures from the superstitious glosses of the Scribes and Pharisees, and also what a fervent desire of promoting God's glory our fathers have shewed afore us, that we may be good scholars of our schoolmaster Christ Jesus, and obedient children, walking in the steps of our fathers. Our Lord and Saviour Christ, coming into the temple and finding it full of buyers, sellers and changers, was grieved to see God's house so misused, gat a whip and drove them all out, saying, "My house is a house of prayer, but ye have made it a den of thieves:" so surely all Christians, which unfeignedly bear the name of Christ, and zealously love the building of his house, would gladly see sin punished, and lament that the whip of God's discipline is not shaken in God's house to the driving out and confusion of all greedy thieves, which if they cannot get in at the door by lawful means, will climb in at the window, and for a little money will sell the bodies and souls of Christ's sheep, and make God's house the pope's market place. But as she that had so much work to do, that she could not tell where to begin, sat her down and left all undone: so I say, worldly wise men see so many things out of order in God's house, and so little hope of redress, that

Rom. xv.

John ii.
Luke xix.

they cannot tell which to correct or amend first, and therefore let the whip lie still, and every man to do what him lust, and sin to be unpunished.

And not only this evil reigns, but the world is come to such a dissolute liberty and negligent forgetting of God, that men sleeping in sin need not so much a whip to drive any out of the church, (so few come there,) but they need a great sort of whips to drive some few thitherward. For come into a church on the sabbath day, and ye shall see but few, though there be a sermon; but the ale-house is ever full. Well worth the papists therefore in their kind: for they be earnest, zealous and painful in their doings; they will build their kingdom more in one year with fire and faggot, *Zeal in correcting sin is godly.* than the cold gospellers will do in seven. A popish summoner, spy, or promoter will drive more to the church with a word to hear a latin mass, than seven preachers will bring in a week's preaching to hear a godly sermon. If this be not true, remember the late days of popery, and see who durst offend him that ware a shaven crown. Who looked so high then, but he would give place to a priest's cap? and now who regards the best preacher ye have? O what a condemnation shall this be to all such as have the whip of God's correction in their hand, to see the wicked so diligent and earnest in their doings to set up antichrist; and christian rulers and officers of all sorts, having the whip of correction in their hand both by God's law and the prince's, so coldly behave themselves in setting up the kingdom of Christ, that neither they give good example themselves in diligent praying and resorting to the church, nor by the whip of discipline drive others thitherward! Where appears in any Christians, in these our days, this earnest zeal of Christ, to promote God's glory by such correction, that we may say we be his followers? I fear rather that Christ, of whom we more talk, than diligently follow or earnestly love, for this cold slackness that he sees in us will say unto us, "Because ye be neither hot nor cold, I will spew you out of my mouth." Woe be to that realm where God is compelled to take the whip in hand to punish sin, because the rulers will not! great shall be the plague thereof. Phinees turned away God's anger from his people, because so zealously he avenged God's quarrel, and punished that wickedness which other winked at. David, seeing God's glory defaced, and his enemies so contemptuously to forget the law of the Lord, was so grieved that he said, "the earnest love that he bare toward God made him to pine away, because his enemies had forgotten the word of God." Elias fleeing from cruel Jesabel, threatening to kill him because he had destroyed Baal's priests, lived in wilderness, desired he might die, for he was weary of his life to see how many were fallen to idolatry, and how few (or none, as he thought) worshipped truly the living God. Though Jehu was an evil man otherways, yet God gave him a worldly blessing, and commended him for his earnest zeal in rooting out the posterity of Achab, pulling down Baal and his sacrificing priests, making a common jakes of the house where they worshipped him. St Paul, seeing the Corinthians rather rejoicing than lamenting or punishing that filthiness committed among them, that one of them had defiled his stepmother, writes unto them, rebukes them all sharply, because they did not correct him, and wills them all to assemble themselves in the name of God, to excommunicate and give him to Satan that had done this wickedness, not to eat and drink with him, that he might be ashamed, repent and amend. So whereas this great zeal and love toward God and his house building stands either in correcting evil and lamenting the defacing of God's glory, or else in wishing and

_{Rev. iii.}

_{Num. xxv.}

_{Psal. cxix.}

_{1 Kings xix.}

_{2 Kings x.}

_{1 Cor. v.}

doing good thereto, and furthering it to our powers: for the first part to be earnestly followed, these few examples shall serve; for the other there be so many, that it is harder to tell where to end, than where to begin.

Zeal to promote God's glory pleases him.
Exod. xxxv.

Moses in the wilderness, willing to make a tabernacle and place where the people should resort to worship their God, had the princes and people so liberal to offer and bring to the making thereof gold, silver, precious stones, silk, purple, hair, iron, brass and timber, of all sorts such plenty, that they would have given more than needed. David, earnestly desiring to build a house for the Lord, (if God would have suffered him,) left his son Salomon so great plenty of all things necessary to that building in a readiness, that he finished that costly building in seven years. Good King Cyrus restored again to God's people all that covetous Nabucho[1] had robbed from them: Cyrus, Darius, Artaxerxes, and his princes gave out of their treasures to the building

Ezra vi. vii.

of the temple and maintenance of their sacrifices according to the law of Moses sufficiently, that they might pray for the king, his children, and the commonwealth. Constantinus the first, worthily called Magnus, a christian emperor, gave great liberty to the bishops and other ministers. Justinianus, Theodosius, Carolus Magnus, Ludovicus Pius, &c., augmented and increased the same with lands and laws. This zeal and earnest love to build God's house and

We are unlike our fathers.

punish sin was in our fathers: this liberality was in princes and rulers, that understood not God's benefits and mercies so plentifully as we do. They pacified God's wrath in correcting sin, and we provoke his plagues with heaping up of sin. They were grieved and weary of their lives, when they see God's enemies despise his word; we wink and cloke it, we laugh and smile at it, and think it not

[[1] Nabucho: Nabuchodonozor, or Nebuchadnezzar. ED.]

to be a fault. They were offended if wickedness were unpunished, and the party not ashamed that sinned; and we be offended if any man go about to see it punished, or the offender ashamed. They were liberal in giving, relieving and maintaining the ministry; we are greedy in snatching and plucking away from them. They were ready to defend with privileges the ministers, that they should not be withdrawn from doing their duty; and we bind them to such clogs that they cannot do their duty: they restored all that was taken from them; and we study daily how to get more from them. When I compare these doings together, and see how good success the one had, and God's church was gloriously builded that way, both under the law and the gospel; it makes me to quake, when I look what shall fall upon us, going so far clean contrary way. Surely both they and we go not in the right way. The Lord for his crucified Christ's sake, which came down from the bosom of his Father to teach us to build him a house here, that afterward we might reign in glory with him there, grant us all, in all degrees from the highest to the lowest, such an earnest simple love to the true building of his house, as the prophet here teaches us, that uprightly we might walk the right way that he hath gone afore us.

If the prince and nobility will maintain that honourable estate that God hath called them to, and avoid the bondage of foreign powers; if the bishops and clergy will feed God's people with the lively food of our souls, God's doctrine and discipline, and not with man's inventions; if the people will truly serve God and obey their prince, flee from idolatry, and escape God's plagues; let us jointly together earnestly abhor popery, correct sin, turn unto the Lord, delight in his word, reverence his ministers, be diligent in prayer, that we may be lively stones, meet for his building, and become the temples of the Holy Ghost, where he with the Father and the Son, three persons and one God, may dwell and be praised[1].

I. P. L. C. D[2].

My earnest love to God hath pined me away, because my enemies have forgotten thy words. Psalm cxix.

I have been earnestly zealous for the Lord God of hosts, because they have forsaken thy covenant. 1 Kings xix.

[1 In the first edition, 1560, it is added:
Among many other things that I, a poor workman in God's house, would have said to encourage other workmen, and specially those that should be the chief builders and pillars of his church, these few things at this time shall serve, because the printer makes haste, and I have not leisure.
James Pylkynton, Maister of S. John's Colledge in Cambridge, to the readers.
Then follow the two verses quoted above. ED.]

[2 These letters need explanation. In the first edition, on the title page immediately after the passage from Numbers, followed the initials, I. P. L. C. and the Preface was signed by the Author as Master of St John's College, Cambridge. See the preceding note. Here we find, in the second edition, the Preface signed like the title page of the former edition, only with the addition of D.—the Author having in the mean time removed from the Mastership of St John's to the Bishoprick of Durham. It seems therefore, the initials are to be interpreted: James Pilkington, Lancastriensis, (he was a native of Lancashire,) Cantabrigiensis, Dunelmensis. ED.]

THE PROPHET AGGEUS[3].

Chap. I.

v. 1. *In the second year of king Darius, in the sixth month, and the first day of the month, the word of the Lord was sent by the hand of Aggeus the prophet unto Zerubabel, the son of Salathiel, ruler of Juda; and unto Josua, the son of Josedec, the chief priest, saying.*

INASMUCH that the year, month and day, when this pro- *Noting of circumstances is a token that the thing is true which is telled.* phecy was spoken, be so diligently noted of the prophet; and also that in which king's days, by whom and to whom it was preached, is so diligently mentioned, it makes much for proving the truth of the prophecy, and that we should the rather believe it. For they that will teach lies, use not so exactly to declare the circumstances wherein things were done, lest, in examination of the same, things be proved contrary, and they found liars. But chiefly this *The deferring of God's punishment declareth his long suffering and our slothfulness in well doing.* long time here appointed of forty years teacheth us the patience and long sufferance of God, who will not punish so soon as we do a fault, but tarry and look for our repentance and amendment, as he did here so long bear the Jews. And also it setteth before us the unthankful disobedience and slothful negligence of God's people, which after so merciful a deliverance, and bringing them home again from Babylon to their own country, (from whence they were led prisoners by Nabuchodonozor) had so long and many years left off the building of that house, which God willed them so straightly to restore, and the good king Cyrus had given *Ezra i.* them liberty to do the same, and restored their old ornaments to do it withal. And in them also we learn our own slothfulness to the fulfilling of God's laws: for of ourselves we be no better than they, nor more diligent in well doing, except God stir us up by his undeserved grace.

[3 Aggeus and Abdias (sometimes written Obdias) are the Greek forms of the Hebrew names, Haggai and Obadiah, which the Bishop uses according to the practice of his day. So Micheas, Esdras, for Micah, Ezra, &c. ED.]

The Jews for their disobedience to God and his prophets preaching his word, according to the prophecy of Jeremy, had their country spoiled, their city Jerusalem burned, their temple destroyed; they themselves were many killed, some for hunger in the besiege of the city did eat their own children or dung, and the rest were led prisoners to Babylon by Nabuchodonozor, and there kept threescore and ten years in great bondage. After these years ended, by the good king Cyrus they had licence in the first year of his reign to go home and build their temple, as many as would, and all other might freely aid them with money toward that great costly work. Some good amongst them (but few in comparison) as Zorobabel, Josua, Nehemia, Mardocheus, and other whose names are reckoned in Esdras, took in hand to be captains of this worthy work: and after they came to Jerusalem, they builded an altar to serve for to make their offerings and their sacrifices on, until the time that the temple was builded. The first and second years of their coming home to Jerusalem, they were something diligent about their building, and laid the ground-work of the temple. But after, partly for complaints of the rulers in the country (which were strangers, and placed there long afore by Salmanasar, and had accused them to the king, saying, "if they were suffered to build their city, they would rebel, as they were wont, and pay no more taxes;") and partly for slothful negligence of themselves, they left off building unto now, this second year of Darius, God sent this his prophet to stir them up to their work.

By this we may learn that when we lie long on sleep in sin, we cannot wake up ourselves, until God stir us up by his prophets, his word, or holy Spirit. For David, after he had committed adultery with Uria's wife, and caused her husband to be slain, lay without remorse of conscience, without repenting for his evil doings, or asking mercy, until the prophet Nathan came and rebuked him for the same. Therefore let us not lightly regard the warnings of God sent unto us by his preachers, but thankfully embrace them, praising his holy name, that not only he hath so patiently borne us so long, and not suddenly destroyed us wallowing in sin, and forgetting him without repentance; but now lastly hath called us, by the preaching of his word and restoring his gospel by our gracious queen, to a new life, which God grant us for his Christ's sake.

The Jews had now lien after their coming home almost forty years, not regarding the building of the temple; wherefore God most lovingly sent his prophet to warn them of their duty, rebuke them of their negligences, and stir them up earnestly to go about that work. And although the counting of these years be hard to count, and are diversely reckoned of divers men, because they would make the Greek histories to agree with the scriptures; I shall let all other histories pass, because they be too troublesome, and follow that only which the scripture teacheth; for that is the easiest and plainest to understand, and without all doubt true.

In John we read that the Jews asked our Saviour Christ what marvellous sign he would work to persuade them, that he might do such things as he did. And he said to them: "Destroy ye this temple, and in three days I will build it again." He spake of his own body, which he would raise up the third day after they had put him to death: but they understood him of that great costly solemn temple of lime and stone, which now they were building, and therefore said: "Forty and six years was this temple in building, and wilt thou build it in three days?" Here we see how long this temple was in building: although some expound this place otherwise: yet this is not meant that they were continually working on the same so long, (for partly they were forbidden and stopped by the kings that ruled after Cyrus, and partly they were negligent and careless for it,) but that there were so many years from the beginning of that work unto the finishing of the same. In the second year of king Cyrus, which was also the second year of their returning home to Jerusalem from Babylon, they laid the foundations of the temple. In the second year of Darius, as this present place teacheth, they are willed by Aggeus to take in hand their work again; and in the sixth year of this same Darius they finish it: so that from the second year of Cyrus, unto the sixth year of Darius, must be forty-six years wherein they were building, as St John saith. This was a great negligence of God's people, and unthankfulness, so

John ii.

This temple was XLVI years in building.

Ezra iv.

Ezra vi.

long forgetting the building of the temple, and their duty to God, after so merciful and late restoring them to their country: but this is all our crooked nature bent unto, except God do not only begin the good work in us, but also continually lead us in the same to the end. Therefore have we need to look diligently unto ourselves, and pray that God would not turn his merciful eyes from us: for if he never so little withdraw his hand from us, and do not every minute guide all our doings, we fall into a forgetfulness of him and our duties.

<small>If God rule us not every minute, we forget him and ourselves. Philip. i.</small>

Many doubt also which Darius this was, that is here named of the prophet, because the Greek histories make mention of divers of that name, as Darius Histaspis, and Darius Longimanus, with other more. But because the scripture makes mention of none after Cyrus' time, but this one, I will seek no further, nor trouble you with such hard shifts as many do, to make the scripture and those histories to agree. The scriptures make mention of no more kings for this building time, but of Cyrus, Assuerus, Darius and Artaxerxes: therefore in their days must this whole history, and those six and forty years mentioned of St John, be fulfilled. Assuerus I take to be husband to Queen Ester, and this Darius to be her son; whereunto also the Hebrew commentaries agree: and although other think otherwise, yet I see no scripture that they bring. Cyrus gave first licence to the Jews to go home and build this temple. Assuerus moved by the accusations of the rulers, did forbid them to build any more. Darius brought up in the fear of God by his mother Ester, and seeing the wickedness of his father, made a vow, that if he ever reigned after his father, he would build the temple; and so in his second year he gave the Jews free liberty to go home and build their temple, renewed their commission, and gave them money liberally to do it withal. Artaxerxes in his seventh year sent Esdras home again with great gifts, and gave liberty to as many as would go with him; and so the work was finished.

<small>Under what kings the temple was builded.</small>

<small>Ezra iv.</small>

<small>1 Esd. iv.</small>

<small>Ezra vii.</small>

Many do think probably, and to whom I can well agree, that the seventh year of Artaxerxes was the seventh year of this same Darius here named, and that Artaxerxes and Darius is both one man. For Artaxerxes was a common

<small>Artaxerxes.</small>

name to all the kings of Persia, as all the kings of Egypt were called Pharao first, and Ptolomeus afterward, what time so ever they lived in: and as all the emperors are called Cæsar, although they have proper names of their own beside. But I will not enter further in this matter, for it is more subtile than profitable, and little edification is in the searching of it: every one judge as the scripture will best bear, and as God shall teach him. *Pharao. Ptolomeus.* *Cæsar.*

The Jews in reckoning their years and months have divers sorts. For sometimes March is their first month and the beginning of their year, and specially when they count their solemn feasts, as God bad Moses, that the moon wherein they came out of Egypt, should be the first moon in the year. Sometime was September, when all the fruits of the earth was gathered into their barns. Sometime they reckon from the day of the coronation of their kings, as we use diversely to reckon also, and sometime to begin at New-year's day, sometime at the Annunciation of the Virgin Mary, commonly called the Lady-day in Lent, sometime from the day of coronation of our kings, and sometime when they pay their rents, as Michaelmas, Martinmas[1], Helenes day[1], &c. But their moons were reckoned to begin ever from the change of the moon, what day soever of our moon it changed, and not by the calendar (for then there was none made), as we do. So that the first day with us in the calendar might be far from the change of the moon with them, as the 12th, 14th, 19th, 24th, or so forth. Their months for a long time, and their days always, had not proper names given them by men, as we have now, to call them Monday, Sunday, Wednesday, Friday; and January, March, August, July. But they reckoned both their months and days, thus: the first, the second, the third, fourth, &c. Nor we read[2] in the scripture any names given to months unto the time of Moses; and then had they no heathen names, as our days *Exod. xii.* *Divers sorts of reckoning years and months, and names of days and months.*

[1] Days observed in the Roman church, the names of which only are retained in our calendar: St Martin's day being November 11, and Helen's day, or the *Invention of the cross*, May 3, on which latter day Helena, the mother of Constantine the great, was fabled to have found the *true cross*. ED.]

[2] Nor we read: nor read we. ED.]

and months have now. So by this reckoning, this prophecy was spoken in the second year of Darius's reign, beginning the year of the time of his coronation, whensoever it was; and in the sixth month from March, which is our August, and the first day, which is not Lammas, as we count, but the first of the change of the moon, what time soever it changed. The marking of this reckoning shall help you to understand divers places of scripture, if they be remembered, for because they use another manner of reckoning than we do.

And although it seem to many but a small matter, by what names the days and months be called; yet if we consider it well, there is a great thing in it. The Latin men and many other more give names to every day in the week of some one of the stars, commonly called the planets, as though the stars ruled all things; as Sunday of the sun, Monday of the moon, Saturday of Saturne: and the months many have their names of emperors, as July, August, for a vain glory that their name should not die with them. And divers other have their names of as light causes.

<small>It is hurtful to call days by heathen names.</small>

If we remember the beginning of the names of two most solemn days in our week, Wednesday and Friday, we shall better perceive the rest. Fabian and other chronicles tell, that when the Saxons invaded this realm, and there were seven kings ruling here at once, they brought with them two idols, the one called Woden, and the other Fria: or else, as other write, it was a noble captain and his wife, which for their worthiness were made gods; and when they had overcome the Englishmen, they made two days in the week to be called Wednesday and Friday by the names of their false gods or captains, and so to be worshipped; and those names we keep still. Why then may it not be thought to be in remembrance of those idols or captains, if every thing have their name after their beginning? And this may be thought the beginning of the Wednesdays and Fridays to be holier than the rest; what pretence soever was found after to fast or hallow them. So this good can come by using the names of strange gods, that idols with false worshipping of God were set up.

<small>Wednesday, Friday.</small>

We never read in the scripture, nor in any ancient

writer on the scripture, that I remember, that either months or days were called by names of stars, men, idols, or false gods, but Feries, as Augustine often doth use to call them: yea, the pope's Portus[1] calleth the days in the week thus; the second, and the third Fery, &c. But now in time it is come to pass, that every day in the year is called by the name of some saint, and not in all countries alike, but as every country is disposed to worship their saints.

In the New Testament I find no days named, but the first of the sabbath, &c., and the Lord's day, which I take to be the Sunday, when John saw his revelation. Thus superstition crept into the world, when men began to forget calling on the true and only God, and made them gods of every dead saint as they list. *Rev. i.*

What can we say for ourselves, but that we put great superstition in days, when we put openly in calendars and almanacks, and say, These days be infortunate, and great matters are not to be taken in hand these days; as though we were of God's privy council? But why are they infortunate? Is God asleep on those days? or doth he not rule the world and all things those days, as well as on other days? Is he weary, that he must rest him in those days? Or doth he give the ruling of those days to some evil spirit or planet? If God give to stars such power that things cannot prosper on those days, then God is the author of evil. If stars do rule men those days, then man is their servant. But God made man to rule, and not be ruled; and all creatures should serve him. *Astronomers do evil in calling some days unfortunate.*

What shall be the cause? If astronomers say true, every man at his birth by his constellation have divers things and desires appointed him. Why then, how can so many divers constellations in so many men at your birth agree, to make one day unlucky in your life to all men? Either let him prove it by learning; or for shame and sin hold your tongue. Stars may have some power on the natural qualities and actions of the body, and for physic; but on the civil voluntary actions of Christians' minds, none.

St Paul says, the children of God be led with the Spirit of God: why then, not by stars. It is faithless superstition *[Rom. viii. 14.]*

[¹ Portus: breviary. ED.]

[PILKINGTON.]

to teach or believe such things; that either at the birth or after we be ruled by stars. All astronomers could never tell why Jacob and Esau, brother twins, born in one moment, should have so contrary natures. What star ruled when Sodom and Gomorrah were burned, and the next towns escaped? were all born under one star that then perished? or all Noe's flood? was not then divers sorts, men and women, young and old, good and bad? Doth not the scripture say that God made seven days, and when he had made all things, he did behold them all, and they were very good? Why shall we then be bold to call them evil, infortunate, and dismal days? If God rule our doings continually, why shall they not prosper on those days, as well as on other? God blessed the seventh day: and yet we dare call that infortunate, evil, and cursed, which he blessed.

Although it be impossible to redress this old common error, so deeply rooted in all tongues and countries; yet it is not unprofitable to note the beginning of these things, that this superstition may be something known. When God made seven days, he called them the first, the second, third, fourth, &c.; but the last day he called the sabbath, which betokens rest, and hath not the name given to be called of any other creature, man, saint, star, or idol; but as the name sounds, so should we on the seventh day rest from all bodily labour, except need compel, but specially from all filthy sin. This is not the right way to make holy men to be remembered, nor surest to avoid idolatry. It were better to be done by writing the chronicles, lives and deaths, of such as were godly indeed, and not every rascal, as *Legenda aurea*, the Legend of lies, does. Pope Boniface the VIII., finding them of Farrare worshipping twenty years one Hermanius as a saint, digged him out of the ground, and burned him for a heretic and author of the sect called Fratricelli, and forbad to worship such evil men[1]. So I

Holy men are better remembered by writing than calling days by their names.

Boniface VIII.

[1 Hæresin Fraticellorum, sacramenta et potestatem ecclesiasticam contemnentium, promiscuos concubitus exercentium, animarum purgatarum beatitudinem ad extremum judicii diem usque differri docentium, condemnavit [Bonifacius Papa VII. vulgo VIII.] Corpus cujusdam Hermanni, qui, ut scribunt Platina et Sanderus, Fraticellorum dux erat, Ferrariæ exhumari et cremari jussit, licet pro sancto cole-

think we, scraping together a number of saints as we list, worship many evil persons. What holiness was in Thomas Becket, which had gotten two days in the calendar called by his name, and priests must evermore mumble him one wicked memory in matins and evensong? If papists, rebels, and traitors to their kings, as this stout champion of the pope was, may be thus rewarded, it is no marvel if many rebel against their kings as he did. *Thomas Becket of Canterbury.*

In that that he saith, "the word of the Lord was sent by the hand of Aggeus the prophet," it teaches the duty both of the hearer and the preacher. For neither must we teach any thing of man's devices, nor the hearer must regard him so much which preaches, that for his cause we must either more or less believe the thing which is taught, (for the preacher takes his authority of the word of God, and not the word takes his authority of the preacher;) but only because it is the word of God, of whose truth we must not doubt, but with obedience receive it. Unto the preacher saith St Peter, "He that speaks, let him speak as the words of God:" and Aggeus being but a poor Levite, keeping this rule, was not to be despised more than the priest. And whereas preaching and believing the things preached is the highest and most pleasant service and worship of God; what thing should be taught, and what punishment is for them which do it not, the scripture teaches plain. St Matthew saith: "They worship me in vain, teaching learnings which are the commandments of men." And the false prophet, which runs before he be sent and deceives the people, speaking in the name of God that which he was not commanded, or else speaking in the name of false gods, shall be put to death. Therefore let the prating pardoner, or the popish priests, *The word of God is only to be taught and believed.* *1 Pet. iv.* *Deut. xviii.*

retur. Concil. Tom. xxviii. p. 675, Paris. 1644.—But the true name appears to be *Fratricelli*, as given in the Bishop's text, and in the following extract: "This Hermann lived at Ferrara in this century, and was highly esteemed for his sanctity; and after his death, in 1269, he was magnificently entombed in the principal church of Ferrara, and was long held by all for a distinguished saint, whose sanctity God had demonstrated by numerous miracles. But as the *inquisitors of heretical pravity* had long been suspicious of him, &c. &c." Mosheim's Ecclesiastical History, Book iii. Cent. 13, Part 2, Chap. ii. Ed.]

take heed in whose names they speak, and what they teach, when for the greedy gaining of a little money they condemn themselves, and set out to sell heaven, purgatory, and hell, as they were all in their power to give at their pleasure. In the pope's name they promise forty, sixty, an hundred days of pardon; and for a trental[1] they may be brought from hell. The true prophets of God, as appeareth in their writings, always use to say: "Thus saith the Lord," "the word of God was spoken to me," &c.; but the pope's creatures, as pardoners, priests, friars, &c., say: "Thus saith pope Alexander, Gregory, John, Clement, or some such other like;" and nothing will they do without money. Let the true preacher teach the mercies of God, that "God hath so loved the world, that he gave his only begotten Son, that every one which believes in him shall not be damned, but have life everlasting;" and yet shall the drunken pardoner and Sir John Lacklatin be better believed than Christ, which spake these words, and promised it: yea, rather the people will buy forgiveness of their sins at the pope and such his messengers' hands, than take it freely at Christ, paying nothing therefore; such is the brutish, blind unthankfulness of the world. "Come and buy freely without money," saith the prophet: and again, "It is I, it is I that put away thy sins for mine own sake;" then it is not for thy money, nor the pope's bulls nor pardons. Let the world therefore take heed; for "if the blind lead the blind, both fall in the ditch." This miserable common excuse, which is so often in their mouths, shall not excuse them, when they say, Thus we are taught, our ghostly fathers say so, and our fathers before us have so believed: Christ says, ye shall both fall in the pit. Believe no doctrine that teaches to go to heaven otherways than by Christ freely, or which is not written and contained in the bible: for that only is the perfect word of God, and which only teaches true salvation. Look the pope's testament throughout, called his decrees and decretals, and you shall not once there be taught to seek comfort at Christ in any trouble of mind; but only to set out his vain glory, and that he is lord of heaven and earth, purgatory and hell; and if thou live never so wickedly,

John iii.

Isai. lv.; xliii.

Matt. xv. Vain excuses.

[1 Trental: trigintal, a service of thirty masses. Ed.]

he and his chaplains have full authority to bring thee from purgatory, so that thou bring them money. I think it hath not been oft heard tell of, that any priest ever said trental without money, or hired any said for themselves: but if they were good, why should they not have them for themselves? If they had charity, they would say them for the poor as well as for the rich: they would not suffer so many poor souls to lie broiling in purgatory, as they think do; no, they would do nothing night nor day all their lives but say masses, if they had such love towards their brethren as they should, and if they were able so to deliver them. For what charity is in him that may help his brother, and will not by all means possible? But they shew by their doings their meaning well enough, when they turn them to the people and say: Of your devotion and charity pray ye for the soul of N.; as though they should say: We pray for money without charity, but ye must do freely of devotion without money. These false prophets, papists, and members of antichrist, came not in the Lord's name, nor speak his word; therefore they be accursed.

<small>Priests pray not without money, nor hire any for themselves.</small>

Also in that he saith, "the word was sent by the hand of Aggeus," we are taught how to esteem preaching ministers by this Hebrew kind of speaking. For as the hand serves to do more things withal than any part of the body; so when they will signify any thing to be done by the ministery and service of any man, they used to say, It was done by the hand of such a man. Therefore the word and message which he brought was the Lord's, and Aggeus was but the servant that brought it. So must we think of the preachers: they be but servants, though they be never so good and learned preachers, and their message is the word of the Lord. Thus says Christ: "It is not you that speak, but it is the Spirit of your Father which speaks in you." St Paul also teaches how we should think upon him and others such preachers, when he says: "Let a man judge and think thus of us, that we be the servants of Christ, and dispensers of God's secret mysteries." Therefore they which seek rather to be lords than servants, and be hinderers of preaching God's word, rather than faithful teachers of God's holy will to his people, are not to be counted amongst the

<small>Preachers are but servants, and must not go before they be sent; but their word is God's. Matt. x.</small>

<small>1 Cor. iv.</small>

servants and ministers of Christ, but rather enemies, seeking their own glory more than God's.

And as Aggeus did not go with this message afore he was commanded and sent by God, and therefore was a true prophet; so they which thrust in themselves to teach, not called by God, nor sent by man ordinarily, come often afore they be welcome, and are not true prophets. For it is written: "Let no man take honour unto him, but he which is called of God, as Aaron was." And if the worser learned be preferred afore the better to the ministery, if they be both true teachers, let not the better disdain him, but know God to see further than he doth, and that there be just causes why the other is preferred afore him.

<small>Heb. v.</small>

Whereas Zerubabel is first named here, and set in order afore Josua the high priest, and the prophet Aggeus was sent by commission from God to the civil magistrate first; it teaches the pre-eminence the temporal rulers have afore priests, by what name soever they be called. If the pope should have received such letters as these be, and seen a layman preferred and named afore him, he would not have been well content; and specially such a man as Zerubabel was, being neither king nor emperor. What a railing letter wrote Pope Adrian the fourth, an Englishman, to Frederick the emperor, because the emperor in his letters had set his name afore the pope's, writing thus his superscription of his letters: Frederick by the grace of God emperor, &c. unto the holy father Adrian, pope. If he had written thus: To the most reverend and holy father the pope Adrian, God's vicar here in earth, &c., your poor and humble servant Frederick, by the grace of God emperor of Almaine, &c., and had placed the pope's name before his own, all had been well. Because he did not, he called the emperor traitor and rebel against God and St Peter, &c.[1]

<small>The civil ruler is above the priest.</small>

<small>Adrian IV.</small>

[1 Hadrianus Episcopus servus servorum Dei, Friderico Romano Imperatori, salutem et Apostolicam benedictionem.

Lex divina sicut parentes honorantibus longævitatem promittit, ita maledicentibus patri et matri sententiam mortis intendit. Veritatis autem voce docemur, quia *omnis qui se exaltat humiliabitur*. Quapropter, dilecte in Domino fili, super prudentia tua non mediocriter admiramur, quod beato Petro et sanctæ Romanæ ecclesiæ non quantam deberes exhibere reverentiam videris. In litteris enim ad nos missis

The commonwealth of the Jews was ruled first by judges, from Moses unto Saul; then by kings, from David to their captivity in Babylon; and now last, from their returning home unto Christ, by princes of the stock of Juda. Their judges were raised up of God to deliver the people, sometime of one tribe or kindred, some time of other, as pleased God; and the children did not succeed the father in such authority. Kings were always of the stock of Juda only, and the son was king after the father; but these princes, although they were for the most part of the stock of Juda, and the succession was by heritage, (except the Machabees,) yet they had not a kingly majesty, crown and power; for they were but as mayors or dukes, and head men amongst the people, as the Hebrew word signifies, *pachath;* and yet they be preferred before the high priest. By which we must learn chief power in all commonwealths to be joined with the temporal sword, though he be but a mean man; and that every man, as St Paul says, "must be subject under him." Chrysostom notes well, writing on that place, that every man must obey the civil power, whether he be apostle, evangelist, prophet, or by what name soever he be called². St Peter himself (being bishop, as they say, at Rome, and of whom they claim all their authority to be above princes, kings, and emperors) was not only obedient to the civil rulers himself, but left written in his epistle, that we should all obey the king, as chief and highest ruler above all other. And although kings and rulers in commonwealths were then infidels, and not christened, yet he bids obey them as the chief and highest; and neither wills any to be disobedient, to pull the sword out of their hands, nor to set up himself

Judges.

Kings.

Princes.

Rom. xiii.

nomen tuum nostro præponis: in quo insolentiæ, ne dicam arrogantiæ, notam incurris. Acta Conciliorum, etc. Tom. vi. Pars ii. p. 1339. Paris. 1714.

The emperor was Frederick Barbarossa, and the circumstance took place about the year 1155. Ed.]

[² Καὶ δεικνὺς ὅτι πᾶσι ταῦτα διατάττεται, καὶ ἱερεῦσι καὶ μοναχοῖς, οὐχὶ τοῖς βιωτικοῖς μόνον, ἐκ προοιμίων αὐτὸ δῆλον ἐποίησεν, οὕτω λέγων· πᾶσα ψυχὴ ἐξουσίαις ὑπερεχούσαις ὑποτασσέσθω· κἂν ἀπόστολος ᾖς, κἂν εὐαγγελιστής, κἂν προφήτης, κἂν ὁστισοῦν· οὐδὲ γὰρ ἀνατρέπει τὴν εὐσέβειαν αὕτη ἡ ὑποταγή. Chrysost. in Rom. xiii. 1. Paris. 1837. Tom. ix. p. 752. Ed.]

above them, but humbly to obey them in all things not contrary to God's truth and religion. But if they command anything contrary to God's word, we must answer with the apostles: "We must rather obey God than man." And let no man think that in displeasing God he can please man: for God, who hath all men's hearts in his hand, will turn his heart to hurt thee, whom thou would please and flatter by displeasing and disobeying God; nor we owe any obedience to any man in such things wherein God is offended and disobeyed. If England had learned this lesson in the time of persecution, we should neither for fear at the voice of a woman have denied our Master with Peter; nor for flattery have worshipped Baal, nor rashly rebelled; but humbly have suffered God's scourge, until it had pleased God to have cast the rod in the fire: the which he would sooner have done, if our unthankful sturdiness had not deserved a longer plague. The Lord for his mercies' sake grant, that both we and all other may hereafter beware from like pulling on our heads the righteous scourge of God for our wickedness, and the unpatient bearing of the same when it comes.

Obey God rather than man.

v. 2. *Thus saith the God of hosts, saying: This people say, The time is not yet come to build the house of God.*

The text.

The prophet dare speak nothing in his own name, or of his own device, but always names the Lord who sent him, and whose message he brought; which thing all preachers must follow most diligently, or else they are not to be believed. St Paul saith: "If I, or an angel from heaven, should teach you any other gospel, beside that which you have received, cursed be he." And mark that he says not, if he teach contrary to that which ye have received, but besides and more than that which ye received: for the pope and his clergy think that they may for our salvation add more to the gospel, so that it be not contrary to the gospel. But St Paul says, besides or more than that which ye received. And Moses saith: "Thou shalt neither put to nor take away anything from the word of God," but content thyself only with that which he teaches; for he only is true,

The scripture is only to be taught.

Gal. i.

Deut. iv. [2.]

and all men be liars, and no man is of his counsel, to teach thee what pleases or displeases him, except he speak himself. And although rulers may ordain some things for an order in the church, yet none of their decrees are articles of our faith; but they may and ought to be changed, when they be hurtful, or turn to any misuse or superstition.

And for all that, that the people had grievously sinned in not building the Lord's house so many years; yet while God did vouchsafe to speak unto them by his prophets and rebuke their sin, there was hope enough of forgiveness, so that they would amend and turn unto God. For like as long as the physician doth appoint the sick man what he shall do, how to diet himself, and what medicines to take, there is hope of life; but if he forsake him, and will not speak unto him, we look for present death: so as long as God of his goodness lets his word be among us, there is good hope of forgiveness; but if he take away his word, there is no comfort left. Saul, when Samuel was dead, asked counsel of God, but he would not speak to him, neither by dreams, nor at the ark of God, nor by visions or prophets; and then he runs to witches: so we, when God teaches not, but are left to ourselves, seek such unlawful means.

While God lets us have his word, it is a token of his love; and the taking it away, of his displeasure. 1 Sam. xxviii.

The Jews had lien almost forty years in this negligence of building God's house: it is almost as many years, since we under pretence of receiving the gospel, and building God's house, have pulled it down: and to root out all the rabble of monks, friars, nuns, canons, &c., we for the most part have sought to enrich ourselves, and one (like thieves) robbed another, and have not of pure love destroyed God's enemies, nor provided for the poor, and furthered learning, nor placed preaching ministers in place of dumb dogs, after the rule of his word, as we should have done, and builded his house.

And what remedy do the wicked papists find to redress this withal? They pull away God's word, and say it was never good world since it came abroad, and that it is not meet for the people to have or read it, but they must receive it at their mouths. They are the nurses, they say, and must chew the meat afore the children eat it. Woe be unto such dissemblers, as under pretence of chewing eat all up; or else, that little which they give (for they say it

Pambo. is not necessary to preach often, by the example of Pambo[1], which when he had heard one lesson, the first verse of the thirty-ninth Psalm, which begins thus, "I thought with myself, I will keep my ways, that I offend not in my tongue," would hear no more until he had in many years learned to practise that one: which example rather proves that we should diligently learn, than seldom preach); it is, I say, so poisoned in their filthy mouths and stinking breaths, that it poisons and feeds not the hearer. David *Psal. cxix.* says: "By what things shall a young man amend his evil ways?" and he answers: "by keeping the sayings of God." And how shall we see to do this? "Thy word, O Lord," he says, "is a lantern for my feet, and a light to my paths." But these thieves that take away the word of God from the people, which is the lantern and light to teach them to go aright, would have them in darkness still, that they should neither see their own faults nor others'. When the fault is not seen, how can it be amended? And how can it be seen, seeing it is in darkness, except the light of God's *Deut. vi.* truth do open it unto us? Moses bids the fathers tell their children the law of God oftentimes, and to study on it in *Psal.lxxviii.* their houses, in going by the way. David bids the same, *Ephes. vi.* and the children to ask the fathers. Paul bids fathers bring up their children in the nurture and learning of God; and *1 Cor. xiv.* wives, if they will learn anything, ask their husbands at *All sorts must learn the scriptures.* home. Then if the father must teach the son, and the son must ask the father, and the wife must learn of the husband; how shall those fathers and husbands teach, except they be learned? and how can they be learned, having none to teach them but Sir John Mumble-matins, nor cannot be suffered to read themselves? But it is true that St John *John iii.* saith: "He that doeth evil hateth the light, and will not come to the light, lest his evil doings be reproved." And this to be true their common sayings declare, when they said, it was never good world since every shoemaker could tell the priest's duty. They were ashamed of their faults, and therefore would have you in blindness still, that ye should see neither your own faults, nor tell them of theirs;

[1 Pambo: a monk of great reputed sanctity in the 4th century. Palladius, Hist. Lausiac. Cap. x. Ed.]

for that specially they cannot abide. But our good God when he blessed his people, and offereth his pardons, he sends many teachers and opens divers ways to learn; and when he is most angry, he takes away his word, that they shall not see how to amend, as Amos sayeth: "I will send a hunger unto the earth, not a hunger of bread, but of the word of God, that they shall seek it from east to west, and not find it." Therefore they which take away his word, or be hinderers thereof, are nothing else but instruments of his wrath and God's scourge to his people. Amos viii.

And that they should the more diligently mark the message which he brought, he tells them in whose name he spake, and saith, "The Lord of hosts spake those words," or, as the Hebrew is, JEHOVA: which is as much to say as, that God of might, majesty and power, which hath his being and substance of himself, and by whom all other things stand and be, and without whom all things fall to nothing if he do not uphold them, he speaks these words. The other word joined withal, when he calls him the God of hosts, is a word of fear and reverence, as JEHOVA is a name of love and power: so that if either they loved him as a father and God of power, or else feared him as a Lord and master, and one that had many hosts of soldiers to conquer them withal, if they did rebel against him still, they should receive and obey this message. In like manner God by Malachy rebukes the people, which called him father and master in words, but in deeds would nothing do as he taught them, and saith: "If I be your father, where is my love that you owe me? If I be your master, where is the fear that is due to me?" This word and name is seldom read in the New Testament, to call him the God of hosts, because it is a word of fear more than of love, and rather threatens than comforts, which the New Testament doth not commonly. St James says: "The withholden wages of them that have reaped your fields cries vengeance in the ears of the Lord of hosts." It is as much to say in this place as, Thus says that mighty Lord of hosts, whom if ye hear and obey, he will make all his creatures to serve and obey you: but if you be disobedient to him still, he hath many armies and hosts to fight with against you, and all his creatures What Jehovah signifies. Exod. iii. [14.] Acts xvii. [28.] Psal. civ. [29.] Malach. i. James v. Why God is called the Lord of hosts, and how he useth his weakest creatures to pull down the proud withal.

from the highest to the least shall be harnessed against you. Think not, that if ye escape one plague, that ye shall escape the rest: for deferring or escaping one is but to see whether ye will amend before the next come. His arrows and thunderbolts are never spent, but he hath new in store: and in the end the victory shall be his, and all disobedient shall perish. And for the better understanding of this to be true, the scripture hath set out divers examples, where God hath fought against man with all his creatures, to let him see how divers kinds of hosts he hath to beat him down withal. The angels destroyed Sodom and Gomorrah with fire and brimstone, and killed with pestilence in three days' space seventy thousand for David's offence; and also in one night destroyed in the tents of Sennacherib one hundred and eighty-five thousand. The sun at the commandment of Josua stood still, giving him light, until God's enemies, the Amorites, in the chase were killed by him, so that one day was as long as two. In Egypt the stars and sun gave no light to the Egyptians; but the darkness was so great, gross and thick mists, that no man stirred out of his place, and men might grope the mists, and feel them with their hand: but where the children of Israel were, the sun shone bright and pleasantly. Against Sisara God fought out of heaven. The water drowned the whole world, save eight persons under Noe. The Red Sea suffered God's people to pass, but it drowned Pharao and all his host. The earth swallowed up quick Dathan, Corah and Abiron, and all those rebels with them. In Egypt storms of hail killed the Egyptians' beasts, and destroyed their corn; but harmed not the Israelites. So the tower in Siloe fell and killed eighteen within it. Such drought was in the time of Elias, that it rained not for the space of three years and a half. Such hunger in all countries, that Jacob with all his house went into Egypt; and there also the Egyptians for hunger sold their land, their cattle, wives, children, and themselves, to be bondmen and slaves to their king.

In the besiege of Samaria for hunger an ass's head and dove's dung was sold dear, and women did eat their own children. Joel threatens that God will send four hosts, one of grasshoppers, another of caterpillars, blasting, and locusts, to devour all the fruit of the ground; and all that which one of these left the next should destroy. In Egypt, mark *Exod. viii.* what mighty men of war God chose to fight withal: it rained frogs even into the king's privy chamber and his bed, and flies[1] fought against Pharao and the whole country, and made them weary, and a murrain fell among the beasts; but by these means God gat the victory. When the ten *2 Kings xvii.* tribes were led away prisoners, the wild beasts increased, so that they devoured the dwellers in the country, because they feared not God. God closed up the wombs of all *Gen. xx.* Abimelech's women, that they should not bear children, because he had taken Abraham's wife. When the Philistians *1 Sam. v.* had taken the ark of God and misused it, God smote them with emorraides in their secret parts[2]. Herod and divers *Acts xii.* emperors were worried with lice. Arius sitting on the privy avoided all his bowels[3]. Nabuchodonozor of a king *Dan. iv.* was made a beast, eat hay, and lived in woods.

Gedeon with three hundred men, knocking their pot- *Judg. vii.* sherds together, made his enemies (which were so many, that they lay as thick as grasshoppers use to lie on the ground) so afraid, that they strove who might run away first; and if his fellow stood in his way, he killed him straight. The *Josh. vi.* walls of Jericho fell without violence or hand laid on them: the Syrians thinking they heard a noise in the night, and *2 Kings vii.* that their enemies came against them (where there was none such indeed), ran all away. Judith, a weak woman, *Judith xv.* cut off Holophernes' head. Jonathan and his man alone *1 Sam. xiv.* put to flight all the Philistians, whereof many were slain

[[1] In the second edition *flees*; in the first the former vowel is indistinct, *e* or *i*. ED.]

[[2] The expression of Scripture, 1 Sam. v. 9, is here substituted for the word used by the Author. ED.]

[[3] This word is also a variation from the original.—The historical fact is recorded as follows: Σύν τε τῷ φόβῳ τῆς γαστρὸς ἐκινεῖτο χαύνωσις, ἐρόμενός τε εἰ ἀφεδρῶν που πλησίον, μαθών τε εἶναι ὄπισθεν τῆς ἀγορᾶς Κωνσταντίνου, ἐκεῖσε ἐβάδιζε. λαμβάνει οὖν λιποθυμία τὸν ἄνθρωπον. καὶ ἅμα τοῖς διαχωρήμασιν ἡ ἕδρα τότε παραυτίκα ἐκπίπτει, καὶ αἵματος πλῆθος ἐπηκολούθει, καὶ τὰ λεπτὰ τῶν ἑτέρων [ἐντέρων]. συνέτρεχε δὲ αἷμα αὐτῷ τῷ σπληνί τε καὶ τῷ ἥπατι. αὐτίκα οὖν ἐτεθνήκει. Socrat. Eccles. Hist. lib. I. c. 38. p. 190. Paris. 1544. ED.]

Gen. xi.

1 Sam. xvii.

in the chase. The proud enterprise in building the tower of Babel was stopped by confounding their language, that one could not understand another. David, a young man with a sling and a stone, kills Golias so strongly harnessed. A bishop of Mentz[1], being persecuted with rats from house to house, fled into a tower he had standing in the midst of the river, lying a mile from any land: but the rats followed him and swam over; neither doors nor stone walls could keep them out, but they worried him for his unmercifulness to the people in a year of dearth. Thus our God may well be called the Lord of hosts, which hath so many weapons and divers to punish us withal, as fire, water, earth, darkness, frogs, lice, grasshoppers, caterpillars, pestilence, hail, drought, &c.; so that there is no help to be disobedient and strive against him, for he will have the victory. There is ways above and beneath us, within us and without us, to throw us down at his pleasure: there is no remedy but to obey him, either willingly and be rewarded, or else against our wills and be punished. His power is not yet minished, but he fights still with his enemies, that all glory may be his. He hath foughten sore of late with his utter enemy, the pope: and with what weapons? with a goose-feather and old clouts, (whereof be made pen and paper); and such simple men hath he used to do this feat, as the world hates and despises. But he hath so shaken his seat, that his fall is begun; and every man which is not wilfully blind sees it. His abominations and his wickedness is opened to the world, as the prophet saith: "I will shew thy filthy parts in thy face, and will set forth thy nakedness to people."

Nahum iii.

These be the ordinances[2], great guns, and bulwarks, that he will set up his church with and pull down antichrist; that all victory may be his, which by such small and weak things throws down the glory of the world. And although their faults were grievous, yet our good God is content with a little rebuking of them, and doeth no more but cast in their teeth their unthankfulness, and saith: "This people

To be rebuked of unthankfulness is the greatest grief to a loving heart.

[1 A popular legend of that day. See the wonderful tale in Jo. Wolfii Lect. Memorab. Tom. i. p. 343. Lauingæ, 1600. ED.]

[2 Ordinances: i. e. ordnance. ED.]

says, It is not yet time to build the house of God:" as though he should say, This people whom I chose amongst all the world, and in respect of whom I seem to regard no other people but them, bestowing on them only or chiefly my blessings; whose fathers I brought out of slavery in Egypt, and made them lords of this plenteous land, destroying the dwellers of it, and subduing their enemies round about them; to whom I send my prophets in all ages to teach them my will and pleasure; and whom now of late, when they were led prisoners to Babylon, I brought home again, and restored to them their land, and willed nothing of them but to build my house and keep my laws; this unkind people, I say, says, It is not yet time to build God's house. This stiff-necked people, that will neither be overcome and moved with gentleness to do their duties, nor yet fear my plagues and threatenings, will not diligently go about to do that which I willed them so straitly to do. The rod is sharp to the flesh, when we be beaten; but to a gentle heart there can be no sharper rebuke than to have his unkindness cast in his teeth. "My people," says God by his prophet, "in what Mic. vi. thing have I offended thee, that thou dost so disobey me? or what have I done to thee? tell me." And that we should better consider our unthankfulness, he compares us to beasts, and says: "The ox knows his master, and the ass knows Isai. i. his master's stable and manger; but my people will not know me." So saith Jeremy: "The turtle, swallow, and the stork Jer. viii. know their times of the year to come; but my people know not the judgment of the Lord." If a king should marry a poor woman, and make her queen, and when she displeased him, should say unto her, "When thou wast but a poor woman, and never looked to have been married to me, I forsook all other women for thy sake, and made thee my wife and fellow; hath it becomen thee to do this fault against me?"—if she have any honest heart in her, it will make her burst out into tears, and ask forgiveness: so will it move any christian heart that fears God, when he hears his unthankful disobedience laid to his charge; and specially if he consider what goodness and how often he hath received at God's hands, and how forgetful he hath been again to so loving a Lord God. The Lord for his mercies' sake grant us such tender hearts, that we may burst out into tears, when we consider his goodness and our wickedness, his undeserved mercy, and our great unthankfulness! What a bitter grief shall this be, to hear him lay our unkindness to our charge! 'I gave you a good king, many true preachers, my word plenteously, my sacraments purely, rooted out idolatry, delivered you from strangers, with all wealth; and yet you would not fear me.' What can we say for shame, but condemn ourselves? God grant we may! for then he will not condemn us.

I do not doubt but many of them had great excuses to lay for themselves, if they had been asked why they did not build God's house, as well as we have for our negligence in the same doing. . Some would say, We are forbidden by the king and his officers, (and so they were indeed, as appears in Esdras). Some, We must first provide a house for ourselves to dwell in, for our wives and children: other, We are unlearned, we know not how to do it: other, We be poor, and not able to take in hand such a costly work: other, Let the rulers begin, and we will help: other, We shall lose our life and goods, if we disobey the king's commandment. But God would allow no such excuse, but casts in all their teeths their disobedient unkindness, and says: "This people say, It is not yet time to build God's house." The priests would say, It is not our duty to build, but to offer sacrifices and sing psalms, as we be appointed. The rulers might say, their office was to see the commonwealth well ruled, and not to meddle in such matters. The people might say, it belonged not to them, being such a costly thing, that required wisdom, learning, riches, and power; but they must apply their husbandry, merchandise, &c. Even as they said in the gospel: "I have bought a farm, or, five yoke of oxen, that I will not come; hold me excused. Or, I have married a wife, that I cannot come." So none could or would take God's work in hand. Therefore, that one sort should not think themselves blameless, and the other to be in fault; or that one should not despise another, because that they were more holy than the rest, and would have builded God's house more gladly than other, the prophet is sent to rebuke them all, for all were guilty in not building. And he says

Excuses of our negligence be vain. Ezra iv.

1 Chron. xxiii. [30, 31.]

Luke xiv.

not, The rulers say, It is not yet time to build God's house; or, The priests say so, or the merchants, or husbandmen: but generally, All this people of all degrees say, It is not yet time to build God's house. And so, because the rebuke is general to all sorts, young and old, poor and rich, learned and unlearned, they may understand that it is their duties to build God's house, what manner of men soever they be.

What a comfort is this for the poor unlearned man, when he heareth that God refuses not, but requires and takes in good worth, that little service which he can do, and wills him to build his house as well as the rich; that he should not think God loves not poor men, nor we are not able to serve him, but he loves only the rich and learned, and they must serve him! Nor again, he must not think, I may do what I will, God cares not for me, nor he hath no work for me to do in his house.

It is in building God's spiritual house, as it is here with us in our buildings. In buildings there be master-masons and carpenters, which do devise the work, draw out the fashion of it, and set their men on work: there be also some that fell trees, carry stones, bring mortar, and make clean the place, &c. So in building God's house there be rich and learned, there be poor and meaner learned; but the lowest and meanest of all, as he is the creature of God, and made not himself, so God hath some work for him to do and requires his service. If he be not a ruler or a preacher, yet he hath wife and children whom he must see live in the fear of God, and that God will require of his hand: and though he be not married, but both lame and blind, yet he hath a body and soul which Christ died for; and they be the house of God and temple of the Holy Ghost, which we should build, and of that thou shalt make account. He that hath received greater gifts hath a greater charge, and more work shall be looked for of him: but if he have no more but life in him, and be not able to stir any part of him, neither hand nor foot, yet God will look that his mind shall be continually occupied in prayer for himself and others, that he be no drunkard, glutton, &c.; and think not but this is the highest service that the best man living can do to God. Such a loving God is our God even to the poorest man

God accepts and requires the service of the simplest.

All things to salvation are given indifferently to the poor and rich.

living, that he gives him as well as the rich all things indifferently, which should bring him to heaven; as baptism, faith, hope and charity, repentance, prayer, fasting, avoiding whoredom, theft, murder, anger, &c., all are as common and as easy to come by, or rather more easy, for the poor than the rich. He disdains not, but thankfully takes, the poorest service that the least creature he hath can do, so that he do it diligently and willingly; and will reward that little so done as liberally as he doth the greater. He that hath received much shall make account of much; and he that hath but little, yet shall make account of that little.

But this is marvellous, that where all sorts of the people were in fault, the prophet is sent by commission from God namely[1] to Zerubabel the chief ruler in the commonwealth, and to Josua the high priest; as though they had only sinned, or they could or should remedy this matter.

What reason seems this, that when many do offend, a few shall be rebuked; and when all the people be negligent, the chief rulers, both in civil matters of the commonwealth, and the chief priest and highest in matters of religion, are blamed? This is the high wisdom of God, that man's wit cannot attain unto: and there is great reason, if it be well considered, why it should be so. God our heavenly Father, knowing the crookedness of man's heart and how ready we be all to evil, hath appointed rulers in the commonwealth to minister justice, punish sin, defend the right, and cause men to do their duties: and in his church he hath placed preachers to teach his law, to pull down superstition and idolatry, and to stir up the slothful and negligent to serve and fear him. If either the one or both of these rulers be

The rulers and ministers are to be blamed, if the people offend through their negligence. For as brethren they must agree to promote God's glory.

negligent in their office, the people (which be always ready to seek their own ease and pleasures) fall from God: but God will punish the rulers for their negligence, that neither they did their duties themselves nor see the people do theirs; and they shall be guilty of the sins of the people, and partakers of their wickedness, because it was done through their negligence in not punishing and seeing the people do their duties, both to God and man.

Exod. iv.

When God gathered his church first, he appointed Moses

[1 Namely: expressly, by name. ED.]

and Aaron, two brethren, to be the chief rulers of the people, the one in religion, and the other in civil matters: to teach us, that these two kinds of rulers be lawful and necessary in a commonwealth, that they should love and stick together like brethren, and that the one with the word and the other with the sword should jointly build God's house, pull down antichrist the pope, and set up the kingdom of Christ. When the children of Israel had committed idolatry in Baal-peor, and fallen to adultery with the women of Moab, Moses in the name of God commands all the rulers of the people to be hanged on gallows against the sun, because they did not their duties in keeping the people from such mischief. To the preachers saith Ezekiel: "Thou son of man, I have made thee a watchman to the house of Israel: thou shalt hear words of my mouth, and shew them from me. If I say to the wicked, Thou wicked, thou shalt die the death, and thou wilt not speak to him that he may keep him from his wickedness, the wicked shall die in his wickedness, but I will require his blood of thy hands: but if he will not leave his wickedness when thou tellest him, he shall die in his wickedness, and thou hast saved thine own soul, because thou hast done thy duty in warning him." By these punishments we may see, that it is neither the duty of civil rulers, by what name soever they be called, to be negligent in their duty, or to set in an evil deputy for them to gather up the profits, that they may go hawk, or hunt, game, or keep whores; for God, that gave them that authority, will look for account for it of them: nor that it is lawful for bishop, dean, archdeacon, prebendary, or parson, to set in a parish priest to make conjured water, and serve the people in a strange tongue, which neither he nor they understand: for by these means the people be not amended.

_{Numb. xxv. [4.]}

_{Ezek. iii. xxxiii.}

Hely, having complaints made to him of the unhappiness of his children, fell and brake his neck, because he would not punish them; and they themselves were killed in battle, and the ark of God was taken by God's enemies: so shall the fathers of the people perish, if they punish not faults of the people.

_{1 Sam. iv.}

"He that desires a bishop's office," saith St Paul, "desires a good labour:" he calls it not a good lordship, nor

_{1 Tim. iii.}

idleness and wealth, but labour. What a man the labourer should be, Ezekiel tells particularly, saying: "Woe to the shepherds of Israel, which feed themselves, and not my flock! ye have eaten the fat, and been clothed with the wool; but ye have not strengthened the weak, nor healed the sick, nor brought home the stray, nor sought the lost, but ye have ruled over them with sharpness." These be the duties of good shepherds and their labours, and not masking masses, mumming matins, and babble they know not what: and he that either cannot or will not do these things, seeking his own ease and wealth, and not bring the people to God, is a thief and murderer. Also, the patron of a benefice or bishop, which admit any such as cannot do these duties to have cure of souls, are partakers of his wickedness; and, as much as in them lies, murder so many souls as perish this ways for want of wholesome doctrine. St Paul says to Timothy: "Lay not thy hand rashly on any man, nor without good trial appoint him a minister, lest thou be partaker of other men's sins." We must neither do evil ourselves, nor consent to other to do it, but, as much as in us lies, stop it: for both the doer and he which agrees to it are worthy death, as St Paul saith. But he that places an unworthy or unable minister wittingly in a benefice, consents to the evil which he doeth, because he might stop him from it if he would; and therefore is he worthy death also.

A tailor that is not cunning to make a gown may mend hose; a cobbler that cannot make shoes may mend them; a carpenter which is not cunning to make the house, yet may he square trees or fell them: but an unable priest to teach is good to nothing in that kind of life or ministery. "Ye are the salt of the earth," saith our Saviour Christ; "but if the salt have lost his saltness, wherewith shall it be salted? it is not good enough to be cast on the dunghill (for so it would do good in dunging the field); but it is meet for nothing but to be cast in ways to be trodden under our feet."

So these priests, which have not the salt of God's word to season man's soul withal, are meet for nothing in that kind of life, but to be put to some occupation which they can do, and get their living with the sweat of their face, and not occupy a place among God's shepherds, seeing they be rather dumb and devouring dogs than good preachers.

Are not we in England guilty of the like fault? When God stirred up our kings as chief in the realm, and Thomas Cranmer, archbishop of Canterbury, with others, for matters in religion, to drive the buyers and sellers of masses, pardons, trentals, &c. out of God's house, which they had made a den of thieves, was not this in all our mouths: It is not yet time to build God's house, the people cannot bear it; we fear strange princes and rebellions?—as though God were content to suffer idolatry for a time, and would not or could not promote his own matters without our politic devices. And almost as many years have we lien loitering as these men did, and not builded God's house, but pulled it down; builded our own houses goodly without any stop or fear, where rebellion most should have been feared, because it was done oft with the injury of others, as by extreme raising of rents, taking great incomes and fines, &c., by these means seeking our own rest and profit. It wants not much of so many years since king Henry began to espy the pope; and yet God's house is not built. What marvel is it then, if we have been thus grievously plagued for our negligence in thus doing, and that every one hath been sought out to death, that was judged to love God's word? When the good king Cyrus had given free liberty to the Jews every one to go home that would, the most part had so well placed themselves in strange countries and waxed so wealthy, that they would not go home when they might to build God's house. What marvel was it then, if God, to punish this great wickedness, stirred up king Assuerus by the means of Haman, to make proclamation through all countries, that it should be lawful for any man to kill all the Jews he could, to take their goods, and order them at their pleasure; that if gentleness could not drive them home to serve God, yet sharpness should compel them to go build God's house?

And hath it not been so in England taught, that all gospellers should be destroyed, and should not leave one man alive[1]? And this thing God of love and mercy did unto us, that where we would not know him by gentleness,

We are like the Jews in long negligence.

Ezra ii.

Esther iii.

[¹ The phrase used by the author is as in 1 Kings xxi. 21. ED.]

we should be compelled by the rod and sharpness to seek him. All faults in our late popery (were they never so great) might be pardoned, save this, to love God's word. But as God took Haman in his own device, and the vengeance light on him and his; so God hath mercifully delivered many in England from the persecutors, gloriously called many to be his witnesses in the fire, and turned the devices of his enemies on their own heads, and sharply destroyed them which murdered his saints, when they thought most to have enjoyed the world at their will. Therefore let us think that God speaks to us by his prophet, saying: This people of England, to whom I have given so plentiful a land, delivered them so often, and sent them my preachers; and whom, when they forgot me and their duty, I punished, sometimes sharply of fatherly love, and sometime gently that they might turn to me; yet they say, It is not yet time to build God's house, for fear of their own shadows: they would lie loitering still, and not be waked out of this sleep. Let us consider what benefits we have received daily of our good God, and see what a grief it is to be unthankful, and have our unkindness thus cast in our teeth. Poor cities in Germany, compassed about with their enemies, dare reform religion throughly, without any fear, and God prospers them: and yet this noble realm, which all princes have feared, dare not. We will do it by our own policies, and not by committing the success to God; and so we shall overthrow all.

The Text. *v. 3. And the word of God was sent by the hand of Aggeus the prophet, saying:*
4. Is it time for you that ye should dwell in your ceiled houses, and this house lie waste?

This is most worthy to be noted, that the prophet dare speak nothing of his own head, but always in the name of God, and as he received it of God's mouth; and for our example, most diligently it is to be followed, seeing he durst not so much as rebuke sin, but as God taught him. But of this enough is spoken afore in the first and second verses.

This prophet, having a gentler spirit than many of the other prophets, doth not so sharply threaten utter destruction of them and their country for their disobedience; but chiefly sets before them their slothfulness towards the building of God's house, and their shameful and shameless scraping and scratching together of goods, their polling and pilling, their labour, diligence, and pains taken to build costly gorgeous houses for themselves: as though he would say, Is it not a shame for you to take so much labour and spend so much money in making yourselves ceiled and carved houses, and can find no time nor money to spend on God's house? Do you love yourselves better than your God? Do ye set more by your own pleasure than God's honour? Will you first satisfy your own lusts, and then, when ye can find any leisure, peradventure God and his house shall have a piece bestowed on him? Is not this to set the cart before the horse? Ye should first serve God, seek his will, and after look to your own necessities, and not vain pleasures. The heathen poet could reprove this in heathen people, saying: "O citizens, citizens, is money to be sought first, and then virtue after riches[1]?"—as though he should say, Nay, not so. This is spoken to all: "First seek the kingdom of God and the righteousness thereof, and all other things necessary shall be given you." *Matt. vi.*

God's house is to be built before our own.

But was this so grievous a fault in God's sight, to build their own houses afore God's house, that they were so plagued for, as appears in the second verse following? Or was there not other as great sins as this amongst them? Yes, truly, there were other heinous sins amongst them, and which God abhors as well as this. They had gotten into their hands all the lands and goods of their poor brethren by usury; and not content with that, they had so handled the matter, that the poor sort had sold themselves, their wives and children, to be bondmen and slaves to the rich. And yet their usury was but little in comparison of ours, which we can more wisely and worldly, than wisely and godly, defend to be lawful. They took but one at the hundred; of a hundred shillings one, of a hundred pounds one; and yet Nehemias

Usury unlawful.

Nehem. v.

[¹ O cives, cives! quærenda pecunia primum est,
Virtus post nummos. Hor. Epist. i. i. 53-4. Ed.]

makes them to restore all again. But we can defend ten at the hundred to be charitable and godly. Surely, if they could not keep it, but were compelled to restore it again, it was theft and robbery so to get it, or yet to keep it: for he is as well a thief that keeps that which is evil got, as he that got it or took it. And if they did make restitution, taking but one at the hundred; I see no cause why our usurers should not be compelled by authority to restore that which was so gotten by ten or sixteen at the hundred. This was our gospelling in England, when we should have builded God's house, as they should have done here.

<small>All sin is forbidden alike, if it let God's house.</small>

The prophet speaks here of building houses namely[1], but under that one sin he rebukes all such like: as when we say, "give us our daily bread," we desire under the name of bread as well drink and cloth, as all other things necessary to live withal. And he saith as well to the drunkards,

<small>Drunkards.</small>

Is it time for you to drink until ye be thriftless and witless, and God's house lie unbuilded? It is written by the prophet,

<small>Isai. v.</small>

"Woe be to you that rise early in the morning to drink, and to follow drinking till it be evening!" He saith likewise to the dainty sluggard, that lies wallowing in his costly beds and soft pillows: Is it time for you to lie slovening in your couches night and day, and God's house unbuilded?

<small>Sluggards.</small>

Is it not written, "Woe be unto you which sleep in your costly beds, and play the wantons in your couches?" And he saith likewise to the greedy carle and prowling poller, that is never filled, but always heaping together: Is it time for you that ye scrape and scratch together all ye can lay your hands on, and God's house lie unbuilded? Do ye not know it to be written, "Woe be to you which join house to house, and land to land, and never cease?" Thus must every man think that God speaks to him still by this his prophet, and says to the ambitious prelate: Is it time for thee, which should chiefly build my house, to gape for promotion, to join benefice to benefice, prebend to deanery, &c., and my house lie unbuilt? Remember thou not Paul's saying, "If we have meat, drink, and clothes, let us be content therewith"? Thou that chiefly should further this work, dost hinder and pull down my house, as much as in thee is.

<small>Amos vi.</small>

<small>Pollers.</small>

<small>Isai. v.</small>

<small>Ambitious.</small>

<small>1 Tim. vi.</small>

[¹ See note, p. 34. Ed.]

Let the merchant, that spares not to sail through all jeopar- *Merchants.*
dies on the sea and travail by land, so that he get much
gains, think that God says to him still: " Is it time for thee
to run and ride, buy and sell, and my house lie unbuilt?"
Let the unthrift think that God speaks to him, saying: "Is *Unthrifts.*
it time for thee to hawk and hunt, card and dice, and
follow whores, and God's house lie unbuilt?" Think not it
is enough to say, I am a gentleman; what should I do but
take my pleasure? it becometh not me to take such pains.
Yes, truly; for God hath no more allowed thee to waste *God allows the rich nothing more to misuse than the poor.*
unthriftily thy goods, nor to misspend thy time, than the
poor man. For like as thou hast the same baptism, faith,
Lord, God, and Father in heaven with him, and hopest for *Ephes. iv.*
the same kingdom that the poor man doth; so hast thou
the same law given thee to live after, and by the same shall
we all be judged.

Why, will no excuse serve, but that every man must lay
his helping hand to the building of God's house? No, verily:
remember them which were called to the feast, and one excused himself, saying, "I have bought a farm;" another, "I *Luke xiv.*
have bought five yoke of oxen;" and both said, "I pray thee
hold me excused:" and the third had married a wife, making
no excuse, but flatly denying he could not come. But it skills
not whether he make excuse or not: all were shut out, and
had no part of the feast.

And so shall all that build not God's house, though they *No excuse is allowed in not building God's house.*
seem to themselves to have good excuses: God allows none at
all. Why, they were forbidden by the king to build any more,
as appears in Esdras, and must they not obey? they should *Ezra iv.*
have run in the king's displeasure, been in jeopardy to have
lost life, land, and goods: should they have been rebels and
traitors to the king? No, surely; this is not treason to kings
to do that which God commands. When Daniel did pray *Daniel vi.*
thrice a day to God contrary to the king's commandment,
and the apostles did preach contrary to the wills and com- *Acts iv.*
mandments of the rulers, it was neither treason nor rebellion.
So must we do always that which God commands: and if *God is rather to be obeyed than man.*
the rage of the rulers go so far as to kill or cast us into
lions' dens, as Daniel was, or whip and scourge us, as the
apostles were; we must suffer with Daniel, and say with the

apostles, "We must rather obey God in doing our duty, than man forbidding the same;" knowing always, that God hath ever ways enough to deliver us out of their dangers, if he will, as he did Daniel and the apostles; or else will strengthen us to die in his quarrel, whether soever shall be more for his glory and the edifying of his church. If the sheriff should bid thee one thing, and the king command thee another, wilt thou obey the lower officer afore the higher? So is the king God's under officer, and not to be obeyed before him.

<small>Luke xiv.</small> It is written, that "if any man come to Christ, and hate not father and mother, wife and children, brother and sister, yea, even his own life," rather than forsake and offend God, "he can be none of Christ's scholars." Christ takes all excuses <small>Matt. v.</small> from us when he saith: "If thy right eye let thee, pull it out; if thy hand offend thee, cut it off; for it is better to go into life with one eye and one hand, than to be cast into hell with both thine eyes and hands." In the ninth of Luke, when Christ called two disciples to follow him, the one said, "Let me go and bid them farewell at home;" and the other said, "Let me go and bury my father, and then I will come." But our Saviour Christ would suffer neither of them both to go to do so little things and honest, as reason would judge, but saith: "Let the dead bury the dead; and he that puts his hand to the plough and looks back, is not meet for the king- <small>Luke xvii.</small> dom of God." "Remember," he saith, "Lot's wife," how she for looking back was turned into a pillar of salt. Therefore there is no excuses admitted in not building God's house, and that earnestly.

<small>Princes may have houses to their degree, so they build God's house first.</small> Yet is not this so spoken of the prophet, that it is unlawful for noblemen to have costly houses, so it be not above their degree, nor built with oppressing the poor, or that they take not more pleasure and pains in building their own houses than God's; but that they should study and take more pains <small>2 Sam. vii.</small> to build God's house than their own. For David, Salomon, and other good kings, had gorgeous houses according to their estate: but when David had builded him a goodly house, he sat down, looked on it, and remembered how the ark of God, and the treasures that God had given them, were but in tents covered with sackcloth, made of goat's hair; he was sorry, <small>Psal. cxxxii.</small> sware an oath, and made a vow to the God of Jacob, that he

would not go into his house nor his bed, and that he would neither nap nor sleep, nor take rest, until he had a place for the Lord to dwell in, and builded his house. Such a desire have all good men to the building of God's house in all ages, that they will prefer God's matters and the common profit of many afore their own.

But here in this people, as among us also, the rich men would not, the poor could not; the priests had forgotten the law, and followed their own fantasies; the unlearned knew not how to do it; young men were given to pastimes, old men to greediness, noblemen greedily to get[1], and unprofitable to spend it; the common sort, as men without guides, followed their own wills: summer was too hot, and winter was too cold: so that no sort of men nor time was given to the building of God's house; but every man followed his own will, and either they could not, would not, or durst not go about the building of God's house. Thus we in England, while we have lien following our own fantasies, and seeking vain excuses under pretence of religion, have destroyed religion; and in pulling away superstition did seek our own profit and promotion. To pull down abbeys, colleges, chantries, and such dens of thieves, we are ready enough, because we hoped to have part of the spoil ourselves; but to maintain schools and hospitals was not for our profit: to take away masses, idols, unpreaching prelates, we durst not, sometime for fear of the king's displeasure, sometime for rebellion or insurrections of the commons; otherwhiles, to bear with the weakness of the people, or for loss of life or goods, or some such like excuse, we would not. *Vain excuses in not building God's house be not allowed.*

But Salomon, to pull away all fond, feigned excuses, teaches divers good lessons and worthy to be noted. To the sluggish fearful man, that feareth and casteth perils to do that which God commandeth him, he saith, mocking and rebuking him thus: "There is a lion in the way, saith the slothful man (when he is willed to do his duty), and he will worry me if I go:" which is as much to say, Cast no perils in serving God; go diligently about to do thy duty; and God will defend thee, though thou go through lions, wolves, bears, bishops, and all wild beasts: and that we should more *Fearful.* *Prov. xxii.*

[1 The first edition reads, *noblemen to ambition, and*— ED.]

boldly do our duties to God without fear of man, St John in his Revelation, xxi., saw: "The fearful, unbelievers, abominable, murderers, &c., shall have their part in the lake that burns with fire and brimstone, which is the second death." To the slothful delicate man, which will not forego his pleasures, he saith: "As the door is turned in and out upon the hinges and gins, so is the sluggard rolled about in his bed from one side to another:" as though he should say, As the door when it is opened or shut, it stirs in and out, but it stirs not out of his place, but is on the hinges still; and the sluggard that rolls himself from one side of the bed to another, is a sloven still, and lies slovening in his bed, taking no pains to do good: so they that be given to any kind of pleasure, if they stir to any thing, it is so little that it doeth no good; they roll but from one side to another, from one pleasure to another, to seek where they may find most ease. They move as the snail doth, always creeping and never the further. Unto them that seek excuses, that either they dare not or cannot, he saith: "He that watches the winds doth not sow, and he that marks the clouds shall never mow:" as if he should say, As he that waits for a good wind to sow in, or whether any clouds arise betokening rain, or there be none at all but great drought towards, that he may mow, shall never sow nor mow: for either blows the north wind, and that is too cold; or the south, and that is too hot; or the east, and that is too dry; or the west, and that is too wet; and the wind is ever in one of these corners, and ever is it drought or clouds like to rain when the wind is so: so he that waits when he may build God's house, and have the world with him without displeasure of the rulers, the people, the clergy, or the laity, shall never do his duty; for ever the gospel hath some enemies. Therefore he concludes, saying: "Sow thy seed in the morning and in the evening, and let not thine hand cease;" meaning, that evening and morning, early and late, fair weather and foul, with favour or with displeasure, we should not cease to build God's house. Do ye not know that God and the world are enemies; and he that will please the one shall displease the other; and impossible it is to please both? Never look to have the world to favour thee, when thou goest about to serve God: and if

Margin notes: Prov. xxvi. Slothful. / Worldlings. Eccles. xi. / Eccles. xi. / The gospel is never without enemies. / Matt. vi.

thou wilt seek the friendship of the world, thou shalt be an enemy to God. So saith St Paul to Timothy: "Preach the word, be earnest, reprove, rebuke in season and out of season;" spare no time, place, labour, nor person; lay it amongst them, tell them their duty, let it work as God will. Do thou thy duty, and as much as in thee lies; and let God alone with the rest. God requires nothing of thee but thy labour: the increase belongs to God alone to give as he thinks good. St Paul, comparing himself with the other apostles, saith, he "laboured more than any of the rest, and filled all places and countries with the gospel betwixt Jerusalem and Illyricum;" but he never tells how many he converted to the faith, for that is the work of God, and neither he which grafts, nor he which waters, is anything, but God which gives the increase. *James iv. 2 Tim. iv. 1 Cor. xv. Rom. xv. 1 Cor. iii.*

And although the scripture require that a preacher, which is a steward of God's house, must be ware as a serpent and simple as a dove, and the weakness of our brethren that have not learned their liberty, must be borne with for a time; yet are we not bidden always to do it, nor be so wise that to please man we displease God. When our Saviour Christ had taught that it was lawful to eat all kinds of meats, at all times, for all men, in all places, the Pharisees were angry with him, and his disciples told him of their anger; but he answered: "Let them alone; they be blind guides of the blind:" he passed not for the offending of them, for they might have learned the truth if they had lust. So must we bear with the weak until they be taught sufficiently: and if they will not learn, we must not lose our liberty for their foolishness, but answer them as Christ did. And as the faithful husband is not bound to the unfaithful wife, if she will not abide with him; so is not our liberty bound to the froward superstitious papists that will not learn. It is better to offend, says Gregory, than to forsake a truth: and Chrysostom[1] teaches, that when more commodity comes by offending than hurt, we must not care for the offence: but this commodity that he means is not worldly, *How far the weak is to be borne withal. Matt. xv. 1 Cor. vii.*

[1 Διὰ δὴ τοῦτο, ὅταν μὲν ἴδῃ πολὺ τὸ κέρδος καὶ τῆς τοῦ σκανδάλου βλάβης μεῖζον, καταφρονεῖ τῶν σκανδαλιζομένων. Contra eos qui subintroductas habent virgines. Tom. I. p. 284. Paris. 1834. ED.]

but godly, and bringing many to Christ. "I had rather never eat flesh," saith St Paul, "than offend my brother:" but that is spoken for the weak, that have not been sufficiently taught, and all doubts they can lay, taken away; but to the stubborn, sturdy, stiffnecked papists (which teach that some meats at some times are unclean and unholy for some men to eat, and so makes man to serve creatures in conscience, that he dare not handle that over which God made him lord) he never said so, but contrarily, "Let them alone; they be blind guides of the blind." Like is to be said in marriage of priests, handling their chalice, corporas[1], and such other burdens as they lay not only on the bodies, but miserably on the consciences, of them which will believe them. "Stand in the liberty to the which ye be called," saith St Paul, "and be not subject to such yokes and beggarly ceremonies:" let not such Cayphas tread you down; but keep your consciences in knowledge free to use freely all the good creatures of God made for your use, according to the scripture, with soberness and thanksgiving.

Thus all the people is chid here for their disobedience, that they built not God's house, although they were forbidden by the king, or could make like excuses. God sent them all home to do this work, and required it of them all; and yet they were all so far from doing it, that they let it lie, not only unbuilded, but waste, desert, never regarding it. There was work for all sorts of men, the costly pieces for the rich, the meaner for the common sort, and the felling of trees, carrying mortar, &c. for the poorest and simplest.

When Moses should make the tabernacle and tent, wherein they should resort to serve God until the temple was builded, the rich sort offered gold, silver, brass, iron, silk, and such like; but the poorest when they came and brought but goats' hair, it was thankfully taken, and did good service in that work; for the uppermost cloth, that covered the tent, was made thereof to keep away rain and storms. And to the younger sort, that they should not think themselves unmeet, saith St Paul, "Let no man despise thy youth;" and generally to every man he saith, "It is now time to rise out of sleep." Bring

[1 Corporas: the cloth on which the consecrated wafer was deposited. ED.]

so much to this building as you can; let no fault be found in you for lack of good will. God will take in good part the little ye can do. Let not the simplest think, I am unworthy to do such things, God needs not my labour, I am too vile to serve him; or it belongs not to me: for he only is worthy whom God makes worthy, and he only is welcome whom he will vouchsafe to take in good worth. Of ourselves the best man living is unworthy; and the more unworthy that thou thinkest thyself unfeignedly, the more worthy thou art afore him. Gedeon, when he was taken from threshing his corn, and made a captain to deliver God's people, said: "Who am I, the youngest and least of all my brethren, or what is my father's house, that his stock afore all the rest should be taken to this honour?" So said Saul also, taken from the plough following his oxen, and made a king: and as long as he continued in this lowliness of mind, and did his duty, he was a good king. So Amos keeping beasts, an herdman, and pulling mulberries off the trees, when he was called to be a prophet, wondered that God would call such a simple man as he was to that high office. So the Virgin Mary, when the angel saluted her, wondered that God would call such a poor maiden and virgin to be the mother of his Son. But ever he that thinks himself unworthy, God takes him as worthy; and those that think so highly of themselves that they be worthy, God refuses, and makes unworthy. Therefore let every man that feels himself in conscience withdrawn from doing his duty to God by any kind of sin, say thus to himself: Is it time for thee to delight thyself in this or that kind of sin, and God's house unbuilt? Think that God hath left this in writing to rebuke him, and stir him up to be more diligent in repairing his house wherein God dwells. And let every man comfort himself that God not only requires, but takes in good part, the least service that the poorest man living can do.

And as he said afore in the second verse, "This people saith, It is not time to build," &c., noting the unkindness of that people, to whom he had so often and long been so loving a lord and master; so he saith now, "This house lies waste," to set out before them the greatness of their disobedience; that they did not neglect and leave unbuilt a common house,

[margin: He that thinks lowliest of himself is meetest afore God to build. Judges vi. 1 Sam. ix. Amos vii. Luke i. Every man think this to be spoken to himself. The worthiness of the place maketh the fault greater being neglected.]

a bishop's palace, or an abbey; but that house wherein God himself said he would dwell, where only they should offer their sacrifices, which only not out of the whole world, but among the places, towns, and cities in all Jewry, he chose by name to be worshipped in; in which only he was most delighted, and made promise to Salomon in the dedication of the same, that he would hear the prayers of them that there called upon him in faith. That house, they did not only suffer it to decay, but were so forgetful of it that they let it lie waste, desolate, laid no hand to it, as though it belonged not to them, nor it were their duty; they had so far forgotten God, which willed them so straitly to do it. The Lord for his mercy sake grant, that the same unkindness may not be laid justly against us, which leave that house unbuilt, yea, tread under our feet like filthy swine, wherein not the sacrifices of Moses are offered, but for the salvation of which Christ offered his body a sacrifice to be killed, and his blood shed, and in which his Holy Spirit dwells, if through unthankfulness we drive him not away. This house is the holy church of Christ generally, and our own bodies and souls particularly, which be not only members and parts of his mystical body, but the temple and house where the Holy Ghost dwells, and wherein he will chiefly be worshipped.

v. 5. And now thus saith the Lord of hosts: Consider in your hearts your own ways.

6. You have sown much, and brought in but little; ye have eaten, and not been satisfied; ye have drunk, and not been filled with drink; ye have been clothed, and not kept warm; ye have wrought for wage, and put your wages in a purse with a hole in the bottom.

Although ye have lien long without consideration of your duty toward God and his house building; and have been sore punished of God, and not known the cause of it; and have sought your pleasure and profit, but not obtained them, being so blinded in fulfilling your worldly lusts; yet now the mighty Lord of hosts and power, whom all other creatures (except you) obey, gives you warning now to consider better in your heart your time past, and not so negligently weigh the working of God with you; for he hath long punished you to have had you to amend, and ye regard it not at all. Sin of itself is darkness, and whosoever walks in sin walks in darkness, and knows not what he doeth: and if a man give himself to be ruled by sin, it makes of fools madmen, and darkens so the reason, that it knows not what to do or say. They had thus many years been plagued, and knew not the cause why, but laid it on some other chance than not building God's house, which was the chief cause; or else, like insensible beasts without the fear of God, regarded it not, as though it had come of some natural cause, and God had not plagued their sin. But as his disease is most perilous, which lies sick and feels not his sickness, nor cannot complain of one part more than another, (for then the disease hath equally troubled the whole body;) so they which lie wallowing in sin, so forgetting God and all goodness, that they feel no remorse of conscience, are desperate and almost past all recovery: yet God, most mercifully dealing with this people, sends his prophet to warn them, and stir them out of their sleep, that there they should no longer so lightly weigh God's displeasure towards them, but deeply weigh why and wherefore these plagues were thus poured upon them. The schoolmaster corrects not his scholar, nor the father his child, but for some fault, and for their amendment: no more hath God sent these plagues to you so many years, but to remember you of your disobedience towards him, and that ye should turn to him. But if the lewd scholar or unthrifty son do not regard the correction laid upon him, nor consider not the greatness of his fault, nor the displeasure of his father or schoolmaster, there is no goodness to be hoped for of him: so is it with you, if ye thus lightly or else not at all consider your life past, God's dealing with you, and how evil things have prospered with you all the time ye thus have disobeyed God. "When the life of man pleases God," says Salomon, "all things prosper and go forwards with him:" but when he offends his God, all creatures turn to his hurt and hinderance. "If thou hear the voice of the Lord thy God," saith Moses, "and keep all the commandments which I teach thee, the Lord will make thee greater than all other people: thou shalt be blessed in the city and in the field; thy children, the fruit

marginal notes: 1 John ii. Sin maketh us without feeling of God and his plagues. — Prov. xvi. [7.] — Deut. xxviii.

of the earth, and all thy cattle, thy sheep and oxen shall be blessed, and increase: but if thou hear not the voice of the Lord thy God, and keep his commandments, thou shalt be cursed in the town and in the field; thy children shall be cursed, and the fruit of the earth, and the fruit of thy cattle, thy sheep and thy oxen: the Lord will send upon thee need and trouble and destruction on every thing thou goest about, until he destroy thee," &c. These plagues, when they fall in any country, are not lightly to be considered.

<small>The cause of God's plague is diligently to be searched.</small>

But as the physician, seeing in a glass by the water the disease within the body, by the learning searches out the cause of the disease, and ministers good things for the same; so in looking in the glass of God's word, the diseases and sins which are in commonwealths, we shall soon perceive the cause of these plagues, and wholesomely minister some profitable and comfortable remedies for the same. God is here so good to his people, that he makes them judges themselves, and mistrusts not the cause but, if they would consider it well, it would move their hard hearts: therefore he sends them not to any strange judges, but bids them be judges themselves, weigh it well first, and then judge; for the thing of itself is so plain that, if they had not altogether been blind, they should in the midst of these plagues have perceived God's anger and their own wickedness, neither of which they had yet worthily considered. "Ye have sown much," saith the prophet, "and brought into your barns but little:" ye have wrought and toiled, ye have spared no labour, thinking to have enriched yourselves thereby and filled your barns: but all was in vain, for ye sought not first to be reconciled with God, which ye ought to have done, and fulfilled his will and not your own.

<small>Psal. xxiv.</small>

"The earth is the Lord's, and all the plenty on it;" and it obeys the will of God in serving him, and giving her fruits to them that love the Lord their God, and not to them which disobey God, that made and rules both man and the whole earth. Let the greedy carle think then, that though he be the owner of the land and field by man's law, yet he is not the lord and master over him whom the earth will obey in bringing forth her fruit. Let him dig, ditch, and delve, weed, stone, harrow, plough, sow, mow, clot and roll, root up trees and bushes, water, hedge, and water-furrow, or what other

<small>Our labour is in vain except God bless us.</small>

thing soever he can devise to make the ground fruitful: yet there can no fruit grow, nor increase come, but by the gift and blessing of the living Lord. It is written of king Kaun- *Kauntus.* tus[1], king of this realm, that as he was standing by the water side after a great rain, marking how the water did rise, by leisure so it increased that it met his foot where he stood: and he being so proud in his heart, that he thought whatsoever he said every thing would obey, straight commanded the water that it should rise no further, nor wet his master's feet any more: but when he saw that the water rose still, and would not obey him, but ran into his shoes, he perceived his foolishness, and confessed there was another God and king above him, whom the waters would obey: so shall all greedy churls well perceive, when they have wrought themselves weary, and gotten little, that all increase comes from the Lord, and not of themselves. For David saith, that pro- *Psal. lxxv.* motion comes neither from the east nor the west, but the Lord is judge. It is not the way to wax rich, to get much, but to get it rightly; "for it is better," saith David, " to *Psal. xxxvii.* have a little righteously gotten, than to have the great riches of sinners:" nor it is not the way to be filled, to gather much together, but thankfully to take and use that little which thou hast, and be content therewith.

These rich gluttons, which the prophet rebukes here, did eat and drink so well, so costly, so finely, and so much as they could devise; and yet they were never full, but the more they drank, the dryer they were, and one good feast provoked another, and their study was how to fill their greedy stomachs. A drunken man is always dry, according to the proverb; and a gluttonous appetite is never filled, but the more daintily he is fed at one meal, the more desirous is he at the next. All greedy affections of man's heart are *No desires can be ruled* unsatiable, if they be not bridled with the fear of God. And *but by grace and keeping* the way to rule them is not to follow their lusts and de- *it under.* sires, but to keep them under and not let them have their full desire. The dropsy desires drink, and drink increases it: so evil desires if they be followed, they increase, and in refraining them they decay. *Crescit amor nummi, quantum* *Ovidius.* *ipsa pecunia crescit:* that is to say, "as thy money increases,

[[1] Kauntus: Canute. ED.]

so does the love of it." Therefore, if thou wilt have thy meat to do thee good, and thy drink to slake thy thirst, take it soberly with thanksgiving at God's hand; acknowledge it to be the good creature of God, given to nourish thy necessity, and not to fill thy beastly appetite. So St Paul saith, "Whether ye eat or drink, or whatsoever ye do, do all to the glory of God:" as though he should appoint how much a man should eat and drink; that is to say, so much that the mind be not made sluggish by cramming in meat, or pouring in drink, that it cannot lift up himself to the praising of God.

1 Cor. x.

Eat not so that it make thee unlusty to serve God.

Therefore he that eateth until his belly ache, or that he lie down to sleep that he cannot praise God, which hath fed him; or he that drinks till his eyes water or his tongue begin to swerve, swear, stut or prate, he doeth it not to the glory of God, which is his duty, nor to the nourishing of his weak body, which is lawful and necessary: but he kindles such an unnatural heat in his body, that it stirs up his appetite to desire more than it should, and is not content with enough, (and that be called here not to be filled nor satisfied in eating and drinking;) or else it overcomes the stomach, and is undigested, and fills the body full of sluggishness, makes it unlusty and unmeet to serve God or man, not nourishing the body but hurting it, and last of all casts him into many kinds of incurable diseases and desperate deaths. Look the end of the rich glutton in the gospel, feasting every day with his brethren, and at length cast into hell fire without hope; but the poor beggar Lazarus, that was content to gather up the crumbs (if he might have had them) which fell from the glutton's table, was carried up by angels to the bosom of Abraham to joy without end. Daniel taken prisoner to Babel, being but a boy, and having a fine diet and costly meats appointed for him by Nabuchodonozor the king from his own table, because he was born of the king's stock, desired his tutor to give him coarse meat, brown bread, pottage and water: but when his tutor said he durst not, because the king had given contrary commandment; and if he through eating such coarse meat should not be so well-liking as his fellows, then the king would be angry with him: "Well," said Daniel, "prove me but ten days, and if I look

Luke xvi.

A thin diet with the fear of God is better than feasting.
Dan. i.

not so well and lusty as my fellows, then I will desire no more:" but God blessed him and his meat, so that he was so well fed as they which had all dainties, as lusty, as healthful and well-liking as his fellows. For except God bless thy meat and give it strength to feed thee; and except God strengthen thy nature to digest thy meat, and thee to take profit of it; either it shall lie wallowing in thy stomach, and thou shalt vomit it up again, or else it shall lie within thy body unprofitable, stinking as in a sink or kennel, and engender infinite diseases within thee. But if God bless thee and thy meat, though it be never so coarse and thou so hungry, thou shalt digest it, and it shall feed thee, and make thee as lusty, as strong, as healthful, as well liking, as he which is fed with capon, partridge, quail, pheasant, or the finest dishes he can devise. And as God here by this prophet willeth them to consider well in their own hearts whether these things were true indeed; so God bids us now look ourselves, and judge whether it be not so amongst us to this day. *[If God bless thee and thy meat, it skills not how coarse it be: if not, the best cannot feed thee.]*

Look how many of your poor neighbours eat brown bread, drink thin drink, have little flesh, live with milk, butter and cheese, lie on the straw without mattress or feather-bed; and judge yourselves whether they be not more lusty, strong, healthful, and well-liking than thou, when thou art crammed full of all dainties which thou can invent or desire. Thus we may see what it is to eat and drink, and not be filled therewith, as the prophet saith in this place.

We wonder much at the great miracles of God, when he changed water into blood and plagued Egypt, when he turned water into wine at the wedding in Cana of Galilee, and such other, because they were done but seldom. But surely to feed our bodies with meat is as great a miracle, if it be well considered, as any other such thing that God works. What is more marvellous, than to see the flesh of the sheep or ox, beast, fish or fowl, which thou did see yesterday running in the fields, flying in the air, or swimming in the water, this day to be changed into thy flesh and blood, and the substance of thy body? We are not nourished only with accidents and qualities of things, as smells and tastings; but with the substance of that thing which we eat and drink. Nourishing is defined of the physicians to be a changing of *[Exod. vii. John ii. To feed our bodies is as great a miracle as any. Nourishing.]*

the nourishment into the substance of the body which is nourished. All the works of God, if they be well considered in their own nature, are miracles and above all reason: but our dull blindness is so great, that because we see them daily, we regard them not; and because we be cloyed with them, and plenty is no dainty, we consider them not worthily. But surely, if we had these great miracles of God afore our eyes, as we ought to have, how by his mighty power he changes the substance of that which we eat and drink into the substance of our flesh and blood; we should eat and drink with more reverence than we do, more diligently thank him that he would vouchsafe to feed us, and wonder at his mighty power that he can, and praise his merciful goodness that he will, work such a miracle so oft, and so wonderful a work upon such vile worms, greedy gluttons, and unthankful creatures as we be, and sustain our sinful nature by feeding us so marvellously, and changing the good nature of his other creatures, which never sinned, and yet are killed for us to feed us; changing them, I say, into the substance of our bodies, which can do nothing of themselves but sin. Elias, fleeing from Jezabel, found a therfe[1] cake baked in the ashes, and a dish full of water at his head, when he waked out of sleep, and was commanded by the angel to rise and eat, for he had a long journey to go. And when he had eaten, he walked in the strength of that bread forty days and forty nights, eating nothing else. So shall all they which fear the Lord, as Elias did, in their persecution be able and strong to do great things by slender meat and drink (as we this day have proved), God blessing them and their meat, be it never so coarse and simple: and they that seek to strengthen themselves by dainty meats, forgetting God, shall not be filled in eating and drinking, nor have profit of that which they receive; but the more they have the more they shall desire, and never think they have enough, as the prophet here saith.

The commonness of God's works makes them to seem no miracles, which of themselves be wonderful.

1 Kings xix.

Sin reigning in a man will let nothing that he hath do him good.

Such is the stinking nature of sin, that while it lies lurking in the heart of man, ruling him, and not ruled of him by grace, but stirring him to a further forgetting of God

[[1] Old editions *therse*. *Therf* is the word used by Wickliffe and others for *unleavened*. ED.]

and his duty; that it will not let the corn grow in the field and increase, it will not suffer the meat and drink to feed thee, but it shall go through thee unprofitably as through a sink (which as it avoids one filth, is ready gaping to receive more); it doth not quench, but rather increase thy appetite. God will not bless any thing thou goest about; thy clothes will not keep thee warm, nor thy money will abide in thy purse, but shall waste away, thou not weeting how nor when, as if there were a hole in the bottom. To a good man every thing shall serve and prosper; but to an evil man nothing shall do good. What a wonderful thing is this, that the more a man eats and drinks, the more he shall desire and not be filled; the more clothes he putteth on, the colder he is; yea, if he have never so warm a fire nor soft feather bed, he shall be more grieved with cold, than they which fare coarsely, be homely apparelled, and lie hard! Let every man judge how true this saying of God is. These fine fingered rufflers with their sables about their necks, their fine furred gowns, corked slippers, trimmed buskins, and warm mittens, they chill for cold and tremble when they come abroad; they cannot abide the wind to blow on them; yea, and always the more tenderly they keep themselves, hurting or not helping the poor, by the just punishment of God the more are they pierced with cold themselves: contrariwise, the labouring man can abide in the field all the long day, when the north wind blows, with few clothes on him, and never grieved with cold: he hath his health, feeds savourly on brown bread, thin drink, and a poor supper: yea, many poor beggars run from door to door with few clothes on them and torn, dining with a piece of bread under a hedge when they can get it, and at night lapping themselves in a little straw, not once in a week filling their bellies; yet they look more lusty, healthful, strong, than thou which hast thy cieled chamber, furred stomacher, long gown, and good cheer. And what can be the cause of this, but that God blessed the one which is content with his poor kind of life, and thanks God for it, thinking it better than he is worthy; and the other, which thinks so highly of himself, that nothing is good enough for him, taking no care but how to cherish himself most tenderly, God doth not bless

<small>Costly apparel, and above their degrees.</small>

him, nor those things on which his pleasure is set? The Israelites in wilderness desiring flesh had quails great plenty given them; but when the meat was in their mouths, the plague fell on them: and after repenting, they were so blessed of God, that their shoes and clothes lasted them forty years; and those clothes which the fathers had worn, the children were content to use afterward. But these tender pernels[1] must have one gown for the day, another for the night; one long, another short; one for winter, another for summer; one furred through, another but faced; one for the work day, another for the holy day; one of this colour, and another of that; one of cloth, another of silk or damask; change of apparel, one afore dinner, another after, one of Spanish fashion, another Turkey; and to be brief, never content with enough, but always devising new fashions and strange: yea, a ruffian will have more in a ruff and his hose than he should spend in a year. I read of a painter that would paint every country man in his accustomed apparel, the Dutch, the Spaniard, the Italian, the Frenchman; but when he came to the Englishman, he painted him naked, and gave him clothe, and bad him make it himself, for he changed his fashion so often, that he knew not how to make it: such be our fickle and unstable heads, ever devising and desiring new toys.

But what? would ye have all apparel alike? There be divers degrees of authority, and so better apparel for them. I do not wish all alike, but every one according to his degree. Give a king cloth of gold and silver, a duke velvet and silk, a marquis satin and damask; then an earl, a lord, a baron, a knight, an esquire, a gentleman, a yeoman, according to their degrees; and see whether those shall not be compelled to go in a russet coat, which now spend as much on apparel for him and his wife, as his father would have kept a good house with.

God grant every one might be brought to his degree! Our Saviour Christ bad his disciples, they should not have two coats: but we, because we will be most unlike his scholars, have our presses so full of apparel, that many know

[1 Pernels: pimpernel, a flower that always "shuts up its blossoms before rain." ED.]

not how many sorts and change of raiment they have. We are in the number of those rich men, to whom St James saith, "Woe," because they had so great plenty of apparel, that the moths did eat them, and their poor neighbours went cold and naked, wanting them. [James v.]

And although those be wonderful and strange kinds of plagues that God laid upon them for their sins, that neither the corn nor the fruit of the earth could increase, their meat would not feed them, nor drink fill them, nor their clothes keep them warm; yet this is most marvellous, that the money which they had in their purses, would not abide with them, but wasted away, they could not tell how, not profiting them, but even as though it had fallen out at the bottom of their purses, or that their purses had been torn so fast, it went from them as they gat it, they did not thrive by it. But such is the wisdom of God, that which way we think to enrich ourselves, displeasing him, the same is turned to our own hurt, and we be catched in our own snares. A man would think his money sure enough when it were in his purse: but lay it where thou wilt, under lock and key, yea, in stone houses if thou wilt; if it be wrongfully gotten, or niggardly laid up, and not bestowed to relieve the need of other, as occasion requires, rather than thou shalt enjoy that wicked mammon, the rust and canker shall eat it, thieves shall steal it, or fire shall come from heaven, if it cannot some other ways, and destroy thee and it, rather than thou shalt continue wealthy contrary to God's will, disobeying him. It is with money as in corn and other fruits: for as he that sows much, and that in good ground, reaps much, so he that liberally bestows much of his truly gotten goods on the needy members of Jesus Christ, shall be enriched much of Christ: for the poor are the good ground that brings thee forth much increase by the blessing of God. "I have seen," saith Salomon, "some give their own goods, and they waxed richer: other scrape that which is not their own, and are ever in need." So he that will thrive, must first get it righteously, and after spend it liberally: for that which is evil gotten, though it be after dealt in alms, displeases God. When blind father Toby heard a kid blea in his house, he bids them take heed that it be not stolen. He saith also to his [Evil gotten goods never thrive.] [Prov. xi.]

<small>Tob. ii.</small>
<small>Tob. iv.</small>

son: "Of thine own substance give alms" (but that which is evil gotten, is not thine own), "and if thou have much, give much; and if thou have but a little, yet give it willingly." These men whom the prophet here rebukes, did none of all these things: for neither it was well gotten, nor liberally spent. What marvel was it then, though it fell out of the purse bottom, and consumed away they wist not how, nor yet did them any good?

This greediness was so far grown into all sorts of men, that the poor labouring man, which wrought for his day's wage, was not content to work a true day's work, but would loiter and be idle, make his work subtle and full of craft and deceit, have a greater wage than his work was worth.

<small>Jer. vi.</small>

It was true now also, that Jeremy complained on in his time, saying: "From the highest to the lowest, from the prophet to the priest, all study for covetousness and deceits."

<small>Evil gotten goods waste that which is truly come by.</small>

But I would wish all such greedy guts to mark this similitude of Chrysostom, where he compares a penny evil gotten, and laid amongst the other silver which is truly come by, to a worm that lies at the heart of an apple. For as she first corrupts the heart of the apple, and that once being rotten, it rots the next piece unto him, and so forth every piece that which is next unto him, until the whole apple be rotten (though for a great space it seem on the outside to be a fair hard apple and sound); so that evil gotten penny, saith Chrysostom, shall infect that which lies next him, and so forth every one his fellow, until all be wasted. Thus the plague being general, that all sorts of men were punished, and nothing did go forward with any kind of men, because generally all sorts had sinned; and God requiring generally of all sorts that his house should be built; it proves that every one had a portion to do in the building of God's house, and that none could be excused from this work.

So we in England all be guilty, all have been punished, because every sort of men should have laid his helping hand to the building of God's house, reforming his religion, restoring and maintaining his gospel, which none or very few have earnestly done: and therefore all these plagues have fallen upon us that these people felt, yea, and more too; for all that would hold fast their profession, either were cast into the fire or banished. No country has more belly cheer than we, and we eat as though we were hungry still. None has more store of apparel, and yet we be a-cold. How our money has wasted, if I seek but only of the sundry falls of money, many can remember, and yet feel the smart of it; though I trust much good shall follow on it. The Lord for his mercy open our eyes, that we may see and consider the cause of these plagues which he hath laid on us so long, and speedily turn us to amend those faults for which we be punished! For even from the highest unto the poor labouring man we have all sinned, and one plagued another: yea, servants have sought to wax wealthy by great wages taking and little working: but, as this prophet saith, their wages was put into a bottomless purse, and they have not thriven by it. What hath been the end of ambitious and covetous men, from the highest to the lowest, which never being content with enough desired more; he which is not blind may see it more among us than all Christendom.

v. 7. *Thus saith the God of hosts: consider in your hearts your own ways.* The Text.

8. *Go up to the hill, and bring home timber, build this house; and I will have delight in it, and I will be glorified, saith the Lord.* Targ. dwell in it with glory.

The prophet hath never done enough in beating[1] in the authority and majesty of his God that sent him with his commission to his people, and never speaks things in his own name; but in the beginning and ending of these short verses addeth the glorious name of God JEHOVA, calling him the Lord of hosts, at whose commandment all creatures be, and who will arm all his creatures to fight against all such as either do not build his house and hinder his glory, or else stop them which would further it. With such words of fear and power must all stubborn stomachs be pulled down: and they which will not be overcome by gentleness to do their duty, must be feared with authority. Thus must preachers An example for preachers. learn to temper their tongues, never to speak but that which they find in God's book: and where the people be hard-

[[1] Second edition, *bearing*. See p. 84, *repeat and beat in.* ED.]

hearted to believe and stiff-necked to hear, they must use such words of God's majesty and power, which will make stony hearts to tremble; and where fear reigns, there to comfort and raise them up by the gentle loving mercies of God offered to the world in his Son Jesus Christ our Lord. And yet once again he refers them to their own judgment, and bids them consider in their own hearts their own ways, and be judges themselves. As if he should say: Hitherto have ye followed your own desires, and have had no profit in so doing; but being sundry wise plagued ye have not considered it. Nothing that ye have gone about hath prospered with you: your fruit of the earth hath not increased; your meat and drink hath not fed you; your clothes hath not kept you warm; your money wasted in your purse, ye could not tell how. But now build my house, and mark your own doings well, whether every thing shall not be blessed and increased that ye go about. I will be delighted in your building, and I will shew my glory to the whole world among you, in defending you, and that my house and worship there. I will be your God, and ye shall be my people, and no enemies shall overcome you: the earth shall be fruitful unto you; your meat, drink, clothes and money shall feed and nourish you. Choose you whether ye will let my house lie unbuilded still, and still be plagued; or ye will repair it diligently, and be blessed.

"Go up to the hill, bring home timber, and build this house:" these three things God requires of them, and he promises them two blessings for them; first, that he will be delighted in that house building, then that he will shew his glory amongst them. For these causes, rather than for worldly profit, they should be more earnestly stirred to do their duty, when they were certain that they pleased God in so doing.

Ezra iii. The hill that he wills them to go to is Libanus, as appears in Esdras[1], which is not within the bounds of Jewry, but of Tyrus and Sidon: for there grew the fairest trees of any
1 Kings v. country. From thence had Salomon trees in his time also for the same building. This figure doth teach us, that as

[[1] Esdras: Ezra. It is here and elsewhere quoted by the author as the 1st book of Esdras, according to the practice then in use of calling the book of Nehemiah the second book of Esdras or Ezra. See the 6th Article of our Church. ED.]

God's temple was then builded of trees that grew amongst the heathen people; so when the full time was comen, Christ's church should be builded of the Gentiles and heathen people, when the gospel should be preached through all the world. And this is comfortable for us, that although we be not born of Jews, yet we be trees meet to build God's house on; and God wills us to be brought home to him by the preaching of his word, that we may be partakers of that house, wherein he will dwell, and be delighted in us, and among whom he will shew his glory. He bids them climb up the hill, draw home trees, and build the house; which all be words of great labour and pains, and speaks nothing of the easier sort of work, as devising, casting the work, framing the posts, &c., but wills them not to refuse the greatest labour that belongs thereto, and that nothing should be thought painful that God commands. And he bids them not look for any great worldly wealth when they had done, (although God of his goodness would give them that beside;) but think this a sufficient reward, that God was pleased in their doings, and would shew his glory among them. *[The heathen be called to be members of Christ's church.]* *[The painful labour must be borne without respect.]*

This is the greatest reward that we can look for, when God is delighted with us: and happy is that people to whom it falls. What have the angels in heaven more, than that God is delighted to be among them, and shew his glorious majesty to them? Thus in building God's house we may make of earth heaven, and of men angels. For where God shews himself glorious, there is heaven: and we shall be like angels, delighting ourselves in praising our God; and God will be delighted and dwell with us, shewing his glorious majesty to us, be our God and bless us.

When they had fallen these trees and carried them home, lest they should turn them to their own use, and build their own houses with them, he saith, "Build this house," meaning the house of God and temple which God had chosen among all other places, and where only he willed them to offer their sacrifices. In which we are taught, that we should not turn to our own pleasure those things which God will have dedicate to himself and to the building of his house. If England had not been so greedy to turn to their own use church goods, which should have necessarily been bestowed *[Necessary church goods are not to be taken away.]*

to the building of God's house, we should not have felt God's rod so sharply, but God would have been pleased, and shewed his glory among us.

But when men would not give lands fast enough to abbeys, then the pope, rather than his chaplains should want, would rob many parishes to feed his monks. God grant that the gospel may restore that justly, which the pope took wrongfully away, and gave them yet a right name of impropriations, because improperly they be taken away, and properly belong to the parishes. The workman is worthy his hire: he that serves the gospel, must live of the gospel. Therefore those impropriations, which take away the preacher's living, be against the word of God.

But what, doth this belong to us or our time? doth God require of us to build him abbeys, nunneries, chantries, &c.? No, surely; but this was an outward exercise for that gross, hard-hearted people for a time to be exercised in, that they should not build temples to idols; and teacheth us to build God's spiritual house, wherein we may offer spiritual sacrifices and prayers to him, wherein he is well delighted and will shew his majesty. This house is now for us to be understood generally the whole church and company of Christians, and the body and soul, the heart, mind, or conscience of all Christians particularly, wherein God dwells by his holy Spirit, as St Paul saith to the Corinthians: "Do ye not know that your bodies be the temples of the Holy Ghost," and which he hath sanctified to be kept holy for himself alone by baptism, and for the which Christ hath died that we might live by him, whom he hath redeemed with his blood, and washed clean from all sin, that we should live no more to our own lusts and desires, but to him that hath redeemed us? It is written, that God dwells not in temples made with hands, nor is worshipped with any work of man's hands; but he is a Spirit, an invisible substance, and will be worshipped in spirit and truth; not in outward words only of the lips, but with the deep sighs and groanings of the heart, and the whole power of the mind, and earnest hearty calling on him in prayer by faith. And therefore he doth not so much require of us to build him a house of stone and timber; but hath willed us to pray in all places, and hath taken away that

Marginal notes: God's house generally is the whole church, or every particular person. — 1 Cor. vi. — Acts vii. — John iv. — 1 Tim. ii.

Jewish and popish holiness, which is thought to be more in one place than another. All the earth is the Lord's, and he is present in all places, hearing the petitions of them which call on him in faith. God is worshipped in spirit and all places.

Therefore those bishops, which think with their conjured water to make one place more holy than the rest, are no better than Jews, deceiving the people, and teaching that only to be holy which they have censed, crossed, oiled, and breathed upon. For as Christ said to the woman, thinking one place to be holier to pray in than another, "Woman, believe me, the time is come when ye shall worship neither at Jerusalem nor in this hill; but the true worshippers shall worship God in spirit and truth:" so is it now said, the place makes not the man holy, but the man makes the place holy; and ye shall not[1] worship your idols, stocks and stones, neither at Walsingham, Ipswich, Canterbury nor Sheen[2]; for God chooses not the people for the place sake, but the place for the people's sake. But if ye be in the midst of the field, God is as ready to hear your faithful prayers, as in any abbey or nunnery; yea, a thousand times more: for the one place he hates, as defiled with idolatry, and the other he loves as undefiled and clean. If the good man lie in prison, tied in chains, or at the stake to be burned for God's cause; that place is holy for the holiness of the man, and the presence of the Holy Ghost in him, as Tertullian saith. John iv.

2 Macc. v.

Yet there should be common places appointed for the people to assemble and come together in, to praise our God: for where the apostle rebuked them, which would not resort with the rest of the Christians to make their common prayers together, to hear his word and receive his sacraments; it proves they had some common place to resort to. And where St Paul requires that all things should be done in a comely order, what can be more comely or agreeing to good order, than to have a time appointed, and a place to resort unto together, to worship our only God? Nay, how shall they come together, except place and time be appointed? How shall they know when and whither to resort, unappointed? Common places of prayer are to be appointed. Heb. x.

1 Cor. xiv.

[¹ The first edition is followed: the second has *do worship*. ED.]
[² An old hamlet of Richmond, where was formerly a Carthusian convent. ED.]

How can the shepherd teach his sheep, if he have not a fold to gather them together in? In the apostles' time, when the rulers were not christened, they resorted into private houses and chambers, and by the waterside, to worship their God; but when princes became christened, they had churches appointed for them: yet all these prayers and preachings that were privily in parlours and by the waterside, were as pleasant to God (yea, better peradventure, for commonly they came of a greater and better love and faith) as ours be now. Those also which then were buried in no hallowed church nor churchyard, nor christian moulds, as they be called (when it is no better than other earth, but rather worse, for the conjuring that bishops use about it) were no worse than they which were buried with all solemnity. It appears in the gospel, by the legion living in graves, the widow's son going to burial, Christ buried without the city, &c., that then they buried not in hallowed churchyards by any bishops, but in a several place appointed for the same purpose without the city; which custom remains to this day in many godly places. As that then was lawful and no hurt to the dead, so is it now; and one place is as holy as another to be buried in, saving that comely order requires the bodies not to be cast away, because they were the temples of the Holy Ghost, and shall be glorified at the last day again, but seemly to be buried, and an honest place to be kept, several from beasts and unreverent using the same, for the same use. It is popish to believe that which the bishops do teach; that place to be more holy than the rest which they have hallowed, as they say, with washing it with their conjured water, crossings, censings, processions, &c., and that God will hear our prayers afore one idol or image rather than another, or in one abbey, as pleases them to appoint him, rather than another. Where it pleases them to grant many days of pardon, there God must hear their prayers sooner, and work more miracles: so God is become their servant, and shall be where they will appoint him. But blessed be that God our Lord, which by the light of his word doth confound all such wicked and fond fantasies, as they can devise to fill their bellies and maintain their authority.

Churches be God's school house, the preacher is a schoolmaster sent from God to teach us his word, we be his scholars, and thither must resort to learn our lessons and his holy will, to amend our lives, to make our prayers to him, desiring mercy for our wickedness past, and beg grace and strength for that which is to come; to thank him for all his goodness so mercifully poured upon us, to receive his sacraments, and profess our faith which we have in him. For these causes must we have churches as common places to resort unto, and use them with such comeliness as becomes men professing Christ, and not to bind any holiness to this church or that church, as though it lay in us to make holy or unholy when and what we lust: as St Mary's in Cambridge was holy enough to say mass in for three year space, and all that would not hear it must be prisoned, although Bucer was there buried; but when it pleased the Carnal's commissioners[1] to say it was not holy, because he lay buried there, then the heretic must be digged up and burned, or their masses were worth nothing: all other might lie still, and not hurt their masses, though they were of his opinion.

The house of God, now for us left to build, is sometime called in scripture generally the whole company of Christians, and sometime every particular man; as St Paul teaches Timothy how to live in the house of God, which is the church and congregation of God, the pillar and seat of truth. And to the Hebrews it is written, "You be the house of God:" particularly also it is said to every man, "Do ye not know that your bodies be the temple of the Holy Ghost? and he that defiles the temple of God, him will God destroy." Again: "Ye be the husbandry of God and the building of God." And St Peter saith, "Ye are built like lively stones for a spiritual house of God." This spiritual house must be diligently builded of us; and the building of this house of wood and stone among the Jews was a figure of this spiritual house building for our days. This is that which St Paul calls so often edifying or building one another; and that edification which he speaks so much of in all his epistles, that is as much to say as one to stir up another to virtue and godliness. For

God's house general: particular.

1 Tim. iii.

Heb. [iii. 6.]

1 Cor. vi.

[1 Cor. iii. 9.]
1 Peter ii.

Edifying.

[1 The commissioners sent down to Cambridge by Cardinal Pole, anno 1557, to purge it of heresy; by whose direction the bones of Bucer were dug up from St Mary's Church, and those of Phagius from St Michael's, and burned in the market-place.—For *Carnal* see note p. 77. ED.]

[PILKINGTON.]

as the building goes forward and increases by laying to one stone after another, and one post or tree after another, until the house be finished; so we, by going forward daily in the fear of God and godliness, shall at length be a meet house for God to dwell in. This house is the body and soul of man, which must be built with daily hearing God's word, prayer, mercy, and faith, with godly exercises; as St Paul saith, "Ye be citizens with saints, and of God's house, builded on the foundation of the apostles and the prophets." God, because he would have us always praying and calling on him for his help, hath so ordered the matter, that this earthly house of ours, wherein he dwells, should always be in building or repairing; and that we should not be idle, and think we had done our duty, but ever desiring him to help forward the building of this his house. If we overcome one evil affection, straightways rises another; and after one temptation cometh another; and the devil never ceases to throw down our house. David saith, "Except the Lord build the house, they labour but in vain which build it."

The spiritual house of God.

Eph. ii.

This house needs continual repairing and helps of all degrees.

Psal. cxxvii.

Let us do all we can therefore, and pray the Lord to further our work; the rulers with the sword defend the good and punish the evil; the preachers with the word, the schoolmasters by their teaching, the fathers by bringing up their children, the masters by correction of their servants, the people in obeying their heads and neighbourly love: and every one defend true religion to the uttermost of his power, drive away the pope and his baggage; and, as occasion requires, guide the ignorant, rebuke crooked stomachs, amend faults in the fear of the Lord, and bring into the right way all such as run astray, that they may be meet houses for God to dwell in. Thus hath every man a part in building God's house: but the greatest portion is left to every man, which is his own conscience, to amend that he finds amiss in himself, because every man knows himself best. Great faults only do appear unto the world, and by rulers must be punished: but the privy hid faults which every man knows in himself, for the most part (for no man knows all that be within himself) must be corrected within himself, by prayer, sighing, repentance, and asking forgiveness. David saith, "Who knoweth his own faults? Lord, cleanse me from my privy, hid, and

Psal. xix.

secret sins, and spare thy servant from other men's sins." Thus must every one himself severally, and jointly all together, climb up to the hills, that is, our lofty minds, and cut down the peevish desires of our hearts, though it be painful: and also correct the highminded, which are called often in the scripture hills; and cut down the high trees, growing on the tops of them: that is to say, to bring into good order the high men of the world, which should give good example for the people to follow, and to punish their faults, and rebuke them as well as the lower sort. They must neither for fear nor flattery leave them unpunished, nor say that is good which is evil afore God. For as God hath given one law for all men, high and low, to live after, and like a righteous judge will punish all that break it; so must all indifferently be punished here (if rulers and ministers do their duty) that break his laws. God hath given no more liberty to sin to the rich than to the poor, nor hath not willed the one to be punished and the other to escape; but generally and indifferently hath said to all, "That soul which sins it shall die:" and, "In judgment ye shall regard no person," but justly judge that which is just, neither condemn the poor because he is poor, nor deliver the rich because he is rich. So must the preacher tell every man his duty; spare neither high nor low; neither flatter the rich for rewards, nor fear the mighty for high looks or bitter words: for when he does his worst, he cannot hurt thy soul, but a little punish thy body.

All offenders must be corrected indifferently.

Ezek. xviii. Deut. i.

Exod. xxiii.

Matt. x.

These are hard hills to climb, and crooked trees to frame meet for any work: yet it must be done, and God requires this of every man's hand, to bring something to the building of his house, and according to his power.

And if we mark these words well, we shall see our own nature set afore us. For as trees growing on the top of hills have a rough bark, crooked knots, long boughs, and therefore unmeet for any building, until they be fallen, pilled, squared, drawn home; and can do nothing of all these themselves: so we, as long as we be wandering in the mountains and wild woods of this world, being highly minded and in great wealth or authority above others, as on an hill, we have froward proud minds, and not meet for God's house, until we be made lowly in our own sights, and fall flat down

We are like to trees.

at Christ's feet, and have the rough bark of our old Adam pulled off, and our crooked affections cut away, be mortified, and drawn home by the learning of his word and working of his Holy Spirit. For that which is high and set by amongst men is abominable afore God; and, as St Paul saith, "We are not able of ourselves as of ourselves to think a good thought;" much less then to cast away all this frowardness of our corrupt nature, until God bring us home, and make us meet for the building of his house, which he doth by preaching, as it is written: "How shall they hear without a preacher? for faith comes by hearing, and hearing comes by the word of God;" and our Saviour Christ saith by St John: "No man comes to me, except my Father draw him." As the scripture calls a good man the good tree that brings forth good fruit, and the evil man the evil tree with evil fruit; so the philosopher defines a man to be a tree with the root upward. For as a man receives at the mouth nourishment for the whole body, and has his head decked with hair; so the tree by the root draws nourishing to it, and decks his boughs with leaves: and as the head of man is upward, so is the root to the tree, though the unlearned believe it not. Many other things there be wherein they be like the one the other: but I will not stand to rehearse all.

2 Cor. iii.

Rom. x.

Joh. vi.

God grant us such preachers that we may hear, and so to hear that we may believe, and so to believe that we may bear good fruit, and be drawn home like good trees, all frowardness cut off, and we made meet for the building of God's house!

God is much delighted in the building of his house.

Now briefly to consider how God performed his promises, in being delighted in that house, and shewing them his glory; the whole history of the Machabees and other like do declare and tell the great glory which appeared in them. The king sent Heliodorus to bring him the treasure of the temple: but Onias the good high priest would not deliver it, but with his fellows stood still looking for help from God, in their priestly apparel, according to the law; and that God was delighted in their doing, trusting and calling on him, it appeared then: for he shewed his mighty glory in defending them that maintained his religion, not yielding to tyrants;

Heliodorus.

2 Mac. iii.

and punished Heliodorus for laying violent hands on the money, which was laid up there for the fatherless and widows. Likewise Alexander the Great, which conquered all countries about him, after he had gotten Tyrus and Sidon, sent to Jerusalem for a tribute, thinking it too small a thing, and not worthy the cost and labour to carry his host thither for the winning of it, and that they would yield unto him for a word: yet when the high priest, fearing God more than him, denied to be his subject and tributary, Alexander came with all his power, purposing to have destroyed all; but the priests meeting him in their priestly apparel, not to fight, but to see how God would defend his people, Alexander lighted off his horse, worshipped the high-priest[1], and confessed him to be the only God whose priest he was, and that in his country, afore he came forth, he saw a like vision bidding him do no wrong to such men: and afterwards he granted them great liberty, and did them no harm.

Alexander.

But most wonderfully this glory appeared, that where every man must go thrice a year to Jerusalem to worship and sacrifice, God promised and performed it, that he would defend their land until they came again. Their land was compassed round with their enemies; they left none at home but women and children; yet God was so well delighted in this their doing, that as long as they did it, they prospered, and no enemies durst invade their land, while they were worshipping God: but when they did it not, they were overcome, and lost their land. If all men in England should go thrice in the year to London, leaving none at home but women and children,

[1 Josephus's account states that he worshipped the name of God inscribed on the high priest's mitre:

Ὁ γὰρ Ἀλέξανδρος, ἔτι πόρρωθεν ἰδὼν τὸ μὲν πλῆθος ἐν ταῖς λευκαῖς ἐσθῆσι, τοὺς δὲ ἱερεῖς προεστῶτας ἐν ταῖς βυσσίναις αὐτῶν, τὸν δὲ ἀρχιερέα ἐν τῇ ὑακινθίνῃ καὶ διαχρύσῳ στολῇ, καὶ ἐπὶ τῆς κεφαλῆς ἔχοντα τὴν κίδαριν καὶ τὸ χρυσοῦν ἐπ᾽ αὐτῆς ἔλασμα, ᾧ τὸ τοῦ Θεοῦ ἐγέγραπτο ὄνομα, προσελθὼν μόνος προσεκύνησε τὸ ὄνομα, καὶ τὸν ἀρχιερέα πρῶτος ἠσπάσατο.   *   *   *   *

Then after the account of Alexander's dream the narrative proceeds:

Καὶ ἀνελθὼν ἐπὶ τὸ ἱερὸν θύει μὲν τῷ Θεῷ κατὰ τὴν τοῦ ἀρχιερέως ὑφήγησιν, αὐτὸν δὲ τὸν ἀρχιερέα καὶ τοὺς ἱερεῖς ἀξιοπρεπῶς ἐτίμησε.—Antiq. Jud. Lib. XI. cap. 8. ED.]

as they did to Jerusalem, and tarry there eight days (for so long continued their feast), we would think the Scots and all round about us would invade our country: but if we were as earnest in religion as they were, God would defend us as he did them, and no enemy should hurt us. When we kept religion, we won Bullen[1]: when we fell from it, we lost Calais.

But the great glory of all was shewed in this temple, and God declared himself to be well delighted in it, first when our Saviour Christ came and sat disputing with the doctors in it, healed the sick, preached the will of his Father, and drove out the buyers and sellers: after also, when the apostles did the like: and when the eunuch of queen Candace, moved with the glory of God and that temple, came so far off to worship there: which all and other like do declare sufficiently, what opinion of God's glory was there commonly judged to be. And how God is now delighted with our assemblies, when we come to pray unto him, and hear his word, Saint Paul teaches, saying, "If ye speak in a strange tongue, and an unlearned man come in amongst you, he will say ye are mad: but if ye expound that which is read, he is rebuked of all, and he will fall down, worship God, and say God is amongst you." Such an earnest defender of his glory is God, that he will give it to no other: and so loves he building of this his house, that if there be but two or three gathered in his name with fear and reverence of his majesty, seeking his glory and not their own, he will be amongst them.

How God hath been delighted in all ages in the building of this his spiritual house by the preaching of his gospel, the glorious deaths of all his holy martyrs from time to time do declare: but now lately in England, by the cruel persecution of the bloody bishops for the maintaining of their wealth, their idolatry, and their antichrist the pope, whose hangmen they were, we all have seen it, yea, and all good

Luke ii.

Acts viii.

1 Cor. xiv.

Matt. xviii.

[1 Bullen, i.e. Boulogne. It was ceded to the English in the year 1546, as a security for the money which the French king stipulated to pay to Henry VIII. in the treaty of peace then concluded. Calais was taken from the English in Mary's reign, in 1558, after having been in their possession two hundred years. The mortification occasioned by this loss is supposed to have hastened the Queen's death. ED.]

consciences hath abhorred their madness in burning the innocents, pulling up the dead, and have praised God for strengthening his poor creatures against all their mad rages and furious rebelling against God and man. The Almighty God grant us like grace, strength, and boldness, to offer our bodies to death without fear for the building of God's house, rather than to see it lie waste and trodden under feet! What greater comfort can any Christians have, than in giving their bodies to death for the building of this house, when he hears God say that he is delighted in their so doing, and that he will shew his glory in them? What greater promotion can a man come to, than to be one such instrument wherein God will be delighted and shew his glory? Death of the body is grievous to the flesh, but death of the soul is a thousand times more fearful to a good man: the one is a little painful for a time, the other hath grief without end. Therefore Christ saith, "Fear not them which kill the body, and cannot hurt the soul; but fear him which can cast both body and soul into hell-fire." Such an earnest love should we have to the building of God's house, both the hearers and teachers, both to build and be builded by all means possible, because he is so well delighted in it; that we should fear neither loss of goods, nor yet death of body, no, nor displeasure of man, so that we may please God, and have him delighted in our doings. To please man is but a small thing; but to please God is the greatest good thing that can be. "He that honours me," saith God, "I will glorify him;" and "he that confesseth me before men, I will confess him before my Father: and he that is ashamed of me, I will be ashamed of him; and he that denies me before men, I will deny him before my Father in heaven." *Most happiness is to have God delighted in us, though we suffer death for it.* *Matt. x.* *1 Sam. ii.* *Matt. x.*

v. 9. *Ye have looked for much, and behold it is but little; ye have brought it into the house, and I have blowen on it. And why so? saith the Lord of hosts: because this is my house which lieth waste, and ye run every one to his own house.* The Text.

The chiefest reasons to persuade an evil man to leave any wicked ways, be to set before him, and often to put him in remembrance, how God hath been angry with him, *The evil be rather moved with threatenings.*

when he did such things, and punished him as long as he lay in such forgetting of his Lord God; and also to threaten him with greater plagues, if he do continue in them still. Both these kinds of counsel doth the prophet here use, to stir them up to building of this house of God. He both sundry times calls to their remembrance the great plagues, which they suffered oft and long aforetime for not building God's house; and also bids them not think that all their sorrow was at an end, but more and greater scourges was hanging over their heads, if they would not build his house earnestly: and if they ceased not to sin, God would not cease to punish them; and if they continued still not regarding the building of his house, God would continue still increasing his curses on them. Ye have been greedy desiring much, saith the prophet; ye have scraped and scratched together all ye could lay your hands on; ye have spent your money and wrought yourselves weary, thinking to enrich yourselves by such means; but behold and mark it well, and it is come but to little.

Behold. Where the scripture uses to say, "Behold," there it tells some notable strange thing, as this is here; that their labour wasted away unprofitably, they could not tell how. That way whereby all other wax wealthy, hath done you no good; and those means which God uses to work by in other and bless them, in you it hath not gone forwards according to your expectation and looking for: yea, and that which is most marvellous, your corn and other fruits hath not only not increased in the field, but when it hath been brought into the barns, it hath consumed there, you could not tell how. A man would think his corn were sure enough when it is in the barn; (for whilst it is in the field, it is subject to many dangers, as blasting, mildews, frost-biting, thunder-beating, laid with a rain, or shaken with the wind, stolen or eaten with beasts, &c.), but even in your barns, *No strength can put away the plague of God.* saith God, I have blown on it. It is as easy for me (saith God) to waste it in the house, as in the field: for if I but blow on it, it is not able to stand in my sight. And as afore he said, their money fell out of the purse bottom, so now in their houses their fruits were not sure. No, lock it up in stone houses, if ye will; it is as easy for God to consume it there, as to blow a blast with his mouth: yea, nothing shall withstand him, whatsoever ye devise, but he will take it from you: ye shall not have your pleasure by displeasing God, nor anything shall prosper with you, until ye build him his house; that is to say, maintain his pure religion, defend his honour, forsake your vain pleasures, and refrain your greedy covetousness. The defending of true religion with a good and godly life is now the true building of God's house, now commanded unto us: and that man, city, or country, which doth not build this house so, hath and shall have the like plagues fall on them, until they earnestly build this house of the Lord's. For as a king is stablished in his kingdom, when his godly laws are taught and kept; and that realm is strongly builded and blessed of God, where good order is maintained: so is God's church and congregation well and surely builded, where God's word and religion is purely taught, sin punished, and virtue embraced. God can no more suffer his laws to be contemned or his honour given to idols, than kings can suffer their kingdoms to be betrayed to their enemies. For as in the whole history of the Jews' commonwealth, in the book of the Judges and the Kings, while the people lived in the fear of the Lord, kept his religion given them from God, they were defended by God from all enemies round about them, were they never so many and so strong; but when they would worship God, either as they lust themselves, or not at all, or else as he did not appoint them, then they were given into the hand of the Philistines, Ammonites, Chaldees, Egyptians, &c., sometime for the space of forty years, sometime eighteen, sometime seventy, and when they were least, three years: so shall all they that build not, or pull down God's true religion, and set up the pope's, taught by man and not of God, likewise be punished, or worse, either with hunger, pestilence, sword, or blind ignorance, not knowing God, and be given up to their own lusts, without remorse of conscience or any fear of God, which is the greatest plague that can be.

<small>God's house.</small>

<small>False religion is the common cause of plagues.</small>

Mark out of our own chronicles what was the estate of this our realm, when we were made tributaries to the Romans by Julius Cæsar, and so continued 400 years and more; or afterward, when the Saxons divided this realm into seven

<small>Romans.</small>

<small>Saxons.</small>

kingdoms, drove out all or most and best of the Englishmen, and ruled as long; or when William Conqueror subdued all to himself at his pleasure: and ye shall find that the same wickedness reigned then, that was now like to have made us slaves to the pope and strangers. The rulers were ambitious dissemblers, the bishops lordly and unpreaching prelates, the people covetous, God's word unknown, and in no degree of men was there any truth. Thus for our sinful disobeying of God, not defending his true religion, have we been given into the hands of all countries round about us; to the Romans and Normans from the south, to the Saxons from the east, to the Danes and Scots from the north: what danger was of late from the west[1], he that would not see should have felt, if God had not holpen in time.

<small>Normans.</small>

And lest they should think these plagues to be laid on them for some other causes, the prophet tells them in God's name here, what was the cause of all these sorrows, and should provoke also these other which follow to be poured on them, if they did not amend. "Because this my house," saith God, "lies waste," unbuilded, not regarded of you, "and ye run every one into his own house," seeking his own pleasure and profit. God will not suffer his honour to be given to any other, or any other (no, not ourselves) to be preferred before him. The lawyer in the gospel asking our Master Christ, which was the first and greatest commandment, when he heard this answer, "Thou shalt love the Lord thy God with all thy heart, with all thy mind, with all thy soul, and with all thy strength;" he did allow it, and said that was the chiefest indeed: and shall we christian men think other things to be preferred before God's will, or our own desires to be more loved and more earnestly fulfilled than God's? Nay, mark what great plagues fell on any country; and we shall see and find this to be true in all ages, that forgetting God's true religion hath pulled God's anger always most grievously upon the people. What causes the Jews at this day to be driven out of their country, their city and temple utterly destroyed, and they themselves abhorred of all men, but denying Christ to be their Saviour, and not receiving his gospel

<small>Matt. xxii.</small>

<small>False religion hath caused all countries to be plagued.</small>

[1 The allusion seems to be to the troubles in Ireland, excited at the beginning of Elizabeth's reign by O'Neil and his followers. ED.]

nor building his house? What causes most part of those people to whom St Paul wrote his epistles, which we have to this day, and many other countries too, among whom the other apostles preached, to be given up now into the Turks' and heathen's hands, but that they fell from their faith, which they first received by the apostles' preaching, and forsaked their christian religion? What caused those grievous plagues in Egypt, but that Pharao would not let the people worship God, as Moses sent from God did will him? What caused Nabuchodonozor of a mighty king to be made a vile beast, and eat hay as oxen do, but that he would not know God and his own wickedness, and set up idols, and killed them which would not worship them? What caused the children of Israel to have such wealth for the most part under David, Salomon, Josaphat, Ezechias, and Josias, which were good kings and restored religion; and other times to be plagued under Jeroboam, Athalia, Achab, Manasses, and other wicked kings, of whom it is so oft written, and of every king in Israel, that they walked in the way of Jeroboam, maintaining idolatry? Nothing surely, but the good kings defended God's true religion, set forth his word, builded his house, and God blessed them therefore: the other pulled it down, set up idols, persecuted his prophets, burned or hid up his scriptures and holy word, following their own fantasies and the teachings of the false prophets and preachers, and God plagued them therefore. *Exod. viii. ix. x.* *Dan. iv.*

And if ye mark the history of the pope and Mahomet, ye shall find that at the same time that the pope in the west part of the world began to get authority over kings and countries, to set abroad his superstition, and the people received it, forsaking God's religion, Mahomet then began in the east part to grow in authority, and conquer countries, and hath evermore so done since that time, because the people fell from true religion: and the more that countries have fallen to following of superstition and forsaking Christ, his word and religion, the stronger waxed the Turk and pope, as God's plagues to punish us, and be like to do every day more and more, until they be driven out of God's church, and Christ's word, religion, and sacraments, be restored to their simplicity, as Christ did ordain them. *Mahomet and the pope began their authority at one time.*

Gregory.

He that desires to be above all bishops is antichrist.

When Gregory[1], the first pope of that name, had denied John archbishop of Constantinople, striving with him afore the emperor Mauritius, that Constantinople should be the chief church, and that the bishop there should be the chiefest bishop, in authority above all other bishops, and said that whosoever desired that blasphemous name or authority, was the forerunner of antichrist; Phocas[2], the next emperor following, granted by much suit Boniface the Third, about the year of our Lord 607, that the bishop of Rome should be the chiefest bishop of all other; and therefore is he the blasphemous forerunner of antichrist, as Gregory said full well. It was a worthy grant of such a wicked emperor, to set up a bishop like himself. Phocas murdered his lord and master, Maurice the emperor, killed his wife and children in his own sight, and made himself emperor. Afterward he made Boniface the pope head bishop over all, and in Rome the chief. Thus our holy father gat his supremacy by a wicked emperor, and not from Peter, as he says; but one thief set up another. Peter, Acts iii. says, "Gold and silver I have none:" but the pope says, as the devil said to Christ when he tempted him, and shewed him all the kingdoms and riches of the earth, "All these are mine, and I give them to whom I lust; I will give thee them, if thou wilt fall down and worship me." So says the pope: but he lies, as his father the devil did.

The bishop of Rome is granted to be above all other bishops.

[John viii. 44.]

This thing once granted, the twelfth year of Heraclius, the next emperor after Phocas, Mahomet the great prophet

[1 Ego autem fidenter dico, quia quisquis se universalem sacerdotem vocat, vel vocari desiderat, in elatione sua antichristum præcurrit, quia superbiendo se ceteris præponit. Gregor. Registr. Epist. Lib. vii. Ind. xv. Ep. 33. ed. Bened. Paris. 1705.

Sed absit a cordibus christianis nomen istud blasphemiæ, in quo omnium sacerdotum honor adimitur, dum ab uno dementer arrogatur. Id. Lib. v. Ind. xiii. Ep. 20. Ed.]

[2 "Cujus rei causa factum est, ut cum ex more litteras ad eum Phocas imperator scriberet, in odium Cyriaci Constantinopolitani patriarchæ professus sit Romanum pontificem esse dicendum œcumenicum, nempe universalem, episcopum, Constantinopolitanum nequaquam: id quidem ipsum Bonifacium ab eo obtinuisse, Anastasius his verbis testatur. 'Hic,' inquit, 'obtinuit apud Phocam, &c.'" Baronii Annales Eccles. Tom. viii. p. 200. Ed.]

of the Turks invaded Christendom the year of the Lord 623, Honorius being pope, and almost drove the emperor out of his empire, and made him glad with money to buy peace unhonourably. And since that time the Turk hath grown bigger and bigger in the east countries, subduing all to himself, but the emperor weaker and weaker; and the pope hath taken from him most part of his empire, and rules in the west parts, and is emperor indeed, the other having only the name of an emperor.

The religion and authority of Mahomet, the Turks' great prophet, and the pope's religion, or rather superstition, and supremacy, began thus in one age within sixteen years together: and as it were dividing the whole world betwixt them, the one in the east, the other in the west, have waxen great rulers, that a man could scarce tell whether was the mightier, as just scourges sent of God to punish the world for not maintaining his word. But now the pope's wickedness and subtilty by God's word being declared and opened to the world, his power waxes less, and the Turk's power increases, because he keeps his people in ignorance: so that if God's mercy be not much more than our deservings, it is to be feared that he shall overcome Christendom. For the cold slackness of the people and princes to build God's house and true religion will care for no religion at all, if they may not have the old dirty dregs of popery. So God gives up unto all blindness them that forsake his light; and forsakes them that forsake him and cast him off.

But many would have not long ago said, What need we to fear these plagues? are not we come home again to our holy father the pope, and to our holy mother the church? is not our old little God come home again to us? have we not our altars, copes, masses, and trentals, that will bring us through purgatory for a little money, how wickedly soever we had lived? Our holy father the pope by his legate the cardinal or by his pardons will absolve us *a pœna et culpa*, that is, from all punishment, from sin, yea, and from all fault or guiltiness of sin, and give us as many days and years of pardon as we

Carnal fool[3] and the pope's church.

[[3] Carnal fool: a play upon the name, Cardinal Pole.—In other places in this work the old editions have *Carnal,* for Cardinal. See p. 65. Ed.]

list. What should grieve our conscience, having thus many ways to heaven? Are not we much better than our holy brethren, which will none of all these to save them, but only Christ, and think him only sufficient for the sins of the whole world? Is not this house well builded, that hath so many strong pillars? Can God be angry with us, that have bought and brought him so many things into the church to delight him withal? We have gilded many goodly images, pleasant to look at and delight the eyes: if he will have any mirth, we have goodly singing and striving who can fet[1] the highest note: we have sweet organs for the ear, and sweet frankincense for the nose: what would God have more? Were not the churches before like barns, bare and naked; and now are they trim, that any God would dwell in them?

<small>Acts vii.</small> Have we not done God good service, trow ye? No, surely; for God dwells not in temples made with hands of wood and stone, but in the heart of man: nor yet is worshipped with man's inventions, but as he willed and taught himself. And this is it that pulls all these plagues on our heads. For as the Jew is most stiff in his religion, so the Turk defends his by might and power; the pope maintains his with fire and faggot; the Anabaptist, Arian, and libertine, are as busy in corners to turn many unto them: and yet all these be enemies to Christ, seeking to serve God another way than he taught them, and to save themselves by some other means, than by only faith in him which was sent to teach us his <small>Matt. xi.</small> Father's will (which none knew but only he, and they to whom he hath taught it), and to save them all which shall be saved; so these and all other which build their religion other ways than God appointed, are traitors unto him, and procure his vengeance. For "he that is not with me," saith Christ, "is against me; and he that gathereth not with me, scatters abroad."

<small>No religion is to be had but that which Christ taught. Exod. xxv.</small> Moses, when he was in the hill with God, had the fashion of the tabernacle and tent shewed unto him, like unto the which God willed him to make another, where the people should resort to worship him, until the temple was builded by Salomon. And lest he should devise any thing of his own head, or invent another fashion, God gives him warning, say-

[¹ Fet: i.e. fetch. ED.]

ing, "See that thou make it like unto that fashion which was shewed thee in the hill;" devise nothing of thyself, neither put to, take away, nor change any thing; but only content thyself with that which I shewed thee. This is so notable a lesson, that it is repeated in the seventh of the Acts, and the eighth to the Hebrews, because it should be kept in memory, and diligently observed of all men in all ages; that they should not be curious in devising a new way to serve God of their own imagination, but submit their wit to God's wisdom, and be content with that which he hath appointed: for that only is good, and all inventions of man (as they be of man) displease him. Likewise David, when he would have builded God a house to have been worshipped in, God appeared unto him and told him he should not do it, but Salomon his son should build it. God shewed him also the fashion that he should build it after, (which fashion David taught Salomon, and prepared all metals necessary to do it withal in his life time,) lest they should have devised some fashion of their own: as man's brain is never content to be ruled by God's wisdom, but pleases himself in his own inventions better than in that which God teaches him. And this temple also that the prophet speaks of here, which they were sent home to build by King Cyrus (whose mind God *Ezra vi.* moved to restore them to their country, and so liberally to help them to the building of so costly a work), is appointed to them by commission, how broad, wide, long, high, and thick it should be, as it was unto Salomon before. If none of these, Moses, David, Salomon, Esdras, nor none of the people, might build these temples and houses of wood and stone, so high, wide, long, thick, broad, or any other fashion, as they lust themselves, but must follow (and are straitly charged often and sundry times so to do) that pattern, copy, example, and fashion, precisely, which God appointed them; much less in this spiritual house of God's building, which is chiefly by the preaching of his word, may we devise anything of ourselves, but exactly follow that which God hath taught us, and content ourselves therewith; thinking that most sufficient learning, able to save our souls, most true and holy, and all other to be dreams, lies, fantasies, and vanity, in comparison of this. "The law of the Lord," saith David, *Psal. xix, xii.*

"is pure, turning souls: the witness of the Lord is true, and gives wisdom to little ones," &c. And again: "The words of the Lord are pure as silver, which is tried seven times."

But how many ways hath the pope devised to build his house and authority, that a man may choose which him lust to follow, so that he follow not Christ! For (saith he in his heart) every one is as good or better than that which Christ ordained. This to be true a man may easily prove him to think; because he persuades men to follow his devices, and persecutes them that love Christ and his word, or will not believe him and his doings to be above the scripture: all these things he would not do, except he thought his ways the better. How many orders of monks, friars, nuns, canons, hermits, pilgrimages, pardons, relics, saints, masses, holy water, hath he set in his church (which all the scripture casts away as nought, because they be not taught us by God, but invented by the pope) for his vantage and vain glory! What diversity is among them (although they charge the gospellers with that falsely), when they put their holiness in their coats; and some say a white cowl is more holy, some say a black, another sort a grey! Some say mass of requiem is best; other say, of *scala cœli:* some, of the five wounds; some, of our Lady. Some pray to one saint, as more in God's favour, and some to other. Some use Trinity knots, and other St Katharine's. Some have St Tronion's fast, other our Lady's, and many the golden Fridays. In the schools some hold of St Thomas, some of Duns, and other of Gabriel, or Bacon[1]. Some hold of Francis in religion; some of Dominick, some of Augustine; but the holiest was St Benet[2]: for, as *Fasciculus temporum* says, he was so holy that he brought to heaven friars 5555, popes 24, cardinals 2000, archbishops 7000, bishops 15000, deans 5000, abbots 74, beside many nuns and holy sisters and priests. O holy St

The pope thinks his laws better than Christ's.

Papists differ among themselves in opinions of holiest things.

[1 Of these distinguished leaders in scholastic theology the first, Thomas Aquinas (of Aquino) flourished about 1260; John Duns Scotus, 1300; Gabriel Biel, 1480; and Roger Bacon, 1270. ED.]

[2 St Benet: or Benedict, founder of the order of Benedictine monks, as the three immediately preceding were respectively of the Franciscan, Dominican, and Augustine religious orders. ED.]

Benet, that was more holy than so many popes, friars, cardinals, &c.! and wretched popes, that can bring other to heaven, and not themselves! Some priests say matins, mass, &c.³ after York's use, some of Sarum, some Bangor, and other of common *sanctorum*. But never one seeks Christ as he should according to the scripture.

They have made them schoolmasters, whom they will follow, of their own devising; whereas God the Father hath appointed his Son Christ, and said, " This is my well beloved Son, in whom I am well delighted; hear him." And he is that prophet of whom Moses wrote, saying: " The Lord your God will raise a prophet from among your brethren, like unto me: him shall ye hear; and that soul which will not hear him, shall perish." He is the wisdom of God the Father, by whom he hath shewed his mercy and power to the whole world, and by whom he hath confounded the mighty and wise of the world: and he is God without beginning. These other which they call saints, or rather make them their gods, are found of late, and it is not many years since they lived. It is not since Francis, Augustine, and Dominick lived, much above 300 years: and if those be the pillars of God's church now, how did it stand afore their days? If these be the means to bring us to heaven now, how do they that died before that these men were born and known? God witnesses of his Son Christ, that he is the Lamb which was slain from the beginning of the world, and that by his death the sins of the whole world are forgiven, and that whatsoever we ask him in his name he will give us.

We have no such promise made us in any other creature: and therefore if we ask any thing in their names, God needs not to give it us; for he hath not bound himself by any promise, as he hath to his Son Christ. God hath not found a new way of late for us to be saved by, but hath appointed one means for all ages, by which only we shall please him: that is, the merits and death of his dear Son,

Christ is the only schoolmaster of his scholars, and the papists agree not in themselves.
Matt. xvii.
Deut. xviii.
Acts iii.
1 Cor. i.

Francis. Dominick.

Apoc. xiii.

John xvi.

Salvation only by Christ.

[³ The second edition reads, *mass, and after*—in the first the passage is wanting. The &c. may easily have been mistaken for & (*and*).— The sentence refers to the different forms of service used in different cathedrals. ED.]

Christ Jesus our Lord. He is the strong rock, upon whom what house soever is builded, shall stand: all other be builded on the sand, and therefore shall fall.

<small>England, repent.</small>

Therefore, England, how canst thou escape the great plagues written in this book, that had banished the word of God, that the people might not have it nor read it? The sheep heard not the voice of the true Shepherd, but the strange language of wolves, hirelings and thieves: yea, thou wast come to such a shamelessness and hatred of God's word, that thou could not suffer the clear light of the gospel to shine, nor the shrill trumpet of God's most holy word to sound in thine ears, which would confound all such enemies of God to have any place at all in thee. Mark well, England, in how miserable an estate thou wast, that thou mightest not hear God speak to thee by his word, nor believe what he teaches thee, but whatsoever pleases the pope to command thee, or the parliament to decree. What are those bishops worthy to have, which in one year space confirmed the preaching of the gospel of Christ and pure ministring of God's sacraments; and the same men within the same year, with the same impudent mouths and blasphemous tongues, brought in the pope, set up idols, banished Christ and his holy supper appointed for all men that will to receive it together, took away his holy gospel and sacraments; and placed by their authority the mass for one shaveling to eat up all, and bless the people with the empty chalice, and burned his preachers to fill their bellies? Moses commanded such blasphemers of God's name to be stoned: and yet they bear the name and title of ministers in Christ's church!

If the Jews deserved all these vengeances, because they did not build God's house, what had thou, O England, deserved in this defacing and pulling it down; and hast thus changed God's house into a den of thieves, and made it the pope's market place, to buy and sell heaven, hell, and purgatory, to deceive christian souls, and deface the death and passion of our Saviour Christ? Thou didst set up idols to be worshipped, and sought help at stocks and stones. Therefore how much need hast thou to pray unto God, that he would give thee good rulers! for thou must believe as they do: and if they love not God, thou shalt not[1] hear him speak unto thee by his word; and[1] if they will not worship God aright, thou shalt not be suffered to do it, if thou would.

Can any people escape unpunished, that thus mocks God? Or if God's mercy were not unspeakable, could he have holden his hands thus long, but have poured out his vengeance, and thrown his thunderbolts in every corner of thee, to destroy thee before these days?

If thou wilt not glorify God in repenting, he will glorify himself in destroying thee. Mark how many days God hath forborne to punish thee; and so many days hast thou had, of his endless mercy, granted thee to repent in: and if thou do it not by times, look not for the contrary, but thou shalt be made an example to the whole world, a laughing stock to thy enemies, a prey and slave to all countries round about thee.

What can be thought of those, which will ever follow that which the prince desires, but that they seek their own pleasure and profit with all diligence, which the prophet calls here to run to their own houses? that is as much to say as, With all their wit and power they do satisfy their own lusts, seek their pleasures, hunt and gape for their own profit, to enrich themselves, build costly houses, and lay land to land, and never think they have enough. *All build their own houses rather than God's.* Would to God they which preach Christ were not guilty in not building God's house as they should, as well as others be! If it be taught of contention, ambition or vain-glory, Paul saith he is glad that Christ is preached; but woe be to him that teaches for such causes, and preaches not for pure love and duty to his Lord God, seeking his own glory! *Phil. i.* All preachers must say (be their gifts never so great), "Not unto us, Lord, not unto us, but to thy name give all praise and glory." *Psal. cxv.* And all the hearers must say, "We do not believe the word, because such a man teaches it, but because God spake it:" for the authority of the gospel hangs not on the messenger which brings it, but on God's majesty which sends it. *The praise is God's.* For as Peter and John, when they had healed the blind beggar, and the people marvelled, said, "Why do ye wonder, as though *Acts iii.*

[1 *Not* and *and* are wanting in the second edition: they are here inserted from the first. ED.]

we had done this by our own power and holiness?"—so must all preachers say, Wonder not at us, but praise God whose messengers we be, and him whose Spirit he hath given to speak in us. For it is not we that speak, when we speak any truth: but it is the Holy Spirit of God that speaks in us, whose instruments we be.

Thus have all parts been guilty of not building God's house: the Lord for his mercies' sake forgive us all that which is past, and stir up our minds to do our duties more diligently from henceforth, that we may escape the plagues which follow!

The text.

v. 10. *Therefore the heavens are shut up from giving their dew upon you, and the earth is closed from yielding their fruit.*

11. *And I will call a drought upon the earth, and upon the hills, upon the wheat and upon the new wine, upon the oil, and upon whatsoever the earth bringeth forth, upon man, and upon beast, and upon all the labour of your hands.*

Now follows the other kind of persuading, which the prophet uses: that is, of the great plagues that hang over their heads, if they did continue in this stubbornness, and would not build God's house. For although they had suffered great things, yet these were much greater which were to come; and God would not hold his hand, until they went earnestly about to build his house, as they were commanded. In the further verse he repeats the plagues in other words, which he spake of before; and doth more plainly tell[1] the cause of all the scarceness that was among them, and why of so great labour they had so little fruit and increase. Here we may see how necessary it is often to repeat and beat in one lesson, because we be so dull to learn. And although many be weary to hear one thing often, yet St Paul saith to the Philippians: "I am not weary, and it is profitable for

It is profitable to repeat one thing oft.

Phil. iii.

[1 This is the reading of the first edition: the second, which was revised by the author himself, and which is generally followed in this reprint, except in typographical errors, has: *and more plainly took the cause.* ED.]

you, to repeat one thing often." "The heavens," saith he, "have been locked up from giving any dew or rain to you; and the earth hath been so hard and dry by that means, that no fruit could grow." Marvel not if the earth be barren, when moisture comes not from heaven: for nothing can multiply here, except it be blessed from heaven. And this is true not only in worldly things, but also in spiritual gifts of the soul; to teach us to look up to heaven, and from thence to beg and look for all goodness from God's hands. "What hast thou," saith St Paul, "which thou hast not received of God?" And St James saith, "Every good gift and every perfect gift is from above, coming from the Father of light." For as the rain and dew from above watering the ground makes it fruitful; so the grace of the Holy Ghost, coming from God the Father for his Son Christ's sake, stirs up our minds to all goodness. Thus by outward blessings God will teach us to look up to him for all goodness. For as it is betwixt the earth and the clouds, so is it betwixt God and our hearts: both be unfruitful, except they receive blessing from above. *All good things from heaven.* *1 Cor. iv.* *James i.*

But it had been among them now, as it was in the time of Achab, when Jesabel did so persecute the true prophets, that they were compelled to hide themselves in caves and dens of the earth. Elias told the king, that there should be no dew nor rain in all the country, but at his word when he said it should be, (for God had given that privilege to the prophet, to set forth his doctrine;) and it rained not of three years and a half, nor was any dew, but great hunger, famine and scarceness of all fruits in the country. So now, when God's house lay unbuilded, the heavens did not water the earth, but great barrenness was of all things. This is one of the plagues that God threatens to send on all countries for contemning his word, saying, "I will make heaven as hard as brass over your heads, that ye shall not wring out of it a drop of dew or rain to comfort the earth; and I will make the earth as hard as iron, that it shall not give her fruit." And so, for false worshipping of God, all countries have been divers times thus punished.

England hath had many great droughts and dearths, both in the time of popery and the gospel: but if ye mark it well, you shall find great diversity betwixt them. In the dearths under the gospel it was not for want of things, that God did not send them plenteously; but through the wickedness of man, which in so great plenty and blessings of God made a needless dearth. For farms were raised, that farmers might not forth to sell as they were wont. Many things were gotten into few men's hands, and they would sell as they list, and not as things were worth according to charity, being content with a reasonable gains. Corn was carried out of the realm, or sold through many hands or[1] it came to the markets; and every one would raise the price, and have some part of gains: some would feed their hogs with it, else let it foist in their barns and be eaten with mice, rather than they would bring it to the market to pull down the price. Men of honour and worship were become sheepmasters and graziers; tillage was turned into pasture, and towns into granges; and all not to make things cheaper, which might have been suffered, but dearer, which was and is hurtful and not tolerable. But since the pope was restored, ye have had unseasonable weather both in wet and drought; the earth hath not brought forth her fruit, and strangers have devoured much of that which ye had. All your Latin processions and singing of gospels under bushes, nor yet your *Ora pro nobis*, could get you God's blessings, but rather increased his anger. When were ye compelled to eat acorns for bread, but in your popery and falling from God? When was Calais lost, but in popery? When was Bullen gotten, and the Scots vanquished so manfully, as under the gospel? But this is the greatest plague of all, and least regarded of you, that the heavenly comfort of God's word was locked up from you, and comfortable dew of God's favour did not fall on you, nor your earthly hearts could bring forth good fruit and works of repentance. And so that curse was fulfilled on you which is written: "I will send a hunger into the earth, not a hunger of bread, but a hunger to hear the word of God, that ye shall go from the east unto the west to hear it, and shall not find it." The good men and true prophets of God, feeling what a grief it was to want this dew of God's word, and seeing heaven locked up from the plentiful preaching of the same,

Amos viii.

[¹ Or: i.e. ere, before. So in p. 91, &c. ED.]

and desiring the coming of Christ and comfortable promises
of his gospel, cry out: "O ye heavens, send down your dew *Isai. xlv.*
from above, and let the clouds rain righteousness; let the
earth be opened, and bring forth the Saviour." But God be *Choreb, drought.*
merciful unto us, and soften our hearts! we are come to such *Chereb, sword.*
a hardness of heart, that those things which good men most
desired, we most abhor; and the gospel which they thought
most happiness and treasure, we are weary of it and would
not have it.

The second verse the Hebrew now reads thus: "I have
called a drought upon the earth and the hills, &c."; and
then it should be nothing but a repeating, or an exposition
in more words, of that dearth and scarceness that was among
them, and so often spoken of before: but the Greek, which
I had rather follow, reads thus: "I will bring the sword
upon the earth and hills, &c." If our Hebrew books were
without points, as theirs were which turned it into Greek,
these points might be well joined to, which signify so as the
Greek is: or else, these points a little changed, it may be
so translated also as the Greek reads it. I think it better
to be an increasing of the plague, which God threatens them
withal to stir them up to this building, rather than an often
rehearsing of these plagues which were past. And where he
names here the hills, if we read it *a drought*, as the Hebrew
now pointed is, it is not so great plague or marvel to see
the hills barren and dry: but if with the Greek we read
the sword, that is to say, their enemies should come and
utterly destroy all, and they which fled to the hills to save
themselves, should not escape, nor their castles and towers,
which they had builded in the top of mountains, should defend them; it were more wonderful, and would strike a greater
fear into them, and stir them up sooner to build this house,
that they might avoid these great dangers ensuing. Thus
he would pull them from trusting in their strong holds on
the mountains, or else from that holiness which they put in
those hills within Jerusalem, where they thought no enemies
could prevail.

In Jerusalem were two hills; Moria, on which was builded *Moria.*
the temple, and Sion, where was the king's palace; unto *Sion.*
which both God had promised many blessings, and therefore

they might think themselves sure there. The city was compassed aforetime about with three walls: within the innermost was the temple and the priests' lodgings; within the second wall were the Levites' houses, the king's palace, and the university, houses of learning three hundred or more; within the uttermost were the merchants and the people: and yet their enemies with the sword should destroy all these. There is no place so holy, as to defend a wicked man; nor the place makes the man holy, but a good man makes every place wheresoever he be holy. When Jeremy preached that God would destroy the temple for the wickedness of the priests, the priests could not abide to hear that, but cried out, "The temple of God, the temple of God;" yet Jeremy said still, he would do unto that house as he did unto Silo, and destroy it. There is no creature of God so holy, but if a man do abuse it, God will give both him and it to his enemies' power, if they do not amend. God suffered his holy ark, wherein were the tables written with his own finger, and Aaron's rod, and a pot full of manna, with other reliques, to be given into the Philistines' hands for the wickedness of the people and the priests which bare it, Ophni and Phinees, Eli's sons. So likewise should these holy hills and all of them be devoured with the sword, if they builded not this house of God.

As long as they kept God's true religion, God defended them and his temple, after it was builded: but when they forsaked God's word and religion, God forsaked them, and gave them into the hands of Antiochus, which defiled the temple, set up idols in it, made a school of fence and heathen learning of it, and killed all those that would not follow him. So was this prophecy and curse then fulfilled, and they destroyed; but specially when Titus and Vespasian with the Romans destroyed it, according as Christ said, there should not be one stone left standing upon another: so there should nothing save them, except they would not only build this house, but also defend and maintain his word and true religion. Those with all other like are written for us, to keep us in due fear and reverence to God and his word, lest we suffer the like plagues as they did for falling from his holy word.

But here let us chiefly mark the goodness of God in this and all his other threatenings: for he doth not tell us this, because there is no remedy to escape it; but that in hearing this we should repent and so escape it. All the threatenings of God are to be understood with this condition, if ye do not repent and amend; as Jonas coming unto Nineve said, "Yet forty days and Nineve shall be destroyed:" presupposing, if they did not ask mercy; but they asked it and escaped. Jeremy saith, "If this people repent them of their evil, I will repent also, saith God, of that evil which I purposed to send upon them." If God were disposed to plague as often as he threatens, he would never give warning nor time to repent in, nor promise mercy to them that repent, but would suddenly come and destroy without all mercy. *God threatens that we may avoid them. God's threatenings have in them a condition ever. Jonah iii. Jer. xviii.*

And where he works all for our comfort, it were a double sorrow, both to be punished, and know it so certainly aforehand that it cannot be escaped: but he gives them and us this warning, that we might turn and by repentance obtain mercy in time. God never sends plague into the world, but he gives warning before it come, that they may repent and escape, as Amos saith: "The Lord will do nothing, but he sheweth it first by his servants the prophets." Before he drowned the world, he stirred up Noe, whom Peter calls the eighth preacher of righteousness; who as he was making his ark a hundred and twenty years, and told them the anger of God towards them for their sins, that they might amend and avoid the danger coming by repentance, so some laughed at him, and few cared for him, and therefore were all drowned save eight persons. Lot preached in Sodom, and when they would not amend, fire from heaven destroyed them. Before the destruction of Jerusalem by Nabuchodonozor God sent many prophets many years to warn them beforehand, whose writings also we have, as Esay, Jeremy, Osee, &c.; and before the last destruction by the Romans Christ himself came, and also sent his apostles to teach repentance: but when all was in vain, then they utterly perished. Have not we in England been as diligently warned by our preachers, and almost all in vain? What shall we look for then, but destruction, if we amend not? Thus God *God gives warning before he plagues. Amos iii. 2 Pet. ii. Gen. xix.*

of his endless mercy never cometh suddenly upon us to destroy us; but mercifully warns us, that we be not taken in our sins, and so perish: and ever he stirs up the sluggish, either by his Spirit, word, minister, or else his gentle correction, to call for his mercy.

<small>Calling.</small>

And where he saith, "I will call a drought or the sword upon the earth, &c.," this kind of speaking is often used in the scripture, and betokeneth nothing but the power of God, that he is able to do it so easily, as to speak a word or call for it; and that as soon as he spake it, so soon it should be done, as when one of us cometh at another's calling. God doth all by his word: and to say a thing is to do it with him; and as soon as he saith the word, so soon it is done with him. Saying and doing are two divers things with us, and much pain we take to do a thing after it be spoken: but with God it is not so, but as the psalm saith, "He spake, and all things were made; he commanded and they were created." Moses speaketh more plainly in the making of the world, and saith: "God said, Let there be light made, and let there be made the sun and stars, beasts and fishes; and they were made straightways." So when God brought Nabuchodonozor to destroy Jerusalem and the country, he said he would call and hiss or whistle him from the north, and he should come: God called, and he came. So all other things, drought, hunger, plague, sword, do tarry and wait for God's calling; and as soon as he whistles, they come straight, and nothing dare or can withstand his calling, as David saith: "Fire, hail, snow, ice, and tempests which do his commandment." Seeing therefore his threatening is not to destroy, but to save and bring us to repentance, let us turn by time, that he be not weary of calling; and desire him not to order us according to his justice, but after his endless mercies: for else shall that be true of Salomon, "I called, and ye refused, and therefore I will laugh at your destruction," saith the Lord.

<small>As soon as God calls, all things obey.</small>

<small>Psal. cxlviii.</small>

<small>Gen. i.</small>

<small>Isai. v. [26.]</small>

<small>Prov. i.</small>

<small>The horribleness of this sin not to build God's house is proved by the plagues.</small>

And where God threatens to destroy wheat, wine, oil, all fruits of the earth, and labour of man, yea, man himself and beast, for not building his house: let us consider the horrible filthiness of this sin especially in not building his house, that it will not let any creature of God serve man, so long as he thus displeases God. This sin doth not only stop the fruits of the earth, but it flieth up to heaven, and locks it up, and so hardens the clouds that no rain nor dew can be wrung out to moisten the ground withal. Such is the just judgment of God, that where God of his mercy made all things in heaven and earth, sun, moon, stars, cattle, fish, fowl, corn, herbs and trees, to serve man, so that man would serve him, reverence, fear and worship him as his only Lord and God, Maker and Saviour; so when he did disobey him, and served God of his own devising, or brake his commandments, he should have those creatures which God appointed to serve him at the first, to disobey him, to rebel against him, and as it were to avenge God's quarrel upon that man which disobeyed the living God, their Lord and Master; and they would not willingly serve him, which would not willingly serve and obey their God and King. When Adam was in paradise, as long as he obeyed God, so long all creatures obeyed him, as appointed of God to be their lord and ruler, as the psalm saith, "Thou hast made all things subject under his feet, sheep and oxen, and all beasts of the field, birds of the air, and fishes of the sea:" but so soon as he brake God's commandment, and eat of the fruit which God forbad him, all things began to disobey him, and as it were would avenge that disobedience done against God their maker. *Through sin no creature would willingly serve man.* *Psal. viii.*

The earth would not bring forth her good fruit willingly, but weeds, brambles, and briars: no kind of beasts would obey him, but waxed wild and rebelled against him. The tokens of this just punishment remains on us to this day, and shall to the world's end. The earth will bring forth no good fruit willingly, but with much labour, toiling, tilling, dunging, harrowing, sowing, &c.; as though it should say to man, I will not serve thee, nor yet willingly give thee any fruit at all. So neither horse, dog, ox, nor sheep, nor any other living thing, is tame at the first to obey man; but it must have many stripes, or it will be brought to any good order to serve him. And many beasts, as lions, bears, wolves, be so wild, that they will not serve man at all, but still remain his continual enemies, always ready to devour him. As often as we see any of these fierce beasts, which are so cruel, we should remember the first cause why they were so *The disobedience of creatures should remember us of our fall and God's anger toward sin.*

turned, and be so fierce against us; and we should then lament our sin, which was the only cause of this so great a plague and change. God hath left them amongst us to be our schoolmasters, that when we see and consider them to be so ready to take vengeance upon us for our disobedience to God, we should much more fear God himself, which is a more righteous judge, and both is able and will punish us more grievously than they do or can, if we repent not and ask mercy by time. These cruel beasts are set before us for examples of greater things; that as we fear to fall into the danger of these ravening beasts, so we should much more fear to fall into the hands of the Almighty and living God, whose anger is a thousand times more grievous than the cruelness of any beast.

And it is not only with one creature or two, that they disdain to serve us willingly, but every one, as St Paul saith: "The creature is subject to vanity not willingly, but for his cause which hath made it subject under hope." Here we see that no creature would serve us willingly, but for God's cause who hath so pointed them to do. So that of themselves we can get no profit nor service of those that have no life without much labour, and taming them by strength and violence which have life: yet for the hope they both have to be delivered from this service, for the time they do obey us according to God's ordinance.

<small>Rom. viii.</small>

<small>God's majesty is declared in his creatures, and saints do not rule them.</small>

Also in the destruction of these his creatures, that they should not serve such evil men, God declares himself not only to be the mighty Lord in making and creating them, but also a merciful God in blessing them with fruitful increase, when his people served him rightly; and also a righteous judge in taking them away for our sins, when they be not so plentiful as they have been to us. For as plenty of them is a token of his mercy and favour, and that it is he only which regards, loves, feeds, nourishes and increases the least creatures which he hath made; so the taking them away, or the barren unfruitfulness of them, is a sign of his anger and displeasure. It is not, as ye commonly say, St Anthony save my hog; St Loy, my horse; St Blase, my house; St Apollony help in the tooth-ache; St Roche for the plague, &c.: but he that made all saves all, guides all, rules all, feeds all, blesses all, and increases all; and takes them from us at his will and pleasure, as Job saith: "The Lord gave it, the Lord took it away, &c." <small>Job i.</small>

These were lessons that the heathen people, and we also, might and should have learned by the making and ruling of the world, that God did rule all things; and because they did not, they were justly punished. Shall then we christian men think God to be weary of ruling his creatures, and put them to some Romish saints' hands, that are more able and willing to rule them better than he can and will? If this were true, saints should be more merciful, able and willing to help, than God himself, which can do nothing but love, and hates nothing that he made: but so to think were most horrible blasphemy against his majesty; for he should be an evil Lord and master, if he so lightly regarded his servants, his creatures, that he would put them to other men's ruling. "God hath not left himself without witnesses," saith St Luke, "giving rain and fruitful times." As these works were sufficient witnesses to the heathen of God's goodness, and that he ruled all, and that their just condemnation followed, if they did not believe; so is unseasonable weather, with taking away his fruits, just tokens of his anger for our sins. Therefore, where we have the same works sufficient witnesses unto us both of his anger and good will, and also his wonderful works written in the scriptures to teach us; what can we say for ourselves, if we do not worship him our only God, seeking help at his only hand, in whom only it is to be found and received? God doth not only make all things, but ruleth them also according to his good will and pleasure: he is not weary of well doing, but guides even the least of his creatures. He makes grass to grow on the hills, and herbs to serve men: he giveth meat to the cattle and to the young ravens; yea, he feeds the birds of the air, which work not nor spin, sow nor mow, reap nor carry into the barns. And briefly to speak: "all things doth look," saith David, "that thou shouldest give them meat in due season: if thou open thy hand and feed them, they are full of goodness; but if thou withdraw thy hand, they fall, vade away, perish and turn into earth, whereof they were made." Thus must all wheat, wine, oil, fruits of <small>Acts xiv.</small> <small>Psal. cxlvii.</small> <small>Psal. cxlv. & civ.</small>

the earth, and beasts perish for the sin of man, and not building God's house: but they prosper and increase to them which love him, maintain his true religion, and fear him.

The two last words, where he saith, Man and all handy labour shall be destroyed also, they be more notable in the Hebrew, than can be well expressed in one word in English. For where the Hebrew hath divers words to signify a man, as *Isch*, and those be noblemen; *Aenosch*, and they be so called of their sorrows and infirmities they be subject to; here is written *Adam*, which betokens the common sort of people. The word that here signifieth *labour*, betokens not every kind of labour, as that which is easy or for pleasure; but it signifies that labour, which the poor man doth until he be weary, even the vilest and sorest drudging labour. By the which both we are taught, that God would not spare the simplest and basest man living; but as they had sinned in not building his house, so should they perish: lest they should think or say, We did not this fault, but our rulers; or, we were not able to take it in hand; or, if they had begun, we would have followed; or such like fond excuses. God requires his house to be builded, his word and religion to be kept and maintained, as well of the lowest as the highest; and they which do not, shall not escape unpunished. Therefore wicked is that saying under persecution, "Let the preacher stand to it; what doth it belong to me?" If the master must teach, ought not the scholar to learn? May the scholar deny or dissemble with God, and the master must not? What privilege has the scholar more to do evil, than the master? That is sin to the one and the other. "He that denies me afore men," says Christ, "I will deny him afore my Father."

Man hath this general name given him to be called Adam, of another Hebrew word that signifieth the earth, *Adama;* which word was placed afore, when he said he would destroy all that the earth bringeth forth: and in Latin man is also called *Homo ex humo;* which allusion and likeness in words we cannot well speak in English, but it is as much to say: Man is called earth, because he is made of earth, as Jeremy saith, "Earth, earth, earth, hear the word of the Lord." And Abraham talking with the Angel of God, and demanding divers questions, said: "Let not my Lord be grieved <small>Gen. xviii.</small> if I yet once again ask my Lord, seeing I am earth and ashes." This should put us in remembrance, that is, as <small>It is profitable to remember whereof we be.</small> oft as we hear this name Adam, that we are earth and ashes, and are come of the sinful seed of Adam our first father, who was made of the earth, and for breaking God's commandment returned into earth again, from whence he came, as we shall all at our appointed time. If this were well considered, it would make our proud peacock's feathers to fall, when we remember from whence we come, and whither we shall, and how we be not able to think of ourselves a good thought; but that all our goodness is given us of God, and unto him we be traitors and thieves, if we be proud of his gifts, and give not him worthy thanks for them, but take the praise to ourselves.

Thus by degrees doth God increase his plagues and threatening; not destroying us at the first, but by laying on us one little rod at the first he biddeth and warneth us to beware of the next, for that will be greater if we amend not. This he doth by his other prophets also. In Osee <small>Hosea v.</small> he compares himself to the moth and lion in punishing: for the moth doth not eat up clothes hastily, but by leisure and by little and little; but the lion devoureth up all at once. So, saith God, I will be no more only as a moth in clothes, in punishing you so gently and by leisure; for by that gentle kind of punishing ye wax worse and worse: but I will come now as a lion, and destroy you quickly; for ye abuse my gentleness, and I cannot hold my hands any longer beside you.

Lord, soften our hard hearts, that where we be guilty in the same fault of negligent building thy house, we may hear and fear those great threatenings towards us; we may dread thee, and obtain mercy for our sins past, and hereafter be more diligent to serve thee.

v. 12. *Then Zerubabel the son of Salathiel, and Josua the son* <small>The text.</small> *of Jehozadac the high priest, and all the remnant of the people, gave ear unto the voice of the Lord their God, and unto the words of Aggeus the prophet, inasmuch that the Lord their God sent him: and the people were afraid in the sight of God.*

Angel.   13. *And Aggeus, the messenger of the Lord, said in the messages of the Lord to the people, saying: I am with you, saith the Lord.*

Hitherto from the beginning hath been nothing but chiding and threatening for their great negligence in building God's house: now follows the profit and commodity that came by such a sharp kind of rebuking. They began to "give ear unto it," mark it, and were afraid to hear and consider those plagues, which yet hanged over their heads: they believed those sayings to be true, which Aggeus said unto them, and they feared God. This is the ordinary way that God useth to teach by, and which the scripture sets before us to learn to believe in God and fear him: first, to rebuke sin and declare the anger of God towards sinners, and preach repentance, *Matt. iii.* as John Baptist and our Saviour Christ began to preach: *Rom. x.* "Repent; the kingdom of God is at hand." "Faith cometh by hearing," saith St Paul, "and hearing by the word of God:" therefore he that will believe, and have his faith increased, must be diligent in the scriptures, to hear sermons, and mark what God saith unto us there. What marvel is it if the papists have so little faith, seeing they read not the scripture, and hold opinion that it is not necessary, yea, not to be suffered that the scripture should be much read or taught, but the pope's laws, customs and decrees?

Law.   The whole scripture hath these two chief parts, into the
Gospel. which it is divided, the law and the gospel. The law contains properly the setting forth of sin, threatenings, curses, God's anger toward sin, remorse of conscience for the same, damnation, hell, despair: the gospel contains comfort, hope, forgiveness, mercies in Christ, heaven, salvation, agreement with God. *Rom. iv.* Thus teaches St Paul, saying, "The law works anger" within a man in conscience towards himself, for displeasing his Lord God; and also declares what is sin, and the anger and just *Rom. iii.* judgment of God for sin. "By the law comes the knowledge *Rom. vii.* of sin." Again he saith, "I had not known coveting, lusting, and desiring for any unlawful thing to have been sin, except the law had said, Thou shalt not lust nor covet." *Rom. i.* The gospel "is the power of God to save all that believe" *Matt. xi.* in Christ, which saith, "Come to me, all ye that labour

and are laden, and I will refresh you:" and, "Thus God loved the world, that he gave his only begotten Son," &c. with many such like promises: as, "If any man sin, we have an advocate with the Father," &c. This profit came here to this people, by preaching the law of God and threatenings unto them, that they which were afore so forgetful of their duties, now hearing the great anger and vengeance of God that hanged over their heads, ready to fall on them, it stirred them up to do their duties and fear God. Thus may we here see the fond and tender ears of them, which would not hear nor have the law preached, but altogether the sweet comfortable promises and mercies in Christ; nor cannot abide the anger of God and just judgment for sin to be taught, saying, It brings a man into despair, and that it is not now in the time of grace meet to be preached. John iii.
1 John ii.

A man as he is made of body and soul, so hath he the law given him to beat down the lusts of the flesh, and keep him in due fear to his Lord and God: and lest the soul should despair, when it considers the greatness of the sin which the flesh and mind draws him to, he hath the comfort of Christ offered unto him in the gospel. So, lest we be proud and forget God, we have the law given to set before us the righteousness of those things which God requires of us, and our weak unableness to fulfil the same, and the righteous sentence of death and God's anger pronounced upon all that fulfil not the same law. But lest we should despair, we have the unspeakable mercies of God offered unto us in his Son, which by his death hath conquered death, and paid the full price for the sins of the whole world. He biddeth us, when we feel our own weakness and unableness to fulfil his law, to come unto him, ask help and mercy at his hands, and doubt not thereof but it shall be granted. For as we see in judgments here amongst us, there is a royal seat set where the judge sits; he that is accused stands at the bar, holds up his hand, hears his indictment read, witness is brought in against him, and he justly condemned to death: so we shall see Jesus Christ, the righteous Judge of the world, that will not be bribed, sit in his seat of majesty at the last day, and all the company of angels about him; and we shall stand at the bar, as accused and indicted for breaking that righteous Law.
Gospel.
Galat. iii.

[PILKINGTON.]

law of his word: the devil, which enticed us so to do, shall bear witness that to be true, yea, and our own conscience also: the fear of that fearful sentence, "Go, ye cursed, into everlasting fire, which is prepared for the devil and his angels," shall make us to tremble. And of mercy there is no hope at all, except we do as we read of a woman, which when she stood before Alexander the Great, and was condemned, she said, "I appeal from thee, O king." Alexander wondering at her said, "Thou art a mad woman: dost thou not know that every appellation is from a lower judge to a higher? but who is above me?" Then said she, "I know thee to be above thy laws, and that thou may give pardon; and therefore I appeal from justice to mercy, and for my faults desire pardon." So we, when we look into the righteous law of God's word, and see him ready to condemn us, and our conscience witness that we have deserved death; we must appeal from justice and our deservings unto his pardon and forgiveness, and both call and trust to be partakers of that salvation, which he hath purchased and offered to the whole world. His mercies do pass all our miseries, as far as God is greater than man; and his pardon can forgive all that call on him.

This is not to be lightly considered, that it is said, "They heard the voice of the Lord their God, and the word of Aggeus the prophet." What needed both to have been written, seeing they were both one? for the words of Aggeus were the same that the Lord bad him speak, as he hath said divers times before. Here in this example we shall learn two good lessons; one for the preacher, and another for the hearer. The preacher must not be afraid to rebuke sin in all sorts and degrees of men, as here Aggeus did rebuke both Zerubabel, the chief civil ruler in the commonwealth, and Josua the high priest and chief in religion, and also the whole people beside, and threatens the plagues indifferently to all without any flattery or respect of person. So do all the prophets, as Esay calls the rulers fellows with thieves, and princes of Sodom and Gomorrha, because they followed their wickedness. And when Achab a king asked Elias, whether it was he troubled all the country, (because it was so long a drought, for the space of three years and a half without any rain or dew,) he answered the king boldly, and said, Nay, it is thou and thy father's house that hast pulled this righteous plague upon thee and thy whole realm. Where all have sinned, all must be rebuked: for as God, a most righteous judge, will punish all sin, so must his preachers indifferently warn and rebuke all sorts of sinners; or else God will require their blood at their hands, if they perish without their warning, as Ezekiel saith. The hearer must not disdain to learn of the simplest preacher that he heareth, as Josua the high priest here doth not disdain to hear the rebuking of Aggeus, being but a poor Levite and a simple man in comparison of him: no, nor yet Zerubabel, the chief ruler, and born of the stock of Judah, the king's stock, disdains him. If a preacher should rebuke the pope, a cardinal, an archbishop or bishop, a doctor, or a babbler in divinity, would they not disdain to hear such simple men? Would they not say, as hath been said of late to many, when they were examined before Annas and Caiphas, Becomes it thee to speak thus to my lord bishop? art thou wiser or better learned than he? shall he become thy scholar? Was not the like said to our Saviour Christ, "Dost thou answer the high bishop so?" What would the pope or cardinal say, if a man should threaten such vengeance of God towards him, as Aggeus doth here to the high priest? Paul, the second pope of that name, when he had wrongfully taken lands and offices from divers, and cast them all in prison, and would not hear any suitors speak for them; at length by much ado when Platina himself came to him, and could get no help, at the last he required of the pope that he might be heard and judged by his own law. Then the pope looking cruelly on him said: "What tellest thou me of the law? Dost thou not know, that whatsoever I say is law? Am not I St Peter's vicar, and all laws are within my breast, and I cannot err whatsoever I say? Am I not pope, and may disannul the decrees of my predecessors, and do what me lust? Thus it shall be, thus I am determined[1]." Thus speak holy popes, when simple men ask their right, or tell them of any faults: their proud stomachs cannot abide to be rebuked of any man.

Ezek. iii.

Disdain not to hear and learn of the simplest.

John xviii.

Paul II.

[1 The account is given by Platina himself, De Vitis Pontificum, p. 297, Colon. 1540. ED.]

Was not this common also in England in the papists' mouths, when the gospel was preached, to deface the truth: "Who are your preachers now, but young men, unlearned and not skilled in the doctors? And who teaches the other old learning, but my lord bishop, master doctor, ancient bachelors in divinity, and prove it by the ancient writers?" These are gay glorious words indeed, if they had been true: but although young men did teach, yet their doctrine was most wholesome and approved by the scriptures and all good writers; which is most to God's glory, that opened the mouths of younglings, to confound the doting of old fools. Simple men confirmed with their blood and constant deaths that which before both master doctor and my lord bishop also allowed and taught with mouth and hands subscribing, until contrary rulers arose: but then, for flattery and their belly, they destroyed the same with all their might and power that they taught before.

Papists change with the world.

So, when and how often soever the world shall change, the most of them, as men without conscience, will be ready to do the like, and make a face as though they believed the same to be true; but not one of them will adventure his body to be burned for the dirty dregs of popery: and yet are they not ashamed to teach and maintain the same with fire and sword, so long as the world is on their side.

The elder must not disdain to learn and hear his fault of the younger.

There is scarce a more certain argument of an obstinate papist, than to look how simple a man he is that preaches, and not to believe his doctrine for the simpleness of the man; nor to look at the thing which he teaches, how true it is and spoken by God. Let all Christians hear and be content with Christ's holy word, as most and only sufficient doctrine to save our souls; and disdain none that brings it, be he never so simple. St Paul saith, "Christ died for our sins, and rose for our righteousness:" and where this is one of the greatest treasures that we have by Christ, to be made righteous by him, mark who were the first preachers of it. Mary Magdalene and the other women, which went early in the morning with ointments to the sepulchre, they see Christ first of all other after his resurrection, and were sent to teach it to the apostles and Peter. Should we not believe this resurrection, because that women taught it first?

Rom. iv.

Luke xxiv.

Apollo, a mighty learned man in the scriptures, submitted himself to be further taught in true religion of Priscilla and Aquila, a simple man and his wife. Timothy and John the evangelist were both very young when they were called to be preachers. Peter the elder apostle is content to be rebuked of Paul his younger. Judith, that good woman, corrected the elders, priests and rulers in Bethulia, mistrusting God's help and providence for them, when they would yield up the city. David, a man according to God's own heart, hears most willingly the prophet Nathan rebuke him, who was of much less estimation than he. And king Ezechias heareth Esay rebuke him of his faults. These and such other examples be written to teach us, that the elder, in what authority soever he be, or by what name soever he be called, should willingly suffer the just rebuke of the younger, bringing the word of God for him. *Acts xviii. 1 Tim. iv. Galat. ii. Judith viii. 2 Sam. xii. 2 Kings xx.*

Further, where he adds this twice, saying, "The Lord their God, the Lord their God;" it is very comfortable for all sinners that have long lien in sin, that they should not despair of God's mercy, but speedily turn by repentance. The long-suffering of God is far above our deserts, and had suffered this people thus long to lie in sin, and yet had not cast them off; but doth vouchsafe to send his prophet to them, to rebuke them and stir them up to their duties, calling himself their God, which had forgotten and forgiven all their former disobedience; who now was and would continue their good, gracious, and merciful Lord and God still. Who can despair to obtain grace and pardon for all his great offences, seeing set before him the loving gentleness of our good God and Master, which offereth undesired his mercies so plentifully to so hard a hearted and disobedient people, his free pardon *a pœna et culpa*, from all pain due to sin or the guilt thereof; which also calls himself their God, and by continual earnest crying of this his prophet awakes them out of this dead sleep of sin, wherein they had lien so long, and left his house unbuilded? "It is commonly said," saith Jeremy, "if a man put away his wife for adultery, will he take her again? yet thou", saith God to his people, "although thou hast played the harlot with many whores, yet turn unto me, and I will receive thee again, saith the Lord thy God," *Mercy is ready to all repentant. Jer. iii.*

Rev. iii.

O merciful Lord, praised be thy holy name for thy gentle offers and liberal promises offered unto us in thy Son Christ Jesu our Lord. Thou standest at the door of our conscience, knocking to be let in, offering thyself to dwell with us if we would receive thee. There is no time so long that a man hath run from God in, nor any time so short to ask forgiveness, but if he will turn, God is ready to forgive him. The Gentiles had lien in sin above four thousand years from the beginning of the world to the death of Christ, without any true teaching or knowledge of God: and yet, when they received the gospel by the preaching of the apostles, they were most gently received of Christ into the number of his people. The thief hanging on Christ's right hand on the cross, asking mercy in the hour of death, obtained it. So that neither the greatness of sin, nor the long time that man hath continued in it, nor the shortness of time to ask forgiveness in, can stop the great unspeakable mercies of God, to pardon the sins of the whole world. Why should we then mistrust the goodness of our God, seeing he is the maker of the same law whereby we shall be judged, and also able to dispense withal, and pardon the breakers of the same law, if he will; who also shall be judge and executor of the same law, as pleases him?

But that the people should rather believe his word, he saith, the Lord their God sent him; no strange God, but the mighty God of hosts, and the living God of Israel: nor he ran not before he was sent, but soberly looked for the calling of God, and then did his message faithfully.

Ministers must not thrust themselves in office.

This is an example for all ministers to follow, that they do not with bribery or flattery thrust themselves into any office, but patiently tarry the calling of the Lord their God, which can and will call them at such time as he judges them necessary to serve him. Who would be so bold to buy a benefice, or flatter for a bishoprick, if he did think them to be offices in God's house, and that they must make account to God for his people? He that comes before he be sent for, oftentimes comes before he be welcome: and he that climbs in at the window is a thief; for the door is made to come in by. But because these popish prowlers seek not the profit of the flock, but to fill their bellies, they care not how they come by it, so they may have it; and think they have done God good service, and the people well content, when they teach them never a word of scripture, but have said mass, made conjured water, or sung an antiphone of our Lady. If they had this true stedfast opinion of God, as they ought to have, that he were a loving Father to his household, and a wise Master that could and would set wise stewards over his house, and that whosoever presumed to take any office in his house uncalled, were a thief, and should be sharply punished; a man could not hire them for money, to take any cure of teaching God's people, until they were inwardly[1] moved of God to do it for love to the people, and not for their own gain. They would also provide to be ordinarily called by man, lest he which should teach and see others keep good order, should be proved the first breaker of all good laws and orders. If a stranger should violently thrust in himself to be the shepherd of thy sheep, thou wouldest ask him who sent for him, what he had to do there; and thou wouldest rather think him to be a thief and a murderer of thy sheep, than a trusty servant: so surely, if thou come to take charge of God's people, before he inwardly move thy conscience to pity his people, and outwardly by order call and place thee where he thinks good, he will judge thee a thief, a wolf, a devourer, and not a feeder.

After they heard that the word of God was sent unto them by Aggeus, and had weighed and considered diligently how true his sayings were, that so many years they had suffered so great plagues; they began to fear, and believe that the threatenings following would also prove true: and then they humbled themselves in the sight of God, and were afraid indeed. This profit had they by hearing the word of God, that they acknowledged their own sins, that they had offended the gracious goodness and majesty of God in not regarding his house so many years; and for fear then they began to take in hand again that work wherewith they were so straitly charged.

Thus faith comes by hearing the word of God; and by hearing and giving ear to his threatenings, our slow and sluggish dulness is raised up to take in hand God's work, and build his house. How necessary fear is, David teaches,

[1 So the first edition: the second, *inward moved*. Ed.]

saying, "Fear of the Lord is the beginning of wisdom." So now, when they feared these threatenings, they waxed wise and turned to the Lord. Truth it is, that the anger of God is not always to be taught, and that it brings not a man to perfection: for David calleth the fear of the Lord[1] but the beginning of wisdom, and not the perfection thereof; and St John saith, "Perfect charity casts out fear." But yet it is the ordinary way to pull down proud stomachs, and to bring them to know their own vileness; and it also stirs up slothful minds to be more diligent to do their duties. St Paul saith, "The law is a schoolmaster to bring us to Christ;" that where we see ourselves justly condemned by God's righteous law, and that we be not able to stand in judgment with him, nor answer one thing for a thousand that shall be laid against us, we should run to Christ for pardon, confessing our faults, and ask mercy.

Thus they had the right use of the law, not bringing them to despair with all these threatenings, but comforting them to go to God and confess their sins, and hope for mercy in Christ. St Augustine compares fear to the bristle, which is on the shoemaker's thread: the bristle goeth through the hole first, but it draws a long and a strong thread after it: so the fear of God's vengeance first goeth before, and throws down a man in his own sight; and then followeth the long thread of God's mercies in Christ offered to the whole world.

The scripture teaches two sorts of fear: The one which is godly, when we fear our God with love and reverence, and would not displease him for the love we bear him; and this remains for ever, as David says, "The holy fear of the Lord continues for ever." Another kind of fear is, not to do well for the love of God and goodness itself, but that we may escape punishment; as the thief will not steal, not for love of any righteousness or reverence to God, but to escape the gallows. This is that fear which cannot stand with perfect charity, but is cast out. Fear in a man's mind is like the thunder in the air: for as when the air is covered with clouds, the sun darkened, tempests begin to arise, lightnings and fire fly from heaven, rumbling and noise is in the air, the clouds burst, and the thunder-crack comes, the rain falls,

[1 Both editions have *fear of the God*. ED.]

and straight follows sunshine and fair weather; so when a man, for fear of his sins, in conscience lies flat down in the sight of God, confessing his sin, as one oppressed with the burden and vileness thereof; complains to God, accuses himself, groans, sobs, and sighs like the thunder-crack, dare not look up towards heaven for his wickedness, but condemns himself; at the last bursts out on weeping, and the tears like rain-drops come trickling down his cheeks: straightways follows quietness of mind, God offers him pardon and clearness of conscience, with wondering and praising the unspeakable goodness of God for his mercies and comfort in Christ his Son offered to such a troubled conscience.

In the latter verse is first declared the worthiness, authority, high title and rule given to the preachers, for the commendation of their office. Aggeus here is called "the angel of the Lord," as some in English do translate it, or the messenger, or embassador, which signify all one thing unto us. So these names with such like are given to preachers in the scripture, to set forth the highness of their vocation and authority that God calleth them to. The worldly-wise men, considering the decay of the living of bishops and priests, *Worldliness decays the ministery.* and that they be not so much esteemed and as wealthy, as when they were loitering, lordly, unpreaching prelates, and ruled all, would say, 'Shall I make my son a minister, and when I have spent all I have on him, he shall neither be able to help my other children, nor yet scarce able to live himself, but shall be disdained of all sorts of men; and if he preach the truth, he shall be in jeopardy of his life? Or shall I marry my daughter to a priest?'—with such like uncomely sayings: 'nay, I trow not; there is more profit by the law or physic: yea, if he be but a pen-clerk, an auditor or receiver[2], I will provide for him better any of these ways.' The goods of the church are the goods of the poor: woe therefore be to them that rob the church so by impropriations, that neither the minister nor the poor can be relieved! For by that means the necessary food of the preacher is given to idle bellies: and these worldlings declare themselves to desire nothing but worldly wealth, in thus doing or so saying. But if they mark this and other places of the scriptures, and

[[2] Both editions have *deceiver*. Ed.]

The preacher's office is worshipful. would have their children made worshipful, they shall find more worshipful names given to the preaching minister, than to any one sort of men.

The noblest creatures that God hath made be the heavenly spirits and angels, which be always in heaven most happy for the continual beholding of his glory; and for their office' sake are chosen and called angels, because they be sent on his message, and do most willingly go at his commandment. *Angel.* This word "angel" betokens not the substance of the creature, but the office; and is a Greek word signifying a *messenger,* or *embassador :* this name "angel" was commonly used to be given to these heavenly messengers, whom God sends [on] his message from his holy place of majesty: as Gabriel the angel was sent to the virgin Mary, and other to *Preachers be angels.* Joseph, Daniel, Moses, &c. This name is also given to the preachers for the heavenly comfort that they bring to man *Rev. i. ii.* from God, whose messengers they be. In the Revelation St John writes to the seven angels, that is to say, to the seven ministers, of the seven congregations or churches in *Mark i.* Asia. John Baptist was called the angel of the Lord, or embassador, sent to prepare his ways. And whom do kings use to send embassadors, but such as be faithful and trusty, whom they love, and [to] whom they dare commit secret and weighty matters unto? What can be more worshipful than to be God's embassador, and in such trust with him that *Eph. vi.* God will vouchsafe to send him on his message? St Paul desires the Ephesians to pray for him, that he might have utterance given him to speak and preach the gospel freely, for the which he was sent embassador. 2 Corinthians v, he saith his embassage stood chiefly in this point, to reconcile us to God.

Stewards. Is not the steward's office an high office, and of greatest credit in great men's houses, and at their commandment and appointing all things be done? They provide and give all in their master's house meat in due season, &c. St *1 Cor. iv.* Paul therefore saith, "Let a man thus think of us, that we be the servants of God and stewards of his secret mysteries," *Matt. xxiv.* which be meat for our souls. St Matthew in a parable calls the preachers stewards, appointed over God's house, to give *Mark xiii. Porters.* their fellow-servants meat in due season. St Mark calleth them porters in God's house, having in commandment to watch that no thieves nor unruly persons come in to trouble the house. They be called "the light of the world," to lead other the right way: they be "the salt of the earth," to season us, that by corruption we do not smell evil before God: they be God's soldiers, to fight for his people, as St Paul says, "No man goes to war on his own wages." They be watchmen, to give warning when enemies come. They be dogs, to bark and awake us out of our deadly sleep, when we forget God. They be the mouth of God, that where we were not able to stand in the sight of God, if he should speak unto us in his glorious majesty, he doth vouchsafe to speak unto us by the mouth of his minister, being a man as we be, and whom we should believe to be sent from God as long as he teaches Christ and his word. Light. Salt. Matt. v. Watchmen. Dogs. Isai. lvi.

These names of trust and credit are given to preachers for the commendation and setting forth of their office, which they bear in God's house; and that they should not think it a vile, but a most worshipful room. And to make them more regarded, the Lord counts those injuries done to himself, which be done to his preachers, saying: "He that despises you, despises me; and in what town soever ye come, if they will not receive you, shake the dust off your feet, and it shall bear witness against them in the day of judgment." Matt. [x.]

And because he joins to the next saying, "In the messages of the Lord;" it doth us to weet the faithfulness of this prophet in his duty, that he speaks nothing but the words of the Lord truly, which sent him; which rule all true preachers should follow. But of this is enough spoken in the verses before.

Now follows the glad tidings of the gospel to comfort this people withal after the great threatenings of God, which the prophet here pronounced in the former verses. For as God works in his creatures, that after winter comes summer, and after a storm fair weather: so in the spiritual doctrine of our souls, first he teaches repentance, preaches the law, threatens vengeance for sin, casts down man in his own sight, and lets him look even into hell with fear of conscience for his disobedience; but afterwards he comforts him, raises him up, and heals him, that this may be found true that is said of our Saviour Christ, "I came not to call the righteous, Matt. ix.

but sinners to repentance;" and "they that be whole need not the physician, but the sick."

<small>The law is first to be taught, and then the gospel.</small>

All the prophets use the same trade in teaching, as Esay in his first chapter calleth the Jews worse than beasts; for "the ox would know his master, and the ass his master's manger, but they would not know their God:" and the rulers he calls the "princes of Sodom," and "fellows with thieves." Jonas also in the beginning of his prophecy saith, "Within forty days Nineve shall be destroyed." Sophony's[1] first words be, that God "will destroy man, beast, fowl, corn, and fruit of the earth." But afterwards every one of them prophesies of Christ, promises blessing from God, with increase of all wealth and goodness. Likewise John Baptist began his preaching: "Repent, for the kingdom of heaven is at hand." And our Saviour Christ began his preaching with the selfsame words. Peter in his first sermon, after they received the Holy Ghost, rebuked the Jews sharply for crucifying Christ the giver of life, and for asking Barabbas a murderer to be delivered unto them: but when their conscience pricked them, they asked what they should do; and he comforts them, bids them repent, and be baptized every one of them in the name of Christ. So here, after the sharp preaching of the law, and threatening of God's plagues, followeth the sweet comfort of the gospel; for he saith, "I am with you, saith the Lord:" as though he should say, Let nothing grieve you, neither the greatness of the sin, that ye have been so negligent in forgetting the building of this house so long; nor the great cost, as though ye were not able to bear and perform it; nor be not afraid of the king's officers which stopped you; for "I am with you, saith the Lord," whose power they cannot withstand, whose mercy passeth your misery, and who can pardon and forgive more than you can sin, and who shall be judge of your doings, and am able to forgive all things trespassed against me. All the riches of the earth is mine, and I bestow it as pleases me: the hearts of kings and rulers be in my hand, and I rule them as I think good: when I will, they shall shew you favour and friendship; and when they lust they shall not stop, hurt, nor hinder my work according to their desire or pleasure, as

<small>Matt. iii.</small>

<small>Acts iii.</small>

[1 Zephaniah's. ED.]

much as they would: but those that fear and love me, I will bless, and they shall not have any harm, and my works shall prosper and go forwards in their hands, as I think good, in despite of all their foes: therefore let nothing fear nor trouble you; for I, whom all things do obey, am with you, saith the Lord.

These are but few words in number, but they are mighty in operation and working, where they be received with an earnest faith; and so mighty, that whosoever hears and believes them to be spoken of God, is not afraid to attempt anything, be it never so great and hard. When Jacob was doubting and afraid, whether he should go into Egypt to his son Joseph or no, God spake to him and said, "Jacob, be not afraid; for I will go down into Egypt with thee, and I will bring thee out again also." Then Jacob, fearing neither the death of his son Joseph, nor the displeasure that might come to him and his, if either he or yet Joseph offended the king; nor yet lest Joseph should lose his authority by a new king, as it is commonly seen; nor the jeopardy of the journey, no, nor yet any other worldly thing that could or might chance, [but] went into Egypt boldly with all his children and substance, and was defended by God. When Moses keeping sheep saw the fire in the bush, and God said unto him, that he would send him to king Pharao to deliver his people, he was afraid and marvelled that he, being but a shepherd, should be sent on such a message to so mighty a prince: but after that God had promised him that he would be with him, he was encouraged, and took in hand to go to Pharao on his embassage, and to lead God's people out of Egypt. When God sent his angel to Gedeon, threshing his corn, and said he should deliver the people from their enemies, which invaded their country and lay as thick in number as grasshoppers do in the field; Gedeon doubted at the matter, until such time as God said unto him, that he would be with him. And after trial of his faith in that promise made unto him, he durst with three hundred naked men, having no weapons but earthen-pots, a fire-brand and horns in their hands, set on their enemies which fled all away, as soon as they heard the potsherds knocked together.

marginalia: Gen. xlvi. — God's help promised stirreth us up to enterprise great things. — Exod. iii. — Judg. vi.

Matt. xxviii.   Our Saviour Christ, after his ascension, sending his apostles into the whole world to preach and baptize, addeth no greater thing to comfort them withal in this great and dangerous enterprise, that so few unlearned men should conquer the whole world, but saith, "Behold, I am with you, even to the end of the world." What good success their preaching had, we at this present day yet feel and see: and also, how he is present always with his, even to the end; and
John xvii. how true his prayer is, that he did not pray only for his apostles, but for all that should believe on him by their preaching.
Rom. viii. When St Paul saith that he was persuaded, that neither nakedness, prison, hunger, persecution, nor life, neither death, angels, nor powers could pull him from the love in Christ Jesu; he had nothing to strengthen himself withal,
Acts xxvii. but that God promised that he was with him, and then he boldly said, "If God be with us, who can be against us?" All be but dust, worms, and vileness in his sight: nothing can prevail against those, whom he doth assist with his grace.

Therefore, when we doubt to take in hand any good work, which agrees with the word of God, for any worldly reasons or carnal fear; let us stir up our faith, and hear God speaking and saying unto us, "I am with you, be ye not afraid." If thy conscience bear thee sure witness, that thou seekest nothing but the glory of God, and the profit of his people; no doubt God will assist thee in such enterprises, and offers this his promise to thee also, saying, "I am with thee: be not afraid," but go on forwards, and I will bless thy doings, seem it never so hard or impossible to thee.

The text. *v. 14. The Lord waked up the spirit of Zerubabel, son of Salathiel, prince of Juda, and the spirit of Josua son of Josedec the high priest, and the spirit of all the remnant of the people: and they went and wrought in the house of the Lord of hosts, their God,*

15. In the twenty-fourth day of the sixth month, in the second year of king Darius.

This is a notable metaphor, and worthily sets forth the nature of sin, in that he saith, "The Lord waked up the spirit of all this people:" for sin is a sleep of the soul, having no fear nor feeling of God, so long as a man lies in it. "It is now time," saith St Paul, "to awake out of sleep," meaning sin. God in his word by such outward bodily things declares unto us the nature of spiritual things, both good and evil. As the dead body lies rotting and stinking in the grave, fearful to look on, and grievous to remember; so when we lie buried in sin, we stink in the sight of God; he cannot abide to look at us, nor will remember us. And as we, when the body lieth on sleep in the bed, which is an image of our grave, can neither see, feel, hear, taste, smell, understand, nor yet move out of the place, until we be awaked, nor can take any pleasure at all in any one creature of God; so when we lie wallowing in sin, we neither see the majesty of God with the eyes of our faith, nor feel his mercies offered unto us in his dear Son and our only Saviour Christ Jesus, nor yet can we taste at all how sweet the Lord is. Our ears are stopped from hearing good counsel; we perceive nothing at all of God's goodness towards us; his word is not savoury unto us, neither yet be we moved or stirred up to do any one good work of charity. But now it pleased the Lord, pitying their misery, to wake them up out of this dead sleep, and set them in hand with building of his house again.

Rom. xiii.

Sin is a sleep and death of the soul.

But where he had preached to them both the law and the gospel, threatenings and comforts; with the plagues they were moved to nothing but fear, as is said in the verses before: but after they heard the glad tidings of the gospel, that God promised to be with them; then they were awaked out of their sleep, and wrought lustily. So it is the gospel that quickens and gives life; but the law kills, fears, and threatens. For as after sleep the body being awaked, it is fresh, lusty, strong and courageous to do his work; so after the fearful threatenings of the law when we hear the glad tidings of the gospel, that God will be our Lord and dwell with us, the mind is comforted, strengthened, and moved up to do his duty. And as a man is judged to be waking when he can do the office of a man, as talk, work, write, or such like; so is man awaked out of the sleep of sins, when he lives in charity, fears God, and walks according to his law in his vocation.

The law kills, the gospel quickens.

Further, as when a man lies in his dead sleep, he cannot awake, except some noise awaken him, or some other call him; so can we not arise out of sin, except the Spirit of God, or his preacher, which is his watchman, with often crying unto us awake us. "Cry" therefore "and cease not," saith Esay the prophet; "Lift up thy voice like a trumpet, and tell my people their wickedness." So that it is the trumpet of God's word continually sounding in our ears, which is the only way to awake us out of this sinful sleep. But the papists turn the order, and say, Cease and cry not; hold thy peace, and say nought; live in rest and be still; and so let all go to havoc, and the people perish.

Isai. lviii.

Thus we may learn here the necessity of preaching, and what inconvenience follows where it is not used. "Where preaching fails," saith Salomon, "the people perish:" therefore let every man keep himself in God's school house, and learn his lesson diligently; for as the body is nourished with meat, so is the soul with the word of God, as St Matthew saith: "A man doth not live by bread only, but in every word that comes from the mouth of God." This is then the ordinary way to keep us in the fear of God, and continual remembrance of the last day, often and diligently to read and hear God's word preached unto us: for that is it which doth and will kill sin in us, as it is written, "Remember the last end, and thou wilt not sin."

Prov. xxix.

Preaching is most necessary.

Matt. iv.

Ecclus. vii.

Faith is kept and increased by the same means that it is gotten: it is gotten by hearing, and hearing comes of the word: let us therefore hear and read it diligently. What is the cause that the papists lie so sound on sleep in their abominations, but that they care not for preaching, nor think it so necessary; and because they would not be told of their faults, that they might amend them? Where sin is not rebuked, it is not known to be sin: nor it will not be amended, without much crying on. David the good king and true prophet of God, after he had gotten with child Urias' wife, could not awake out of that sleep of sin, until he was warned by the prophet Nathan, notwithstanding all and singular such great gifts, which God hath endued him withal; but invented one policy after another to cloke his whoredom and naughtiness withal. First, he sendeth for

Rom. x.

2 Sam. xi.

Urias home, being his faithful soldier in his wars, willing him to go home to his wife; thinking that, if he had lien by her, the child might have been called his. But when he saw that Urias would not go home to his wife, he devised to send him with letters unto Joab the captain, that he should be set in the fore front, when the town should be assaulted, and that his fellows should flee from him, that he might be slain. This policy David wrought so privily, that he thought no man should espy it: for who durst open the king's letters? But at length cometh Nathan the prophet, and telleth him a parable, how there was a rich man, that had many sheep, and a poor man his neighbour had but one, which he loved most dearly: the rich man took this one sheep from the poor man, and Nathan asked what this man had deserved. Then answered David in anger, and said, he deserved death: then said Nathan, Thou hast given a very good sentence: it is even thou thyself that hast done this deed; thou shalt die. For thou hast many wives, and couldest not be content with them, but hast taken thy poor neighbour's, Urias' wife." Then cried David, "I have sinned;" and made that worthy psalm fifty and one: "O God, have mercy on me according to thy great mercy, and according to thy many mercies wash away my wickedness. And yet more wash me from my wickedness, &c." But before Nathan came, he lay without feeling of his sin, or yet any remorse of conscience at all knowing that he had done evil.

So when the good king Ezechias, being restored to his former health, had letten the embassadors of the king of Babel, which came to rejoice for his recovery, see all his treasure and jewels, being very proud of them; Esay the prophet comes unto him, and asketh what they had seen: he told him: Well, saith Esay, even from thence a king shall come to rob and spoil all these treasures that thou hast been proud of. Then the king knowledged his fault, but not before he was rebuked by the prophet. Peter, until he was rebuked of Paul for his dissimulation with the gentiles, did not leave it. Joas was a good king, as long as Jehoiada the high priest lived; for he followed his good counsel: but after he fell from God, when he would hear no good counsel at all.

2 Kings xx.

Gal. ii.

2 Chron. xxiv.

Thus we see how necessary it is for us to be kept in God's school, and hear the trumpet of his word sounding continually in our ears, to awake us up out of this deadly sleep of sin, and stir us forward to a diligent doing of our duties. What a pride is this for us to think so highly of ourselves, that we be so far more holy, strong, wise, learned, more able to stand, than these good men were; and that we need not such continual teaching and counsel, but that we may well enough want it! These men fell when they heard not the voice of the prophets: and yet we, that are not so much worthy as once to be compared unto them in the gifts of God, think we shall stand of ourselves.

<small>To hear preaching all men ought.</small>

Many will say, What should I do at the sermon? I know as much before I go, as I shall learn there: I can read the scripture at home, and comfort myself sufficiently. These are better than they that will neither hear nor read, but say, I know there is no more but do well and have well: I know this is all that can be said, Love God above all things, and thy neighbour as thyself: I can say my pater noster and my creed as well as he; and further I know, that in the one is contained all things necessary to be asked at God's hand, and in the other all that is to be believed: and what can or should a man have more than this?—These sayings, although they be true, yet are they most brutish, and nothing else in very deed but naughty excuses to cloke our slothful wickedness withal; and signify plain that we would not in any wise have preaching, because we would not hear our faults rebuked, nor yet our minds exercised in meditation of God and his goodness, of our own sin and misery. St Paul to <small>Phil. iii.</small> the Philippians saith, that he was not ashamed to write one thing often to them, and it was for their safety. The <small>Matt. xxv.</small> parable of the five foolish virgins and the five wise teacheth plainly, that both the wise and the foolish did both nap, slumber, yea, and fall hard on sleep; wherein is set before us all our natures, whether we be foolish or wise: we fall on sleep forgetting God, when we should watch for his coming, though we think never so highly of ourselves, if we have not the light and burning lamp of God's eternal word burning in our hearts.

What a foolishness is it to think that we can or shall

stand, where as every one hath fallen that is gone before us; or that we shall escape, where every one else hath been taken! There is not the best learned man, but he needs often to hear the preachings and counsel of others, although he can comfort himself in his private studies and in reading the scriptures never so well. For as the physician, when he is sick, cannot heal himself, nor hath not his judgment so perfectly as he had before he was sick, but seeketh help at another physician's hand; so the learnedest man living, as long as he liveth, and beareth sinful flesh about with him, shall have sinful and froward lusts and affections reigning in him, which blindeth his sight, that he seeth not his own sins, until he be warned of them by others. St Peter saith he would put them in remembrance of their duty, as long as he lived, although they knew it well. What should move Paul so often and so earnestly to write unto Timothy and to Titus, having such worthy gifts as they had, if they need not to be warned of their duties? For what cause should either David have had the prophet of God, Nathan, sent of God himself unto him, or yet Ezechias the prophet Esay, either the apostles to be sent forth by couples together, or yet to meet in counsel at Jerusalem, and there to decree hard matters, if one should not learn at another? 2 Pet. i.
1 Tim. iv.
Titus iii.
2 Sam. xii.
Acts xv.

And mark here that he saith, all were fallen on sleep, and lay still on sleep, until the Lord awaked them up by this his prophet Aggeus; both Zerubabel the prince and chief ruler in the commonwealth, Josua the high priest and chief in religion, and all the people also: not so much as one from the highest to the lowest that did his duty herein, but were all fallen on sleep.

What would the pope say, if a man should tell him he were on sleep and fallen from God? Would he not straightways rage, fret and fume, and say that he was God's vicar, or at least Peter's successor here in earth, and that he could not err, but every thing which he did or said was both good and also godly? Surely this high priest, otherwise a very good man, bearing the figure of Christ, and much commended in Zachary the prophet, and having his authority given him of God, and coming unto it by descent also according to the law of Moses, had thus foully fallen on sleep, and forgotten *The pope errs.*

God: and shall we think that the pope, living in the puddle of sin, given to follow all pleasure, and usurping authority against God and his saints, cannot do or say amiss?

And as I noted before, so it is not to be lightly considered, that where so often the prophet here rehearseth the names of Zerubabel and Josua, the two chiefest rulers; yet he evermore setteth in order the civil magistrate and power before the chief priest, to signify the pre-eminence and preferment that he hath in the commonwealth and other matters, more than the chief priest, by what name so ever he be called, whether it be the pope, archbishop, or metropolitan.

The civil ruler is above the priests.

When they were thus awaked, "they went and wrought in the house of the Lord their God." This is a sure argument that a man is awaked, and not still on sleep, when he can and will go work about his business. It is not enough to say he is awaked and will work, but to work indeed. So differs the hypocrite and dissembler from the true charitable man, that the one hath nothing but fair, glosing words, and the other, as oft as he hath occasion offered, doth it indeed, without boasting or cracking of it: for he that doth not work in very deed, is on sleep still, what fair face soever he make on it. The gospel saith plainly, that "by their fruits ye shall know them." And the two sons, whereof the one, when his father bade him go work in his vineyard, said he would and did not, the other said nay, and went, only he that wrought did his father's will. So only be they awaked, which work in the Lord's house: the other either slumber, dream, or else be hard on sleep, and do not their due work in building the house of the Lord our good God.

They that build not the Lord's house sleep in sin.

Matt. vii. & xxi.

When they began to lay the foundation of this temple, the people of the country, which were placed there by Salmanasar, would have holpen them to build, and said they worshipped the same God that they did, (because they perceived that the good king Cyrus favoured them at that present;) but after that Assuerus, the next king following, had stopped them from building any more, they were most earnestly against them. The good men that were amongst them perceived their dissembling, and would not suffer them to work with them. So many amongst us, which be papists indeed,

2 Kings xvii.

when they see that they shall please the rulers, will cry most earnestly for the building of God's house, and pretend as though they would work most stoutly: but if they see the world turn, they will be the first and most earnest destroyers of the same. Such false brethren must be most diligently taken heed of, and not be suffered to join themselves with the true workmen, lest they betray all the good; as we both feel and see our papists to have done, to the slander of God and his word, our hurt and shame. St Paul telleth often how great dangers he was in; but he complaineth of none more than of false brethren, which make a shew of godliness, and yet are most wicked within, even very wolves in lambs' skins. 2 Cor. xi.

But these men, after they were thus awaked by the preaching of Aggeus, went and wrought, now no longer about their own houses, as before, seeking their own profit and commodity; but in the house of the Lord of hosts, whose power now they feared, and mighty hand they had felt so long, and yet not worthily regarded the heaviness of his displeasure, nor his great plagues that he had laid upon them so many years. It was noted in the verses before, why God is called the Lord of hosts, which is for the great, mighty, sundry, and divers ways that he hath conquered, and uses to conquer, those which rebel against him. This is the strength and power that comes by the word of God; that where it is diligently heard and faithfully believed, it maketh us altogether new men, of loiterers workers, and altogether lusty and courageous, and afraid of no displeasure, so that we may work in the Lord's house. Preaching maketh us new men, and of cowards bold.

If we mark in what sort and case these people were, we shall better perceive what effect this little short preaching took in them. They had lien many years not regarding the building of God's house, for fear of the king's displeasure, who had commanded the rulers in the country to stop the building of that house: but now, partly for fear of the plagues which the mighty Lord of hosts had threatened to lay on them, and chiefly that God had promised that he would be with them, they were so stirred up that they regarded not now their own gain and pleasure, nor they feared not the king's officers' displeasure, which had forbidden them to build any more; but straight without suing for a new commission or licence of the king, or speaking with the king's officers, they set up their work, knowing that he which promised would be with them, and that they should prosper well in it, for he was able and would perform it. In Esdras it appears what bold answer they make, when the king's officers asked them by what authority they began to renew their old work; and that letters were sent to king Darius, to know whether they should be suffered to go forward in their building or not. But God so moved the king's heart, that he gave them not only liberty to build, but money also to do it withal: and by the strength of God they had not only given the enterprise, but also went forward in their building, asking no licence at all of any man, before they were complained on.

<small>Ezra v.</small>

This strength hath God's word when it is worthily received, that it maketh a man to forget his own profit, yea lands, wife, children, goods, and life, and manfully to bear death, prison, fire, and displeasure of princes, so that he may do his duty to his Lord God, and escape his displeasure. Peter, who denied his Master at the voice of a handmaid, after he had received the Holy Ghost, was bold to confess him before lords and princes even to the death. Paul, in furious rage of his persecution, was stricken down, and of a wolf rose up a lamb. Nicodemus, that afore durst not be known to be Christ's disciple, or bear him any good will, after durst ask the body of Pilate, and boldly buried it. Thus where true faith is given to God, commanding any thing to be done, or to the preaching of his word, it makes of haters lovers, of fearful bold, of persecutors preachers, and doth wholly change the nature of man, as David saith, "The law of the Lord is without spot, turning the minds of men." This was neither treason nor rebellion against the king, to do that which God by his prophet so straitly commanded, as was declared and noted before; but they were rather traitors to God, that had not of so many years gone more earnestly about that building of God's house, as God willed them to do.

<small>Acts ix.</small>

<small>John iii. & xix.</small>

<small>Psal. xix.</small>

And where he calls God their God yet after so great and long disobedience; it commends unto us the long suffering and merciful goodness of our God, that will not forsake us for a fault or two, nor in a year or two, but continually beareth with us, calling us to him by all means possible, and would not one of the least to perish. "All the day long," saith God by his prophet Esay, "I have stretched out my hands to a people that speaks against me, and faithless." But of this is enough spoken before. God is long-suffering.

Isai. lxv.

And where he addeth this, and saith, "They went and wrought in the Lord's house the twenty-fourth day of the sixth month, and the same second year of Darius;" it teaches us the earnestness of them towards their work, now after they were thus awaked and stirred up out of their sleep. They had but three weeks and three days, both to hear this preaching of Aggeus, and to make ready their tools to work withal; which time had been little enough to have prepared their tools in, although they had not had any other business to have been occupied withal. The prophet was sent from God the first day of the sixth month, as appears in the first verse; and now, the twenty-fourth day of the same month, they began to renew their work with a lusty courage: so the whole time both to hear the preaching, and prepare all things necessary for their great work, was but three weeks and three days. So earnestly doth true faith work, where God is truly feared, and his commandment reverently obeyed, that they cannot be quiet until they have done that which God commands. There is nothing now that can hinder them from this work, neither the fear of the king's displeasure, nor the costliness of the great work, nor the greediness of their own profit, which they sought so much before, neither the greatness of their disobedience in so long forgetting their Lord God; but with one mind and courage they set up this great costly work, manfully continuing in it, and happily finish it in four years' space, notwithstanding the great lets, hinderance, and accusations that were made against them to the king, and other divers ways many. This promise that God had made them, that he would be with them, had so encouraged them, that nothing could stop them from their

Faithful love seeks no delays.

work: but as David, going to fight with Golias, was not afraid of all his strength, harness, nor yet his power and might, but said, "Thou comest against me trusting in thine own strength, and I come to fight with thee with this little sling and few stones, in the name of the living God of Israel;" so they were bold in him only to set on this great work.

1 Sam. xvii.

If they were thus stirred up by this little preaching, what dulness shall we think to be in ourselves, that after such continual crying and calling cannot be awaked to do our duties! Is it any marvel that God doth so often and so grievously plague us, seeing we should without all excuses do it, which he commandeth us; and yet in so long time we cannot be brought to fear him as we should do? We may also learn, what a treasure it is to have God's word amongst us, seeing it is the ordinary way that he hath ordained to bring us unto him by; and what a grief it is to want the continual preaching of the same: and also the wickedness of the papists, that thus do rob the people of it, and would make them to believe that it were not necessary for them, but brings them into heresies, and that it is the mother of all heresy and mischief, and that there was never good world since the scripture was in English, with such like blasphemies.

Scripture is necessary for all men, and no cause of evil.

But if we mark the scripture throughly in all ages, we shall find that in good kings' days, which maintained God's word and his true religion, as David, Salomon, Josaphat, Joas, Ezechias, Josias, in Juda only there was more plenty of all worldly blessings, than there was in all Israel beside, where as the scripture was not regarded. Again: if ye mark well all the ancient heretics, even from the beginning, as Arius, Pelagius, Valentinus, Marcion, Sabellius, Donatus, Eutyches, &c., you shall find none at all, or very few, that were unlearned, but all for the most part were great clerks; and by this reason then the learned, rather than the unlearned, should be kept from the scriptures, if reading the scripture make heretics. For men fall chiefly into heresies, when they trust to their own wits and learning, forsaking or not submitting their wits unto God's wisdom contained in his infallible word and truth. If they will let the people hear the scripture in sermons, I cannot tell why they should not be suffered to read it. Why should rather heresy come by reading than by hearing? Nay, this is their meaning, they would have no preaching, nor yet reading, saving of their dirty dregs[1] of popery, which maintains their idle lordliness; whereas the scripture setteth out their wickedness, which they will not have known, nor yet once touched. The Lord, for his mercy's sake, defend us from their tyranny! Amen.

A PRAYER.

Most mighty Lord and merciful Father, which didst stir up the Jews to the building of thy house by the preaching of thy prophet Aggeus: we thy miserable creatures, oppressed with sin, and living in blindness, beseech thee for thy mercy sake, have mercy upon us, and thrust out diligent workmen into thy harvest; send out faithful preachers, which may by the hard threatenings of thy law, and comfortable promises of thy gospel, awake all thy people out of their dead sleep, wherein they lie wallowing, forgetting thee and their duty. We have all sinned from the highest to the lowest, in not earnestly professing thy holy word and religion; both the princes, rulers, and magistrates, bishops, ministers of all sorts, and all the people: no state nor condition of men hath done their duty herein unto thee, our only Lord and God. Therefore we all with heavy hearts fall down flat afore thy throne of grace and majesty: we beg, crave, and ask thee forgiveness of our great sins: open our eyes, O good God, that we may

[[1] Old editions *dragges*, which is a form sometimes used for *drugs*. But see p. 100, l. 22. ED.]

consider the plagues, which thou hast laid on us so long for our great disobedience towards thee and thy word. Give us new hearts, and renew thy Holy Spirit within us, O Lord; that both the rulers may faithfully minister justice, punish sin, defend and maintain the preaching of thy word, and that all ministers may diligently teach thy dearly beloved flock, purchased by the blood and death of thine own and only dear Son our Lord, and that all people may obediently learn and follow thy law, to the glory of thy holy name for Christ's sake, our only Lord and Saviour.

Chap. II.

v. 1. *In the seventh month, and the twenty-first day of the* The text.
   month, was the word of the Lord sent by the hand of
   Aggeus the prophet, saying:
2. *Speak to Zerubabel, the son of Salathiel, ruler of Je-*
   huda, and to Josua the son of Josedec, the chief priest,
   and to the remnant of the people, saying:
3. *Who is left amongst you, that hath seen this house in*
   his former glory? and what a one you see it now! is
   it not like as it were nothing in your eyes?

As concerning the reckoning of years, months, and days enough was spoken in the first chapter: and what it is to be sent by the hand of a prophet, whoso lust, there he may read.

This message sent now in the seventh month, and the next that comes in the ninth, declare the good will of God towards them that build his house, and how ready God is to further all their doings. They began to work the twenty-fourth day of the sixth month, and had continued to the twenty-first day of the seventh month; and then, lest the fear of the king or the rulers should discourage them, they had need to be comforted: therefore Aggeus is sent unto them again to encourage them, lest they should have fainted or left off working. Again, in the eighth month is the prophet Zachary sent unto them, and in the ninth month Aggeus is sent twice; and all because they should not let their work slip, but with a courage finish it; and that also they might see how true it is, that "to every one that hath it shall be given," and for them which work courageously in the Lord's vineyard, how well the Lord is delighted with them and blesses them. God sends preachers to them that serve him.

Thus God knowing the weakness of this[1] people, every month sends new messages unto them, that they may understand what a care he hath over them, and that they should trust in him which had all things in his hands to rule at his

[[1] First edition *his*. Ed.]

pleasure; and not to trust in themselves, which of themselves could do nothing. Let us therefore work in the Lord's house, and no doubt he will send us comfort enough.

Now, where he is bidden speak to Zerubabel the prince, to Josua the chief priest, and to the remnant of the people; and so often rehearses them in this same order in this prophecy; it doth us to understand, that there is one doctrine of salvation to be taught unto all sorts of men, and that all sorts are bound to hear and learn the same: and besides that, it teaches the preferment of the civil magistrate or ruler to the priest, as was noted before.

And herein we shall chiefly learn the wickedness of them that withhold the scriptures from the lay people, saying, it is not meet for them to be so much occupied in hearing the same. For the prophet saith here sundry times, that he was sent to all the people as well as to the rulers; and therefore it was their duty to learn and hear his message as diligently as it was the rulers'. And this is a great occasion, why that all rulers should behave themselves lowly towards the people, seeing God hath made all things, as concerning salvation, common and of one sort both to poor and rich, that by this means he might increase brotherly love betwixt both parts. "There is one Lord God," saith St Paul, "of all," both poor and rich, one Holy Ghost that makes us all holy, "one baptism, one faith" that we believe, one Saviour Jesus Christ, one Father in heaven unto whom we pray, one everlasting kingdom which we all look for, one scripture and word to teach us, one sacrament for us all; we be born, gotten, die, and buried all in like; and a great knot it is of love amongst us, seeing we speak one language, being of one country or town, and one air which we receive, one fire, sun, moon, stars, earth, herbs, trees, corn, cattle, fish, fowl, that we be fed on: we go, stand, sleep, work all alike, &c.

<small>All things to salvation are given to all sorts of men in like.

Eph. iv.</small>

All the difference that is betwixt us is this: that one is higher in authority, better clad or fed, hath a prouder coat or a softer bed, or more store of money, lands, or servants, than another hath; which thing helps not to salvation. But what vain things these be to rejoice in, or to despise one another for that wants them, the things themselves do declare.

For he that wants all these not necessary things to salvation, is commonly better man, more lusty, strong, and healthful than the other, as is said in the verses before. And to rejoice in ancient blood, what can be more vain? Do we not all come of Adam, our earthly father? and say we not all, "Our Father which art in heaven, hallowed, &c."? How can we crack then of our ancient stock, seeing we came all both of one earthly and heavenly Father? If ye mark the common saying, how gentle blood came up, ye shall see how true it is:

> When Adam dalve, and Eve span,
> Who was then a gentleman?
> Up start the carle, and gathered good,
> And thereof came the gentle blood.[1]

And although no nation has anything to rejoice in of themselves, yet England has less than other. We glory much to be called Britons; but if we consider what a vagabond Brutus was, and what a company he brought with him, there is small cause of glory. For the Saxons, of whom we come also, there is less cause to crack. So that of Brutus we may well be called brutes for our brutish conditions, and of the Saxons *saxi*, that is, stout and hard-hearted: but if we go up to Cain, Japhet, and such other fathers of us gentiles, we may be ashamed of our ancestors: for of all these we come, that knew no God.

Tully, a heathen philosopher, telleth how many ways men came first to have great possessions, and waxed more wealthy and mighty in the earth than others did: either by coming into void places, (saith he) where as none did dwell, and then every man took to himself as much ground as he would; or else they got it in the wars by power from others; or bought it; or else by gift, or descent. So that at the first we were all alike, not one better than another: and we shall be also all alike angels at the last. For in heaven there is no higher place for rich men, nor lower for the poor; but every man according as he hath done, so shall he receive. If the

How authority began.

[1 The last two lines are wanting in the second edition. In both editions the first line has *dalve*, as here printed: Chaucer uses *dalfe* in the preterit tense. ED.]

poor and rich man's blood were both in one basin, how should the one be known to be better than the other, seeing we crack so much of it? Yet doth this derogate nothing from that honour and dignity, which is due to all princes and magistrates in this life of all sorts of men: but it is only spoken how all sorts shall obtain the life to come, and that we should not overmuch rejoice in worldly vanities, but in God alone, that we have him for our God.

And whereas the prince, priest, and people, have all one lesson taught them, and no difference at all is made betwixt them, how to please God, we may see the wickedness of our priests, that by their trentals and other masses can help, as they say, others to heaven, but they themselves care not for such baggage, and buy none of them for themselves, because they think them unprofitable; or else they see there is another way to heaven than this, and therefore will not use this at all for themselves, but deceive others therewith: or rather they care not for heaven, but will here live at ease, and enrich themselves, they care not how, not hoping for another life. But the prophet here, and all the scripture throughout, teaches one way of salvation for all sorts of men, whatsoever they be, how to live and die and enjoy heaven.

The effect of this message now is to comfort them, that they should not faint in their work, but manfully go on forwards, and luckily finish the building of God's house, being discouraged at nothing. Many there were that, beside the fear of the king's displeasure, which had forbidden them to build any more, seeing the gorgeousness of the old temple builded by Salomon, and how slender a house this would be in comparison of that, were sore grieved at it and discouraged. Esdras writeth, that when the ground-work and foundation was laid, some which had seen the old temple, how costly, great, and solemn it was, were very sorry to see this, how slender a work it would be in comparison of the old; and therefore they fell on weeping when as they considered it. The younger sort which had not seen the old temple, that was destroyed by Nabuchodonozor, and now seeing this go so well forward, took their instruments, sang psalms, and praised God that had given them so good and prosperous

Ezra iii.

success; and were right glad that they might have such a house to resort unto, to make their prayers and sacrifices in, although it were not so costly and pleasant as they would wish. In which two sorts of men the one, as Esdras saith, wept because this house was not costly enough, nor becoming the majesty of God their Lord; the other did sing and rejoice, that they had one so good a house as this was. We may learn the sorrow which good christian hearts take, when they see God's true religion, not only coldly set forth, and negli- *Divers good affections in religion.* gently followed, but also if it be not in such perfection as it ought to be, and as they have seen or yet would wish. Also we be taught how we should rejoice, when we have any honest little house and religion granted unto us, to serve and worship our Lord and God in, so that it be according to his word: for the primitive church was glad, if they could get private houses to teach in. The noise was so great, as Esdras saith, that a man could not discern whether was greater, the noise of them that sung, or of them which wept: therefore the prophet saith to them, which were so sorry and heavy for the slenderness of this building, that although this house seemed nothing in comparison of the other in beauty in their sight, yet it should appear a more glorious house afore God than the first. And so it came to pass, as afterwards it shall appear.

Let us note also where he saith, "Which of you hath seen this house in his former glory, &c.", the strong patience and longsuffering of the people of God, that had borne their cross so long, and were not weary of it; but were very sorry that they could not have God worshipped so solemnly as they would. *The cross must be borne strongly, though it seem long.* There was none that could have seen the first temple of Salomon standing in his glory, and now this second temple beginning to be renewed, but he must at the least be fourscore years old, and yet be not past ten years old, when it was destroyed by Nabuchodonozor.

The years of the captivity in Babylon were seventy, as Jeremy promised, and the foundation of this temple was laid under Cyrus, the second year of their returning: so that if we take these years besides those seventy years of captivity, they must have so many also after they were born, that they might be able to remember the temple standing, which can be no less than ten years, or twelve: so that, all counted, they could be no less, but rather more, than fourscore years old: but if we reckon to this second of Darius, they must be anno 130 years old at the least. This I speak to note, how manfully they had borne their banishment under heathen kings, where they were prisoners, mocked, and evil entreated: whereas we are so tender, that we cannot abide a little sorrow for Christ's sake under christian rulers, nor cannot depart from our flesh pots and belly cheer. We call the Jews sturdy and stiff-necked people: but if we compare ourselves to them in many points, we shall find ourselves much worse. They Ps. cxxxvii. sat on the water-banks of Babylon seventy years weeping, and hanged their harps in the willows, instead of the temple, when they had sung their psalms: they were mocked, and yet manfully did they bear all sorrows: we being banished or punished under christian rulers, yet cannot be content with necessaries; but grudging that we want our old flesh pots of Egypt and our superfluous dainties, murmur and grudge at God's doings, and provoke his vengeance upon us.

Matt. xxiv. The apostles coming to our Saviour Christ, and shewing him the goodly building and workmanship of this temple, which they now builded, wondered at the costly fineness of it: but these old men, which had seen the first temple of Salomon's building, wept because it was not good enough, nor to be compared to the first. Notwithstanding all the fineness of it our Saviour Christ told them that the days would come, when their enemies should come, besiege it, destroy it, and not leave one stone standing upon another: and so it came afterwards to pass by the Romans. The first house, if ye mark in the life of Salomon, where is described all the fashion of it, length, breadth, thickness, and height of the walls, the wideness of the house, and what things and jewels were in the house, it is much more gorgeous, costly, and pleasant than this second temple is, whose greatness Esdras telleth in the sixth chapter: but the things that were done in this second house by Christ and his apostles, were much more wonderous than those which were done 1 Kings x. in the first. It was great glory that the queen of Saba came from the utmost part of the earth to see the first temple: but it was much more glorious that into the second temple came the Son of God from heaven, to preach his Father's will and the glad tidings of the gospel.

As in the restoring of this second temple many old men did weep, because it was not so great, gorgeous, costly, and glorious as the first was; so now in the restoring of the gospel many weep, when they see not the churches so well decked and furnished as before. The pope's church hath all things pleasant in it to delight the people withal: as for the eyes, their god hangs in a rope[1], images gilded, painted, carved most finely, copes, chalices, crosses of gold and silver, banners, &c. with relics and altars; for the ears, singing, ringing, and organs piping; for the nose, frankincense sweet, to wash away sins (as they say) holy water of their own hallowing and making; priests an infinite sort, masses, trentals, diriges, and pardons, &c. But where the gospel is preached, they knowing that God is not pleased but only with a pure heart, they are content with an honest place appointed to resort together in, though it were never hallowed by bishop at all, but have only a pulpit, a preacher to the people, a deacon for the poor, a table for the communion, with bare walls, or else written with scriptures, having God's eternal word sounding always amongst them in their sight and ears; and last of all, they should have good discipline, correct faults, and keep good order in all their meetings. But as they wept to see this second house no more costly nor pleasant to the eye; so our poor papists weep to see our churches so bare, saying they be like barns, there is nothing in them to make curtsey unto, neither saints nor yet their old little god. But hereafter it appears, whether of these churches God is more delighted withal. For although these ceremonies in the old law were given by Moses for the hardness of the people, to keep them exercised, that they fall not to idolatry of the gentiles; yet is there no mention of any of these in the New Testament, nor yet commandment now, neither to us nor them, but forbidden to be used of all, both of us and them. We be no longer under shadows, but under the truth: Christ hath fulfilled all, and taken away all such dark kind of cere-

The diversity of the pope's church and Christ's.

Ceremonies.

[1 The pix, or box with the consecrated wafer, hung up by a cord over the altar. ED.]

monies, and hath placed the clear light of his gospel in his church to continue to the end.

But the pope hath thrust the church full of more blind and wicked ceremonies, than ever Moses did: and where Peter said (when the apostles were consulting how many ceremonies should continue for a time) that it was not meet to lay on the gentiles' necks the yoke of Moses' law, which neither they nor their fathers could bear; yet the pope, with cracks to be St Peter's vicar, contrary to St Peter's saying will lay on all people such a heap of his own ceremonies, and that under pain of cursing, as the Jews had never the like in foolish blindness, nor more in number. St Augustine saith, that Christ in the New Testament was content with few sacraments in number, but which were in signification most worthy, as baptism and the Lord's supper[1]: but the pope hath made so many as pleased him, and that such as no scripture can allow. Thus we are taught here, not to esteem the goodness of things by an outward and glorious shew, but to be content with the homely simpleness that Christ taught us in his church, and used himself: for that is more pleasant than all the gorgeous device of man's brain. The wit of man is never content to submit itself to the wisdom of God, but pleases itself more in his own inventions, than in that which God commands: but the gospel saith plainly, that that which is so excellent in the sight of man is abominable in the sight of God.

Acts xv.

Luke xvi.

The text.
    v. 4. *But now be strong, Zerubabel, saith the Lord, and be of good courage, Josua, the son of Josedec, the chief priest, and pluck up your courage, all people of the earth, saith the Lord, and work; for I am with you, saith the Lord of hosts.*

    5. *I will perform the promise which I made with you, when ye came out of Egypt; and my Spirit shall dwell in the midst of you: be not afraid.*

[1 Sacramentis numero paucissimis, observatione facillimis, significatione præstantissimis, societatem novi populi colligavit; sicuti est baptismus Trinitatis nomine consecratus, communicatio corporis et sanguinis ipsius. Epist. II. 54. Tom. II. p. 186. Paris, 1836. ED.]

Lest we faint in the midst of our work, where dangers be great and lets many, there is need of great comfort. The king's officers asked them oftentimes, who gave them leave to renew this building, and what commission they had: the work was great and costly, and their own rulers and brethren by bribing and usury had polled them so sore, that they might well think they were not able to finish it accordingly: their sins and negligence were great, that they had deserved such plagues. Therefore to comfort them withal, God sends his prophet to encourage them all generally, and particularly those by name which were chief in the commonwealth and religion, as Zerubabel and Josua, which had offended most, because they, being rulers, did neither their duty themselves, nor yet caused others to do theirs, which both they should have done; first, in giving good example themselves, and after in seeing others to have done their duties in this building. But as our Saviour Christ, after that he arose from death, sent Mary Magdalene and the other women to the disciples generally, and to Peter chiefly by name, both to comfort them all together (because they all had forsaken him), and to encourage namely Peter, because he cracked most that he would never betray him, but afterward fell the foulest of them all, and therefore had need to be comforted more than all; so now Zerubabel and Josua by name are comforted of the prophet, because they had been more negligent than the rest, and should have been better than the rest. "Tell my disciples," saith our Saviour Christ to the women, "and tell Peter, that they go into Galilee, and there they shall see me, as I told them before." Such a loving God is our Lord and Master, that lest weak consciences should despair, except they have comfort of forgiveness, he sends unto them by name, he speaketh to some by name. The rest of the people are bidden be of good courage, for the Lord God would be with them, pardon and forgive them, aid them and further their doings; but not by name, as these other were, because their offences were not so great as the rest were.

_{They that have fallen most are most to be comforted.}

_{Mark xvi.}

So God hath yet in his church both general absolution, and forgiveness of sins offered unto all by preaching his word, and promise made in Christ to the believers; and also par-

_{Absolution.}

ticular, to comfort the weak conscience withal, when as he applies to himself the promise declared unto him, and believes the same. Work on still, saith the Lord, and be not dismayed of any trouble which ye see towards: for although ye think that many hosts of men be against you, yet fear ye not; for I the Lord of hosts, which have all my creatures ready harnessed to fight against them that strive against you my people, I say, I am with you. Who can prevail against you, when I am on your side? How can any creature, that is but vile worms and ashes in comparison of me the everlasting God, prevail against me their God and Creator? Mark before, and ye shall better perceive here, why he doth so often call himself the Lord of hosts; which is chiefly, because in such dangerous enterprises they had need of some strong man to take their part; and where he had so many hosts ready to defend them as all his creatures from the highest to the lowest, they should not fear, for they had one stronger on their side to fight for them than all others could be that should fight against them.

The selfsame words of comfort that were given them at the beginning to enterprise the building withal, are now repeated again, that they should more manfully continue in the same. Even so is it the selfsame doctrine, faith and belief, by the which we are received into the number of God's people first by baptism; by the which we increase and go forwards in the same faith; and by the which also we shall enjoy heaven at the last: for even as in a child, when[1] he grows to be a man, remains the same substance that was in the child before, but now is made stronger by age, and casts away all childish toys; so in the same faith, which we profess in our baptism, must we grow and learn the full understanding of it, that it may be felt sweeter unto us daily more and more while we live, even to our last end. And as the words are all one here, to comfort the rulers and people withal; so that faith is one also, by the which we shall all be saved. God hath not appointed one way nor gospel for the rich, and another for the poor; but all have one, as is said before: and so is he with all alike, as well with the people as with the rulers. He is not a partial God, but he

It is one faith by which we are received into God's people, by which we also grow in the fear of God, and by which we be saved; and that in all sorts of men.

[1 *When* wanting in the second edition. ED.]

is with all and defends all alike, providing for all indifferently; and will defend the simplest as well as the highest, the people and subjects even as well as the prince. For as a natural father provides for and loves every child, and a good prince will not so look to one piece of his realm that he neglects the rest; so God, our heavenly King and Father, will not so love some of his people that he will hate the rest, nor so provide for a few that the other shall want; but most lovingly provide for all, and saith he will be with them all that work his work. With whomsoever God dwells, he can want nothing, no more than he that stands in the sun can want light: for in God is the well of all goodness, and he gives part thereof to all them that be his, and that he takes into his tuition.

What comfort is in these words, and what it hath caused all faithful men to take in hand when God so promised them, enough was said before. Almost all the notable things in the scripture were taken in hand by the comfort that was taken in these few words, "I am with thee," and by the sure faith that was given to God by them. And as God requires nothing here of them but to work, and other things he himself would care for; so in all other our doings he reserves to himself the success and going forward of things, and nothing shall be ours but the work. He will give increase to all good things that are taken in hand in his name, as he thinks best. Let not us therefore be so careful for that: only let us work as be biddeth us, and he will bless it to his pleasure. "Neither he that plants nor he that waters is anything, but God that gives the increase," saith St Paul. And again: "Your labour was not in vain in the Lord." He gives increase to some thirty, sixty, or an hundred, as his heavenly wisdom thinks good: yet all must work most earnestly in his vineyard, referring the end of their labour and profit to him whose work it is, who will see no necessary thing fail them which be not loiterers in his building. Little things, that are taken in hand in the Lord's name, shall grow to great things to them which work diligently, as the scripture saith, "That which is weak before God, is stronger than men; and that which is most glorious before men is abominable before God." Jonathan and his page

[margin: Let us work, and the profit commit to God.]

[margin: 1 Cor. iii. xv.]

[margin: Matt. xiii.]

[margin: 1 Cor. i.]
[margin: Luke xvi.]

discomfited all the host of the Philistians, and then Saul following the chase destroyed them. Eliseus and his boy being in the city, when his boy was afraid, he desired God to open his boy's eyes, that he might perceive how many more were with them than against them; and then the boy saw the hill full of angels harnessed to defend them both, and God so blinded his enemies that they followed the prophet, whom they sought to kill, into the midst of his country, where he might have destroyed them if he had lust.

<small>1 Sam. xiv.
2 Kings vi.</small>

God made divers promises to them, after they came out of Egypt: but because he beginneth to entreat of Christ in these sentences following, I think he means that promise chiefly, where Moses said, "The Lord would raise up unto you a prophet like unto me; him shall you hear." This prophet was Christ Jesus, like to Moses in many points, being born amongst them, and of their brethren of the stock of Judah and David, of whom afterwards the Father said with a voice heard from heaven, "This is my well-beloved Son, in whom I am well pleased; hear him." Or else it may well be taken for the promise which is written in the twenty-third[1] of Exodus, where it is said, "Behold I will send my angel (or messenger) before thee, and he shall lead thee in the way, and shall drive all thy enemies out before thee, whose land thou shalt possess." This angel was Christ Jesus, who is called the Angel of the great counsel, because he brought from the bosom of his Father the secret counsel of God, and preached his great love to the world. An angel is no more but a messenger or embassador from God, to declare and preach his will and pleasure to the world. And that Christ was present with the Israelites, and guided them in the wilderness, St Paul telleth plain, that they tempted Christ, and murmured against him; and Christ was the rock. The meaning and effect of this promise is no more, but that as God was present with their fathers, when he brought them out of Egypt, and delivered them out of all dangers, were they never so many nor so great, and brought them into the land that he promised them; so he would now be present with them, deliver them, and finish their work, if they would work earnestly, neither mistrusting his mercy

<small>Deut. xviii.</small>

<small>Matt. iii. [xvii.]</small>

<small>Christ promised was present with our fathers before he was born.</small>

<small>Isai. ix.</small>

<small>1 Cor. x.</small>

[¹ Both editions, 22. ED.]

but that he would be with them and defend them against the rulers which hated them, nor fearing his power but that he was able to perform his promise unto them. If we mistrust either his good will towards us that he will not, or his power that he cannot, deliver us, we provoke his anger to devour us, and cannot look for help at his hands to save us: for nothing offends his majesty more than mistrust, unfaithfulness, or doubting, as St James saith, "He that doubts is like a wave of water driven with wind to and fro; and that man which so doubts, can look to obtain nothing at God's hands." He gives all his gifts to them that be faithful, and believe that he is both a true God, performing all that he promises, merciful and willing to help all which in their need call upon him, and able to fulfil all that he saith. They that either doubt or deny his offered mercy or power to help, deny him to be a God. ^{James i.}

Therefore fear not, but believe me to be your God, and I will deliver you and defend you, as I did your fathers; and ye shall finish this temple by my protection, as I did bring them into the land which I promised them, drove out their enemies, and gave them the land to dwell in. So according to this promise it came to pass to this people now; for in four years' space next following they finished that temple, as Esdras teaches. So good speed had they after that they believed his promise, and that he would be with them. ^{Ezra vi.}

But here may be moved a great question, how this is true that God saith by this prophet here, that he brought them out of Egypt, when this people never came there, but about a thousand years before Moses brought out their fathers through the Red Sea, where Pharao was drowned, after that he would not believe the great wonders wrought in his sight, nor fear the Lord, that had so often and grievously plagued him for handling his people so cruelly. The scripture uses oft to give that which was done to the fathers, as though it were done to the children: as, when Melchisedec took tithes of Abraham, he is said also to have taken tithes of Levi, which was not born of many years after, because he was contained in the loins of Abraham, and afterward born of his stock and seed. So likewise saith St Paul: "By one *That which the fathers had is also said to be the children's.* *Heb. vii.* *Rom. v.*

man sin entered into the world, and by sin death, and hath gone through all, in whom all have sinned." So we all, that now live or hereafter shall do, and all before us, have sinned in Adam, and broken God's commandment, as well as Adam did, because we were contained in his loins and as it were part of him, and took our sinful nature of him in his seed and posterity. As we see those rivers, which spring out of little wells, are of the same nature that the head and spring is whereof they come, though they run two or three hundred miles off through divers countries; and as those crabs are sour this day, that grow on the crab-tree which is two or three hundred years old, because the first root and plant was sour: so we all be sinful that be born of Adam, and sour as he was, because he the first tree was such a one, and the spring whereof we come was corrupt and filthy. So likewise God saith, he brought this people out of Egypt, which never had been there, because he delivered their fathers thence, in whose loins they were contained, and should have been born there and subject to the same slavery that their fathers were, if God of his great mercy and mighty power had not delivered their fathers thence, and brought them into the land which he promised them. And as the mercy which hath been received in times past is a token and argument of like mercy and grace, to be shewed whensoever we stand in the like need and distress; so here, that they should look for a sure help at God's hand now in these dangers that they were in, he putteth them in remembrance of that great deliverance, which not their fathers only, but they also had before out of Egypt, that they should not be afraid now, but look for sure help. The danger was greater before, out of which they were delivered, and yet they escaped it: so now, God's power and good will being no less toward them than before, they should look for the like help of God as before.

Mercy received aforetime is an argument of like to be shewed in trouble to come or present.

He promises them here, that his Spirit should dwell with them, and therefore they should not be afraid. For as before he sent his angel to guide them in the wilderness; so now he would send his Holy Spirit unto them to dwell with them, which should teach them all things that they doubted of, or were ignorant in; should comfort them in all dangers and distress, and deliver them from all perils that were toward them, and therefore they should not fear.

But as the other part of the promise concerns Christ, which should come to deliver them out of spiritual bondage and slavery of sin and the spiritual Egypt; so this part here concerns the sending of the Holy Ghost, whom Christ said he would send to dwell with us and be our Comforter to the end. And as the building of this second temple betokens the church of Christ builded by the preaching of the gospel; so here is the Holy Ghost promised, which he said should not come, except he went away from them. This Spirit is called a Comforter, because he strengthens us in all our trouble: he is the Spirit of truth, because he leads us into all truth, and putteth us in remembrance of all things which Christ himself taught before, but no new doctrine he brings of his own. And because our Saviour Christ is taken from us in his bodily presence, he promises us that this Spirit shall dwell with us, not for a time, but to the end, and therefore we should not fear. *The Holy Ghost is promised to the builders. John xvi. John xiv.*

But is this a sufficient cause to persuade a man that he should not fear the power of kings or worldly trouble, because the Spirit of God dwells with him? Yea, truly; for what spirit can prevail against the Holy Spirit, which is the power of God? It is written of Gedeon, when he enterprised that venturous act to fight against God's enemies, that the Spirit of the Lord did clothe and defend Gedeon, as our clothes do us; and so he obtained that noble victory, with so few against so many. And not to be afraid in such trouble is the work of the Holy Ghost, as Esay called him the Spirit of boldness, strength and wisdom. Peter, when he denied his Master for the words of an handmaid, after he received the Holy Ghost, did and durst confess him to the death before princes and rulers. So said our Saviour Christ to his apostles: "When ye shall stand before kings and rulers, take no thought what or how ye shall speak; for in that hour it shall be given unto you what you shall speak: For it is not you that speak, but the Spirit of your Father which speaketh in you." *Judg. vi. Isai. xi. 2 Tim. i. Matt. x.*

And although to worldly wisdom this Spirit seems but a small thing, yet it is most true that St Paul saith: "That which is foolishness before God is wiser than men, and that *1 Cor. i.*

which is weak before God is stronger than men." And he that hath this Spirit dwelling in him needs not to fear any power, be it never so great: for "if God be for us, who shall be against us?" and if he take his breath and spirit from the mightiest princes, they are troubled and vade away.

<small>Rom. viii.
Psal. civ.</small>

<small>The text.</small>   v. 6. *For thus saith the Lord of hosts: Yet one little time shall be, and I will trouble the heavens and the earth, the sea, and the land.*
7. *And I will trouble all people, and the Desire of all people shall come; and I will fill this house with glory, saith the Lord of hosts.*

The prophet goeth on forth with this comfort to all people, and promises not only that God would be with them in this building, which they should finish in few years following; but into the temple also, which they did now build, God would send his Son Christ Jesus to preach his Father's will, whom all people looked for and desired his coming; and he would fill that house with glory, that they should not need to care for the smallness of it: if they would only with courage work, God would fulfil the rest. And that they should know him to be able to fulfil his promise, he calls himself by the glorious name of the Lord of hosts so often here in these verses, that they may understand all creatures to be at his commandment, and that none could prevail against that which he would have done, as is said before.

But this is a strange kind of comfort to tell them of such a trouble, as should trouble heaven and earth, sea, land, and all people; and yet they should be glad of it, and that it should come not long after. The time when this trouble chanced was about five hundred years after that this prophet had thus spoken; and yet he calls it but "one little time." And this may well be called a little time in respect of God, with whom all things are present before his sight without time, and a thousand years with him is as yesterday which is past, and he himself is before all times, not contained in time, but living for ever without time. Or else it is called a little time in respect of that long time, wherein their fathers had so long looked for the coming of Christ, and so much desired

him, and yet see him not. It was now above three thousand *Great trouble for Christ is joy to the good, and though it be long it seems short; but the evil be vexed sore at it.*
year since he was promised to Adam; about two thousand since he was so often spoken of to Abraham; and one thousand since it was renewed to Moses, and after to all the prophets from time to time: in respect of which five hundred may well be called a little time.

This trouble which he saith should trouble heaven, earth, sea, land, and all people, is described by these mighty words, to set out the greatness of the trouble by the figure called hyperbole; and not that the trouble was such that heaven, earth, sea, and land, should feel it and be troubled therewith, which are insensible creatures, and can feel nothing that troubles them; but thus by these words the scripture uses to tell the greatness of anything that it speaks of. Moses *Deut. xxxii. Isai. i.* and Esay, because the people were hard-hearted and would not hear their saying, to set forth their hardness of heart, and the greatness of that message which they had from God to speak, say thus: "Hear, ye heavens, and give ear, thou earth, &c." St Paul saith by the like figure, "Every *Rom. viii.* creature groans and travails, looking for the last day, wherein they shall be delivered from this vain corruption wherein they serve;" not because dead creatures can groan or travail, but for the great desire that they have to see that day of our redemption fulfilled, as the woman which travails groans, and desires to be delivered out of her pain, and to be restored to her former quietness: or else it may be taken, that all creatures in all these places should be troubled.

But if this trouble should be so great, how can it be a promise of joy and comfort? Who can be merry to hear tell of such a great trouble? Surely this is not promised to the evil, but to the good. For as our Lord and Master Christ saith, speaking of the trouble that should be in the destruction of Jerusalem and the latter end of the world, "Woe be to them that be with child, and give suck in *Luke xxi.* those days! and the wicked shall wish the hills to fall on them and hide them; they should seek for death, and it should flee from them:" so he saith to the good in the midst of all that desperate sorrow, wherein the evil man cannot tell what to do, "Lift ye up your heads and be merry, for *Matt. xxiv.* your redemption and deliverance is at hand." So after this short time that he speaketh of, this great trouble which shall be at the birth, preaching, miracles, and death of our Saviour Christ, should be but only to the wicked. For the good men should as much and more rejoice, because that day of salvation and redemption was comen, and he whom all people looked for had now appeared to the comfort of all good men.

And this trouble should not be so much to the bodies and goods of the wicked men, as to the mind and conscience: nor this joy should not be so much worldly and outward to the good, as to the soul and inward. Great worldly peace was in all the world, when our Saviour Christ Luke ii. was born: but that peace which the angels sang, "Glory be to God in high, and in earth peace," is rather the peace of conscience, because God and man were now reconciled, and peace was made betwixt us and God; because his Son had taken our nature upon him, and was made man: Isai. xlviii. but unto the wicked it may always well be said, "There is no peace to the wicked, saith the Lord." What a trouble was Herod in, when the wise men came and asked, "where was he that was born king of the Jews?" The scripture Matt. ii. saith, that "Herod and all Jerusalem was troubled" at this question. Herod thought he should lose his kingdom, and the scribes and Pharisees thought that their authority was gone: which thing grieved them so much, that they had rather have had no Christ than lost that authority. But Herod devises a policy to save himself withal, and kills all the children that were two year old and under, thinking amongst them all he should have killed Christ: and he had rather have killed all, than that only Christ should escape. What a trouble was he in, when he caused such a murder for fear of a young child! What reason is it that such a king should so much fear a young child? But God provided well enough for his Son, and was as wise, ready and merciful to save and deliver his Son Christ, as the other was subtle and cruel to murder him: for Herod had rather slay all the children than that one Christ should escape. God bad Joseph take Mary and the child Jesus, and flee into Egypt, and tarry there until he gave him contrary word.

What trouble were the scribes and Pharisees in, when for his doctrine, preaching, and miracles, which were so wonderful that they could not tell what to say, but sometimes said, "Do we not say well that thou art a Samaritan, and hast a devil?" another time they would have thrown him down of the hill; and again they say, "It hath not been heard of from the beginning, that any man hath opened the eyes of him that was born blind;" and again, "A manifest wonderful sign they have wrought, we cannot deny it;" and also, "If we let him alone thus, the whole world will follow him." How was the other Herod (which beheaded John Baptist) troubled, when he heard of his miracles, and would have had him to have wrought some in his sight! How was Pilate's wife troubled in her dream for him, and sent her husband word that he should not meddle with him! How gladly would Pilate himself have delivered him, washed his hands to declare his innocency, and said he found nothing worthy of death in him! How were all the priests afeard, when they heard tell that he was risen from death, and gave money to the watchmen to say his disciples came and stole him away when they slept! Why should they fear a dead man? If he were a man only, he could not hurt them: if a God, they could not withstand him. What trouble were the priests in, when they forbad the apostles to preach any more in Christ's name, and followed the counsel of Gamaliel, saying, "If it were of God, they could not abolish it!" Why should they be afraid of a dead man? John viii.

Acts iv.

Matt. xiv.

Luke xxiii.

Matt. xxviii.

How was king Agrippa troubled, when Paul had defended his cause, and said to him, "Thy great learning, O Paul, maketh thee mad!" How were the great learned philosophers in Athens troubled, when Paul preached the resurrection of the dead, and of Christ, and said, "What means this sower of new doctrine? he seemeth to teach new Gods!" What a trouble was the emperor Tiberius in, when Pilate wrote to him of the preaching and miracles of Christ, and he demanded that the whole parliament of Rome would worship him as a God[1]! Acts xxvi.

Acts xvii.

[[1] Tiberius ergo, cujus tempore nomen Christianum in seculum introivit, annunciatum sibi ex Syria Palæstina quod illic veritatem illius divinitatis revelaverat, detulit ad senatum cum prærogativa suffragii sui. Senatus quia non ipse probaverat, respuit. Cæsar in sententia mansit, comminatus periculum accusatoribus Christianorum. Tertullian. Apologet. adv. Gentes, cap. v.—See note A. at the end of the volume. ED.]

But they, considering that he is a jealous God, and that he will have no other worshipped with him, but all honour must be given to him only, denied him to be a God, or yet to be worshipped there as God. What caused pope Leo the Tenth[1] to be so afraid, when Zuinglius began to preach the gospel, but that he perceived the light of God's word would deface his pomp aud pride, and set abroad all his wickedness to the world to be laughed at? and lest he should go forward in preaching and rebuking his abomination, he sent his letters to him sealed under his bull of lead, willing him to hold his peace, and preach no more of such things, and he would give him what living and as many bishoprics as he would, yea, to be a cardinal, and whatsoever he would ask, except his own seat to be pope. But he like a true preacher went on forwards in his business, setting up Christ, and pulling down popery.

Papists fear the gospel, and indeed deny Christ.

What makes the pope at this day and his clergy to burn, persecute, and imprison all that love the gospel, but that they fear to lose their lordliness, make their bellies their God, and would live at ease like lords of the land? What makes them to deny Christ to be a God, not so much in plain words, as in doctrine and deeds covertly; but that they see they get much riches by relics, pilgrimages, saints, masses, pardons, &c., which do as much in effect as deny Christ to be God, because they seek help by these means in their troubles, and forgiveness of sins with comfort of conscience, which all belong so unto Christ, that whosoever seeks them other ways or elsewhere, than at his hands only, do as much as in them lies as to make Christ no God, rob him of that honour which is due to him only, and give it to gods of their own making? What marvel is it, if they follow that old decree of the Romans in their parliament, where they denied Christ to be received and worshipped for a God, because he should not have all honour alone, as it is due to him only?

Thus we see, what great trouble it is to the wicked to have Christ and his doctrine to come abroad; and how true

[1 It was pope Adrian VI. anno 1523. Leo X. had died the year before. Hottinger. Hist. Eccles. Sec. XVI. P. ii. cap. iii.—See note B. at the end of the volume. ED.]

this was that the prophet saith here, and what trouble hath been, and shall be to the end, where the gospel is preached. "The father shall deliver the son to death, and the son shall rise against the father; so shall the mother against the daughter, and the daughter against the mother, brother against brother, &c.," which things we all see at this day to have come to pass. How many wives, rather than they would forsake God, have suffered death, forsaken husband, children, goods and country, and willingly banished themselves; and so have many good husbands also! How hath one brother persecuted another, one friend and familiar another, even to the death! How hath one bishop deposed and burned another, not to be an earnester preacher than the other was, but more lordly and cruel persecutor! But this is ever true, that Christ our Saviour said should follow the preaching of his word; that whoso will be his disciple must forsake himself and all pleasures of the flesh, and those which be of his own house shall be his enemies. Matt. x.

Although this is marvellous, that in such trouble there should be joy and comfort; yet this is more marvellous, that after all people were thus troubled for the gospel, they should come unto it, believe it, and receive it, not regarding any sorrow which was joined therewith,—no, not fearing the loss of their lives, so they might enjoy it. Fear maketh a man to run away, and not to come: but this is the nature of the gospel, that the more it is persecuted the more it flourishes, as David saith: "The righteous man flourishes like a palm-tree." The palm-tree is such, that if a great weight be laid on it, the broader it spreads and flourishes. And as camomile with treading on it and walking waxes thicker; so the good man, the more he suffereth for his Christ, the more is his faith increased. And as the husbandman that will reap much must sow much; so the more that die for the word of God, the more increase to follow the same: as we commonly say, Of the ashes of hereticks rise up a new sort. It cannot be, but when men see one so constantly stand in defence of his opinion, that he gives himself to the death for it, they will begin to consider what a thing it was that he died for, and that no man will rashly cast himself away: when they see the truth of it, and God opens their eyes to per- Psal. xcii.

Persecution increases the gospel and boldeneth men.

ceive, they are moved to offer themselves to the same death and jeopardy also.

Cyprian writes, that the blood of martyrs is the seed of the church[1], whereof rise and increase more, as of the seed in the field springs new corn. Augustine likewise saith of them that were persecuted for Christ and his word: "They were tied in chains and torments; they were whipped, slain and burned; they were imprisoned, they were killed and torn in pieces; and yet they increased[2]." They were so far from fear, that not only they denied him not; but the more sorrow they had, the more believed on him. And when St Laurence see his bishop Xistus[3], being then pope, to be drawn to death, he said: "*Quo is, pater, sine diacono, quod non soles?*" That is to say, "Father, whither goest thou without thy deacon, which thou wast not wont to do?" "Well," saith he, "thou shalt follow me not long after." And so it came to pass indeed; for he died for Christ too. It is written of one notable woman, which when she heard tell of the day of execution, and that many should be put to death for Christ's sake, she took her child in her arms uncalled for, and runs thither that she might profess her faith, and be put to death with them. As she was running, she met the officer going to see them put to death: he, seeing her make such haste, asked her whither she went; and she told him: "Why," saith he, "knowest thou not that there shall be a great number put to death, and that I go to see it done?" "Yes," saith she, "I know it well, and therefore I go that I may die with them." Then said

Marginal note: De Civitate, liber xxii. cap. 6.

[1 The sentiment is Tertullian's, Apologet. adv. Gentes, cap. XLVI. fin. Plures efficimur, quoties metimur a vobis. Semen est sanguis Christianorum. Augustine also has: Pro ipsis idolis adversus nomen Christi repleta est terra martyribus: sparsum est semen sanguinis; surrexit seges ecclesiæ. Serm. 109. De Temp. cap. 4. ED.]

[2 Ligabantur, includebantur, cædebantur, torquebantur, urebantur, laniabantur, trucidabantur, et multiplicabantur. Non erat eis pro salute pugnare nisi salutem pro Salvatore contemnere. De Civ. Dei, Lib. XXII. Cap. VI. § 1. fin. ED.]

[3 Xistus, or Sixtus, bishop of Rome, was put to death in Valerian's persecution, anno 257. St Lawrence (Laurentius) three days after was broiled on a gridiron by a slow fire. The beautiful story connected with his death is referred to below, p. 157. The whole narrative will be found in L'Abbé Fleury's Ecclesiastical History, Book VII. Chap. 38, 39. ED.]

the officer, "Why dost thou carry thy child with thee?" And she said, "That it may be a martyr to die for Christ." The officer marvelling that the Christians did not fear death, sent the emperor word, that he would not go to put them to death; but he should send another, if he would have it done.

Likewise in the Acts, when the priests forbad the apostles to preach any more in Christ's name, and whipped them, the more they preached, and thought themselves happy that they were thought worthy to suffer such things for his name's sake. And for all the cruelness of the rulers, Peter turned two thousand at one sermon, and three thousand at another, which came, saying, "Brother, what shall we do?" and being pricked in conscience ran not away, but came as the child to the father when he is afraid. When Paul and Silas had been whipped all day, and locked in the stocks at night in the deep dungeon, and were watched with soldiers; the chains fell off them: the keeper perceiving the prison door open by itself, and thinking the prisoners were escaped, would have killed himself: but after that he see they were all there, and perceived the great work of God, he fell down, desired them to go into his house, washed their stripes, believed in Christ and was baptized. *Acts v.* *Acts ii. iv.* *Acts xvi.*

There is no people under heaven, but they have once received the gospel; and that cannot be said truly of any other kind of learning in the world. "Their sound hath gone through the whole world," saith the psalm. The philosophers never agreed all in one kind of learning, but had many sects amongst them; nor the whole world never received them: nor any heresy was generally received; but only the scripture hath been universally taught and received, which is a sure argument of the truth of it. "Ask of me," saith God the Father to his Son Christ, "and I will give the people for thy heritage, and the uttermost parts of the earth for thy possession." Many such general promises there be, wherein the turning of all people on the earth to the gospel is contained, and since the coming of Christ perfectly fulfilled. The heresy of transubstantiation, purgatory, priests not to marry, ministering the Lord's supper in one kind, the pope's supremacy, &c., the Greek church never received, nor yet do. And although at the council at Flo- *No doctrine hath been generally received but the gospel. Psal. xix.* *Psal. ii.*

rence a few seemed to agree to it, yet were they shent[1] for so doing, when they came home, and it would not be received. Before the death of our Saviour Christ, God had chosen to him but only the Jews to be his people; but after they had refused to receive him for their Redeemer, he bad his apostles go into the whole world, and preach to all creatures. Now was the time come that all were called; and of all sorts, degrees, countries, and states, many were turned unto God.

<small>None can be excused by ignorance. Rom. i.</small>

There is no people under heaven that can excuse themselves by ignorance, but they have been sufficiently taught: for St Paul saith, that the heathen before Christ was born were without excuse; for where they knew God, and worshipped him not as God, therefore God gave them up to their own lusts. By the creature his invisible power and majesty may be known, that he is a God. And therefore the most unlearned is without excuse: for this is sufficient to teach them to know there is but one God, and to worship him as God, though they never read the scripture; and whosoever doth not worship him by this natural knowledge, is justly condemned.

<small>Antony.</small>

We read of Antony, that holy father, which lived in wilderness, and, being so far unlearned that he could not read, was asked of his friend how he passed the time away, seeing he lived alone and had no books: "Yes," saith Antony, "I want no books; for all the creatures of God are my books, and I read and learn his majesty out of his creatures, as you do out of your books[2]."

<small>The creatures of God are rather laymen's books than images.</small>

And surely they be goodly books to be looked on and to behold, the sun, the moon, stars, birds, fishes, beasts, herbs, corn and grass, trees, hills, rivers, &c. And he is worse than a beast that can go look at all these, and not love, praise, and wonder at his strength, power, wisdom, and goodness,

[1 Shent: blamed, from the old verb, to shend.—The council was held A.D. 1438. Dr Delahogue's account of the result of its proceedings is: "Facta est unio ecclesiæ Græcæ cum Romana; sed cito disrupta fuit a Græcis in patriam reversis." Tractatus de Ecclesia Christi. Append. II. ED.]

[2 Τὸ ἐμὸν βιβλίον, ἔφη ὁ Ἀντώνιος, ὦ φιλόσοφε, ἡ φύσις τῶν γεγονότων ἐστί, καὶ πάρεστιν, ὅτε βούλομαι, τοὺς λόγους ἀναγινώσκειν τοὺς τοῦ Θεοῦ. Socrat. Eccles. Histor. Lib. IV. Cap. xxiii. ED.]

which hath made all these to serve us. The stars keep so good an order and course in their movings, the virtue of herbs help diseases, and all fish, fowl and beasts feed and serve man: which things come from him who is Lord of nature, and not of themselves. These may better be called laymen's and the unlearned people's books than images and idols, which be like unto whomsoever it pleases the painter to make them like. If all the images of any one saint were laid together, they would all be unlike one to another in many points; and what a monster should he be that should be like all these! If the relics, as arms, head, legs, scalp, hair, teeth, &c., were together in one place, that are said to be worshipped in many, some should have two or three heads, more legs and arms than a horse would carry; their gilded coats and painted faces should teach rather to be proud and to play the harlot, than soberness, simplicity, holiness and lowliness, as becomes the godly and saints indeed.

After when he adds, "The Desire of all people shall come," there is prophesied the coming of Christ in our flesh and nature to redeem us from the bondage of hell, sin, and death, which thing all good men from the beginning have desired. It was a joyful thing to perceive Christ to come by the eyes of faith, and happy was he to whom it was given to understand and believe in him to come: but more happy did they think themselves, which did not only believe in him to come, but see him present in flesh. Simeon, a righteous man always occupied in prayer, desired to live till the day when he might see the Lord: which request God granted him; and when the child Jesus was presented in the temple by his mother, he took the child Jesus in his arms, praised God, and said, "Lord, now lettest thou thy servant depart in peace, according to thy word; for mine eyes have seen thy saving health;" and so was well contented to die after he had his desire. John Baptist, being young in his mother's womb, leaped for joy as soon as his mother heard the salutation of the virgin Mary coming unto her. Anna, the prophetess, a widow, living in fasting and prayer continually, chiefly desired to see the day of his coming. "Many kings and prophets," saith St Luke, "have desired to see that day, and have not seen

[margin: Christ is desired of all good men.]
[margin: Luke ii.]
[margin: Luke i.]
[margin: Luke x.]

it." Such a great desire for the increase of their faith have all good men had to see Christ in our flesh and nature, that we might by his death be delivered from the slavery of hell, sin, and death. What a misery is it to be in bondage of conscience for our sins, and God's righteous judgment! and what a comfort is it to know, that God is reconciled to us by the death of his Son! This is the desire of all good men, which is fulfilled to us in Christ. And he is called "the Desire of all people" by the Hebrew phrase, which is as much to say as "most desired." So St Paul calls him not only righteous and peace-maker, but righteousness and peace itself: for so have such words more strength when they be pronounced like substantives, than the adjectives have. What a desire had Esay the prophet, when he cried: "Would to God thou wouldest burst the heavens and come down!"

1 Cor. i.

For this peace, that God saith he will "fill this house with glory," much was said afore: but there he said only he would shew his glory; and now he saith, he will fill it with glory. And this is to comfort them that were so sorry, because this house was little in comparison of the other old one, and nothing so costly and glorious. The fulness of this glory appeared when Christ preached his Father's will, healed diseases, wrought miracles, rebuked the scribes with their traditions, &c. as was said before. What greater glory can be, than to do good to them which be his enemies, to help them which cannot help themselves, and to do it so freely that he looks for no reward in so doing; but even of free pity, which he had on us, seeing us lie in such misery, did shew such mercy as to redeem us, to take us for his children, lovers and friends, to teach us, help us, and give us grace to do his will, worship his majesty, fear him, and love him, know our own weakness; and pardon our negligence, our infirmity, our forgetful and unthankful disobedience? Great glory was shewed in this house, when as Alexander the Great, called Magnus, submitted himself to the high priest, God's minister, confessing his God to be the true God, where afore he was purposed to have destroyed Jerusalem[1]: and also, when Judas Machabeus with his bre-

The glory of Christ in his church.

[[1] See above, p. 69. ED.]

thren, after many noble victories, restored God's religion. But none of these filled this house with glory, but some part of it: only Christ our Lord, in whom is the fulness of the Godhead, filleth this house with glory. Christ filled this temple so full of his doctrine and miracles, by himself and his apostles, that the fulness thereof ran through the whole world: for there it began as in a spring, and now hath filled the whole world therewith. So liberal is he that he giveth not only a part, but full and heaped measure, even to the top that it flows over. What a glory of God was shewed in this house, when out of all countries under hea- Acts ii. iv.ven were gathered devout men to worship God there; and after that the apostles received the Holy Ghost, when Peter in his sermons converted five thousand! How far spread was this glory, when the eunuch of queen Candace, moved Acts viii.with the great report of that gorgeous temple, came thither for to worship! But this the mighty Lord of hosts works, which hath all things at commandment, and truly fulfils all his promises even unto the end.

> v. 8. *Gold is mine and silver is mine, saith the Lord of* The text.*hosts.*
> 9. *Greater shall be the glory of this later house, than of the further, saith the Lord of hosts. And in this place will I give peace, saith the Lord of hosts.*

There were two chief reasons which discouraged them from this building, which were meet, yea, and necessary to be pulled out of their minds: and therefore the prophet chiefly touches these two. The first was the kings beforetime, who had forbidden to build, and their officers, which were as diligent to stop them: the second was poverty, for that by the great usury, bribery and oppression of the rulers they were so needy, that they were not able to finish it. For the first, God sets himself against the king, as though he should say: 'Though the king's power be great, yet I am greater: though he forbid, yet I bid: though he be against you, yet am I with you, saith the Lord of hosts. What harm can they all do unto you, when I am with you? Who can hurt, when I will defend?' For their poverty, they should not fear; for 'all gold, silver, riches and treasure is mine, saith the Lord; and I give as much and as little, when, where, how long, and to whom I list. All be my stewards, and to me shall make an account: it is not their own to spend as they will, but as I appoint. Although churls be niggards and will not part with it; unthrifts do waste and misspend that which they have; and neither of them will further this my work; yet fear not ye, for I (in whose hands are all hearts and all riches) will so move their minds, and bring the matter so to pass, that my house shall not lie unbuilded for lack of money. I ask no more of you but to do as much as in you lieth: put your good wills to, and work; let me alone with the rest: although ye know not how to come by money, I have ways enough, and will not see you want.'

<small>God will not see his builders want.</small>

And although this promise be made to this particular people, in this present matter of building God's house; yet it serveth not for that only case, but it is a sufficient comfort for all them which take the Lord's work in hand (what kind thing soever it be, so that it be to set forth his glory, and not our own), that in such godly enterprises we shall not lack, but have enough to finish it and do it withal.

And besides that, if we believed this to be a true saying, that God did speak it, and would perform it, it would work much goodness in us.

<small>If we believed all riches to be the Lord's, we would neither get them wrongfully, nor spend them wastefully.</small>

First, It will work such a fear in us towards God, that for no need or vantage we would take or yet get one penny wrongfully, either by flattery, perjury, usury, bribery, lying, stealing, deceit, false weights and measures, or by any other unlawful means. For who durst take one half-penny, if that he were persuaded that it were God's, his Lord and Maker, who hates and punisheth all falseness? Who dare be a thief and a traitor to God that is in heaven, who made and rules all in earth? But because he thinks it to be such a man's, and that God seeth him not, and man shall not perceive it; without all shame he deceiveth man, and robbeth his Lord God and heavenly Father. Therefore, when the devil puts in thy heart to get any thing wrongfully, think with thyself: 'What shall I do? shall I be a thief to my Lord God, who made me and saved me? these goods be not this man's only, but they be my Lord God's, who hath made him his steward over them, and unto whom he must make account of them. And although I can deceive man in getting of them, yet God seeth all things, and nothing is hid from him.' If true faith considered these things thus, no man would nor durst use any deceit in any kind of thing.

Secondly, If this saying were duly considered that all gold and silver is the Lord's, who durst misspend or waste one farthing of it unthriftly upon things not necessary? God hath given man all his creatures to serve for his necessary use: but to be a drunkard, a whore-hunter, a gamer, a swash-buckler[1], a ruffian to waste his money in proud apparel, or in hawking, hunting, tennis, or in such other unprofitable pastimes, but only for necessary refreshing of the wit after great study or travail in weighty affairs, he hath (I say) not allowed thee one mite. Read the scriptures through, and thou shalt not find where gentlemen be allowed to waste their money upon vain pastimes or unprofitable, more than the poor simple man is. In all good commonwealths there be no laws that give more liberty to sin to the rich than to the poor. God our heavenly Father, like a rich wise steward, deals his money abroad to us his servants, some more, some less, as he thinks good; and saith unto us all, "Work until I come," and increase this portion that is given you. Poor and rich hath this said unto him, and every one shall make an account unto him, and it shall be said to every one, "Make account of thy stewardship." Look in the law of God, and there shalt thou find how to bestow thy money: and if thou cannot find it agreeing with God's word, it is evil, howsoever thou bestow it. For as a rich man giveth his man money, sends him to the market, and bids him not bestow his money as he list, but appoints him how to do it, thus much upon such things, and thus much upon other; so God hath given us his scripture as a rule to follow in bestowing his money or other gifts. And although men or things be not there named, whereon to bestow it; yet the degrees and sorts of both, as the poor and necessaries, be often beaten into our heads. Gentlemen and young rufflers may not say as they com-

No degree be allowed vainly to waste his goods.

Luke xix. & xvi.

[1] Swash-buckler: swaggerer. ED.

monly use, 'Is not my money mine own? May I not spend it as me lust? who shall correct me? what would ye have me to do? Shall I build castles and towers with it? I have more than I can get spent: the next rent day is at hand. Shall I be a lout, and sit in a corner? Nay, it becometh a gentleman to make merry and ruffle it. Shall I not make good cheer, that other may fare the better? Let me make merry when I am young: I will wax sad, wise, and thrive, when I am old.' But thou which thinkest thus, remember the evil steward, which when he was called to account, and could not discharge his reckoning, gave away his master's goods that he might maintain his idleness. But he was put out of office, as all they shall be cast from God's face, which likewise unprofitably spend that portion which God hath given them. Thinkest thou that God will allow this account, if thou say, 'Thus much is spent upon whores, this at cards, this at dice, this on masking, this on mumming, this at bear-baiting, &c.?' Nay, nor yet on massing, gilding of saints, painting of stocks and stones, setting up roods, buying of popish pardons, giving money to this cloister of monks, and that house of friars, with such like. Who would spend one penny so evil, if he thought that it should bear witness against him and condemn him at the last day? It is for lack of faith, that such unthrifts do misspend God's, their Master's money; because they think it is their own, and not the Lord's, as the prophet saith here.

Thirdly, If this were believed as it ought to be, it would make us neither to grudge against God, that gives plenty many times to the evil men, and the honester sort lives more barely; nor we should not disdain to see one preferred before ourselves, in more wealth or authority. We should also content ourselves with that portion which God hath given us, not murmuring nor sorrowing that we have less than other. This thing hath often grieved Job, David, Jeremy, Abacuk, and other holy men, that they did see evil men in wealth, and good men in trouble; and they could never satisfy themselves in this, what should be the cause of it, until they entered into the sanctuary of the Lord, and there they spied that the riches of the earth is the Lord's, to dispose at his holy will and pleasure. And because it

Marginalia: Luke xvi. — Job xxi. Psal. lxxiii. Jer. xii. Habak. i.

pleases God to bestow so much or so little upon this man or that man; it is just, and I should content myself therewith, knowing that whatsoever he doeth, it is good because he doeth it, and no man must grudge or disdain thereat. The will of God is the rule of all justice and righteousness: as because God will have it so, therefore it is good, just, and righteous. God's will is the first and chief cause of all things: so that, when we see that God will have it so, we must not ask, why he will have it so; but be content therewith, sit down and quiet ourselves, praising his goodness, and marvelling at his wisdom, that rules all things so well and wisely. And with that little portion that it hath pleased him to give us, we shall content ourselves, when we consider that he owes nothing to any man, but that which he gives, he gives it freely and liberally, and so much as he knows better than thou thyself what is meet for thee to have.

To refer all to God's wisdom stays the mind in all trouble.

Thou which hast little, think thus with thyself: 'My good God and Father, who hath ruled and doth rule all things at his own will and pleasure; whose wisdom I am not able to perceive, and whose unspeakable love towards me in giving his only Son to die for me I cannot understand; he that loves me better than I love myself; he, I say, knoweth that if I had more riches and wealth, I should be too wanton and so displease him; and if I had too little, I should deal untruly and blaspheme him. Therefore praised be his wisdom, which doth not overload me with more than he will give me grace to discharge; nor lets me want necessaries, that I fall not to any falsehood or untruth. How can I love him enough, that gives me all necessaries, and doth not charge me with superfluities?' The evil men which have such plenty of all things, he would win them with gentleness, and by gentleness draw them unto him: but in thee that hast less, he will let all the world know that thou lovest him not for any great wealth which he giveth thee, (as evil flatterers many time do,) but even as duty, and that thou wilt bear the cross of poverty willingly, rather than forsake him.

What a misbelief is it, to think that God doth not give and dispose his goods so well and wisely, but that many can devise it better! And if we had once this faith rooted in our hearts, that he doth all for the best; it would make us

say, howsoever we ourselves or other have much or little,
1 Sam. iii. "It is the Lord that doeth it; let him do that seemeth good in his sight." And if we lose it by fire or robbery, we shall
Job i. be content to say with Job, "The Lord gave it, and the Lord took it away; and as it pleases the Lord, so it is done: the name of the Lord be praised." What a pride is this in man, to think that he could deal his goods better than God hath done; or that it were better for such men and such to have more or less than they have: as though
Isai. lix. we were wiser than God, and if things lay in our hands, we could do them better than he can or doth! Our Saviour
Matt. vi. Christ calls it lack of faith, when we mistrust the power of him that he cannot, or the goodness of God that he will not, provide necessaries for us, chiefly if we seek the kingdom of God and the righteousness thereof, and saith, "Mark the birds of the air, how they neither sow nor mow, nor gather into the barn, and yet your heavenly Father feeds them: how much more will he do you, ye of little faith!"

There is nothing can grieve that faithful heart so, which constantly believes that gold and silver is the Lord's, but it would undoubtedly look and hope for all necessaries by God's provision to be given him; and if ordinary means did fail,
1 Kings xvii. that the ravens should feed him, as they did Elias; the
Exod. xvii. stones should flow out water, as in the wilderness; or water
John ii. should be turned into wine, as in Cana of Galilee; or that little which they have should so increase, that it should be
1 Kings xvii. sufficient until plenty came, as the handful of meal of the poor widow's; or else one slender dinner should strengthen
The faithful cannot lack necessaries. them so, until they came where they might have more sufficiently, as Elias walked in the strength of one therfe cake forty days, eating nothing else. For it is as easy for God to provide for his people by some one of these ways or other
2 Kings vii. like, as by any other ordinary means; as in the besieging of Samaria, where they eat their own children and dung, and the next day such plenty, a bushel for a groat. But this is ever most sure, that those which be of God cannot
Rom. viii. lack. For, as St Paul reasons: "He that hath not spared his own Son, but hath given him for us all; how can it be, but with him he hath given us all things;" and for his sake he will deny us nothing meet for us? How can he deny

us a piece of bread, meat, or a coat, that hath given his only Son Christ Jesus to die for us? Can a worldly earthly father, if he see his child want, weep, and ask him meat, deny him? will he not rather spare it from his own belly, than see him weep or want? And shall we think that God hath less pity and love toward us, than one of us hath towards another? Which things all considered, they and all we, which have God's house to build, should not discourage ourselves for poverty or lack of ability: for the Lord of hosts saith, all gold and silver is his; and he will give sufficient to his own building.

And although many of them thought that this later house would be nothing so pleasant, gorgeous and costly as the first; and therefore they wept when the ground work was laid, as was said before; yet to comfort them with, that they should with better courage and stomach go about it, he promises them, that "the glory of this later house" shall be more than the first, and they shall not only have enough to build withal, but it shall be a more gorgeous house in the sight of God than the first was.

The first temple had in it the golden candlestick, the golden censer, the golden altar, the cherubins, the golden ark of the Lord, wherein was the tables of Moses, the rod of Aaron, and the pot of manna, the golden table: it had also Urim and Thummin, with divers other relics, which all or many of them were destroyed by Nabuchodonozor and others which spoiled the temple: so that, although other jewels and ornaments were restored by the good king Cyrus, yet we do not read, (and the Rabbins also think,) that these were not in the second temple; and of Urim and Thummin Esdras seems to speak plain that they were not there. *Ezra ii.* What should make then this house more glorious than the first, seeing it wanted these outward glorious and pleasant things to the eye, and in such ornaments was nothing to be compared with the first? Surely nothing but this, that we spake of before, that our Saviour Christ presented himself therein, preached his Father's will and the glad tidings of the gospel, rebuked the traditions and ceremonies of the scribes and Pharisees, healed all diseases. Therefore may we gather here this necessary argument upon these words of

What things make a temple to please God best.

the prophet; that the church is more pleasant in the sight of God, where the gospel is preached, God's majesty and his mercy declared, than where all the ceremonies of Moses or the pope do shine so gloriously to the sight of the world. Let the papists examine well by these words, whether their copes, chalices, vestments, crosses of gold and silver, their singing, ringing, censing, their images, relics, pardons, conjured waters, &c., be more pleasant service to the Lord our God, than where the trumpet of God's word sounds in our ears, to stir us up to the praising of God, and pulling down of our own crooked froward nature and stomachs. There can be nothing found in this second house, but it was all and much more to be had in the first, save the preaching and miracles of Christ and his apostles. For this point only therefore, wherein it did excel the first, it did please God more than the first: therefore must it needs follow, that those companies and churches please God better, where his lively word is preached, and the sacraments without great pomp commonly and purely ministered, than where they go about with dead ceremonies to serve him, though they be never so glorious outwardly.

Let us be ashamed then of these lewd sayings: 'What should I do at the church? I may not have my beads: the church is like a waste barn: there is no images nor saints, to worship and make curtsey unto: little god in the box is gone[1]: there is nothing but a little reading and preaching, that I cannot tell what it means: I had as lief keep me at home.' This is a woeful saying, that because we may not worship God as we lust ourselves, we will not worship him at all. This is idolatry, to leave that kind of worship which he hath appointed us in his word, and devise a new sort of our own, which God shall either be content withal, or else be without. The heathen people would say, when they see the people so foolish to think that God would be worshipped with gold and silver, *Dicite, pontifices, in templo quid facit aurum?*[2]—which is to say, 'Tell us, O ye bishops, what good doth gold in the temple?' Ambrose saith: "The sacraments look not for gold; and those things which are not bought with gold,

[1 See above, p. 129. ED.]
[2 Persius, Sat. II. 69. ED.]

cannot please with gold³." And the best writers do witness, that it was better when the Lord's supper was ministered in wood and glass, and the priests were pure as gold and did preach, than when the priests were wood and the cups gold,—that is to say, dumb, unlearned, unpreaching prelates, and yet would minister the sacrament in cups of gold and silver. The riches and treasures of the church belong to the poor; and upon them should all the goods of the church be bestowed, which is remaining of the preacher's livings, and not to feed idle belly-gods withal, as monks, friars, priests, &c. Such a godly answer made the godly and true deacon Laurence, when as the emperor sent his man to spoil the church of the treasure that there was. He commanded Laurence in the emperor's name to deliver him all the treasure in the church: Laurence required a few days' respite to gather all the goods together; which being granted, at the day appointed he gathered all the poor folks in Rome together. When the emperor's servant came, thinking to have received the whole treasure, and calling for Laurence asked where the treasure was, Laurence shewed all the poor people, and said, "Behold the treasure of the church⁴!" Thus was the goods of the church then bestowed, and not to maintain the pope, nor yet his carnal cardinals in their ruffian rout and idleness, &c.

The peace which he promises to send, "in this place," is not so much an outward peace, although they had that peace as long as they feared the Lord: but here is meant the peace of conscience, which Christ brought from heaven; as the angels sang at his birth, "Glory be to God on high, and in earth peace, &c." And he is not only the peacemaker betwixt God and man, but peace itself, as St Paul calleth him, saying, "He is our peace, which hath made of both one," as was noted before. It is more to call him the peace itself, than to call him the peacemaker betwixt God and man, pacifying the Father's wrath for our sins, and purchasing

Luke ii.

Eph. ii.

[³ Quid enim dices? Timui ne templo Dei ornatus deesset? Respondebit: Aurum sacramenta non quærunt; neque auro placent, quæ auro non emuntur. De Officiis, Lib. II. cap. 28. T. IV. p. 61. Paris. 1632. ED.]

[⁴ See above, p. 144, and the note. ED.]

pardon for all our wickedness. The peace of conscience when we believe God to be our Father for Christ's sake, forgiving all our sins, and bestowing all his goodness on us, is the greatest comfort that can be, though the world rage never so much against us; as our Saviour Christ saith, "In the world you shall have affliction and trouble, but in me you shall have peace": and again, "I leave my peace among you, and I give my peace unto you, &c." And although the church of God is often more forgetful of his goodness received, when they have worldly peace, (as the prophet saith, "In this outward worldly peace my bitterness is most bitter",) and therefore necessary it is to be tried by adversity, heresies, imprisonments, death, and other cruelties; yet in the midst of all trouble they shall find present comfort and peace patiently to bear all such sorrow as shall be laid on them.

<small>John xvi.

John xiv.

Isai. xxxviii.

Worldly peace is most grievous, and in persecution the conscience is quiet.</small>

When as emperors were not christened, great was the persecution, and yet could they not prevail. When heresies began to spring in the church, then God raised up Augustine and others to withstand them; and the more that they were, the more was the truth tried out and flourished: but after that the pope had conquered all, good learning decayed, and the devil thereby had lulled all on sleep; then came this outward worldly peace, where the most part submitted themselves to the beast, and his peace was the bitterest thing that could be before God, and greatest trouble to all good consciences. For then outward peace brought in lordly pride, which harmed more than any persecution, as Bernard saith. But now, after that the light appears again, with what peace of conscience can and do men offer themselves to the fire, though the pope and his clergy rage like lions or mad dogs! What great learning hath God revealed in our time more than before! And chiefly it hath been done because of errors, heresies, sects and controversies that be abroad, that God's chosen people should not live in blindness still, and that his goodness may be known. And although persecution be great, yet God strengthens his to die for his truth in most quiet peace to the shame of their persecutors. Where there is no striving, there is no victory: where there is no victory, there is no praise nor reward: therefore God of his great love, that his people may have most noble victories and greatest reward, suffereth them to be troubled by the devil and his ministers, but not to be overcome. Where the tormentors rage, because they cannot overcome the simple souls, holding fast the faith which they would pull from them, and for the which they strive; God so strengthens his, that they suffer all torments with more peace of conscience, than the tormentors do lay it on them, which devise the deaths for them.

But not only this inward peace, but an outward also was given them, as long as they displeased not the Lord. God commanded that every man amongst the Israelites should come thrice a year to Jerusalem to worship him there: and Exod.xxxiv. lest they should grudge, saying, 'Who shall defend our country when we are gone so far from home? our enemies will invade and destroy us;' God promises that he will defend their country in the mean time, and that they should have no harm. Thus they believing God were bold to go to Jerusalem to serve God, leaving none at home to keep their goods and lands, but a few women and children. So we, if we would serve the Lord aright, and maintain his true religion, our enemies should not hurt us, but women and children should be able to defend us: if we will not serve him as he hath appointed, there is no worldly power able to defend us, but we and they shall perish all together.

v. 10. *In the twenty-fourth day of the ninth month, and the* The text. *second year of Darius, was the message of the Lord sent by the hand of Aggeus the prophet, saying,*

11. *Thus saith the Lord of hosts: Ask, I pray thee, the priests the law, saying,*

12. *If any man bear holy flesh in the lap of his garment, and do touch with his lap bread or broth, wine, oil, or any kind of meat, shall it be made holy? The priests answered and said, No.*

13. *And Aggeus said: If he that is defiled in soul do touch any of these, whether shall it be defiled? The priests answered and said, It is defiled.*

14. *Aggeus answered and said: So is this people, and so be these folk before my face, saith the Lord, and so is all the work of their hands; and whatsoever they bring hither, it is defiled.*

For the reckoning of months, years, days, and such other particular words, we said enough before. Now is the prophet sent to appose¹ the priests in the law of God, and make them give sentence against themselves. "The lips of the priest keep knowledge, and they shall ask the law of his mouth," saith Malachy: and therefore, to see what knowledge they had in the law of the Lord, and what answer they would make, he was sent to examine them; and he puts forth his question so wisely, that he makes them to condemn themselves by their own judgment. He is bidden ask them out of the law of God, and not out of the pope's law, nor yet any man's law, which often through bribes is ended as a man is friended, but out of God's book, which without partiality speaks indifferently on all parts, and neither fears the rich for his might and authority, nor hath foolish pity on the poor for his poverty, but uprightly judges right, and condemns sin, wheresoever it is found. If the priests in Moses' law had this charge given them, to be so cunning in the scriptures, that they should be able to answer all doubts, which could be asked them; how much more should our priests now be able by the scripture to teach all which be ignorant, and answer all doubts that can be moved! for St Paul saith, a minister "should be able to exhort with wholesome doctrine, and confute false." But if ye want one to keep a cur rather than a cure, to be a hunter or a falconer, to be an overseer of your workmen, to be your steward, or look to your sheep and cattle, to be your gardener, keep your orchard, or write your business, who is meeter for any of these businesses than Sir John Lacklatin? What a wickedness is this, that they should take such pains to be so cunning in these things that God looks not for of them; and in those things which God hath charged them withal, they can say nothing at all! they be dumb dogs, not able to bark in rebuking sin; and blind guides, not able to rule their flock. But if the world be on their side, then can they play the wood² dogs, biting and snatching at every man near them, and let no honest man dwell in rest by them; but accuse, burn, and condemn all that speak against their mis-

[¹ Appose: question, *pose*. ED.]
[² Wood: mad. ED.]

chiefs. If there be a trental to be said, or any money to be gotten for masses, diriges, relics, pardons, &c. then who is so ready as they? They can smell it out a great sort of miles off. But if a man want comfort in conscience, would understand his duty towards God, or God's goodness towards us; they be blind beasts, ignorant dolts, unlearned asses, and can say nothing but make holy water, and bid them say a lady's psalter.

The questions which he putteth forth here tend to this purpose, that by one thing which is like he may prove another like. For like as hallowed flesh did not hallow these things which it touched; so did not the goodness which was in some of them make the rest holy. But like as he who is defiled in soul did defile all the works that he taketh in hand, even his prayers and sacrifices, &c. so they did also defile all which kept company with them by their evil example. This kind of teaching by parables and similitudes, *Similitudes be a good* which be like in matter, consequence and truth, although *kind of teaching.* divers in words, is pithy to persuade, and is used sundry times in the scriptures, to bring a man to give sentence against himself. As when Nathan told David the similitude 2 Sam. xii. of the rich man that had many sheep, and the poor man that had but one; and that the rich man had taken the poor man's one sheep; David said he had deserved death, not understanding that Nathan did mean David himself to have done this thing, who gave this sentence of death against himself, because he had so many wives of his own, and yet could not be content with them, but took Urias' wife also. So when the woman of Thecua feigned herself 2 Sam. xiv. to be a poor widow, and her two sons had the one killed the other, and the officers would have put the other to death for murdering his brother; she makes supplication to the king David, desiring that her other son might not be put to death, for she had rather lose the one son which was killed, than have the other now put to death also; for then all her comfort was gone: when David had granted her request, that her son should not die for this murder, then said she, "Why should not the king bring home again his son Absalon, which killed his brother Ammon, but suffer him to die also banished?" Thus David was deceived by the woman, which under the names of her own sons made suit for Absalon, the king's son, by the counsel of Joab: and David thought in reason he should be as ready to shew pity to his own son Absalon as to another, and gave sentence so against himself. So the priests here, granting that whatsoever touches him who is defiled in soul, that thing is also defiled too, prove and give sentence against themselves, condemning all their own deeds to be naught and defiled, because they themselves were wicked and defiled. What wickedness were in this people, Esdras tells, when he divorces such a number as had married heathen wives contrary to the law; and Nehemias, when he tells how by bribery and usury they had polled their poor brethren, and gotten their goods and lands into their hands: and how they had all offended God in not building this temple, this prophet teaches here plain. These with divers other gross sins had defiled this people; and therefore all that they did and touched was defiled. Sin is so vile and filthy, that it defiles even those things which God himself hath commanded. Esay saith, "Your sabbath-days and other feasts my soul abhors;" and yet God had commanded them his own mouth to observe such feasts. Esay saith also, "He that offers an ox is as if he killed a man, and he that sacrifices a sheep is as though he brained a dog:" and again, "Sacrifice and offering for sin thou hast not required." But Esay addeth a reason why God should hate that which he once commanded, and saith, "Your hands are full of blood; ye do not hear the widows' and the fatherless' cause," &c. Seeing then sin hath such a strength in it, that it makes God to hate those things which he ordained himself; how much need have we to take heed what we do, lest in thus offending God we make him to forsake both us and all that we should have good of!

Holy flesh. That is called holy flesh which was offered to the Lord, and whereof sometime the whole was burned, and sometime that part which remained was eaten of the priests and them that brought it to be sacrificed. If that flesh then, which was thus hallowed by the commandment of God, had not this strength in it, to hallow the lap of a garment wherein it was carried, and so the lap to hallow what thing soever it should touch; how can the pope's conjured water, which he calls holy, make the man or house where it is sprinkled so holy, that no devils dare enter? The devil durst tempt our Saviour Christ; and yet they say he fears their conjured water, as though it were holier than Christ himself. Where hath he any promise from God of such foolishness? What can their holy ashes, holy palms, holy crosses, holy bells, holy cream, relics, moulds, chalice, corporas, fire, candles, beads, or that which is their most holy relic, their oil, wherewith they anoint their shavelings, priests, and bishops, do? They would make men believe that the oil hath such holiness in it, that whosoever wanteth it is no priest nor minister. Therefore in the late days of popery our holy bishops called before them all such as were made ministers without such greasing, and blessed them with the pope's blessing, anointed them, and then all was perfect; they might sacrifice for quick and dead: but not marry in no case, and yet keep whores as many as they would. If any of their such greased disciples were traitor, felon, or heretic, that he had deserved death, (in token that their oil was so holy, and had entered so deep into the flesh, but bringing no holiness with it; for then their anointed should not have fallen so sore as they did, and do;) before any such offender could suffer death, he must first be deposed of all that he received from the pope of his orders and apparel, and have all that skin of his crown and fingers pared off or scraped, because they were greased with their oil.

<small>Popes have no scripture for their hallowing of things.</small>

What oil used the apostles in making ministers, or what scripture is for it? The holy flesh which was offered to God by his own commandment had not this power to hallow the things which it touched; and yet their holy water and grease must have it. Is this like to be true? doth not all their false feigned holiness, which they put in things made holy by their own hallowing only, and not by God, fall by this one sentence of God's mouth? can any thing be more plainly spoken against all their juggling than this? For the same reason that is against flesh, is against all their holy toys, by what name soever they be called. If they will not believe God and his scripture, let them believe the priests, their elders and predecessors; yea, and that which they crack so much of, that is a general council, which they think can-

<small>Nothing hallowed by the pope's tradition can hallow another thing.</small>

not err. The prophet here is sent to all the priests; and here is answered in all their names by general consent and counsel, that holy flesh cannot hallow that thing which it touches. If it be so in one hallowed thing, as it is in this flesh, why should it not be so in all other likewise?

<small>Christ only maketh us holy, and only hath the fulness of holiness.</small>

<small>1 Cor. xii. John iii.</small>

There is no creature which can give that holiness to another which is in itself: this thing belongs to Christ alone; for "of his fulness all we have received," as St John saith. And where we have gifts of the Holy Spirit by measure, so much as pleases God of his goodness to give; Christ our Lord and Saviour had the fulness of the Spirit without all measure, that of his fulness we all might receive part. Christ hath the fulness of the gifts of the Spirit so much, that although he give part to us all, yet he hath nothing less himself. For as the sun gives light plentiful to the whole world, and yet keeps the self-same light within itself; so our Saviour Christ, God and man, hath the perfect fulness of all goodness in himself, and yet gives part to us as he thinks good, not losing any piece of that he hath himself, but lightning our darkness with that light which he hath within himself. St Paul saith, he "is our wisdom, righteousness, holiness, and redemption," because he gives us all these things.

<small>1 Cor. i.</small>

As it is in flesh, so it is in all other creatures; although a probable objection to the contrary may be made out of the scriptures themselves. Our Saviour Christ, saying, "Woe to the scribes and Pharisees," which taught that "he which swore by the temple or the altar was nothing, but if he swore by the gold of the temple, or the offering on the altar, he was in fault," seems to teach contrary; for he adds unto more, saying that the temple makes the gold holy, and the altar the offering; and that he which swears by the altar, sweareth by it and those things which be on it; and he that swears by the temple, swears by it and him which is in it; as though the temple and the altar made other things holy. St Paul, speaking of the marriage of the faithful and the unfaithful, saith that the unfaithful part is made holy by the faithful. But here you must mark, that this holiness, which St Paul speaks of, belongs nothing to the salvation or forgiveness of sin of the unholy party; but teaches that such marriage to continue is not unlawful and

<small>Matt. xxiii.</small>

<small>1 Cor. vii.</small>

whoredom, and the children so born be not bastards and heathens. That other holiness in the temple and the altar is but such a holiness, as Moses teaches in his law, which then was a ceremony, but is now taken away, and therefore belongs not unto us. Any thing is called holy by the law of Moses, which is dedicated to serve God in any kind of ceremony or service in the temple, and is no more turned to serve man in any kind of civil matter, or in his house; or else, which by his institution signifies some holy thing unto us. But these be called holy, not because any holiness for salvation is in them, or that they can give holiness to other things; but because the end and use whereunto they be turned is holy. Nothing beside man can receive this true holiness: for faith is the instrument and means whereby true holiness is received, which profit to salvation, whereof the prophet speaks here chiefly. Holy.

But it is not so with the evilness and sin of man: for that doth not only defile the man, when it is in him, but all that the evil man doth is evil also; as all that touches the thing which is defiled, is defiled also. For as a carrion doth not only smell evil itself, but infects all that come near it; so that man which is defiled in soul doth defile all things that he takes in hand. Valentinianus[1], a christian man, turned from idolatry to the knowledge of Christ, and afterward made emperor, when other had cast upon him such holy water as they made to their idols, he was angry with them that they defiled his coat, and smote the priest that gave him the holy water and moved him to sacrifice. For he thought (as truth is) that whatsoever was consecrated to idols was so filthy, that it defiled whatsoever it Sin defiles not only the man himself, but every thing that he doth and all that use his company.

[[1] Καὶ γὰρ Βαλεντινιανὸς ἐκεῖνος, ὁ μικρὸν ὕστερον βασιλεύσας, (χιλίαρχος δὲ ἦν τηνικαῦτα,) τῶν περὶ τὰ βασίλεια τεταγμένων λογχοφόρων ἡγούμενος, ὃν εἶχεν ὑπὲρ τῆς εὐσεβείας οὐκ ἀπέκρυψε ζῆλον. ὁ μὲν γὰρ ἐμβρόντητος ἐκεῖνος [Ἰουλιανὸς] εἰς τὸ τῆς τύχης τέμενος εἰσῄει χορεύων· ἑκατέρωθεν δὲ τῶν θυρῶν εἱστήκεισαν νεωκόροι, περιρραντηρίοις τοὺς εἰσιόντας προκαθαίροντες, ὡς ἐνόμιζον. Ἐπειδὴ δὲ τοῦ βασιλέως ἡγούμενος τῇ χλανίδι ῥανίδα πελάσασαν εἶδε Βαλεντινιανὸς, ὁ βασιλείας ἑκατέρας χάριν τούτου τετυχηκὼς, πὺξ ἔπαισε τὸν νεωκόρον, μεμολύνθαι φήσας, οὐ κεκαθάρθαι. Theodoret. Eccles. Hist. Lib. III. Cap. 16. Paris. 1544. ED.]

touched, if it was received with such opinion of holiness as they thought.

Some read here, "if he that is defiled by the dead do touch," &c.: the sense is both one of this and that. Many unclean things were in Moses' law, that whosoever touched them should be unclean also: as he that touches a dead body shall be unclean seven days; and he that hath the flux of seed shall be unclean; and he that touches the bed where such have lien, or sits where they have sitten, shall be unclean also. But this is not so much for the uncleanness which is in the dead body or the seed by nature (for both be the good creatures of God), as that under this figure God would teach us, that we should not as much as touch sin, which is the death of the soul: likewise the evil lusts, which reign when the flux of the seed is, be the causes which make them unclean which suffer such diseases and affections. So that, whether we read, "he that is defiled in soul," or "he that is defiled by the dead," it is sin that both do mean: for that not only defiles, but kills the soul which doth it. And sin is such, that it defiles all that touch it; as Sirach saith, comparing it to pitch, "He that touches pitch is defiled with it." St Paul saith also, "Evil communications corrupt good manners." David saith, "The sinner's prayer is turned into sin." The good man therefore makes all his works good; and the evil defiles every good thing he takes in hand.

This verse teaches plain, that the whole life of an evil man, whatsoever he doeth, is defiled. For as St Paul requires of a good man, that "whether he eat or drink, or whatsoever he do, he should do all to the glory of God;" so the evil man, if he eat, drink, sleep, wake, talk, work, or be idle, all is defiled before the Lord. For an evil tree cannot bring forth good fruit, nor figs grow on briars: yea, let him study, pray, fast, give alms, buy trentals, give his body to be burned, or do what he can devise, and it is defiled. "If I had all faith," saith St Paul, "so that I could make mountains to stir out of their places; if I know all secrets, give my goods in alms, and my body to be burned, I am nothing better, it profits me nothing, if I lack charity." All evil men lack charity; for "by this shall ye be known to be" good men, and so " my scholars, if ye love one another," saith our Saviour Christ: therefore whatsoever they do, it is defiled. The good man if he eat or drink, he doth it with thanksgiving to God for such sustenance righteously gotten, and soberly takes it to refresh his weak nature, that he may the better serve his Lord God. If he work, use merchandize, or any other kind of life, he doth it not so much[1] for his own, as for the common profit. But the evil man either gives not due thanks for his meat, or gets it wrongfully, lays it up niggardly, or else spends it unthriftly; and in all his labour seeks his own profit with the hurt of others; and therefore it is sin.

By this is also proved this great controversy, whether we be made righteous by works or faith. For if works should make us righteous, then the good works which an evil man doth should make him righteous. But the prophet saith here, that whatsoever the evil man doth, it is defiled. Therefore the man must be good before the work be good, as our Saviour Christ saith: " Either make the tree good and the fruit good; or make the tree evil and the fruit evil." And as the fruit makes not the tree good, but shews and gives it to be a good tree; so it is in the evil fruit and the tree. The sour crab-tree makes the crabs bitter, and not the crabs makes the tree evil. As the tree is, so is his fruit; and as the man is, such is his life. " A good man out of the good treasure of his heart brings forth good things; and an evil man out of the evil treasure of his heart brings forth evil." But the heart and the man is evil, before the deed be evil, not in time, but in the order of nature. For as in a well-spring, look what taste the water hath at the head of the spring, the same it hath when it runs forth; so if the heart of man be defiled, which is the spring whereof comes whoredom, adultery, murder, and all other our doings, the deeds must needs be naught which come out of such a defiled head and spring. So that, if we will do any good deed, we must be good men and trees before in God's sight and election of God, that our fruit and deeds may be good: for out of an evil root cannot come good fruits. God loves the deeds for the man's sake which doeth

We be not made righteous by works properly.

Luke vi.

The work is good for the man's sake.

[1 Second edition, *doth it so much.* ED.]

them, rather than the man for the good works that he doeth.
Gen. iv. As God looked first at Abel and then at his gifts, but to Cain and his offerings he looked not: because Abel was a chosen vessel of God, therefore God received his offerings; and Cain's were not received, because he was not of that number. For as a schoolmaster will take in good part the diligence that his scholars can do; and if he see them put their good wills thereto, he will bear with their faults, and teach them their lessons; but to stubborn and froward he will shew no gentleness, but cast them off: so God with those whom he hath chosen in Christ before the world was made, will bear with their infirmities, and wink at their little faults, teach them to do better, and praise their well-doings, and gently correct their faults; but his enemies and outcasts, because whatsoever they do is hypocrisy, he loves them not, but even their prayer is turned to sin, and whatsoever they do is defiled, because they be not grafted and
Wisd. xiv. chosen in Christ Jesus, as the wise man saith, "The wicked man and his wickedness are hated in like of God."

Thus the man makes the work good, rather than the work makes the man good, in God's sight and judgment, be it never so godly to the outward shew in the eye. So if the heart of man and conscience be defiled, it defiles the good creatures of God which otherwise be good and lawful.
Titus i. St Paul speaking of meats saith, "All be clean and lawful to them which be clean; but to the unclean nothing is clean, but their minds and consciences be defiled." For if a man eat but a piece of bread, and think that it is not lawful for him to do so, he sins, because he doth it not of faith; and so
Rom. xiv. the conscience wanting faith is defiled. "For whatsoever is not faith is sin:" and he, wanting true knowledge that God made all things to serve man, now through superstition and a defiled conscience serves that creature which should serve him, and so defiles that which of itself God hath created holy, clean, and meet to be eaten at all times with thanksgiving. All this comes by reason of sinful superstition in the man, which not believing the scriptures, that all meats be lawful for all men at all times, wants faith, and so hath his conscience defiled, which defiles the meat which he eats.

Whereas they commonly reason, Our evil works condemn

us, therefore our good works save us; this place of the pro- ^(Sin condemns, but) phet teacheth the contrary reason. For all the priests in ^(good works save not.) their general council grant, that he which is defiled in soul defiles all things which he doth; yet they deny that if a holy thing touch another thing unholy, that it maketh it holy also: so that sin hath greater strength to defile other things, than goodness hath to make other things holy. St Paul, reasoning of the same matter, teaches us how to conclude, saying, "The reward of sin is death;" and then he saith ^(Rom. vi.) not, the reward of virtue and good works is everlasting life, but he saith, "Everlasting life is the free gift of God." Thus must we reason then, both as the prophet doth here, and St Paul in the same case; that our evil is more able to condemn us, than our goodness is to save us.

This should also be a sufficient warning for us to beware ^(Evil company is to) what company we join ourselves unto: for sin in one man ^(be avoided.) is of so great force, that it defiles all the company he is in. Thus teaches St Paul: "Evil communication corrupts good ^(1 Cor. xv.) manners." The wickedness which is in these men, it creeps ^(2 Tim. ii.) like a canker, which infects always the next part unto it, until it have run through and infected the whole body: so the wicked never cease, until they have drawn unto them all such as keep their company. What is a more dangerous thing than to keep company with unthrifts? Have not many, which before they knew such unthriftiness were sober and honest, but after they have been tangled with such evil men, sold house and land, some became beggars, and many hanged? Have not many honest young men, by keeping company with swearers and whore-hunters, become open blasphemers, and give themselves to all unhappiness? So in companying with papists, and to please the world, many have forsaken the truth, which they knew and professed, and are become open enemies and persecutors of God and his people. Did not Salomon fall to idolatry with marrying heathen ^(1 Kings xi.) wives? Did not God forbid marriage with the heathen, lest ^(Deut. vii.) they should entice us to idolatry? Was not Sampson over- ^(Judg. xvi.) come in keeping company with Dalida[1]?

What a proud presumption then is this to think, I am strong enough, wise enough to take heed to myself, in what

[1 The Greek form of the name *Delilah*. ED.]

company soever I shall come! For except you be wiser than Salomon, or stronger than Sampson, thou shalt be overcome as they were. When thou shalt sit among papists, and hear them blaspheme thy God and praise their idolatry; how canst thou escape with a safe conscience undefiled, if thou hold thy peace? Yea, and if thou have not greater grace and learning to judge good and evil, thou shalt hear some crooked reasons which shall deceive thee, and peradventure entangle thee and bring thee from God's truth. If thou sit by, hear the truth spoken against, and will not defend it to thy power, thou art guilty to thy Lord God: for Christ saith, "He that is not with me is against me." If thou speak in God's cause, thou shalt be in danger of thy life and goods, or both. These things well considered would make them which have the fear of God in them to mark this lesson well, and fly evil company: for whatsoever the evil man, who is defiled in soul, touches, it is defiled.

<small>Matt. xii.</small>

Where the prophet saith here, that "the people and the works of their hands and all that they brought thither to offer, was defiled also," it moves this hard question: whether the evilness of the minister do defile his ministry, and God's sacraments which he ministers? First mark, that the minister, if he be a drunkard, an adulterer, or covetous, &c. he doth not hurt the strength of the sacrament which he ministers; neither yet defiles any man that receiveth at his hands: but to himself he ministers damnation, as St Paul saith, "He that eats and drinks unworthily, eats and drinks his own damnation." But he saith, *sibi ipsi*,[1] "to himself" (for so is the Greek, and not "to thee") he receives judgment. If we should flee ministers because of their sin, whom shall we then hear? for who wants sin? So in preaching, as long as they say true, hear them, though their doctrine condemn themselves: for Christ saith, "In Moses' chair sit the scribes and Pharisees; do as they bid and teach you, but do not as they do." So he that is baptized of an evil minister, is as well baptized as he that receives it of the good, and as much doth it profit him: for else so much difference should be betwixt their baptisms, as is betwixt the goodness of the ministers; and the baptism of the better minister should ex-

<small>An evil minister makes not the sacrament or word evil.
1 Cor. xi.</small>

<small>Matt. xxiii.</small>

[¹ Κρίμα ἑαυτῷ ἐσθίει καὶ πίνει. Ed.]

cel the baptism of the worse: and then might we well say, "I am Paul's, I am Apollos', and I am Cephas';" which Paul forbids. The goodness of baptism hangs upon God who did institute it, and not on the minister which gives it.

^{1 Cor. i.}

Let them look therefore, which will be so holy, that rather they will sit at home than here pray or communicate with such a minister as pleases them not, what scripture or example they follow. Esay, Jeremy, Aggeus, yea, Christ and his apostles, forsaked not Jerusalem, but diligently kept the feasts appointed by God, and offered their sacrifices according to the law; though the temple was full of evil[2] priests, scribes and Pharisees. As long as God's institution in his sacraments and sacrifices was kept, they did not so much respect the goodness or evilness of the minister: no more ought thou to do.

Then, if the evilness of the minister do not hurt me which receives the sacrament, why am I forbidden to communicate with papists at their mass? Surely, not so much for the evilness of the men themselves, as the wickedness of the order and thing which they minister. For when thou comest to the communion with the papists, and, according to St Paul, would eat of that bread and drink of that cup; they will neither give thee bread nor wine according to Christ's institution, (for they say the substance is changed, and there remains no bread;) but they will give thee an idol of their own making, which they call their God. They come not together according to Christ's rule, to break the bread; but they creep into a corner, as the pope teaches them, to sacrifice for the quick and the dead, to sell heaven, harrow[3] hell, and sweep purgatory of all such as will pay. They come not to communicate with the people, but to eat up all alone. Therefore, because they have changed Christ's ordinance in his supper, broken his commandment, and set up their own device, we must not meddle with them in such things as they have done contrary to God and his word. Their baptism, although it have many evil things blend in among, yet

We may not communicate at popish masses.

Baptism of papists is not so evil as the mass; and yet faithful ministers are to be preferred to baptism.

[² Second edition, *Civill* (the *c* imperfect) *priestes:* the passage is not in the first. ED.]

[³ Harrow: plunder or destroy. Chaucer and Spenser both speak of Christ as having *harrowed hell*. ED.]

because they keep the substance of the sacrament, the words and fashion that Christ himself used, it is nothing so evil as their mass is: although it be as much to be abhorred of all good men as may be; and good men ought to seek as much as may be to have their children christened in a christian congregation and of a godly minister, where no such conjuring nor misuse is practised. Yet if he cannot come by such a one as he would wish, let not the christian parent think his child to be worse baptized, because the minister is wicked: for every one shall sink in his own sin, and the father shall not die for the child, nor the child for the father, nor the minister for him which receives at him, nor he that receives for the evilness of the minister; although that minister, which so wickedly corrupts the good sacraments and holy ordinances of God, doth minister them to his own damnation and judgment.

Ezek. xviii.

Then, to conclude this place: the prophet here exhorts the people to the building of the temple. For although they had an altar to sacrifice on for the time, yet because they left undone that building which God sent them home to do, and willed them so straitly to do it, they brake his commandment in not building, and so were defiled with sin of disobedience. And the heart being once so defiled, all their works which came from such a defiled heart must needs be defiled also. When Saul was commanded by God to destroy all the Amalekites, and all that had life among them, and to spare none; he was moved with a foolish pity and covetousness, and saved the fairest and fattest cattle to sacrifice unto God: but God because of his disobedience cast him and all his posterity from the kingdom; and Samuel tells him, that "obedience is better than sacrifice." Some would think it cruelness to kill the beasts which made no fault; and other would think it holiness to save for God's sacrifice the fattest and fairest: but that is not cruelness which God bids, neither is that good which he forbids, whatsoever worldly reason can say to the contrary. Therefore let us without all excuse do that which God commands, and seek no starting holes; for then we deceive ourselves. These people might allege poverty, the king's authority who forbad them to build: but nothing can defend us, where that is left undone which God

Marginalia: Disobedience to God defiles all our doings. 1 Sam. xv. God's commandment must be kept without excuse.

commandeth, but it is sin. And where this sin of disobedience reigns, there the man and all that he doeth is defiled. Therefore, if they would that any thing which they did or took in hand should please God, they must wash away this filthy disobedience, build this temple, and all should be well.

If we would apply these things to ourselves and our times, we should with hearty repentance build God's house much more diligently than we do. And truly, although we have had great plagues, yet is there greater behind, if we do it not throughly without halting: for "the servant which knoweth his master's will, and doeth it not, shall have many stripes."

v. 15. *Now consider, I pray you, in your hearts from this* The text. *day backward, afore one stone was laid upon another in the house of the Lord.*

16. *While they were so, they came to a heap of corn of twenty bushels, and there was but ten; and ye came to a wine press to draw fifty gallons, and there was but twenty.*

17. *I have smitten you with blasting winds, and mildew, and with hail, all the works of your hands, and you would not turn unto me, saith the Lord.*

18. *Consider now in your hearts from this day backward, from the twenty-fourth day of the ninth month, from that day when the ground-work of the temple was laid, consider it (I say) in your heart.*

19. *Is your seed yet in the barn? or have your vineyards, fig-trees, pomegranates and olive-trees not yet flourished? from this day forth will I bless them.*

The prophet calls them here to an earnest and diligent consideration of the years past, and the plagues which they suffered so many, so divers, so grievous and strange. As though he should say unto them thus: Ye are too negligent in marking God's working towards you, which hath wrought so wonderful great things among you, to the intent that ye should return unto him, and be more diligent in building his God's doings should teach us, whether they be good or plagues. house, which he[1] so straitly charged you to do. Mark them now more diligently; for God did it to teach you your duty, if

[[1] *He* is wanting in the second edition. ED.]

ye would have learned. God doth not only teach us by his word and writing, by prophets and preaching, but by his deeds also and working: if they be good and blessings, to love and thank him for all his goodness bestowed on us such misers; and if they be sharp and painful, to bring us home again by repentance, to ask forgiveness of our faults, and beware that we no more offend him. Therefore these strange plagues which ye have suffered so many years; that the earth did not yield her fruit; your meat and drink did not feed you; your clothes did not keep you warm; your money wasted in your purses, ye could not tell how, as though it fell out of the bottom; your corn in the barns consumed, ye wist not how; yea, when it came to fanning and winnowing, a man thought in one heap he should have had twenty bushels, he found but ten, the half; and in the wine-press, where ye thought to have had fifty gallons, almost three parts lacked and were consumed, and there was but twenty gallons;—(a good husband that hath much experience, when he comes to an heap of corn or a press of wine, will guess within a few bushels or gallons, how much is contained in the whole; but here in the corn to be deceived the half, and in the wine three parts, was very strange, and could not be but as God said before, that when it was brought into the house, he did blow it away, and so it consumed;)—what a negligence was this to suffer such plagues so many years; and yet to be so hard-hearted, that they weighed them not, but lightly let them pass, not considering wherefore God sent them, nor what fault was in them to be amended, which provoked God's anger so grievously against them! But such blindness is in us all, that when we be under the rod, we feel it not, if God open not our eyes to see his displeasure; yea, rather of nature we murmur against his gentle corrections.

We cannot worthily consider God's plagues without a special grace.

Or else, if God withhold his heavy hand for a time, to try whether we will amend with little correction, before he lay on us a greater, we fall to our old fashions, and forget God, his rod, our duty, and his reverence, attributing such plagues to unseasonable weather, pestilent airs, or some evil chance, as though they came not from God. As when we had the sweat, where so many died so suddenly, that men were astonied at it, so many sick that there was not whole folks enough to keep them: then for that time we could call on God, repent, restore evil gotten goods, give alms, and be sorry that we had not been more liberal before time; but as soon as it ceased, we were as evil or worse than before. So in the late days of bloody persecution and cruel popery, how oft with tears desired we God once again to restore us, and we would no more so wickedly live! and yet we be worse than before. How many sweats, rebellions, dearths, unseasonable years have we had; and yet we have forgotten them, as though they came not from God, nor yet that God had not sent them to teach us to turn to him by them!

The workings of God, whether they be in blessing or plaguing, present or past, to ourselves or others, particularly or to a whole country generally, are deeply to be considered: for he would teach us many things by them, if we had that grace, wit, and eyes, to consider them. St Paul teaches the Corinthians by examples past long before, that they should not murmur, be idolators, nor tempt Christ, as their fathers did, lest they should be destroyed as their fathers were. How often doth the scripture put the Jews in remembrance of their great deliverance out of the vile bondage in Egypt; and bids them not trouble the stranger, for they were strangers in Egypt themselves, and knew the griefs which strangers suffered. In particular examples and plagues he saith, "Remember Lot's wife;" lest in looking back, and desiring your old lusts in Sodom, ye perish as she did. So in good things also, he teaches us by examples past: "Ye see the suffering of Job, and the end how the Lord rewarded him," saith St James, moving us to patience in trouble. And generally it is said to us all: "What things soever are written before hand, they are written for our learning, that by patience and comfort of the scripture we might have hope."

God's doings are diligently to be considered.

1 Cor. x.

Levit. ix.

Luke xvii.

James v.
Rom. xv.

So in things done in our time, when we see God's anger poured upon the whole realm, or one country or house, as war, plague, hunger, dearth, sickness, fire, loss of lands or goods, sweat, loss of friends; look what grievous and notable sins then reigned in such men or places, and learn to avoid the same, lest the like fall on thee. For by that plague God teacheth all which hear of it to avoid the like wicked-

The plague of one is a warning to the rest.

ness, lest like plagues fall on them. If they will not learn, what marvel is it if they sink in their own sin?

So, if thou see thy neighbour punished, rejoice not at it; but pray for him, comfort him, and learn the goodness of God towards thyself; that where thou hast deserved more to be punished than he, yet God spares thee, and gives thee warning by his punishment to amend betimes, lest thy course be next; and then shalt thou be more grievously plagued, because thou didst not learn to amend thy faults by his correction and punishment.

If thy neighbour be in wealth, and thou in trouble, learn to amend thy faults by his, that God may bestow his benefits on thee, as well as on him. Disdain not his wealth, nor be not sorry for it, whether he be good man or evil: for if he be evil, God would win him with gentleness; if he be good, follow his doings, that God may bless thee also. Thus shall we learn of God's doings to comfort ourselves, and amend our own lives. How diligent we should be to search out for what cause God plagues us, we are taught by Josua in casting lot with the people when they were plagued, who had angered God so grievously, that he punished them so sharply, and so tried by the lot, that Acham was in the fault. So Saul tried by lot, that his son Jonathan had offended, when God so sharply punished them. Jonas running from God was tried by lot, cast into the sea, and the tempest ceased.

Josh. vii.

1 Sam. xiv.

Offenders must be tried and punished, that the plague may cease.

Thus must not God's plagues and works be lightly passed over, but deeply considered wherefore he punisheth, and the offenders tried out and punished that God's plague may cease: for before it will not. If the rulers be negligent in punishing sin, as their duty requires, God must needs take it in hand himself; for sin must needs be punished, and he is a righteous God, and will as well punish the sinner as reward the good: but if man do punish the fault, God will not; for he punishes not twice for one fault. Therefore let us no more be so negligent in not regarding God's plagues, lest in despising little gentle ones we provoke him to pour his whole wrath on us, as these men did.

He bids them look backward, not at one year or two passed, but even from the beginning "whole forty years, since one stone was laid on another in the foundation of the temple," and till all that time that they left off their building; and to remember how unfruitful and unseasonable years they had. The corn did not yield the half that men looked for, or yet judged it to be; the wine not three parts of that they hoped for in thus many years together: therefore they should have known, that all was for their disobedience in not building the Lord's house.

But how came all this to pass? who was the worker of these plagues? was it wind, mildew, hail, storms or tempests, which did all this? Indeed they had all these and many more; but God saith, "I smote you with blasting winds, and mildew, and hail, all the works of your hands." In which he teaches, that wind, hail, mildew, storm and tempests, be his servants, go his messages, where he will, destroying so much and so little, when and where as it pleases him, as David saith, "Fire, hail, snow, ice, and tempests, *Psal. cxlviii.* which do his commandment." And because no such harm comes by chance or by the ruling of the stars, but all be his creatures, serve and obey his holy will and pleasure; he calls it his own deed, and saith, "I smote you." Therefore by his just judgment it is done, whatsoever is destroyed: and murmur or grudge we must not at his doings, thinking him to do us wrong, or deal like a tyrant with us; but thankfully bear it, knowing that by such light punishment he wills us to amend and escape a greater. We must say with Job, "The Lord gave it, and the Lord took it away: *Job i.* as the Lord willeth, so let it be: blessed be the name of the Lord now and ever."

Although God use his creatures in punishing, yet he calls it his own deed.

If we could thus with a reverent fear acknowledge God's working in all his punishing, we would not seek unlawful means in danger of fire; as St Aga's letters[1], the holy candle, or a hawthorn in lightning, the hallowed bell to ring in thunder, &c.: and it would be a great quietness to our minds, that we should patiently and willingly bear all crosses that he shall lay upon us, lest we seem to grudge

[[1] "St Agathe's letters" are mentioned in one of our Homilies, (Sermon on Good Works, Part 3,) in an enumeration of various kinds of "papistical superstitions and abuses." Agatha was a martyr of the third century. ED.]

at his doings, which were no small fault. When Job had lost all that he had, yet he accused neither devil, enemies, nor any other man, but said, "If we received good things at the Lord's hands, why should we not suffer evil also? The Lord gave it, and the Lord took it away." Though the devil of malice stirred up such men to commit such robbery against Job, and they of covetousness or envy did spoil and rob the good man, and so both the devil and his members in all their doings heap their own condemnation, because they do it of such a wicked mind and for so evil a purpose and end; yet the good man in such plagues hath a further respect to God, thinking that he which ruleth all, and suffereth these things, by such means trieth his patience: and therefore he thankfully taketh it. So in one deed God's love, with just punishment for our sins and trial of our faith and patience, do appear; and also the malice of the devil towards us, and the frowardness of us one towards another. But because the end and purpose wherefore it is done be so far divers, we work our own damnation willingly, when we do any wickedness one towards another: and God is not the cause nor yet the enticer of us to any evil, but a just punisher of all sin.

<small>God's love and justice, the devil's malice, and man's cruelty, appear in one deed.</small>

Mark here diligently the merciful goodness of our good God and Father in punishing his people; how he destroys not utterly first their wives and children, or plagues them with extreme diseases, but begins gently with their corn and other fruits, far off from them, whose loss they might better bear: yet nevertheless by these little ones he gives them warning to amend; or else he will punish them more grievously, and come nearer unto them in such things as they love more dearly; and at length they and all theirs should perish, if they would not amend. Thus saith God, "I will visit you in the rod of men," that is to say, gently: and David in God's name saith, "I will visit their wickedness with a rod, and their sins with a scourge; but my mercy I will not take away from them, nor I will not hurt them, as I am a true God." Thus, like a father and not like a tyrant, he punishes to amend and not to destroy, to save and not to condemn, for love and not for envy, to pull us from our wickedness to him, and not to make us to hate

<small>God begins first gently to punish.</small>

<small>[2 Sam. vii. 14.]
Psal. lxxxix.</small>

him or run from him, first by little ones, that we may avoid greater, and not in them utterly perish.

The end of God's punishing this people so long appears here, when he saith, "You would not turn unto me, saith the Lord." For this cause then, that they should turn to him, did he send these plagues; and not for hate or harm to his people. But what a wickedness and hard hearts were these men of, that among so many threatenings, so great plagues, and in so many years, they would not turn unto the Lord! Here appears, how true it was that he said before, that all were fallen on sleep, both prince, priest and people, until the Lord awaked up all their spirits to see their great disobedience, and to go about their building. And also this declares, how unable and unwilling we be to do good, until God stir us up by his grace. God deals with us as the shepherd doth with his sheep: if a sheep run from his fellows, the shepherd sets his dog after it, not to devour it, but to bring it in again: so our heavenly Shepherd, if any of us his sheep disobey him, he sets his dog after us, not to hurt us, but to bring us home to a consideration of our duty towards this our heavenly Father and loving Shepherd. *God punishes for our profit, and suffers long.*

God's dogs be poverty, banishment, sickness, evil rulers, dearth, death, war, ignorance, superstition, loss of goods or friends, &c. Who could have holden his hands beside such a sturdy people, and not utterly have destroyed them; where no sort of men among such a number, for so many plagues, in so many years, would turn to their Lord God? Here therefore may appear the long-suffering of God, who doth not suddenly in a rage take vengeance on us, as soon as the fault is done, as one of us doth towards another; but tarries so long to look for our amendment and repentance. Also it is evident, how true that is which God saith, "All the day long I stretched out my hands to an unfaithful and rebellious people." Our Saviour Christ saith, he stands and knocks at the door, and would come in, and we will not let him in. *God suffers long. Rom. x. Rev. iii.*

The Lord for his mercy's sake soften our hearts, that we despise not such gentle callings, and be found in the number of such hard hearts; lest we be given up to our own lusts, and so perish in our own wickedness. When we read and hear this sturdy disobedience towards God, we think this people to be the worst under heaven; and if we had been in their case, we would not have been so disobedient: but if we look at ourselves, and without flattery examine our own consciences and behaviour towards God, we shall find that we have been plagued no less than they, and have had God's long sufferance and benefits shewed towards us no less than they; and yet we have not learned so much, yea, less than they. God of his goodness amend it in us for Christ's sake!

And because they had been so negligent in not considering God's plagues and works among them so many years; yet twice again in this verse he wills them not lightly to consider it, nor forget it any longer, as they had done beforetimes, but deeply to weigh why those plagues had fallen upon them. God works nothing in vain, but for our learning and great profit, that we may remember our duty the better, and more reverently worship him hereafter. It is no small fault so lightly to consider God's works towards us: for that we might the better do it, he hath given man only reason as a chief treasure, that we may do the same; and also taught us by his word to do so. Therefore, if we do it not, we are worse than beasts, which have not reason to consider such his workings.

No kind of fruit, corn, vines, figs, pomegranates, olives, had prosperously increased of all these years; which could not be but for some great cause: and yet they passed but lightly on it, neither fearing God the more, lest he should increase the plagues, nor amended their lives, that he might hold his hand from plaguing them any longer. Often and earnest remembering of our disobedience towards God, and considering his scourges for the same, works in all good hearts an earnest amendment of life. The unthrifty son in the gospel, that had spent all his portion of goods unthriftly, when he was driven by hunger to remembrance of himself and his misbehaviour, comes home to his father, submits himself, confesses his fault, saying, "Father, I have sinned against heaven and thee, and am not worthy to be called thy son;" and so is received to mercy. The publican, acknowledging his

Remembering our sins and plagues work good in us.

Luke xv.

sins, went home righteous. St Paul, remembering how he was a persecutor, cruel, a blasphemer, is kept in an humble and lowly knowledge of himself. Esdras and Daniel, confessing their disobedience and sins of the whole people, knowledge their misery, God's justice in punishing, and so obtain mercy. Moses, to teach the Jews to be pitiful to strangers, bids them remember, how they were strangers in Egypt and slaves to Pharao: for in so considering their old estate and heavy case that they were in before, they should learn the better to pity strangers and consider their heaviness. This by remembering diligently, our case and state past with God's punishment for our sins, we shall learn our misery, call for help of God, and be more ware hereafter, that we fall not into the like sins, and so procure God's anger and heavier hand, heaping our own damnation. God sends such things to teach us our duty; and if we do not learn, he will cast us out of his school. No good schoolmaster will suffer such lewd scholars in his school as will not learn, when they be sufficiently taught both by gentleness and sharpness, by things past and present, by example of others and experience of themselves.^{1 Tim. i.} ^{Dan. ix.} ^{Exod. xxii.}

And where these plagues began to fall upon them, even after the ground-work of the temple was laid, and when they left off building; a man would think God dealt extremely with them, which would not spare them any thing at all, but for the first fault punishes so sharply and continues so long. But, as the Machabees teach, when he hath reckoned the cruelty and persecution of Antiochus, lest a man should think God hated his people for dealing so sharply with them, he saith, "God did it for love, and that he loved them more than all other people, because by correction he would so soon call them back, and not let them live in sin still, as he did other nations." The Gentiles whom he punished nothing so sharply, but let them live at their pleasure, they knew him not, worshipped him not; he gave them not his word nor his prophets, but let them take their pleasure, as though he cared not for them. David, considering the divers plagues and sickness which God laid on him, said, "It is good for me that thou hast corrected and humbled me; for before I was cor-

2 Macc. vi.

God's punishing is a token of his love.

Psal. cxix.

rected, I sinned." For as a man[1] will suffer those beasts which he appoints to be killed, to go where they lust in the best pastures, and to break his hedges, that in so doing, the sooner they be fat, the sooner they may be slain; so God, those people which he loves not in Christ his Son, he lets them take their pleasure, corrects them not for their amendment, but lets them work their just condemnation, in giving them up to their own lusts. " Every father," saith the apostle, " corrects his children; and those which he corrects not be bastards." And although correction of God seem sharp and bitter for the present time, and seems to come of hate and not of love; yet the end is sweet, loving, and profitable, that he may give us his holiness. A vessel, if it be foul, must be scoured before wine be put in it; and he that will make his ground fruitful, must first pull up the weeds, before he sow good seed: so by these sharp medicines of God's correction must the body be purged, that the mind may bring forth his due fruit in fear and reverence.

Let us in England therefore remember God's plagues, which we have suffered of God's good will, so long and many, for our amendment; and let us lament our hardness of heart, that have been so grievously and long punished, and yet have not duly considered the heaviness of God's hand, nor the greatness of our sins which have so provoked his anger upon us. We are sufficiently taught by all examples before us, if we will learn, and by these present plagues that we feel, what a grievous thing and horrible sin it is in God's sight to leave God's house unbuilt: and yet, like unreasonable beasts and unsensible, we neither fear our good God as a Lord, nor love him as a father, as Malachy saith, " If I be your Lord, where is the fear ye owe me? If I be your father, where is the love that is due unto me?"

<small>Malac. i.</small>

From henceforth God promises " to bless their fruit and works:" and they had not so great scarceness before, but now they should have as great plenty. So that when man turns unto God, God turns unto him: when man amends, God

<small>God turneth to us, when we turn to him.</small>

[1] The first edition reads, *the butcher will*—altered in the second to *the a man will*—where the first word appears to have been left by mistake. ED.]

looks cheerfully on him, where before he was angry: when man leaves sinning, God leaves plaguing: when man builds God's house, and maintaineth his true religion, God blesseth his house and all that is in it. As Moses teaches: "If thou hear the voice of the Lord thy God, to do his commandment, thou shalt be blessed in the city, in thy house, in the field, &c." Deut. xxviii.

And how came all this to pass, that they were so amended? By preaching rather than plaguing: for that which could not be obtained in forty years' plagues, was gotten in three weeks' preaching. Aggeus came the first day of the sixth month, and the twenty-fourth of the same they began to work; so they had no more time to preach in, nor to prepare their tools in, but three weeks and three days. Such a strong thing is the word of God, sharper than a two-edged sword, and piercing to the division of the mind and soul: and where it is earnestly received, it makes many to fear no death nor displeasure, nor to think any thing painful, so that he may please his God. Therefore let us have it in reverence, use it, hear it, read it, mark it, remember it, and practise it: for in it is shewed unto us all the counsel of God; and it is set for a sufficient doctrine to us, to stir us up to the doing of our duty and salvation of our souls, to the worshipping of God, and understanding his goodness offered unto us. Preaching moves more than plagues. Heb. iv.

Also a worthy example it is to be followed of all that have correction of other, that when the rod will not serve, to prove words and counsel: for often many be such, that they will do more for a word than a stripe; and often strokes harden the heart, when gentleness wins and persuades. Gentleness is oft better than sharpness.

v. 20. *The word of the Lord was spoken the second time unto Aggeus, in the twenty-fourth day of the month, saying,* The text.

21. *Speak to Zerubabel, the ruler of Juda, saying, I will trouble heaven and earth also.*

22. *And I will destroy the seat of the kingdoms, and I will break in sunder the strength of the kingdoms of the heathen, and I will throw down the chariots and the riders in them: the horses shall fall down, and the riders on them; and the noblest shall be slain by the sword of his brother.*

23. *In that day, saith the Lord of hosts, I will take thee, Zerubabel, son of Salathiel, my servant, saith the Lord, and I will put thee as a signet; because I have chosen thee, saith the Lord of hosts.*

God blesses them that build his house, and sends them preachers.

The people of God, now going diligently about to build the Lord's house, and working at it now three full months, did so well please the Lord, that he sent his prophet twice on a day to comfort and encourage them in their doings, lest they should faint or be slack in going forward, as they were before. Such a loving Lord is our good God unto his people, that he will maintain and set forward all such as go about diligently to walk in their vocation, and build his house to their power. Every month, from the beginning of the restoring of this temple, they had one message or other from God by his prophet, to will them to continue and go forward in this well doing and building God's house.

In the sixth and seventh month came this prophet Aggeus with God's message unto them, as is said before. In the eighth month comes Zacharias the prophet. In the ninth month comes this prophet again twice on a day from God, with comfortable promises: in the eleventh month comes Zachary again. So while they were thus diligent to do their duty, God was as ready to shew them mercy; and will be to all which do the like, as he hath promised that "to every one that hath it shall be given." Therefore, if we be desirous to have increase of the Lord's blessings, let us be diligent to increase that little which we have given us first, and it shall be increased to much more. He brings the Lord's message and not his own, like a true servant; not for money, as the pope's pardoners and priests do, but freely and willingly comes twice a day, as the Lord appoints him. Contrariwise, if the people follow not that which they be taught, God takes his word and prophets from them. It is written of a holy father called Felix, which when certain desired him to preach, he said, "In time past, when men did as they were taught, God opened many preachers' mouths: now the people will not learn; therefore God stops their mouths[1]."

Zech. i.

Luke xix.

Felix.

[1 Vitæ Patrum. Lib. v. Libell. iii. 18. p. 566. Antverp. 1615. The sequel is: Quæ cum audissent fratres, ingemuerunt dicentes, Ora pro nobis, pater. ED.]

He is now sent to Zerubabel, the prince and chief ruler, specially by name; but not as though this promise pertained to him only, and not to the rest of the people, but by him to the rest of the people. Under the name of Zerubabel is contained here all his posterity and kingdom: for to him it was never performed. As what league, truth, or promise of favour soever is made to any king, in the same is his kingdom contained, and his subjects are also partakers of the same: so the promises made to Abraham, Isaac, Jacob, and David, belong not to them only, but to their children also, successors, heirs, people and subjects. "I will restore the decayed houses of David," saith the prophet, meaning the kingdom of Christ and Christians to the end, whom he calls David, by the preaching of the gospel. Promises made to rulers pertain to their successors. Amos ix.

For this "troubling of heaven and earth" enough was said before; and this is that which the apostle saith to the Hebrews, "Yet once I trouble heaven and earth:" meaning, that those things which are thus troubled perish, and those which be not continue; and that those kingdoms that set up themselves against Christ shall fall, but Christ's kingdom shall stand for ever; as David saith, "This kingdom is an everlasting kingdom." It is as much to say, that he would fill the world with war betwixt the Persians and the Grecians, that they shall trouble the earth. Heb. xii.

This prophet in the verse following tells of the destruction of the kingdom of the Persians, under whose dominion the Jews were now, and to whom they paid great taxes, as Nehemias tells. He calls it "the seat of kingdoms," because many kingdoms were subject unto them, and that all the greatest kings feared them, served them, were in league with them, or sought friendship at their hands. And although this is now told, yet it was not fulfilled of a hundred forty and five years afterwards, or a hundred thirty and four years, as some do count. It is spoken to comfort the Jews, and answer to two privy objections, which they might have laid against God and his prophet.

After that they had now wrought earnestly at the building of God's house three months, God was so well delighted with them, that whereas heretofore he had so long plagued and sharply punished them, he said, "From this day forth will I bless you;" and your olives, vineyards, pomegranates, and other fruits, should increase and multiply, which all before had been unfruitful. But to this the people might have said, "What are we the better to have all these fruitful and plenteous? Are we not tributaries to the Persians? and what plenty or profit soever we have, they take it from us by their great taxes. All is one matter whether we have much or little, plenty or scarceness, good cheap or dearth: for if we have much, we pay much; and if we have but little, we pay little: so all is one thing to us, except this could be amended." Therefore our most merciful God, which will take all doubts from us which we can object, and comfort us in all points that we can fear, saith thus unto them: 'Be not afraid of this great power and kingdom of the Persians, under whom ye now be, and pay tribute unto; for rather than my people shall be still oppressed, I will pull down the whole kingdom and strength thereof; the chariots, horses, the riders on them, and horsemen, all shall fall; yea, the chiefest man among them, even the king himself, shall be slain by the sword, not of a stranger, but of his own countrymen, brother and servant. And although this shall not come to pass nor be done in your time and days; yet be ye sure it shall be done at the time appointed, when God shall think it best for his glory and your commodity.'

God's promises satisfy the conscience in all doubts.

Dan. ii. vii.
Daniel in his visions was often taught of four kings and monarchies which should come: first, of the image which had the head of gold, the arms and breast of silver, the belly of brass, the legs of iron; and again, by the image of four beasts, a lion, a bear, a leopard, and the fourth for cruelness wanted a name, which with his teeth should tear all, and tread under his feet, &c. By which all were noted, first the kingdom of the Assyrians and Babylonians, the second of the Medes and Persians, under which the Jews now were; the third was the Grecians, and the fourth of the Romans; which all should reign in course a time, and should continue to the world's end; but every one more cruel and worse than the other, as is now the Romish pope, under whom we be. He is emperor in deed, usurping the fourth kingdom; and rules like a prince on earth above kings;

The pope is emperor in deed, and his ruling is worse than the rest.

and hath driven the emperor almost out of Italy, and taken the lands and possessions of the empire from him; and makes him content with a corner of the world in Germany, where the revenues of the empire is not now so much as divers lords have. Every one of these kingdoms was worse than the other before them, as these beasts and metals were worse than the other. By the which we may learn, that the kingdom of the pope is worse than the others were; and that it is worse to be under him, than the other which were heathen, and knew not God. God hates them worse, which bear the name of christian men, and make a shew to love God, and in deed do nothing else but hate and persecute the good men, as the pope doth. "The servant which knoweth his master's will, and doeth it not, shall be worse beaten than he which offends by ignorance."

The kingdom of the Assyrians was now pulled down, and given to the Persians: and this is that kingdom now, which the prophet saith God would destroy, and give over to the Grecians. This came to pass in the time of the last Darius, who in divers battles fought with Alexander the Great, suffered the worse, and was overcomen. Where Alexander, first taking Darius' wife the queen, his mother and his children prisoners, used them gently as his own. Darius, seeing such gentleness, and thinking to find like favour for himself, sent embassage to Alexander, and said, if he would let him keep his kingdom still, all other things should be at his pleasure. But Alexander answered, that he could not suffer him so; for the world could no more abide two kings to reign, than to have two suns to shine: therefore there was no remedy, but yield himself, if he would live. Then Darius seeing that prepared himself to the field, where he was traiterously slain by his servant Bessus. So is this true, which the prophet sayeth, "the chiefest man by the sword of his brother should be slain." So would I translate the Hebrew word *Isch*, rather than "every man," as some do. For every man was not slain by his brother, but the king namely, as the history tells. This is common in the scripture, to put the word "brother" for one that is of the same country, kindred, or religion; and not always for those which have one father and mother. So it may well stand that he was slain of his brother, that is to say, of his countryman, as the history calls Bessus his servant. Alexander finding king Darius thus deadly wounded of his servant, for justice sake to punish such traitors, bended down the tops of two young trees, and tied the legs of Bessus to them, and let them swing up suddenly again, and so rent him in pieces. Likewise David, when one came unto him, telling him how he had slain Saul his enemy, thinking thereby to pick a thank and get a reward of David, he was by the commandment of David slain: and so should all traitors, which be false to their masters, be served. Thus the king being slain, the kingdom was brought from the Persians to the Grecians, as the prophet telleth here.

Brother.

Traitors.

2 Sam. i.

Where God saith by his prophet, that he "will destroy the kingdom, throw down the horses and horsemen," &c., we be taught that God maketh kings, pulleth down, and "changes kingdoms from one people to another," for the sins of the people, as Sirach saith, and maketh to rule whom pleaseth him. The land spewed out the rulers and people in it for their sins, and God gave it to the Jews. Therefore let not princes trust in their great strength and power; for it is the Lord God that giveth victory, as he thinketh good: whether they be good rulers or evil, they be set up of God, as Salomon saith in the name of God, "By me kings do reign;" and our Saviour Christ said to Pilate, "Thou shouldest have no power over me, except it were given thee from above." If they be good rulers, it is God's good blessing and free mercy: if they be evil, it is of justice to punish our sins, as Job saith, God makes hypocrites to rule for the sins of the people.

Ecclus. x.

Princes stand not by their own power.

Levit. xviii.

Prov. viii.

John xix.

Job xxxiv. [30.]

What cause have we then in England to complain, that God deals so sharply with us; that where we have been long hypocrites afore him, he punished us of late awhile with hypocrites to be in authority over us? When the Saxons invaded this realm, drove out the Englishmen, and ruled as kings; the state of the commonwealth was much like to these our days, and the like sins reigned in all sorts of men, both high and low, nobility and people, rulers and subjects, prelates and clergy: the most part were great hypocrites, and superstitious, cruel, covetous, proud, gluttons, whore-hunters, and ambitious. Therefore let us amend, or we shall be given up to the Spaniards, Scots, Flemings, or Frenchmen, as we were then to the Saxons. God gave his people into the hands of the Babylonians, and other people round about them, which were then the common scourges of the world: and so will he do with us, as he hath done to our fathers afore us, if we do not amend; for he hateth sin in all ages, and will punish it.

But as God comforts his people here, now building his house, and saith, he will throw down that kingdom which then troubled them; so he will be as good unto us, if we worship him truly, and he will destroy them that trouble us. His love to his people is greatest, as he saith, "He that touches you touches the apple of my eye." So tender is our God over us, as we be over our eyes, which be the tenderest parts of us: and he will most assuredly revenge all displeasure done unto us; for he can no more see his people take wrong and be oppressed now, than aforetimes. He is no changeling, nor his love waxes not cold nor old: we be his children and the members of his mystical body, as they were now, to whom he promiseth this help: he is our Lord God and Father, loving his children and members in all ages, and pouring his blessings on them, for Christ's sake, in whom he hath chosen them. Therefore he will shew the like mercies unto us, and of justice revenge all displeasures done to us for his sake. *God's love in all ages is greatest to his people. Zech. ii.*

The last verse maketh answer to another objection, which the Jews might have made against the prophet, saying, 'If this kingdom shall be thrown down, and so great war shall be, as though heaven and earth should go together, then shall we be destroyed: we are but few in number; there is but few of us come home again; and what shall we do then? how shall we escape? Being compassed about with so strong and many enemies, we shall be devoured.' To this God maketh answer, and biddeth them not be afraid: for "in that day," when this great trouble shall come, "I will take thee, Zerubabel, my servant," whom I love, saith the Lord, "and I will keep thee as my privy signet, and thou shalt not perish, saith the mighty Lord of hosts, because I have chosen thee." So good a God and *God delivereth his in greatest dangers.*

comfortable Lord is our God to all his people in all ages, that he will leave no doubt untaken away, that can discomfort his children; but he will satisfy all which can be said, and pull all fear from us. Therefore Zerubabel is here promised to be delivered out of all dangers of that great war, and translating of the kingdom from the Persians to the Grecians, so that he should catch no harm.

But here riseth a hard question, how this should be true, that God would deliver Zerubabel in that day of so great trouble, seeing that he lived not so long, but died within fourteen years after this prophecy. Zerubabel was the first prince of Juda, which ruled the people, after their returning home from Babylon: he came home with the people, was their captain, and had now ruled a forty years: he ruled in all but fifty-two years, as the history saith; and this destruction of the kingdom of the Persians was not fulfilled of one hundred and forty-five years afterwards, or near hand so much. How could he then be delivered in that day, and died so long afore? Unto this may be answered that which was said afore; that promises made to kings and the[1] fathers are not to be applied to themselves only; but they be made also to their children and subjects, and shall be fulfilled in long years afterwards, rather than at that present: so will God exercise our faith in patiently looking for his coming, when his holy wisdom shall think good, and not when our foolish rashness shall wish and desire him to come. Promises made unto Abraham, Isaac, David, and Jacob, &c. were not fulfilled in their days, but to their children long afterwards. So God makes promise here to these princes and rulers, that all the subjects may know that they be contained also in the same truce and league of God, and that the promise concerns them also; and they shall be delivered in that day from all the danger of war and enemies that shall come upon them. And it is as much as though the prophet should say: 'Thou Zerubabel and thy kingdom, all thy people and subjects, be not afraid; for in those troublesome days I will save you and keep you as diligently as my ring and private seal.'

And that they might the more earnestly believe it, he

Promises made to the father belong to the children.

[¹ Second edition, *that*. ED.]

called him "servant:" whereby he might well assure himself, that if earthly lords and masters will defend their servants, much more he that was King of heaven and earth, and Lord of lords, most tender and loving of his subjects, would not see his servants oppressed, violently trodden under foot, nor thrown down; but he would be their mighty deliverer, and revenge their wrongs. What can be greater comfort to any people, than to hear God vouchsafe to call himself their Lord God and master, and them his servants? If this be thought so great a promotion, that an earthly lord will take us to his service, speak cheerfully to us, set us in some office, or let us wear his livery; it is much more to be esteemed to be servant to Jesus Christ, to bear his cross (for that is his livery), to fight under his banner, and have him for our captain. Men do commonly sue to be servants unto noblemen, and wear their liveries, that whosoever seeth their coat may fear them, and under their master's name they may rule in their country, like lords of the land, do wrong when they lust, and every man shall call it right; and though they were slaves afore, yet now they shall be every gentleman's fellow: but they which wear Christ's livery, be obedient and loving to all; do no wrong, but suffer; pray for them which persecute them, and do good for evil. This livery we must wear if we will be the Lord's servants, and partakers of his promise and deliverance in the day of trouble. *God delivereth his servants, if they will wear his livery.*

This similitude, which the prophet useth, of a ring, that God would keep him as safely as his ring, is taken of kings and princes, which among all things keep their seal, signet and ring most surely, either themselves, or betake it to some most trusty friend to keep. If the seal should be counterfeited, stolen, or blanks sealed with it; what hurt or treason might be done thereby! Their lands, offices, or treasure might be given away; the subjects stirred to rebellion; or the destruction of the whole commonwealth might follow thereon. Therefore, that they might most certainly persuade themselves, that in that troublesome time of war and destruction of the kingdom of the Persians they should be most safely kept; he saith, he will keep them as his ring and seal, that is to say, most safely. And as when a friend send his ring or seal for a token to his friend, it *God saveth his people in all dangers.*

signifieth that he loveth him most dearly, to whom he sendeth such a pledge of love and friendship; and also teacheth him, that where he seeth his friend's ring, he should not deny him his request, nor doubt of the message that it should be counterfeited; so when he names his ring here, they should not doubt of his love towards them, nor mistrust his promise. For as with us when doctors be created, they have a ring given them, as a ceremony of honour and authority; and in marriage the husband giveth his wife a ring for a sure pledge of love: so God our Saviour under this similitude of a ring commends his honour, that he hath called us unto, to be his servants and children, the love he bears unto us, in that he hath married us unto him in his Son Christ by the wedding ring of faith; and the wedding apparel appeareth, when Osee saith, "I will marry thee to me in faith, justice, judgment, mercy, and many mercies."

The scripture is God's indenture, and the sacraments be seals.

Hosea ii.

Seal.

Under this name of a seal he commendeth unto us also both his outward visible sacraments, and the inward grace of the Holy Ghost, working in our consciences by them. St Paul calleth circumcision (a sacrament of the old law) "the seal of the righteousness of faith:" and as that was a seal in that time to our fathers of righteousness, so be our sacraments to us in these days seals of God's promises unto us, and all have one strength and virtue. The scripture of God is the indenture betwixt God and us, wherein is contained both the promises, grace, and mercy, that God offereth to the world in his Son Christ, and also the conditions which he requires to be fulfilled in our behalf: the sacraments are the seals set to his indenture, to strengthen our faith, that we do not doubt. For as it is not enough to write the conditions of a bargain in an indenture, except it be sealed; so God for our weakness thought it not sufficient to make us promise of his blessings in writing in his scripture; but he would seal it with his own blood, and institute his sacraments as seals of the same truth, to remain to be received of us in remembrance of him and strengthening our faith.

Rom. iv.

Baptism is a sacrament sealed by God, and sealing our consciences that God taketh us for his children and servants; and we offer and bind ourselves to serve him only as a Lord and Father. The supper is also a sacrament, wherein he feeds us spiritually, thus taken into his service, with his own precious body and blood; and we, reckoning with ourselves wherein we have offended him, ask mercy, nothing doubting to obtain it, and renew our bond to him which we have so often broken, and promise to do so no more. So that, when God giveth these his sacraments to us by his ministers, and we receive the same, the bargain is full made betwixt God and us, the writing sealed and delivered: we are become his people, and he our God; we to serve, love, honour, and worship him; and he to help, deliver, defend, and provide for us all necessaries.

This inward sealing of the conscience, which is the second sort of sealing, is where God poureth his love so plentifully into our hearts by the Holy Ghost which is given us, that he beareth witness to our spirit that we be the children of God, and stirreth up our minds to call him "Father, Father:" we have a taste and feeling that God hath chosen and sealed us for his people with the Holy Ghost promised, as St Paul saith. This is a sure token to a faithful heart, that he is the child of God, and God his Father: and of this he takes so great comfort, that in what trouble soever he fall, he knoweth that God doeth it not of hate, but of love; trieth his faith, that other may know the same, how earnestly he loveth his God; and that nothing can be so strong to pull him out of his God's hands,—not for his own strength, but that God which holdeth him is stronger than all. Of such as were thus sealed St John in his Revelation speaketh, when he saith, that of every tribe there were twelve thousand sealed; and St Paul teacheth Timothy, that this groundwork stand strong having this seal, "The Lord knoweth who be his." For as noblemen and princes bear a love to their servants, and for a witness of the same will give their outward cognizance, badge, and livery, whereby they may be known from others, and stirreth up their minds to love him again by such tokens: so God will both by his Spirit pour his love into our hearts, and let us see the care that he taketh for us; and will also by outward sacraments, as badges, mark us for his people, and by the same seal us surely to himself, and stir us up to love him again and look diligently to our duty. If earthly lords and princes will so safely defend

Rom. v. viii.

God sealeth the consciences of his people with the Holy Ghost.
Eph. i.

Rev. vii.

2 Tim. ii.

their servants; let them not doubt but God, that is Lord of lords, will defend his people from all dangers and wrongs, be they never so many and so great, if they would earnestly in faith call upon him in the day of their trouble, forsake their own strength, wit and policy, and trust in him only. David saith well: "The Lord is not delighted in the strength of an horse, nor the strong legs of man; but the Lord is well pleased with them the which fear him, and with them that trust in his mercy."

<small>Psal. cxlvii.</small>

There is no way sooner to provoke God's anger, and make him to forsake us in trouble, than to trust to ourselves, and in our own wit, strength, and policy: for that is as much as to take the praise to ourselves from him, and mistrust God that he cannot or will not defend us. And although we must not trust in ourselves, yet we must use all means which he hath ordained for our defence. For as we must be diligent to do all good works, and not put our trust of salvation in them, but say with St Luke, "When ye have done all that I commanded you, say ye be unprofitable servants;" so we must use all ways lawful to defend ourselves, and yet say, "Our help is from the Lord, which hath made both heaven and earth:" he hath ordained such means to save us by, and works by the same our deliverance when pleaseth him; and sometimes, to shew his power, he delivereth us without such ordinary means.

<small>Although we must use all lawful measures, yet trust only in God.</small>

<small>Luke xvii.</small>

<small>Psal. cxxiv.</small>

And why will God thus save them? for any goodness in them, which had so long forgotten him and his house? or for their good works, who had so long been so disobedient? No; but even "because I have chosen thee, saith the Lord." This is the first and chiefest cause, why he bestoweth his goodness upon any people; even because he hath chosen them in Christ afore the world was made: and for this cause he continueth bestowing his blessing to the end upon them whom he hath once chosen.

<small>God helpeth us for his own sake, and not for our goodness.</small>

St Paul, reasoning of this matter, putteth two causes, wherefore God should love, justify, and choose us: either freely of grace and mercy, saith he, or for the goodness of our works. If it should be for our works, then (saith he) it cannot be of grace: and if it be of free grace, love and mercy, then is it not for our works, neither past nor to come; for

<small>Rom. ii. iv.</small>

then grace should not be grace, saith he, if it were not thus freely given. If God should choose us for any goodness in us, then he should but do one good turn for another, and freely without reward do nothing; which is most against his nature, that doeth good for evil, yea, and where he seeth no possibility of goodness or reward to be looked for. "Who hath given him any thing first, and he shall be recompensed again?" saith St Paul; as though he should say, No. "I have chosen you, and ye have not chosen me," said Christ to his disciples and apostles. And as he thus chose them, so he chooses all which be chosen: and so he will declare his free grace, love, and mercy, to all which be his, freely, even because it pleased him to choose them, and they deserved not to be chosen of him, but rather to be cast away from him. When God promised to deliver his people in like distress by his prophet, he said, "For mine own sake, for mine own sake I will do it." And not only thus in bodily deliverance, but in forgiveness of sins he says likewise, "It is I, it is I, which forgiveth thy sins for mine own sake." Thus freely God our heavenly Father, for the love which he beareth to us in his Son Christ, in whom he had chosen us from the beginning, and for whose sake he continueth his favour to us,—he, I say, bestows all his blessings freely on us both in body and soul, in this life and after. *Rom. xi.* *John xiii.* *Isai. xlviii.* *Isai. xliii.*

The will of God is the first cause of doing all good things: and when he will, all things work and obey him; and when he will not, they stay and cease. So because his choosing of us cometh of his free will and mercy, it is the first and chiefest cause of our salvation. If he should be stirred to choose us for our goodness, which he foresees in us, that is ever imperfect; or if for any other cause within us or without us, then he should not be the first cause and mover of all things. But St Luke saith, "In him we live, be, and are moved." That which moves another thing is in nature afore that which is moved; and also it is better, stronger, and wiser: but to say that anything is stronger, wiser, or better than God, is treason and blasphemy to his majesty: therefore his will is the first cause of all our goodness. *God's will is the first cause of all.* *Acts xvii.*

Thus our good God teaches us, and comforts his people,

that all things shall turn to the best to them which love him, be the troubles never so many and great, that man's wit cannot tell how to escape. Let kings and princes fall together by the ears; kill, murder, shew what cruelty they can; get or lose kingdoms; war, fight, or what they can devise: God will save and deliver his people, if it please him, out of all their hands. When Pharao persecuted the Jews through the Red Sea, God saved his people and drowned the Egyptians. In the wilderness when Seon and Og, two mighty kings, denied them victuals and passage, God destroyed them both, and gave their lands to his people. After they came to the land promised, he drove out seven mighty people, and dealt it to the Jews: and when all the heathen people, which dwelt round about them, made war against his people, he destroyed them all. In Babylon, when they were prisoners under Balthazar, king within the city, and Darius, king of the Medes, with Cyrus, the king of the Persians, besieging the city round about, that none should escape; when the city was taken, God did not only deliver his people from all the cruel hands of these three mighty kings; but gave them such favour in the sight of Cyrus, that he not only hurt them not, but set them at liberty, sent them home to their country, gave them licence to build this temple, restored their jewels, which Nebuchadnezer took away, and gave free licence to every man to help them with money as much as they would. Who could have thought God's people should have been now delivered out of the hands of three heathen kings, being all their enemies, and might have slain them like sheep? When Haman had gotten licence of the king to destroy the Jews, and made a gallows for Mardocheus; God sent queen Ester to save his people, and Haman was hanged on his own gallows. When Darius was slain by Alexander, and the kingdom brought to the Grecians; Alexander coming to destroy Jerusalem, because they denied him tribute, God so turned his heart, that he entreated them well, submitted himself to the high priest, meeting him with the other priests in their priestly apparel, and confessed their God to be the true God. When the Romans conquered the Grecians, and the Jews were under the rule of the Romans, they did not greatly harm them, until they crucified Christ and denied him to be their God, saying, "His blood be upon us and upon our children!" In the cruel persecutions afterwards, the more sorrow that was laid on God's people, the more they increased. *Matt. xxvii.*

Thus in all ages God delivered his out of trouble; or else taketh them to himself by some glorious death. In these our days, when the mightiest princes of the world strive and fight cruelly who shall be the greatest, rather than godliest, God provideth always some corner for his to flee into, where they may serve him. And if they be persecuted from one place, he prepares another to receive them. And although persecution was great amongst us, yet God shewed himself more glorious, mighty, and merciful in strengthening so many weak ones to die for him, than in so mercifully providing for them which were abroad; although both be wonderful. What glorious cracks made proud persecutors, that they would make God's poor banished people to eat their fingers for hunger! but they had plenty for all the others' cruelty: God's holy name be praised therefore! What a mercy of God is this, that where we deserved to be cast from him for ever because of our wickedness, he now corrected us gently, and called us to this honour, that he punished us not so much for our own sins, as that he called us to the promotion of bearing his cross, witnessing to the world his truth, and vouchedsafe to prove, teach and confirm others in this his truth by our witness bearing. He called us to the same honour that he called his own Son Christ Jesus, in suffering for his name's sake; that "whereas we suffer with him, we shall be glorified" and reign with him. *Rom. viii.*

Let the cruel papists consider therefore, how God hath delivered his people out of their hands, fulfilled this his promise, and kept us safely, like his privy signet, in these miserable days of their persecution. Let the bloody bishops, void of all religion, and changing with the world to fill their filthy bellies, (although they would now make men believe they would be constant, and stoutly confute that which afore they proved true by oaths and doctrine,) let them, I say, consider whether they, or the simple souls which they tormented, have gotten the victory. The simple soul offered himself to die, rather *God's people have the victory by suffering.*

than to offend God by superstition or idolatry: the proud Caiphas threatened fire and faggot, if he forsook not his true faith. Thus whilst they strive for religion, and not for life, the poor members of Christ hold fast their faith; and the proud prelate with his torments cannot overcome God's simple sheep. They strive not for life; but the simple man offers it willingly, rather than forsake the truth: and so God ever confounds the wisdom of the world, and is glorified in the fools and abjects. God for his mercy's sake grant all his like boldness to withstand their cruelty, whensoever God shall try us!

A PRAYER.

MOST righteous Judge and merciful Father, which of love did punish sharply thy people, being negligent in building thy house, that by such sharp correction they might be stirred up to do their duty, and so have pleased thee: we acknowledge and confess before the world and thy divine majesty, that we have no less offended thee in this behalf than they have done, and that, for all the sharp plagues which thou laid upon us, we could not awake out of our deadly sleep and forgetting the earnest promotion of thy glory and true religion; but rather consented to the persecution of our brother, thy true and faithful people, until now that of thy infinite goodness, by giving us a gracious Queen and restoring the light of thy word, thou hast let us taste the treasures of thy mercies in our extreme and desperate miseries, when for our wickedness we durst not, and for the great power of thy enemies we could not, hope nor look for any such help or redress at all. We fall down flat therefore before the throne of grace, desiring pardon of this great negligence and of all our former offences; and pray thee, that thou will not deal with us as we have deserved: but as of thy own free will thou promised thy people, falling earnestly to thy work and restoring of thy temple, that from thenceforward thou would bless all their work and fruits, overthrow their enemies, and save thy people; that thou wouldest make that house also more glorious than the first, by the preaching of thy gospel; so we desire thee for Christ's sake, thy Son and our Saviour, to be no less good and gracious, Lord, unto us, yet once again going about to restore thy true religion, trodden down and defaced by the cruel papists. Send forth, O Lord, many such faithful preachers, as will set out thy glory unfeignedly: open the hearts of thy people, that they may see how far more acceptable unto thee is the lively preaching of thy holy word, than all the glittering ceremonies of popery: deliver us, we beseech thee, from all our enemies: save and preserve our gracious Queen as thine own signet; endue her and her council with such reverent fear of thee and thy word, that, all policy which is contrary to thy word set apart, they may uprightly seek and earnestly maintain thy true glory, minister justice, punish sin, and defend the right. Confound, most mighty God, and bring to nought all the devices of such as go about to overthrow thy word and true worship: open our eyes, that we may see how dearly thou hast loved us in Jesus Christ, thy Son our Lord. Hold us fast, O Lord of hosts, that we fall no more from thee: grant us thankful and obedient hearts, that we may increase daily in the love, knowledge, and fear of thee: increase our faith, and help our unbelief, that we, being provided for and relieved in all our needs by thy fatherly care and providence, as thou shalt think good, may live a godly life to the praise and good example of thy people, and after this life may reign with thee for ever, through Christ our Saviour; to whom with thee and the Holy Ghost, three persons and one God, be praise and thanksgiving in all congregations, for ever and ever. Amen.

Here endeth the prophet Aggeus.

ON

THE PROPHET

OBADIAH.

A PREFACE

TO ALL THE ENEMIES OF GOD, HIS WORD, PEOPLE AND
RELIGION, TO LEAVE THEIR WICKEDNESS: AND
TO COMFORT THE GOOD MANFULLY
TO BEAR THEIR MADNESS,
AND PATIENTLY TO
LOOK FOR GOD'S
GOODNESS.

LIKE as in Aggeus my endeavour and purpose was, that those that fear the Lord should be stirred up to an earnest building of God's house, loving of his word, and maintaining of true religion; so in this short prophet my travail and meaning is, that the wicked, understanding how vainly they strive with all their wit, power and policy against the poor simple innocent crucified Christ Jesus, the almighty Son of the living God, the wisdom and power of God, his Father, might cease their raging madness; and not only that, but also how they shall be overthrown in their own devices that they imagine against true Christians, the mystical members of his body and church, or against his word and religion; as all their fathers have been from the beginning, whose steps they follow in hating and persecuting God's people. Their stomachs be stout, their policies great, their might is strong, their wits are wile, yea, all the world is on their side; yet in the end they shall serve dastards, ignorant, helpless, witless and misers: for, as the wise man says, "there is no wisdom, polity nor counsel against the Lord." The more wisdom, sublety, strength or power that a man has, the more he has it to his own destruction, if he have it not and use it to the glory of God and comfort of his people. For as wild beasts, the more fierce and cruel that they be, the more it harms them, and causes men to hunt and seek ways how to destroy them; so, the more that the wicked set up themselves against the Lord, and oppress his people, the readier is God to help and deliver his, and overthrow the

_{Prov. xxi.}

other. Can they find any rebels against God, his word and people, from the beginning to this day, that has prevailed against the Lord and his chosen folk? If there be none, (as it is most true none to be,) how can they look to be the first? Why may not true Christians boldly say with David then, " Why do the heathen fret and fume, and the people imagine vain things against the Lord and his anointed, saying, Let us brust in sunder their bonds, and cast their yoke away from us?" But it follows, " He that dwells in the heavens will mock them, and the Lord will laugh them to scorn."

<small>Psal. ii.</small>

In the two first sons[1] of Adam, and so orderly in all ages to these days, it appears how the wicked continually malice and persecute the good, but to the hurt of themselves and the praise of the godly. Cain killed his brother Abel, and thought he should have been blameless: but Abel's innocent blood and such like cried vengeance on Cain and his followers from that day to this; and the righteous God revenges it daily, and at length will condemn the obstinate utterly. Cham mocked his father Noe, and his seed the Canaanites persecuted God's people the Jews, that came of Sem his brother: therefore his posterity was accursed of God to the world's end. The proud giants with their captain Nimrod, building the tower of Babel, to get themselves a name in earth, were overthrown in their own device by God from heaven. Carnal Ismael sought to destroy the promised Isaac, but in vain. Bloody Edom or Esau, whom this prophet describes, sought the death of his brother Jacob; but the God of Abraham their father saved them. Joseph was sold into Egypt by his brethren, and by the false accusing of his mistress was wrongfully prisoned: yet he that sits on high looked down to the low dungeon of the prison, and raised Joseph to be ruler and saver of the land. The Egyptians oppressed God's people for a time; but the Lord of hosts drowned Pharao and his company for their cruelty against them. The froward people, murmuring often against their captain Moses, some were swallowed up with earth quick, some burned with fire. The Philistines and seven nations

<small>Matt. xxiii.</small>

<small>Gen. ix.</small>

<small>Gen. xi.</small>

<small>Gen. xxvii.</small>

<small>Gen. xli.</small>

<small>Exod. xiv.</small>

<small>Num. xvi.</small>

[1 In the only preceding edition it is *sinnes*, an evident misprint. ED.]

round about God's flock kept continual war against them; yet they could never devour them, but were devoured at the length. Saul and his flatterers banished and pursued poor David, whom his God of a shepherd made a king maugre all his foes. The ten tribes of Israel with their kings were enemies to Juda and Benjamin evermore: yet though they were the stronger and more in number, they were sooner rooted out. The Chaldees, Assyrians, Persians, Grecians and Romans, the mightiest princes on the earth, oft subdued the Jews, forsaking their God: but the Lord, their old Saviour, ever restored them again when they sought him, unto[2] they utterly refused Christ their Saviour. The Jews crucified Christ Jesus our Lord, thrust him to the heart with a spear, buried him and laid a heavy stone on him, thinking he should never rise again a conqueror; but in vain was all their spite, and their labour lost.

The emperor many years cruelly tormented all that believed in the Lord, fondly thinking to have by that means overthrown them. The pope in process of time conquered almost all princes, except the Grecians, unto of late the Lord, opening the eyes of some, brake his snares, and delivered his folk. Monks and freres[3] by man's traditions would have overwhelmed true religion: papists of late have banished, burned and persecuted many godly men so cruelly, as no history speaks of the like this thousand year, willing to have feared all from ever acknowledging their Lord and Christ. Many heretics have laboured to have defaced God's truth; but all is in vain. God (his name be praised therefore!) has overthrown them in their highest ruff, laughed them to scorn, and raised up that which they would most gladly have utterly oppressed. For as death and the grave could not prevail against Christ our head; no more shall it against his body and members. As Nimrod therefore, Pharao, Jeroboam, Nebuchadnezzar, Darius, and Alexander, with all their kingdoms and partakers, be now vanquished and subdued by the Turk, the Sophy, and the Soldan, prester John, and other heathen princes; their countries made waste, strangers possess them; their religion altered from evil to worse; their cities, towns

[2] Unto: here and elsewhere used for *until*. ED.]
[3] Freres: friars. ED.]

and temples (as the prophets did tell afore) are made dens of wild beasts, owls and other filthy birds: so since Christ, that which emperors manfully conquered, the pope by subtlety devoured, made himself a prince of princes; but now by the power of God's word preached he is made a laughing stock to all those whose eyes the Lord has opened to see his abominations; and all realms that afore feared him, now God visiting his people, fall from him. For as the woodbine leaning to a tree climbs up and spreads itself over all the branches, unto it have overgrown and killed the whole tree; and as a strong heady stream, undermining great high banks, at length makes all to tumble into the water, and washes it away: so the pope, first seeking aid at princes' hands and finding favour, overwhelmed them all at length, as the wood-bine, and undermining them, as the heady waters, has thrown them down these many years, unto it pleased God to open the eyes of some few to consider their estate and seek for remedy.

No kingdom, people, nor religion, that withstood God and his truth, can be found, but it has been overthrown. Babylon, the first and worst, continued longest; yet it had an end by the Persians. The Persians, Grecians and Romans cannot all together compare in time with Babylon, and yet they be vanquished away. Popery has troubled God's church a long time; but now, through God's mercy, it melts away like snow afore the sun. But Christ saith, our religion and people professing the same, without all kind of popish superstition, have been from the beginning, continued in all ages from time to time; and at these days (the Lord's name be praised therefore!) whole countries do abhor his abominations. In the midst of all mischief, when every kind of flesh had so defiled himself, that God of justice drowned the whole world except eight persons, yet was there found kept undefiled, and calling upon the living God with true faith, holy Seth, Enos, Enoch, Noe, &c. In idolatrous Chaldee was faithful Abraham, Sarai, Nahor and Lot, &c. In superstitious Egypt lived innocently Jacob and his sons, Moses, Aaron, &c. In the wilderness wandered in God's fear Josue, Caleb, Phines, Eleazar, &c. When the number of God's people increased in the time of the judges and kings, there were so many godly men found among the people, beside men of power, as Gedeon, Jephthe, David, Josaphat, Ezechias, Josias, that they cannot be numbered. Against Jesabel stood up Elias, Eliseus, Abdias, &c. In the captivity were Esdras, Daniel, Aggeus, Nehemias, with many more. Against Haman and Holophernes stood Ester, Mardocheus, Judith, and Alier. What valiant warriors the Machabees were against bloody Antiochus, the ancient father Eleazar, and the manly mother of the seven brether so cruelly murdered, the history declares. From Christ's time to consider God's stout soldiers, it is harder to tell where to begin than where to make an end. The apostles and martyrs, so cruelly tormented, be so many and so well known, that they need not be rehearsed. What storms then can the pope devise with his clergy to oppress, deface and overthrow God his word, religion or people? Can they be more cruel than Nero, Diocletian, Domitian? Can they pass Jesabel, Nebuchadnezzar, Antiochus, or such like beastly tormentors? In the spite of all the mighty persecutors, God blessed his. Surely their mischievous malice and blood-thirsty tyranny pass all these in madness: and yet, if they could pass themselves in cruelty, all is vain. He is stronger that is with us, than any can be against us. The devil is cruel in his members, but the loving Lord forsakes not his. Let not the wicked then triumph, nor God's people be dismayed.

God our Father for love will try his people, what they will bear for his sake; but of mercy he will not lay too heavy loads on us, nor forsake us: the Lord of strength and power will shew his glory in our weakness, that by his mighty hand such weak bodies may be strengthened to suffer that that passes reason. The oftener that the goldsmith tries his gold in the fire, beats and knocks it with his hammer, the finer is the gold: the more that God tries our faith in the furnace of temptation, the more he loves us, and the more we glorify him. The stormy winter cannot overwhelm the fruits of summer. Weeds be many, yet the corn is not devoured. Wild beasts be cruel; yet God defends the shiftless sheep. Many fishes be raveners; yet the young fish increases. The hawks be greedy; yet shifts the little birds. Dogs hunt and follow the chase most greedily;

yet escapes safely the fearful hare. Summer is raging hot; yet the leaves make a comfortable cold shadow: the winds blow boustously; yet stand fast the low bushes, when the great oaks are overthrown. The waves of the sea are rough and huge; yet safely slips away the sliding ship. The rage of fire is swaged with water; the heady streams are kept in with banks. Unruly people are bridled by laws: hot burning fevers are cooled by medicines. Thus ever against an extremity God has prepared a remedy, that fearful man should not mistrust God's careful providence that he takes for him. How should proud popery then think to conquer all by might and cruelty, that God defends so fatherly? and why should God's people be afraid at every storm? He that smites, heals; and he that sends trouble, gives strength. Let us therefore pluck up our stomachs, and pray with St Augustine, *Da quod jubes, et jube quod vis*[1]: "Lord, give me strength to do and bear that that thou commandest, and command what thou will."

It is wonderful to consider the foolishness of the wicked, which in polity would seem so wise. The higher that a man climbs, the nearer and more dangerous is his fall: the greater weight that is cast on, the sooner it breaks: the faster a man runs, the sooner he is weary: the further that the bow is drawn, the sooner it flies in pieces: the heavier that the cart is loaden, the slower it goes: the hotter that the fire is, the less while it continues: the more grievous that the disease is, the shorter it is. Tyrants reign not long: wild beasts, the crueller they be, the more they be hunted and killed. In sum, no violent thing can long endure. Yet foolish papists think with cruelty to wish their will to reign like lords of the land, and stablish their kingdom on earth, and to bring it so to pass, that not only men dare not or will not withstand them, but willingly believe, follow, do and practise whatsoever they command them. They cannot be so ignorant to not know these things; and wilfully to wish against knowledge and conscience must needs be a great madness. God's word, christian faith and religion is of that nature, that the more it is persecuted, the more it thrives; the more it is hated, the more good men love it; the faster

[[1] Confess. Lib. x. Cap. xxix. Ed.]

that they be pulled from it, the more they run unto it. Let them therefore consider, how God has wrought in other kingdoms, overthrowing them all that set up themselves against him; and how yet he works in the natural course of things, to teach us by them his like working for us spiritual things: and let them look for no less an overthrow at God's hand in his appointed time.

If these things cannot persuade them to stay their rage, I would they would consider to whom they make themselves servants, that they might be ashamed to serve so vile a master. They "give place to the devil," (for all cruelty is of him:) they become his instruments, whereby he works his feats: they be his slaves and drudges at commandment to do that he bids, but were made to serve and fear their Lord God: they be driven and led of him like brute beasts, forgetting him that made them, and their sely[2] tormented brethren, that pray for them: unnaturally forgetting themselves to be men, they regard not man's life, but unmercifully spills and spoils them. And for what end or purpose? to satisfy (if they could ever be full) their bloody appetites, to fill their idle bellies, to rule like kings, to be glorious in the world, to oppress the simple, to deceive the ignorant, and deface God's truth, to feed the people with lies, to set up their god the pope, to deface Christ and his merits, to hide his word, and set up superstitious idolatry: where they should do all things to the contrary, because in such their doings all true Christians abhor them.

But in these our miserable days, where it pleased God of his undeserved mercy to stay their rage in burning and prisoning God's sely souls, that mischief, which their bloody hands and cruel hearts dare not attempt, their poisonful tongues spue out. Now ceases fire and faggot, yet their slanderous lying lips are not stopped, where they dare not blaspheme the doctrine so freely as they be wont: now they inveigh against the teachers and professors of it with such terms as please them, though never one be true. But, as Samuel said to the people, when he had anointed Saul king, "Speak here afore the Lord and his anointed king, whether 1 Sam. xii. I have taken any man's ox or ass, or have oppressed any one

[[2] Sely: simple, inoffensive. ED.]

of you, or taken bribe; and I will restore it;" and they were not able to charge him, and yet were weary of him: so I doubt not, but they be not able justly to burden the preachers with such lies as they devise against them: and if any be, for my part I wish them not to be hid. This kind of persecution is as grievous to an honest heart as the other is: but a justified mind in this case will turn himself to the Lord, bear his cross thankfully, and knowledge that the scholar is not above his master. If Christ our Lord escaped not these tongues, but they called him Samaritane, and said he had a devil, let no Christian look to be free. David felt these pangs when he prayed, "Lord, deliver my soul from wicked lips and from a deceitful tongue." If they remembered God's threatenings to all such, they would not be so talkative. "What shall be given thee, thou crafty tongue?" says David: "Even sharp arrows and burning coals," answers the Holy Ghost. And again, "The Lord will destroy all crafty lips and proud tongues." Would God that these wicked men understood these threatenings to be true, and that God would faithfully fulfil them to their confusion! If they did believe them, they would tremble and quake for fear of them, and not be so ready to speak what please them. Many think their tongues to be their own, and that they may speak what they lust, and words to be no grief nor kind of persecution: but blessed David is of contrary opinion, when he compares such tongues to swords, poisonful stinging of serpents, sharp razors, &c.

Psal. cxx.

Psal. xii.

Psal. lii. lviii.

Thus be we fallen in such miserable days, where under popery we be tormented and persecuted with all extremity, and under the gospel we be slandered and reviled, that we may justly say with the apostle, "We are counted as sheep appointed to the slaughter daily."

If these fearful examples and grievous overthrows of the wicked, and so many from the beginning, cannot persuade these cruel haters of God and his word, murderers of his saints and their brethren, to abate their pride and swage their malice; if this particular prophecy written for that purpose (to teach all bloody butchers and proud Caiphas, that a like destruction will fall on them, as it did on Edon) can not help; then let them mark the manifold threatenings of the Lord, where he thunders against such wicked doers. "Be not

Isai. xli.

afraid," says the prophet, "thou Israel my servant, for I am with thee; and fear not, for I am thy God that strengthens thee and helps thee. Behold, they shall be ashamed and confounded all that fight against thee, and all that gainsay thee shall perish and be brought to nought, &c." Again: "Thou art the hope of Israel: all that forsake thee shall be ashamed, and they that go from thee shall be written in the earth," and not in heaven. But this seed of Esau in our days is worse than old Edon, as their deeds will declare. When Jacob was banished twenty years, Esau was content to meet his brother Jacob returning homeward, to forget all old grudges, to take and use him as his friend and brother: but our Edomites would not receive their banished brother returning home, forget no old malice, nor use any friendship toward them; but with word and deed shew all cruelty they could devise against them, and yet so continue. ^{Jer. xvii.}

To this some of the wiser sort peradventure will say, There is just cause why they should do so: they be not used as Jacob did his brother Esau: Jacob sent great gifts to his brother Esau, took nothing from him, but let him live where he lusted. Indeed this may be a great cause: for they are so well pleased with gifts and wealth, that in the midst of their rage a little bribe would have loosed heavy chains of iron, and quenched hot flaming faggots. But now, though many things may be suffered in temporal matters, yet the discipline of the gospel will not suffer persecutors to occupy the place of feeders, nor wolves the room of shepherds. If true discipline might take place, not only murderers and apostates, forsaking that religion which afore they professed and taught, should be deposed from their office; but all turn-tippets, that turn with the world and keep their livings still, should have no office in Christ's church, until they made satisfaction by open repentance afore the congregation. But alas for pity! for lack of sharp discipline they lie lurking and looking for that day when they may turn to their old vomit again, enking[1] their hands in blood, and laugh in their sleeves to see such coldness in religion to serve the living Lord, where they were so earnest, bold, and diligent to set up their own devices.

Yet, all things considered, it is no marvel why the good

[[1] Enking: inking. So used by Wickliffe, 3 John, 13. ED.]

men, succeeding in the place of such evil persons, be so evil spoken of at these days. For as he that rips in a dunghill is infect with the smell thereof a long time after, though he were never so clean afore; and he that comes to a house infected with the pestilence is soon taken therewith, though he be never so sound afore, (yea, the better complexion, the sooner smitten;) so good men now, searching the festered cankers and ripping the stinking duddles[1] of popery, for a time smell evil in the noses of the wicked, and seem to be infected with a worse plague than the other. Their places may be well termed with the scriptures *Cathedræ Pestilentiæ*, "the seats of pestilence," because they either infect the good, or else sore assaults them. This misery good men must be content patiently to bear: for this is our nature more than any other people, always to repine and be grieved with the present state. In the late days of persecution those which now be eyesores to look on, were much desired and wished for; and those that now be lamented, were then commonly cursed of the greater and better sort. Then all cried, "Lord God, deliver us this once, and we will be most ware ever hereafter, how we offend thy divine majesty;" but now being delivered, we are worse, more unthankful and disobedient than ever afore: which wickedness surely the righteous God will not let escape without heavy plagues.

To make an end: if any natural pity or mercy of man were in them, or if like men they would be ruled by reason, these threatenings and examples of the wicked might move stony hearts: but seeing many of them be so blinded in their wickedness, that it needs not or boots not to speak unto them; to the rest, whose hearts God has something touched, and are not altogether cast of God, I say thus much: Consider for God's love, and health of your own souls, who they be that ye hate and persecute: they be God's creatures and his handy work, made like to his own image and similitude: they whom ye murder so innocently, be those that Christ loved so dearly, that he would die with most bitter pains for them, rather than they should perish: they be many of them your kinsfolk, the most part your neighbours; but every one is your countryman, speaking the same language that ye do,

[[1] Duddles: bundles of filthy rags. ED.]

true subjects to the same prince that ye should faithfully obey, and members of the same commonwealth: they saved your lives and goods, not seeking your undoing, when it lay in their hands. Consider how unnatural a thing it is thus to fight against nature: remember how dangerous in God's sight it is thus unthankfully to provoke his anger. Think on how in your late raging madness God suddenly cut you off, and yet patiently tarries to see if ye would have new hearts. When that day came which ye so long looked for, ye had not every thing after your own will, but many heavy plagues God laid on you; and surely, whensoever God sends the like again for our unthankfulness, and not for your goodness, all can not fall as ye would wish. Surely, if God like a father sharply correct his children, what can his enemies look for? Give place to nature, fear God, love your brother in Christ, live quietly like friends and subjects to one prince: wash your bloody hands and hearts with bitter weeping tears: take to you pitiful minds: love them that wish you good: leave your raging madness, lest ye perish in your obstinate blindness: so shall God the Lord bless both you and us, contrary to our deserts, for his own mercies, and not for any our goodness, through his dearly beloved Son Christ, who offered himself a sweet sacrifice for us all, that we should sacrifice ourselves to him, mortifying all carnal lusts, that we may live and die to him, and afterward be glorified with him; to whom with his Father and Holy Spirit, three Persons and one God, be glory and praise in all congregations, now and ever. Amen.

Psalm cxxxvii.

Remember, O Lord, the behaviour of the children of Edon, in the day of Jerusalem, when they said, Down with it, down with it, to the ground!

THE VISION OF ABDY.

v. 1. *Thus saith the Lord God to Edom: We heard a voice from the Lord, and a message was sent to the heathen, saying, Rise, and let us go fight against her in war.*

This prophet is not long in words, but he is pithy in sentence: he entreats not many nor divers matters; but this one is weighty and deeply to be considered. For even as apothecaries use to put their costliest medicines, and rich men their greatest jewels, in some little box or chest; so God, our heavenly schoolmaster, uses many times to teach in short writings so much of his heavenly wisdom, as many other times ye shall not find in long books. Likewise of learned men in one witty sentence and figure will declare as much wit and eloquence, as the common sort will do in long volumes. And as a little gold is worth a great deal of brass, and a small diamond is better than a number of right stones; so in this short prophet is more learning, comfort, and godly wisdom, than ye shall find in searching long and sundry sorts of the learnedest philosophers or eloquentest[1] orators.

<small>Why prophecies are called sights, and prophets seers.</small>

The prophets use to call their writings *visions* or *sights*, for divers causes: *first*, because none should take in hand to be God's messenger to teach his people, but he that is lightened of the Lord, and has his eyes and sight opened to see the mysteries of God. For unto the blind sinner says

<small>Psal. l.</small>
God, "Why dost thou declare my righteousness, and take
<small>Luke vi.</small>
my testament in thy mouth?" and again, "If the blind lead the blind, both fall into the pit." *Secondly*, because they open the eyes and give sight to the blind; as David says,
<small>Psal. cxix.</small>
"The declaring of thy words lightens and gives understanding to the simple ones:" and also, "Thy word is a lantern to my feet, and a light to my paths." *Thirdly* and last of all, because of the certainty of the things which they writ: that is to wete, they were not tales which he had heard of

[¹ The old edition, *cloquence*. ED.]

our[2] men, but which he saw himself by the eyes of faith. Things that a man hears of others oft be false; but of those which he sees himself, no man doubts, as the poet says, "One witness that sees it with his eye, is more to be believed than ten that heard it by report[3]." For this certainty, prophets were called *seers* commonly of all men. "In old time," as it is written, "when they went to ask counsel of God, they said, Come, let us go to the seer." But how can he see those things which were not done in his lifetime, but long after? He saw them not in a dream, nor in a conjuror's glass, nor by the vain foresight of the stars, as astronomers, deceiving the world, would make men believe they can tell them their destinies and things to come: but he saw them by the eyes of faith, when God, which can not lie, had shewed these things unto him aforehand, and proved them true afterwards in deed. This is the surest way of knowledge and seeing; for those things which I believe, and see with the eyes of faith, be surer than those that I see with my bodily eye, or feel with my hand. God is truth itself, and therefore those things that he teaches must needs be true; and that faith and credence, which is given to his word, can not deceive, but must needs come to pass, and be as true as if I see them with my eye. When Thomas Didymus would not believe, except he see the print of the nails, Christ said, "Blessed be they that believe and see not."

1 Sam. ix.

Sight by faith is surer than the eye.

John xx.

O notable example for all true prophets and teachers to follow, that they teach nothing but that which they see in God's book, and not man's learning, (for that is full of deceit;) and that they may call their preachings visions and sights for the certainty of them, that they be seen by a true faith, and found in God's book which can not lie; and therefore they be as true and to be believed, as if we saw them with our eyes! Man's learning is darkness, and therefore can not be called visions, or things seen, but feigned, as Ezechiel says, "Woe be to the foolish prophets, which follow their own spirit, and see nothing!" But of God's word it

Ezek. xiii.

[2 Qu. *other* men. ED.]

[3 Pluris est oculatus testis unus quam auriti decem. Plautus, Truc. II. 6. ED.]

is said contrariwise: "We have a surer writing of the prophets, to the which when ye give attendance, as to a candle shining in a dark place, ye do well, unto the day shine and the day-star rise in your heart." Thus St Peter attributes thus to the scripture and writings of the prophets, that they lighten our hearts and eyes, as a candle doth a dark place, unto a fuller knowledge be given unto us by the Spirit of God, to drive out ignorance, as the day-star or day itself drives away darkness.

<small>Pet. i.</small>

Abdia, or Oabdia, as the Hebrew calls him, is as much to say as *the servant of God*: wherein we learn, who is he that writes this prophet, and from whom he comes, and the goodness of our good God toward his servants, that he lets not them wander in ignorance, but declares his whole will and pleasure unto them, that they perish not with the wicked world. But he was not of such sort of servants, which St John writes of, "The servant knows not what his master does;" for such be rather slaves, which know not their master's pleasures, and serve not of love, but fear. But he served the Lord his God in true worship: for such sort of servants the Hebrew word signifies; and that kind of service is true freedom, as St Paul says, "Ye be made free from sin, but ye are servants to God." Thus Paul and Peter call themselves not only apostles, but also servants of Jesu Christ. Therefore the Lord vouchsaved to declare his whole will unto him, his faithful and beloved servant, concerning things to come, and the estate of the cruel Edomites, which did so cruelly handle God's people, and had persecuted them so long; and, like a true servant that loves his fellows, he keeps it not close to his self, but comforts others therewith.

<small>Abdias.</small>

<small>John xv.</small>

Names in the scripture be not given in vain, but that so often as they hear or think on their own name, so oft they should consider what they be taught by it. Abdia in thinking on his name should remember, that he should serve the Lord his God: Abraham, on the blessing of God, which made him a father of many people: Zacharia, that according to his name he should continually remember the Lord: Peter, that his faith is the strong rock, whereon Christ will build his church; for so the word signifies by interpretation: and so forth in all others. Therefore fathers do well in giving

<small>Names are not given in vain.</small>

<small>Abraham. Zacharia. Peter.</small>

their children such christian names, as may remember them of their duty to God ward, and call them not by heathen names or feigned foolish saints, which can teach them no goodness.

Many doth think this Abdias to be the steward of Achab's house, which had an hundred prophets of God in caves, and fed them, fifty in one company, and as many in another, in the time of Jesabel's cruel prosecution; and now by God's providence feeds many thousands with his wholesome doctrine. And although the holy scriptures do not plainly shew, that he was the same Abdias in deed, yet probable enough it is, as many learned men think: unto whose mind also I can well agree, that it is the same man. He was one that feared the Lord, as he said to Elias; and was a stranger born in Sychem of Idumea, as some think, and not a Jew born, but turned after to the law of the Lord, forsaking the wickedness of his people. His writing is so much more notable, because, being a stranger, he prophesies against his own country; and therefore the truer belike also it is, and without partiality spoken; because none will willingly threaten such destruction to his native country, as he does here: but he that is a true servant of God, without sparing will speak his master's message freely and truly against his dearest friends, if the Lord God send him.

1 Kings xviii.

This prophecy is more meet also for these our days, because we were under the like persecution that he was, or worse: for the true prophets of God were not suffered to hide themselves in dens and wilderness, as they might do then under cruel Achab and Jesabel; but were most cruelly thrown into the fire; yea, the madness of God's enemies was so much, that they could not be satisfied with the blood of them that were on live, but, that which was seldom read of among the heathen, they pull up the dead bodies which were buried many years before, to burn their bones, and straw their ashes abroad, as Master Bucer, Paulus Fagius, &c. yea, of thieves[1], for praying God to deliver us from the

[[1] i. e. the dead bodies of thieves: referring to the case of John Tooley, who was hanged for robbing a Spaniard at St James's, June, 1555, and having at his execution spoken against the pope, and called upon the bystanders to pray for deliverance "from the tyranny of the

tyranny of the pope. These Edomites, against whom he writes, were not so cruel as our men were and be. And therefore your destruction shall be the greater at the appointed time, than this other was. Let us not flatter them nor ourselves, because they be our countrymen, or because we would not see the destruction of our country. For the Lord is a righteous God, and will sharply punish sin, wheresoever he finds it, if we do not earnestly beg his pardon, mercy and forgiveness, with amendment of life. But it is to be feared, that as Abdias did no good to his country folks, because they would not hear him; so much labour is lost in our country, because they stop their ears, and will hear nothing but that which pleases them: for it is true that our Saviour Christ says, "There is no prophet without honour and credit, but in his own country." Yet nevertheless lift up your voice, blow the trumpet of God, and tell the people their faults, lest they perish and their blood be required at your hands: discharge yourselves, rebuke them earnestly, and let it take root and profit as God will, which gives all increase as he thinks good. If they hear not, they perish in their own sins, and thou art free.

<small>Matt. xiii.</small>

The preface that he puts here before gets him great authority and credit with the hearers, and declares him also to be a true prophet of God, because he speaks nothing in his own name, but says the Lord God had put these words in his mouth, and he was author, and Abdias but the messenger to speak them to his people. A worthy example for all teachers to follow, that they never say things but out of God's book, and that they may say for every thing that they teach, "Thus says the Lord." This saying is most common in all the prophets, and to be followed of all preachers; as St Peter says, "If any man speak, let him speak but the words of God." But of this enough is said in sundry places of Aggeus.

<small>1 Pet. iv.</small>

Edom, unto whom the Lord speaks here, is all the people of Idumea, being so called of Edom their first father,

<small>bishop of Rome and all his detestable enormities," was "first suspected and condemned after his death, and then digged out of his grave, and given to the secular power, and so burned for a heretic." Foxe's Acts and Monuments, Vol. vii. p. 90, &c. 1838. ED.]</small>

as the scriptures uses to call the people by the name of the father. So were the Jews called Israel of Jacob, which was called Israel, their old father: likewise Ephraim, Joseph, Jehuda, of these their old ancestors. This Edom is Esau, Jacob's brother, as he is called in Genesis, "Esau, he is Edom;" and had that name given him for his colour that he had when he was born, or of the colour of the pottage, for the which he sold his birth-right for unto his brother Jacob, when he was hungry. Esau was also called Seir, which signifies *rough*, because of the roughness of his skin· and for this cause these people of Edom, and their country, is sundry times in the prophets called Seir also. Or if we seek further, Edom may have his name of Adam; for they be written both with one letter in Hebrew, save that they differ in points: *Adam* signifies to be red; wherefore Edom for his cruelty in shedding blood may well be so called. As our cardinals in their red scarlet robes, which be the followers of these Edomites, do well declare in their apparel the blood-thirsty minds within, and their outward deeds have declared them to the whole world: but they say, their red apparel signifies they should abide by the truth to their blood-shed. *Adam* also betokens a man, and one of the common sort: so these men were not noble afore God, which is only the true nobility, but enemies to his word and his people. *Adama* signifies also *the earth;* so that from whence soever we shall derive this word *Edom*, and all that be derived like it, they signify no good people, but earthy, worldly, cruel, blood-thirsty, mortal and abjects. Of the two brethren, Jacob and Esau, came these two people, the Israelites and the Edomites. And as Esau did ever hate and persecute his brother Jacob, so his stock and posterity did continually hate and persecute the children of Jacob.

 This is the secret judgment of God, that of one good father, Isaac, came two so contrary children; the one so wicked, the other so good, and this wicked hatred to continue in the hearts of their children's children, so many ages after. But this is to teach us the free grace of God, without any deserts on our part, whensoever he calls any to the true knowledge and fear of him; and that [it is] neither the goodness or evilness of the father that makes a good or an

[marginalia: Edom. Gen. xxxvi. Gen. xxxvi. Seir. Adam. Adama.]

An evil father maketh not an evil son, nor contrary; and so the good.

evil child; for many good fathers have had evil children, and evil fathers good children. Adam had good Abel and wicked Cain: Noe had good Sem and evil Cham: Abraham had both the carnal Ismael and the spiritual Isaac: Isaac had the beloved Jacob and the hated Esau: David had both proud Absalon and wise Salomon: so that the soul of the father

Ezek. xviii.

is the Lord's, as well as the soul of the son; and the soul that sins shall perish, and not the father for the son, nor the son for the father, as the prophet says: but every one shall die in his own sins. So has there been from the beginning, in the house and children of one father, both good and evil, both carnal and spiritual, where the one has persecuted the other: as there is now in the outward church of Christ and company of them that call themselves Christians, both true people and faithful, and also hypocrites, dissemblers and cruel persecutors of their brethren, as these late days well declared, where the father persecuted the son, and the son the father; the man the wife, and the wife the man: which all and such other our Saviour Christ declares to be consequents to the gospel. Therefore can none doubt of the truth of the gospel now taught, and who be the true followers of the same, but he that is wilfully blind, seeing all these and many other true tokens fulfilled in our days.

And where he says, "We heard a saying from the Lord, and a message was sent to the heathen, that they should go fight against Edom;" he declares by what authority these people came to destroy the Edomites: not sent by any kings or the high priest, but it was the Lord God, which would use Nabuchodonozor and his people for a scourge of his justice, to the punishing of these wicked people. It must not be thought strange that God lets one people plague another, seeing the scriptures is so full of it: for as God shews his mercy unto his people by the help and means of other men, (for God works nothing without means,) so he does not plague

1 Kings xii.

other without some means, and lets one people destroy another. When Roboam would have fought against Jero-

All plagues be from God, yet only man sins in plaguing one another.

boam, for withdrawing ten tribes from him, the Lord spake unto him, and bad him he should not fight with him; for the thing was his deed, and he willed it should be so. All God's creatures be but his servants to do his pleasure; to help and comfort where it please him, and to punish, correct, try, and destroy where it please him.

But all other creatures, except man, do not sin in destroying or hurting man, because they have no evil affection of mind in doing it: only man sins in his doings, because he adds to his doings some evil affection of his own mind, or else is stirred to it of the devil. So Job says, "The Lord has given, and the Lord has taken away; the Lord's name be praised." He calls it not the deed of the Sabees or Chaldees that robbed him, but the Lord's; and yet they sore offended God in so doing: for they did it not to try Job, as God would have had it, but of a greedy covetousness to rob him, and a malicious mind, because he was so wealthy, which thing they disdained. Joseph says that his brethren, which sold him to the Ismaelites, were not the cause of his coming into Egypt, but the good will of God; for the Lord turned the malice of his brethren both to the promotion of Joseph and all their comforts. Job i. Gen. xlv.

The Lord therefore now, when the sin of this people was ripe, and when he had tried long enough for the amendment of them, and they would not turn unto God, but abused his patience and long-suffering; he sends forth his messenger to the heathen about, to come and justly to punish these obstinate people for their long disobedience. It is as well the property of God to shew justice and punish sin, as mercifully to help the weak and repentant heart; and mercy is not so in God, that justice is banished. As the Lord said, he would whistle and with hissing call for Nabuchodonozor, to come and destroy Jerusalem; so now he sends messengers to come bid them fight against Edom. Yet Nabuchodonozor, in justly punishing the Jews and Edomites, and that by the commandment of God, sore offendeth God, because he was proud of the victory, cruel in murder, and covetous of spoiling, ambitious in raveing [ravening], and never thought he had enough: and therefore was his kingdom afterwards destroyed by the justice of God. So the deed, as it is of God, is good, pure and just: but being defiled of us, with adding our evil affections to it, as when good wine is put into an evil vessel, it is sin and damnable; and yet is God free from all our sin and wickedness, and no causer thereof, but a hater and revenger of all wickedness. Isai. v. vii.

But here is doubted, who these be that heard this voice of the Lord, and how this message was sent to the gentiles. To the first part I had rather say, that the prophet speaks of himself in the plural number, as though they were many that heard it: which kind of speaking is common in the scripture; as Paul says, "If we have sown you spiritual things, is it much?"—or else, that the other prophets, which prophesy against Edom, heard the same saying from God as well as he did, and they all together, or Abdias alone in their names says, "We heard a saying from the Lord, &c." And so this saying should be true and the rather believed, because so many did agree in one saying. Against Edom prophesied Esay, xxi. xxxiv. Jere. xlix. Ezech. xxxv. Amos i. But most plainly, earnestly, and orderly agreeing with this Abdias, and almost word for word, does Jere. xlix., whose words if ye compare with this present prophecy, ye shall see the agreeing truth of God's Spirit in his scripture, and a great light shall be ministered to this place thereby.

It is no less doubt how this message was sent, and who was the minister that carried it: for some think that Abdias was sent with this embassage himself to stir up Nabuchodonozor and his people to destroy these Edomites; but other, to whom I had rather agree, think that the devil by God's sufferance put into the mind of them to work his will and justice upon them. God calls Nabuchodonozor his servant for such causes, although the devil moved him to it, and says that he did him good service in executing his judgment; as the hangman serves the king in punishing offenders, and the jailor in prisoning them, as well as other do in their kind and office: yet is God no more the cause of their sin and evil doing, than the king is of the offences and robberies of the people: but God, like a righteous judge, of justice must needs punish such faults as other magistrates do in their commonwealth. But like as this voice of the Lord was not heard by the ears of the body of the prophets, but put into their minds by the work of God, as he thought good; so I think this message was not sent by any man: but as when embassadors be sent, or rumours of war be certainly spread, kings prepare themselves to war; so these people, stirred up of God by justice to punish their sin, and set forward of the devil to satisfy their wicked desires, rise up all together to fight against Edom, and destroyed it. So the Lord used the devil as his jailor and hangman to be a lying spirit in the mouth of Achab's prophets, and sent him to war that he might there perish, and God's righteous sentence be executed, where he said that the dogs should lick his blood where they did lick up Naboth's. Thus God in his scripture, speaking to men, uses to speak as men: for as men by messages or rumours of robberies are stirred up to war; so the Lord by some meet mean, as though it were by messengers, would stir up the Chaldees to destroy Edom. _{1 Kings xxii.}

The cause of this war and destruction was, as Ezechiel says, xxxv, because the Edomites, which should have been helpers unto the Israelites in their trouble, (because they were not only neighbours, their kingdoms joining together, but also they came of two brethren, Jacob and Esau, which thing should have knit them in brotherly love,) they did not only not help them, but cruelly persecute them continually: "I will destroy thee," says the Lord, "and make thee desolate, because thou hast had a continual hate against the Israelites, and didst fear them with the sword in the time of their trouble." Amos tells the same cause likewise, and almost with the same word. *The cause of this war.*

So this is the case of God's people, that for their religion they shall have enemies of their own house, kinsfolk and friends, as this day well declares. And our Saviour Christ said, "He came not to set peace, but to divide the father against the son, &c." Where hatred falls betwixt brethren and friends, and specially for religion, it is the cruelest hate that can be. This hate began betwixt Jacob and Esau for losing his blessing; but it continued and increased with the time in their children and posterity. The eldest son, as the Hebrews write, had their privileges afore the younger, as they have commonly now. The eldest then succeeded in his father's authority, was reverenced of his brethren: he had also double portion of his father's goods, as other say, and also enjoyed the priesthood. Where worldlings, that care for nothing so much as the world, have lost their worldly honour and authority, how do they rage and sin! Esau, when he had lost and sold these things, he sought *Religion causes nearest friends to be extreme foes.*

The privilege of the elder brother.

his brother's death: as our papists, that would be counted the elder brethren, losing their worldly estimation, their belly cheer and lordliness, their wealth and proud priesthood, they fret and fume, burn and kill all that gainsay them, as the Edomites did.

God refuses the elder and glorious in the world to choose the younger and abjects.

But as then for Cain the wicked and his seed, although the elder brother, God chose Abel, the younger, Seth and Enos; for Ismael the elder, Isaac the younger; for Esau Jacob; for Ruben Juda and Levi; and David, the youngest of seven brethren, and as of no reputation in respect of his other brethren, but set to keep sheep; so God, to pull down the pride of man in these days, also chooses the abjects to set forth his glory, refusing the proud Pharisees, and disdaining holy hypocrites, and at the length will destroy them, as he threatens here the Edomites.

The wicked shall not ever prosper, nor the godly be in misery.

For God, to comfort his people, that the wicked should not ever prosper, and the chosen people live in continual misery, lest they fall away from God through over great adversities, threatens to destroy their enemies, and deliver them, if they will abide his leisure. But as destruction is here prophesied to Edom for their cruelty; so shall all haters of God's people perish at the length.

No true love is where religion differs; but enemies will join to overthrow it.

Where as difference is in religion, there can be no true heart nor stedfast love. For seeing God is love itself, that love which is not in God, but raised of carnal and worldly reasons, when the world turns, must needs change, and shew itself what a love it was, and where it was grounded: but that which is builded on God will continue, because he changes not, and all their[1] change with time. These Edomites joined themselves with Nabuchodonozor, when he came to destroy Jerusalem; as Pilate and Herod, which afore were enemies, agreed to crucify Christ our Lord, and as our papists did now with the Spaniards, to destroy the gospel and his professors.

The Text.   v. 2. *Behold, I will make thee a little one among the heathen; thou shalt be very much despised.*

3. *The pride of thy heart has deceived thee, because thou dwellest in the open places of the rock, and in the height is thy dwelling, and says in thy heart, Who shall draw me to the earth?*

[¹ Qu. *other*. Ed.]

4. If thou will climb up as high as an eagle, and if thou will make thy nest among the clouds, from thence I will make thee come down, says the Lord.

Where as the scripture uses to put this word, "Behold," it betokens some notable thing to follow; as when the prophet said, "Behold, a maid shall conceive and bear a son," he signified that it should be a notable birth and conceiving of a child, and contrary to the course of nature, and that the child which was born should be wonderful. So says David, "Behold, I was conceived in sin;" betokening the great corruption, infirmity and defiling of our nature in our conception. "Behold, as the eyes of the servants are at their masters' hand," says David, signifying that he would be more diligent in watching what the Lord God would do, and what were his holy will for him to do, than the lowest and diligentest servants would be to watch what their masters would will and command them to do. In the same sense says the prophet here, "Behold," and mark it well, what I will say unto thee; for it is no small matter, and truly it shall come to pass. Likewise in the threatenings in our own tongue we use to say, 'Mark what I say to you, take heed to yourself, for I jest not; remember my words well; for I will be even with you, and I will do it in deed,' and such like sayings. "Behold, mark well," says the Lord, what I say: "I will make thee a little one among the heathen:" thou that thinkest so highly on thyself, and thinkest thyself to be so strong, so mighty and greater than thy fellows, "I will make thee a little one among the people" where thou dwellest, and less than any people about thee. Thou flatterest thyself of thy strength, might, power, multitude, strong holds, and to be greater than thy neighbours, people or countries about thee; and thinkest none is able to conquer thee, or pull thee down, or worthy to be compared unto thee: but I will pull thee down, says the Lord; I will cut thy comb; I will abate thy strength, pluck down thy courage and high stomach; I will throw down thy castles and strong hold; and whatsoever thou rejoicest in, I will take it from thee, and make thee more vile and slave, less and weaker than any people round about thee. Thou shalt well know that there is a God, which can and will be avenged on all high minds, and will let all such lusty stomachs see what it is to be proud in their own eyes, and rebels against him and his people.

God casts in their teeth that, where he had given them a narrow place to dwell in among the hills, they were proud of it, as though it were the plenteoust place in the country. They were proud of a thing of nought in comparison of other places, as Malachi says, "The Edomites I have placed in the mount Seir." He speaks not all these words in number and order, but so many in effect and purpose; and to the same meaning he writes them in the preterite tense, as though the thing were done and past: for so all the prophets use to speak by the preterite tense such things as shall not be done of many years after, and yet shall as certainly come to pass, as though they were now done and past. In this sort said David, "They have wounded my hands and feet;" as though the thing were done and past, which was not fulfilled unto Christ our Lord had suffered. Also of the murder of the children by Herod spake Jeremy, as though it had been done and past: "A noise was heard in Rama, weeping and much lamenting;" with infinite such other like, which were not fulfilled of many years after. And because the whole country and people pleased themselves so highly, and stood so much in their own conceit, God threatens them further, that they shall be much despised.

The righteous judgment of God is commonly to punish us by the same parts wherein we offend him. The rich glutton, that sinned so grievously in his feasting and banquetting, now desires a drop of cold water, and cannot have it. Adonibezec, which had cruelly used his victories, and had chopped off the hands and feet of sixty kings, whom he conquered and made them gather up the crumbs under his table with the dogs, was used after the same sort himself, when he was overcome by the Israelites. Thus teaches the wise man: "By what thing a man sins, he shall be punished by the 'same." This people had much and many years despised the Israelites without cause: they had highly avanced themselves in their own conceit: therefore justice requires that they should be despised again, and should understand how vile a thing pride is in the sight of God, and how horribly it procures his great anger to fall upon us, when we one despise another. And although Nabuchodonozor was the worker of this destruction, and minister executing God's justice upon this wicked people of Edom, yet the Lord says himself that he will do it, and it shall be counted his deed. So Job says, that the Lord had given and taken away his goods, although the Chaldees and Sabees robbed him, as we noted afore. Thus must we in all things that be done, whether they be good or evil, (except sin, which God hates and causes not,) not only look at the second causes, which be but God's means and instruments whereby he works, but have a further eye, and look up to God. If they be good things that he bestows upon us, think not nor marvel not so much at the man or the means whereby it is wrought, but lowly praise the Lord God which has vouchsafed to use such a way to thy comfort: and if it be evil adversity that is fallen upon thee, do not so much murmur and grudge against him or the thing by which it was done, but look up to thy Lord God, which author, being displeased with thy sin, will this way correct thee, and bring thee to repentance, amendment of life, and the knowledge of thyself, thine own vileness, and his holy majesty, mercy, and power, whom thou hast provoked so to punish thee, and yet in mercy, and not as thou hast deserved; or else he will try thy patience, and declare thy faith and hope that thou hast in him to the world, that his might may be praised in thy weakness, which although of thine own self thou be not able to suffer such adversity, yet by the strength of his Spirit thou both can and will.

In all things look up to God which rules all.

In the next verse is declared the cause of this great destruction, and God's vengeance so grievously poured upon this people. It was the same sin that drove Adam out of paradise, being not content with his own state, but would be fellow with God; and out of which, as out of a root, springs all mischief. "The beginning of sin is pride," saith Ecclesiasticus, x. when a man leaves considering of his own vileness, and the mighty power and majesty of God, (which author of both is able to work lowliness in any honest heart,) and begins to flatter and please himself in any good gift that he has within him or without him, in body or soul, in

Pride.

worldly wealth or wisdom; for then he forgets God and himself, runs headlong to all mischief, offending God and hurting himself.

The pride of this people was both sundry and great, both of mind, wisdom and polity, strength of body, holds, castles and towers, wealth and plenty of corn and cattle; that it might be well said of them, that which proves true in all, wealth makes wanton. We will entreat of all these in order, as the prophet does, and set them out something more at large. The kind of pride that here is touched, wherein they rejoiced so much, trusting in themselves and offending God, was their strong holds, their high castles, builded on the top of the rocks so strongly, that they were sure enough, as they thought, from all hurt and danger, that they should not be overcome. These be pleasant things to a worldly wit, and therefore we are soon taken with the love of them. To declare the inexcusable pride of this people, the prophet says, "The pride of thine own heart has deceived thee;" as though he should say, 'It is not God, nor the devil only, nor any other man's counsel or persuasion, that has taught thee this or beaten it into thy head; but it is even thyself, thine own device and free will, thine own proud heart, and vain trust that thou hast taken in thine own strength and goods.' It is a notable word, that the Holy Ghost puts here, when he says, "The pride of thine own heart has deceived thee;" and well declares the nature of pride, and well-spring of all sin to begin in thy heart and thine own free will. "From the heart come evil thoughts, murder, adultery, theft, &c." as St Matthew says, xv. And well may that be said to deceive man, that under the cloke of godliness, honesty, profit, or pleasure entices a man to it, where in the end it proves wicked, hurtful, and displeasant. For except it had in the beginning some fair shew of some goodness in it, no man would be allured to it. If it were good in deed, it were no deceit; but because it is not, it may well be said to deceive.

Pride is only of good things. Pride among all other sins has this property, that it ever rises of some good thing that a man has given him of God, and takes the praise of it himself. For no man is so foolish to rejoice in any thing that is evil of itself, except it have some appearance of goodness in it. When God gives a good gift to any man, then the devil and his own froward nature makes him not to give God due thanks for it, but to rejoice in himself, as though he himself were worthy all the praise for finding out or using well such a gift. Thus the Pharisee, being proud of his own righteousness in fasting, holiness, and paying his tithes, abuses the good gifts of God, and takes part of the praise to himself, which should be given wholly to God alone; and also in pride he contemns the poor publican, which sat praying by him, because he was not so holy as he was. So strong holds and castles is the good gift of God; but to rejoice in them, not putting his whole trust and deliverance in God, is a great pride and unthankfulness to God, which has given thee such gifts to stir thee up rather to praise him, which has taught thee to find out the profitable use of such things. But it is hard for a worldly man to have these, and not be proud of them; and therefore he says, "Thy pride has deceived thee." Beauty is the good gift of God; but because in outward appearance it seems good, it soon deceives man, enticing him to evil, rather than to praise God in it. The wise man says, "Look not in the face of a maiden, lest ye be enticed with her beauty." Towers, castles, holds, bulwarks, be ordained by the provision of God to defend his people: but yet must we ever know, that in vain labours the watchmen, be they never so many, wise and strong, to defend the city, except the Lord defend it, as David says. Beauty.
Ecclus. ix.
Holds.

Psal. cxxvii.

What an unthankful pride is this toward God, that when he has given us wit to devise such engines of war to defend ourselves withal, and liberally bestowed on us men and money to make such things withal; and then we do rob him of his due glory, and take that praise to ourselves which is due to him, and rejoice in ourselves! Because they dwelt and builded their holds on the tops of hills, they thought no man should be able to climb up to hurt them, except he could fly: and though undermining will hurt many times, and throw down great castles; yet where the building is on the hard rock of stone, as this was, they can not mine through the rock: so that above, except they could fly, they could not come near them; nor by low they could not pierce the hard stones of the ground-work, being so many, hard, deep and strong. Wine is pleasant to look on, sweet to taste and cheer the hearts of man; yet in drinking it soon deceives a man, and overcomes the brain, and therefore the wise man counsels, saying, "Delight not thyself in looking on the wine, when it shines merely in the glass." The words of women are sweet, yet oft full of poison. Riches is the good gift of God, yet the apostle calls them the nets of the devil, because under a fair pretence we be soon tangled with the desire of them. So generally to speak of all the creatures of God, when they be loved or trusted in for themselves, and not for his cause that made them, they deceive us.

Consider not therefore the beauty, strength, wealth, commodity and pleasure of any creature in itself, for then it will surely deceive thee: but lift up thy mind to him that made them for thy use and commodity, and praise him for his great care that he takes for thee, in making of them and giving thee the use of them; and so shalt thou not be deceived by them, but receive profit thyself, giving him his due honour, when thou knowledgest thy God to work thy salvation, pleasure, or commodity by such his creatures. The Lord has given herbs divers strength to heal divers diseases; but if in sickness we trust in the physician or his medicines, we be deceived in his good creatures. For, as David says, "It is the Lord that heals our diseases," and is at our bedside when we be sick. So these people, having received a strong and plenteous country at the merciful hands of God, forgat him that gave it them, trusted in their own strength, wisdom and polity; and so be[1] the fair outward shew of these things, pride crept in, deceived them, and made them to trust in themselves. And well it may be said to have deceived them, because it crept in under such a fair pretence, and also because, when they looked to have been saved by them, they were soonest deceived; their holds wherein they trusted were thrown down, their country conquered, and the people spoiled and destroyed. Thus does all worldly things, with a goodly outward shew, deceive a man when he trusts most in them.

"A horse is a deceitful thing," says David: and again, "Some trust in their chariots, and some in the horses; but we trust

[¹ Qu. *by*. ED.]

in the name of our Lord God." When the people would have gone into Egypt for succour, the prophet said, "Egypt is but a reed." Golias trusted in his harness and strength; but David in God's name overthrew him. Trust not therefore in any worldly thing; for it will sure deceive thee, when thou lookest for help of it. No, trust not in princes, be they never so mighty: for Nabuchodonozor, walking in his gorgeous palace, considering his mighty strong city of Babylon, containing sixteen miles square, as Pliny teaches, his many kingdoms and people that were his subjects, thought he should never have fallen; and then suddenly was he cast out of his kingdom, and lived and eat grass with beasts. What could be devised stronger than the tower of Babel? but how suddenly vanquished [vanished] that vain hope away! *(margin: Isai. xxxvi. Princes. Psal. cxlvi. Dan. iv. Gen. xi.)*

That which is added, "Thou sayest in thy heart, Who shall draw me down to the earth?" teaches us thus much, that it is not only these gross outward sins, as murder, theft, whoredom, and such like, but even the fine thoughts of our own hearts, which we think that none knows but ourselves, which God will judge and be avenged of them. They did not so much blasphemously crack openly, saying, "Who shall draw us down?" as they thought it in their hearts, and privily laughed in their selves at God's people, being so few, hated, oppressed, and despised of all round about them; and thought themselves so strong, that none durst be bold to touch them. Likewise speaks David, "The wicked man said in his heart, There is no God:" meaning not so much, that there was no God, or that they did so openly speak of him, as that they thought God had no care over them, or knew not things done on earth; as he says in another psalm, "Is there knowledge in the height? or who sees us even in these gross sins?" Our Saviour Christ says, "He that looks at a woman to lust for her has committed adultery." Therefore let us not deceive ourselves, saying, "Thought is free;" or, "I may think what I lust," or, as the psalm says, "Our lips are our own, and who is our God?" for as God has create and made our hearts and all our powers of our souls, so will he have a count of them, be served with them, and have them to think on his majesty, mercy and goodness, and be praised that ways as well as in our out- *(margin: Psal. xiv. lxxiii. Matt. v. Sins of the mind be damnable. Psal. xii.)*

ward deeds: and if we do use them for other purposes, it deserves damnation.

In the last verse the Lord makes answer: What shall become on Edon for all their great cracks, proud looks, strong holds, or any thing that they rejoiced in? And he says, I will not only draw thee down to the bare earth, from the tops of the hills, where thou delightest thyself in thy strong holds; but if it were possible that thou could "fly as high as the eagle, and build thy nest among the stars, from thence I would draw thee down, says the Lord." Herein we may see, how horrible a thing it is to forsake God, hang on our self, or trust in any worldly strength. "Let not the wise rejoice in his wisdom, nor the strong in his strength, nor the rich in his riches," says Jeremy.

Jer. ix.

And these things all to be true shall well appear in this prophet, proved by particulars: for the people had all worldly wealth wherein to rejoice; but they were deceived in them all, and destroyed, as hereafter shall appear. But this is ever the wisdom of the flesh, to rejoice in things contrary to God; and therefore is it worthily condemned by his example. The worldly man says, when his enemies come against him, it is good abiding within strong walls, and see whether they can fly over them like birds, or undermine them like conies: but the godly man says with Eliseus, being besieged of the king within the city, and his boy came and told him, "Fear not, for there is more with us than with them." Afterward he desired the Lord to open his boy's eyes, that he might see how many were on their side: the Lord gave him sight, and he saw the hills full of angels and chariots ready to fight for him: and beside that the Lord blinded his enemies, and Eliseus led them into the midst of Samaria, among their enemies, where God bade him feed them, and not harm them; for it was not he that had brought them thither, but the Lord his God. The worldly man, when persecution comes, thinks, 'Shall I leave my country, friends, and goods, go into a strange land, I know not whither, and whose language I understand not?' But the faithful man, hearing God speak to his conscience, as he did to Abraham, "Come out of thy country and from thy friends, into a land that I will shew thee; serve me,

2 Kings vi.

Gen. xii.

and fall not to idolatry;" he will obey with faithful Abraham, knowing that God will guide all those that love and follow him, and that his country is wheresoever God is served, and these be his friends and cousins that fear the Lord; as our Saviour Christ said, "These be my mother, brether,[1] and sisters, that hear the word of God and keep it." The tower of Babel was builded a wondrous height, and Nimrod with his companions would have gotten an everlasting name by it: but the Lord, perceiving their proud enterprise, disappointed them and scattered them abroad into all countries. Satan was an angel in heaven, but for his disobedience is now made a devil in hell. Nabuchodonozor was the mightiest prince, yet afterward made a very beast. Herod was proud of his great eloquence, and straight after was worried of life. Rabsaces, blaspheming the living God of Israel, and avanting himself in his great conquests, as though they had been gotten by their idol's power, had almost two hundred thousand slain in his camp in one night by the angel of God, and without man's power, in the time of good Ezechias. The Madianites, lying so thick as grasshoppers in the field, thought they should have devoured God's people at their pleasure; but God send his captain Gedeon, which with three hundred naked men, unharnessed, having lamps in one hand and earth pots in the other, vanquished them all. Thus it is true that the psalm says, "If I climb up into heaven, thou art there; and if I get down into hell, thou art there also; and there thy hand shall rule me." *Matt. xii. Gen. xi. Dan. iv. Acts xii. 2 Kings xviii. Judg. vii. Psal.cxxxix.*

The whole scripture, if ye go through it, is nothing else but a perpetual teaching, how God always throws down the proud, and lifts up the simple and lowly. Oh, if the papists would be as earnest to set up the true glory of God, as they be diligent spaniels to seek all ways possible to set up that vile puddle of idolatry of their god, the pope! In all ages have been some people that have been plagues to the rest; and yet God has thrown them down at length: so no doubt the papists be now; but their fall will be incurable when it comes, although they be a great scourge almost to all Christendom, and flourish for a time.

[[1] The three forms *brether, brethern,* and *brethren* are used by the author. Ed.]

Mark well the last words of the prophet, "I will make thee come down, says the Lord." The destruction of this people was done by Nabuchodonozor many years after, and yet the Lord calls it his own deed, and says he will pull them down. So, as I have noted afore, &c. that is called the Lord's deed, which is done by his servants, whether they be good or bad: for by such means the Lord will correct us, bring us to the knowledge of ourselves and him. In all such worldly corrections therefore let us not look so much at him that vexes us, or murmur and grudge at him; but look who has sent him, whose servant he is, and wherefore he comes: for he comes from God to do and teach us good: and then we shall patiently bear whatsoever comes. And because they should not flatter themselves, as though these things should not thus come to pass, he joins unto it, "The Lord says:" as though he should say, Flatter not yourselves, I speak not of mine own head: the God of all truth, that can not lie, says thus: therefore most certainly look for it. He that is a righteous judge of all creatures, and both can and will be avenged on all evil doers, and will deliver us his people out of the hands of their oppressors, when he has sufficiently declared the patient abiding and deep sighing of the oppressed, and abiden long enough for the turning of the proud enemies, when he sees no amendment to be hoped for, he will then come in deed, fearful for his enemies, and comfortable for his poor people; as the psalm says, "For the misery of the poor and the sighing of the oppressed I will rise, says the Lord." Who shall be able to stand, when he says he will pull down? yea, who dare be bold to look, when he shews his anger? Deceive not yourselves, he will come.

It is called the Lord's deed that the servants do.

Psal. xii.

The Text. v. 5. *If thieves had come to thee, and if robbers in the night, how should thou have holden thy peace? Would they not have stolen sufficient for themselves? If grape gatherers had come to thee, would they not have left some clusters?*

6. *But how have they searched Esau, and ransacked their hid things!*

After that the prophet has told them that they shall be destroyed, now he tells them after what sort, and of what things they should be spoiled. Edom was a country not only compassed about with hills, that no enemies could enter, and fortified with strong holds and castles on the top of the hills, as appears afore; but it was a plenteous country also of all fruits, and full of wise men of great polity: which all should be taken from them, with all their things that they rejoiced in. And where he uses two similitudes here, one of thieves and of grape gatherers, which both, wheresoever they come, do much harm and take all things at their pleasure, spare nothing, but search all privy corners, where any thing can be hid; yet these spoilers should be much worse, and more cruelly entreat them. This first part of the similitude has two arguments of their cruelness in it; and it is as much as though he should have said thus to them: If thieves should come in the day time to spoil thee, or robbers in the night season, thou could not have holden thy peace, but would have called and cried for help of thy neighbours; thou would have prepared thyself to have foughten with them, to have withstand them, to have defended thine own goods, and to have taken or killed them that thus violently came on thee: but when these destroyers shall come, thou shalt not be bold to whisper, to cry, to call for help; or else, if thou cry never so loud, it is but vain to defend thyself or rescue thy goods; but fearfully like a sheep lie still, and like a coward let them do to thee what they please; it shall be fulfilled in thee, that God threatens to the breakers of his law, that "one shall chase a thousand, and ten men ten thousand:" yea, and that which is more marvellous, they shall be afraid at the fall of a leaf. Deut. xxviii. xxxii. Levit. xxvi.

Or if we read thus, (so the Hebrew word signifies both ways,) "How should thou have been destroyed!" then this is the meaning, that although thieves and robbers would have destroyed them, yet that destruction should not[1] have been like to this: so extreme a plague should this be to them, that these other were not worthy to be compared unto it. The latter token of their great destruction is, that the Babylonians, when they come, should deal worse with them than thieves or robbers would: for thieves, when they come, they do not take all, but the best things they find, lest they should not

[1] *Not* is required by the sense: wanting in the old edition. ED.

flee fast enough away, or be bewrayed by many things when they should be known. And again, they use not to tarry long in robbing a house, for fear lest some should espy them, and come upon them suddenly. But the Chaldees should not be afraid of any company of men, when they should overrun them; nor be content with a few things, but destroy all after them; and that which they could not carry away, they would utterly mar by some means, that they should have no good of that which was left. They would not be content with a few things, as thieves, but they would have all: they would not hastily run away for fear of any help coming to rescue them; but they would without fear spoil, and tarry their leisure, searching all corners, not caring who shall espy them. And, that which is more marvellous, thieves, although they come suddenly upon a man, giving no warning, that a man might prepare himself to stand in his own defence, should not do so much harm as the Assyrians should, coming not suddenly upon them, nor they unprepared, but being prepared, and although they knew of their coming, and had all kind of weapons to defend themselves withal, yet they should not be able nor bold to defend themselves or their country, but should utterly perish, be robbed, spoiled and destroyed.

The latter similitude of grape gatherers declares this more plainly. Grape gatherers, although they search every branch, and peep under every leaf, lest they leave any grapes growing behind them, (and yet they were commanded in the law by Moses to leave some growing of all kind of fruit behind them; and if they let any fall, they should not turn again to take it up, but let the poor come gather and glean,) yet these greedy cormorants, so covetous that they never had enough, so greedy that they were never filled, they would not leave one cluster growing behind them, but so utterly spoil them, that they would leave nothing at all, neither for poor nor rich. They would spare neither man nor woman, old nor young, house nor land, town nor castle; beasts of all sorts without mercy should be wasted, burned, and destroyed.

<small>Levit. xix.</small>

The latter verse shews this utter destruction at large in few words, saying, " But how have they searched Esau, and ransacked their secret things!"—as though he should say to them, Although thieves, robbers, grape gatherers, use to do much harm, wheresoever they come, and nothing can escape their hands; yet it shall be nothing like unto this destruction, that these of Babylon shall do. This destruction shall be incurable; these shall spoil, kill and destroy without mercy. Nabuchodonozor, when he comes with his men, shall search and ransack all your secret places and corners, that nothing shall escape them. In sacking of towns men be wont to cast their plate, money, jewels, and such other treasures into deep wells, to dig them in the earth or some privy place, where none or few uses to come, or few would mistrust any thing there to be hid: but when he comes, hide your treasures where you lust; cast them into jakes, dunghills, cisterns, or blind corners, where please you; it shall not skill, it shall be espied, and shall not escape: ye shall not have profit of any thing ye have. He wonders at the utter destruction of them, when he says, "How have they searched and ransacked the secrets!"—as if he should say, It shall be unlike unto all other doings: no reason would think what great cruelty in searching and spoil shall be shewed unto thee; it shall be so horrible, so contrary to men's looking for, and so far unlike to all that has been shewed to any other people.

And marvel not at this extremity shewed unto you: good reason it is, that they which have comforted themselves in their worldly things beside God, that they should be so corrected of God, that they should understand that there is no help, succour or comfort, but in God; and they which would not know God in prosperity, must now drink of his justice in adversity. He had given plenty to them of all fruits, corn, cattles, and all kind of riches; but this could not move them to knowledge him to be their Lord and God, giver and saver both of man and beast: therefore now must they taste of the rod, to know there was a God whom they had offended. God does not give us his benefits, riches and blessings to make us trust in ourselves or any other creature, but to stir up our minds to heaven, to look on him, trust in him, call on him, and praise him: therefore it was right that all these should be taken from them, to bring them to the knowledge of themselves and his justice, which can not abide such things. This is the reward due for all such as will not shew mercy, but cruelty to them that be in distress; they shall find the same cruelty and measure given them again, when they shall be in need; they shall ask mercy, call for help, but find none.

<small>Gen. xliv.</small> Joseph's brethren, when they would shew no mercy to their brother, when he desired them, were straitly looked on for a time, and sharply spoken unto, when they came into Egypt: and then they could confess that God had worthily rewarded them their unkindness that they shewed their brother Joseph. Nabuchodonozor with all his cruel proud men, which spoiled, conquered and cruelly entreated all countries about them, were served with like measure at Cyrus' hands, when he overcame them: he destroyed their city, and conquered their country. And as our papists, with their spies in all corners, would let no man dwell in rest, but accuse, complain, imprison, and burn them, and had rather fulfil the bloody desires and minds of the cruel murderers and butchers, than shew any gentleness to God's people, (and all to pick a thank or get a bribe of the proud bishops or hard hearted and never satisfied horse-leeches, the lawyers;) so their time will come, when they shall feel God's heavy wrath and displeasure against them with such grief of conscience, that they <small>Rev. vi.</small> shall wish for death, and not find it, desire the hills to cover them from the face of the Lamb, and yet be without comfort. These be the Edomites, that persecute the true sons of Jacob at this day: these be the false brethren, that be moved neither with the fear of God's love to his word, nor natural to their brethren, countrymen and kinsfolk; but, like brute beasts, devour all afore them, satisfying their own lusts and desires, increasing their own condemnation, if they turn not and repent with tears.

<small>The Text.</small> v. 7. *Even unto the border of thy country have they cast out thee, and persecuted all men which were in league and confederate with thee: the men that made peace with thee have deceived thee, and prevailed against thee; and those that eat thy bread have wounded thee privily: there is no wisdom in him.*

8. *Shall I not in that day, says the Lord, destroy the wise men from Edom, and wisdom from the hill of Esau?*

9. *The strong men of Theman shall be afraid, because every one of the hill Esau shall be destroyed.*

This plague, that God threatens to this people now, is of two sorts; and that, because they had double offended. According as it is the policy of princes to join themselves in league and friendship with princes that dwell near unto them, that by their help they might be the stronger and more feared, and also to have wise men of the counsel; so had these Edomites sought the friendship of all the mighty countries about them, and picked out also the worldly-wisest men they could find to be their rulers; thinking that by polity and wisdom of the one, and the strength, power, and riches of the other, they should be able to defend themselves against all men that would proffer them wrong; yea, they should rather under this pretence be bold to do other men wrong, and none should once be so bold to say, Why do ye so? This is a common practice likewise at these days, of such as would hurt other,—but that either they dare not nor can not,—to run always under some great man's wing, to bear the name of his servant, wear his livery, or be one of his retinue, that under this colour he may disquiet the whole country where he dwells, and no man dare be so bold to blame him.

But God hates all such as forsake him, and hang on themselves; takes all such in their own devices, and that wherein they think to save themselves is turned to their own destruction. These people, says the Lord, with whom thou art in league, thinking thereby to save thyself, and be stronger than all other, even the selfsame people shall rise up against thee, take part with thy enemies, and drive thee out of the borders of thy own country. You would think it a great pleasure if, when thou were conquered and overcome, thou might dwell in thine own country still, paying tribute and taxes to Nabuchodonozor and other about thee; but thou, that hast been so cruel to thy brethern, God's people, the sons of Jacob, shall not find so much favour and friendship at their hands, as to dwell in thy own land, but shall be driven not only out of thy strong holds and wealthy places of it, but even out of all the coasts and borders of the same; and that by those which thou takest for thy friends, and in whom thou puttest thy trust.

Such shall be the case of all those that forsake the Lord, and put their trust in themselves or their friends. When the people of God would have gone to Egypt again for succour, when Nabuchodonozor had subdued all the country, Jeremy cried still, No, they should not do so; for where they looked for help, they should find woe: for Nabuchodonozor overcame Egypt also, and then all that fled thither were in worse case than if they had tarried in their country still. "Egypt is a reed," says Isaie, "and they that flee thither shall perish." In dangerous times there is no succour to be found, but at the Lord's hands: for when the Lord sees that in prosperity we forget him, he sends us adversity, that for fear we should be compelled to look for help at his hands. Such a loving God is he unto us, that he would win us by all means possible; but if we can be drawn to him by no way, he gives us over, that we may work justly our own condemnation without excuse, having nothing to lay for ourselves.

Moreover those that made peace with these people deceived them, and those that eat their bread wounded them privily. This is the reward of worldly wisdom, that when they trust most in them, they shall be soonest deceived; and when they look for help of them, they shall be the first that shall wound them. There can be no true love, which is not grounded in God and for his sake: for where as God only is sought for, there is love and truth itself; wheresoever he is not, there is neither truth nor true love. That love which is grounded on worldly causes, when the world changes, it fails too. If it be for beauty, profit, or friendship, as soon as these be gone, farewell love, friendship is gone. Nabuchodonozor, whom they feared, and looked for promotion at his hands, was now comen to destroy Edom; and therefore all the country about was not only ready to fall from the Edomites, with whom they were in league afore, giving them no help; but were the first and cruellest enemies that they had, ready not only not to help them, but to drive them out of their own country. Who pretended a greater love to Christ than Judas, and who sooner betrayed and denied him? How many examples is England able to give of such as, while they were in authority, they were feared rather than loved, (although it was called love, fair faces were outwardly, promises, oaths, bands, marriages were made, and all devices that could be, to make it sure;) but when they fell, they which were thought dearest friends were become open enemies, accusers and condemners, in hope to climb into his room, or catch part of his goods or lands. David complains _{Psal. xli.} of such as made fairest face of friendship, and did eat of the same dish, and yet soonest deceived him.

These words in the Hebrew be written in the preterite _{Preter tense.} tense, but spoken that so it should come to pass as sure as if it were now done: according as the custom of the prophets is, to speak that which is to come as though it were done, where other languages use to speak such things in future tenses.

But the latter end of the verse, where he says, "there is no wisdom in him," (that is to say, in them, or all the Edomites, by a common figurative speech in Hebrew, where the singular is put for the plural, as in the 89th psalm, "I will visit their wickedness with a rod, &c. but my mercy I will not take from him," them,)[1]—is most marvellous; for who will believe, or who can judge the contrary, but that it is great wisdom and policy to the strengthening, defence, and maintaining of a country, to have strong holds in it, and to be in league with their neighbours round about them, as these men were? But God says, "there was no wisdom in them," nor in this their doing: not because it is not lawful for God's people to have, use, or make such things in their commonwealth for their defence and keeping out their enemies, but that they may not do these things to put their trust in them; or when they have them, to despise their Lord God, seeking no help at his hands, but trust in their own strength, thinking themselves able to defend themselves against all enemies; as though God did nothing, nor victory and defence were not of him. And again, when they have such strong defence, they may not use it to the hurt of God's people; as these wicked proud Edomites did both against God, their brethren and the people of God.

This is right wisdom to forsake himself and hang upon

[1 The old edition is confused: *take from him*. *Them is most*. ED.]

God, to know that no policies are good which is against God's people, nor to think themselves strong by hurting others. The conjurers that stood afore Pharao working miracles, thought they should have defaced Moses and set up themselves: but Pharao was drowned with his host, Moses with his people was delivered, and the conjurers granted that the living God wrought in Moses. Achitophel, counselling Absalon to follow his father David that same night he began to rebel, lest in deferring time he should escape, thought Absalon should have been a king: but God proved his worldly-wise counsel to be foolishness; for when he see that he was not beloved nor his counsel followed, he went and hanged himself: but David escaped, and Absalon was slain. When Haman had obtained a proclamation for the destroying of all the Jews, and made a gallows for Mardocheus, he thought himself wiser than all the world; and that he should have been promoted himself, and the people of God spoiled and destroyed: but Haman was hanged on the same gallows, Mardocheus promoted, and the Jews delivered. When Saul promised David his daughter for the killing of an hundred Philistines, not for love, but thinking David should have been killed himself afore he had killed so many, he thought he had done politicly; but David killed them all, married his daughter, and was king after him: for which thing only Saul abhorred him. The scribes and Pharisees, thinking, if Christ were once dead, they should be safe, and never hear tell more of him: but after his death, the apostles wrought more miracles in his name than he did himself, being alive, and more believed in him after his death, than ever did when he was alive.

Thus all the scripture proves plain, that that which worldly wisdom thinks best to set up themselves by, and to destroy God's people, is proved to be the destruction of all those that trust in it; and when they look for most comfort of their device, it turns to their own hurt: as we see it has chanced by God's merciful providence to our papists for bringing in the Spaniards, trusting by that people to maintain their superstitious popery and idle lordly authority. "The wisdom of this world," says the apostle, "is foolishness afore God." The wiser thou art afore men, not having the glory of God afore thine eyes, ever studying how to set forth his will to the world, the more fool thou art: the craftier thou art to set up thyself, the sooner thou workest thine own destruction. How many of the worldly policy men have been trapped in their own snare here among us! Have not they, when they were highest in authority, suffered death by the same their own laws? Thus ye see that all worldly wisdom against God is nought; and that it is no wisdom indeed, but foolishness. And although worldly wits do many things well for a time, yet when they trust in it most, and stand most in need of it, they shall be deceived, as the next verse says: "Shall I not in that day destroy, says the Lord, the wise men from Edom," &c? And as it is in worldly wits and policies, that they be all vain when they strive against God; so is it in the spiritual kingdom of Christ, in his word and church: for the dregs of popery, with their canons and decrees, shall be thrown down, and cannot always maintain those idle belly gods, the pope's chaplains; but as they have been cast down by times ever, so shall they at length be trodden under foot to their confusion. Like is the case of subtle schoolmen with their distinctions, defacing Christ and his truth; neither setting forth the majesty of God and his Son Christ Jesus, nor edifying with comfortable promises the weak consciences, nor opening the mysteries of the scripture; but with foolish glosses defacing the mercies of God taught in his holy word, and burdening men with traditions, unwritten verities, or rather vanities, their own dreams and fantasies; all which God abhors, and says, "All that worship him, teaching man's doctrine, worship him in vain." These and all such like, coming of "the wisdom of the flesh," be everlasting death, as Paul says, and "sensual, carnal, and devilish," as James terms them, and mere ignorance of God and his mercies: for a "natural sensual man perceives not the things of God." *Matt. xv. Rom. viii. James iii. 1 Cor. ii.*

And to conclude, generally all wisdom that sets up itself in any kind of things, whatsoever it be, it is no wisdom; it shall confound all that use it or trust in it; and when they would most gladly enjoy it, they shall surely not have it. "There is no wisdom nor counsel against the Lord," says *Prov. xxi.* Salomon. The pope with all his rabble is not so wise to throw down Christ, as the scribes and Pharisees were in their time: and as they were confounded, so shall all that rebel against the Son of God, which by the might of his Holy Spirit, in the mouth of his true apostles, disciples and ministers, being but poor simple abjects and a despised people in the sight of the world, has overthrown tyrants, stopped blaspheming mouths, confounded the wise and learned, and declared his strength in our weakness, that there is no power, wisdom, strength nor policy that prevails against him or his people: and because they did glory so much in their wisdom and policy, the Lord counts it a glorious thing to throw them down; and because the glory may be given to him alone for such a noble victory, he says, "Shall I not throw them down?"—as though he should say, No man shall have the praise of it, but I myself; I will destroy them with mine own hands in that day when they look not for it, and trust most in themselves. The tower of Babel, the cities Nineve and Jerusalem, being great and mighty, were suddenly overthrown when they thought not on it. The wisdom of God purposes one thing, and the wisdom of man another: so wisdom shall overcome wisdom, and the pride of man shall be overcome by the mighty hand of God. God tarries long to have his enemies to turn by repentance, to see their own folly, and ask forgiveness: but when he sees there is no remedy nor hope of their amendment, he comes like a sharp and righteous judge, and utterly overthrows them.

But not only their wisdom and wise men perished, but their "strong men shall be afraid also, because every noble man among them should be afraid," as the last verse says. What a case shall these people be in, when neither wisdom nor strength shall serve! Theman signifies by interpretation *the south*, and it is also the name of one of their chief cities; and therefore some translate, "Thy strong men shall be afraid of the south," because Nabuchodonozor came with his host from the south; for so Babylon stood southward from them: or better, "the strongest men of Theman," thy chief city, shall be afraid; and so Jeremy uses it, "There is no more wisdom in Theman." It is thought of many learned, and that probably, that Job dwelled in this country afore Esau was born, and married Dina, Jacob's daughter, as Philo says; and that Eliphas also the Themanite[1], one of Job's friends, which came to comfort him as he sat on [Job ii.] the dunghill, dwelled in this city Theman, and thereof was called the Themanite[1]: and well it may be so; for in his counsellings and comforting of Job he speaks oft more worldly than godly, although wittily and wisely.

The latter end of the verse some read, "Every one of the hill Esau;" some, "the noble men," as the Targum reads; but both well enough. For *Isch* signifies both *every one*, and also [Isch. a man,] but such one as is noble. Therefore I join them together, and say, "every noble man;" and so I express both their meanings. So here is plainly taught, that neither wisdom nor strength can prevail against the Lord. All glorying, cracking, rejoicing or boasting, that any man has of himself, or any thing beside God, is vain and wicked: for this must always be afore us, "He that glories, let him glory in the Lord;" and Cyprian says well, "We must glory in nothing, because nothing is ours: we have received all from God, and therefore all praise must be given to him, that gives all[2]." "What hast thou," says St Paul, "that [1 Cor. iv.] thou hast not received of God? and if thou have received it, why crackest thou on it, as though thou had not received it?" What a proud soul is he that will be proud of his borrowed coat, or painted sheath! God clothes us, and covers our filthy nakedness with his godly gifts: what unthankful treason is it then, to take the praise from him to ourself, and not render due thanks to him for them!

Mark here the difference betwixt true wisdom and bold- *Godly-wise.* ness, and earthly worldly wit and power. When danger *Worldly.* comes, the godly-wise man will commit himself wholly to God, looking for help and deliverance at his hands; or else patiently bear it without any dismaying, whatsoever God lays on him: for he knows well that things are not ruled by fortune, nor that any thing can fall on him without the good will of his good God and loving Father. But the worldly-

[1 Old edition, *the Aminites*. ED.]

[2 In proprias laudes odiosa jactatio est; quamvis non jactatum possit esse, sed gratum, quicquid non virtuti hominis ascribitur, sed de Dei munere prædicatur. * * * Dei est, inquam, Dei omne quod possumus. De Gratia Dei, ad Donatum. Pag. 2. Oxon, 1700, ED.]

wise man, when he sees worldly wit, power and polity fail, he thinks all the world fails, and things be without recovery: he trusteth not in God, and therefore no marvel if he be left desolate. Of the good man's fear in the time of adversity writes Jeremy: "Blessed is he that trusts in the Lord, for he shall be a tree planted by the waters, and in the drought he shall not be careful, nor cease to bear fruit." And David also says, "Thou shall not be afraid of fear in the night, &c." The wicked contrariwise shall be afraid at the fall of a leaf: one shall chase a thousand, and [two] ten thousand, as God threatens in Deuteronomy by Moses. He will lie, flatter, swear, and what ye will have him to do, rather than lose his profit. The like says Jeremy of them too: "They shall be a reed shaken of the wind. They shall dwell in dry wilderness, in a salt ground." The people which dwelt in the land promised to the Israelites, when they heard tell what wonders God wrought in the wilderness and the Red Sea for his people, and seeing them come near unto them, and hearing the victories they had against the kings, See and Og, their hearts melted in their bodies like wax, as Rahab confessed to the spies which Josue sent; but Rahab herself she plucked up her heart, trusted in God, and was delivered where the other perished. So the good Gabaonites that feared God yielded themselves to Josue, and were saved: the other that trusted in their own strength, and would try it with the sword, for all their brag were faint hearted and overcome. So the Philistines, seeing Goliath their grand captain slain of David, being but a child in comparison of him, fled away post; where the Israelites afore were so afraid that they durst not stir. Thus God turns the course of things when pleases him, that those which afore were dismayed, pluck up their courage and win the victory; and those that were stout, bragging of themselves afore, now be made cowards, run away and fly, thinking the dangers greater than they be indeed.

One wicked plagues another.

It does evidently appear here also, how the Lord raises up one wicked to plague and throw down another. These Edomites had joined themselves with their neighbours to trouble poor Jacob's seed and his people: but now the matter is so turned, that one wicked persecutes, destroys and plagues another, and Nabuchodonozor destroys Edom. Wicked

Jehu was raised to throw down cruel Jesabel: and all the kings of Israel, called the ten tribes, being all evil, every one murdered his predecessor, and was killed of his successor. How many popes have used the same practice in poisoning one another, that they might come aloft, it were more long and tedious to tell, than hard to find. In twelve year space under one emperor were eight popes, whereof every one almost persecuted another, being dead and digged up out of the earth, and beheaded them, as Formosus, Stephanus, &c. Some other reigned but a month, and poisoned one another, as Crantz[1] writes.

2 Kings ix.

The Text.

v. 10. *For the violence toward thy brother Jacob, shame shall confound thee, and thou shalt be destroyed for ever.*

11. *In that day did thou stand against him, even in that day when strangers did take his goods, and when strangers entered his gates, and when they cast lot for Jerusalem, thou also wast one of them.*

12. *Thou shalt not look in the day of thy brother, nor in the day when strange things shall happen him; nor thou shalt not rejoice against the children of Juda in the day of their destruction, nor thou shalt not open thy mouth boastingly in the day of their trouble.*

13. *Thou shalt not enter the gates of my people in the day of their destruction; nor thou shalt not look on their trouble in the day of their misery; nor thou shalt not stretch out thyself upon his goods in the day of his destruction.*

14. *Nor thou shalt not stand in the cross ways to kill them that flee; nor thou shalt hem them that be left in the day of their trouble.*

15. *For the day of the Lord over all people is at hand: as thou hast done, they shall do unto thee; like punishment shall fall upon thine own head.*

16. *As ye have drunken upon my holy hill, so shall all people drink continually: they shall drink and swallow up, and shall be as though they were not.*

Now follows the declaration of the causes of God's anger and heavy displeasure against Edom, lest any man should

[[1] Albert Crantz, or Krantz, a celebrated historian of the 15th century. ED.]

think God unjust in his doings, or too sharp in his punishings. Some would think a less punishment might have sufficed to have corrected them withal: but when they shall consider how great and grievous the sins of them were, it shall be judged too little a punishment for so many faults.

The first verse contains generally that which the verses following declare by particulars. The pride, violence, injuries, wrongs and robberies, that they shewed toward their brother Jacob, be the causes of this their destruction. Jacob and Edom are not here taken for the two brethren, the sons of Isaac; but for the whole seed, stock, posterity, children, and issue born of them both: so that, as hatred began in Esau against Jacob in their father's life, yea, in their mother's womb, insomuch that Esau persecuted his brother Jacob to death so sore, that Jacob was caused to flee to his uncle Laban; so the hatred, persecution and enmity did continue in their children unto this time, was fulfilled that the prophet speaks of here, when the posterity of Esau was utterly destroyed. And this is comfortable both for the long-suffering of God afore he do extremely punish, and also a true proof of his justice, that although he do defer his punishing long, yet he is a righteous judge, and will come at the length, and be avenged on his enemies, and deliver his children that have been so long oppressed under their enemies. Therefore, as the good need not to be discouraged, as though their God cared not for them; so the wicked shall not triumph, as though they might do what they list, and God would not call them to account.

They had thus persecuted Jacob and his posterity above a thousand years, and that continually, afore they were destroyed, and could never be satisfied of their cruelty: therefore, partly to stop their raging, and bring them to the knowledge both of God and themselves, and partly to fear other for following the like example, if they should be unpunished, but specially for the crying of the poor oppressed people, whom God takes into his custody to be their tutor, the Lord will rise to shew himself glorious, mighty, and merciful, pull down his enemies, deliver his oppressed, as David says, "For the misery of the poor, and the sighing of the wretched, I will rise, says the Lord, &c." Why should God's people then be dismayed when they be persecuted, seeing they have so mighty a judge, that can and will deliver them when it shall be meetest for his glory and their comfort? "Refer ^{Rom. xii.} the vengeance to me, says the Lord, and I will revenge it." Let us therefore submit ourselves under his hands, and patiently look for his coming; for no doubt he will come. When Moses led the people through the wilderness, and came near the bounds of Edom, he asked licence to pass through ^{Num. xii.} their country, keeping the highways, hurting them in no behalf, insomuch that they would pay for the water that they drank: but they, more like no men than cousins, coming of the same stock and father, being not content with this churlishness, to deny them passage, threatens them further, that if they would not pass by all their country, and not once be so bold as to enter within their coasts, they would by and bye fight against them with all their power. So Moses, to ^{Deut. ii.} keep peace, led the people by a great compass round about; and what said God to this? did he bid destroy them? No; but clean contrary, he bade them not to fight against them; not only them, but he says unto them, "Thou shalt not harm Edom, because he is thy brother."

Note here the patience and long suffering of God's people, that would not once attempt to revenge such displeasures, unkindness and injuries done unto them. And again note the churlishness of feigned friends, hypocrites and dissemblers, which will shew no gentleness to God's people, though they may do it without their hurt or displeasure of any man. Is not the world full of such unthankful, unkind, and unnatural folk at this day? St Paul complains of such as cast off all natural affection, that should be among men: as when they which be all of one house, stock and kindred, coming of one great grandfather or ancestors, be so cruel one against another, that nature, which works in brute beasts, has no place in them, one to love or help another: he calls them *sine affectu;* as though he should say, if ^{Rom. i.} nature can not work or move them, which moves stones, trees, herbs, and beasts, what hope is there that the gospel, which is so far above and contrary to nature, should take any place in them? So St Paul calls them which do not provide for them and theirs, "worse than infidels." ^{1 Tim. v.}

Wherefore it was necessary, some great plague to fall on this people that had so far forgotten nature, that they would not let them pass through their country, nor drink of their waters, which they would pay for.

But this is the mark betwixt God's chosen and the devil's, the gospeller and the papist, the true Christian and an hypocrite; that the one will suffer wrong, do good for evil, pray for them that hate him, be content with a little, not murmuring; but the bloody papist is proud, cruel, murdering, oppressing the innocent, merciless, hating without reconciliation, ever seeking to hurt, that they may live like lords of the land and idle belly gods. What a comfort is this for God's poor afflicted people, that although God do long suffer them to be vexed of their enemies, yet he will not suffer them to be overwhelmed; but he will utterly root out the wicked, when he begins to execute his justice on them! "He that touches you," says God to his people by the prophet Zachary, "touches the apple of mine eye." What part of man is more tender than the eye? or which part do we take more care for than that? Yet, if the eye be sore or dim of sight, we will lay sharp biting waters or powders in it to eat out the web, pearl, or blearedness. So will God, although he love his people so tenderly, lay sharp biting salves, purging medicines, corrosives, lancings, letting blood, yea, and cut off rotten members, lest the whole body perish or rot away. But all that is for fatherly love, to drive us unto him, to make us weary of the world, to purge carnal cares, eat out the dead rotten fantasies of our minds, let out the bruised blood, or cut away by death some for the example of other, to strengthen them boldly to confess the truth and glorifying of his name by such constant witness of our weak natures. A little worldly shame, as it is thought of worldly, but not godly men, may light on God's people for a time; but everlasting shame shall confound their enemies for ever afore God. A short temporal punishment may grieve God's children for a time; but their haters shall be utterly destroyed for ever. The Israelites were ashamed for a time in their captivity, when Esau joined with Nabuchodonozor to destroy them; and yet afterwards were brought home again: but now should these be utterly destroyed for

[margin: The godly be corrected for a time, the wicked for ever.]

[margin: Zech. ii.]

ever without recovery. The Philistines for a time made the Israelites ashamed: but after that David had slain Goliath, the Philistines were vanquished, slain, and every day more and more rooted out. [1 Sam. xvii.]

The verses following declare the cause of the destruction of Edom. First, because when Nabuchodonozor sacked their city Jerusalem, entered the gates and cast lot on Jerusalem, who should have the best part, spoiled their good, burned their houses and temple, beat down their walls, and made havoc of all, "Thou, Edom, stood among them," took their parts, robbed as fast as the best, cast lot with them which should be thy part; and when other would have shewn pity, thou cried, as the psalm says, "Down with it, down with them, even to the bottom;" leave not one stick standing, leave not one stone upon another. O what cruel words are these, that they which were cousins, and should have been friends unto this people, when their enemies would have shewn pity, they cry, Down with them, down with them; leave not one piece standing! The Scots invading England made a like brag among themselves, to destroy all afore them; and the morning afore the battle was fought, they played at dice for all the dukedoms and great cities in England, who should have them: but God turned them in their own pride; for their king was slain in the field, and all the host discomfited to their great loss and shame[1]. [Psal. cxxxv]

Where brotherly love required that thou should have holpen thy brother Jacob and his seed, thou stood by and looked on, and would not help, when such strange things and destruction fell on him: yea, not only that, but ye rejoiced at their harm, and stood boasting and cracking against them, where thou should have been a comfort, and delivered of them. It is hard to tell whether he offends God more that does the wrong and oppresses another, or he that stands by laughing, mocking and scorning, and may help and will not; but sure both be damnable. David complains of such as hurt the oppressed, "They have persecuted him whom thou hast smitten, and they increased my sorrow:" and again, "They sang rhymes against me, as they sat drinking wine." They that stood mocking at our Saviour Christ, hanging on [Psal. lxix.]

[[1] The battle of Flodden Field, A.D. 1513. Ed.]

the cross, were as guilty of his death as they that crucified him: "Thou that destroyest the temple of God, hail, king of the Jews! Let him save him, if he will have him." They which consent to any wickedness are as well guilty as they that do the deed. It is against all humanity that, when God punishes, man should also lay on more sorrow beside. No beast, if another stick fast in the mire or fall under his load, will stand mocking or hurting him, or laying on more weight to hold it down: and what beastliness or worse rather is this, that man should rejoice at another man's harm! it is against nature of man. God bids by Moses, that if ye see thine enemy's ass fallen under his load, that thou shall not pass by, but thou shall help to lift him up: and surely God does not command this so much for the ass's sake, as the man's; as St Paul says in a like case, in muzzling the labouring ox, "Has God care for oxen?" And if we be taught thus to shew this friendship to our enemy and his ass, much more it will be required at our hands for our friends and neighbours. But they had so far forgotten all gentleness, that they were more ready to do them harm than their open enemies were and strangers. "They burst open their gates, and went in with the first, laid hands upon their goods, and spoiled them as fast as the best." Yea, they were not content to stand by, look on, and rob them; but they stood in the cross ways, that if any escaped, ran away, or made shift to save himself, they either were ready to kill him, or else take him prisoner, and bring him and deliver him into the hands of his enemies. O miserable cruelness, that would not let them live which had once escaped danger, nor would not let them flee away which were once delivered from their enemies! What a pleasure had these wicked men in murdering and robbing their brethren, that could not suffer them to escape which had once escaped!

Yea, all this cruelty they shewed when the Lord had forbidden them: for so the Hebrew reads all these cruel parts negatively, forbidding them so to do. And because they had done so cruelly to their brethren, and contrary to God's commandment, the plagues fell on them which the next verse speaks of. The Chaldee targum reads them all affirmatively, saying, "Thou did stand against thy brother; when the heathen robbed him, entered his city, cast lot for Jerusalem, thou took their parts, stood looking on him in the day of his destruction, and spake boastingly against him; thou robbed him, and stood in the cross ways to kill them that ran away to save themselves." The sense and meaning is all one, whether we read them affirmatively or negatively; for the one casts in their teeth their cruelty, and the other forbids them it, and shews that for this their unkind and wicked behaviour toward their brethren, God's people, they should drink such as they had given other. This is the common practice of the world, that when a man is down, then even those which were his feigned friends afore, will be the first that shall work him displeasure. When Absalon had gathered a great company, and driven out his father, then those that were David's counsellors and flattering friends, were the first that forsaked him; saw the world change, ran to Absalon, and thought there was most profit to get to be gotten that way. 2 Sam. xv.
1 Kings xv.

But if I should apply this to antichrist, the pope, and his pigs, we shall easily perceive how true it is not only afore, but in these our miserable days. When Vertiger, king of this realm, would forsake his lawful wife the queen, and marry the daughter of Hengist a Saxon, then to defend that naughty deed must the Saxons be brought in contrary to the people's mind; and so at length they conquered all, and made themselves kings, driving out the Englishmen. Of what one cruel point can our unmerciful papists excuse themselves at this day, but they have been as cruel against the brethern in this realm for religion, as Edom was against Jacob? For the maintaining of the idolatries, when they see that the most part of the realm had espied their wickedness and proud tyranny that they would exercise against the people of God, they see there was no way to keep their pomp and feed their idle bellies, but by might, power, and strong hand. So these caterpillars, caring not how they come by it so that they had it, better they think it to danger the whole realm, than idolatry be not maintained, their pope honoured, poor souls bought and sold, their greedy ambitious desires set aloft, that they may rule like lords. When they see their brethren cast in the fire, they stand by laughing, boasting their false doctrine, cracking to root out all

Papists are worse than the Edomites.

that love the gospel, and not to leave one alive that is suspect to love any good religion. These greedy cormorants, if they see any that had a good living that they list to have, by and bye they set one of their promoters or other to accuse him, and never ceased unto they had driven him out. Yea, when the pope's spaniels some would speak against such cruelty, and wish more gentleness to be used, they would most earnestly be against it, and yet call themselves spiritual.

Nero. Nero, when any evil chanced, or he had done any mischief himself and set fire in Rome, would say the Christians were cause of it, or had done it, to bring them in hatred with the people. So our papists, if there was unseasonable weather, or any thing did displease the people, they said it was because these gospellers were not yet rooted out, but suffered to live: when any was content to forsake country, house, wife, lands, and goods, according to God's commandment, rather than defile himself with wickedness, submitting himself to their abominations, they would rail on him, calling him runagate, traitor, heretic, and what pleased them. And because they would be like Edomites in all points, which watched their cross ways to kill those that escaped; so the papists, if any gospeller had escaped their hands, they would send commandments into other countries to call them home, lay watches and spies in all corners to catch such as they lust to have, and bring them home like prisoners, which never had offended. What strait watch was laid in every haven to catch them that came in or out, though they were but poor afflicted men, and banished members of Christ! What rejoicing, if any was taken; and what strait commissions to search what goods any such banished person had left behind him, and in whose hands it was, that it might be taken from them! What great cracks their great Nimrod[1] and captain made, that he would

[1 "Seeing the professors were fled out of their bloody hands, they thought to be even with them by endeavouring to hinder all supplies of money and provisions to be sent them; saying that they 'would make them so hungry, that they should eat their fingers' ends.' These words Gardiner in great passion had uttered in Calais, being there embassador with Cardinal Pole and others." Strype, Memorials, Vol. III. i. ch. xxxi. p. 403. 8vo. where he proceeds to illustrate this by a quotation from Bishop Pilkington. See the passage at p. 197 of this edition. ED.]

bring all such runagates (as it pleased him to term them) to such need, that they should eat their fingers for hunger, it is not unknown to the world: that they might thus prove themselves true Edomites, in robbing their poor brother Jacob. But that we may perceive our papists to be the true seed of the spiritual Edom, mark the beginning, and it shall more easily appear.

Edom, which is Esau, lost his father's blessing, by which he should have had authority over his brother; and that was the chief cause of hatred toward Jacob: so our papists, because the gospellers teach them to be humble, as Christ was, and to leave their lordliness over God's flock, they persecute them to death. Esau, to fill his belly, lost his birthright, by which he should have had double portion of his father's goods, to his brother: so our popes, because they may not have double honour, promotion, riches, and wealth to other, as their father the pope has, they hate all that gainsay them. Esau was rough skinned, a wild man of conditions, and a hunter: so our hypocritical popes be of cruel and rough conditions, hunters for promotions, yea, hawkers and hunters in deed, and given to all pleasure, rather than to feed God's sheep. We read in the scripture of two notable hunters, and they were both naught, Nimrod and Esau: but among the popish priests ye shall find few but he can keep a cur better than a cure, can find a hare, keep a kennel of hounds or a cast of hawks, better than many other; and because they will be cunning in their occupation and all kind of hunting, they hunt for pluralities of benefices *a tribus ad centum et tot quot*; yea, they can hunt whores (for they say, it is better to have a whore than a wife) so cunningly, that they may teach a school of it. Edom hunted for venison and good cheer: so can our belly gods, the popes, Sir John Smell-smoke, smell a feast in all parishes near him, sit at ale house, carding, dicing, bowling, drinking from morning to night, thinking he has served God well when he has mumbled his matins, some piece roasted over the fire, some sod over the pot, some chased over the fields, some chopped, some chowed; that if their God were not coming, he could never set them together. Other of the higher sort can sit drinking with their malvesey, marmalade, sucket, figs, raisins, and green

A comparison betwixt the Edomites and popes.

ginger, &c. and say they fast, punish their bodies, and go the right way to heaven: even as right as a ram's horn.

Esau, because he had lost authority over his brother, persecuted him so sharply, that he lived banished twenty years: so our Edomites (I had almost said, Sodomites) banish their brethren for ever, if they can; yea, curse them to hell, because they may do much there by their many friends, not leaving them any room in their purgatory, because they be lords of the soil, and none shall dwell there, except he take a lease and pay rent to them. Esau, because he would not obey but displeased his parents, married divers wives of the heathens round about him, contrary to God and example of all his good forefathers: so our papists, abhorring lawful marriage, follow carnal whores; and living in spiritual adultery, worship false gods, images, stocks and stones, the works of man's hands, and follow all men's traditions in all countries about, gadding from country to country a pilgrimage, to buy pardons, and rob Christ of his due honour.

But I must make an end of their ungodliness, which has no end; and let them which would see more of their doings, confer the life of Jacob and Esau together from the beginning to the end; and then they shall easily see how truly these antichrists do resemble their father Edom, that all things which is here prophesied may be well and truly applied to them. It shall be sufficient for me thus briefly at this time in these few things to have compared them together, and have opened the way and given an example for the ruder sort to follow, in comparing them further together, and setting out worthily their wickedness, if any tongue or pen could sufficiently do it.

What shall be the end and reward of such cruelty, pride, rejoicing, robbing, killing their brethren, the two last verses declare. The day of vengeance over all people that have so violently handled God's flock is at hand: God has borne long enough, he will not see his sheep any longer devoured: he has tarried sufficiently for their repentance, if they would have turned: he sees there is no hope of amendment; he will now be avenged of his enemies, and that most justly. For "even as thou, O Edom, hast done to him, it shall be done to thee;" and "what measure thou hast given other, the same shall be

Luke vi.

measured to thee again." Such punishment shall it be, that it shall extend even unto thy infants, which in all other destructions are wont to find favour, and thought to be innocent; yet now they shall be as extremely punished as the rest.

And as ye have drunk and made merry on my hill Sion and Moria, where the temple was builded and God worshipped, and ye laughed to see it destroyed, burned and cast down; so shall your enemies drink, laugh and make merry on your hills, where your strong holds were builded, when they shall throw them down, conquer your lands, and lead you captives and prisoners, make you slaves, rob your goods and treasures, laugh you to scorn, and work their pleasure on you and yours: they shall swallow you and yours up so clean, leaving nothing behind them, and devour all your goods, as though ye had never been dwelling there, and as though no such things had been. This is the just judgment of God, to do again the same things to his enemies that they did to his people, and reward like with like.

If he should shew sharper punishment, men would call him cruel: if less, many would judge that he could not, would not, or durst not. Therefore he renders even the same again, that both his enemies and his people may call him a righteous judge: for few will or justly can blame him that does but like for like. So says David: "Let the people rejoice, for thou judgest thy people righteously." Psal. lxvii. Adonibezec, a heathen, that chopped off the toes and fingers Judges i. of seventy kings which he conquered, was so served himself when he was taken; and then confessed he God to be righteous in doing to him as he had done to other. Absalon killed his brother with the sword violently, and perished with 2 Sam. xiii. the sword himself. Joab smote Abner unjustly, and David xviii. iii. ii. i. commanded him to be likewise handled. He that came bringing word to David that he had killed Saul, thinking thereby to have picked a thank and gotten a bribe of David, was commanded by David to be slain for laying his hand on the anointed of the Lord, contrary to his expectation.

Thus by these few and such other examples the righteous judgments of God and merciful dealing in his punishing appear, that although his enemies rage and fury in their

[PILKINGTON.]

doings and in their madness, care not what cruelty they shew; yet God, although he most justly might, according to their deserts, revenge with more sharpness, he will not but reward with like. Let all cruel papists and persecutors of God's people take heed therefore, what violence they shew: for although God seem to suffer for a time, yet he will come at his appointed time to deliver his, and reward them with the like measure that they have shewed to other. And of all causes and injuries God can suffer none worse unavenged, than that which is counted against Jerusalem, his temple, his religion, and where he is honoured: for that touches his own person. "His honour," he says himself, "he will give to no other:" he is a jealous God, and the first and chief commandment is, to worship him alone, to have no other Gods but him; for else he punishes to the third and fourth generation of them that hate him. Can any country or people be found from the beginning, which rebelled against God and his people, but God has thrown them down? Can then our antichrists, or any later, mocker of God or his people at this day, by what name soever they be called, look for any less than to receive the same measure that they have given other? Nay, nay; for surely the more examples that they have had to teach them, and they will not learn, the greater shall be their condemnation.

Among all injuries God will not suffer his religion specially to be defaced.
Isai. xlviii.
Exod. xx.

And let them not think that this day of vengeance is so far off, seeing that so many things cry on the Lord to hasten his coming. Every creature in heaven and earth, quick and dead, groans and travails, looking for our full deliverance. The souls under the altar cry, "How long, O Lord, is it that thou revengest not our blood?" And these be not few in number; for "from the blood of righteous Abel all innocent blood shall come on you." "The Spirit and the spouse cry, Come, and he that hears cries, Come." Mercy to help his oppressed, and justice to revenge, cry, "Come, Lord Jesus, quickly." Can God stop his ears from all these cryings? No, no: let them assure themselves, their days be at hand: they shall perish everlastingly, if they repent not, and God's people shall be delivered to his glory. "Come, Lord Jesus," let all cry, and he will come. The church of Christ is the spouse of Christ; and he is our husband, he

Rom. viii.
Rev. vi.
Matt. xxiii.
Rev. xxii.
The day of vengeance is not far off.

our head, and we his members and part of his mystical body: he our father, and we his children; he our God, and we his creatures; he our king, and we his subjects; he our Lord and master, and we his poor servants; Christ our brother, and we fellow heirs with him; he loves us better, and takes more thought for us, than we do for ourselves. Great is the love of the mother toward her children; yet greater is God's love toward us. Although "the mother can forget the child," says the prophet, "I will not forget thee:" yea, as the hen will fight for her chickens, so will our God for us against all our enemies. "How oft would I have gathered thee under my wings, as the hen her chickens!" says our Saviour Christ. Our bodies are the temple wherein he dwells; yea, we are the lively stones, whereof his house is built: we be of his household, citizens, burgesses, and freemen in heaven; his familiar friends, whom he loved so dearly, that his Son should die that we might live. And that we should not doubt of his good will, but that he has given us all his treasure, he says, "He that spared not his own Son, but gave him for us all, how can it be but he has given all things with him, &c.?" *Isai. xlix. Matt. xxiii. 1 Cor. iii. 1 Pet. ii. Eph. ii. Rom. viii.*

Let no man therefore doubt of God's good will towards us, seeing God himself has declared so many ways his exceeding great love towards us by so many similitudes: and let no papist rejoice nor triumph against God's people, as though God cared not for them, had cast them away, or would not deliver them. For he will come in deed, and not be slow. Peter says, "The Lord is not slow in coming, as some think, but patiently tarries for us, &c." Can any husband see his wife take wrong? or any man hate or neglect his own flesh? Can the father deny his child any thing he asks; or "if he ask bread, will he give him a stone?" Is any more ready to help his people than God? Will not a king defend his subjects, the master his servant, or lord his tenant? Will not brotherly love move him that is love itself, as St John says, to have pity on us? He has bought us too dear to see us cast away. Will he do less for us than the hen for her chickens, or the brute beast for her young ones? No man will see his house pulled down over his head, but he will restore it. A good burghmaster and *2 Pet. iii. Matt. vii.*

ruler of a city will provide necessaries for his, that he has rule over. Therefore, seeing our God has taken all these names and offices on him, doubt not but he will do his part for us, if we do not run from him. He sets not deputies to do his office, nor is not weary of well doing: he bears not the name of these offices, and refuses the labour, as men do; but he says by Salomon, "My delight is to be with the children of men;" and by David, "He neither slumbers nor sleeps, that watches Israel."

<small>Prov. viii.
Psal. cxxi.</small>

<small>The Text.</small> v. 17. *But in the hill Sion shall be escaping, and there shall be holiness; and the house of Jacob shall possess the inheritance of them which possessed his.*

18. *And the house of Jacob shall be fire, and the house of Joseph the flame, and the house of Esau for stubble, and shall burn them, and shall devour them, and there shall be no remnant of the house of Esau: for the Lord has spoken it.*

19. *They shall possess the south part of the hill Esau, and the plain country of the Philistines, and they shall possess the country of Ephraim and the country of Samaria: Benjamin shall possess Galaad.*

20. *And the captivity of this host of the children of Israel, those which be the Canaanites unto Zarphat; and the captivity of Jerusalem, which be in Sepharad, shall possess the cities of the south.*

21. *And there shall come saviours into the hill Sion, to judge the hill Esau; and the kingdom shall be the Lord's.*

Mark here the diverse end of the good and bad, the persecuted and the persecutor, the true Christian and the hypocrite, the gospeller and the papist. The wicked flourishes for a time, but his end is everlasting damnation: the man of God, looking for another kingdom than on the earth, is content to bear the cross here, under hope of that which is to come. The stock of Esau has hitherto triumphed against Jacob, God's people; but now, when his wickedness is ripe, the Lord rewards[1] him according to his deserts. The hill Esau afore rejoiced in his strong holds, wealthy country,

[1 Old edition, *rewarde*. ED.]

and the leagues made with all neighbours round about them: but now in the hill Sion shall be safe escaping, when Edom shall have no place to flee unto. In Sion, that is Jerusalem, and God's elect beloved people, shall be holiness, the true worshipping of God, the holy sanctuary and temple where God's holy name shall be called upon: whereas Esau in the mean time is defiled with idolatry, and given up to the hands of the gentiles. Yea, and furthermore Jacob shall possess the land of them that possessed his.

And although God have promised to godliness, not only in the world to come, but in this life also, great blessings, as appears by Job, Abraham, Isaac, Jacob, David, Josias, Ezechias, Josaphat, which were of great riches; yet this place do I not think to be so understand, that Jacob should ever possess the lands of Esau, although the scripture says that David and Jacob overcame the Edomites. But I think rather under this outward kingdom to be prophesied, that the kingdom of Christ, as the prophets use by worldly prosperity to declare the spiritual felicity, by the preaching of the gospel should be enlarged in those countries, which were now enemies to God and his people; and so the spiritual seed of Jacob, the Christians, should by preaching conquer[2] and possess Esau his land and the gentiles, which so sore hated and persecuted them afore. This is the nature of God's people, to be good to them which hate them, and to win them all to God, which have done them most displeasures: and this is the nature of God, to call them which be his utter enemies, and soften their stony hearts to make them meet houses for the Holy Ghost to dwell in; and in the midst of their raging persecution to smite them down, as he did Saul, raise them up and make them Pauls, of wolves sheep, and of haters lovers of the truth. Thus shall Esau be destroyed, when his idolatry, superstition, false gods, and such wickedness shall be taken away: and Jacob shall possess him, when he shall turn him to the true worshipping of the living God, forsaking their idols and superstitions, and follow true religion. What can be counted a greater conquest than to conquer the devil, and make all people subject to Christ?

After rebuking their sin, and threatening them just punish-

[² Old edition, *confer*. ED.]

ment for the same, now follows comfort; as ever after the law preached follows the gospel, and after correction comes grace and pardon. Sion is the church and congregation of Christ and faithful men believing in him; so that whosoever flees thither shall be safe, and whosoever is not under his wings and in the number of christian people, shall perish in the day of his wrath: as all living creatures, which were not in the ark with Noe, did perish with the waters, so all that be not of God's household shall be cast into outward darkness. This other promise, that God makes here unto the faithful seed of Jacob, that has his faith, is most notable and comfortable: "In the hill Sion, the church of Christ, there shall be the Holy One," as the Seventy read; or "holiness," as other; or "the sanctuary," as some, and holy place to worship God in purely. It skills not much which we read; for the sense is all one, and the meaning is, that the church and faithful people of Christ shall not want the true religion and knowledge of God. For the church of Christ is the spouse of Christ and his mystical body: and if mortal men love their wives and bodies so dearly, that they will not forsake them or leave them comfortless, much less will Christ our Saviour not forsake us after that he has redeemed us, seeing he bought us and love us so dearly, being his enemies. This is then the greatest token of God's love to his people, when he gives them his true religion, and therefore most earnestly to be embraced of us. And this is the blessing taken from Esau and given to Jacob.

If we read "the holy one," he is Christ, which promised to be with us to the end of the world: he " is made to us of God our Father righteousness, holiness, wisdom and redemption;" because that whosoever is holy receives it of him, and none is holy that has it not of him, though he have bulls, calves, pardons, relics, holy water, holy ashes, holy palms, holy cross, yea, and all the holiness that is in Rome, if he have not the Spirit of Christ. I am sure, they will not say they sell the Holy Ghost when they sell pardons, for that were simony: therefore they buy no holiness in them. If we read "holiness," then it is an upright life, true faith with pure worshipping of God. "This is the will of God," says St Paul, "your holiness." As they have but one God, so they will worship him only, and as he has taught them, and not after the device of man: they will also study for a holy life, as God commands, "Be ye holy, for I am holy." And if we read "holy place," or sanctuary to worship God in, it is Levit. xix. true also: for in all persecutions, and in the spite of the pope and all antichrists, there has been in all ages and shall be (for God so saying can not lie) true professors of God, although the most part of the world was blinded. So Christ comforts his, saying, "Fear not, thou little flock." Luke xii.

Thus in Christ's church, in spite of their foes, shall ever be Christ the head, knit to the body necessarily; and as he is holy, so shall he make them holy that hang upon him, and so govern them by his Spirit, that they shall ever follow a holy kind of life, fleeing mischief and uncleanness; and so shall they have also his sanctuary and holy place where to resort In all persecutions God to worship their God, hear his word, and call upon him. defends his, Abraham, Isaac, Jacob, David, in their wanderings, called and provides a place for them to upon their God, taught their children to fear the Lord, made worship him in. their sacrifices; and God revealed himself to them again, and never forsaked them. In the captivity of Babylon, though not in the temple, yet they could by the water-banks sing Ps. cxxxvii. psalms on their instruments. When Christ was crucified, the disciples kept them together in a chamber, praying and Acts i. ii. looking for the coming of the Holy Ghost. After, when persecution began, some went to other countries, some from house to house, teaching, praying, communicating and dealing to the poor. Paul says at Philippos, "By the water Acts xvi. side they were wont to pray:" and in the midst blindness of all popery has there ever been some good men teaching true doctrine, and opening their blasphemies: for this cannot be false, that Christ promised his church. "When the John xiv. x. Spirit, which is the Comforter, shall come, he shall lead you into all truth." "I will be with you unto the end of the Matt. xxviii. world." "He that is of God heareth the words of God; and you hear not, for because ye are not of God." "And my sheep hear my voice; a stranger they do not follow."

Therefore let all that be under the cross and persecution, see they assemble together to praise God, and openly confess him, if it be possible, or at the least as much as they may, following the example of the faithful Christians in the beginning, which in spite of their foes could not be holden from assembling together with prayers and songs, afore the day was light. Nor let any papist rejoice against God's scattered and persecuted flock; for this is the state and condition of God's people, and preaching the gospel, that they shall not want a cross: and yet God will perform this promise, that "in Sion the Holy One, Christ, will be" with them, to govern them in holiness of life, pureness of religion, and an earnest faith, trusting in God, and will give them a place to call upon him in, that his might, mercy and grace to his people may appear to the world in the sight of his enemies. When Abraham and Jacob fled into Egypt, the Egyptians learned God, which afore never heard of him. In the captivity of Babylon the Chaldees, Assyrians, Babylonians, Medes and Persians, with all other people among whom the Jews were scattered, learned God of them. When persecution began in Jerusalem after Christ's ascension, the disciples scattered by persecution went and preached Christ to the heathen, which afore heard not of him. In England, after Wickliffe's death, when persecution arose, some died for the truth constantly; some fled into Bohemia and brought the gospel thither, where it continues to this day, although both emperor and pope with all their might, many sharp battles and blood shedding, would have rooted it out. What great assault the poor Waldenses have suffered at divers French kings' hands, going about to have destroyed them for their religion, being a few in number, and yet could never deface them this three hundred and sixty years, it is piteous to hear.

Persecution spreads the gospel abroad.

Thus is this ever true, that in Sion, the true church of Christ, shall be the "Holy One," Christ, sanctifying all that believe in him: there shall be "holiness" in faith, religion and manners, to the praise of God: there shall be also "a sanctuary and holy place" with assemblies, in spite of their foes; and persecution does not hurt, but rather increase and further true religion, though not in the greater, yet in the better part of men. For whosoever the Holy Ghost does inflame with an earnest zeal to his religion, they can not keep it within them; they can not abide to see their God and his word blasphemed; they will brast[1] out and declare their faith, and say, "The

Psal. lxix.

[[1] *Brast, brust*, and *burst* are used indiscriminately in this author. ED.]

earnest love towards thy house has eaten me," as our Saviour John ii. Christ did: when he see the temple, his Father's house, so misused, and his religion contemned, he gat whips and drove them out. Jeremy says, "the word of God was to him as Jer. xx. a burning fire in his heart, and closed within his bones, that he was not able to keep it" within him, but would brust[1] out.

This victory is set out more at large in the next verse following, where he says, "The house of Jacob shall be fire, the house of Joseph the flame, and the house of Esau the stubble, &c." Here is no description of horse, harness, guns, any great host, or such other worldly things, wherein princes do conquer and triumph. As the house of Jacob is spiritual, and the kingdom of Christ, so be the weapons, soldiers, and victory. The swords, wherewith they fought, were, as the apostle says, "the word of God, which is sharper than any Heb. iv. two-edged sword," and pierces more the soul, conquers the affections, and pulls down high stomachs, deeper than the sword can the body.

The guns were the apostles' words, as James and John Mark iii. were called "the sons of thunder," because with such great power they thundered terribly, preached and feared carnal minds more than the thunder does, and threw down sin more than any guns could the walls. When Peter at two sermons Acts iv. xv. converted five thousand, and Paul filled all countries from Jerusalem to Illyricum with the gospel, what emperor is able to be compared of such men of war? When Charles the Fifth, emperor, began to reign, Luther and Zuinglius began the same time to preach: and whether he has thrown down, stopped and hindered the gospel more with all the help that his ghostly and superstitious prelates could give, than they with their scholars have set it forth, and shewed the wickedness of popery and defaced his pomp, let themselves judge. The pope with his partakers have had strength, power, polity, wit, wisdom, armour, guns, horses, harness, men, and money, and whatsoever they could devise: these other have foughten with preaching, writing, and giving themselves to the fire for the truth. Their weapons were their tongues, pen, ink and paper, never shedding blood but their own, and ever seeking how to save other men's souls, sparing no labour, nor fearing any

Preaching conquers more [than] fighting.

displeasure. So mighty weapons is "the undefiled law of the Lord," turning souls and hearers, that "neither life nor death, angels nor powers, things present nor to come can pull them from the love of our God, offered in Christ Jesus."

This fire, that he speaks of here, is the might of the Holy Ghost, which came on the apostles in fiery tongues, and so kindles the hearts of all that receive the word, that it burn up all carnal affections and worldly lusts, so that for the glory of God they care not what they suffer. David prays oft for this fire: "Burn my reins and heart." And John in his Revelation says, that these which be "neither hot nor cold, God will spue them out of his mouth." It is therefore a good fire that burns up the stubble, which is false doctrine, superstition and all evils, as St Paul calls it, "If any man build hay, wood, stubble, it shall perish, &c." The house of Jacob and Joseph shall be the preachers; and Esau shall be thus happily burned up from his former filthy life, and turned to the Lord. The house of Joseph contains two tribes, Ephraim and Manasses, which were the children of Joseph, but chosen and taken of Jacob to be as his own sons, when he blessed them all, lying on his death bed, and made them equal inheritors with his own children of the land promised. And because Jeroboam, which first set up the golden calves in Dan and Bethel, (and so provoked all Israel to sin and idolatry, in which they continued so many years,) was of the house of Joseph and stock of Ephraim, lest they should think themselves to be cast away of God, and their sins could not be forgiven, he says, they shall be so hot followers and setters forth of Christ, that they shall be like the flame, and shall turn Esau and the gentiles, heathen and wicked men, to the knowledge and worshipping of the true God. Such a merciful and loving God is our Christ, that even those that have been most traitors and enemies to him, he will call them to most high honour. Peter and all the rest of the apostles denied our Saviour Christ, when he was taken of the Jews, and ran away from him: but he forsaked not them, nor cast not them out of their apostleship; but sent them into all the world to preach the word of life, grace and salvation, and gave them more fulness of the Holy Ghost than they had afore. And because it is uncertain in the scripture, whether any of the apostles were of the tribe of Ephraim; yet in the latter end, and when all sort of Jews shall be converted to the Lord, and so "all Israel shall be saved," if this be not yet performed in them or but partly performed, it shall be afore the last day more fully. Rom. xi.

"Thy word is fierce," says David; and therefore it is no marvel, if it burn them up, that hear and receive it. The word of God is not like other histories or learning, which do not move, or else but little stir the hearers: but such grace and strength is given by it to the ministers and hearers of the same, that either it turns them that hears it to a godly zeal and love toward his glory and an upright life, or else it casts them into the burning fire of hell; as the apostle says, "He makes his angels spirits, or wind, and his ministers a flaming fire:" and again, "The preaching of Christ's cross is foolishness to them that perish; but to them that be saved it is the power of God." In the disputations against the Arians, where all the learned men could not confute Arius, a man unlearned stood up, making a simple confession of his faith openly; and where, as long as they thought to overcome him by disputing and by reasons, he ever had to answer them withal, when this simple plain man, trusting not to eloquence nor learning, but in the might of God's Spirit, and only seeking the glory of God, began to speak, he see such grace in his words and power joined withal, that he was not able to withstand it. Arius granted his own[1] error, and the other to say true[2]. So St Paul, writing against false prophets, says, his "preaching was not in eloquent words of man's wisdom, but in power of the Spirit;" and although he was not eloquent in words, "yet not ignorant in knowledge." Thus shall hypocrites, antichrists, and unbelievers be overcome by the might of God's word and the Holy Ghost working withal, and not by any worldly wit, strength or polity; as the apostles' preaching took place and turned the whole world to receive their doctrine after the same sort. Psal. cxix. Heb. i. 1 Cor. i. Ruffinus. Lib. i. cap. iii. 1 Cor. ii. 2 Cor. xi.

[1 Old edition, *one*. ED.]

[2 Auctores Ecclesiasticæ Historiæ, Lib. x. (Ruffini I.) cap. iii. p. 219. Ed. Basil. 1535, where the story is told not of Arius, but of "quidam insignis in arte dialectica," and the conclusion is thus stated: Ita obstupefactus virtute dictorum, mutus ad omnia, hoc solum potuit respondere, Ita sibi videri, nec aliud verum esse quam quod dixerat. ED.]

But where he says, "there shall be no remnant of Esau left," that shall be fulfilled in the latter day, where the wicked shall be cast into unquenchable fire: for in the mean time the good and bad shall be blend together, so that wicked hypocrites, idolaters, shall be consumed both in this world and after, but in the fulness of time, when God has appointed, and not when we think; for they shall prevail a time, as this wicked seed of Esau did, for the trial of the good, and exercise of their faith, that all men may know that the godly love the Lord unfeignedly. Thus the house is put for them that be of the house of Jacob and Joseph; and not so much for the carnal seed, as for them that have and follow the faith of Jacob and Joseph, which be only they that be ordained to life.

And because they should not doubt of the performance of the thing, he adds, "The Lord has said it." As though he should say, This is no man's tale, but the living Lord God, that made both heaven and earth, and have all things at his commandment, which is truth itself and cannot lie, which is both able and will perform it, has said these words; therefore they must needs come to pass. "All men be liars," but God only cannot be deceived nor deceive; and whatsoever he has said, that he will perform. Can ye find anything that he said he would do, since the world was made, but he has done it? Believe him therefore in this thing too; for he will do it in deed.

The next verses, which contain so many people by name, I think do not signify these people only to be counted (for that is to "possess" them) to the faith; but all gentiles and people should receive the word, and these be put by name, specially because they were the next countries about them, and always their open enemies. For if these, which were ever most bitter enemies, should be converted by them; much more other countries, that were not so earnest haters of them,

<small>Canaanites.</small> should rather be turned to them. The Canaanites be called
<small>Zarphat.</small> of some men the Germans: Zarphat is thought to be France,
<small>Sepharad.</small> and Sepharad Spain, by the Rabbins: so that even the utmost parts of the world shall follow them. For into these parts it is written of some that the apostles came, or at least
<small>Psal. xix.</small> their doctrine; as David says, "Their sound went out into

the whole earth:" but whether they or their scholars came to teach the gospel, it skills not: the thing is proved plain, that these countries once received the word and faith of Christ, howsoever they be now drowned in popery, or fallen to heathen idolatry, which shall be rooted out at length too, notwithstanding their maliciousness now. Have not all the wicked tyrants and idolaters, which reigned once in all these countries, been driven out by the light of God's word? Their cruelness could not stop the faith of the Christians, neither with fire, sword, nor any cruel death they could imagine: yea, the more cruel they were in persecuting, the more earnest were they in professing; and the more they put to death, the more increased, as Augustine says[1], "Christian men were bounden, cast in prison, beaten, racked, burned, cut in pieces as butchers cut their flesh, killed; and yet notwithstanding all this they multiplied and increased." *Civitat. Dei, Lib. xxii. cap. vi.*

The last verse promises saviours to come and judge, and the kingdom to be the Lord's. This is notable to consider in the kingdom of Christ, that which is contrary to earthly kingdoms. Worldly princes, when they go to conquer a country, they go with fire and sword to destroy all that withstand them: but in Christ's kingdom there come saviours to preach salvation to rebels, his enemies and haters, if they will repent. Earthly princes come with guns, horse and harness: Christ's disciples come to conquer the devil and his members without bag, staff, or money. Mortal princes come with might and power of men: the preachers of Christ's kingdom come in the might of God's Spirit, which opens the eyes of the blind, and softens stony hearts, and turns them to the Lord. Worldly princes do much by flattery, bribery, or threatening to win the people: but Christ's ministers come in meekness of spirit, praying and beseeching, seeking not their own vantage, but the turning of the poor stray sheep, that they may bring them home to the fold again. Earthly princes fight for an earthly kingdom: but the preachers of Christ's gospel teach the way to heaven, peace of conscience, the love and favour of God, purchased by the death of Christ Jesus. So in all points, as heaven and earth are contrary, so are the kingdoms, the ministers *The diversity of Christ's kingdom and earthly.*

[¹ See the passage cited before, p. 144. ED.]

and subjects of them both, the way to conquer and compass them both, the means to enjoy them both, and the pleasures in them both when we have gotten them. Yet, notwithstanding all things in them be so contrary, and worldly men by all ways possible go about to stop and hinder the getting of the other heavenly kingdom, to withdraw men from it, and envy the glory and increase of it; yet "the kingdom shall be the Lord's" in spite of all his foes, and their malicious enterprises shall come to nought.

<small>Saviours.
Judges.</small> They be called *saviours*, because they teach the word of salvation; and *judges*, because they will be righteous, and neither for gifts, bribery, nor partiality deliver the wicked, and condemn the innocent, but uprightly according to the scripture preach salvation to the penitent, and condemnation to the hard hearted. Their judging shall not be in worldly matters, no more than their preaching and saving: but as their ministery is spiritual, so shall their commission, judgment, and deliverance be. In Esau is meant hypocrites, persecutors, false teachers and all evil doers. St Paul says <small>1 Tim. iv.</small> to Timothy, that "in doing these things," which he taught him, "he should save himself and these that heard him." <small>James i.
Rom. i.</small> St James called the gospel the word that "can save their souls;" and to the Romans it is called "the power of God unto salvation of every one that believes," because the mighty power of God, how he saves us, is declared in it. But Christ is only the Saviour, properly speaking; and other be <small>Acts iv.</small> but ministers and teachers of the same: for "there is no other name," as St Luke says, "under heaven, in which we must be saved." Thus in the church of Christ, Sion, shall be ever salvation preached, judgment ministered, and sin punished.

Woe then be to them that flatter, lay pillows under their elbows, teach false doctrine, &c. and yet will have the rooms and names of preachers in the house and church of Christ! They be wolves, hirelings, and devourers of the flock of <small>John ix.</small> Christ. Christ says, he came to the judgment of the world, to condemn the works of the world; and so for the same use he gives his Spirit still to his ministers, to set up his kingdom, and condemn the works of the world, antichrist and his enemies. A kingdom cannot stand without ministering of justice, punishing sin, and maintaining the truth, delivering the innocent repenter, and condemning obstinates. So the ministers of Christ's kingdom have power spiritual to loose and bind, as they see the scriptures teach them, "Receive ye the Holy Ghost: whose sins you forgive, they are forgiven;" but not whensoever Sir John Lacklatin will for money lay his hand on his head, whisper *Absolutione et remissione*, &c. in Latin, that neither he nor the other weak conscience understands, it is not, I say, by and bye forgiven; but unto them it is said, "I will curse your blessings," and I will bless your cursings. If the absolution be not given to the penitent heart, oppressed with the burden of sin, and seeking comfort in Christ, it is no more profitable than baptism or the communion is to a hypocrite or unpenitent sinner. Yea rather, it is to the condemnation both of the giver and receiver, if it be ungodly done, because they misuse the good ministry of God. Therefore they that in absolving judge not, according to the commission of God's word committed unto them, be not saviours of the people, but deceivers. {John xx.} {Mal. ii.}

And where he says, "the kingdom shall be the Lord's," he condemns all that teach any doctrine in the church, to set up any other king or kingdom, but the word of God, which be his laws, given to his people, that they may live according thereto, knowing them to be his subjects, and him their king; that so his kingdom may increase and be ruled by his laws, as earthly princes rule by their laws. Therefore the pope, teaching his decrees, setting up himself and his kingdom, as though he were lord of heaven and earth, purgatory and hell, and bringing the people to his obedience, as the chief ruler, is traitor to God and deceives the people. And to St Peter, whose vicar he says he is, he must needs be proved most unlike, and a traitor to Christ for drawing men from him, and willing them to buy his pardon and forgiveness of sins at his hands, as though he were set to gather up Christ's tolling money; when St Peter teaches, "Ye be not redeemed from your vain and false superstition with gold either with silver, &c." If we be not redeemed with money, then the pope lies, saying our sins be forgiven, if we buy pardons to forgive sin. St Peter says, money does not for- {The Pope is most unlike St Peter.} {1 Pet. i.}

give sins, but the blood of Christ Jesus: the pope says, Yes, or at least he will not do it without money. St Peter had his own wife; the pope will none, nor let his clergy, but whores as many ye will. St Peter said, he had neither gold nor silver; the pope will do nothing without gold or silver, as it is said, *Quicquid Roma dabit, nugas dabit, accipit aurum:* "Whatsoever it be that Rome will give, trifles it will give, but gold it doth receive." St Peter was subject himself unto Nero, a wicked infidel tyrant, and teaches other to be so in civil matters; but the pope will rule all christian princes by rigour, depose them at his pleasure, and obey none, but his own lusts. Therefore it is plain to see, what is to be thought of his kingdom, and of such men as will rule with rigour over the flock of Christ, and will not feed God's sheep with his word, that the Lord may rule in his own kingdom by his own law and word, and his sheep hear the voice of their own true Shepherd, and flee from strangers, hirelings and wolves. It is not meet that God should be king, and the pope to make laws for him to rule by; but God rules by his own laws.

"Pray therefore the Lord of the harvest, that he will thrust out workmen into his harvest," that they may work truly for the setting up of his kingdom, and pulling down the pope's; and that we may grow to good corn, to be laid up in the Lord's barns, and be not light chaff, blown away with every puff of doctrine; but grounded upon the rock Christ Jesus, may surely stand against all storms; that we be not cast into outward darkness and everlasting fire, but may enjoy that unspeakable joy that he has prepared for them that love him and look for him. Amen.

A PRAYER.

Most righteous Judge, God of all mercy and comfort, which by thy secret judgment and wisdom suffers the wicked to triumph and increase for a time, for trial of the faith of thy well beloved little flock, and the mortifying of their lusts, but at length to the utter confusion of the enemies, and joyful deliverance of thy people: look down, we beseech thee, on thy dispersed sheep out of thy holy habitation in heaven, and strengthen our weakness against their furious rages; abate their pride, assuage their malice, confound their devices, wherewith they lift up themselves against Christ Jesus thy Son, our Lord and Saviour, to deface his glory and set up antichrist. We be not able of ourselves to think a good thought, much less to stand against their assaults, except thy undeserved grace and mighty arm defend and deliver us.

Perform thy promises made to Jacob, and stop the mouths of the cursed Edomites: call them to repentance whom thou hast appointed to salvation: bring home them that run astray, lighten the blind, and teach the ignorant: forgive all those that wilfully and obstinately rebel not against thy holy will; let thy fearful threatenings parse[1] our stony hearts, and make us tremble at thy judgments. Make the examples of them, whom thou hast overthrown in their own devices, to be a warning for us, that we set not up ourselves against thy holy will. Grant free passage to thy holy word, that it may work effectually in us the blessed hope of our salvation, to the eternal praise of thy majesty, through our Mediator Christ Jesus, to whom with the Father and the Holy Ghost, three Persons and one God, be praise and thanksgiving in all congregations, world without end. So be it.

Jaco. P. Ep. D[2].

[1 Parse: pierce. Ed.]
[2 Jacobus Pilkington, Episcopus Dunelmensis. Ed.]

Anno,   1562.

¶ Cum priuilegio ad Imprimendum solum.

EXPOSITION

UPON CERTAIN CHAPTERS OF

NEHEMIAH.

TO WHICH IS ADDED

DR ROBERT SOME'S

TREATISE OF OPPRESSION,

AS INSERTED BY THE ORIGINAL EDITOR.

A GODLIE EXPOSITION

VPON CERTEINE CHAP-
ters of *Nehemiah*, written by that worthy
Byshop and faithfull Pastor of the Church
of Durham Master IAMES
PILKINTON.
(*)

AND NOW NEWLIE PVBLISHED.

In the latter end, because the Author could not finish that treatise of Oppression which he had begonne, there is added that for a supplie, which of late was published by ROBERT SOME D. In Diuinitie.

Psal. 127. 1. Except the Lord build the house, they labour in vaine that build it: except the Lord keepe the citie, the keeper watcheth in vaine.

Psal. 122. 6. Praie for the peace of Ierusalem: let them prosper that loue thee.

Psal. 80. 14. 15. Returne, we beseech thee, O God of hostes: looke downe from heauen, and behold and visit this vine, And the vineyeard, that thy right hand hath planted, and the young vine, which thou madest strong for thy selfe.

A PREFACE

OF

M. JOHN FOX,

TO THE CHRISTIAN READER.

As it is greatly to be rejoiced, and the Lord highly to be praised, for the happy enterprise of the godly work of Nehemiah, begun by the reverend and vigilant pastor of Christ his church of famous memory, M. James Pilkington, Bishop of Duresme; so again it were to be wished that, if the Lord had thought it so good, his days might have continued to the full perfiting of the same, which now is left unperfect, only containing five chapters by him expounded. For the setting out whereof, being requested hereunto, I thought to add these few lines in recommending the same to the godly reader, trusting no less than that whosoever will take pains in reading thereof, the same shall find his labour therein not altogether lost. And that for divers causes. First, for the better explaining of the chapters whereof he entreateth. Secondly, for the opening of ancient histories intermixed withal, much needful to be known. Thirdly, for the opportunity of the time well serving for the purpose present. For as Nehemiah then by God's providence was set up for the re-edifying of the material temple of Jerusalem, destroyed by the Babylonians; so in like sort the spiritual church of Christ, in this spiritual Babylonical captivity, being in long time in ruin and decay, standeth in great need of godly helpers and good workmen; as, blessed be the Lord! some we have seen, and do see, right zealously occupied to the shedding of their blood in repairing Christ his temple.

Yet notwithstanding, the matter being of so great importance, and the time so dangerous, it shall not be amiss in these our days to be taught by the time before us.

First, that the outward temple in Hierusalem, destroyed by the Babylonians, did lie waste for many years, it cannot be denied. Which being granted, it must needs follow, that either the said material temple doth bear no representation of the spiritual church of Christ (which cannot be denied,) or else that the same church of Christ must necessarily suffer some captivity and apostasy for a time by certain spiritual Babylonians in latter times: which being so, then must it likewise follow consequently, that as that former temple of God in Hierusalem, after long captivity, at length was restored again by the mighty hand of God; so the like is to be accomplished in Christ his church, after long wrack and decay to be repaired again, as we see now come to pass. For what oppression, what tyranny, what darkness hath overwhelmed the poor church of Christ these many years by the Romish Assyrians, who is so blind that seeth not? Wherefore much deceived be these our pope-holy pretensed catholics; who, dreaming in their fantasies no other true church to be in earth but only their holy church of Rome, falsely so persuade themselves, because the outward state of their Romish church so gloriously and richly shineth in the world, and therefore the true church of Christ is at no time to be blemished with ignorance and darkness, but continually flourish without spot or wrinkle in the eyes of men, never to suffer any wrack or decay, but perpetually to be preserved from all ruin or distress. By which ruin if they mean the perpetual or final desolation of the true church of Christ, true it is that the same shall never finally be forsaken nor overthrown; but for a time the same to suffer violence and oppression by enemies, it cannot be denied. For antichrist, by the secret permission of God, must have his own course, and reign here in the church for a time; in which time, by the assured testimony of St Paul's epistle, there must come a defection and apostasy: whereby is signified, no doubt, a spiritual and, as it were, a general departing from the right faith of the gospel for a time and space, till it shall please the Lord again to give his book to the mouth of his prophets, and to send down by his angel his measuring-reed, to measure the wasted temple of the Lord for the re-edifying again, as we read Revela. x. xi.

Howsoever, antichrist in the mean space doth flourish in this world, sitting in the temple of God, boasting himself as God, and drawing the faith of the people from God to himself. Certainly with the true church of Christ it standeth much otherwise, which must be brought down by antichrist, not to final destruction, but for a time to be oppressed till it shall please God again to repair it, as we by experience have good proof to declare. Wherefore let no man marvel at the decayed state of Christ his church, which hath been so long time continued; nor think the worse of the gospel now preached, as though it were a new faith or a new religion lately erected. If this gospel now preached were not taught by Christ himself, by Paul and other apostles, let it be counted for new. If the pope's doctrine be not agreeing to the same, then let every man judge which is new and which is old. Briefly, let us take example of the ancient tabernacle or house of God, first set up by Moses, afterward more magnificently framed to the like proportion in timber and stone by Salomon, which house or tabernacle the Lord promised to stand for ever: yet notwithstanding the same temple of God (exemplifying no doubt the spiritual church of Christ here in earth) was utterly overthrown by the Babylonians for a certain space, and afterward repaired again by God's people with much difficulty and hardness of times; and after that the same again miserably despoiled and destroyed by wicked Antiochus. In like manner the spiritual church of Christ, although it have the true promise of Christ to endure for ever, as it doth and ever shall do, yet lacketh not her Babylonians, her Antiochus, her overthrowers and temporal oppressors; yet not so oppressed, but at length by labourers and artificers of God is to be repaired again, albeit sent in great sharpness of time: we see it now come to pass.

Which being so, let us therefore, comparing time with time, look well to the matter every man what he hath to do. Such as be builders may take example of those good builders there, of whom we read, that with one hand they builded and with the other they held their weapon, that is, the spiritual sword of God's word to keep off the enemy. Such workmen the Lord send into his vineyard to be diligent labourers, not loiterers; not brawlers, but builders, labouring and working, not with one hand, but with both hands occupied. And likewise upon these labourers the Lord send good overseers, such as this good Nehemiah; who, not regarding his own private charges and expences, bestowed all his care in tendering and setting forward the erection of the Lord's house, to encourage the workmen, to provide for their necessities, to defend them from enemies, to keep them in good order from strife and variance. For as every good building there best goeth forward, when the workmen in one consent join themselves together; so contrariwise, nothing more hindereth the setting up of any work, as when the workmen are divided among themselves. Albeit during the time of Nehemiah we find no great stirs among the people; or if there were any, it was soon composed by the wise handling of that good governor, as in the fifth chapter may appear. Wherefore for the better example to be taken of those distressed days, I thought it not amiss, in this so dangerous building up of Christ's church in the perilous latter times, this treatise of Nehemiah, compiled by the right reverend and famous prelate, M. James Pilkington, of blessed memory, to be published and commended to Christian readers; whereby all good labourers and overseers of Christ his church may receive some fruitful advertisement to consider in these so great affairs of the Lord his business, what is to be done and looked unto.

THE BOOK OF NEHEMIAH.

Benigne fac, Domine, *in bona voluntate tua Sion, ut ædificentur muri Jerusalem.*

Non nobis, Domine, non nobis, sed nomini tuo da gloriam.

Non moriar, sed vivam et narrabo opera Domini.

THE ARGUMENT UNPERFECT, AND SO MUCH THEREOF AS WAS FOUND IS HERE PUT DOWN.

AND because both the books of Ezra and Nehemiah entreat only of such things as were done under the kings of Persia, which few other parts of the scripture do; it is not amiss something to touch the manner of living and behaviour both of the kings, people, and nature of the country, that thereby things may better be understood; as Strabo in his book, Leovicius in his *Varia Historia*, and others have left them in writing.

Susia was that part of the country which lay towards Babylon, wherein was also the chief city Susa, which was like in building unto Babylon. These were a quiet people, never rebellious, and therefore kings loved it the better; and Cyrus was the first that made his chiefest abode there. Other houses the king had, which were strong and costly, and where their treasure was kept. At Susis they lay in winter, at Ecbatana in summer, at Persepolis in harvest, in the spring at Babylon: Pagasabia, Gabis, and other houses were not neglected, although destroyed with the kingdom shortly after by Alexander Magnus. The riches of the kings were great; for when all was brought to Ecbatana, men report that there were 180 talents. This country of Susia was so fruitful, that their barley and wheat would bring forth an hundredfold or two hundred as much as was sown.

Their kings be of one kindred; and whosoever obeyeth not, he hath his head and arm cut off and cast away. They marry many wives and keep many harlots. The kings yearly give rewards to them that have gotten most sons. The children come not in their father's sight before they be four years old. Their marriages are made in March. From five years old unto fourteen they learn to shoot, pick darts, ride, and chiefly to speak truth. Their schoolmasters be men most sober, applying all things to the profit of their scholars. They call their scholars together afore day by ringing of a bell, as though they should go to war or to hunt. They make one of the king's sons their ruler, or some great men over fifty in a band; and command them to follow their captain thirty or forty furlongs, when he runneth afore them. They ask account of those things that they have learned, exercising their voice, breath, and sides to heat, cold, rain, and passing of rivers. They teach them to keep their armour and clothes dry, and to feed and live hardly like husbandmen, eating wild fruits, as acorns and crabs. Their daily meat after their exercise is very hard bread, cardanum, salt, and flesh roasted. Their drink is water. They hunt on horseback with picking their darts, shooting their shafts, or casting with their sling. In the forenoon they are exercised with planting of trees or digging up the roots, or make harness, or apply themselves to working of line, or making of nets. The kings give rewards to those that get the best game at running and other games, which they use every five year. They bear office and play the soldiers on foot and horse, from twenty years old unto fifty. They be armed with a shield made like a diamond. Besides their quiver they have their crooked faulchion and daggers; upon their head a steeple cap, upon their breast a coat of plate. Their princes have their breeches triple-fold, and a coat with wide sleeves lined with white inside[1] to the knee, and the

[1] The old edition reads, *and syde to the knee*. But the passage in Strabo, which is here translated, is: χιτὼν δὲ χειριδωτὸς διπλοῦς ἕως

outside coloured. Their apparel in summer[2] is purple, or else of divers colours; in winter of divers colours. Their caps like unto the mitres of their soothsayers; their shoes high and double. The common sort wear a lined coat to the mid-leg, and about their head a roll of sindal[3]. Every man useth his bow and sling. The Persians fare daintily, having many and divers kinds of meat, and their tables shine with their plate of gold and silver. They debate their weighty matters at the wine. If they meet their fellows or acquaintance by the way, they kiss them: if they be poorer, they make curtesy. Their soothsayers they leave unburied to the birds. The greatest riches that the kings had were in buildings; and they coined no more money than served the present need. The people were temperate in their living, but their kings passed in excess. The king's attire of his head was of myrrh and other sweet gums. They kept commonly three hundred women, which slept in the day, and sang and danced all the night. If the king would go to any of them, the floor was covered with fine arras. He rode seldom but in his chariot. If he suffered any man to come to his speech, he sat in a throne of gold, standing on four pillars, with precious stones. At the head of his bed were five thousand talents of gold, which were called the king's pillow; at his feet were three thousand talents of silver, which was called his footstool: over his bed was a golden vine with golden branches and grapes drawn with precious stones.

Thus far the Argument was
finished, and no more
thereof found.

γόνατος· ὁ ὑπενδύτης μὲν λευκός, ἄνθινος δ' ὁ ἐπάνω. Lib. xv. Tom. ii. p. 1042. Oxon. 1807. ED.]

[² Old edition, *some:* the correction is supplied by the original passage of Strabo, as before: ἱμάτιον θέρους μὲν πορφυροῦν ἢ ἄνθινόν, χειμῶνος δ' ἄνθινόν. ED.]

[³ Sindal: sindon, fine linen. ED.]

AN EXPOSITION

UPON

PART OF THE BOOK OF NEHEMIAH,

BY

MASTER JAMES PILKINGTON,

LATE BISHOP OF DURHAM.

CHAPTER I.

The word of Nehemiah the son of Hachalia.

ALTHOUGH there be divers opinions, whether Ezra or Nehemiah wrote this book; yet for my part I rather believe, all reasons considered, that Nehemiah wrote it, as Wolfius well proveth it. But whether so ever the one or the other wrote it, if the authority of the writer may give any strength to the writing, or man's worthiness add any thing to the credit of God's holy scripture, it skilleth not much; for they were both the true, learned, and faithful servants of God. Yet surely this worthy man Nehemiah, which in English is to say, *a comfort sent from God*, to comfort his people in those troublesome times, should not be robbed of his well deserved thanks. But first God should be chiefly praised, that raised up so worthy a man, whose pedigree is unknown, and his father's too, in so ill a time to do not only so great things both in the commonwealth and religion, in peace and war: and then should Nehemiah also be worthily next commended, that so faithfully obeyed the Lord his God, so painfully travailed for the wealth of his country; also attained such learning that he could, and was so diligent in study among all his great affairs that he would, to the great glory of God and comfort of all his church unto the world's end, put these his own doings in writing. A worthy example for all that love religion, be servitors in the court, attend on the prince, bear office in the commonwealth, or captains in the wars, to follow. For in all these things was Nehemiah famous: in religion earnest; in great favour with his prince; with all uprightness of life towards all; in war skilful, courageous, and painful; and with his pen so learned, that he could so clerkly put it in writing. Gentlemen therefore and men of the world are not born to live in pastime and pleasure, as they list, and many do, no more than poor men; but first to serve the Lord, promote his word and religion earnestly, minister justice severely, maintain peace quietly, defend the commonwealth stoutly, relieve the oppressed mightily, follow learning and study diligently; that so they may increase in virtue and honesty, as Nehemiah did, and after all these great travails refresh themselves with honest pastimes measurably. Among the heathen princes such a one was Julius Cæsar; in the wars cunning and happy; in government of the commonwealth commendable; and in learning so excellent, that no man hath written more eloquently. Such like were Alexander Severus and Marcus Aurelius, emperors. But I will not persuade much in God's cause with profane examples.

And to return to our purpose, I would not have men think that the scripture taketh his authority and credit of the man that writeth it; but the writer is to be credited for the Holy Ghost's sake, who inspired him with such heavenly knowledge, and whose instrument he is for God to speak by. Scripture cometh not first from man, but from God; and therefore God is to be taken for the author of it, and not man. The gospel saith, "It is not you that speak, but the Spirit of your Father that speaketh in you." And St Peter saith, "Prophecy came not in old time by the will of man, but holy men of God spake as they were moved by the Holy Ghost." Augustine saith well, "The scripture is a letter sent from God the Creator unto man his creature[1]." Therefore, when thou readest this book or other parts of the scripture, do it as gladly and reverently, yea, and much more too, than thou wouldest use and read the prince's or thy friends' letters, seeing it is a letter sent to thee from

Matt. x. 20.

2 Pet. i. 21.

[1 Et de illa civitate, unde peregrinamur, litteræ nobis venerunt: ipsæ sunt scripturæ, quæ nos hortantur ut bene vivamus. Enarr. in Psal. xc. Tom. IV. p. 1387. Paris. 1836. ED.]

thy God for thy salvation. God then is the chiefest author of this book, as he is of the rest of the scripture, and Nehemiah the pen or writer of all these mysteries. David said of himself, "My tongue is the pen of a writer that writeth swiftly;" meaning the Holy Ghost to be the writer, and his tongue the pen. So Nehemiah was the author of this book, as David of the psalms. And because they should know which Nehemiah he was, he saith he was "the son of Hachalia." For there were divers others of that name, but not his sons.

<small>Psal. xlv. 2.</small>

v. 1. *It came to pass in the month of November, and in the twentieth year, that I was in the castle of Susan.* <small>The Text.</small>

2. *And there came Chanani, one of my brethren, he and men of Juda; and I asked them for the Jews which scaped and remained of the captivity, and for Jerusalem.*

3. *And they said to me, The remnant which remained of the captivity there in the country be in great misery and reproach; and the wall of Jerusalem is broken down, and the gates of it are burned with fire.*

4. *And it came to pass when I heard these words, I sat down and wept; and being sad certain days, I fasted and prayed before the Lord of heaven.*

The scriptures use not to reckon their months after the order of our calendars, but by the exchange of the moon; for our calendars are not of that anciety that the scriptures be by many years. The first month in the year with them began at the next change of the moon, whensoever it fell, after the 22nd day of March, when the days and nights be both of one length. And then was March called the first moon of the year, whereas we make January our first moon. So this moon here, which is called Casleu, was the 9th month from it, and fell in the latter end of November, what day soever the moon then changed. The twentieth year that he speaketh of here, was of the reign of king Artaxerxes, as appeareth in the beginning of the 2nd chapter; of whom ye shall hear more there. Susan was the chief city of all the kingdom of Persia, where the king had both his palace and a strong castle also of the same name, where his treasure was kept. This city (as Strabo writeth) was long, and in compass 15 miles about.

Who this Chanani was, it appeareth not; but belike some honest man of good credit, and more earnest in religion and love to his country than others, because his name is put down in writing, and the others are not. And where Nehemiah calleth him *brother*, it is not necessary to think that he was of the same father and mother that Nehemiah was; but either further off in kindred, or else of the same country and religion. For this word *brother* in the scripture signifieth all those sorts of brotherhood, that be any ways kinsmen, or else of any country and religion. St Paul saith, "I wish to be accursed from Christ for my brethren and kinsmen after the flesh, which be the Israelites." Where he calleth all the children of Israel his brethren, because they came all of one father, Jacob, long ago, and now were of one country and professed one God.

Rom. ix.

What occasion these men had to come to the court, it appeareth not, and therefore not necessary to be searched; but belike some great suit for their country, because they took so long a journey in the winter and so unseasonable a time of the year, which men commonly use not to do for small causes. And by this we may learn a good lesson, that no time is so troublesome, no journey so long, but good men will not refuse it to serve God and their country.

And where Nehemiah, walking abroad about the court, beginneth to examine them of the estate of the Jews, how they did, and of the city of Jerusalem, in what case it was, it declareth the great love that he had to his people, country, and religion. O worthy example for all courtiers to follow; sometimes to walk abroad, to see what suitors there be, and learn the state of the country from whence they came, and help to further their good causes! The contrary is too commonly used: they lock themselves up, and will not be spoken with; their doors must be opened with silver keys, many means and friends must be made, and a long time of attendance, afore ye be heard, except some servant about them have some gentle remembrance to help you to their speech. And this is more common in the meaner sort than the higher. Yet I say not that all walkers abroad and talking with suitors be ever good men. For "Absalon walked afore the court gate, took them by the hand and embraced them, asked what suits they had, pitied their causes;" but for an ill purpose, to bring the king his father in hatred with the people, saying, "there was none about him that would hear and help them;" and to bring himself in favour with the people, saying, "if he were king, he would do them justice, hear their causes, and they should not wait so long but be quickly despatched." God deliver us from such courtiers! for by this means he robbed the hearts of the people from their natural and liege prince, and by flattery won the people so to himself, that they rebelled against their king and set up Absalon. *2 Sam. xv.* *2 Sam. xv.*

We need not at these days to complain of all courtiers, that they be so hard to speak to, and that many times the master is not at leisure, until the servant be pleased with something, though the master bid the contrary. For there be too many, that when suitors do come, they will learn too diligently what suit they have, out of what country they come; and then, if they will faithfully declare unto them, what office is there void in the country, or what good farmhold is to be had there at the prince's hand, or rather at any church, they promise they will help to further his suit diligently: but when they have learned all that they can, then they know him not when they meet him again the next day; or else give him fair words, with strange looks and many delays. By these means and such like they are so cunning in all corners of the realm, that they can perfectly tell what the prince or any man in the country hath: and if it be not presently void, they are content with a reversion, though it be many years to come; yea, and often sue for the same thing that the poor man came for, saying, another would have had it, if he had not stayed it; and so under a cloak of friendship make him pay more than he needed. We seek what should be the cause of such needless dearths as the realm is full of: and surely, though many be given, yet I think none greater than this. For when these leases be granted, the landlord hath but his old rent, and the tenant no more but his old farmhold: but the leasemonger, that is crept in

[PILKINGTON.]

betwixt the landlord and the tenant, goeth away with the sweet from them both. For first he racks the rent and sacks the tenant so, that he is not so able to sell his things so reasonably as else he might, nor serve the prince nor his landlord as he should; nor the landlord, paying so dear for all things, is able to live as his elders did before. This undermining micher[1] liveth better than they both, and taketh no pains at all for it, that they both should live on, and the one relieve the other.

Haman walked afore the court gates, to see who would reverence him, as he passed by, and who would not: poor Mardocheus, because he would not, was brought in great danger of his life, and all the Jews with him; but God, that overthroweth such courtiers, deliver us from the like, and raise us up some godly Nehemiah to favour the commonwealth and religion, as he did! The miserable end of Absalon, Haman, and such as we have seen in our days, maketh wise men to take heed how they live and behave themselves in the court: for none is so high, but by like offending of God they may have as great a fall. As this toucheth not the honest sort of courtiers, so the good ones will not be offended; and those that be guilty, God grant them to amend it!

3. *And they said.* After that Nehemiah had of good will towards his people and country so diligently inquired how they did, and in what case they were, Chanani and the other Jews that came with him declared in what miserable case the people were, in hatred and despised of all people about them, and that "Jerusalem, their city where God was chiefly worshipped, lay waste and burned and unbuilt." Thus God bringeth good men together, one to comfort another; and things are not ruled by chance: for both Nehemiah and these Jews lamented the miserable state of their people and country, and by their talk God provided a remedy. Nehemiah was in good state to live, and in great favour with the king; and needed not to trouble himself with the cares of his country, if God had not otherwise moved his mind to pity with talking with his countrymen. This good, then, courtiers, lawyers, and great men may have by talking with poor suitors,

[1 Micher: pilferer. Ed.]

Marginal note: Esth. iii.

that if there be any spark of grace in them, they will be moved with the lamentable complaint of poor suitors. Surely thou that art in authority, or hast learning, oughtest to think that the poor suitor cometh not to thee by chance: but the same God, that gave thee thy authority and learning, hath sent this poor man to thee to be relieved by thee. Look therefore upon him, hear him, as Salomon teacheth, saying, "The good man Prov. xxix. heareth the cause of the poor." Hide not thyself from him, consider his complaint, pity and help him; and not so much for money as for charity's sake; for so did good Nehemiah.

What can be a greater grief to an honest heart, than to have all things that he doeth or saith, be they never so good, to be taken in ill part; to be hated and ill spoken of by all his neighbours; to be slandered and belied, and to have displeasure where none is deserved? In this case were the miserable Jews, then the beloved people of God, though now justly cast off for their wicked hate to our Christ, the Son of the living God. Beside that, their "city was burned, the gates stood open," that enemies might rush in, murder and spoil them when they list, except they should keep a continual great watch, which was too troublesome and costly for them.

4. *And it came to pass.* What good cometh by hearing poor men speak, appeareth here plainly in them that fear God. For that pitiful state, which he understood his brethren the Jews and that famous city Jerusalem to be in by their report, did so move his heart and grieve him, that he "sat down, and wept certain days, was sad for them, fasted, and prayed unto the Lord of heaven" for them. Hearing and seeing be two senses, which bring into the mind of man to consider all things that be painful or pleasant to others; for except we see them or hear them, we cannot learn or understand them, much less pity them, or be glad of them. St Paul saith likewise in God's cause, "Faith cometh by Rom. x. hearing." For when thou hearest the preacher declare the glorious majesty of God, his sharp punishing of sin, the wretched estate of man, that of himself can do nothing but sin, and the everlasting pains appointed for all hard-hearted sinners; it maketh him to quake, to enter into himself, condemn himself, ask for mercy, and from thenceforth to become a new man: so when he heareth God's great mercy

declared to man in Christ, it maketh him to believe, love, obey, and follow so loving a Father. This profit then cometh by hearing the poor man's complaint, that it moveth them to pity, to tears, to fasting, and praying the Lord to relieve the misery of thy oppressed brother. Turn not therefore thy face from the poor; but hear them and pity them, as thou wouldest be heard and pitied thyself. So in religion, if thou wilt learn to fear God aright, to know thyself, amend thy life, and what blessing God hath prepared for thee, run not from the church, as many do, some for one cause, some for another, but none for good: but humble thyself in the sight of thy God and his people; hear his word reverently, believe it stedfastly, obey it diligently, pray earnestly; and God shall heap his blessings on thee plentifully.

And that we may the better understand how this miserable case of his brethren and country did touch his heart inwardly, he sheweth it by his behaviour outwardly: for the affections of the mind declare themselves openly in the face and behaviour of man, when they grow great in the heart. As, if we be sorry, our countenance is heavy, sad and cloudy; if we be merry, our face hath a good colour, and sheweth itself pleasantly; when we be ashamed of ill doing, we blush; in fear we be pale, in anger high coloured and swollen in the face, &c. So this sorrow for his brethren did so pinch him at the heart, that he could not stand, but sat down; as a man's legs in heaviness are so weak that they cannot bear him: his heart was so burdened, that he could not forbear, but brast out into tears; for certain days he could not be merry, eat nor drink, but fasted; and in the end found no other remedy, but turned himself unto the Lord, fell unto prayer, assuring himself that God would hear him, and relieve them in his due time, when he thought good.

By this we may learn how coldly they pray, that cannot bend nor kneel when they speak to the Lord; or if they kneel, it is but on the one knee, and that must have a soft cushion under it, and a softer under his elbow. Weep he may not, for disfiguring his face; fasting is thought hypocrisy and a shame: and when his paunch is full, then, as priests with their drunken nowls[1] said matins, and belked

[[1] Nowls: nolls, noddles, heads. ED.]

out, *Eructavit cor meum verbum bonum*[2], with good devotion, as they thought; so he blusters out a few blustering words, without due consideration of them, and then he thinketh he hath prayed well. O wretched man, that forgettest thy God and thyself! Remember what thou art, a lump of earth, a sink of sin, worms' meat; and that belly which thou carest so much for, is but a stinking dunghill. Down, proud peacock! consider, when thou prayest, that thou speakest to the Lord of heaven and earth, at whose beck the devils do tremble: his thunderbolts fly abroad to punish thy sin: who in his anger drowned the whole world, except eight persons; Gen.vii.xix. burned Sodom and Gomorrah with fire and brimstone from heaven, to pull down thy proud heart, and teach thee to fear his majesty. Learn of the poor publican, which was so ashamed of his wicked life, that he durst not look up unto heaven, but condemning himself cried, "O God, be merciful Luke xviii. unto me a sinner:" whereas the proud Pharisee stood stoutly, cracking of his holiness, as thou doest. Learn of the woman of Chanaan to be earnest in prayer: go not away from the Matt. xv. Lord, until thou feel thy conscience comforted and mercy promised: for no doubt the Lord will hear such a prayer. These outward things, as kneeling, weeping and fasting, are good helps and preparations unto prayer; as Sara continued Tobit iii. three days in fasting and prayer, that the Lord would deliver her from that shame: and so Toby maketh a general rule of it, saying, "Prayer is good, joined with fasting." Ecclesiasticus saith, "The prayer of him that humbleth him- Ecclus. self pierceth the clouds, and she will not be comforted until xxxv. she come nigh, nor go her way, till the highest God have respect unto her." God grant us here to learn to pity our poor brethren, and thus to prepare ourselves to pray for them, that our prayer may be heard in their need!

And although I noted afore the disordered life of some lewd courtiers, which make so much of their painted sheath, esteem themselves more than all the world doth besides; and when they think they deal so cunningly that they be not seen, many one espieth them, and laughs full drily in

[[2] The vulgate translation of Ps. xlv. 1. which our version renders, "My heart is inditing a good matter." Literally, "hath belched out." Ed.]

their sleeves at them; yet now in this godly gentleman appeareth a contrary dealing, and he may be a worthy pattern for all courtiers to follow. The court is not ill of itself, but a man, if he will, may serve the Lord uprightly, and also defend his church, and profit the commonwealth mightily; and good men may live in it honestly. It is a dangerous place, I grant, to live in, and many occasions of ill are offered daily in it; yet not so wicked, but good men living in it may take great occasions to do much good in it. Joseph in Pharao's court, a godless king, provided for all the country in the time of their great dearth and scarcity; relieved his father and brethren, then the only known church of God, in their necessity. Moses in the same court, though not under the same king, learned all the wisdom of the Egyptians, and delivered all the people from the slavery that they lived in. Abdias hid and fed a hundred prophets in caves by fifty in a company, whose lives Jesabel sought for, himself being in the wicked court of Achab and Jesabel. David feared the Lord in the court of Saul, though he escaped oft not without many great dangers. Daniel, an ancient courtier, in three kings' days kept the law of God his Lord diligently; and being in great authority with the king, had the charge of divers countries committed unto him, which he ruled faithfully, and relieved God's people mightily. So did his three companions, Sidrach, Misach, and Abednago. Mardocheus in the court of Assuerus saved the king's life, whom his chamberlains would have murdered; and delivered all the Jews, which were appointed all by Haman on one day to be slain. Jerome in his epistle commendeth one Nebridius, who, living in the court, and being nephew to the empress, behaved himself so virtuously, that all his suits were for the relief of the poor.[1] The place therefore maketh no man ill, but his illness cometh of his own wicked and crooked mind. The dangerous life of courtiers, if they will rebuke sin, and not sing *Placebo*, the example of John Baptist, who lost his head for telling the truth, may suffice to teach. But let not good men be afraid:

[1 Quicquid ab Imperatore poscebat, eleemosyna in pauperes, pretium captivorum, misericordia in afflictos erat. Tom. I. Epist. ix. Francofurt. 1684. Ed.]

for God hath the heart of princes in his hand, to turn as pleaseth him. Do thou thy duty in the fear of God; and he will defend thee, as he thinketh best.

v. 5. *And I said, I beseech thee, O Lord God of heaven, thou great and fearful God, which keepest covenant and mercy for them that love thee and keep thy commandments;*   The Text.
6. *Let thy ears hearken, I beseech thee, and thy eyes be open, to hear the prayer of thy servant, which I pray before thee this day, night and day, for the children of Israel thy servants, and knowledge for the sins of the children of Israel which they have sinned against thee; yea, I and my father's house have sinned.*
7. *We have outrageously sinned against thee, and have not kept thy commandments, and thy ceremonies and judgments, which thou commandest Moses thy servant.*

As a man that is earnestly bent to prayer hath commonly these outward things joined withal that were spoken of afore, as sitting or kneeling, weeping, a grieved mind, sad countenance, fasting and abstinence: so necessarily he must have a charitable mind and pitiful towards his brethren, and an earnest and lively faith towards God, (which both appear in Nehemiah;) for without these two his prayer can not be heard. His loving mind towards his brethren appeareth, in that he, leaving all other pastimes, so diligently inquireth of their estate and their country, and disdaineth not to hear them: but it is seen more evidently, when he weepeth and mourneth, fasteth and forbeareth dainties, as though he were in misery with them; but specially, when he taketh so great pains and travail to do them good, as appeareth hereafter throughout this book. His earnest faith appeareth, in that he prayeth, and that only "to the God of heaven," and with such vehement and meet words, as do declare his full mind, that he doubted not but God both could and would help them. In trouble no man asketh help but of him whom he thinketh will do him good: and because there is none so merciful to hear, and so willing to help, as God himself is, in all our griefs we must turn unto the Lord of heaven alone: for other saint there is none that will help or can help. The apostle saith, that "he which will come to the Lord must not only believe that there is a God, but also that he is a rewarder of them that seek him." This faith therefore let us bring with us when we pray. This faith did continue in Nehemiah, though he had lived so many years amongst the unbelieving Persians; which was a special gift of God to him in such troublesome times. In prayer let us ask only such things as may stand with God's good pleasure. For where many times foolishly we ask things to our own hurt, God of his wisdom and fatherly goodness doth not grant them; as St James teacheth us, saying, "Ye ask, and receive not, because ye ask evilly, to spend it upon your lusts."

<small>Heb. xi.</small>

<small>James iv.</small>

I am afraid to enter into the opening of this prayer, because it is so perfect of itself, that it cannot be amended: yet for the help of the unlearned, for whose cause only I take these pains, I shall in few words open it more plainly.

O thou Lord God of heaven and earth, which of thy mere love towards man madest heaven and earth, the sea, with all the furniture in them, as the sun, moon, and stars, fish, fowl, herbs, trees, corn, fruit and cattle, and appointed them to serve him, that he might serve, honour, and obey thee; which not only rulest, feedest, governest and guidest them all according to thy good pleasure, but hast made heaven thy seat and the earth thy footstool, that from hence, out of this vale of misery, we should look up unto thee our only God, where thou reignest in thy majesty above all the heavens, and from whence we should look for our deliverance out of all troubles: O thou great and fearful God, whose creatures pass all powers of princes, against whom to strive is mere folly, and with whom to wrastle is extreme madness; whose might, wisdom, and justice is infinite; whose mercy, goodness, and pity hath no end; which art so great, that thou fillest all places, and not concluded in any, but art present every where, and seest all things; whose majesty surmounteth all creatures so far, that it cannot be contained or ruled of any: thou great and fearful God, which in thy anger threwest thy angels that offended thee out of thy glorious presence in heaven into everlasting darkness of hell;

who in thy rage drownedst all the world except eight persons; which burnedst up Sodom and Gomorrah with fire and brimstone from heaven; which didst cast Adam and us all out of paradise for eating the forbidden apple; who causedst the man to be stoned to death for gathering a few sticks on the sabbath day; which man would judge to be but small faults, yet were great because they were contrary to thy commandments; who killed Uzzah for upholding the ark being ready to fall; which plagued Pharao with frogs, flies and hailstones; which made Nebuchadnezzar of a mighty king a vile beast to eat grass, and made Herod to be worried with lice: O thou great and fearful God, at whose beck the devils do tremble, the earth doth quake, and the heavens shoot out hot fiery thunderbolts, the clouds pour out great storms and tempests, to destroy thine enemies: O thou God of heaven, thou great and fearful God, I thy poor wretch, vile worm, and miserable creature, void of all goodness and full of all wretchedness, I forsaking myself, and trusting on thy goodness, am bold to creep in at a corner, and present myself before thy throne of mercy, quaking and trembling at thy fearful judgments and sharp justice against sin. I offer unto thee this poor soul and carcase, the work of thy own hands, made glorious by thee, but foully defaced by me. I, Lord, I, God, do most humbly with a heavy heart and troubled mind beseech thee; I most earnestly with bitter tears beg and crave of thee, to cast me not away out of thy sight, but graciously to hear my prayer. For although thou dwellest in thy high and holy place in heaven, yet thou lookest down into the earth, to hear the sighing of the poor and deliver the oppressed; and though thou be great and fearful in all thy works, yet I know thou art great in mercy and rich in goodness. For although thou hast punished sharply, yet thou savest more mercifully. Adam was cast out of paradise in justice, and yet had mercy offered unto him in great plenty. The enticing of a woman made him to offend thee, and the blessed Seed of the same woman hath bruised the serpent's poisonful head, and delivered us. Thou therefore, that art a God of truth, and keepest promise, and shewest mercy to them that love thee and keep thy commandments, look pitifully on us, which forsaking ourselves hang upon thee, and though we see thy deserved rod, yet we fly to thy promised mercy. Though we have not kept our promise made unto thee in our baptism, " that we should forsake the devil, world and flesh, serve, honour, and faithfully obey thee our only Lord and God, with all our heart, strength, power and soul;" yet art thou a true God in keeping thy promise and not casting us off. When we run from thee, thou callest us again; and not destroying us suddenly, tarriest for our amendment. When we hate thee and become thy open enemies, thou, remembering thy promise made to Abraham, David, and our fathers, seekest by all means to bring us home again to thee. Though we be unfaithful, thou art true: though we forget thee, thou rememberest us. Though we deserve to be cast away from thee, without all hope of redemption, yet when thou fatherly correctest us, in the midst of thine anger thou rememberest thy mercy, and receivest us again to thee. We grant, O Lord, that we do not love thee, nor keep thy commandments, as we ought: yet, Lord, thou that art love and charity itself, and lovest all things that thou hast made, and in thy dear Son Christ Jesus dost embrace us, not looking at our deserts, but at his worthiness, who hath fulfilled the law for us, and made us partakers of thy righteousness; Lord God, hear us and have pity on us. O thou Lord God of all mercy, which never didst cast any away that fled unto thee, open thy ears and hear the prayers of me thy humble suitor. Shall I be the first whom thou wilt not hear? Is thy mercy all spent, and none left in store for us? Open thy eyes, O God of our salvation, and behold the miserable state of thy poor people. Our city lieth waste, the walls unbuilt; our enemies rush in on every side, and we are a laughing stock unto them. Thou heardst the crying of Agar, being cast out of her house; thou lookedst at the oppression of Egypt; thou pitiedst the woeful sighing of Anna; and when thy people were oppressed of any enemies round about them, thou raisedst up one judge or other to deliver them. Consider, O Lord, I beseech thee, our woeful state. We are spoiled on every side: mark and hearken to the prayer, which I thy poor servant make unto thee, which seest all secrets this day, continually crying night and day with a simple and unfeigned heart, not for mine own self, whom thou hast so well placed in the court with plenty of all things, but for my brethren, the children of Israel thy servants, the offspring of thy dear beloved Jacob, which be in great heaviness. While they be in misery, I cannot be merry. Their grief is my sorrow, and their welfare is my rejoicing. I grant, O Lord, we have grievously offended thee; yet have we not cast thee off, nor forsaken thee to be our Lord: we be thy servants, though unthrifty, unthankful, and miserable; and thou art a God rich in mercy to all that turn unto thee. I confess, O gracious God, that the children of Israel have sinned against thee; yea, not only they, O Lord, but I and my father's house have heinously broken thy commandments: and yet we despair not to obtain thy favour again, as children that have offended their loving Father. There is none of us free: we plead mercy, and not justice; we stand not in defence of our doings, but yield ourselves[1] into thy merciful hands. While thou givest us a heart to pray, we continually believe thou wilt hear us in the end. O Lord, correct thou us after thine own good will and pleasure; but give us not up to the lust of thy enemies which blaspheme thee, saying, Their God hath forsaken them, their God cannot nor will not help them: they hate us, not so much for our own sins, as for that we be called thy servants. O Lord, let not thy holy name be ill spoken of through our wickedness: rise and defend thine own cause; cast not away thy servants in thy heavy displeasure. What vantage canst thou have in giving us over to thy foes? They shall laugh, when we shall weep: they will slander thy goodness for our forgetfulness of thee. Thou promisedst, O Lord, by the mouth of thy prophet, that in Ezek. xviii. what hour soever the sinner did repent, thou wouldst no more remember his wickedness, nor lay it to his charge. We weep, we confess and acknowledge our manifold wickedness, wherewith we and our fathers have offended thee: we call for mercy; we pray night and day, not doubting but thou wilt keep thy promise in delivering and hearing us in thy due time. Though we have broken our promise in disobeying thee, yet if it please thee thus to try our faith and exercise our patience by laying on us thy heavy hand and

[[1] Old edition, *yourselves*. ED.]

sharp correction, thy good will be done: give us strength to bear that thy wisdom will lay upon us, and lay on us what thou wilt. Thou gavest us thy law to be a bridle, to rule our wicked desires, and keep us within the compass of them; but we, like madmen, or rather wild and untamed beasts, that cannot be tied in chains nor holden in any bands, have outrageously broken all thy commandments. No laws could rule us, no saying compel, nor correction could stay us; but wilfully we followed our own fantasies. There is nothing, O Lord, that thou canst lay to our charge, but we willingly and frankly confess ourselves guilty thereof: for we have neither kept thy commandments, which thou gavest us by Moses thy servant, wherein privately we might learn how to direct our lives both towards thee our God, and also toward all men; nor the ceremonies, sacraments and sacrifices, which thou appointedst us to keep in thy religion, and in them to worship thee, we have not duly regarded and kept, but cast them away, and followed the fashions of the heathen people about us, and such as we devised ourselves. Our priests and prophets have taught us lies and devices of their own heads; yet have we been more ready to hear, believe and follow them, than thy holy will and word, declared unto us in thy book of life. The civil laws, by which thou appointedst thy commonwealth to be ruled, we have broken and disobeyed, living at our own lust and pleasure. Our judges, rulers, and lawyers have sought their own gain more than justice to their people, oppressing them wrongfully. There is no goodness in no sort of us: prince, priest, people, judge, ruler, and all sorts from the highest to the lowest, we have all run astray: we deny it not, but with many tears and grievous heart we fall before thy throne of mercy, earnestly craving and faithfully believing to find mercy, grace and pardon at thy hands.

With these and such like words he poured out his grief before the Lord. For no doubt he spake much more than is here written; but these may suffice to teach us the like.

The Text. v. 8. *Remember, I beseech thee, the word that thou commandedst Moses thy servant, saying, Ye will offend, and I will scatter you among the heathen:*

9. *And if ye turn unto me, and keep my commandments, and do them; if ye were cast to the uttermost parts of heaven, from thence I will gather you, and will bring you to the place which I have chosen to set my name there.*

10. *They are thy servants, and thy people, whom thou hast redeemed in thy great power and with thy mighty hand.*

11. *I beseech thee, my Lord, I pray thee, let thy ear be bent to the prayer of thy servants, which desire to fear thy name; and give good success, I pray thee, to thy servant this day, and grant him mercy in the sight of this man. And I was the king's cup-bearer.*

Give me leave, Lord, I beseech thee, to speak unto thee, and put thee in remembrance of those things which thou seemest to us to have quite forgotten. Thou forewarnedst us by thy faithful servant Moses, that if we offended thee, thou wouldst drive us out of that pleasant country which thou gavest us, and scatter us among the heathen people in all countries; yet, if we would turn unto thee again, and keep thy commandments, there was no part under heaven so far off, nor none so mighty or cruel against us, but thou wouldst bring us again and settle us in that place which thou hadst chosen and appointed us to call on thy name there. The first part, O God, we find too true: we have sinned, and thou hast punished us: we have broken thy laws, and thou hast scattered us into all countries: and if we lived among a people that knew thee, or loved thee, our banishment and loss of our country would be less grievous unto us. But, alas, good God! we live amongst them that hate thee, and laugh at us: they worship gods of their own making, and think them to be of greater might than thou, the almighty and ever-living God, art. This grief we cannot digest: this is so tedious unto us, that we cannot be merry until thou restore us. After our long captivity by Nebuchadnezzar in Babylon thou seemedst to remember us something, and movedst the good king Cyrus to give licence to as many as would to go home and build thy temple again; and this was some good token of thy love and favour towards us: but yet, alas! O Lord, there be as many years or more past,

Deut. iv. xxxii.

since Cyrus began this our deliverance; and yet we live among the unbelieving Persians, a people as cruel and wicked as the Babylonians and the Chaldeans were: thou changest our captivity from one kingdom to another, and from country to country; yet we never a whit the better. We are not brought to thy promised place and holy land: our city is burned up, and lieth uninhabited; the walls are pulled down, and the gates lie open, that our enemies may rush in on every side, spoil and murder us at their pleasure. By thy good servant, king Darius, thou didst build us a temple to call upon thy name in it; and that was some good hope that thou wouldst fully deliver us from our enemies, and mercifully restore us to our undeserved country. Thou seemest, O Lord, to have kept part of thy promise; but yet the greatest part is behind. Remember, O God, I beseech thee, thy promise, and bring us home again; finish the thing that thou hast so prosperously begun. Thy enemies will think that either thou canst not or wilt not perform thy promise: arise, O Lord, and deliver us fully, that the world may know thou art a true God in keeping thy promise: let thy enemies see that there is no people so strong to hold us, nor country so far off, but thou both canst and wilt destroy them that rebel against thee, and fully deliver us and bring us home again. Pardon my rude boldness, gracious God, which so saucily speak unto thee; the grief of my heart is so great, it brusteth out, I cannot hold in, but talk unto thee as one doth to another. The faithful hope that I have in thee, that thou wilt perform thy promise fully, maketh me thus boldly to speak; yet the greatness of our misery and the weakness of our faith maketh many to think that thou hast forgotten us. Bear with our weakness, and pardon our impatience. The sick man that lieth in great pains, and looketh for the physician's coming, thinketh he cometh but slowly, when he maketh all the haste he can; and when he is come, except he give him some ease quickly, he thinketh that either he cannot or will not help him. But the wisdom of the physician is such, that if he should purge or let him blood presently, it were great danger; or if he should satisfy his fantasy, letting him eat and drink what he list, it would increase his pains; and therefore he tarrieth until he see better occasion given: so we, O Lord, lie in great pains, and think thou tarriest long: we would gladly have our desires fulfilled; but thy wisdom seeth the time is not yet come. Give us patience, O God, to tarry thy leisure, or rather a speediful deliverance. Our weakness is such, that we cannot but murmur and grudge at our delays, and think thou hast forgotten us. Bear with our foolishness, O Lord, which cannot understand the secret wisdom of thy doings: we judge thee according to our own wits, as we think good, and submit not ourselves to thy wisdom, which knowest what time is best and meetest for us to taste of thy undeserved goodness. We think thou hast forgotten us, if thou speedily satisfy not our desires. Arise, gracious God, and deliver us, that the world may see that thou rememberest thy promise made so long ago to thy faithful servant Moses. This profit we have by reading thy scriptures, left unto us by thy servants the prophets, that our faith is increased, our hope faileth not, but manfully tarrieth with patience for thy coming. Faith doubteth not, and hope is not weary, though our grudging nature cannot be contented. Increase our faith, O gracious God, our hope and strength, that we fall not from thee: pardon our murmuring and mistrusting of thee: though our state be despised when we look at ourselves, yet when we remember thy promise, we cannot despair. We follow our father Abraham, who, contrary to hope by reason, hoped in thee that thou wouldest fulfil thy promise to him, though reason could not see it. And that thou mayst the more willingly do it, O Lord, consider who we be. We be thy servants; other lords and masters we seek none: we are thy people, and thou our God and King. Can any master forsake his servant, or any king his subject, that humbly submitteth himself unto him? Though we have sinned and deserved to be cast away from thee, yet art thou, O Lord, rich in mercy, a King of great power, and thy glory shall shine in our deliverance. Is any fault so great, that thou canst not forgive it? Is any man so hard-hearted, but at length he will be entreated? and shall any wickedness overflow thy goodness so far, that thou wilt not be entreated? So many years' punishment would satisfy a stony heart, and forgive and forget all that is past: think on us, O Lord, what metal we be made of, and deal not with us in the balance of justice, but in mercy. We are by nature earth, dust and ashes, and therefore heavy, sluggish, and forgetful: we are born of sinful parents even from the beginning; and therefore of ourselves must needs follow their trade in ill doing: we be no angels, and therefore cannot serve thee as we should do. Take in good part, O Lord, our simple good will: that that wanteth in us, thy Messias, thy Son, our Lord and Christ, hath fulfilled for us, and made us partakers of his righteousness. Look at him, O Lord, and not at us, who redeemed us with no gold nor silver, but by his own precious blood; and let that price satisfy thee, and deliver us. I grant, O Lord, thou deliveredst our fathers from their bondage and slavery in Egypt, wherein we should have continued, if thy mighty hand, great power and strength had not made us free. And not only then, O Lord, we tasted of thy goodness, but ever since, when the Philistines, Ammonites, Moabites, or other enemies round about us oppressed us, thou heardst us, thou deliveredst us; and shall we now be clean forgotten? Arise, O Lord, speedily, and let thy people know that thou rememberest them, and hast a care over them. How shall thy goodness be known, if thou have not a people to praise thee? I beseech thee, Lord, pardon my importunity. I cannot depart, until I obtain my suit at thy hands: though thou seem to deal hardly with us so many years, yet I will say with patient Job, "Although he kill me, yet I will trust in him still." I know thou lovest us, whatsoever thou doest unto us; and therefore I will trust in thee still. Though thou hast seemed hitherto, O Lord, to look strangely on us, yet now bow down thine ear, and hear the prayer of me thy poor servant, and the prayers of all the rest of my sorrowful brethren, thy servants; which would gladly, so far as the weakness of man's nature will suffer us, fear thy name. Thy Holy Spirit giveth us a desire to serve thee; but the rebellious flesh, which we received of our first father Adam, withstandeth all such motions, and draweth us from thee. Deal not with us, therefore, O God, in the rigour of thy justice, but in the unspeakable measure of thy mercies. Rule thy servant this day, and grant me to find grace and favour in the sight of this mighty king, Artaxerxes, whose cup-bearer

I am. It lieth most in him to help and to hinder us, to set us at liberty or keep us prisoners still, to build our city or to let it lie waste. I see, O Lord, the fierceness of his nature, and how little he understandeth thy goodness towards him: but yet I know, O God, that the hearts of princes, even infidels, are in thy hands to dispose as thou thinkest good. Have pity therefore, O God, on thy people, and bend his mind to pity them. Other friends I do not seek; for without thee all suit and labour is in vain.

A PRAYER.

Lord God, which of thine own mere good will inspiredst thy prophets in old time with the knowledge of thy secret mysteries, and of thy great love towards us thy servants hast caused them to be put in writing, and hast preserved them from destruction by thy mortal enemies, that we might learn in them thy mercies, shewed to our fathers and promised to us; give us, we beseech thee, a willing mind with reverence to hear and read thy holy word, declared in this book, and a diligent care to follow the same. Raise up, we pray thee, in these our latter days such faithful servants about the prince in the court, as Nehemiah was, that would pity the miserable state of the poor people and afflicted church, rather than seek their own ease, wealth, and profit. Grant us, we pray thee, to weep, fast, and pray with such love to our brethren and sure faith in thee, as Nehemiah had, and not to cease, until we have obtained some grace in thy sight, as he did. Our need and misery in these latter days are as great as was in his time; and yet we see it not. Thou correctest us, and we feel it not: thou teachest, and we will not learn. Thou hadst brought home part of the Jews from their captivity, and yet many remained behind: so, Lord, thou hast in our days opened the eyes of some, and delivered us from that Romish slavery wherein we were so long drowned: but, alas! O Lord, many of our brethren lie blind and will not see, have ears and will not hear. Open their eyes, O God, and fully restore us, that we and they may jointly fear thee as our Lord, and reverently love thee as our dear Father, to the confusion of Satan and his partakers, and the everlasting glory of thy blessed name, and comfort of thy poor people, through Christ thy Son, our Lord and only Saviour. Amen.

CHAP. II.

v. 1. *It came to pass in the month of March, in the twentieth year of king Artaxerxes, that wine was afore him; and I took up the wine, and I gave it to the king, and was not sad afore in his sight.*
2. *And the king said to me, Why is thy countenance so sad, and thou art not sick? It is nothing else than a heavy heart. I was very sore afraid.*
3. *And I said to the king, O king, God save thy life for ever. Why should not my countenance be sad, when the city and the place of my fathers' burials lieth waste, and the gates are consumed with fire?*
4. *And the king said to me, For what thing dost thou ask? And I prayed to the God of heaven.*
5. *And I said to the king, If it be thought good to the king, and if thy servant find favour in thy sight, send me into Juda to the city of my fathers' burials, that I may build it.*
6. *And the king said to me, the queen sitting by him, How long will thy journey be, and when wilt thou return? And it was thought good in the king's sight, and he sent me; and I appointed him a certain time.*

The month Nisan, as it is called in the Hebrew here, is the first month of the year, as the scripture useth to reckon, and answereth unto our March, beginning at the first change of the moon after the twelfth[1] day of March, when the days and nights are both of one length. And although many doubt who this Artaxerxes was, I take it certainly to be him that was called Longimanus, *Long-hand*, because the one hand was longer than the other; as Edward the First was called Long-shanks because of his long legs. I love not to fill up books with moving doubt unto the unlearned, for whose cause specially I write; and namely such doubts, as be harder in searching than profitable in understanding. The learneder sort, that list to try their wits, may search many men's writings, and see divers opinions; but a most apparent truth

[1 Old edition, 12. Compare p. 287, "22nd day of March." Ed.]

simply told is best for the unlearned. Yet in the fourth chapter of Ezra[1] I have fully enough opened the matter, which I think after good consideration will be best liked of most men.

Among many things, which prove the good disposition of Nehemiah, these certain times that he appointeth of his doing most clearly declare the same. In the ninth month, November, in the latter end of the year, reckoning the year by the course of the sun, he received these heavy news of the misery of his people and country: and in the first month of the year following, (yet both these months fell in the twentieth year of the king Artaxerxes,) God gave him this occasion to speak for the relief of them to the king. It oft falleth out, that the latter end of the year by the course of the sun is the beginning of the year by the reign of the king: as our gracious queen Elizabeth began her happy reign in November, yet March in the year following is part of the same year of her reign that November was in the beginning. All this while, four months at the least, from November to March, was Nehemiah sad, weeping, fasting, praying, and seeking some good occasion to seek to the king for the relief of his country. After this sort will good men commend their suits unto princes, first by weeping, fasting, and praying unto God; because they know the prince's heart to be in God's hand, to dispose and turn as he thinketh good: but the wicked worldlings, that have not God afore their eyes, nor think not God to rule the world and princes too, seek clean contrary ways; and by rewards, by him and by her, by flattering and dissembling, make their way, and break their suits unto princes. When queen Ester should speak to the king for the deliverance of the Jews her people, as Nehemiah should here, she bade Mardocheus go and will all the Jews to fast and pray for her, that she might find favour in the king's sight, and obtain her suit for them: and by these godly means both Ester and Nehemiah prospered in their requests.

Esth. iv.

But because every one cannot have access to speak unto the king, and break his suit himself, (nor it is not fit that it should so be,) it is not amiss to use the means of some good man about the prince to open the suit unto him sim-

[1] It does not appear that the Exposition on Ezra was ever printed. ED.]

ply in the fear of God, committing the success thereof by earnest prayer to God's good will and pleasure. And better it shall be for them thus simply to walk in the fear of God, and to fail in the suit, than by lying, flattery, or bribery to obtain it. A hard lesson for courtiers to follow, but a most true and godly way! When Absalon was out of favour with his father David, by the means of Joab and the woman of Thecoa he was brought in again; but by practice rather than upright dealing, and therefore it prospered not. 2 Sam. xiv.

Nehemiah had hitherto kept his inward sorrow so secret, that the king perceived it not: but it overcame him now, and he was not able to cover it any longer. What earnest love was this in him toward his country, that thus long fasted and prayed! and we are so nice, that what danger soever hangeth over us, we cannot forbear a dinner, that by some abstinence from the belly we may more earnestly give ourselves to prayer. They that with reverence will consider God's secret providence and care that he hath for his people, how he governeth all things, yea, even those that seem outwardly of no value, after such a sort, that his heavenly wisdom and fatherly love doth most manifestly appear in them toward those that seek him, may here see a manifest example of it. Not by chance (for so nothing falleth out,) but by God's great providence, the king had wine afore him, was dry, and called for drink. Nehemiah also, as God had appointed, stood by; and as his office required, being his cupbearer, took up the cup, tasted and gave it to the king to drink, looking very sadly, which he was not wont, and princes love not to have any to do so about them. Upon this sad look falleth out all the matter, which otherwise he durst not open. The king demandeth what maketh him so sad: Nehemiah openeth his grief: the king asketh what he would have: Nehemiah maketh his petition: the king granteth it, and sendeth him to build Jerusalem, and giveth him liberally things necessary to the doing of it. A weighty matter to rise by occasion of a sad countenance: but thus our God of small things can bring forth great matters. David used to sit at king Saul's table, until he fell in displeasure with him: when he saw his place empty, Saul would ask where he was, that he came not to dinner. And if he spake angrily, Jonathan, Saul's son, would let David know, that he might keep him out of Saul's danger: thus by an empty place at the table David's life was divers times saved. Ester, when she would go to speak for her people, and of long time afore had not seen the king, nor might not come in his presence except she were sent for, putteth on her costly apparel, and standeth afore the king's window, where she might be seen. The king, seeing her, sendeth for her; and she, spying her time, maketh her suit to the king for her people, and delivereth them. Thus of small occasions God worketh great things, that we may know that he ruleth all things, be they never so small in man's sight.

But among many great tokens of God's providence and good will toward Nehemiah, none is greater, than that he, being a prisoner, a stranger born, and one not of their religion, serving idols, but worshipping the true living God, should be called to such a place of credit and worship, to be the king's cup-bearer and taster. None useth to put any to such offices of trust, but such as be thought to be of great honesty, truth and fidelity. No doubt many of the Persians desired that office, and disdained that Nehemiah, a stranger, should enjoy an office of that credit and authority, where he might have free access to the king, and take occasion to move his suit for himself or his friend. Yet this is God's accustomed goodness, that when his people be in trouble, he always provideth some to be about the prince, which both may and will help to defend them. In this long captivity, under king Darius was Daniel and his fellows in great authority with the king; under king Assuerus were Ester and Mardocheus; under king Cyrus were Ezra, Zorobabel and others; under Artaxerxes was Nehemiah in great favour: which all, being Jews born, did wonderfully relieve and comfort the oppressed people in this great extremity under heathen kings. A strange work of God, to cause heathen princes to favour and defend the religion that they knew not, and to defend that people which their subjects hated! But such a loving Lord is our God to us, that though he punish his own people sharply for a time, yet he casteth them not away for ever; and if he lay on heavy load, yet he giveth them strength to bear it.

Here may be moved a hard question on these men's doings, whether it be lawful now for a christian man to serve a heathen prince or no, as they did then. Let the case stand as it doth here, and it is easy to answer. These men all were prisoners, taken out of their own country by violence; lived under heathen kings; and therefore ought faithfully to serve and quietly to obey them. So lived Joseph in Egypt under Pharao: so Daniel, Mardocheus, Ezra, Nehemiah, and others. So did Jeremy and Baruch the prophets teach them to live, saying unto all the Jews, then being captives under infidels, "Pray for the life of Nebuchadnezzar and Baltasar his son; seek the peace of that country whither ye be carried away prisoners, and be not troublers of the commonwealth." So St Peter taught the Christians in the beginning of their receiving of the gospel, that servants should not forsake their masters, though they did not yet believe, but serve them faithfully and obey them reverently; yea, though they were hard and froward to them. So St Paul and Peter both biddeth the faithful wife not to leave her unfaithful husband, but behave herself more honestly, that by her well doing the husband may be won to the Lord, and God's holy name not ill spoken of through them. What good could a rude unfaithful people think of that God or religion, that would teach the servant or wife to run away from their masters or husband? The scripture teacheth no such thing, but all faithfulness, duty, and obedience toward all men, so far as we offend not God. But in these days, if any should leave the company of christian people willingly, and go serve an infidel king for vantage sake, that were ill done, and differeth far from the case of these good people, and may not be done, except it were to go and preach. Good men afore rehearsed dissembled not their God nor their religion; but among the infidels boldly confessed it, as all Christians ought to do in all places, and afore all men, though they be cruel against them.

Jer. xxix. Baruch i.

1 Pet. ii.

1 Cor. vii. 1 Pet. iii.

2. *And the king said.* The good will of the king toward Nehemiah appeareth, in that he marketh the countenance of his servant so diligently, (which kings use not commonly to do, but to such as they love dearly,) and asketh the cause of his sadness. Some would rather have chid him,

and bid him go out of the king's presence; for princes may not have any occasion of heaviness shewed before them, but all devices that can be to make them merry: yet God would by this means move the king's heart to pity his man, and by granting his suit comfort his heavy heart. The king, belike, was a wise man: for by a heavy countenance he could perceive the heaviness of his heart. A good kind of reasoning and seldom untrue. The heart is the beginning and well-spring of all affections and motions of the body, and by outward signs sheweth what it thinketh inwardly. Momus[1], which is one that findeth fault with all things, when he was willed to tell what fault he could find in the fashion and shape of man, sayeth, Man was not rightly made; for that his heart was locked up secretly in his breast, that his thoughts could not be espied: he should have had some glasses set there, that his thoughts might be seen. But he that will diligently mark the countenance and behaviour of a man, shall easily perceive what the heart thinketh. Hypocrites may dissemble and cloak them for a time; but time will soon descry them to a wise man. Salomon sayeth, "A merry heart maketh a cheerful countenance, and by the sorrow of the heart the mind is heavy." Ecclesiasticus saith, "A wise man is known by his countenance;" and the next verse is, "A man's garment, laughter and going declare what a man is." Gregory Nazianzen, when he saw Julianus Apostata, the emperor, first, by his countenance and foolish moving of his body conjectured truly of his wickedness and falling from God, which followed afterward; and cried out, "O Lord God, how great a mischief is nourished in the empire of Rome!"[2] Other affections likewise, when they grow much, as this sorrow of Nehemiah

Prov. xv. 13.

Invectiva 2. Niceph. x. cap. 37.

[1 An allusion to Lucian, *Hermotimus*, sec. 20. Tom. i. p. 759. Hemsterh. ED.]

[2 Τοῦτον πρὸ τῶν ἔργων ἐθεασάμην, ὃν καὶ ἐπὶ τῶν ἔργων ἐγνώρισα. καὶ εἴ μοι παρῆσάν τινες τῶν τηνικαῦτα συνόντων καὶ ἀκουσάντων, οὐ χαλεπῶς ἂν ἐμαρτύρησαν· οἷς, ἐπειδὴ ταῦτα ἐθεασάμην, εὐθὺς ἐφθεγξάμην, Οἷον κακὸν ἡ Ῥωμαίων (γῆ) τρέφει! Orat. iv. (Invectiva in Julian. ii.) Tom. i. p. 122. Paris. 1630. Nicephorus, as referred to by the author, cites the passage, supplying the γῆ, which is wanting in Gregory. ED.]

did, work greatly. When Ophni and Phinees were slain, and the ark of God taken, Eli their father, hearing the news, for sorrow fell off his chair, and died: and Phinees' wife, being near the time of her childbirth, hearing the death of her husband, fell on travail, and died for sorrow. When the blessed virgin Mary came to salute Elizabeth, "the child sprang in her womb for joy." So much a merry heart can do.

I cannot tell, whether the wisdom of Nehemiah in bridling his affection, that in so great a sorrow he cried not out like a woman, or the good disposition of the king that so pitied the sorrowful heart of his man, is worthy more praise: but surely both are to be followed of all Christians. Affections must be holden under, that they grow not too much; and heavy hearts would be comforted. For as the king, seeing the sad countenance of his man, diligently searched out the cause of his sorrow; so Christians, when one seeth another in heaviness, should brotherly comfort him, and "weep with them that weep," as though we were partakers of the same sorrow, according to the rule of St Paul, "If one member of the body, be it never so small, be in pain, the rest of his body is grieved" also, and every member seeketh to ease it as they may, so they be naturally linked together. So should all Christians, being members of Christ's mystical body, one bear the grief of another, and help to relieve him. *Rom. xii.* *1 Cor. xii.*

When Nehemiah had been thus long sad, weeping, fasting, and praying, he was now cast into a very great fear, by reason of the king's earnest requiring the cause of his sadness. Thus one sorrow followeth another, and a christian man's faith and patience is continually exercised: when one grief is ended, it hath another straightways following. The king said, "This sorrow must needs come from a heavy heart, seeing thy body is not sick." This toucheth a man near, when he must needs open the secrets of his heart to a king, whom he cannot tell how he will take it, or what opinion he hath of him. Many thoughts and suspicions rise in good men's hearts, as well as ill men's, and cast them into great fear: for every man is subject to affection, of his own nature. Nehemiah might fear lest the king had heard some accusation against him, or had taken some displeasure with him, or would not grant his request, or some other would hinder his suit, or might lose his office, &c. and therefore no marvel if he were sore afraid: but a strong faith will boldly pass through all such cares, and trusting in God, will continue his good purpose. "The troubles of the righteous be many," saith David, "but the Lord will deliver him out of them all."

<small>Psal. xxxiv.</small>

3. *And I said.* After that he had something overcome his fear, and recovered his spirits, he declareth unto the king the cause of his sadness. The majesty of a king will make any good nature afraid to speak unreverently, though they be daily in company with him and favour, as Nehemiah was. And though the courtesy of a prince be such, that he will abase and humble himself familiarly to use his subject; yet the subject should not over boldly nor saucily behave himself toward his prince. Diogenes said, A man should use his prince or peer as he would do the fire. The fire, if he stand too near it, will burn him; and if he be too far off, he will be a cold. So to be over bold, without blushing or reverence, bringeth in contempt of both sides; for the king will think him too saucy, and the subject will forget his duty: and to be over strange and afraid will cause the king to think him to be of an ill nature, and not bearing a good heart towards him. Therefore Nehemiah, not over bold with his prince, with most humble obeisance wisheth the king good life, as the common phrase of the scripture useth to speak, and plainly telleth the true cause of his sorrow and sad countenance. Here we may learn the duty of Christians, that live under heathen princes: that is, they may not only serve them, but ought humbly to obey and reverence them. For surely this kind of salutation in Nehemiah, to pray for the king's life, was not holy water of the court from the teeth outward, *Saluta libenter;* but from an unfeigned heart desiring it. St Paul, who lived under the emperor Nero, as wicked a man as ever the earth bare, biddeth to pray for all "kings and them that be in authority," (which then were all infidels,) "that under them we may live a quiet life with all godliness and honesty." And if thou thinkest such ill men are not to be prayed for, yet for the quietness of God's church thou must pray for them, that God would so rule their hearts, that under them we may live a peaceable and godly life. For

<small>Diogenes.</small>

that is the reason that St Paul yieldeth, though such wicked men will not learn their own salvation themselves.

After that Nehemiah had thus dutifully behaved himself to the king, so that there could be thought no just cause of any evil suspicion in him toward the king; then he boldly declareth the cause of his sadness, and saith, "the city where his fathers lay buried lay waste, and the gates were burned." And is this so great a cause why Nehemiah should be so sad, weep, fast, and pray so long? had he not seen nor heard of greater cities and countries than it was, which were destroyed as miserably as it was? Babylon, which was much bigger than Jerusalem, was conquered not long afore by Cyrus; Samaria, their neighbour, by Sennacherib and Salmanasser, &c. But this city had a greater cause to be lamented for than others. For it was taken from wicked men by God's mighty hand, and given to God's people: it was increased with many benefits from God, beautified with religion, priests, a temple to worship the living God in; strengthened by many worthy princes and laws; and was a wonder of the world. It was "the holy city," because it was dedicated to the Lord's service; though the people were evil that dwelt in it, and misused it. The gospel saith, the devil tempting Christ our Saviour "took him into the holy city, and set him on a pinnacle of the temple;" and Christ our Lord, foreseeing the destruction of it to be at hand, wept for it. Matt. iv.
Luke xix.

This was then the cause of Nehemiah's sorrow, that God was dishonoured; for that this city, which was dedicated to his name, and given to his people to serve him in, was now defaced by heathen princes; his religion decayed, and people subject to strangers. A zealous man cannot abide any thing without great grief, that seemeth to deface the glory of his God. But if these causes were not, yet the natural love to his country had been sufficient to move him to tears. For as it is a pitiful sight to see a prince or nobleman to be cast from his dignity, to be spoiled of his honour, lands and goods, and become a carter and drive the plough, or lie tied in prison; so surely it must needs move any heathen man, to see the city where he and his elders were born and buried, to be overthrown, lie open to all enemies, unfenced with walls or gates, and be inhabited with a few cottages, and no better than the poorest ragged hamlet in a country: much more Nehemiah must needs be touched for this city, which was so famous throughout the world. There may be good reasons alleged beside these, why he should weep for his city and country; as because it was a great relief and succour in all needs, to all that lived in it from time to time, and a great strength to the country about it.

But what is that, to be sad for the place where his elders were buried? Is there any holiness in the ground, that it is better to be buried there than elsewhere? or the dead men any thing the worse, if they be pulled out of their graves? What is the cause? Indeed it was called holy in divers places of the scriptures, as other outward things be, that are appointed and consecrated to a holy use. St Matthew saith that divers dead bodies, "after the resurrection of our Lord and Master, Christ Jesus, rose out of their graves, came into the holy city, and appeared to many." This holiness came not by holy-water casting, or hallowing of popish bishops which hallowed church or churchyard; but by God's appointing, and choosing it for his dwellingplace, where he would be worshipped, as the psalm teacheth, "The Lord hath chosen Sion, he hath chosen it for a dwellingplace for himself: this is my restingplace for ever; here will I dwell, because I have chosen it." So on God's behalf and appointing it for a place where he would be worshipped, it was holy, though the wickedness of the people had defiled it, and justly procured God's anger to destroy it. Christ Jesus our Lord, finding his temple full of all usurers, buyers and sellers, gat a whip, and drave them out, saying, "My house is a house of prayer; but ye have made it a den of thieves." So, by God's appointing it was "a house of prayer," and by man's misusing of it "a den of thieves." And he, seeing the wickedness of the people in it, wept for it, and said, "Jerusalem, which killest the prophets, and stonest to death them which are sent to thee, how oft would I have gathered thee, as the hen doth her chickens under her wings, and thou wouldst not!" The prophets of old time for the wickedness of the people in it have likewise rebuked Jerusalem sundry times: "How is this faithful city, which was full of justice, now become a harlot!" And again: "Hear, thou harlot," speaking to Jerusalem. Thus one thing, by God's appointing it to a holy use, may be called holy; and by man's misusing of it become most unholy. But the place itself maketh nothing holy, as it is written: God chose not the man for the place sake, but the place for man's sake; and therefore this city did not make the dead men holy that were buried in it, nor any thing the worse if they were buried out of it. Therefore the papists are both wicked in teaching the people, that one place is more holy than another to be buried in, as in the church rather than in the churchyard, and near the high altar rather than in the body of the church; and they are thieves also in picking poor men's purses for the same. In these were many abuses, as in any one thing.

But he that will keep these three rules shall not err. First, *that he do not cast out the dead bodies unburied*, to be devoured of wild beasts; nor bury them in dunghills, ditches, or such like places, where none else is buried. Diogenes, when his friends asked him, How he would be buried? bade them cast him out, it skilleth not how. "Why," say they, "the beasts will devour thee." "Nay then," saith he, "lay my staff by me, and I shall drive them away." A barbarous saying, and meet for a heathen man[1]! Yet I think the laying of the meteyard in the grave with the dead man came upon some such like cause, or else to drive away devils. Socrates, when he was asked the like question, answered more honestly, and bade bury him so as were most easy for his friends.

The second is, *to avoid great cost and sumptuousness*, as shrines, tombs, tapers, torches, candles, mourning coats, feastings, &c. which do no good to the dead, and are too chargeable and unprofitable to their friends. Yet, if civil policy add some solemnity to princes and noblemen, as their coat, armour, flag, sword, head-piece and recognizance, I dare not utterly condemn it; and yet would wish it more moderately used than many times it is. As there was difference in them, while they lived, from the common sort and state; so there may be in their burials for policy's sake, but for no religion or holiness at all.

[[1] Yet not so barbarous, if the remainder of the story be told: Qui poteris? illi: non enim senties. Quid igitur mihi ferarum laniatus oberit, nihil sentienti? Cic. Tusc. Quæst. I. 104. Ed.]

The third thing to be observed is, *that no superstition should be committed in them;* wherein the papists infinitely offend: as in masses, diriges, trentals, singing, ringing, holy water, hallowed places, years', days' and month-minds[1], crosses, pardon-letters to be buried with them, mourners, *de profundis*, by every lad that could say it, dealing of money solemnly for the dead, watching of the corpse at home, bell and banner, with many more than I can reckon.

These three abuses taken away, remaineth that comely order which christian charity requireth: as, to have neighbours quietly to accompany the corpse to the grave, as it was in the poor widow's son of Naim; brotherly to comfort those that lost their friends, as the Jews did Mary and Martha for their brother Lazarus; to confirm faith in the resurrection of the dead in the selfsame body, that there is put in the earth; to prepare themselves to die daily, not knowing when our course shall come; to praise the Lord, that granted the man so long a life among us with honesty, and in the end gave him a stedfast faith to seek his salvation only in Christ Jesus, who hath conquered death, hell and sin, by his own death, and by his rising from death hath justified us, and will raise us up from the grave in the end to live with him in heaven without end. The comely using of these in God's church is a great comfort to all good Christians, and the want of them a token of God's wrath and plague. Abraham was promised burial in his ripe age, as a blessing from God: Josias was promised that he should be buried in peace, and not see the plagues that should follow. The Gabeonites are praised of God, and rewarded also of David, for that they buried king Saul and his son, though the father was an ill man. Contrariwise, to king Jeroboam and Achab was threatened for a plague, that he and his posterity should not be buried, but devoured of beasts; and to king Joachim was foretold it, that he should be buried as an ass for his falling from God. Tobias was chiefly commended for burying the dead bodies of his countrymen that were cruelly slain.

Thus burial is commended; and to want it was great re-

[¹ The minding or remembrance of the dead, attended with feasting, at particular periods after their decease. The "month's mind" was generally used in our country; the "day's mind" &c. elsewhere. ED.]

proof. Jeremy threateneth them, that for their wicked life they should be pulled out of their graves. The place of burial needeth no bishop's blessing nor popish hallowing; but every comely place is holy enough, so it be reserved for that use only. It is called in the Greek *Coimeterion*, (κοιμητήριον,) that is, a sleeping place, and in the Hebrew *Beth-haiaim*, that is, the house of the living; thereby to teach us, that the body sleepeth, and the souls live, as Salomon saith, "The earth shall go to the earth from whence it was, and the soul shall return to him that gave it." Abraham bought a field to bury his in, and there was he and his posterity buried: and that was a common custom, continued long after by the judges and kings of Judah. So Gedeon, and generally the rest, were buried. It is said of king Osias, that he was "buried in the field where the other kings afore him were buried," in a place kept for that use only. And the gospel teacheth, that with the money which Judas sold Christ our Lord for, they "bought the potter's field to bury strangers in." These places were sometimes within cities, sometimes without, as Jesus Christ our Master was buried in a garden without the city Jerusalem; and he met the poor widow of Naim at the gates of the city, going farther to bury her son. It was long after, afore they used either church or churchyards.

Likewise mourning for the dead would be bridled, that it be not too much, and seem to grudge at God's doings in taking our friends from us. David wept for his child, and prayed whilst it was sick; but after it was dead, he wept no more. Our Saviour Christ cast the minstrels and mourners both out of the doors, when he raised up the young woman in her father's house. By which we are taught, that we should not dance with minstrels (for that is too barbarous and against nature,) nor to be grieved with the death of our friends, nor desperately mourn with the heathen, as though there were no life after this. "I would not have you ignorant," saith St Paul, "of them that sleep in death, that ye mourn not, as they that have no hope" to rise again. Sirach appointeth a reasonable time for reasonable mourning, saying, "Mourning for the dead is two or three days;" and before he addeth, "or seven days at the most." The cost that is made for the dead is rather, as St Augustine saith full well, "a comfort for the living, than help for the dead[1]." For sure it is comfortable to all good folk to see our friend in his life-time to have behaved himself so honestly, that his neighbours bear him so good will after his death, that they will see him buried; and it strengtheneth our faith of the resurrection, when the bodies are not cast away, as beasts' bodies be.

And although this general doctrine of comeliness be most true and comfortable, yet many times the case falleth out so, that many a good man cannot enjoy this kind of burial. In persecution many good martyrs have been devoured of wild beasts; many torn in pieces, and hanged on gibbets; many burned, aad their ashes cast into the water: yet these good men were nothing the worse for wanting their grave. For the kingdom of God standeth not in outward things, but in true faith in God by Christ. For as it profiteth not an evil man any thing at all to be solemnly buried; so it hurteth not a good man to want it in these cases, if he cannot get it. Every one shall receive then, as he hath done in his life; and not after his death, nor his costly burial. We read of the rich glutton, that he "was buried," and no doubt costly, as all his life was gorgeous; but poor Lazarus gat little cost at his death, that could find so little mercy in his life: yet was the glutton "in hell" for all his pomp, and poor Lazarus "in Abraham's bosom" in joy.

2 Cor. v.

Luke xvi.

But among all other foolishness in popery, I cannot but marvel at this, that in their great solemn singing for the dead they would not use, but forbid Alleluia to be sung. If the Romish church be the true church, and all well that they command, why should the late synagogue of Rome deface that which the best bishops of Rome allowed of? Jerom writeth in his thirtieth Epistle, called *Epitaphium Fabiolæ*, that at the burial of that noble woman "the people of Rome were gathered to the solemn funeral; and there the psalms did sound aloud, and Alleluia, rebounding with his echo on high, did shake the gilded ceilings of the temple. On one side a company of young men, on another side were old

Jer. Ep. 30.

[[1] Proinde omnia ista, id est, curatio funeris, conditio sepulturæ, pompa exsequiarum, magis sunt vivorum solatia quam subsidia mortuorum. De Civ. Dei, Lib. I. cap. xii. ED.]

men which sang forth the praises and deeds of that good woman. And no marvel," said he, "if men rejoice of her salvation, of whose conversion the angels in heaven were glad." The like is written in the twenty-seventh Epistle *ad Eustochium* for her mother Paula. In this I note the old church of Rome, that at such solemn funerals they sang Alleluia on high, as the papists do now on Easter day. Then they praised God for the dead, for so *Alleluia* signifieth; and now they pray God for the dead to get money withal. Then they rejoiced of their salvation; and now they weep for fear of the pope's purgatory. "Blessed are they that die in the Lord," saith St John. Why, then they go not from pains here to misery there. Why should the new Romish synagogue mislike that good ancient order? The one of them must needs err; which many think cannot be, and specially in this our age.

There be other controversies in these our days abroad, which might have been very well left untouched, if the quietness of God's church had been dutifully sought, as it ought to be: as, "whether the ministers should bury the dead, as the common order appointeth; and whether burial sermons are to be suffered and used, &c." This place giveth no great occasion to entreat of such matters, and therefore I shall let them pass. I love not contention, but do earnestly require every one in his calling for God's cause to seek peace with all their might; and those that profess Jesus Christ, I desire the Lord that they would join with their brethren in pulling down the Romish antichrist, the common enemy of all God's doctrine and religion, leaving such unprofitable contentions which breed division. And if they have too many burial sermons in the city, God grant us some more in the country!

Thus much have I spoken by occasion of Nehemiah's mourning for "the place of his fathers' burial;" not for the loss of the houses, city or walls; or that he was troubled with such superstitious opinions of thinking any holiness in the place, or that the dead folk were any thing worse in wanting their covering in the earth; but that he was grieved to see the city, which God chose himself to be worshipped in, and those good men, whose bones did rest there, or had faithfully served the Lord in their life, now to be given to heathen men's hands, God's religion neglected, the state of the commonwealth and good laws overthrown, God's enemies to triumph over them, as though their God could not or would not restore them. This should grieve all Christians in all ages, when they see the glory of the living God any ways blemished. God grant us this zeal unfeignedly!

4. *And the king said.* After that the king understood the cause of his sorrow and sad countenance, he both pitied the case and his man's heavy heart; and God so moved the king to favour his suit, that he asked him "what he would have?" When Nehemiah perceived the king's good inclination towards him and his suit, afore he would declare his petition, he turned him unto the God of heaven, and prayed him that he would so guide his tongue, that he should speak nothing which might justly offend the king, and also that he would so move the king's heart that his request might be granted. A worthy example for all Christians to follow in their suits making to the prince. He goeth not to any great man, nor to any other which was in favour with the king, to desire him to speak for him, to commend his cause, to persuade the king to grant his request; which he might lawfully have done. Also, he offereth no rewards nor like pleasure to any man; but turneth him to the God of heaven, as the chiefest governor of all goodness, which setteth up rulers, and putteth down kings, and is King of kings, and prayeth him to prosper his suit. He prayeth to no idols nor saints, though he lived among that idolatrous nation; for he knew they could not help him; but faithfully called on the living God, which his good fathers had worshipped of old time. This prayer was not so much in speaking or kneeling, but a lifting up of his mind towards God, and desiring him to further his suit. Anna made like prayer, when she poured out her sorrow before the Lord, moving her lips, but speaking never a word; in so much that the high priest thought she had been drunken. For it falleth out oft, that in great sorrow a man cannot let a tear fall, the heart being oppressed with grief, and yet he at another time will weep tenderly: so in prayer ofttimes, the more earnestly that a man prayeth, the less he can speak, his heart being so earnestly given to call on the Lord. As when Moses was in great heaviness, and prayed for the children

1 Sam. i.

of Israel, being in that great distress, God said unto him,
"Why criest thou unto me?" and yet there is not one word Exod. xiv.
written, that he cried or said. It is the praying and crying of the heart, that God is so much delighted withal; and
yet never the worse, if it burst out into words, and shew
itself. Let no man then excuse himself, and say he cannot
pray, except he were in the church or in his chamber alone;
for in all places he may lift up his mind to God, though
he were in the market or mountain; and with hearty prayer,
though he speak not at all, desire the Lord to hear him,
as Nehemiah doeth here in the presence of the king and
many others. And no doubt, if he pray in faith and for
such things as further the glory of God, the Lord will hear
him. Let us learn here to begin all our doings with prayer
unto the Lord, and we shall speed so much the better.

5. *And I said.* When Nehemiah had made his short
prayer in so earnest a faith, and perceived the king's good
will towards him, then with all humbleness, not appointing
the king what he should do, but referring all to his consideration and wisdom, desireth him, that if he thought it
good, if Nehemiah himself were thought a fit man for the
purpose, or his service had been acceptable to the king, that
it would "please him to send him to Jewry," to the city
where he was born, and his elders lay buried, that he might
"build it up again." No marvel that Nehemiah was afraid,
and prayed earnestly for good success in his suit: for he
knew well that the Jews were counted a rebellious people,
and hated of all countries about them; and the king might
think him to make his suit for building of Jerusalem, that
they might settle and strengthen themselves against him and
other kings, and claim their old liberties that they had afore.
But God so moved the king's heart, that he had no suspicion of any such enterprise by Nehemiah, his faithful and
trusty servant.

With such modesty princes would be dealt withal, and
not roughly nor unreverently: for so Nehemiah doth here
most dutifully. If many men had their choice at the king's
hand now a days, to ask what they would, as Nehemiah
might have done here, would they not have asked castles,
lands, offices, and authority for them and their issue, that

they might have been great men in the world; and not the building of a city, which would have been a trouble and cost unto them rather than any profit, and when they had finished it, it had not been their own, but other should have enjoyed it, and they little the better for it? But such is the zeal of them that love the Lord, that they will seek to build and not to pull down, as many do, and will prefer all things that may further the glory of God, though it be with their own loss, rather than seek their own profit with the hinderance of it. Terentius, a nobleman, captain under the emperor Valens, when he had been in wars and sped well, the emperor, liking well of his good service, bade him advise himself what he would make suit for, and he would reward him liberally. Terentius, being a zealous man in religion, and perceiving the great heresy of the Arians to be much favoured, (and the emperor himself being thought to be infected therewith,) could not abide such blasphemy against Jesus Christ our Saviour, put this supplication in writing, and with most humble reverence and earnest desire required the emperor to grant him his request, and he would think his service fully recompensed. The effect of his supplication was, "that it would please the emperor to grant the true Christians a church to serve and worship the Lord Jesus in separately from the Arians, which dishonoured him; for it was not fit among the Christians to hear such blasphemy against the Lord Christ, as they spued out." The emperor, reading his supplication, and considering the effect of it, was very angry, pulled it in pieces, and threw it away, chid with Terentius, that he could devise nothing to ask but that. Terentius gathered up the pieces of paper courteously, and said, "if he could not be heard in God's cause, he would not make further suit for his own profit[1]."

Theodor. Lib. iv. cap. 32.

Niceph. xi. cap. 49.

O noble captain! where is thy fellow? Who hath done the like, but Nehemiah here, Ester, and some few other? God increase the number of such religious men about princes! and then they will not gape so fast as they do, to pluck

[1 Ὁ δὲ τῆς ἱκεσίας συλλέξας τὰ ῥήγματα, Ἐδεξάμην, ἔφη, ὦ βασιλεῦ, καὶ ἔχω τὸ δῶρον, καὶ ἕτερον οὐκ αἰτήσω· σκοποῦ γὰρ κριτὴς ὁ τῶν ὅλων κριτής. P. 334. Ed. Paris. 1544.—Nicephorus merely repeats Theodoret. ED.]

and pull away from God and his ministers all that they may scratch or scrape, to the dishonour of God, defacing of his glory, decay of the ministery, religion, and all good learning; thinking most highly of themselves, that they be worthy to have all things, where in deed they deserve least, and the more they get the less are they satisfied. It is a full contentation to all good men, when they see God glorified in his church, word, and ministery; for then they know, if they dutifully seek, that the Lord will not see them lack that which shall be necessary for them; and they will content themselves with that portion that God giveth them, and will not greedily seek for other men's things wrongfully, to the dishonour of the high God.

6. *And the king said.* When the king had considered his request, he advised himself well, and was both loth to deny him his suit, and also to forego so faithful a servant; asked him how long he would be absent, and when he would return. So did the queen too, which sat by the king: they both loved him so well, and would not have him long from them. A special gift of God, to see a stranger born, of that religion and people which were hated of all the world, to be in such favour with the king and queen, and to find such favour and grace in their sight, that he gave licence and all other necessary things to build that city, which had been noisome to so many kings about them. But such is the merciful goodness of our God towards his church and people, that he will make strangers and their enemies to defend and help them: as Pharaoh and Assuerus did, by the good means of Joseph and Ester, &c.

Gen. xlvii. Esth. viii. ix.

And because "the queen sat by," it is like that there was some solemn feast that day; for the queens of Persia used not to come into the king's presence, but when they were called for by name, as it is written in the book of Ester: and Strabo writeth, that the Persians "used to debate of weighty matters, when they were refreshed with wine." This might be a great cause of the great fear that Nehemiah was in, as he said before, to see the queen present, and many other great men beside, no doubt, as is commonly used at such solemnities. It will make any good nature afraid to speak to a king, but much more in the presence of so many estates, who might be hinderers of his suit, and counsel the king to the contrary. But when God will pity his people, and have things forward, he will so move kings' hearts, that nothing shall hinder that he will have done. And so the king did grant him his request, gave him leave to go build that city, and sent him away honourably, and rewarded him liberally, as followeth. Nehemiah appointed the king a time of his return to him again; but when, it is not here mentioned; yet such a time as the king was content withal. In the last chapter of this book it appeareth, that in the twelfth year following Nehemiah returned unto the king, and yet gat licence again to go to Jerusalem. But whether this was the time that he appointed to return, it is not written, and therefore uncertain; and being unwritten and uncertain, it is not so necessary to be known, nor curiously to be searched; but we may content ourselves to be ignorant of it, as of all uncertain, unwritten, and unnecessary truths.

The Text. v. 7. *And I said unto the king, If it be thought good to the king, let them give me letters to the captains beyond the river, which may convey me until I come into Jehuda;*

8. *And letters also to Asaph, keeper of the king's woods, that he may give me timber to make beams for the gates of the palace, which is near the temple, and for the walls of the city, and for the house which I shall enter to. And the king gave me, according to the hand of my God, which was good toward me.*

9. *And I came to the captains beyond the river, and gave them the king's letters; and the king sent with me captains of the army and horsemen.*

10. *And Sanballat the Horonite and Tobias, that servant and Ammonite, heard of it, and they were grieved with great sorrow that a man was come to seek any good for the children of Israel.*

Nehemiah was a glad man, that the king had granted his request; and sleepeth not his purpose, nor letteth the time slip; but with all diligence prepareth things necessary for his journey. And first, because the journey was long, and dangerous for enemies, that hated him and all the Jews, lest he should have some displeasure done him by the way, he desireth the king, that his council and secretaries might give him a passport, and grant him men to conduct him safely into Jewry. A bold request for so mean a subject, being but the king's cupbearer, a stranger, and born of that people and country which all the world hated. What could have been done more for the noblest man in the country, or for the best servitor the king had? I cannot tell whether it is to be more marvelled at, that either he durst ask it, or that the king would grant it. But Nehemiah perceived God's good will and the king's favour toward him, and was bold to ask: God prospered his suit, that the king granted his request.

And as afore, so here mark also, that he doth not boldly and rashly appoint the king what he should do, but with all modesty referreth his request unto the king's wisdom and discretion, to grant or deny, and saith, "If it be thought good to the king." Again, he doth not with bribes or flattery procure the king's letters to be signed privily, (as many do, that make unhonest suits, and would not have their matter debated by the wiser sort, lest so it might be denied;) but he requireth, that they which are appointed for that purpose, and do such things by good advice, as chancellors and secretaries, might give him letters to the captains beyond the river Euphrates, (for that is meant by the river, because it was more notable than any other river in the country, and did divide the kingdom of Persia from other countries about it,) over which into Jewry he might pass.

It might be thought strange to some, that Nehemiah here asketh not only of the king his letters of passport, but also a number of soldiers, to conduct him safely into Jewry. For Ezra, when he had licence of the king to take the same journey, and build the temple, neither asked nor had any to conduct him safely on his way, though the danger was as great then, and he was afraid as well as Nehemiah was now. Why should Nehemiah ask now, seeing he served and trusted in that same God that Ezra did, and was as earnest and zealous in religion as he was? why should this be lawful or commendable in the one, and not in the other? Causes may be rendered divers. There was difference in

Ezra viii.

the persons and times. Ezra was a priest, cunning in the law, and had oft taught boldly afore the king and his nobles, how sure and safe they were from all dangers, that put their trust in God alone: and if he should have afterwards been afraid, he should have seemed to have spoken untruly afore, and his God should not have been thought able or willing to defend his people that trusted in him. Nehemiah was a courtier, and in great favour with the king, and had not so openly and boldly spoken of God's providence and care towards his people as Ezra had, (though he believed it as faithfully as the other did,) and therefore might more boldly, without reproach of his God or his doctrine and sayings, ask it.

Yet this proveth not, that preachers may not at any time require a safe conduct of princes, to whom it belongeth to provide in dangerous times, that passage by the high way may be safe and quiet. Paul, as we read, when the Jews had "sworn that they would neither eat nor drink until they had killed him," desired an under-captain to bring his nephew (who told him of that conspiracy) to the high captain, to declare so much to him, and desired that he would provide some safety for him, that he were not murdered by the way: and in this doing Paul neither offended man, nor distrusted of God's providence and care toward him. Again, in that great and long storm that Paul and his fellows were in on the sea, where they looked for nothing but to be drowned, the angel of God told Paul, that "God had given him the lives of all that were with him in the ship," and none of them should perish; yet afterward, when the mariners would have cunningly conveyed themselves out of the ship, "under pretence to have cast anchor," Paul told the high captain, that if he suffered them to go out of the ship, they should all perish: and this he did not say, as doubting of the angel's true message, nor of God's good will and mighty hand, able to deliver them, but to teach us that, although God have made us promise of his mercy, we may not tempt him, lie down, and sleep carelessly, but diligently to look for and use such helps and means, as God hath appointed us to work by. God worketh all goodness in us himself, and yet hath appointed means for us to use and do such things, the which we may in no case neglect; and

_{Acts xxiii.}

_{Acts xxvii.}

yet all praise is due to him, whatsoever we do; for it is he that both ordaineth the end of all things, how they shall come to pass, and also the means, how they shall be brought to pass, and prospereth all them that, forsaking themselves, use such means and hang on him, knowing the beginning, midst, and end to be ruled and come to pass as he appointed.

God inspired the apostles with all knowledge of the scriptures suddenly, which were unlearned and never went to the school; yet may not we think that we will be learned after the same sort, without study and prayer: for then we tempt God, refusing such helps as he hath appointed for us to come to learning by. And though we study and pray never so much, yet we shall understand nothing until he give us his Holy Spirit, the schoolmaster of all truth, to lighten our minds and give understanding of his holy will. We be <small>Isai. x.</small> like an axe in the carpenter's hand, which though it be a good one, yet the praise of the good work that is done with it is to be given to the man, and not to the axe. Such things be we in God's hand, by whom he worketh his will and glory, though not unsensible, as dead things be, yet as unable to work any good thing without him, as the axe is without the carpenter; for of ourselves we "are not able to think" a good thought, as the apostle saith, that all praise <small>2 Cor. iii.</small> may be his, that blesseth and prospereth both us and the means that he hath appointed for us to work by, and bringeth it to a good end. We must think likewise of God's doings and ourselves in all other things, sin except, that he "worketh all in all," yet not without us; that all may say with David, "Not unto us, O Lord, not unto us, but unto thy name <small>Psal. cxv.</small> give all praise and glory."

Thus we see that some man may at some times do that another may not; yea, one man himself cannot do at all times that he may well do at some times. But, this general rule being kept, that God's glory be not defaced by doing of it, it may be done of all men at all times. Paul wrought for his living, when he preached, which others did not, nor are bound to do; and he might have lived of his preaching, as well as others did: yet the time was such, and the people so peevishly bent to slander the gospel of God, that Paul forbare to use that liberty which God gave him, and would not be thought to preach for gains; but wrought for his living, would not be chargeable to any man. Such was the case here, that Ezra might not ask help, and Nehemiah might.

8. *And letters also.* Nehemiah, wisely considering what he wanted yet to the finishing of such a work as he went about, perceived he should need timber; and therefore desired the king's letters of warranty "to Asaph, keeper of his woods, that he might deliver him such trees and so many, as would serve his purpose, both for the building of the gates, the towers of the palace near the temple, the city walls, and the house that he should dwell in himself." And here we shall see the king worthy great praise, though he was but barbarous; that for policy's sake, and wealth of his country, both preserved his woods, and set a keeper over them, that they should not be wilfully wasted. A good example for princes, to foresee the like in their countries in all ages; for commonwealths cannot stand without the use of woods in many kind of things. Nehemiah is also much to be commended, that although he was in so great authority and favour with the king, yet he would not take of his woods without his licence and warrant, as many do. If these two things were kept in this land, that both the prince's woods, and others too, should be preserved, faithful keepers set over them, and none delivered without sufficient warrant, we should not find the great lack that we generally do. What spoil hath been made of woods in our remembrance, wise men have noted, but few gone about to amend it, though many have lamented it. What common dealing hath been practised to get such lands of the prince and other men, as were well wooded, into their hands, and when they had spoiled the woods, racked the rents, and deeply fined the tenants, then to return the same land into the prince's hand again, or sell it over to others, and get as much, it is too well known throughout the realm, and to the hurt of many, at this day.

Nehemiah could ask nothing so much, but the king did grant it speedily. God did so move the king's heart, and prospered Nehemiah's doings, in so much that he giveth all the praise to God alone, and saith, "the hand of his God was good toward him," to set forward his good purpose of building Jerusalem. Nehemiah knew well that God was the common God of all people and nations, both by creation and government of them: but because he seemed to favour him more than he did other, in giving him boldness to open his grief unto the king, wisdom to make his humble suit without offence unto the king, and so good success to have all things granted that he required of the king, so unlooked for, he calleth him his God, as if he loved or cared more for him than for the rest of the world. This is the common use of the scripture, to call him the God of Abraham, Isaac, Jacob, David, and Daniel, because he did both deliver them out of such trouble as none else could or would, or any hath been so oft and wonderfully delivered as they were; and also, did so bless and prosper them and their doings, as the common sort of men were not wont to be. So they that see their own misery, and how little goodness, but rather punishment, they deserve at God's hand, when they see the Lord pity them, remember them, help them, and bless them, they conceive by and bye such a love toward God, that it would please him to look upon them, that for joy they burst out into tears, they call him their God, because they feel his good will and favour so much toward them, and more than to other, yea, much more than they could deserve or be bold to look for at his hands. And as one man useth to help another by putting forth his hand to raise him that is fallen, to give him such things as he wanteth, and to put away and defend him from such things as may hurt him; so it is called "the good hand of God," when he either bestoweth his blessing and good things upon us, or when he putteth away such dangers and evils from us, as might hurt us, as it were with his mighty and merciful hand.

9. *And I came to the captains.* Nehemiah hath now taken his leave at the court, and loseth no time; but when he had provided all things necessary for his journey, he speedeth himself forward, and thinketh all time lost that is not bestowed in relieving his country, being in such misery. A strange example, to see a courtier leave that wealth, ease, and authority that he was in, and go dwell so far from the court, where commonly it falleth out that he which is out of sight is out of mind and soon forgotten, in an old, torn, and decayed city, a rude people and poor country, where

he should not live quietly for his enemies, but take pains to build himself a house, and the city where he would dwell; to toil and drudge, like a poor labouring man, that should work for his living, yea, and many times to be sore assaulted of his enemies, both openly and privily, to the great danger of his life, as the rest of the book following will declare. But this is the case of earnest and zealous men in religion, that they can say with David, "I have chosen rather to be a door-keeper in the house of God, than to dwell in the palaces of sinners;" and, "it is better to be one day there than a thousand elsewhere." God for his mercy's sake raise up some such few courtiers as Nehemiah was, which can be content to forsake their own ease, wealth and authority, and give themselves painfully to travail for the wealth of their country! And because that is to be wished, rather than hoped for, good Lord, give us such as will be no hinderers, and will be content to live in compass quietly, and not seek to trouble others that would serve the Lord willingly. Amen.

_{Psal. lxxxiv.}

The king did not only deal thus liberally with Nehemiah at his departure, but also honourably sent him away with captains and horsemen, safely to conduct him on his journey, that none should hurt him by the way. And where the king used him so courteously, no doubt the rest of the court shewed him much courtesy; for courtiers must needs like and mislike whatsoever the king seemeth to like or mislike, to set up or pull down. Courtiers commonly, when the king speaketh, have lost both sense and wit; for if the king seemeth to favour any thing, they all, as men without understanding, say it must needs be so. If the king will not give ear to hear a matter, they are all deaf and cannot abide to hear speak of it. If the king will not see it, they all cry out, Away with it! So that it is hard to tell, whether is in more miserable case, the king or such dissemblers: for if the king have no judgment of himself, he shall have no help of such; and they, like witless men, dare not speak a truth. Happy is that prince therefore, that hath wise counsellors about him, which will dutifully inform him of matters uprightly, wisely debate the matter with him, without all double dealing, as the other sorts do. When king Assuerus would advance Haman, every man had him in reverence; but when Mar-

docheus was set up, then was there crying, *Crucifige*, on Esth. iii. &
Haman. But thus mercifully doth our Lord God deal with viii.
his church and people, that in every age he hath some about
the prince, that both can and will speak and be heard, though
not for all generally in their rage and persecution, yet for
many, as occasion serveth, which shall be delivered from
such tyranny to glorify their God for his mercy; though
many willingly spend their lives patiently to the praise of the
same God eternally. But no rage shall be so great to root
out God's chosen, but the Lord will ever preserve a number,
even by help of their enemies, openly to worship and serve
him in despite of all their foes.

Plinius, the ruler of a province under Trajan the emperor, Euseb. Lib.
and appointed to punish the Christians sundry ways, seeing iii. cap. 33.
the great number of them, doubted what he should do; and
wrote to the emperor, that "he found no wickedness in them,
but that they would not worship images, and that they would
sing psalms before day-light unto Christ as a God, and did
forbid all sins to be used among them." The emperor, hearing
this, became a great deal more gentle unto them[1]. Sallus- Ruff. Lib. i.
tius, tormenting Theodorus, a Christian, sundry ways and a cap. 36.
long time, to make him forsake his faith, but all in vain,
went to Julianus the emperor, and told him what he had
done from the day-break until ten of the clock; and counselled him that he "should prove that way no more by cruelty,
for they gat glory in suffering patiently, and he gat shame
in punishing so sharply," because they would not yield unto
him[2]. Many more such examples the ecclesiastical histories

[[1] Πρὸς ἃ τὸν Τραϊανὸν δόγμα τοιοῦτον τεθεικέναι· τὸ Χρισ-
τιανῶν φῦλον μὴ ἐκζητεῖσθαι μέν, ἐμπεσὸν δὲ κολάζεσθαι. P. 30.
Ed. Paris. 1544. Pliny's Letter to Trajan here referred to is extant.
Lib. x. Epist. 97. ED.]

[[2] Quod Sallustius, præfectus ejus, non probans, licet esset gentilis,
tamen jussus exequitur; et apprehensum unum quendam adolescentem,
qui primus occurrit, Theodorum nomine, a prima luce usque ad horam
decimam tanta crudelitate et tot mutatis carnificibus torsit, ut nulla ætas
simile factum meminerit. Cum tamen ille in equuleo sublimis, et
hinc inde lateribus instanti tortore, nihil aliud faceret, nisi quod vultu
securo et læto psalmum, quem pridie omnis ecclesia cecinerat, iteraret;
cumque se omni expensa crudelitate Sallustius nihil egisse perspiceret,
recepto in carcerem juvene, abiisse fertur ad Imperatorem, et quid egerit

are full of, where God delivered his people by the forespeech of their enemies: but these shall suffice at this present.

God had now raised up Nehemiah, and had given him favour and grace in the king's sight, to ask and obtain comfort for the deliverance of his church and people, the Jews, which had been so long in great misery and slavery. Nehemiah then passeth on his journey toward Jerusalem with great speed and honour, passeth the river Euphrates, and those thievish and dangerous ways that he was afraid of, safely cometh to the rulers of the country beyond Euphrates, delivereth them the king's commission for timber, and a band of new soldiers for his safe conduct into Jewry, that these might return home again to the king, with thanks that they had conveyed him so far on his way safely.

10. *And Sanballat.* As Nehemiah was glad that God had prospered his doings so well hitherto, so others were sorry. For at his coming into the country Sanballat and Tobias were so sore grieved, that any man found such favour with the king, that he might procure any good thing toward the children of Israel; that, if he had not brought the king's letters with him, he could not have escaped their displeasure. It is not manifest in the text, what country these men be of; but I can well incline to that opinion, which thinketh that Sanballat was a Moabite of the city Horonaim, which Esay in the xv and Jeremy xlviii speak of, and that Tobias was an Ammonite; because the Moabites and Ammonites were ever from the beginning most cruel against the Israelites in their coming out of Egypt and all their doings, though they came and were born of near kinsmen. Abraham was uncle unto Lot: of Abraham came the Israelites; of Lot, when he was drunken, came the Moabites and Ammonites, gotten by his own daughters. And this is commonly seen, that both those which be so bastardly born against nature prove not honest; and when displeasure groweth among kinsfolk, and specially for religion, as this was, it scarce can be forgiven. Sanballat by interpretation signifieth *a pure enemy;*

Gen. xix.

nuntiasse, ac monuisse ne tale aliquod tentare vellet de cetero; alioquin et illis gloriam et sibi ignominiam quæreret. Auctores Hist. Eccles. x. (Ruffini I.) cap. 36. The same account is given by Theodoret, Lib. III. cap. 11. ED.]

and Tobias was a servant, and yet crept into great authority, as the other was. These two points may well agree to the papists, and all enemies of God's truth; for they will lurk privily, until time serve them to shew their cruelty, and then they will rage fiercely: and so will slaves and servants, that come to authority from base degree. Salomon saith, "There be three things that trouble the world," whereof the first is "a servant when he cometh to be a ruler:" for then he waxeth so proud and cruel, that he forgetteth what he was, he disdaineth all men but himself. The papists are bastardly born of spiritual whoredom, serve the pope as slaves in all his superstitions: they come of Agar the bond woman, and not of Sara the free woman; and therefore hate the true children of God, which believing the promises of God are saved, and they will be saved by their own works, contrary to the scripture; and so grieved when they see any thing prosper with them, that for very malice and envy they pine away; as these two wicked imps do here shew themselves, because they would not see Jerusalem restored. Prov. xxx.

As the building of this Jerusalem had many enemies, so the repairing of the heavenly Jerusalem by the preaching of the glorious gospel of Christ Jesus hath many more. The malice and envy of worldlings against all those that set up the kingdom of Christ, and pull down the pride of man's heart, is so great that it can never be satisfied. If malice had not blinded these men, what harm was it to them to see the Jews do well, and God worshipped there? The Jews never went about to invade or conquer their country; and yet they could not enjoy their own country without much trouble of these envious people. Envy ever disdaineth to see other do well, and specially such as live well and serve the Lord Christ, and is glad of other men's mischief and harm, for then they think none shall be able to withstand their pleasures and devices. The people of Canaan, when they heard of Josua and the Israelites coming with so great courage to possess their country, were so dismayed, that their courage melted away like wax at the fire. Herod and all Jerusalem were astonied, when they heard tell that a new king Christ, being but a child, was born; and yet the angels sung for joy. When our Saviour Christ was Josh. ii.

crucified and buried, his disciples were sad, and the Jews rejoiced: but when Christ had conquered death, and was risen again, then the disciples were glad, and the Jews were sad. Thus one thing worketh diversely in divers men. Nehemiah was glad that he had found such favour with the king to build Jerusalem; Sanballat and his fellows were as sorry that any should do it. The gospel hath foretold that it should so fall out with the worldlings and the godly: the one shall rejoice, when he seeth God's glory flourish; and the other shall be grievously tormented in conscience. "The world shall be glad," saith St John, "but ye shall weep; and yet this your sorrow shall be turned into joy:" for God will not see his servants overwhelmed with trouble, but he will deliver them. David, describing at large the manifold blessings that God poureth on them that fear him, in the end of the psalm saith, "The ungodly shall see it, and it shall grieve him; he will gnash with his teeth, and pine away for malice; but the desire of the ungodly shall perish."

Joh. xvi.

1 Cor. x.

Psal. cxii.

There cannot be a greater grief to an ill man, than to see a good man do well. When there was a question moved before king Frederic among his physicians, what was best to make the sight clear, and some said fennel, some saladine, some glass, some other things, as they thought good; Actius Sincerus, a nobleman standing by, said he thought envy was the best: when every man either laughed or marvelled at his saying, he yielded a reason, and said, "Envy maketh any thing that she seeth to appear better than it is; for the envious man thinketh another man's corn to be better than his own, and another man's cow to give more milk, and the least good thing that a good man hath seemeth great in his eye, that cannot see other thrive, and espieth diligently with great grief the smallest things the good man doeth; and that is," said he, "to make the eye sight clearest, when every small thing shall be best espied." Envy is worse than any poison of other beasts. The snake, the adder, the toad, have deadly poison in them, wherewith they hurt others, and yet it hurteth not themselves: but envy is so poisonful a thing, that it killeth him that hath it first, and hurteth not other: for he fretteth with himself, he fumes, he pines away to see others do well; he eateth not, nor sleepeth quietly, nor can be merry until he see some mischief fall on the good man: and as the canker eateth and consumeth hard iron and brass, so malicious envy with fretting consumeth out envious stomachs. When Sanballat and Tobias, hearing but of Nehemiah's coming into the country, and that he had found such favour with the king to build Jerusalem, were thus grieved with malicious envy to see the Jews do well; what sundry attempts they made afterwards to overthrow that building, the residue of this book will declare. How the envious papists, disdaining to see God's gospel take place in any country, do rage, fret, fume, pine away for sorrow and anger; how they have blooded and bathed their hands in their brethren's blood, and yet cannot be quiet, the world seeth it too well, good men lament it, justice crieth vengeance, and God will revenge it.

v. 11. *And I came to Jerusalem, and I was there three days.* The Text.
12. *And I rose in the night, I and a few men with me, and told no man what God had put in my heart to do in Jerusalem: and there was no beast with me, but the beast which I sat upon.*
13. *And I went forth at the valley gate in the night, and before the dragon's well to the dunghill gate; and considered the walls of Jerusalem which were broken down, and the gates which were consumed with fire.*
14. *And I passed over to the well gate, and to the king's fishpool, and there was no room for the beast under me to pass.*
15. *And I went up in the night by the brook, and I considered the well; and coming back I came by the valley gate, and returned.*

Nehemiah hath now done with the court, and is come to Jerusalem, which he so much desired: he was weary of the noise and solemnity of the court, and thought he should live more quietly in his country; but it falleth out clean contrary: for his trouble and danger is double to that it was afore; and he cometh from the court to the cart, and from a pleasant life to a careful. After his long journey he resteth himself and his company three days, knowing the weakness of man's body to be such, that it cannot continually endure labour, but must be refreshed with ease and rest. Thus must good men in authority not overlay their servants with continual labour, but let them have reasonable time of rest: for God made the sabbath day, that both man and beast might rest, and not be oppressed with continual toiling: such a consideration he had of man's weakness. We do not read of any great solemnity that the Jews used to welcome him withal, being their countryman, and coming from the court so honourably, with such a band of men to conduct him, and being in so great favour with the king: it is like, if that there had been any such thing, it would have been declared, as well as his estate was in the court afore. It was but a hard beginning, to have Sanballat and Tobias, two of the greatest men in the country, to lower so at his coming, and no greater rejoicing made of his countrymen, for whose sake he took all those pains: but nothing can discourage him; on forward he goeth with his purpose.

These three days, though he rested with his body, his mind was not yet quiet: he was still devising how he might best and speedily go about his building; how he might open to his countrymen the cause of his coming; how he might persuade them to join with him in that work; and to declare unto them the king's commission and good will toward him, and what favour he found in the court. For they might well doubt, if they should enterprise so great a work without the king's licence, they might run into great displeasure, seeing they had so many enemies in the country about them, that with all their might had sought the hinderance of that building so many years. They themselves had lien so long in despair, followed their own business, sought their own gains, and cared not for building their own city, nor sought any ways how to do it; they had almost so far forgotten their God, oppressed the poor, and fallen to so great wickedness, as appeareth hereafter, that they had no care of religion in the most part of them.

12. *And I rose in the night.* After that Nehemiah had thus long debated with himself, how this work should be taken in hand, he could not sleep, but riseth in the night, taketh a few of his men with him on foot, and he himself

on his mule, and rideth round about Jerusalem, vieweth the walls, in what place they were worst destroyed, and how they might most speedily be repaired. If he had taken his view in the day-time, every man would have stood gazing on him, wondering what he went about, and have hindered it; and not unlike, some would have been offended at him, and his enemies round about would, as much as they durst or could, have stopped his enterprise. The night therefore was thought to be the quietest time to do this in, and he is content to break his sleep for the furtherance of this great good work. A good example for all men, and especially for those that be in authority in the commonwealth, as Nehemiah was now, and for those that have the charge of God's church committed unto them, not to be idle, even in the night season to break a sleep, yea, watch all night, if need be, to set forward the building of God's house and city.

The physician will watch with his patient all night, if need be: the good captain will not sleep all the night long, though he have set his watch afore; but he will sometimes at the second watch, sometimes at the third, arise and see whether his watchmen be fallen on sleep, and what they do, or whether any enemies draw near or no: so should every Christian privately for himself break his sleep, lift up his mind unto the Lord, call upon him by faithful prayer, call for mercy at his fatherly goodness, commend himself and all God's people to his gracious protection, desiring that all stumbling-blocks, which be hinderers of his glory, may be taken away; but specially those that be negligent to watch a whole night in prayer, devising what ways God's glorious name, gospel, and religion may best be increased, his kingdom enlarged, Christ glorified, and antichrist confounded. David saith, he "rose at midnight to give praise" unto the Lord's blessed name. Our mortal enemy, Satan, never sleepeth night nor day, but continually "goeth about like a roaring lion, seeking whom he may devour;" and if we had not as good a watchman to watch for our safety when we sleep, we should be swallowed up every hour. "Behold," saith David, "he neither slumbereth nor sleepeth, that is the watchman of Israel." All praise be to that merciful God, which taketh such care for his miserable people, and watcheth when we sleep, that our enemy devour us not suddenly!

Psal. cxix.

Psal. cxxi.

Luke vi.　　Our Saviour Christ, to give us example of this diligent watching to pray in the night, prayeth the whole night himself in the mount, afore he chose his apostles to preach.
Josh. x.　　Josue marched forward all the night long, to fight with the Amorites, and overcame them. Gedeon in the night season
Judg. vi.　pulled down the altar of Baal that his father had made, and the grove of wood that was near unto it, being afraid to do it in the day time for fear of his father's house and people thereby; and in the night also set on the Madianites, and vanquished them. So good men let no time pass, wherein occasion is given them to further God's glory, night or day, but earnestly follow it until they have brought their purpose to effect. And that this viewing of the walls might be more secretly done, he chooseth the night season rather than the day to do it in; a few men to wait on him, rather than many; no more horse than his own, and all the rest on foot, for making noise. Many men and horses would soon have been espied, one troubled another, made a great noise, and have bewrayed his counsel, which he kept so secret to himself, that he told it not to any man what he went about: and if he had gone alone, he might have fallen into some danger of life, having none to help him. The night is the quietest time to devise things in; for then all things be quiet, every man keepeth his house and draweth to rest; no noise is made abroad; the eyes are not troubled with looking at many things; the senses are not drawn away with fantasies, and the mind is quiet.

Many men would have committed the doings of such things to other men, and would have trusted them to have viewed the walls, and after to have certified him of their doings, in what case they were, and how they might most speedily be repaired: but Nehemiah, lest he should have wrong information given him, though he was a man of great authority, did not disdain to take the pains himself, brake his sleep, and rode about the walls himself,—to teach us that nothing should be thought painful at any time, nor disdainful to any man, of what estate soever he were, to set forth the building of God's city and dwelling-place, which every man ought to do in his calling. David, when the ark of God was brought out of Abinadab's house, played on instruments, and after cast off his kingly apparel, and for rejoicing danced afore the ark in his poor ephod, to glorify his God withal. Michal his wife, looking forth at a window, and seeing him dance, laughed him to scorn, and asked him if he were not ashamed to dance so nakedly afore such a company of women, as though he had been but some light scoffing fellow. But David was so zealous a man and earnest to glorify God by all means, that he forgat himself to be a king, abased himself with the lowest and simplest, and said to Michal, that he would "yet more lowly cast down himself," so that his God might be glorified in his doings. Michal for mocking of him was barren all her life, and had no children; but David for this humbling of himself was blessed of the Lord. Moses forsook to live in pleasure in Pharao's court, and to be called his daughter's son, and chose to live in trouble with his brethren the Jews, and to keep Jethro's sheep, so that he might serve the Lord. Our Saviour, the perfect pattern of all humbleness, did not disdain to wash the miry feet of his disciples, and wipe them: and last of all, as though that had not been base enough, he humbleth himself to the slanderous death of the cross, and to hang on a cross between two thieves for us, being his enemies, as though he had been a third: he loved us so tenderly, that he would go to hell, that we might go to heaven; he would die so vile a death, to purchase us so glorious a life; and suffer the pains due to our sins, that we might enjoy the pleasures of heaven. God grant all estates this humbleness of mind, that for his cause, that forsook all worldly honour, they may be content to abase themselves, to suffer all pains and reproachful things in the world for the furtherance of the building of God's city! Such humble abasing of themselves is the greatest honour that ever they shall get: all worldly pomp without this is vile and shameful.

In that he "telleth no man what he went about, and that God had put it in his mind to do it," he declareth that it was not his own device, nor came from any man, but God himself was the mover of it, and therefore was more earnestly to be followed. He that will learn to keep counsel in deed, let him learn of Nehemiah here to tell no man, not to his dearest friend. Many will come to his friend, and say, I can tell you a secret matter, but ye must keep in counsel and tell nobody. What foolishness is this, that thou wouldst have another to keep thy counsel secret to himself, and thou thyself canst not keep it secret to thyself! Wouldst thou have another man to do that for thee, which thou wilt not do for thyself? Keep thine own counsel, and then thou shalt not need to fear lest other men bewray thee. And if thou wouldst have another man to keep thy counsel, he will think thou shouldst not have told it thyself, and then it had been safe enough: but in telling him, he telleth another friend, and he saith to him as thou saidst to thy friend afore, I can tell you a thing that was told me secretly, but you must keep counsel and tell nobody: so with going from friend to friend, it will be known to all men. Therefore the surest and only way to have counsel kept secret is to follow Nehemiah here, and tell it to no man, though he be thy dear friend; for he hath other friends to tell it to, as thou didst tell it him.

If any do marvel why Nehemiah was thus earnest in this building, and refused no pains nor jeopardy, but with courage went through them all, he telleth a sufficient cause here himself, and saith, his "God had put it in his heart to do it." He taketh not the glory of it to himself, but giveth all the praise to God alone, as we must do in all good things. Whensoever God putteth any good thing into man's heart to do, he driveth him so forward, that he cannot eat, sleep, nor rest quietly, until it be done: he thinketh all time long and lost, that is not bestowed on it: therefore they that be so cold in their work, that they care not whether it go forward or not, are not moved by God. The Holy Ghost, which worketh this great desire in us, is called fire. John Baptist said, he "baptized in water, but he that came after him should baptize them with the Holy Ghost and fire." The Holy Ghost fell on the apostles in fiery tongues; and our Saviour Christ said, he "came to set fire on the earth, and what would he else but that it should burn?" These be spoken to teach us, that those which are moved of God are earnest in their doings. God loveth not those that be "lukewarm;" he "will spue them out of his mouth." You must be either an earnest friend or an open enemy: he loveth no dissemblers; you must be either hot or cold: "he that is not with him is against" him: double dealers are the worst people that be; they are good neither afore God nor man: an open enemy is better than a flattering friend. All which sayings do teach us to be earnest in God's work; or else he putteth it not into our heart. Salomon commendeth plain dealing so much, that Prov. xxvii. he saith, "The wounds that a friend giveth are better than the crafty kisses of him that hateth thee."

This heavenly fire burneth up all desires in man, and kindleth all goodness in him. Jeremiah, when he saw the word that he preached to be contemned of the people, he waxed very sad; he would preach no more: but when he had holden his tongue but a little while, he said "the word within Jer. xx. him was like a burning fire; it burst out, he could not hold it in," and he fell to preaching again: he was so grieved to see God dishonoured, and so earnest to bring the people to knowledge of their duty, that he could not hold his peace, but needs must preach again. When Jesabel persecuted Helias, because he had killed Baal's priests for their idolatry, he fled into the wilderness, and the angel finding him asked 1 Kings xix. him what he did there. Helias said, "I am earnestly zealous and grieved for thee, O Lord God of hosts, that the children of Israel have forsaken thy covenant, &c." Moses Exod. xxxii. loved his people so well that, when God would have destroyed them, he prayed to forgive them, or else to put him out of his book. The Holy Ghost told St Paul, that in every town Acts xx. there were chains and troubles ready for him; but he said he cared not, his life was not dear to him, so that he might run his course. For his countrymen also he wished to be "accursed from Christ," so that they might be saved. The other apostles, when they were whipt for preaching Christ Jesus, went away "rejoicing that they were thought worthy to suffer any worldly shame for his name's sake."

Such an earnest love should every one have, both the magistrate to do justice and punish sin, and the preacher to root out evil doctrine and preach Christ purely, that nothing should make them afraid, but they should build God's city, the heavenly Jerusalem, boldly: nothing should weary them, and all labour should be pleasure, so that they might serve the Lord. Phinees, when he saw whoredom and wickedness Num. xxv.

abound, and none would punish it, taketh the sword himself, when others would not, and killed the man and woman, being both of great parentage, in their open whoredom. God was so well pleased with this zealous deed of Phinees, that could not abide to see sin unpunished, and God's glory so openly defaced, that he blessed him and his issue for it after him. Our Saviour Christ, when he saw God's house appointed for prayer misused, "gat a whip and drave them out." Thus whensoever God putteth any thing into man's heart to do, it pricketh him on forward, that he cannot rest until he have finished it. Nehemiah was here moved by God to this work. God for his mercy's sake inflame many men's hearts with the like earnest desire of building God's spiritual city, that the workmen may be many, strong and courageous; for the work is great and troublesome, the enemies many, malicious, and stout hinderers, in number infinite, and true labourers very few.

<small>John ii.</small>

Gregory saith well, there is no such pleasant sacrifice afore God, as is the earnest zeal to win souls unto the Lord. The men of Jabes Gilead, when the Israelites joined all together to punish that wicked adultery in Benjamin, stood by, looked on, and would take part with neither of them; not knowing who should get the victory, thinking to scape best and pick a thank in meddling on neither part: but for such double dealing the Israelites set on them afterward and destroyed them. A just reward to fall on such as will stand by, and look how the world goeth, meddle of no side for fear of a change, or else ever join with the stronger part. How full the world is this day of such double-faced popish hypocrites, that will turn with every wind, good men lament, and God must amend when pleaseth him. They be the worst men that live. Such men be of no religion: some call them *neuters*, because they are earnest on no side: some call them *uterques*, because they be of both sides as the world changeth: some call them *omnia*, because, if a Turk or any other should come, they would yield unto them all. They be like free-holders; for whosoever purchaseth the land, they hold of them all, though every year come a new master. But they say, best it is that they be of no religion: for as there is but one God, so there is but one religion; and he that knoweth

<small>Judg. xxi.</small>

not the true God and religion, knoweth none at all, although he make himself every day a new God and a new religion, and the more the worse.

13. *And I went forth.* In these next verses is nothing but the way described, by which he went to take the view of the walls, how they were pitifully destroyed, and how they might best and most speedily be repaired. The gates of cities have their names on some occasion outwardly given, as the north-gate and the east-gate, because it goeth northward or eastward: sometimes of them that builded them, as Lud-gate and Billings-gate, of Lud and Billinus: sometimes of things that are brought in or carried out of the city by them, as the fish-gate, the dunghill-gate, &c. This gate that he goeth out at first is called the "valley-gate," because the way into the valley of Josaphat, which lay afore it eastward, betwixt it and mount Olivet, was through it. This valley was called Josaphat's by reason of a noble victory that God gave Josaphat there. Divers people joined themselves together against Josaphat; but God so ordered the matter, that one of them killed another, and Josaphat, looking on, after the slaughter came and took all their riches and spoil, and he delivered without any stroke giving. The "dragon's well" had its name of some venomous serpent lying there: the "dunghill-gate," because the filth of the city was carried out that way: the "well-gate" and "king's fish-pool," because there was great plenty of water ponds, watering places, &c. "The brook" he speaketh of is thought to be Cedron, which is spoken of in the gospel, John xviii. 2 Chron. xx.

Nehemiah, when he had viewed all the walls, returned in at the same gate that he went out at: but in some places he found so great store of rubbish of the broken walls, that he could not pass on horseback; so miserably were they torn and overthrown, and all the gates that should be shut were burned to ashes. O righteous God and miserable people! God of his mercy foretold them by his prophets, that if they fell from him and served other gods, these mischiefs should fall on them: but they, blinded in their own affections, believed it not. O stony heart, learn here how vile a thing sin is in God's sight: for not only the man that doeth sin is punished, but the earth, the country, the stones, the walls, the city, trees, corn, cattle, fish, fowl, and all fruits, and other things that God made for man's necessity, are perished, punished, and turned into another nature for the sin of man: yea, and not only worldly things, but his holy temple, law, word and religion, the ark of God, the cherubims, the pot with manna, the mercy seat, Aaron's rod, with all the rest of his holy jewels, were given unto the wicked Nabuchadnezzar's hand for the disobedience of the people: and God will rather suffer his open enemies to enjoy his wonderful benefits than his flattering friends. When Adam had sinned, the earth, which afore was decked with all good fruits, brought forth weeds to punish them withal. For the wickedness of Sodom God not only cruelly destroyed the people in it, but to this day that pleasant ground, which afore was like paradise, is now barren, full of filthy mire, slitch, tar, &c., and the air of it so pestilent, as divers do write, that if any birds fly over it, it killeth them. The whole country of Jewry, a plentiful land, "flowing with milk and honey" of his own nature, by the disobedience of the people became a barren land, as David teacheth in his psalm, "The Lord turneth a fruitful ground into a barren for the wickedness of the dwellers in it." Jerusalem was not only destroyed now thus piteously by the Babylonians, but afterwards by Vespasian the emperor, and had "not one stone left standing on another," and the Jews driven out of it, who now live scattered through the world, abhorred of all good men, and under God's heavy rod, for crucifying the Lord Jesus Christ, the Son of God, and their continual despising of him.

Psal. cvii.

Let every man therefore learn reverently in the fear of God to live: for sin will not only be punished with everlasting death in the world to come, but even in this life man himself is plagued, and all things that should serve or pleasure him shall be turned to his destruction, because he would not serve his God as he ought to do. What can be a more righteous judgment of God, than so to order things, that no creature of God shall serve a wretched man, which will not serve nor fear the Lord, his God and Creator? Sin is so vile in God's sight, that he will punish those innocent, unsensible, and unreasonable creatures, as the stones in the wall, the house wherein thou dwellest, the earth whereby thou livest, which never sinned, for the sin of thee, wretched man. O consider how God abhorreth sin and disobedience of his word, that he could never be pacified, but by the death of his own dear Son Christ Jesus for thy sins! O miserable man, consider thy wretched state! Thy sins pulled thy Lord Christ from heaven to hell, from joy to pain; thou causedst him to be whipped, and hanged on a tree, thrust to the heart with a spear, by his blood to save thee: thou causedst him to die, that thou mightest live. If thou shouldst deal thus with another man thy fellow, what wouldst thou think thou hadst deserved? And when thou hast thus misused thy Lord and Christ, the Son of God, crucifying him again, and yet continuest in sin, contemning his commandments, "treading the Son of God Heb. x. under thy feet, and esteeming the blood of his eternal testament as a profane thing," how canst thou look up unto him, how canst thou hope for mercy? Wicked men are so horrible in God's sight, that the angels in heaven abhor them, the creatures on earth disobey them, good men fly their company, and devils in hell pull them unto them: and yet malice hath so blinded them, that they cannot turn unto the Lord.

But whatsoever there is in us, O God, forget not thou thyself; shew thyself a God still, though we forget thee. As thou lovedst us when we were thine enemies, so love us still now, whom thou hast made thy friends, and bought so dearly; and turn us, good God, that we may love thee. Remember, O Lord, whereof we be made: from the earth we came, on the earth we live, and delight in earthly things; unto the earth we shall return: thou canst not look for heavenly things to come from so vile a matter; this earthly nature cannot be changed but by thy heavenly Spirit: deal not with us therefore, O Lord, in justice as we deserve, but in thy great mercy, which is our sure salvation, and let thy manifold mercy devour our manifold misery, that our manifold sins be not laid to our charge. Gracious God, forgive us: as our misery is endless, so is thy mercy, and much more large than we can think.

As we see God deal in his anger with this city, for the sin of the people that dwelled in it, so he will deal with all obstinate breakers of his law in all ages and places, without respect of persons. The walls of the city may well be compared to the magistrates, which both defend the people from their enemies, and also govern the citizens within; as the walls keep out other from invading, so they keep in the inhabitants from straying abroad: and the gates of the city may well be compared unto the ministers, which open the door of life to all penitent persons by the comfortable preaching of mercy promised in Christ, and shut heaven gates against all reprobate and impenitent sinners, by terrible thundering of his vengeance, threatened to such in his word. The walls are destroyed, and the gates burned, when the rulers and ministers do not their duty, but care for other things. And as this wretched people had justly, for their disobedience, neither walls left to keep out the enemy, nor gates to let in their friends, but all were destroyed; so shall all godless people be left without godly magistrates to govern them, and live in slavery under tyrants that oppress them, and also without comfortable ministers to teach them, and be led by blind guides that deceive them, and so "the blind lead the blind, and both fall into the ditch," to their utter and endless destruction. They be not worthy to have either magistrate or preacher, that will not obey laws nor believe the word. This Osee, the prophet, foretold them should fall on them, saying, " the people of Israel should sit many days without a prince, without sacrifice and image, without the ephod and teraphim, and yet in the end they should return unto their God." But they feared not these threatenings then, no more than we do now: yet as they fell on them then, so will they fall on us now.

After that Nehemiah had thus diligently viewed the walls, and the breaches of them, he was more able to render a reason, and talk with the rulers how they might be repaired. A good rule for all those that have any charge committed to them, that they should first privately consider the things they have to do themselves, and then shall they be more able to consider who giveth best counsel for the doing of it. Rashly to enter on it, a wise man will not, nor open his mind to others, until he have advised himself privately first what is best to be done: and so shall he be best able both to render a reason of his own doings, and also to judge who giveth best advice.

v. 16. *The magistrates knew not whither I went, or what I did; and to the Jews, the priests, the nobles, the rulers, and the rest of the workmen, I told nothing hitherto.* The Text.
17. *And I said unto them, Ye know the misery that we be in, how Jerusalem is wasted, and her gates burned in the fire: come, and let us build the walls of Jerusalem, that we be no more a reproach.*
18. *And I told them of the hand of my God, that it was gracious toward me, and also the king's word that he spake unto me; and they said, Let us rise and build: and they strengthened their hands to good.*

Nehemiah not only, like a godly zealous man, is diligent to set forward this work, but also, like a very wise man, sheweth in his doings the chief properties of him that hath weighty matters committed unto him. He that hath great matters to do must be faithful and trusty, and also secret, and keeping counsel close, as the poet saith, *Fide et taciturnitate est opus*[1]. And where every sort must be made privy in such a work, hitherto he had opened it to never a one.

17. *And I said unto them.* After Nehemiah had thus long kept his purpose secret, and diligently viewed the walls, how great the breach was, how it might be best and speedily repaired, and was able to talk with all sorts, and render a reason of his doings to every one, both high and low in authority, to the common sort of the Jews, to the workmen, priests and rulers; he now propoundeth the matter unto them all; and in few words, after he had declared the misery that they were in, and how that famous city lay open to all enemies to invade, to their great shame, exhorteth and encourageth them to fall to the building of the walls, and live no more in such shame and reproach, as they had done, but recover their old estimation again; for he had found favour both in God's sight and the king's.

There be two kind of reasons to persuade a man to do any thing: the one is, if he declare how hurtful and shameful

[[1] Terence, Andr. i. i. *Fidelity and secresy are necessary.* ED.]

it is to do or suffer such a thing to be done or undone: the other reason is, to open unto him what good help and encouraging there is to set it forward. The shame was great, that for their great sin and disobedience God's people, who cracked so much of their good God, should live in such slavery under infidels, as though their God could not or would not deliver them. The hope to prosper well in this building was great, for that both God and the king had shewed great tokens of their good wills for the furtherance of this good work. Both these kinds of persuasions he useth here: his words be not many, but effectual. For as the shame was, to lose their city, so the glory should be greater in recovering it; and wise men use and love few words; for either those will serve good men, or more will not. The woeful sight of those broken walls, and this miserable slavery of the people in it, were sufficient to move a stony heart to pity, though never a word were spoken by any man: but those weighty reasons, well considered, made them all to fall to work with great courage. What man had so little feeling of God and honesty, that would not help to build God's city and their own country? Those that love to hear themselves talk, and with many words to colour their ill meaning, may here learn how a simple truth, plainly told in few words, worketh more in good men's hearts, than a fair painted tale that hath little truth and less good meaning in it. An honest matter speaketh for itself, and needeth no colouring; and he that useth most flattering and subtle words, maketh wise men mistrust the matter to be ill. A few words well placed are much better than a long unsavoury tale.

18. *And I told them*. After that Nehemiah had briefly set afore them the misery they lived in, the cruel destruction of Jerusalem, which God chose for himself to dwell in, and what shame it was for them, not to recover by well doing that which their fathers for their wickedness lost; he now declareth unto them, as a full reason to persuade any man that would be persuaded, and saith, "both the hand of his God was gracious toward him in this enterprise, and the king's words were very comfortable." When a man hath both God and the king of his side, what needeth he more? who can hurt him? what should he doubt or be afraid of? what would he have further? God had given him such a favour

in the king's sight, that as soon as he asked licence to go and build the city, where his fathers lay buried, it was granted; and the liberality and good will of the king was so great, that he granted him both soldiers, safely to conduct him to Jerusalem, and also commission to his officers for timber to this great building. What should they mistrust or doubt of now? There wanted nothing but a good will and courage on their side: if they would rise and work lustily, no doubt the work would be finished speedily.

Nehemiah still calleth him *his* God, as though God heard his prayer only, and moved the king's heart to give him licence to build this city, which many, divers times, had wished and laboured for, and could not get it. He thought this to be so great a blessing of God, that he can never be thankful enough for it, and therefore calleth him his God. He that loveth his God earnestly, rejoiceth in nothing so much as when he seeth those things prosper, whereby God's glory may be shewed forth. He careth more for that, than for his own pleasure and profit. And when such things go backward, it grieveth him more than any worldly loss that can fall unto himself. And though some wavering worldlings may say, the king might die, or change his good will from them; and God many times, when he hath given a good beginning for a while, yet in the end he cutteth it off; and by this means discourage other from this work, and will them not to meddle; the time might change, and then they might be blamed; and Nehemiah, although he was in great favour with the king at this present, yet, being absent long from the court, might soon be forgotten; others, that bare him no good will, might creep in favour and bring him into displeasure, (for in the court commonly, out of sight, out of mind;) these and such other reasons would soon withdraw dissemblers from their good furtherance of this work; yet God so wrought with them all, that they all boldly took this work in hand and finished it. God, of his great goodness, for the better exercising of our faith hath thus ordered the course of things, that although, when we look into the world, we shall find many things to withdraw us from doing our duties to his majesty, yet by his Holy Spirit he hath given us faith and hope of his promised goodness, that nothing should discourage us from doing our duties: for we have him on our side that hath all things at his commandment, and whose purpose none can withstand.

Let the world therefore waver never so much; let it threaten never such cruelty; let it counsel and persuade as craftily as it can, to meddle in no such matters of God: yet good men cannot be quiet, until they have shewed their good will, to the uttermost of their power, for the further-ance of God's work and obedience of his will. Abraham, when he was bidden to leave his country and kinsfolk, and go into that place that God would shew him, might have many reasons to stay him: as, that he could not tell how to live when he came there, that he should want the comfort of his friends, live amongst strangers, and those that would rather hurt him than help him: yet none of these could stay him, but he would follow whither the Lord would lead. God bade him sacrifice his son Isaac, having no issue, and yet promised him that "in his seed all nations should be blessed." Abraham could not tell how these two should stand together, both to kill his son and to have issue of him: yet he doubted not in faith but, rather than his promise should not be true, God would raise him from death, to beget and raise up seed after him. When Isaac, going to be sacrificed, asked his father where the sacrifice was that should be killed, (for he had the wood on his back and the fire in his hand,) Abraham, not doubting, though not knowing how, where, nor when it should be done, said, "God will provide himself a sacrifice, my son;" and proceeded to sacrifice his son, until the angel stayed him, and shewed him a ram in the bushes, which he should offer unto the Lord instead of his son. The apostles, when our Saviour Jesus Christ sent them out to preach without bag or wallet, money, or staff, made no question how they should live, or defend themselves against so many enemies, or how they should teach others, that never went to school themselves to learn; but obeying his commandment, and believing his promise, went forth boldly, and did their message diligently, and God blessed their doings wonderfully. When they came again unto him, and told him how well they had sped, he asked them whether they wanted any thing by the way, while they were in his service? and they said, Nay. Thus

marginal references: Gen. xii. Gen. xxii. Heb. xi. Gen. xxii. Luke xxii.

good men will not be withdrawn from serving their God, though many worldly reasons might withdraw them: and God will so increase their faith to go forward, that nothing shall discourage them. They will rather stick to God's promise than any cunning practice of man. A good beginning is a great reason to persuade a man that God will give good success unto the end. David comforteth himself to kill Goliath, because he killed a lion and a bear when he was young, keeping sheep. God never doeth any thing in vain; but when his faithful servants take things in hand of mere love and duty to further his glory, he ever bringeth it to good effect. The good success that God hath given us afore, should persuade us that he will give us more. Hypocrites, faint-hearted soldiers, double-dealers, and those that be not grounded upon a sure faith and hope of his promised goodness, oft fail of their purpose through their own default. God hath promised nothing to such dissemblers, and those that trust him he never faileth. Let all those therefore, that fear the Lord unfeignedly, boldly begin the Lord's work, continue it stedfastly, look for the mighty furtherance of the same faithfully; and no doubt they shall have it. Who ever to this day trusted in the Lord in vain, but he had good success in his doings? Let no man mistrust God's goodness to further those good things that he taketh in hand: let us work diligently, and commit the success unto him boldly; no doubt he will bring it to good pass. ^{1 Sam. xvii.}

When they had well considered Nehemiah's words and his good counsel, they cast all perils away, and said, "Let us rise and build those decayed walls." Let us linger no longer, but speedily fall to labour, and recover that with our diligence that our fathers lost by disobedience. Now they buskle and bowne[1] themselves to this work; they spit on their hands, and take better hold than afore; they buckle themselves to labour with courage, not to be driven from it any more. So much can a few words spoken in the fear of God uprightly by some man at some times do, that cannot be gotten at other times by many persuasions. Aggeus, when they had lain many years on sleep, forgetting the building of God's house, with like few words so encouraged them to

[1] *Buskle*, the same as *busk*, prepare. *Bowne* I cannot explain. ED.]

work, that they finished the temple in four years, which afore had lain almost forty years unlooked at. So can God make them earnest in a short time, when pleaseth him, which afore had been cold and negligent.

And this courage that they gather now came rather by gentle persuasions than by fearful threatenings: for good natures are moved rather with the glad tidings of the gospel than sharpness of the law. The law threateneth correction, the gospel promiseth blessings: the law killeth, the gospel quickeneth: the law breedeth fear, the gospel bringeth love: the law casteth down, the gospel reareth us up: the law layeth our sin to our charge; the gospel saith, Christ hath paid the price for our reconciliation. A gentle kind of preaching is better to win weak minds, than terrible thundering of vengeance. Yet is the law most necessary to be taught, to pull down froward hearts, and bring them to knowledge of themselves. I see divers of the prophets terribly threaten the wickedness of their time; yet I see none of them, that doth so mightily dissuade them from their ungodly life, as Aggeus and Nehemiah with their mild dealing bring so many to repentance. Both be good and necessary; but the gospel more comfortable, and the law fearful. Fear maketh a man many times to fly from ill, but love maketh him willingly to do good. Salomon saith, "Love is as strong as death:" for as all things yield unto death, so nothing is too hard or painful for him that loveth, but he will adventure at all perils, until he get the thing that he loveth. St Paul saith, "Who shall separate us from the love of Christ Jesus? Shall trouble, anguish, persecution, hunger, nakedness, jeopardy, or the sword?" If thou wouldst have a man earnest in any thing, rather draw him to it by love, than drive him to it by fear: bring him once to love it earnestly, and nothing shall make him afraid to stand to it manfully. Fear maketh men cold, discourageth them, and many times turneth them to hatred. That preacher therefore, which will win most unto God, shall rather do it by gentleness than by sharpness, by promise than by threatenings, by the gospel than by the law, by love than by fear: though the law must be interlaced to throw down the malice of man's heart; the flesh must be bridled by fear, and the spirit comforted with

Cant. viii.

Rom. viii.

loving kindness promised. Nehemiah useth both the law and the gospel to persuade them withal.

The seventeenth verse layeth afore them the misery they were in, to live under heathen and strange princes, the pitiful sight of their broken wall, their gates burned, whereby they lived in continual danger of the enemy round about them to be spoiled and murdered: the shame was no less than the loss, that they could not repair and recover by their well-doing that their fathers lost; and they had dwelled so many years in it since king Cyrus gave them licence to go home again: all which were the heavy burdens and curse of the law. But this verse setteth afore them the gracious goodness of God and the king, which had given great tokens of their good will and favour toward the work, of their mere mercy: and so both the law and the gospel laid afore them the misery taken away and mercy offered unto them; they should most thankfully receive the goodness promised, and avoid the great burden of misery that they so long had borne. This kind of teaching is very meet to be followed of all preachers, and those that shall speak unto a people where all sorts of states are to be persuaded; for these kinds of reasons touch all sorts of men, and if it be done in the fear of God, it will work as it did then. Those be the best scholars that will learn without the rod; yet none so good but at times he needeth the rod: and a wise schoolmaster will make such choice of his scholars whom he will have learned, that he shall profit more with gentleness than cruelty; and such asses as must continually have the whip, are meeter to be driven from the school to the cart, than by their loitering to hurt others.

v. 19. *Sanballat the Horonite, and Tobias the servant, an Ammonite, and Gesem the Arabian heard it, and they mocked us, and said, What is this thing that ye do? do ye fall away from the king?* The Text.

20. *And I answered them, and said unto them, The God of heaven is he that hath granted us prosperity; and we his servants will rise up and build: and as for you, there is no portion and right nor remembrance in Jerusalem.*

These men, as they were sad at Nehemiah's first coming, when they see that any man had found such favour with the king to do good to Jerusalem, so now were they almost mad for anger, when they heard that they went about to build the walls of Jerusalem. Openly to withstand them, or forbid them to work, they durst not, because they had the king's commission to do so; but so much as they durst, they discourage them: they mock them, they threaten to accuse them, and of that which would make any man afraid; they lay rebellion to their charge, and say, they would build that city for no other cause, but that they would make themselves strong against the king, fall away from him, set up a king amongst themselves, obey none, but use their own liberty, and rule all about them, as they did afore. These men bare some authority in the country; and like proud braggers, and dissembling malicious enemies to God and his word, they would hinder so much as they could this building. The world is too full at this day of such like dissembling hypocrites. The one sort, if they come up of nought, and get a badge¹ pricked on their sleeve, though they have little, yet they look so big and speak so stoutly, that they keep the poor under their feet, that they dare not rout.² All must be as they say, though it be neither true nor honest: none dare say the contrary. But the dungeon dissembling papist is more like unto them: for he careth not by what means to get it, by fear or by flattery, so that he can obtain his purpose.

These men first mock the Jews, and scornfully despise them for enterprising this building, thinking by this means to discourage poor souls, that they should not go forward in this work: after that they charge them with rebellion. These two be the old practices of Satan in his members, to hinder the building of God's house in all ages. Judas in his epistle saith, that "in the last days there shall come mockers, which shall walk after their own wicked lusts." Peter and Paul foretold the same. Our Saviour Christ, though he was most spitefully misused many ways, yet never worse

2 Pet. iii.
2 Tim. iii.

[¹ Badge: a mark or ornament, usually of silver, shewing that they were in the service of some nobleman or powerful person. ED.]

[² Rout: make a stir, rebel. ED.]

than when they mocked him; both Herod, Pilate, the priests and the Jews. It is thought but a small matter to mock simple souls, and so to withdraw them from God; but Salomon saith, "He that mocketh shall be mocked:" and David, "He that dwelleth in the heavens shall mock them, and the Lord shall laugh them to scorn." This shall be the just reward of such scorners. Prov. iii. Psal. ii.

It is justly to be feared, that as the Jews were given up to Nebuchadnezzar for mocking the prophets and preachers of their time, as it is written; so we, for our bitter taunting, scoffing, reviling, disdaining, and despising of God's true ministers at these days, shall be given into our mortal enemies' hands. What is more common in these days than, when such hickscorners[3] will be merry at their drunken banquets, to fall in talk of some one minister or other? Nay, they spare none, but go from one to another, and can spy a mote in other men, but cannot spy their own abominations. Christ was never more spitefully and disdainfully scoffed at, than these lusty ruffians open their mouths against his preachers: but the same Lord Christ saith of his disciples, that "he which despiseth them despiseth him." What reward the mockers of Christ shall have, I think every man knoweth. Good men with heavy hearts commit themselves and their cause unto the Lord, and pray with David, "Lord, deliver my soul from wicked lips and from a deceitful tongue." Salomon saith, "God will laugh when such shall perish." Michal, wife to David, was barren all her life for mocking her husband, when he played on his harp and danced afore the ark of God. The children that mocked Eliseus, and said, "Come up, thou bald pate, come up," were all devoured suddenly of wild bears, that came out of the wood hard by. David, amongst many miseries that he complaineth of, saith, that "the scorners made their songs of him," when they were at their drunken feasts; and when he seeth no remedy how to escape their poisonful tongues, he patiently turneth him unto the Lord, committeth all to him, and in the latter end of the psalm God comforteth him, and telleth him what sundry mischiefs shall fall on them for their despiteful dealing. When Belshazzar, king of Ba- 2 Chron. xxxvi. [Prov. i.] 2 Sam. vi. 2 Kings ii. Psal. lxix. Dan. v.

[3 In an old allegorical drama, printed by Wynkyn de Worde, *Hyckescorner* is represented as a libertine who scoffs at religion. ED.]

bylon, made his drunken feast to his great men, and called for the vessels and jewels which Nebuchadnezzar brought from Jerusalem, that he and his harlots might eat and drink in them in despite of the living God of Israel, a hand appeared writing on the wall, which Daniel expounded, when none of his soothsayers could do it, and said, his kingdom should be taken from him; and so it came to pass: for the same night Belshazzar was slain, and Darius king of the Medes possessed his kingdom. A just reward for all such drunken mockers of God, his people, religion, and ministers; and yet our merry toss-pots will take no heed.

<small>Gen. xxi.</small> Sarah saw Ismael playing with Isaac her son, and said to Abraham, "Cast out the handmaid and her son, for he shall not be heir with my son." But St Paul, alleging the <small>Gal. iv.</small> same text, calleth this playing persecution, and saith, "As he that was born after the flesh did persecute him that was born after the spirit, so it is now: but the scripture saith, Cast out the handmaid and her son, for he shall not be heir with the son of the free woman." So shall all scornful mockers, jesters, and railers on God, his word, religion and people, be cast out into utter darkness, and not be heirs of God's kingdom with his children. This playing and mocking is bitter persecution, and therefore not to be used of good men, nor against good men and lovers of religion: yet at this day he is counted a merry companion and welcome to great men's tables, that can rail bitterly or jest merrily on the ministers. Such is our love towards God, his word, and ministers: but sure, he that loveth God and the word in deed, cannot abide to hear the preachers ill spoken of undeservedly. I cannot tell whether is worse, the scoffer, or the glad hearer. If the one had no pleasure in hearing such lewd talk, the other would not tell it.

The other thing they charge the Jews withal is rebellion, falling from the king, and setting up a kingdom amongst themselves. <small>1 Kings xviii.</small> When Elias rebuked Achab and the people to return unto the Lord, Achab saith unto him, "Art thou he that troubleth Israel?" "Nay," saith the prophet, "it is thou and thy father's house." Rebuking him and teaching truth was counted troubling of the commonwealth and the king. What was the cause that king Saul and his flatterers hated poor

David so much, and so cruelly sought his death, but that the people sang, after that Goliah was slain, that "Saul had killed 1 Sam xviii. a thousand, and David his ten thousand"? Which was as much to say as, they thought that David was a mightier man than Saul, and meeter to be king. Daniel set open his windows, and contrary to the king's commandment prayed thrice a day unto Dan. vi. the living Lord, and therefore was accused of disobedience to the king, and cast to the lions' den to be devoured of them. The Israelites in Egypt, when God blessed them, and increas- Exod. i. ed them to a great people, were accused that they waxed so many and wealthy, that they would rebel against the king; and therefore, to keep them under, were oppressed by the taskmasters, and set to make brick for their buildings. When our Lord and Master Christ Jesus was born, the wise men Matt. ii. asked, "Where the king of the Jews was?" Herod was mad, and killed all the children of two years old and under, lest any of them should come to be king and put him down. When our Saviour Christ said, his "kingdom was not of this John xviii. world," then said Pilate, "Thou art a king then?" Whereupon the Jews took occasion to accuse him of treason; and said, "Every one that maketh himself a king speaketh against the emperor; for we have no king but the emperor." The apostles Acts v. were accused, that they had troubled the commonwealth by preaching Christ, and filled Jerusalem with their doctrine, contrary to the commandment of the priests and elders. Jason was drawn out of his own house for lodging Paul, being accused that he had troubled the world, and disobeyed the emperor. When St Paul had preached Christ in Athens, Acts xvii. he was accused for troubling the state by teaching his new doctrine. Thus ever the building of God's house by preaching of the gospel hath been charged with rebellion, disobedience to princes, and troubling of the commonwealth and peace. But good men have not been dismayed at such big words, but with good courage have proceeded in their work, having the testimony of a good conscience that they be not guilty of any such thing.

20. *And I answered.* This was the first push, but not the worst, that they had to discourage them for proceeding in this building; and not unlike but it made some afraid to hear such big words, and so great matters laid to their

charge, by men of such authority as they were. But as they were not ashamed so unjustly to accuse God's people, so Nehemiah steppeth forth, as boldly answereth for them all, and defendeth their doings. A worthy example for all those that be in authority to follow: they have not the sword committed unto them in vain; they ought to defend, both by word and deed, in their well doings those that be committed unto them. Their duty is not to suffer God's enemies to invade or hurt, slander or blaspheme, those that they have charge over, but draw the sword, if need be, to drive away such wolves, and punish such wicked tongues. It is not, as we commonly say, when any danger or persecution ariseth for the doctrine, or that the ministers are untruly reported of, Let the preachers defend it, it is their duty and vocation; we are not learned, it belongeth not to us; our care is for the commonwealth only. Religious magistrates will neither do so nor say so: they will not suffer, as much as in them lieth, the church, religion, doctrine, nor the ministers to be ill spoken of, reviled, defaced, nor overrun. They be mouths, to speak for God's people, as Moses was unto Pharao: they be hands to fight for them; they be rulers to defend the good, and punish the evil. Jephthah, when the Ammonites fought against Israel, defended the cause in disputation by words, and after in battle with sword. The good king Ezechias, when he received the blasphemous message and letters from Rabshakeh against God, his temple, people and religion, he seeketh by all means to defend them all, and encourage the people not to fall away from their God in that great danger. When Holofernes railed on God and his people, Achior and Judith defend them, and she cutteth off his head. When the great giant Goliah reviled the people of God, and provoked them to fight with him hand to hand, if they durst, for the victory, none was found that durst do it; but poor David, with no strong weapons, but his sling and a few stones, killed that lusty champion, and delivered his people. When Dathan, Korah, and Abiram, with their fellows, railed against Moses and Aaron, God's true ministers, Moses, committing the revenge of it to the Lord, warned the people to depart from their company, lest they perished with them by that strange death: and straightways the earth

Judg. xi.

2 Kings xviii.

1 Sam. xvii.

Num. xvi.

opened, and swallowed up them and their goods and tents where they dwelt, quick into hell. Nay, women were not spared; for Mary, Moses' sister, was smitten with a leprosy for [Num.xii.] railing on Moses her brother, God's lieutenant over them.

As the magistrate therefore both with word and sword must defend God's cause, his religion, temple, people, ministers and doctrine; so must the preacher and those that be learned, with their pain, prayer, preaching, and all other means that they can: yea, if our goods or lives were required for the defence of it, no state of man ought to refuse it. For this end are we born and live, to glorify our God and set forth his praise: for this purpose are all things given us, and therefore must not be spared, but spent and bestowed, when his glory requireth. For this cause Esaias the prophet gave his body to be sawn in sunder with a saw of iron. For this cause Jeremy was cast into a dungeon of Jer. xxxviii. mire and filth, Daniel into the lions' den: St Paul pleadeth his cause oft in chains at Jerusalem and at Rome, afore Festus, Felix, and Agrippa; and our Lord and Master Christ Jesus, afore Annas, Caiaphas, Pilate and Herod: John Baptist lost his head for this quarrel; and no good man will think any thing too dear to spend in Christ his Master's cause. For this cause Tertullian, Ireneus, Justinus, Athanasius, Chrysostom, Nazianzenus, have written great books against the heathens which railed on our religion. What infinite number of martyrs have stood stoutly and given their lives in the same quarrel! He that hath seen any learning can better tell where to begin than where to make an end of reckoning; the number is so infinite: and our late days have given sufficient proof thereof, under that bloody butcher Bonner, that the most ignorant, if he will open his ears and eyes, might hear and see great plenty.

But alas! the fiery faggots of those days were not so grievous then, as the slanderous tongues be now in our days. Nebuchadnezzar made a law, "that if any did blaspheme the Dan. iii. God of Sidrach, Mesach, and Abednago, he should be slain, and his house made a dunghill." Moses made a law, that every Levit. xxiv. blasphemer should be stoned to death. Seeing God and princes have made such strait laws against such lewd railers, good rulers should see some correction done, and not with silence to suffer ill men to talk their pleasure on God's city, religion, and ministry. While others possibly made courtesy to speak and answer these busy braggers and quarrellers, Nehemiah steppeth forth boldly, defendeth this cause stoutly, answereth their false accusation truly, encourageth the people manfully to go forward with their work, despiseth their brags, and telleth them plainly, that they "have no part nor right, nor are worthy to be remembered in Jerusalem."

The effect of Nehemiah's answer was, that the God of heaven had given them good success hitherto in moving the hearts of king Cyrus and Darius first to the building of the temple, and now of Artaxerxes to restore the city; they were his servants and worshipped him, and he stirred them up to this work; for of themselves they were not able to do such things. They served no idols nor false gods, they needed not to be ashamed of their Master, the God of heaven was their Lord, and they his people, he was their master and they his servants; he their king and they his subjects: they would go forward with their work, they must have a city to dwell in to serve their God, who would defend them in this their well doing: these men had no authority to stop or forbid them to work, they had nothing a [to] do in Jerusalem, nor any authority; they would not obey them, but with all diligence apply this work until it be finished. The apostles, when they were forbidden, preached and would not obey, but said, they must obey God that bade them. Thus must all they that take God's work in hand, confess it to come from God, and that he blesseth their doings, that all the praise may be his, and that they of themselves be weak and unable to do such things without his special grace and assistance.

Psal. cxv. All good men in such enterprises will say with David, "Not unto us, O Lord, not unto us, but unto thy name give all the glory." If these wicked men had had any worldly shame or fear of God in them, they would have quaked and trembled: as the good men rejoiced to have God on their side to further them; so they, when they heard the God of heaven named to be against them, and that it was his doing, they would have forsaken their idols, and have furthered this building, or at least have sitten still and not hindered it. For who is able to withstand his will, or hinder that he will have forward? The devils in hell quake and tremble at the naming and considering of God's majesty; but these wicked imps not only now, but sundry times, as appeareth hereafter in this book, most cruelly, spitefully and craftily go forward in their old malice, and by all means seek the overthrow of this building. So far worse is a devil incarnate in an ill man, than by himself in his own nature. When the devil will work any great mischief, he taketh commonly one man or other, angel or creature, to do it by, knowing that he shall do it more easily that way than if he should attempt it by himself. How is every murder, false witness, whoredom, robbery, &c. committed, but when the devil stirreth up one man against another? Let every good man therefore take heed unto himself, how he yieldeth unto sin: for in that doing he maketh himself a slave to the devil, and his instrument to work by. One devil will not offer that villainy to another devil to make him his slave; but if he can bring man unto it, there is his rejoicing. Take heed therefore, O man.

In that they confess themselves to be " the servants of the God of heaven," it is as much to say as, they wrought not for themselves, nor at their own appointment, nor for their own profit: they wrought for their master's cause, and for his glory. Good servants in all their doings will seek their master's profit and praise, not their own: they live not for themselves, but all the profit of their doings returneth to their masters. If they take any thing to themselves more than their master giveth them, they be thieves unto him, they do him no true service. Let all the builders of God's house therefore, whether they be rulers in the commonwealth, as Nehemiah was now, or of the learned sort in the ministry, or elsewhere, not only confess in words that they be servants to the God of heaven, but most humbly, simply, and boldly shew it in their deeds, that they seek their master's praise and glory, the common profit of their country and not their own; that they work for him, and not for themselves; and that they serve him not for any worldly respect, or gain, or honour, but uprightly for conscience sake serve and obey him, yield all praise to his glorious name, taking nothing to themselves, and being not afraid to go forward in his building for any braggers, knowing that all the pride of man's heart, which setteth up himself against the God of heaven, is vile and vain; and that their God will defend his servants, and confound his foes.

It is no rebellion against princes to do that which God commandeth: for princes themselves are bound, as well as other meaner degrees, to serve the Lord God of heaven with all their might and main; and unto the same God they must make account of their doings, as all other must. For this building they had the king's commission, and therefore it was no treason to do it. It is more glorious to be called God's servants, than to have all the titles of honour and dignity that the world can give. He that serveth the Lord truly is master of sin, hell, death, and the devil, and by the assistance of God's Holy Spirit shall not be overcome of them, but shall overcome and conquer them: which is greater honour than any worldly prince can give. The woman that had an evil spirit in her confessed Paul and his fellows to be "the servants of the mighty God, and that they taught them the way of salvation." See then, how devils are afraid of God's servants. Paul in all his epistles rejoiceth in nothing more than terming himself an apostle and servant of Christ Jesus. The Holy Ghost told Paul, that in every city, where he should come, there were chains and troubles ready for him; but he said, he "cared not for them, for his life was not dear to him, so that he might run his race, and testify the glorious gospel of God." Be not ashamed therefore of thy master; for our Saviour Christ saith, that "whosoever denieth him afore men, he will deny him afore his Father in heaven." Worldly masters will not cast away their faithful servants, but maintain them as they may; and thinkest thou that God will forsake his servants? Thinkest thou a mortal wretched man to be more loving to thee than the eternal God and merciful Father, that made thee, feedeth thee and defendeth thee, when man cannot help thee?—yea, loveth thee better than thou lovest thyself, and stayeth thee from running from him, when thou wouldst willingly seek thine own destruction wilfully. Stand to boldly, forsake him not cowardly. Polycarpus, an old man, when he should suffer martyrdom, was advised by some to have pity on his old age, and not so stiffly to stand. "Nay," saith he, "I have served my master Christ these eighty-six years, and he did me never harm; I will not forsake him now in my last days[1]."

Thus Nehemiah stoutly answering them, and boldly encouraging his fellows, goeth forward with the work, contemneth their mocking and false accusations, and falleth to his building again. So must all good builders of God's house neither be afraid nor weary of scornful mockers' threatenings, accusations or violence; but manfully go forward to the end, knowing that their God is stronger, wiser, and more willing to defend his people, than his enemies shall be to hurt them. "He that putteth his hand to the plough, and looketh backward, is not meet for the kingdom of God," saith Christ our Lord. "And he that continueth unto the end shall be safe." Our Saviour Christ, when he preached that "whatsoever went in at the mouth did not defile a man," was told by his disciples that that doctrine offended the Pharisees: but he answered them, and said, "Every plant that my Father hath not planted shall be plucked up, &c." As though he should say, Their doctrine is not from my Father, and therefore cannot stand: let those blind guides alone, seeing they be wilful and obstinate, and will not learn: go ye forward with preaching of the gospel, care not for them. So every good man must continue, that he may say with St Paul, "I have kept my faith, I have run my race, the crown of righteousness is laid up in store for me, &c."

Luke ix.

Matt. xv. 20.

2 Tim. iv.

After that Nehemiah had thus boldly answered them, and encouraged his countrymen to their work, he now turneth him to Sanballat and his fellows, and sheweth himself to make as little account of them as they made of him, and saith, "As for you, ye have no right, part, nor remembrance in Jerusalem;" as though he should say, What have you to do with us in this building? ye are not Jews born, as we be, ye belong not to Israel, nor are partakers of his blessing:

[[1] Ἐγκειμένου δὲ τοῦ ἡγουμένου καὶ λέγοντος, Ὅμοσον, καὶ ἀπολύσω σε, λοιδόρησον τὸν Χριστόν, ἔφη ὁ Πολύκαρπος, Ὀγδοήκοντα καὶ ἓξ ἔτη δουλεύω αὐτῷ, καὶ οὐδέν με ἠδίκησε· καὶ πῶς δύναμαι βλασφημῆσαι τὸν βασιλέα μου τὸν σώσαντά με; Euseb. Eccl. Hist. Lib. IV. Cap. XVI. p. 38. Ed. Paris. 1544. The passage in Nicephorus is a quotation of the same original, viz. the letter written by the church of Smyrna to other churches. ED.]

ye be Samaritans, strangers to his city and commonwealth; ye be none of God's household; if ye will be doing, meddle where ye have to do. This city God himself did choose for his people to dwell in and serve him. Ye be idolaters, and worship not the true God of heaven. If ye will be building, build ye Samaria, your own head city: ye are no citizens here, nor have any freedom, liberty, or privilege granted unto us: ye be none of our corporation, or denizens; ye shall have nothing to do here. All that build here have their portion of land and living in this city and country appointed for them: they shall have justice, right and law ministered unto them; and for a perpetual remembrance of their faithful service unto the living God, their names shall be registered, that all posterity may know their doings, and praise the Lord that strengthened them to this building. But ye have none of all these. For when the land was divided by lot and measure by Josue, ye had no part appointed for you: under the law ye do not live, but have lived after your own device; nay, ye bear such hatred unto us, that ye will not willingly eat, drink, nor keep company with us friendly: let us alone, trouble us not: get you hence, and let us fall to our building again.

It is no small blessing of God, when he calleth any to be a builder of his house; for both in this world his name shall be had in perpetual remembrance, and he is written in the book of life, where no death can prevail. David saith, *Psal. cxii.* "The righteous man shall be had in perpetual remembrance:" *Rev. xx.* and St John saith, that "he that is not found written in the book of life, shall be cast into the fiery lake." The builders of this city now have their names written in the next chapter following for their perpetual praise in this world, to teach us, that as the builders of this worldly Jerusalem have their names registered here, much more the builders of the heavenly Jerusalem have their names written in the book of life to their salvation. Ill men and troublers of God's building have their names written in this book too. What more blessed then is [he that buildeth than][1] he that hindereth? *Prov. x.* Salomon teacheth and saith, "The remembrance of the righteous is to his praise, but the name of the wicked stinketh." This is then the difference, and thou mayst choose whether

[[1] These words are supplied, as necessary to the sense. ED.]

thou wilt be remembered to thy praise or to thy shame, and with the good will of the living, or hatred.

But by this answer of Nehemiah, when he saith that they "have no part, right, nor remembrance in Jerusalem," it is partly given us to understand, that when they could not hinder this work by big brags and threatenings, they offered themselves to join with them in this building, to take their part and bear their charges fellow-like: for why should he deny them these, except they required it? But Nehemiah, a wise man, would neither be afraid of them as open enemies, nor receive them into his fellowship as feigned friends. Wherein he teacheth all true Christians how to behave themselves in building of God's house; that is, neither to fear the one nor to receive the other. St Paul saith, "Be not yoked with infidels: what hath righteousness to do with unrighteousness, light with darkness, or Christ with Belial?" God's people are knit together with two bonds: the one is Christ their head, who giveth life to all members of the body; the other is brotherly love among themselves. But neither of these can be found in idolaters; for they neither take Christ for their head and live by him, nor they love not Christians as their brethren, but dissemble with God and man. All Christians have one God, one Father, one baptism, one religion, one law to live under, and one heavenly kingdom to look for: but infidels and hypocrites have many gods; all religions be alike unto them; they live as they list; and that is their law and will, to go to heaven after their own device, if they can get it. Yet they have a delight to thrust themselves in among God's people, pretending a love unto them; where indeed it is for no good will, but to learn their secret counsels and purposes, that by such means they may betray them when occasion serveth. But wise builders will admit them into no fellowship nor friendship, as Nehemiah here utterly refuseth them, and will have nothing to do with them. But this case *Ezra iv.* is more plainly propounded to Ezra, and there I have spoken more largely of it; and Ezra plainly determineth the matter there; whoso list to read and consider. God be praised!

A PRAYER.

Whereas of thy great power, most gracious God, thou hast not only made the hearts of all men, but farther of thy plenteous mercy hast taken into thy custody and defence the hearts of all those that thou hast chosen in Christ Jesu to serve thee; grant us, heavenly Father, we beseech thee, such an earnest love to the building of thy house and city, as thou gavest to thy faithful servant Nehemiah; that as he was sad, gave himself to prayer and fasting, and could not be merry, until he found grace in the king's sight to repair thy decayed house and wasted city Jerusalem, so we, by diligent prayer calling on thy name, and humbly submitting ourselves to thy blessed will and pleasure, may not cease crying at thy throne of mercy, until we, by the means of our spokesman Christ Jesus, thy Son and our Lord, may find such favour at thy hands, that by the assistance of thy Holy Spirit, according to our calling, we may every one of us build the heavenly Jerusalem, set up the kingdom of thy crucified Christ, and with one consent pull down the tyranny of antichrist, to thy eternal glory and comfort of our consciences. And as thou then movedst the hearts of heathen kings, not only by laws, commissions, and commandments to give licence to every one that would repair thy house, but also with great gifts and liberal rewards to set it forwards; so now, most loving Lord, move the hearts, we beseech thee, of all christian princes, humbly to throw their sceptre at thy feet, with all their power, laws, commissions and commandments, that they may by the authority committed unto them procure the speedy repairing of thy heavenly kingdom, and with their liberality maintain the builders of the same. And, alas! O Lord, we are so weak of ourselves, and impotent to do these things without thee, that, considering our miserable case, extreme need driveth us impudently to crave thy fatherly goodness, not only to grant us all these thy blessings, but farther to confound the wicked devices of all greedy raveners, that seek the spoil and defacing of thy church; and defend us from thy foes, our mortal enemies, Sanballat and his partakers, that we be not afraid of their proud brags, nor deceived by their subtle practices. Thou, most mighty Lord, mayst not only give us all good things, but also deliver and defend us from all ill; for of ourselves we can do neither of them to ourselves. Raise us up such rulers, O God, we most humbly beseech thee, both in the church and commonwealth, as may and will, with the spirit of boldness, encourage the dull spirits of the fearful and wavering people courageously to go forward in thy building, as Nehemiah did; that neither mocking nor threatening of the Romish Sanballat and his members, nor the crafty practices of the flattering Ammonites, prevail against us, but with all might and main we all may be found true workmen in thy house, so far forth as our vocation shall stretch, to the confusion of thy enemies, thy eternal praise, and our endless comfort in Christ Jesus thy Son, our Lord and gracious Saviour. Amen.

[PILKINGTON.]

CHAPTER III.

Because this chapter standeth most in describing the building of the walls of Jerusalem, by whom they were done, and what part every one did repair, rehearsing the name both of the builders and of the portions of the walls that they took in hand to finish, (which thing seemeth strange, or rather unprofitable, to the people that understand not the mysteries of it, nor the fashion and situation of the city,) I shall in few words pass over things not so necessary for the edifying of the unlearned, and note only such things as may increase the faith of the simple unlearned, for whose profit chiefly this labour is taken; and also in reforming their lives may move and stir them to a more careful building of the spiritual Jerusalem; which thing is chiefly to be learned here, and to the which every one is bound with all his power to employ himself and all that he hath.

The Holy Ghost, who is the author of the holy scripture, hath not put down any one word in writing, whether in the new testament or in the old, that is either superstitious or unprofitable, though it seem so to many; but it hath his mystery and signification for our learning, and either for the plainness of it it may be understood of all men, or else for the deep mysteries that be hid in it is to be reverenced of all sorts of men, and with diligence and prayer is to be searched out, as far as we may. The new building of this old destroyed city by God's enemies putteth us in remembrance, how Satan by his members had overthrown God's city and chosen people; and where now all sorts of men lay on hands lustily to repair it again, it teacheth us our duty, how diligent every one should be in his degree to the restoring of God's city, his church, to his old beauty and strength again.

Gen. xiv. This city Jerusalem was first called Salem or Solyma, where Melchisedech was king, and met Abraham returning with the spoil which he recovered from the king of Sodom and his fellows. Melchisedech, by interpretation of his name, is first called "the king of righteousness," and after, "the king of Salem, that is, of peace," who representeth unto us Christ Jesus, as the epistle to the Hebrews saith, which is the king of all righteousness, and by whom all we are made righteous, as the apostle saith, and is "a priest for ever after the order of Melchisedech," and offered up that sweet and saving sacrifice of his own body and heart's blood, to pacify the wrath of God against man, and make peace betwixt them both, as it is written to the Ephesians, ch. ii. Heb. vii.
1 Cor. i.

This city afterwards was called Jebus, where the Jebusites, one of the nations, did dwell, whose land God gave to his people of Israel. These Jebusites came of the cursed seed of Canaan, whom Noe his father cursed for mocking him in his drunkenness; and inhabited this country until that worthy king David recovered the strongest part of it from them, called Sion, and named it the City of David after himself. That noble captain Josue indeed conquered the whole land, and divided it among the Israelites; but these Jebusites were partly so strong, dwelling in the mountains, that they could not be vanquished in short time, and partly the people so negligent, that they would not drive them out or destroy them, as they were commanded, but suffered them to dwell among them, to their great shame and harm: for they were ever like "thorns in their sides, to prick and hurt them," as it is written, Josue xxiii. Whereby we learn, that as the Jebusites, God's enemies, could not fully be conquered until David came, no more could the kingdom of Satan be clean overthrown, until Christ Jesus, the King of glory, was born of the seed of David, who conquered sin, hell, and the devil, and possessed the holy hill Sion, and made his people citizens of the heavenly Jerusalem. And like as they suffered the Jebusites to dwell amongst them to their great harm, so sin remaineth in our mortal bodies, conquered indeed that it doth not reign over those that serve the Lord, yet not clean taken away, but left for our exercise, who, having our mortal enemy dwelling within us, should fight against sin under the banner of faith in Christ Jesus, who only hath, can, and will continually defend his people, subdue their enemies, and give his children the victory. Josh. xv.
Gen. ix.
2 Sam. v.

How king David won this city from the Jebusites, is fully declared in the 2nd Samuel, v. chapter. And how Christ

Jesus, the Son of God, conquered the whole kingdom of Satan, sin, death, and hell, the whole history of the gospel declareth. And as king David, when he had reigned thirty-three years nobly in Jerusalem, died with great victory; so Christ Jesus, our Lord and grand Captain, after he had preached the kingdom of his Father, gat this noble victory against death and all his enemies in the thirty-third year of his age, by suffering death and triumphantly ascending into heaven, where he reigneth a glorious King for ever.

After that David had recovered this city from the Jebusites, it was continually called Jerusalem, (which is, by interpretation, *The Lord he will see Salem,*) alluding to both the old names joined together, *Jebus, Salem,* and changing one letter only. In the gospel it is called "the holy city," as when the devil tempted Christ, he "took him into the holy city, and set him on a pinnacle of the temple;" which name it gat rather of the holy law, word, and sacrifices, that were taught there and offered, than of that wicked and unholy people that "denied the Lord of life, and required Barabbas to be delivered." But when it was destroyed by the Romans, and not one stone left standing on another, as Christ foretold it should be, Ælius Adrianus, the emperor, for vain glory builded a new city, and called it after his own name, Ælia or Capitolina. And when the heathen had gotten it from the Christians, pope Urban the second kept a council in France, and by his flattering friars stirred up all princes to recover the holy land again, more like a superstitious Jew, putting holiness in the place which then was inhabited with wicked people, than like a true preacher of true holiness. But it cost many princes their lives, lands, and goods, and yet not recovered; whereof England felt his part, when king Richard the first went thither, and was taken prisoner, paid a great ransom to the impoverishing of the realm. As God gave this city and people, falling from him, into his enemies' hands; so will he cast us up, if we frowardly forsake him.

This city Jerusalem[1], after that it was recovered from the Jebusites, was enlarged and fortified by David, Salomon, Ozias, and Ezechias, and other good kings, and had within it two chief hills,—Sion, where the king's palace was built,

[1 See before, pp. 87, 88. ED.]

and Moria, where the temple was. And after, when the people increased, other two hills were taken into it, Acra and Bethera, as Josephus writeth. It had three wards and walls within it. Within the innermost wall was the king's palace, and temple, and the priests' lodging: in the middle ward were the prophets and noblemen, their schools, Levites and doctors. By which we are taught how to place and esteem learning and learned men, schools, universities and preachers, which are not now much regarded. In the uttermost dwell the citizens, merchants and artificers. It was then four miles about, and after enlarged to six. It was most glorious in the time of our Saviour Christ; for Herod and Agrippa had made great cost on it: and Christ wept for it. David in the forty-eighth psalm describeth the beauty and strength of this city, and biddeth them "go round about it, mark and behold it, and count the towers of it," that were many, that the Lord might be praised for it. The uttermost wall had towers ninety; the middle wall had towers fourteen; and the innermost wall had towers sixty: in the whole a hundred and sixty four towers, as Josephus and others do write. But I take it, that it was so rather in the time of Christ than of David, or of this building now: for as it increased in wealth, beauty and strength, so it did in pride, riotousness, superstition, contempt of God, and all wickedness; so that this last and utter destruction was at hand, for refusing, crucifying and condemning the Son of God, their Saviour.

Whensoever the scripture speaketh of any going to this city, it saith commonly " they went up to Jerusalem," because it was built so on hills, that on what side soever thou camest in, thou shouldst go up an hill; which though it seem a small matter to be noted, yet God, which doeth nothing in vain, as he did by other outward things teach that gross people heavenly things, as here in this climbing up to this earthly city they left worldly things beneath them in the valleys; so they that would pray unto the Lord or seek the heavenly Jerusalem, must climb up by faith into heaven to the mercy-seat and throne of grace, casting away all worldly cares, and leaving that behind.

The common opinion is that Adam, our first father, dwelt and was buried here in this city. And the scripture teacheth, Gen. xxii.

that good father Abraham offered his son Isaac on the mount Moria, where Salomon built the temple. Which all were figures that Christ Jesus, the new Adam, should be buried in the same place, where the old Adam was, to restore to us that life which old Adam had lost; and should offer his precious body on the tree for our redemption, a sweeter sacrifice than Isaac, or any bloody sacrifice that was offered in the temple of Salomon.

It is comfortable to consider, and wonderful to behold, how the wisdom of God hath made the circumstances of our destruction by Adam, and salvation by Christ Jesus, to agree. Adam in paradise, a garden of pleasure, offended God, and was cast out for his disobedience, and we all his posterity: Christ Jesus was buried in a garden, and hath by his death restored to us life again. By the enticing of a woman man fell from God; and by a woman that blessed seed, Christ Jesus, was born, and reconciled us to his Father again. By a pleasant apple was man deceived; but by Christ having bitter gall given him to drink man was saved. In that garden had Adam all pleasant things freely given him: and in this garden without the city had Christ our Lord all cruel and spiteful torments that could be devised; that we should go forth to suffer with him, forsaking the dainty pleasures of this city. In the temple no sin could be forgiven without shedding of the blood of some sacrifice; and in this world is no pardon of our wickedness without the blood of Christ Jesus, the innocent Lamb of God. And as by the fall of one man, Adam, we all were condemned, so by the rising from death of one man, Christ Jesus, we are justified. By the corruption of our father Adam we all did perish, and by the innocency of our brother, the Lord Christ, we all be sanctified. Why should not the goodness of the one profit us as much as the illness of the other did hurt us; or rather, much more bless us, being the immortal Son of the living God, and the other being but a mortal man made of the earth?

And as they that had any suit to the king, or sacrifice to be offered by the priest, first entered in at the uttermost gate, where the common sort of citizens dwelt; and then through the second, where the Levites and learned men were;

and lastly in at the innermost gate, where the king and his palace, the high priest and the temple, were built: so they that will go to the great King and High Priest of the heavenly Jerusalem, must first enter the uttermost gates, where all sorts of Christians are born into this world; and then be brought to the second, to be instructed by the ministers in the law of the Lord, and received into the church, and there nourished by the sacraments of God; which being diligently done, he may boldly enter at the innermost gate to the King's palace and temple, to make his humble suit, pray, and offer his body and lively sacrifice to God the Father by Christ Jesus, his Son, King of kings and Lord of the heavens, who also is our High Priest and Archbishop, that offered up that sweet sacrifice of his own blood for our filthy and stinking sins. For as the king and the priest dwelled both together in the innermost ward, and on the high hills; so our King and High Priest, Christ Jesus, hath taken unto himself the kingdom and priesthood, and by his Holy Spirit made us "a kingly priesthood" to God his Father: kings, that we might by him conquer the kingdom of Satan; and priests, to mortify and kill the filthy lusts of our flesh, and offer our souls a living and holy sacrifice to serve him. For as no sacrifice could be offered any where, but in this only temple of Jerusalem; so no prayer nor thankful sacrifices can be offered unto him, but in the name of Christ Jesus, his Son and our Lord.

Lastly, as God of his justice for the wickedness and superstition both of the princes, priests, and the people, destroyed the kingdom, law, and priesthood of Moses, never to be built or restored again, though the Jews sundry times attempted it, and with great sums of money would have gotten licence to have yearly come and lamented the destruction of it; yet both the emperor Ælius Adrianus[1], to withdraw them from it, built a new city in another place, called it after his own name, and graved a swine and his own image over the gates to bring them in hatred with it, and commanded in pain of death they should not come thither; God also with earth-

Niceph. iii. cap. 24.

[1 Εἰς ἅπαν δὲ τὴν πόλιν ἀπομειώσας ἐπὶ τῷ σφετέρῳ ὀνόματι ταύτην ἐγείρει, καὶ τὴν προσηγορίαν αὐτῇ δοὺς Αἰλίαν ὠνόμασεν· ἐν αὐτῷ δὲ τῷ ἀδύτῳ τοῦ ἱεροῦ καὶ τὸ ἑαυτοῦ ἀνίδρυσεν εἴδωλον. ED.]

quakes overthrew their doings, destroyed their tools, and swallowed up the workmen[1]: so in his mercy he hath built a new spiritual Jerusalem, given us the comfortable tidings of the gospel, sent his apostles to preach it through all the world, set up a new kingdom and ministery, not in a corner of the world, as it was then, but through all countries, that all which believe may be saved: and that, not in fear and threatenings, as the law was, but in loving-kindness and mercy, grace, peace and truth in Christ Jesus.

Many of these things are well noted by Wolfius and other learned men: and because there is divers times occasion given in this chapter to speak of these figures and spiritual comparisons, I have once for all set them down, that I need not oft repeat them afterward; and they that list, may briefly here see all set together, and apply them afterward as occasion serveth. I will not in this chapter, as I have done in others, follow verse by verse, nor sentence by sentence, nor word by word, to examine them particularly, because it standeth most of names, wherein the unlearned should not take so much profit as labour in reading of them; (though the learned may with pleasure pick out good lessons of them by allegorical interpretation of the places, &c.) but I will briefly note such things here and there in some verses, as shall give occasion to help the simpler sort to further the building of these walls, for whose cause specially I have taken this labour.

[¹ Τῇ ἐπιούσῃ ἐλθόντων ὡς ἂν τὸν πρῶτον θεμέλιον ὑποθήσωσι, σεισμόν φασι μέγαν ἐπιγενέσθαι, τῷ δὲ πολλῷ τῆς γῆς κλόνῳ ἐξ ἐσχάτων κρηπίδων ἀναδοθῆναι τοὺς λίθους, οὐκ ὀλίγους δὲ καὶ τῶν Ἰουδαίων διαφθαρῆναι. Cap. 32. Δευτέρα γοῦν πείρᾳ ἐπιχειρούντων, πῦρ ἐκεῖθεν λέγεται τῶν θεμελίων ἀναπηδῆσαν, καὶ ἄλλο δὲ οὐράνιον κατασκῆψαν, καὶ πλείους ἢ πρότερον διαφθεῖραι. * * * * τοῦ δὲ πυρὸς, ὡς εἴρηται, κατασκήψαντος, αἵ τε σφῦραι καὶ γλαρίδες καὶ πρίονες, οἱ πελέκεις τε καὶ τὰ σκέπαρνα, καὶ ὅσα πρὸς τὴν οἰκοδομὴν ἐπιτήδεια οἱ ἐργάται προσεπεφέροντο, θᾶττον εἰς χοῦν ἐλεπτύνοντο, τοῦ πυρὸς δι' ὅλης ἡμέρας ἐπινεμυμένου αὐτούς. Cap. 33. Ed.]

Niceph. x. 32, 33.

v. 1. *Eliasib the high priest gat him up, and his brethren* The text. *the priests, and builded the sheep gate.*
2. *And next unto him builded the men of Jericho.*

AFTER that Nehemiah had so stoutly answered Sanballat and his fellows, and encouraged his countrymen to the building of the walls, all sorts of them pluck up their stomachs, and are no more afraid, but lustily fall to their work. And among other, Eliasib the high priest and the rest of the priests also gat them up, and took in hand to repair the sheep gate which went toward mount Olivet, and so the wall all along unto the tower Hananeel. Such goodness cometh by having a stout captain, where the people be faint-hearted. Aggeus complaineth in the building of the temple, that prince, priest, and people were fallen on sleep, until he came with message from the Lord to awake them, and then they fell lustily to work. So now here, after that Nehemiah came with commission both from God and the king, they lingered their building no more, but boldly went on forward with it, though it had lien many years unlooked at; and now in the beginning they had many stout brags.

Chabrias, as Plutarch doth write[2], was wont to say, that "a host of harts should be more feared if a lion were their captain, than a host of lions should be if a hart were their captain;" teaching what profit cometh by a stout captain: and so it fareth in God's cause too. St Paul, considering what a chargeable office was committed unto him, and how fearful a thing it was to preach Christ afore princes and wicked people, desireth the Ephesians to pray for him, that he might have "utterance given him, boldly and freely to do his message in preaching the gospel." He desireth the same thing of the Colossians and the Thessalonians. So that, Col. iv. where we see this boldness in preaching joined with wis- 2 Thess. iii. dom and discretion, we may persuade ourselves that it is the gift of God in such a man, and above the nature of man to do it.

This lesson is given to all good builders of God's spiritual house, that they should "not fear him that will kill the Matt. x.

[2 Apothegm. T. I. p. 744. ed. Wyttenb. Oxon. 1795. ED.]

body, and cannot hurt the soul, but fear him that can cast both body and soul into hell." And St John saith in the Revelation xxi., that "those which be fearful shall have their part in the burning lake of brimstone, with murderers, adulterers, and idolaters." And by the example of Eliasib and the priests, which disdained not to be admonished and learn their duty of Nehemiah, coming from the court, we shall learn humbleness of mind, and not disdain to be admonished of our duty at mean men's hands. They are not offended at him, nor think him saucy to counsel and teach them, which were teachers of others, but are content to join in this work with him and the rest, yea, boldly to begin and give good example to the rest, as their duty was, and to encourage others. So no estate must disdain to be warned of his duty, and to be encouraged, though it be by mean men; for all sorts, high and low, learned and unlearned, are fearful and forgetful of themselves, until God stir them up by his word, Holy Spirit, and messenger.

Rev. xxi.

And reason it was, that as they were shepherds to the people, so they should build "the sheep-gate," which was at the east end of the city where the temple was, in the uttermost wall, where the sheep came in that were offered in sacrifice, and whereof they had their parts according to the law. This gate may well be compared to Christ Jesus, who sought the lost sheep, and was sacrificed as a lamb, and is the gate whereby only we enter, and his shepherds must be the builders of it, and bring the people into the fold.

Many good lessons might be plucked out of the interpretation of the names herein contained, and what were signified by them; but those be meeter for the learned, which can by order of learning keep themselves in compass, and apply all things to the rule of faith, than to the unlearned which have not that judgment. And where the men of Jericho join with the high priest in this building, it teacheth that not only priests and citizens must build God's city, but also countrymen; yea, those that dwelt farthest off, and be least regarded, must put to their helping hand. It is commendable in both, that neither the priests refused their aid, and they that dwelt farthest off were the first that came to work. So must all that be of God's household help to build, even the simplest and basest as well as the best; for as he is God of all, so he will have all to serve and worship him.

If either Nehemiah or any other had taken this work in hand alone, it would have been thought great arrogancy in them, and others would have disdained that they should have all the praise of so great a building alone. Common things would be done with common consent, and the common aid of them to whom it pertaineth would not be refused. Jericho was the first city that Josue overthrew for their wickedness, and it is now the first that cometh to help this building. So great a change cometh when God turneth the hearts of the people. Without this gate was that watering place or sheep-pool, whereof St John writeth in the fifth chapter, and where the sheep were washed that came to be offered.

v. 3. *The fish-gate builded the sons of Senaah; they covered it, and set on the doors, locks and bars.* The text.

5. *The great men of Thecoa put not their necks to the work of the Lord.*

This gate was at the west end of the city, where the fishers came in at the sea-coast with their fish to sell. If a man would stand on figures and allegories, this gate may well signify Christ, who made his apostles and preachers fishers of men, who by him brought and daily bring them into this spiritual Jerusalem; for he is only the door, whereby all must enter into the Lord's city. These men, like good builders, leave nothing undone that might fortify that gate; for they set on not only the doors, but also bolts and locks. So must God's church be made strong by laws, discipline, and authority, that ravening lions nor filthy swine rush not in, and disquiet or devour God's people: and the wholesome doctrine must be confirmed with strong arguments and reasons against false teachers.

Much controversy there is now about discipline, which every man granteth to be necessary, and desireth to have; but whether this, that is so vehemently urged, be the right way to strengthen the Church, as stronger doors, locks and bars, that should keep out all ravening wolves and wild beasts, or they be like to spider's cobwebs, that will catch a weak fly and let the great drones burst through, I leave it to the consideration of the wise. I will be no partaker of these troublesome contentions. And if a man would study for an example of this, I cannot tell where he might find a fitter. These poor men of Thecoa work willingly and diligently, but the richer sort were too stiffnecked, would not stoop nor obey the superiors of the work; for so the Hebrew word signifieth him that is appointed a ruler and master, as well as it doth signify the Lord God; and divers of the best learned do so turn it into Latin.

Every company of workmen had their overseers, appointed to direct and keep them in order, that every one should not do what he list, work when and where he list, nor loiter and be idle: other companies did obey their masters of the work, but these rich men were too proud. This kind of speech, "they put not their neck to the work," is taken of oxen, which being made for the yoke to draw, should teach all labourers in God's building, as well laymen as kirkmen, to be painful as the ox, and not too stately to stoop under the yoke. The scripture sundry times commendeth this painful labouring by the example of the plough and the ox: as, "He that putteth his hand to the plough and looketh, &c.," and, "Thou shalt not muzzle the mouth of the ox, &c." For no kind of people are exempt, neither poor nor rich, learned nor unlearned, man nor woman, but they must bend and bow their necks under the yoke, and be not ashamed nor too stately to work at the building of God's city. The proud pharisaical popish friars and monks, which have so many privileges from their father the pope, may not say, *Domine, nos sumus exempti*, We may not work: the solemn prelate, the fine-fingered dames, nor the surly lords of the land, the dainty and trim courtier, nor the lofty lawyer, are exempt; but every one must bow his neck in his vocation, painfully to work at God's building; as in this chapter ye shall have examples of all these sorts, that painfully wrought at this building.

But I fear me, that if, after the order of this discipline which is so greedily sought, and many do like of it, because it is so gentle, the rich would not care for it, but live as they list; if their consistory of seniors were set in their seats with their pastor in every church, with their full authority in all causes ecclesiast, they should find many proud peacocks, that would not bend their necks under the yoke of such simple silly woodcocks, as every parish presently is able to give. For as yet in few places shall able men be found, that dare and will wrastle with the rich in correction. A proud thacker[1] of Thecoa would laugh them to scorn and contemn their dispiling discipline. For they that will contemn correction, the laws and officers standing as they be, it were also necessary to have the prince's power, doors of iron, bolts of brass, and locks of steel to bind them fast, *ad alligandos reges eorum in compedibus, et nobiles eorum in* Psal. cxlix. *manicis ferreis:* then with such kind of dealing to be mocked, they would stoutly say, *Disrumpamus vincula eorum, et pro-* Psal. ii. *jiciamus a nobis jugum ipsorum.*

We read of Ambrose, that excommunicated the emperor Niceph. xii. Theodosius[2], and how humbly he obeyed it: but whether was more to be praised, he that durst do it or the other that would obey it, I cannot tell; and I know not where in a good cause the like has been done since, though the proud pope for his wicked authority hath attempted and achieved the like sundry times against emperors. Indeed excommunication rightly executed is a fearful bond to all good consciences; for it locketh up heaven gates, and throweth into the pit of hell: yet worldly men, that fear not God nor love his people, are more afraid of prison, iron chains, and fetters here, than of God's eternal wrath there. Such therefore must have a sharper consistory than our seniors be. God for his mercies' sake grant us a worthy discipline for such stiffnecked Thecoites! For the simple ones will be more

[[1] Thacker: a provincial form of *thatcher*. Ed.]

[[2] Ἐπεὶ μετὰ τὴν Εὐγενίου νίκην ἧκεν (Θεοδόσιος) εἰς Μεδιόλανον, καὶ εἰς τὴν ἐκκλησίαν, ὡς ἔθος, εἰσήγετο εὔξασθαι, καὶ πρὸς ταῖς θύραις ἐγένετο, ὑπαντήσας Ἀμβρόσιος, καὶ τῆς ἁλουργίδος λαβόμενος ἐπὶ μέσῳ τῷ πλήθει, τῶν ἱερῶν ἐπιβαίνειν προθύρων ἐκώλυεν, Ἐπίσχες, φάσκων, κ. τ. λ. * * * * Δέχου δὲ τὸν δεσμὸν, ᾧ Θεὸς ἄνωθεν τὴν ψῆφον ἐπήνεγκεν· ἀληθοῦς δ᾽ ὑγιείας οὑτοσὶ πρόξενος. Niceph. Eccles. Hist. Lib. xii. cap. 41. The δεσμὸς, *chain*, was the symbol of excommunication. See the same account in Theodoret. Lib. v. cap. 18; also Ambrose, Lib. v. Epist. 28. Ed.]

easily ruled with a gentle discipline. Such as have the wealth and authority of the country, given them of God to benefit and defend the country withal, are not worthy to live in the country, if they withdraw their helping hand from their country, as these Thecoites did now. The porters of every city and great men's houses are commonly tall, big and bold men, to keep out unruly people: and reason is that it should be so, for else all men would be bold to trouble the gates. So must the ministers and rulers of God's house, whom the Holy Ghost calleth his porters, be more stout men and strong than every realm is able to set up in any parish.

Surely the having of these seniors might do much good in many matters, but in my opinion after another sort than as yet is put down: which I refer to the determination of the wisest. How many papists at this day do contemn the church and all the discipline in it, because it is so soft! and if the fear of the magistrate's sword did not more bridle them than any honest fear, they would daily increase in boldness and contempt of all orders. If ye did but excommunicate them, they would heartily thank you and laugh you to scorn; for they willingly excommunicate themselves, and will come at no congregation; and under pretence of your excommunication they had just pretence of absenting themselves, and never would seek reconciliation. God grant all such obstinate contemners of his church and his word their just and deserved discipline! This overmuch softness that is used, and an opinion of some that be zealous in religion, whereby they think they may not punish an ill man for his conscience and religion, doth much harm, and emboldeneth them in their ill doings. Surely in my opinion they that have authority, and will not correct such wilful dealings, be partakers and maintainers of others' ill doing, and fill both the church and commonwealth with disobedient persons.

The text. v. 6. *The old gate builded Joiada, &c. they recovered it, and set on the doors, locks and bars.*

Because this setting on of locks, doors, and bars is sundry times rehearsed here, it shall suffice once to declare it, and not to fill up books with much writing, and trouble others with often reading of it. "Doors" serve to let men in and out, to shut them in or keep them out: "locks" serve against treasons or conspiracies within, and "bars" serve against open enemies and violence without. So must God's church be fenced and strengthened with sundry doctrine and discipline, to instruct the ignorant, comfort the weak, raise up them that be fallen, encourage the forgetful, bridle the unruly, and confute all errors. This promise God made to his church, Matt. xvi. that "hell gates should not prevail against it." It hath been oft sore assaulted, and yet never conquered; and never worse dealt with than by her own children and feigned friends, rather than by open enemies, as this day well proveth: no force: it hath a watchman that "neither sleepeth nor slumber- Psal. cxxi. eth," which can neither be overcome by strength, having all things at his commandment, nor deceived by treason, practice nor policy, having all wisdom to foresee mischiefs pretended, cunning and great good will to prevent them all; wherein standeth the comfort of all good men, that they have such a grand Captain.

By the right use of this discipline and doctrine is heaven gates set open to all penitent believers, and locked up against all obstinate and double-faced hypocrites. And what- Matt. xvi. soever the true and faithful "porters" of these doors "do bind in earth, it is bound in heaven; and whatsoever they loose in earth is forgiven in heaven:" and whosoever they let in are welcome, and whom they keep out are cast away. Such commission and authority hath God given to his word and ministry for the comfort and correction of his people, that all dissolute behaviour may be banished from amongst his, and all good order, peace and quietness maintained. The Lord for his mercy sake grant his church faithful porters, to open the doors to the sheep and shut them fast against the wolves, and drive from this chargeable office of trust all picklocks and conspirers to betray this city and citizens of the spiritual Jerusalem! For this is the duty of all good builders, not only to set up the walls and house, leaving the doors and windows open; but to make it strong with doors, locks, bolts, and bars, and set true and faithful porters and overseers of the house and all in it. The building of this old gate is the preaching of the old commandments of faith and love, which St John writeth of, as Beda noteth well. 1 John ii.

The text.   v. 7. *The men of Gibeon and Mizpah builded unto the throne of the duke beyond the river.*

Now this work goeth forward, and the towns in the country come and help to work lustily. Such goodness cometh, when God sendeth such a faithful ruler as Nehemiah was: God increase the number! Who this duke was it is uncertain, whether he was a Jew or a stranger; but God is to be praised, that stirred up such to set forward this work. Some think him to be Daniel, that was set in great authority by king Darius; and not unlike to be he, if he lived so long, for he was as zealous towards his country as any other. Divers Jews were in great authority in their captivity and troublesome times, who ever helped them in their great need. So God provideth for his church, that when any doth trouble them, he raiseth up some to comfort them. Mardocheus about this time was in great favour with Assuerus. Sidrach, Misach and Abednego, Daniel's companions, were much accounted of in their time. The river, that he speaketh of here, is Euphrates, which was a great notable river in the borders of Persia, and is ever signified by this kind of speech amongst the people, as Nilus was called "the river" in Egypt, and understood by that name in that country, as they be both called by that name in one sentence, Gen. xv. Some translate *unto the throne*, and some *for the throne*, as Munster and others: both may stand well, and not unlike but this duke, though he was out of the country, yet bare his portion of the charges and builded his part. What cause is there to name him here, if he did nothing to this building?

Dan. vi.

Esth. viii.
Dan. iii.

In the eighth verse come in the "goldsmiths and apothecaries," (for so the Hebrew words signify), and they leave their fine work and sweet spices, and fall to work in rough stones and mortar. None must be too dainty to file his fingers in working at God's building: all sorts, as they be the Lord's, so they must serve the Lord, and the Lord looketh for it of duty.

But in the eleventh verse the Moabites, which is most marvel, (for they were most utter enemies to the Jews,) come and help to build. Thus God, who hath the hearts of all men in his hands, of foes maketh friends, and where great hatred was afore, much love to ensue. And though the greatest part of the Moabites were ever utter enemies unto the Jews, as the Jews be unto the Christians, yet some Jews be turned unto the faith now, as some Moabites were then. And in the twelfth verse Sallum, an enchanter's son, (for so the Hebrew word signifieth,) cometh with his daughters and falleth to work. Wherein I cannot tell, whether I should marvel at the father or the daughters more. The father was a great man of authority in Jerusalem, and therefore no doubt the daughters were as nice and fine as their calling required; and therefore great marvel that they would humble themselves to work in mire and clay. No less marvel that Sallum, having a wicked conjuror to his father, should forsake that science which many great men delight in to their own destruction, and fall to work at such rough work.

But thus God calleth whom pleaseth him, and those that be truly called are neither weary nor ashamed to serve the Lord in the lowest kind of service. Thus David promised, that "the kings of Tharsis and the isles, of Arabia and Saba should bring gifts," and serve the Lord Christ, which all then were heathen people and knew not God. Conjuring was a common thing among the Jews, insomuch that some of the high priests were infected with it, as appeareth, Acts xix.; yet at Paul's preaching they came and brought in their conjuring books, and burnt them. A comfortable example is this to all those that have ill men to their fathers, that the illness of the father shall not hurt the son, if he turn to the Lord, leaving his father's steps. And all dainty dames may here learn of these gentlewomen to set more by working at God's house than by trimming of themselves. Would God they would spend that on the poor members of Christ and citizens of this spiritual Jerusalem, that they wastefully bestow on themselves, and would pity their poverty something like as they pamper themselves! St Peter biddeth them leave their "gold and frizzled hair, and their costly apparel," and so modestly behave themselves, that "their husbands, seeing their honest behaviour, may be won" to the Lord by them; for so Sara and other holy women did attire themselves, &c.

But it is to be feared, that many desire rather to be like

Ezek. xviii.

1 Pet. iii.

[PILKINGTON.]

dallying Dinah than sober Sara. And if the husband will not maintain it, though he sell a piece of land, break up house, borrow on interest, raise rents, or make like hard shifts, little obedience will be shewed. Placilla the empress, the worthy wife of Theodosius the emperor, would visit the sick folks in their houses herself, and help them; would taste of their broths how they were made, bring them dishes to lay their meat in, and wash their cups; and if any would forbid her, she said she offered her labour for the empire to God that gave it. And she would oft say to her husband, Remember what ye were, and who ye be now, and so shall ye always be thankful unto God[1]. It were comfortable to hear of such great women in these days, where the most part are so fine that they cannot abide to look at a poor body, and so costly in apparel that that will not suffice them in jewels, which their elders would have kept good hospitality withal. When Moses moved the people to bring such stuff as was meet for the making of God's tabernacle and other jewels in it, the women were as ready as the men, and they "brought their bracelets, ear-rings, rings and chains all of gold;" and the women "did spin with their own hands" both silk and goat's hair: they wrought and brought so much willingly, that Moses made proclamation they should bring no more.

Exod. xxxv.

Compare this people's devotion with ours that be called Christians, and ye shall find that all that may be scratched is too little to buy jewels for my mistress, though she be but of mean degree; and if any thing can be pulled from God's house or any that serveth in it, that is well gotten, and all is too little for them. God grant such costly dames to consider what metal they be made of! for if they were so fine of themselves as they would seem to be, none of these glorious things needed to be hanged upon them to make them gay withal. Filthy things need washing, painting, colouring, and trimming, and not those that be cleanly and comely of themselves: such decking and colouring maketh wise men to think, that all is not well underneath: content yourselves with that colour, comeliness, and shape, that God hath given

[1] Theodoret. Lib. v. cap. 18. The above is a close translation of the leading particulars of the original. Ed.]

you by nature, and disfigure not yourselves with your own devices; ye cannot amend God's doings, nor beautify that which he hath in that order appointed. Learn of these good women to offer your jewels to the building of God's city: lay to your hands, and spin rough goat's hair to clothe the poor; stoop and work, be not ashamed of it, it is the greatest honour that ever ye shall win. If ye will be partakers of the pleasures of God's city, ye must take part of the pains to build it. If women would learn what God will plague them for, and how, let them read the third chapter of the prophet Esay: and if they will learn what God willeth them to do and be occupied withal, though they be of the best sort, let them read the last chapter of the Proverbs. It is enough to note it, and point them to it that will learn; for I fear few will read, fewer learn, and fewest practise it: but many rather wish it cut out of the book, that they should not be troubled with hearing of it.

And in the thirteenth and fourteenth verses and others following come in the rulers of the country towns, with their people, for to work: wherein we learn that not only the priests and Levites, but the great men in every country, yea, and the country people too, must work at God's building. This "valley gate" that he speaketh of is thought to be the gate that goeth into the valley of Josaphat, which otherwise was called Gehennon. This is a worthy example for all Christians, that they should not live to themselves, but help to bear the burdens of the church and commonwealth. That city and temple were the common places appointed, whither they should resort to serve the Lord, and whither they might fly and find succour against the enemy, where victuals and other necessary provision might be had for all sorts. Therefore, if zeal toward God and love toward their neighbours could not move them to lay to their helping hands, and open their purses wide to set forward this building, their own private profit would move those that had any consideration of themselves, to maintain this city. And that no man should disdain to work at the vilest place in God's city, here cometh a nobleman, and buildeth "the dung gate," where all the filth of the city was carried out, and where all the sinks, canals, and conduits did wash and convey away all the sweepings and filth of the streets into the brook Cedron. As in all great and well ordered cities there be officers appointed for that purpose, which be men of wisdom, painful, and in authority, and have a great care for the health and wealth of the inhabitants, who will daily and duly look that such noisome things be conveyed away out of the streets for infecting the people with pestilent smells and contagions; so in God's church and city must be men of gravity, wisdom, learning and authority, which must dare and will wrastle with the stoutest, and see due correction done, and such rotten members, as would infect the whole body, cut off and carried away from among the congregation, to the comfort of the good, and terror of the evil doers.

In God's house there be both good and ill, as in the field the corn groweth not without the chaff, nor in the garden the good herbs without the weeds. Yet the good husband will carry in the good corn, and winnow the chaff: when the weed overgroweth the herbs, the good gardener will pick out the weeds, and carry the good herbs to his house. So in God's church open blasphemers, notorious wicked livers and teachers must be cast out, that God's holy name be not ill spoken of, as though he loved such ill doings, and would not with justice punish them; and also, that other by their ill example should not fall into the like mischiefs. St Paul biddeth, that "if any brother were called covetous, a fornicator, drunkard, a railer, extortioner, idolater, they should cast him out of company, not eat nor drink with him," that he may be ashamed of himself, when he seeth himself abhorred of all men, and so amend his wickedness.

<small>1 Cor. v.</small>

Excommunication is the common remedy for such disobedient persons, which God for his mercy sake grant that it may be restored to his true use, and that every one may willingly submit himself to godly correction! We have so long contemned the pope's curse, that now we think we may live as we list without blame; and if any due correction be offered, we laugh it to scorn, despise the ministers of it, and by this means shall cause the Lord to take the whip into his own hands; and then "who shall be able to stand?" God will not have sin unpunished; and if we refuse this gentle

correction, that he hath given his church to execute and
bridle ill doers withal, we shall find it "an horrible thing to Heb. x.
fall into the Lord's hands," and he will "rule us with an Psal. ii.
iron rod, and bruise us all to pieces." Such dung and filth
may not be suffered in God's house; and it is as necessary
to have a gate to carry such out at, as it is to have a gate
to bring good ones in: for as the rain from heaven washeth
the streets, so God's grace from above must first wash the
heart, that the mind may be renewed. In worldly matters
prisoners condemned to die are carried out of the city to
suffer execution, as members not meet to be suffered in any
company: so God's city will not suffer such ill doers to live
amongst them, but cast them out.

The "stairs" which be spoken of in the fifteenth verse,
and the "tomb of David" in the sixteenth verse, contain
good lessons in them, if they be well applied: for all outward
things in this worldly Jerusalem's building have a signification in them, to teach us to build the spiritual Jerusalem.
By these stairs the king came down from his palace on the
hill Sion into the lowest part of the city: and by the same
steps all suitors went up into the palace to make their petition. So the merciful Lord Jesus, by taking our nature on
him, and being made man in his mother's womb, came down
from the bosom of his Father in heaven into "the lowest
part of the earth," yea, and humbled himself unto the vilest
death, and hell too; that we by the same ladder, steps and
stairs of humbleness may climb by faith from virtue to virtue
into the heavens, by Christ Jesus our Lord, who is our
only spokesman and mean-maker, unto that high and mighty
King, God his Father. And as David born in Bethlehem,
when he had reigned thirty-three years over all Israel, was
buried in Jerusalem, and great treasures laid in the grave
with him, with part of which Hircanus delivered the city
when cruel Antiochus besieged it; so Christ Jesus, born in
Bethlehem, in the thirty-third year of his age was crucified,
and buried in Jerusalem, in whose grave we find great
treasures of our redemption: for both our filthy and stinking sins are there buried with him; and the sweet "balms,
spices, and ointments" that he was embalmed withal, are
there to be found by faith, and no holiness of the place;

that is, forgiveness of sins and rising with him to life everlasting in heaven.

In the seventeenth verse, and the rest of the chapter following to the end, is almost no great matter to be noted, but the earnest diligence of the Levites and priests (which were some chief men and rulers, as appeareth here,) and their bond servants to set forward this building, and for the most part in repairing the innermost walls in the first and second ward. Whereby we shall learn, that they were not so beggarly as many would make them in our days, if they might have their will, but of good wealth. How vain are those foolish exemptions which the pope giveth to his shameless shavelings, that they should not bear the common burdens of the church and commonwealth! St Paul biddeth them and all others to "pay tribute and taxes to whom they be due," and shew their obedience to the higher powers in all godly things, as well as any of the laity. Our Saviour Christ "paid tribute for himself and Peter," and willed the Pharisees to do the like; but these unprofitable pharisaical drones, because they will be most unlike unto him, will pay none at all.

<small>Matt. xvii.</small>

There is yet remaining here amongst us a sort, not popish, as they pretend, but earnest builders of God's house in their own opinion, where indeed they be the overthrowers of it; which are in effect as ill Pharisees as the papists be. They will take a benefice and cure of souls, promising solemnly to feed the flock; but when they have turned their back, they have a dispensation in a box to lie from it, and flock and flout whosoever would have them to continue there and do their duty, contending by law they may do it, and stand on their defence, *Domine, nos exempti sumus.* God for his mercy sake take away such laws, grant discreet officers, that will not dispense so unadvisedly with every one for small causes, as is too commonly used, and give those unprofitable caterpillars such remorse of conscience, that they will take pains to feed the flock as well as they feed themselves, eating until they sweat again, and become pillars to uphold God's church, and not pollers of his people, nor so greedy to pick their purses and pluck off the fleece, as painful to relieve and comfort the weak both in body and souls with wholesome doctrine and corporal food, as the great

God will ask a strait account of them at the last day, where their dispensation may not be pleaded, nor will be allowed, nor the dispenser can justly excuse himself nor them, but both like wolves and hirelings shall be charged, *Væ pastor et* ^{Zech. xi.} *idolum derelinquens gregem*, and, *Sanguinem eorum de manu tua requiram*, Ezech. iii. Full little do such men consider, what a jewel God hath committed to their charge; and less they regard the charge they have taken in hand. Jesus Christ came down from heaven to preach his Father's will unto his wandering sheep, and shed his precious blood to purchase us heaven: and these idle labourers will not take pain to visit, teach, or feed them whom our Lord God hath bought so dearly. God amend us all!

This "second measure," another part of building which is so oft spoken of here, is thought of the most part of writers to be the second ward and wall, which was called *Secunda*, where the Levites, prophets and learned men did dwell, and was divided into every man his portion to build; or else were they appointed first to build the half height of the wall for a time, to be some succour for them against the enemies. Some were so earnest in building, that they finished the second height unto the top of the wall afore other had built the half height. As in the twentieth verse Baruch "burst out in a heat," (for so readeth the Hebrew,) being angry both with himself and others, that were so slothful in working, and had done no more, and in a fume rose up, and finished his portion in a short time. Such anger is good, when a man is offended with himself or others, that they be so slow in serving their God and building his house: it will make him more earnest and diligent afterwards.

In the twenty-first verse Meremoth is commended, that he built so far as the house of the high priest raught. A small praise, if the house were not of some greatness. And so other priests, against their houses, in the verses following and in the twenty-eighth verse. I do but note it, because that many disdain that any ministers should have a house of any countenance. But among all builders, none are worthy more praise than these Nethinims be. They were no Jews born, but descended from those heathen Gibeonites, which deceived Josue by putting on old shoes, and having fusty bread in their bags, clouted sacks, and broken bottles, feigning themselves to have come a long journey to be received amongst God's people. By law the Jews should have destroyed all heathen people at their entering into the land of promise; but where by this policy Josue had granted them life and liberty, and so could not destroy them for his promise sake, he "gave them to the Lord to serve the priests in carrying water, cutting wood," and such other drudgery works for the sacrifices. So that Hebrew word signifieth them that were freely given unto the Lord; and all this people from that time forth, as long as the commonwealth stood, served the Lord as faithfully as any Jews even in their captivity, never grudging that they were not called to no higher estate, nor disdained not at their drudging; never ran away in any troublesome time, as they might easily have done, nor claimed any liberty, nor wrought any displeasure to the Israelites, where they might have oft betrayed them, and now most earnestly fall to building, and serve the Lord. A strange example, that such a people continued faithful in the house of God so many years, and stood so stoutly in all storms: but when God calleth, he blesseth, and nothing is painful, so they may serve the Lord; as David saith, "I had rather be a door keeper in the house of God than to dwell in the palaces of sinners." Saul would have destroyed this people, but God saved them and plagued him.

Psal. lxxxiv.

If we look unto ourselves without flattery, we shall easily perceive how unlike we be unto them, how cold in serving the Lord, how soon weary of our estate, how desirous to climb higher, how changeable in every age, how fearful to profess our religion, how flattering to men, and how "carried away with every blast of new doctrine." God grant us to see it, to be ashamed of it, and to amend it! Our own days have given us too many examples of such wavering worldlings; and I fear our sins will shortly pluck the same plagues on our heads again: so little tokens of repentance appear amongst us. We be the right Nethinims, made free from sin, and servants to the Lord. God grant we be not found worse, (being called Christians, and living in the time of grace under the bright light of Christ Jesus, declared unto us in his gospel, and by whom we be saved and made free,) than these heathen people the Gibeonites were, living in bondage, under shadows of Moses' law.

Hanum, the sixth son of Salech, wanteth not his praise here; who, being a younger brother, falleth to work, and no mention made of the elder. There must be no courtesy making, who shall begin: God hath oft called the younger to serve him before the elder, as Jacob, David, &c.

Thus the Holy Ghost hath registered unto us the names and diligence of the builders of this earthly city Jerusalem, by the pen of his faithful servant Nehemiah, for our comfort; and to teach us, that much more he hath registered the names of the builders of the spiritual Jerusalem in the book of life, where no devil can scrape them out, but shall be the dear children of the Lord God, defended by him from all ill. Let us therefore cast away this slothful sluggishness, wherein we have lain so long, rise up quickly, work lustily, spit on our hands, and take good hold, that we fall not back again from our Lord God. It is more honour to be a workman in this house, than to live the easiest life that the world can give.

A PRAYER.

As thou didst choose unto thyself here in earth, O mighty Lord, a certain place and city, Jerusalem, whither thy people should resort to worship thee, to offer their sacrifices and make their supplications unto thee; and as long as they did it faithfully, thou didst bless and prosper their doings; when they offended and fell away from thee, thou laidst thy heavy hand and sharp scourge upon them; so grant unto us, O gracious God, whom thou hast made free by thy dear Son,

Christ Jesus, and not bound us to any one place, but hast left us free in liberty of conscience to assemble ourselves and call upon thee in every place and corner of the earth, to preach thy word, learn our duty, and set forth thy majesty, to receive thy sacraments, and offer ourselves, our souls and bodies, a sweet sacrifice to thee: grant us, we beseech thee, O merciful Father, thy loving countenance, to continue thy blessings amongst us, and deal not with us in thine anger, as we justly have deserved to be cast away from thee; but as thou in thine anger grievously punishedst thy people the Jews, burnedst their city, destroyedst their temple, spoiledst the country, leddest a great number into captivity, killedst more, and broughtest them all into bondage and slavery under heathen princes; so, loving Lord, we confess our horrible sins have deserved no less in justice at thy hands, but thy mercy, O God, triumpheth against justice: for as, after a few years' correction, thou movedst divers heathen princes to send home thy people with great gifts, to repair the broken walls, build the temple, inhabit the country, and restore thy religion; and stirredst up also thy people, priests, princes, nobles, worshipful rulers and private men, artificers, women, and of all sorts some, earnestly to work at the building of thy city; so, heavenly King, let us not be cast away in thy heavy displeasure, and be the first that cannot find favour in thy sight; but turn the hearts of christian princes to give free course and liberty to thy word of salvation, and raise up faithful workmen of all sorts and degrees to build thy spiritual Jerusalem: thrust forth true labourers into thy harvest; root out all slothful sluggishness from amongst us, that we be not unprofitable members of the church and commonwealth; and let all magistrates know that by thee they rule, that thou settest them in authority, and maintainest them that fear thee; and make them not only to offer unto thee their bounden duty and service in building and working themselves to the good example of others, but also in encouraging and defending the faithful labourers in thy vineyard, and compelling the froward diligently to set forward thy building. Grant us strong walls and bulwarks to keep out Turk, pope, tyrants, atheists, anabaptists and libertines, with all other hinderers of thy building, that thy simple people may live quietly, and serve thee without invasions or persecution. And as of thy great mercy thou hast left to us in writing the names of all such as were the chiefest doers in this work, for our comfort and example to follow; so we beseech thee, loving Lord, to stir up those whose names thou hast written in the book of life, that manfully they may stand in the defence of thy truth, to the confusion of thy foes, and thy immortal praise, for thy Christ's sake. Amen.

CHAPTER IV.

v. 1. *It came to pass, when Sanballat heard that we builded the wall, he was very angry in himself, and disdained greatly, and mocked the Jews.*
2. *And he spake afore his brethren and the soldiers of Samaria, and said, What do these impotent Jews? will they make themselves strong? shall they offer sacrifice? shall they finish it in a day? shall they rear up the stones out of the dust, where they were brent?*
3. *And Tobias the Ammonite was beside him, and said, Yea, that which they do build, if a fox come up, he shall break down their wall of stone.*

THE last chapter declared unto us the forwardness of all sorts of men, from the highest to the lowest, both of the laity and the ministry, strangers and citizens, to build and repair the broken walls of Jerusalem; and this chapter and divers others following describe the manifold lets, subtle devices, bold enterprises, both of the outward enemy and hypocrites amongst themselves, to overthrow all this building; so that if God had not, contrary to reason, assisted, encouraged, and defended his faithful servants, this work had never been finished. Such hath been, is, and shall be unto the end, the state of God's people and church, that in no age it hath wanted or can want many sore assaults to overthrow it, if it were possible. But let us trust his faithful promise that said, he would "be with us unto the end of the world," and we shall not be overcome.

Let no man marvel therefore in these our days, because he seeth the like troubles fall among us, nor blame the doctrine that is taught, as though that were the cause of all mischiefs: for God is not so gracious to any country in any age to set up his kingdom there, but the devil is as busy and malicious to overthrow it, as much as he may. Let every man also, that will faithfully serve the Lord, think this to be most true, and look into this state of the Jews, as it were in a glass, and he shall find that "by many troubles we

Acts xiv.

must enter into the kingdom of heaven," and that it is a "narrow way" that leadeth thither, as it is written, Matthew vii. only take thou heed that thou deserve not to be persecuted, and the Lord will confound them. The rich glutton went to hell with all his belly-cheer; and the poor beggar Lazarus to heaven, and all his sorrow was no hinderance. Look at the footsteps of all our forefathers, the patriarchs and prophets, Christ Jesus and his apostles, with all other martyrs and good men; and we shall find none, but his whole life was a perpetual warfare, subject to infinite sorrows, and the ending of one was the beginning of a new: "but he that continued to the end was saved." Let us not look to come into heaven, if we walk another way; and be of good cheer, for the end shall be happy. These be spoken and written for our learning, not to discourage us, but rather to encourage us, that we be not found unlike to our forefathers, but manfully to stand in all trials, knowing that we have the same God that they had, that he is as able now and as willing to defend his chosen congregation as he was in the beginning, and will never forsake his dear children. _{Matt. vii.}

In the second chapter, verse 10, Sanballat and Tobias, hearing that Nehemiah was come with commission from the king to build Jerusalem, they were "grieved very sore" within themselves, cast into a dumpish sad heaviness, almost amazed for sorrow that any man should come to do the Jews any good at all: but now that they heard say they did work so lustily at this building, Sanballat first burst out into anger; he stamps, he stares, he frets, he fumes, he rageth, he raileth, and taketh on like a madman, and cannot tell how to stay them; and after that he falleth on mocking and mowing, potting and smiling at them, and flocking and flouting, scorning and scoffing of them, in fingering, fleering, and girning at them, to try them, whether they by this means would be dismayed or afraid to work any more. A shrewd trial for a sort of poor people, which were but lately restored to their country, and yet not well settled in it, to see the greatest ruler in the country to be so angry toward them, to scorn and mock them! If God had not strengthened them, it would have made them to leave their work for fear and run away. Look round about you in these our days; and ye shall see that if but a mean man in authority, or his man with a badge on his sleeve, do but look sourly, speak roughly, or behave himself any thing stoutly, all about them stoop, make low courtesy, run when they are bidden, and dare not whisper nor mutter one word, no, not in their good and just cause: yet where God's Holy Spirit giveth comfort, all these brags are nothing regarded, but in their well doings they will on forwards with their just cause and serving the Lord. Let every man take heed how he falleth into wickedness, for he cannot get out when he would. These men increase in mischief and amend not: so shall all they that yield unto it, and stay not in the beginning.

2. *And he spake afore his brethren.* The malice that the wicked men bear against the godly is so great, that it cannot be forgiven nor forgotten: whatsoever falleth out well to the good man, they are sorry for it; and they think all the posterity [prosperity] of the godly to be their disgracing and overthrow. Cain envied Abel, because God accepted his sacrifice better; Saul envied David, because he was more esteemed of the people. The Pharisees disdained Christ our Lord, because they see their doctrine decay and his received. And what maketh such a stir this day in the church, but that the pope and his partakers see their kingdom decay and the truth appear? These be "written for our learning," that we should not discourage ourselves in these miserable times, but boldly stand and continue to the end.

Sanballat, after that he had thus chafed in himself, and also had scorned and scoffed at their doings, he is so sore vexed in his mind that he cannot hold in, but bursteth out into blustering big words, and saith openly before his fellows and countrymen, which were of the same mind and superstition that he was; and [that] it might be more fearful to the Jews, to discourage them, he "speaketh" and braggeth it out "before the soldiers," which were set there to repress all mischievous attempts and enterprises that any should take in hand. As who should say, that if any went forward with his building, the soldiers should overthrow it and destroy them; for they were as ready to do such a mischief as he was to bid them. And thus he saith, "What do these beggarly Jews," these slaves, peasants, and villanes? what go they about? what mean they? will they take in hand such a building as no mighty prince is able to finish? and that many noble kings afore them could scarce in many years perform, will they on a sudden bring it to perfection? But if they be so foolish to think that they can finish it themselves, are the heathen people so mad to stand by, look on, and laugh, and suffer them to go forward with this building, which hath been of old time a great enemy unto them, and may be now again, if they be suffered to work still? Do they think the gentiles so foolish that they foresee not their meaning? or do they think them such cowards that they dare not, or so impotent and unable that they cannot, hinder and overthrow this work; or so unwilling to help their country, that they will suffer them to go forward in it? Nay, I warrant you, ye shall find them stout men, ready and willing to defend their country, and will not suffer such runagates to strengthen themselves against them. Shall they offer their old sacrifices? Shall they restore their old religion, in despite of us and our conntry, and go about to draw others to their religion? Shall they use their old accustomed solemn days, their great assemblies, and have it for well done? Nay, let them assure themselves, we shall find them otherwise occupied; we shall hold their nose to the grindstone; they shall not have leisure to pray and to be merry, as they look for. They work so lustily as though they "would finish it in one day," afore their neighbours should espy them; but they shall find it far otherwise: we foresee their meaning well enough, we will be heavy neighbours to them: it shall not fall out as they look for. Many kings afore them were busy to build, some one place and some another, and in many years; but these braggers go to it so greedily, as though they could finish it in a day or two. A sort of beggarly vagabonds and proud beggars take this work in hand, as though they were able to go through with it. What will they do? Will they glue the old stones together again? when will they get new stone? The old ones are burnt to powder, knocked in pieces, and will not serve for any building again. They shall find it another manner of work to finish than they look for.

The same miseries is the building of God's church subject to at this day; the same scoffs, mocks, threatenings and jeopardies are daily spued out by such like wicked ruffians and popish imps, some in corners and their drunken feasts, some afore princes and rulers: yet God confoundeth their wicked devices, comforteth and encourageth his poor people to go forward, and the Lord blesseth their doings. God in all ages "hath chosen the abjects of the world" to set up his kingdom by, and to overthrow the pride of man's heart, be they never so worldly-wise.

1 Cor. i.

3. *Tobias the Ammonite.* It was not sufficient for this *Miles gloriosus,* Sanballat, to rail at God's people and their building, as proud Golias and blasphemous Sennacherib did afore him, to their open destruction; but starteth forth another flattering lewd lubber, Tobias, an Ammonite, that slave, peasant, "servant" and bondman, as he termed him afore, ch. ii. 19. and he, not with so many words, but with as bitter scoffs, scorneth as scornfully at them as Sanballat did afore. And he standeth up and saith, If it like your worship, you need not thus to vex and chafe yourself at these vile Jews. For let them go on forward with their building as they have begun; when they have done the worst that they may, "if a fox come up, he shall break down their stony wall," he shall scrape it down with his claws and deface it. What needeth your mastership to care for so small a matter? it can do no harm: quiet yourself, we shall be able to deal with them well enough, and overthrow them: ye are a man of wisdom and authority, and may easily put these vagabonds to flight; we need not so much the strength of a lion, as the subtlety of a fox, to vanquish them. Thus bragging Thraso never wanteth a flattering Gnatho[1], and one jade claweth another by the back, and all to discourage the poor workmen.

Our miserable days can give many like examples, as when the bloody butcher[2] sat broiling God's saints and that glorious disputation at Oxford[3] with God's good and learned ministers, whom after many such like blasphemous mocks the Lord of his mercy took to his rest, and yet suffereth some of his enemies to live in shame, who in so long a time cannot

[[1] The allusion is to two characters in the *Eunuch* of Terence. ED.]

[[2] Bishop Bonner is intended by the term *butcher,* an appellation usually given him for his cruelty. ED.]

[[3] Between Cranmer, Ridley, and Latimer on the one side, and certain divines appointed from both the universities on the other, in 1554. ED.]

repent, but are given up to their own lusts and hardened hearts, so far as man can judge; beside many other young whelps of their teaching, which can bark in corners, and make themselves merry with railing and scoffing at the holy scriptures of God, the ministers and professors of it. Yea, some became so shameless, that they would call their dogs by the names of the first writers and professors of it. But our God liveth, who will defend his own quarrel, and confound his foes, laugh they never so merrily, or brag and scoff they never so bitterly. Salomon saith, "God will mock them that mock:" and David saith, he is "blessed that sitteth not in the seat of scorners." Diocletian, the emperor, as Volateran[3] writeth, had a jester called Genesius, who used to make him merry at his dinner, and amongst other devices would scoff at the Christians with mad gestures; but God plagued him for example of others, that they should not do the like. And yet it is too common at this day: they cannot eat their meat nor be merry, except they have some at their elbow that will blaspheme, scorn and laugh at the religion, scriptures, and lovers of it. A shrewd kind of trial for poor souls: for some are so weak that, rather than they will be mocked, lose their estimation amongst their acquaintance, or have a strange look of many a gentleman, their neighbour, they will forsake God, his word and religion, and say whatsoever a man will have them.

Prov. iii.
Psal. i.

What hindereth more at these days, than such like brags and mocks as these? What will these new fellows do? say they: will they overthrow that faith that ourselves had so many years ago? Nay, let them alone a while; sit down and laugh at them, they will be trapt in their own snare. Do they so turn the whole world into their own fantasies? will such a prince or such suffer it? See ye not this great man and that great man look strangely at it? Do "any of the rulers believe it," but a sort of rude and common people? Are not all countries in trouble about it, and have been many years? Live quietly, and let them alone

[3 Genesius, Arelatensis patria, arte mimus et infamis, Christianos apud imperatorem Diocletianum turpissimis gestibus irridebat, passus tandem et ipse sub eodem. Raph. Volaterranus, Commentariorum: Anthropolog. Lib. xvi. p. 572. ed. 1603. Ed.]

a while, and look for a day, and apply it better when it cometh than ye did: the last was lost for want of good looking to in time.

But the good Christian will with patience go forward, and not be ashamed of God nor his word, nor afraid of such proud brags, nor amazed at their bitter scoffs. He knoweth that "all which will live godly in Christ Jesu must suffer persecution," and that all good fathers from the beginning have suffered the same; and prepareth his back and shoulders patiently to bear all sorrows for his Master's cause. Psal. lxxix. David complaineth in all good men's names, "We are become a mocking stock to our neighbours, a laughing matter and scoffing to them that be round about us." When Peter had preached the fearful last day to be at hand, they mocked 2 Pet. iii. him, saying, "Where is the promise of his coming, that thou hast so long talked of? Since our fathers died, do not all things continue as in the beginning?" But enough was said of this matter afore in the second chapter, nineteenth verse. This is then the remedy that David useth in all these griefs: fall to prayer, commend thy cause unto the Lord, [Psal. xxvii.] fall not from him for any storm, "tarry the Lord's leisure," and play the man; comfort thy heart, look for the Lord's Psal. cxxiii. coming, and say unto him with David, "Have mercy on us, O Lord, have mercy on us, for we are utterly despised. Our soul is full of the slanders of these wealthy worldlings, and despising of the proud." No doubt, the Lord will comfort thee and confound them, as our days have well declared.

The Text. v. 4. *Hearken thou, O our God, for we are despised; turn their shame upon their own head, and make them despised in the land of their captivity.*

5. *Cover not their wickedness, and let not their sin be put out of thy sight; for they have provoked the builders.*

6. *Then we builded the wall, and the whole was joined together unto the half height, and the people had a mind to work.*

After that he had described the mockings and threatenings that they had for their bold enterprise in building, to discourage and drive them from it, if they could, if it had been possible, he now declareth what remedy and comfort he found by prayer at the Lord's hand. Nehemiah, seeing their great danger, turneth him to the Lord, the people praying with him, and saith: Our God, that hast chosen us only, though most unworthy, for thy people amongst the whole world, and whom only we worship, and at whom we seek for help and deliverance in all our trouble, hearken, we beseech thee, O Lord; bow down thine ear and hear our prayers; for thou art a righteous judge and mighty revenger of all thy faithful servants: we, thy poor people, are in a miserable case: we looked for aid at our neighbours' hands, and they are our utter enemies: we hoped for comfort of them, and they utterly despise, mock and contemn us: but thou art a God that never forsakest any that come unto thee, nor castest any away that faithfully trust in thee: hear us, O gracious God, and turn their own shame, that they would lay on us for building thy city, on their own heads: that villainy that they would do to us, let it fall on themselves. If thou let this cruelty scape unpunished, thou shalt be thought negligent and careless of thy people: these Samaritans, that be so cruel against us, be strangers in the country where they dwell, as we were in Babylon; they were brought out of their own country, and placed here by Esar-haddon, king of Assyria: make them, O Lord, to be despised in this land of their captivity, as well as they despised us in our misery. O Lord, let not their wickedness be hid, but make it known to all the world and all ages to come, how despitefully they deal with us for thy sake: others will attempt the like, if this scape unpunished. Forgive not their sins, but ever keep them in thy remembrance: thou shalt not be thought a righteous judge, if thou wink at such wickedness: they hinder not our own buildings, but they provoke the builders of thy house and city. They despise us because we serve thee. They hate us, not for any of our wickedness, but for the hatred that they bear to thy house, religion, and city, which they would have lie waste, overthrown and trodden down. We grant we have deserved to be cast away from thee, if thou deal with us in justice; and yet after thy fatherly correction we obediently return and submit ourselves unto thee; whereas they contemptuously still rebel against thee, and hate us because we love thee. If they did persecute us for our own deserts, we would bear it; but to see thy majesty defaced we cannot abide it: they would have thy city to lie unbuilt, that men might speak ill of thee, that thou were a weak God, not able to defend thy people, that call on thy name, so mightily as their idols do them that know not thee. The shame that they would lay on us shall turn unto thee, O Lord: for it is done unto us for thy sake, and hatred of thee and thy word. Avenge thy own quarrel, O God, and look not at our own deserts: for though we have grievously offended thee, yet we repent, and they obstinately stand in defence of their own wickedness. O Lord, forget not this malicious dealing of them toward us for thy sake; abate their pride, assuage their malice, and confound their devices that they intend against us: comfort and encourage thy poor workmen and builders, whom they provoke to anger, and grant us, that we may, by thy aid, with good success finish that which we have, through thy goodness, so well begun. Amen.

Out of his prayer may arise two doubts: one, *whether it be godly*, and good men may use the like that he prayeth for here, that is, that the same ill may fall on them that they would do unto the Jews; the other, *that their sin should not be forgiven them*. The scripture teacheth both to pray for our enemies, and to forgive them, and also that God would revenge their cause himself in his justice. Our Saviour Christ prayeth for them that crucified him, saying, "Father, forgive them, for they know not what they do." St Stephen likewise. But David many times prayeth the contrary, as, "Let his sorrow be turned on his own head, and let his wickedness fall upon his own pate." Again, "Let them be confounded and ashamed that seek for my life, and let them be driven back and ashamed that seek to do me evil." These psalms and others are full of such like speeches. And where some expound such places to be a prophecy and foretelling of such mischiefs as should fall on them, rather than a wishing or praying that they should fall, it is not ill that they say; but it may be doubted whether it be most agreeing to the text. But howsoever it be, this must be most taken heed of, that in all such prayers nothing be asked of malice against the party, which is hard for our froward nature to do, but only for the glory of God, which is to be sought in

<small>Acts vii.
Psal. vii.
Psal. lxix. cix.</small>

all our doings and prayers, which may be in shewing his justice. In the Lord's prayer we say, "Hallowed be thy name:" we desire not God only that he would direct both every man in his doings to set forth his glory, that his name may be hallowed; but also that he would stay, confound, and take away all hinderers of the same, with all their devices and subtle practices; that, all stumbling-blocks being taken away, his name may be sanctified in all nations. So prayed David, "O my God, make the counsel of Achithophel to seem foolish." So in the commandments, the affirmative is included in the negative, and the negative in the affirmative; as, "Thou shalt not kill:" wherein we are not only forbidden all cruelty, but are commanded to relieve, succour, and help, by all means that we may. Nehemiah hateth not the men, but their wickedness: so we learn to put a difference betwixt the man and the sin of man, and pray for mercy to the one, and justice to the other. Man is God's good creature, and to be beloved of all sorts: sin is of the devil, and to be fled of all sorts. And it is a great difference, whether we pray for revenging our own private quarrel, which may not be in any case; or it be for God's cause and glory, which we would seek the furtherance of by all means we may. *2 Sam. xv.*

6. *Then we builded the wall.* This verse declareth what they got by this short prayer. The people's heart was encouraged to go forward with this work, insomuch that they repaired all the breaches of the wall, and joined it all together, as though it were one whole sound wall, and never had been defaced afore. Prayer is a sovereign salve for all sores: for it will heal not only the wounds of the body and soul, but also hard stony walls. This is the common practice of all good men, when they be scorned for the Lord's sake, to turn themselves unto humble prayer, commit the cause unto the Lord, who will justly revenge his own quarrel, when he thinketh good. David, when he had complained unto God how the "judges did mock him, and the drunkards and minstrels sang their songs against him" to make them merry withal, and could find no remedy, he saith thus, after that he was sore grieved at them, "But I, O Lord, made my prayer unto thee;" and then the Lord comforted him. Likewise king Ezechias getteth him to the temple, when Rabsachis had railed against *Psal. lxix.* *2 Kings xv.*

the living Lord, and written blasphemous letters: he read the letters in the sight of God, falleth to prayer, and desireth the Lord to help him in that extremity; and his God delivered him.

This prayer of Nehemiah is not long; for God regardeth not so much the length of our prayer, as the earnest hearty desire of the mind, with an humble submission of himself to the Lord's good will and pleasure, repenting earnestly for his offences, and faithfully hoping without mistrust for the Lord's comfortable assistance, when and as he shall think good. By this prayer they obtain at the Lord's merciful hand boldness to go forward with their building, and to contemn their proud mocks and brags: they finish the whole length and the height of the wall, in despite of their enemies: and the people were not weary of working, but the more they wrought, the more desirous they were to work still; for the good success that they had in building hitherto did encourage them to go forward with it, and they doubted not but that God was with them, and therefore feared no other. Let us learn therefore at these good men's examples, to be bold and constant in well doing, and not to fear every brag and blast of wind. Let us be as a lusty horse, that goeth through the street, and careth not for the barking of every cur that leapeth forth, as though he would bite him: so let us not be afraid of the barking curs, nor look backward, but go on forth, not changing with every tide: and the mighty Lord will strengthen our weakness with good success to finish his building: for so have all good men done from the beginning.

The Text. v. 7. *It came to pass that when Sanballat and Tobias, the Arabians, the Ammonites and the Azdodites heard tell that a salve was come on the wall of Jerusalem, and that the breaches of it began to be stopped up, they were very wroth.*

8. *And they conspired all together to go and besiege Jerusalem, and to make a scattering in it.*

9. *But we prayed unto our God, and set a watch by them day and night in their sight.*

10. *And Judas said, The strength of the bearers is decayed,*

and there is much mortar, and we are not able to build on the wall.

11. *And our enemies said, They shall not know nor see till we come into the middle of them, and we shall slay them, and make the work to cease.*

As good men go forward with God's work, so the wicked swell for anger, increase in malice against them, and, by all means possible, not only by themselves go about to overthrow all their good enterprises, but they seek all the partakers that they can get, and will refuse no kind of man, be he never so ill, to join with them, so they may obtain their purpose, and hinder the Lord's building. Sanballat and Tobias afore thought with their bitter scoffs, big words, and haughty looks to have dashed these poor souls out of countenance, and made them to leave building: but now, when they see they were not afraid, but wrought more lustily, they make other devices; they will fight for it, they gather a great company of neighbours, as ill as themselves, and will set upon them, kill them, and overthrow their building. Such a thing is malice once earnestly in man's mind conceived, and specially for religion, that it so blindeth a man, that he seeth not what he doeth, nor what will follow of his doings. He that falleth from God wandereth in darkness, and cannot tell what he doeth, where he is, nor whither he goeth; but the farther he stirreth, the farther he is out of the way, and the more darkness he is in; for " God is light," " the way, truth, and life," and he that hath not God for his guide cannot find the true way to everlasting life. Let every man therefore, that will walk uprightly in the fear of God, take heed how he once give place to any wickedness: for if the devil get a little entrance into thee, he will draw thee clean away with him, if God be not more merciful to hold thee. When the devil tempted Eve, he appeared in likeness of a serpent,—to teach us, that as the head of the serpent is the greatest part of the body, and wheresoever the head getteth in, the whole body followeth easily; so the devil, if he once enter into man's heart, he will creep into all parts, and never cease, until he possess the whole man, and bring him to everlasting death with him and destruction in this world, as he did with Judas, entering into him first by little and little, but after that Jesus Christ "had given him the sop," he did so fully possess him, that straightways he betrayed his master, the Lord of life, into the hands of wicked men, to be put to most vile death, and all for greediness of a little money.

Sanballat by the help of Tobias had now gotten a great band of soldiers, of others, and specially of Arabians, Ammonites and Azdodites, to fight for him against these sely souls, and for no other quarrel, but because they heard say that they had repaired all the breaches of the walls of Jerusalem. Their foolish madness appeareth the more, because they rage so fiercely for only hearing how well the work went forward, as though that had been the greatest fault that they could have committed. Wisdom would have tried, whether such tales had been true, afore they had believed them : but anger is so hot an affection, that it cannot abide to be ruled by reason. There is no difference betwixt an angry man and a mad man, but that anger lasteth but for a time, and continueth not still, as madness doth. *Ira furor brevis est,* "Anger is a short madness," saith the poet ; and again,

>Impedit ira animum, ne possit cernere verum:

James i. "Anger letteth the mind, that it cannot see the truth." St James therefore biddeth, "Let every man be swift to hear, but slow to speak, and slow to anger: for the anger of man worketh not the righteousness of God." And though anger ought to be suppressed in all things, that it grow not to any extremity, yet is it most chiefly to be holden down when any correction is to be executed. Tully teacheth well, *Qui iratus accedit ad pœnam, nunquam mediocritatem illam tenebit, quæ est inter nimium et parum*[1]*:* "He that punisheth when he is angry cannot keep that mean, which is betwixt too much and too little." Theodosius the emperor, when he had caused a great number to be slain in his anger at Thessalonica, and for his rashness in so doing was excommunicated by Ambrose, bishop of Milan, after that he knew his fault and openly confessed it, made a law that no execution should be done on any offender, whom he judged to die, afore thirty days were expired, that he might have so long time to con-

[[1] De Officiis, Lib. i. cap. 25. Ed.]

sider in, whether he had judged rightfully[2]. God grant every man a diligent care to foresee that he do nothing in his anger unadvisedly, but with patient modesty may do all things in the fear of God! [Ruffin. Lib. ii. cap. 18.]

Tobias was an Ammonite, of the seed of Ammon, whom Lot begat of his own daughter in his drunkenness; and as they were ever utter enemies to the Jews, though they were near kinsmen, the one being come of Abraham, the other of Lot his nephew, so now, having such a man of authority their countryman to be their captain, as Tobias was, they were more easily drawn to join with them, that by this occasion they might more easily revenge old quarrels against the Jews more bitterly. The Arabians were their next neighbours, a wild mountain people, living much by robbery, and therefore easily brought to such a mischief. The Azdodites were one corner of the Philistines, their old enemies, and would rather run to such a mischief unbidden, than tarry for any calling for. So we may see, how readily one wicked man will be drawn to help another, and how the wickedness of one will infect another that will give ear unto it. But good men are oft left to themselves, without help or comfort at man's hand, as the Jews were here now; and the church of God hath been from the beginning subject to such dangers, and shall be to the end, that God's glory may more evidently shine in defending of it, in despite of all their foes. [Gen. xix.]

The metaphor, or kind of speech that is used here, when he saith, "a salve was come on the walls of Jerusalem," is taken from chirurgeons, who, when they heal wounds, join the flesh together again which afore was cut in sunder: so the new breaches of the walls, which afore lay gaping open, were now joined together and made sound, as though it were one whole sound wall. And as it was such a grief to these wicked men, to hear tell only that the walls went well forward in repairing; so is it at this day the greatest grief that God's enemies can have, when they hear tell that re-

[[2] Lege sanxit in posterum, ut sententiæ principum super animadversione prolatæ in diem tricesimum ab executoribus differrentur; quo locus misericordiæ vel, si res tulisset, pœnitentiæ non periret. Auctores Hist. Eccles. Lib. xi. (Ruffini ii.) cap. 18.—It was done at Ambrose's suggestion. See Theodoret. Eccles. Hist. Lib. v. cap. 18. Ed.]

ligion goeth forward in any country: then they conspire, both by themselves and their friends, and specially by that *bastard Tobias*, their pope, so much as in them lieth, though it be with fire and sword, or any other cruel device, to overthrow it.

8. *And they conspired.* When they perceived that mocking taunts, high looks, nor proud words could not drive them from their building, they will now make open war against them, to dash them out of countenance, put them to their shifts, and scatter them asunder, that being amazed at such a company coming on them suddenly, they should not assemble any more to work there. Thus the wicked never cease by all means to hinder God's building; but as Satan their father "goeth continually about, like a roaring lion, to devour" the Lord's flock, so do they: but our God is as diligent to save us that they do no hurt, and watcheth us when we do sleep, that they overcome us not. Pilate and Herod were not friends afore; but to condemn our Lord Christ Jesus they soon agreed, and were friends afterward. So thus many kind of people, which agree not well many times among themselves, yet now to overthrow Jerusalem they all put on armour, join themselves together, become friends, and agree all in one mischief. David marvelleth to see, how all sorts of people and princes conspire together against the Lord Christ, and crieth out, "Why do the heathen so fret, and the people devise vain things? the kings of the earth have risen together, and the princes have assembled together against the Lord and his Anointed." But when David had considered all their raging madness, he comforteth himself, and saith, "He that dwelleth in the heavens shall mock them, and the Lord shall laugh them to scorn, &c." So shall God's faithful little flock be defended and comforted in all their troubles unto the end, and their proud enemies shall be confounded. But this is all our froward nature bent unto, that we be so ready to mischief and slow to do good.

Luke xxiii.

Psal. ii.

9. *But we prayed.* As Nehemiah declareth the manifold troubles that fell on them for this building, so also he setteth forth their merciful deliverance and God's favour towards them. For if Satan should continually assault us, and the Lord leave us to ourselves, man's weakness were not able to stand; so strong and subtle is he, so unable and wretched

are we. They forsake themselves therefore, and by humble prayer submit themselves to their God, who never failed them in all assays. Prayer is a sure anchor in all storms; and they never perish that humbly fly unto it, and faithfully cleave unto it. Prayer is a salve for all sores, yea, it healeth not only body and soul, but even hard stony walls. No kind of earthly physic that God hath made is good for all kind of folk at all times, and all kind of diseases: but this heavenly physic of prayer in wealth and woe, in plenty and poverty, in prosperity and adversity, in sickness and in health, in war and peace, in youth and age, in life and death, in mirth and sadness, yea, in all things and times, in the beginning, midst and ending, prayer is most necessary and comfortable. Happy is that man that diligently useth it at all times. But he that will so effectually pray that he may obtain the thing he desireth, must first prostrate himself in the sight of his God, as this people did, (for so the Hebrew word here signifieth,) forsaking himself as unable to help himself, condemning himself as unworthy to receive such a blessing at the Lord's hand; and yet nothing doubting but that his God, that never forsaketh them that unfeignedly fly unto him, will deal with him in mercy and not in justice, deliver him and comfort him, not for any goodness that he findeth in him, but of his own mere pity, love, grace, and mercy, whereby he may shew himself a glorious God, a present help and succour to all afflicted and oppressed minds. He that findeth anything in himself, to help and comfort himself withal, needeth not to pray; but he that seeth and feeleth his present want and necessity, he will beg earnestly, crave eagerly, confessing where his relief is to be had. No man will pray for that thing which he hath or thinketh himself to have; but we ever ask, desire, beg, and pray for that we want.

Let us therefore in all our supplications and prayers unto the Lord first confess our beggarly poverty and unableness to help ourselves, the want of his heavenly grace and fatherly assistance; and then our gracious God will plenteously pour his blessings into our empty souls, and fill them with his grace. If we be full already, there is no room left to take any more: therefore we must know ourselves to be empty and hungry, or else we shall not earnestly desire this heavenly comfort from above, which is requisite in all prayer. For he that asketh coldly getteth nothing; and the more that we confess our own weakness, our want, and unableness, the more we confess our God to be almighty, rich in mercy, possessing all things in his own hands, and dealing them abroad to his poor people where he seeth them need, and sending the rich empty away. And as we must thus cast down ourselves in ourselves by faith to our God, and to pray to no other, but unto the living Lord that made heaven and earth, as this people doeth, and therefore call him "their God." For if we seek help at any other, we mistrust him, we do not faithfully believe on him, and then we shall not be heard of him. "Call on me in the day of thy trouble," saith thy God, "and I will deliver thee;" and I ask no other reward but to glorify, praise and thank me, knowing thy safety and deliverance to come from me.

Psal. l.

But these men did not only pray to their God, but according to their duty they put themselves in a readiness to defend themselves against their enemies, which is lawful for all men to do. It is not sufficient to pray, and then to neglect such means as God hath appointed us to use for our defence and comfort, no more than it is to say, when he hath prayed, I will live without meat and drink, and God himself shall feed me. For as the Lord hath taught us to pray, "Give us this day our daily bread," so he hath commanded us to work for it, and saith, "He that doth not labour, let him not eat." So here it was not sufficient to call upon their God, though he was most mighty and loving unto them; but they keep watch and ward, put on armour, take their weapons, not cowardly creeping into corners, but stand forth stoutly on the top of the walls by the workmen's elbows in the sight of their enemies, that they might see that they were not afraid of them, but would manfully defend themselves and the workmen against all assaults they could devise. They had a stronger God to defend them, than any devil could be to hurt them, or overthrow their work.

2 Thess. iii.

So prayer and God's providence destroyeth not policy, but maintaineth it; and when they be joined together, God blesseth them both, as his own ordinance. They knew well how true it was that David said, "Except the Lord defend the city, the watchmen watch in vain that keep it." But when the Lord defendeth it, and the watchmen do their duties faithfully, trusting in the Lord, and not foolishly bragging of their own strength and power, then is that city well and strongly kept. The children of Reuben, Gad, and the half tribe of Manasse, as it is written, when they fought against the Agarens, gat the victory, and all because they joined prayer with their power, not trusting in themselves, but in the mighty Lord of hosts, who heard them and overthrew their enemies. Thus must good captains learn to join prayer with policy, if they look to obtain the victory, and not trust in horse, spear, shield or other kind of weapons. God ruleth those that fear him in battle as well as in peace, and those that trust in their own strength he will overthrow. Constantine the great, that worthy emperor, our countryman[1], taught his soldiers daily to pray thus: "We knowledge thee, O Lord, we know thee for a King: we call on thee for our help; from thee we have the victory, and by thee we are conquerors. We give thee thanks for this present prosperity, and by thee we hope for things to come. We all are humble suitors unto thee, that our emperor and his godly children may be preserved safe, long to live, and we humbly beseech thee that he may be a valiant conqueror, &c.[2]"

Psal. cxxvii.

[1 Chr. v. 18—20.]

Euseb. Lib. iv. De vita Constant.

And that captains may not do what they list, but must learn to defend good causes only, Theodosius, the good emperor, teacheth in his prayer that he maketh for himself, saying: "O Almighty God, thou knowest that I have taken

[1 One traditionary account represents Constantine to have been born in England; but it is very doubtful. Gibbon adopts that which assigns his birth to Naissus in Dacia. His father Constantius died at York. ED.]

[2 Σὲ μόνον οἴδαμεν Θεόν, σὲ βασιλέα γνωρίζομεν· σὲ βοηθὸν ἀνακαλούμεθα· παρὰ σοῦ τὰς νίκας ἠράμεθα, διὰ σοῦ κρείττους τῶν ἐχθρῶν κατέστημεν· σοὶ τὴν τῶν ὑπαρξάντων ἀγαθῶν χάριν γνωρίζομεν· σὲ καὶ τῶν μελλόντων ἐλπίζομεν. σοῦ πάντες ἱκέται γινόμεθα, τὸν ἡμέτερον βασιλέα Κωνσταντῖνον, παῖδάς τε αὐτοῦ θεοφιλεῖς, ἐπὶ μήκιστον ἡμῖν βίου σῶον καὶ νικητὴν φυλάττεσθαι ποτνιώμεθα. P. 150. B. Ed. Paris. 1544. ED.]

these wars in hand in the name of Christ thy Son, for a just revenge: if it be otherwise, revenge thou it on me; but if I come hither in a good quarrel, and trust in thee, then reach forth thy right hand unto thy people, lest peradventure the heathen people will say, Where is their God?[1]" By Moses' law the priests should go to the field with the army to encourage, teach, and comfort them, even when they should join battle. The papist will have his morrow mass priest with him; and yet such negligence is in those that call themselves protestants, that they think the company worse if a learned minister be among them: and if he will rebuke their spoil, gaming, swearing, whoring, they are weary of him; and if he touch any of the better sort, then away with him, or else work him some displeasure. So rashly we cast off the Lord's yoke; so foolishly we enter into wars, as though the victory lay in our own hands, and God did not bestow it on whom he thinketh best. John Baptist, when the soldiers came to him to be baptized, as other sorts of men did, he taught every one how to amend their lives; and to the soldiers he saith, "Do violence to no man, accuse none falsely, and be content with your wages."

God grant all good soldiers to follow these lessons unfeignedly; for the Holy Ghost noteth these as common faults, that such kind of men be infected withal. Many lusty younkers think not themselves brave enough, except they can look big, speak stoutly, and pick a quarrel against every simple man, dealing hardly with all sorts, that they can come by, they think all is well gotten. How common this kind of dealing hath been, I leave it to the consideration of others. And for that divers have fallen to a great sobriety and lived orderly, since they learned religion, God is to be praised; and God increase the number! They be not made soldiers to do wrong, but to correct them that offer wrong. They enter not

[[1] Tum ille, ut conversas suorum acies videt, stans in edita rupe, unde et conspicere et conspici ab utroque posset exercitu, projectis armis, ad solida se vertit auxilia, et prostratus in conspectu Dei, Tu, inquit, omnipotens Deus, nôsti quia in nomine Christi Filii tui ultionis justæ, ut puto, prœlia ista suscepi: si secus, in me vindica. Si vero cum causa probabili, et in te confisus, huc veni, porrige dexteram tuis, ne forte dicant gentes, Ubi est Deus corum? Auctores Eccles. Hist. xi. (Ruffini ii.) c. 33. Ed.]

that trade to live without law, but to bring them in obedience that offend the law. They may not think the prince's coffers to be at their disposition, but must content themselves with wages and that portion that is allotted to them. He that dealeth otherways getteth it unjustly; and though he thinketh he dealeth so cunningly that it cannot be espied, yet the righteous Lord will punish it in this world to his shame, and, if he be not more merciful, most grievously in the world to come.

Thus prayer and policy joined together make a perfect work, and the one halteth if it want the other. David when he fought with Goliah, though he refused king Saul's armour, yet he took his sling and stones in his shepherd's bag, and calling upon the Lord overthrew that giant mightily. So shall it be in God's church, when the ministers and people pray earnestly, the preachers speak boldly, beat down sin mightily, and watch night and day, that Satan by his members creep not in subtilly and disturb the flock of Christ. God grant us so to watch and pray that the Lord's name may be worthily praised in us: for so St Paul teacheth, "Be diligent in prayer, watching Col. iv. in it with thanksgiving." And St Luke saith, "Watch and Luke xxi. pray at all times, that ye may scape all the evils which are to come." This kind of fighting against all fiery assaults of Satan is as necessary in God's church, as open war is against the enemies of the commonwealth.

10. *And Judas said.* This gap was not so soon stopped, but there bursteth forth another worse than that. Open enemies can do little harm, if the other parties within be true amongst themselves; but if the soldiers within the city fall at a mutiny among themselves, disobey their captain, discourage their fellows, or work any treason, drawing parties together, then the danger within is greater than any can be without. The greatest part of the tribe of Judah now wax faint-hearted, draw back, discourage their fellows, murmur against the captains, and would gladly leave working. A perilous practice in such a dangerous time, and able to overthrow all. One coward in an army, breaking the array, running away or discouraging the rest, may easily discomfit the whole army. But here come now a great company, not of the meanest sort, but of the king's tribe of Juda; and they

murmur, they discourage, they dissuade, and hinder the work as much as they may. The Israelites in Egypt, when Pharaoh increased their labour, because Moses and Aaron would have them delivered, they cry out on Moses and Aaron for their well doing. When they were come out of Egypt, and wanted their flesh-pots, they cry out of Moses and Aaron which brought them out, and would return again into Egypt. The spies, that were sent afore to bring word what a people and country they should come unto, were faint-hearted, and discouraged the rest, saying, "The men were great giants, their cities stronger" than they could conquer, though the ground was fruitful and pleasant of itself. Thus Satan never ceaseth to devise something to overthrow God's building.

<small>Exod. xvi.</small>

The reasons that Judas allegeth were great, and able to persuade any man. First, "the workmen were weary," say they; their shoulders ached with bearing so many heavy burdens, their strength was gone, they were not able to bear any more. Secondly, there "was much mortar" to carry away, both of the old rubbish of the broken walls, and also new mortar to be brought in for the new building. The Hebrew word will serve for both, which I had rather follow, though some learned apply it only to the old rubbish of the old walls, and some to the new mortar to be carried for the new building. This troubled Nehemiah more than any brags of his enemies abroad. For of these he looked for help, and of the others none. These should have comforted him, and now they discomfort. Now he must first pacify and please the men, then he must comfort them, and also stir them up to their work, lest others should faint and fall away as well as they.

It is an easy matter to begin a good work, but a special gift to stand in all storms and continue to the end. The proud papist at this day, at whose hands no goodness is to be looked for, neither toward God nor good man, doth not hinder the building of God's church and preferring of his gospel so much, as these faint-hearted protestants, white-livered hypocrites, double dissemblers, and servers of time. When they set them down and look into the world, What? say they, we have wrought ourselves weary these fifty years, and profited little; our shoulders ache; the more popish rubbish we carry away, the more we see remain behind. Our open enemies are so many and so cruel, that they will not let us work, and our friends are so weak, that they are not able to help themselves and us: many of those that seem to be friends are faint-hearted, wax cold, and deal cunningly against a new day and a change do come, and then we shall be left in the briars. So much old popish rubbish is left behind in the church, that it will never be carried out: so much new good order and discipline is to be brought in, that it is hard to tell, whether it be a harder matter to carry out the old dregs, or to bring in new mortar to build new walls. How many have they burned! how greedily do they gape to be broiling again! St Peter in the Acts of the Apostles asketh, "why they would go about to lay that yoke of Moses' ceremonies on the neck of the disciples, which neither they nor their fathers were able to bear?" And if that might be truly said then, of those ceremonies which came from God himself, how much more may it be verified now on those which come from the pope, the father of all superstition! The double dealing of wily worldlings is such, that it is to be feared this popish rubbish will never be clean rubbed off. For we ever keep some Romish room in store to turn ourselves on, so oft as the world shall turn.

And this old Judas may well be a figure of the latter Judas, that betrayed our Master Christ, and all other such hypocrites, which being faint-hearted would betray the building and builders, that God's city should not be finished. There is great striving, who shall be Peter's successor in authority; but I fear Judas hath more followers, which cowardly and greedily for a little money hinder, betray, and undermine both the faithful builders and building. If it be heinous treason to betray one man, whom thou owest duty, reverence, and faithful service unto, it must needs be much more heinous in a city, a camp, a church, or any society, where faithfulness should be found, to deceive, run away, deal dissemblingly, or to dissuade, discourage, and withdraw any or many from their dutiful obedience, labour, diligence, and faithful dealing, to the dishonour of God, the overthrow of religion, and hurt of his people. God for his mercy's sake root out all desperate Judases from among all faithful companies, that they may not discourage others, and

[PILKINGTON.]

specially from among the flock of Christ, whom he hath so dearly bought, that the Lord's building may go forward lustily!

What these Romish rubbish be, I had rather leave it to other men's considerations, than by blotting of paper, and filling men's ears with such filthiness, stand to rehearse them: but among many I think none worse than many lewd dispensations, which such idle lubbers seek for, whereby their duty is undone. But many a good builder will not build on the sand, but dig to the sad[1] earth; and the good husband will pluck up the weeds afore he sow good corn: so surely in God's church ill doctrines, ceremonies, customs, and superstitions must be rooted out, afore good laws, orders, wholesome doctrine and government can take place.

11. *And our enemies said.* The malice of Satan by his members is so great against the building of God's city, that by all means, openly and privily, inward enemies and outward, fair words and foul, sword, fire and faggot, war and peace, teaching or holding their tongue, knowledge or ignorance, undermining or conspiracies, and all other devices whatsoever, they let none slip, but try all, that they may overthrow all, and not so much to do themselves good, as to hinder others; to set up themselves in the sight of the world, and to deface the glory of God; but in the end all is in vain, and our God shall have the victory. They will not yet use any open violence, but cunningly come on them unawares, be on them afore they know it or look for it, secretly prepare all things necessary for their purpose, and steal on them privily, that they shall be in the midst of them afore they wot where they be; they will kill them, shed their blood, mercilessly murder them, and make that building to cease, overthrow the walls, pull down the bulwarks, and so overwhelm them that they never dare attempt any such building any more. O monstrous malice against thy Lord to thine own destruction in hindering his building, and his immortal praise in defending of it! What foolishness is this to strive against the Almighty! a wretched worm on the earth to rebel against the Lord's holy will and determinate pleasure in heaven! Nothing grieveth them so much as to see this work go forward: if this work were laid asleep, their hearts

[1] Sad: firm, solid. Frequent in Wickliffe. ED.]

were well eased: but our God in patience letteth them utter their malice, that in his justice he may overthrow them.

In this *serpentine, crafty, and devilish* dealing of these wicked men appeareth the old serpentine, devilish nature and malice of Satan, that old cankered enemy of God and man from the beginning. God said to the serpent, that "the seed of the woman should tread upon his head, and the serpent should tread upon his heel." Crafty and subtle men, when they will work a mischief, go privily about it, to deceive the good man, as the serpent, if he will sting a man, will not look him in the face, but steal on him privily when he seeth him not. God endued man, when he made him, with such a majesty in his face, afore he fell to sin, that all creatures did reverence and fear him: and although sin hath much defaced and blotted out that noble majesty and grace that God endued him with, yet it is not utterly disgraced and taken away, but some spark and relic remaineth at this day, that no wild nor venomous beast dare look a man in the face boldly, and hurt him; but will give place for the time, and seek how he may privily wound or hurt him, when he seeth him not. It is good wisdom, therefore, for every man that shall be in danger of any such hurtful beasts, always to look them in the face, and beware when he turneth his eye from them, that they suddenly and subtilly leap not on him and hurt him. These crafty and subtle foxes therefore, like the seed of the serpent, would not openly invade nor gather any great power of men against them, but at unawares steal on them privily, afore they should suspect any such thing. This is the nature of wicked men, so craftily to undermine the godly.

Gen. iii.

The next property of the serpent that appeareth in these devilish men is, that they *mercilessly would murder them*, when they had once thus suddenly invaded them. Satan was "a murderer from the beginning," as St John saith; and therefore no marvel if his children be bloodsuckers, like unto the father. When he would not spare the innocent Lamb of God, Jesus Christ, but most cruelly crucified him, why should we marvel, to see him by his wicked children so greedily seek to shed innocent blood still?

John viii.

The last property of Satan appeareth here most plainly in these wicked men, in that they *would so gladly overthrow this building of Jerusalem*, that it should never be thought on any more. Satan is "the prince of this world," and therefore cannot abide another king to reign, nor any kingdom to be set up but his own; and for maintaining of that he will strive by his members unto death.

If a man would describe a papist, I know not where he should find a more lively example than these men be. The papist is close and subtle in going about to work his feat on a sudden, as these men were, afore it be spied, if God utter it not. Their bloody hearts and hands have filled all countries in all ages with shedding innocent blood; but especially this age plainly declareth to them that will not be wilfully blind, how true it is. Those bloody marriages in France of late, which were pretended to be made for peace, love and quietness, shall be witnesses against them of these kind of dealings, (though they rejoice in their mischief,) unto the world's end. St Paul calleth the devil not only a prince, but a "god of the world," because he disdaineth the glory of God, and would have that honour given unto himself. And that ye may easily see who is his truly begotten son, look who "sitteth in the temple of God, boasting himself as God," as St Paul saith; who sitteth so deeply in ignorant men's consciences that they dare not offend him, but think him to be holiest? who taketh in hand to bestow heaven and hell and purgatory at his own pleasure, to forgive sin, and make righteous, which belong to God alone, but the pope and his chaplains? Therefore he that will not wittingly deceive himself, may easily judge whence popery cometh, and whither it leadeth us.

No marvel therefore, if the papists at this day be so earnest to serve their god, the pope, and hinder the building of God's church and city, lest their kingdom, superstition, pride and authority decay. Open your eyes and see, mark the practices of superstitious idolaters from the beginning; and ye shall find them in nothing more earnest, than in hindering the true God to be worshipped as he ought. What made Pharaoh so desirous to stay the children of Israel in Egypt, but that they should not go sacrifice to the Lord, as he had appointed? Wherefore did the scribes and Pharisees so rage against Christ, but that they would not have their traditions to decay, and the true doctrine of Christ Jesus to be

marginalia: 2 Cor. iv. / 2 Thess. ii. / Exod. / Matt.

set up? Why did the high priests and elders whip the <small>Acts v.</small> apostles, and "command them to preach no more in the name of Jesus," but that they would overthrow his kingdom, if that they could? Why were so many thousand martyrs so cruelly murdered in so many ages, but that they would know no God and Saviour but only the Lord Christ? Why doth the pope and his partakers so rage at this day, as Herod did, when he heard that a new king was born, but that he seeth his kingdom and superstition overthrown by the preaching of the gospel?

And as it falleth out thus generally in the building of God's spiritual house and city, that all sorts of enemies most diligently apply themselves, their labour, wit, power, policy and friendship to overthrow the true worship of God; so particularly "Satan goeth about like a roaring lion seeking whom he may devour," and therefore every man hath great need to be wary and circumspect, that he be not suddenly overthrown; but let him watch and "put on all the armour of God," which St Paul describeth, saying, "For this cause <small>Eph. vi.</small> take unto you the whole armour of God, that ye may be able to resist in the evil day, and having finished all things, stand fast: stand therefore, and your loins girt about with verity, and having on the breastplate of righteousness, and your feet shod with the preparation of the gospel of peace, &c." that he may stand stoutly in the day of battle, and through the might of his God get the victory. The devil never ceaseth; for if he cannot overthrow the whole church, yet he would be glad to catch any one that belongeth to the Lord, if he could.

> v. 12. *And it came to pass, when the Jews which dwelt be-* <small>The Text.</small>
> *side them came and told us of their practices ten times*
> *out of all places whence they came unto us,*
> 13. *I set in the low places beyond the wall, and in the*
> *high places also I set the people according to their*
> *kindreds, with their swords, their spears, and their*
> *bows.*
> 14. *And when I saw them, I rose and said to the nobles,*
> *and to the officers, and the rest of the people, Be not*
> *afraid of the sight of them, but remember the great*
> *and fearful Lord, and fight for your brethren, for*

your sons and your daughters, your wives and your houses.

15. *And it came to pass, when our enemies heard tell that it was told us, God disappointed their purpose, and all we returned unto the walls, every man to his work.*

This comfort our loving God hath left to his chosen people, that as the devil ceaseth not by his members to trouble and vex his church and beloved children by all means that he can devise, so the mighty Lord of his own free goodness, by his Holy Spirit, his angels, his creatures all, and most sensibly by the comfort that one good man giveth another, in all our griefs faileth not to aid and comfort us, night and day, privily and openly, that ever we may have just cause to rejoice in him for our deliverance, and not in ourselves.

These wicked Samaritans, Sanballat, Tobias, and their fellows, were not so cunning privily to prepare men and armour suddenly to invade Jerusalem unlooked for, to murder the builders and shed innocent blood, but the living Lord, to glorify himself in opening their subtle practices, which they thought had been kept close from all men, by other of the Jews which dwelt among them, in Samaria, Arabia, and other places, doth bewray their conspiracy, and maketh it known in Jerusalem often times out of all corners of the country. Thus it proveth true, that the gospel saith, "Nothing is hid but it shall be openly known," be it never so craftily devised: nothing can be so privily devised to hurt the man of God, but the wisdom of our God doth foresee it, his merciful goodness doth open it, and his mighty hand doth so rule it, that it overwhelmeth us not. God increase our faith, and help our unbelief, that in all dangers we may humbly submit ourselves unto him, and without grudging or doubting boldly look for his help in due time, and patiently tarry his leisure: for no doubt he will help them that faithfully look for and earnestly beg his aid.

King Saul purposed divers times suddenly to have slain poor David; but God opened his mischievous mind and malice by Jonathan his son and Michal his daughter, and David was delivered. The king's chamberlains had privily conspired

2 Sam. xviii. xv.

to have murdered Assuerus, their king and master; but Mar- *Esth. vi.* docheus openeth his treason, and the king was saved. Benhadad, the king of Syria, made war against Joram, king of Israel, and by counsel of his servants laid ambushments privily to trap Joram, the king of Israel, by the way; but Eliseus the prophet, perceiving that Joram would go the way where the ambush was laid in wait for him, gave the king warning, and bade him go another way: when Benhadad heard tell that his secret purpose and counsel was known to Joram, and he came not that way, he was angry with his servants, and said they had betrayed and opened his counsel to Joram. "Nay," saith one of his servants, "there is a *2 Kings vi.* prophet in Israel, Eliseus, and he openeth whatsoever thou speakest in thy privy chamber." King Herod minding subtilly *Matt. ii.* to kill the young babe, Christ Jesus, craftily bade the wise men go and learn "where the new king was born, and he would come and worship him," as well as they did: but the gracious God, which never faileth at need, bade them go another way, and not tell Herod; for he meant to kill the young babe Christ. The wicked Jews made a "vow, they would nei- *Acts xxiii.* ther eat nor drink until they had killed Paul:" but Paul's sister's son, when he heard their conspiracy, opened it, and the captains set soldiers to defend him, and deliver him out of their hands.

I cannot tell, whether these Jews which dwell abroad in divers countries, and came and told them in Jerusalem of the conspiracy that was intended against them by Sanballat and his fellows, be worthy more praise or dispraise. It was their duty to have come home, stood in storms, and help to build Jerusalem, as well as these other their fellows did: but God, which turneth our negligence and foolishness to the setting forth of his immortal goodness and wisdom, gave them a good will and boldness to further that building as they might, and stirred them up to come often times, and open unto them in Jerusalem the great conspiracy that was intended against them; that they might be ready to defend themselves whensoever they were assaulted. It grieved them to understand the mischief that was purposed, both to have their brethren's blood cruelly shed, and also that building to be overthrown; and though they durst not come and join with them both in battle and working, yet they are to be commended that they so pitied their brethren and the work, that they gave warning of that great conspiracy purposed against them.

Thus God useth the service of all men and creatures to the benefit and comfort of those that fear him truly. So among wicked people many times do good men dwell, both to bring them from their wickedness by their good example and counsel, and also to be a relief to other good men abroad in other places, when occasion shall serve. Thus was Lot in Sodom, Joseph in Pharao's house, and Daniel in Babylon; and if these Jews had not dwelt abroad among the Samaritans and Arabians, this conspiracy had not been opened to the builders in Jerusalem; but they should have been suddenly slain, afore they knew of their coming. Thus is God's providence and care for his people, when they understand not their own danger, to be praised; and this natural love, that these Jews bare to their country and brethren, in forewarning them to defend themselves, is to be followed of all good men. Demaratus of Lacedemon was unjustly banished his country: yet when he heard that the Athenians[1] would make war against his country, he gave his countrymen warning of it, that they might be in a readiness to defend themselves. When the Israelites had made the golden calf, and God in his anger would have destroyed them, Moses falleth to prayer, though they oft rebelled against him, and desireth the Lord to pardon them, or else to put him out of his book. St Paul wisheth "to be accursed from Christ," so that he might win his brethren the Jews to the Lord Christ, though they oft sought his death.

<small>Exod. xxxii.</small>

<small>Rom. ix.</small>

Thus good men will forget displeasures done unto them, and be ready always to help and comfort their country, and specially those that be of the household of faith. This may be a comfort to all good men, that as God opened this conspiracy to his people at this time by the Jews that dwelt far from them, so his fatherly care never faileth them that love him, but he will defend and deliver them: for he maketh his enemies, if they be made privy of any such mischief, so babbling that they will open it, either for vain glory, bribery, malice, or else their own consciences do accuse them, that they cannot quietly suffer such a mischief to be wrought. And although they were

[<small>1</small> The Persians. See Herodotus, vii. 239. ED.]

thus oft, and out of all corners, warned of this conspiracy, yet they could scarcely be brought, many of them, to believe any such thing to be attempted; it was so horrible and incredible. Good men judge others to be like themselves, simple and plain dealers, and cannot easily be persuaded that any man should go about such a mischief. But the gospel teacheth that we should " be wise as serpents, and as simple as doves." The serpent is wise to save his own head, and hide himself until the danger be past; and the dove will not craftily devise any harm to any other: so the man of God must be wise as the serpent, and not be careless of his safety, (for God hath given him reason to defend himself, and foresee mischiefs, and provide for them;) nor he must not be crafty to hurt others, as the dove is not: but he must rather think, that the wicked men, whom Satan hath so possessed, will leave nothing undone that may overthrow the good; and therefore they ought to be as wise, circumspect, and diligent to defend themselves and their country from such mischiefs by all honest means, as the other shall be busy to devise or do them any harm, or else they shall be guilty of their own destruction and many others'; which cannot be defended in conscience, nor the Lord can allow it in justice, being hurtful to so many.

13. *I set in the low places.* Nehemiah by leaving the court, where he lived in ease, is now come to a goodly bargain. First, he was master of the work, set every man in order, that none loitered, nor wrought otherwise than he was appointed, and that none troubled his fellows; daily dabbling in the mire, mortar and clay, as long as he might, and yet would not be weary, with great displeasure and grudging of those that should be his friends and helpers; but now is become a warrior, is driven to put on armour, keep watch and ward night and day, and oversee them himself; to set his people in array, and appoint them their standing places, giving them their weapons, and teaching them what they should do. Such reward shall they have that forsake the world, and will build God's house and city: God and the world cannot be friends; and that maketh so few courtiers to tread this trode. Moses, being brought up in Pharao's house, and might have been called as son to Pharao's daughter, refused the court, and " chose to be in trouble Heb. xi.

with his brethren the Jews," and serve the Lord, rather than to have all the dainties in the court, living in idolatry and displeasure of God. I know not many courtiers, which might have lived in the court with such favour and authority, and would not, to set by these two men. God increase the number, and make many earnest followers of them!

Nehemiah now, like a good captain, "setteth some of his soldiers in trenches," that they could not be seen below, where the walls were lowest, that if any entered there, they should be entrapped by and bye: some he "setteth on the top of the walls with their bows," that they might both be seen far off, and so make the enemy afraid to come near, when they should see them in such readiness; and also that they might shoot far off at them, and hurt them afore they could assault the walls. And like a wise captain, he setteth "all of one kindred" together, that one should be true to another, as kinsfolks will rather than strangers.

It hath been a common practice with us of late to take the soldiers of one country from their captain, whom they know and love, and put them to a stranger whom they know not: what goodness hath come of it, let wise men judge; in my opinion little or none, except it were the private profit of the captain. But sure it is not without great cause, that the Holy Ghost declareth here the order that Nehemiah set them in "by their kindreds" together, teaching us that nature will move one kinsman to be truer in all dangers to another of his kindred, rather than to a stranger; and that one kinsman will open his grief to his friend, and take comfort at his hand, rather than to him whom he knoweth not. He cannot be bold with a strange captain nor a strange soldier, and that discourageth him, and casteth down his spirits; but when neighbours, friends, and cousins are together under a captain whom they love and know, it emboldeneth them, they cleave together like burrs; if one be in danger, the rest will not forsake him: where as strangers every man seeketh to save himself, and careth not for his fellow, but letteth him shift for himself as he may. This godly example of Nehemiah in placing friends together is to be followed, rather than the private profit of one captain. How strangely strange captains have used their strange soldiers, it is strange to remember; and pity it is to see the soldier, how unwilling he is to serve among strangers, and many times doth serve but slowly. I have seen, when a mean gentleman hath gone to the wars, his tenants would strive who should go with him first; and if he refused any to go, he thought his master loved him not: but now, by this dividing of neighbour from neighbour, friends and friends from other, neither the gentleman that cannot have his trusty men about him, nor the soldier having not such a captain and fellows as he loveth, trusteth, and knoweth, both the master and the man seeketh by all means to tarry at home, and so the worst men are thrust out to serve, which is to be lamented. God amend it!

It is possible, some will think me too saucy, to enter into matters wherein I am not skilled: but that forceth not, the truth must be spoken, though some do grudge; and this example of Nehemiah shall defend me, whatsoever is said to the contrary. The scripture teacheth generally every man his duty, what kind of life soever he live; and God will require that every man should frame himself to that rule: therefore the preacher may enter into consideration of every man's duty, so far as the scripture leadeth him, even to the controlling of the mint, as master Latimer of worthy memory, being found fault withal for meddling in such matters, alleged the prophet, saying, "Thy silver is turned into dross." When John Isai. i. Baptist began to baptize, and all sorts of people resorted unto Luke iii. him, amongst whom came the soldiers too, he taught both the soldiers and all the rest how to behave themselves in their kind of life, if they would receive the gospel.

Here may be noted also, what simple kind of weapons were then used in the wars, and how many cruel and subtle devices we have of late devised one to kill another. Here is none other mentioned but the sword, if they joined hand-strokes; the spear to push them away, if they scaled the walls, and the bow to shoot afar off, to keep them from coming near the walls. What glory this realm hath gotten with these weapons, and specially by the bow, all chronicles declare, and all nations for that feared us: but how in shooting the old glory of this land is decayed, and gaming and ale-houses haunted, to the hurt of the youth, wasting of their money, weakening of their strength, and decay of this worthy exercise, good men lament, and few go about to amend. Shooting is a special thing, not given to all men and nations, but chiefly to the Jews first, while their kingdom stood; then to the Persians, who yet can do something with it; and then to the Englishmen, who have wrought great feats by it. Few histories make any mention of other countries, that could or did use it much in the wars; and if there were some few among them that could do something in it, it was to small purpose or none in the battle. Look at our neighbours round about us, even to the Scottish man, which goeth nearest unto us, and coming both of one ancestor; and it will easily appear how true it is. If any shoot ill favouredly, we say "he shooteth like a Scot;" and yet some few of them shoot well too.

Gen. xxi.
2 Chron. xiv.
1 Sam. xxxi.

The scripture, which is ancienter than any kind of learning by many years, maketh mention, that Ismael, Abraham's son, "was a cunning archer:" king Asa had out of one little tribe of Benjamin two hundred and fourscore thousand archers. King Saul was chased with bowmen, and slain with the Philistians. The sons of Reuben, Gad and Manasses were good warriors and bowmen forty and four thousand seven hundred and threescore. Judas Maccabeus set his bowmen in the forefront of the battle. Pliny, lib. vii. cap. 5, writeth that Perses, the son of Perseus, of whom the Persians had their surname, should be the first deviser of shafts; but how untruly it is reported, these scriptures afore rehearsed, which were long afore this time, will testify. By the which the anciety of the scripture appeareth afore all other learning. And yet the papist will stand on his anciety, and say they have all old learning on their side, where their fathers the popes were but yesterday in comparison of the scriptures, which were elder than any of these by three thousand years: but such lewd doctrine is meet to come from them that will not obey the truth.

The Persians loved shooting so well, that they set an archer on their coin of gold which was of great value, as we do the angel: and, as we used to say, when a man hath great suits, and cannot be so well heard as he would wish, that he must make angels to speak for him, and they cannot be said nay, which thing by report is too common and true at this day; so the king of Persia, being offended at Agesilaus, gave the

Athenians thirty thousand pieces of this great coin of gold of theirs; which thing when Agesilaus understood, he said merrily, but yet truly, that "he was driven away with thirty thousand bowmen," (meaning their coin of gold, which had an archer coined on it,) "and how should he a poor man be able to withstand so many archers?" No more, truly, than our men can say angels nay. For the feats of war done by our elders in this land with bowmen, I refer it to be considered by our own chronicles. But I will not enter into a full discourse of this matter, it belongeth not so much to our purpose; this short touching of it shall suffice now. Whoso listeth to see more of the commendation of it in time of peace, may read that learned book which Master Ascham wrote of it.[1]

As these Samaritans ceased not continually to hinder the building of this earthly Jerusalem, so Satan by his members, papists, and Arians, &c. ceaseth not in every age to hinder the comfortable building of Christ's kingdom and spiritual Jerusalem by all means that he can devise, and never more fiercely than now in our days. But as God stirred up Nehemiah then to defend and encourage the people to go forward with their building, notwithstanding their cruel assaults; so the Lord stirreth up some few to stand in defence of this truth, and God's enemies win not at their hands so much as they look for.

And as Nehemiah here "setteth the people in order by their kindreds, with their swords, spears, and bows, to defend the workmen," so should good magistrates place every where stout soldiers of one doctrine and religion, endued with the special gifts of the Holy Ghost, as knowledge of tongues, discerning of spirits and doctrines, able to confute the false and defend the truth with gifts of utterance, eloquence, and persuading, and with government to bridle the unruly and troublesome folk, that the flock of Christ Jesus, which he bought so dearly, be not drawn away headlong by devilish doctrine from their Lord and Shepherd of their souls, the Lord Christ. God for his mercy sake stir up the hearts of magistrates, and specially courtiers, to set this example before themselves, and diligently to follow it; that we be not found more neg-

[1 Toxophilus, the Schoole of Shootinge. Lond. 1544. ED.]

ligent in this our free liberty under the light of the gospel, in serving our God faithfully, than these poor Jews were under the ceremonies of Moses after their captivity. A lamentable case, to see how bold and earnest these Jews were against so many fierce enemies, and how cold, negligent, and careless we that bear the names of Christians be. Lord, increase our faith, help our unbelief, and make us with courage to work at thy building. We are lulled on sleep; we wallow in wealth and forget thee; we seek our own advancement in the world, and care little or nothing for the advancement of thy kingdom, thy glory, thy people, and the wholesome doctrine of salvation declared unto us in thy holy word.

14. *And when I saw them, I rose and said to the nobles.* After that Nehemiah had thus, like a good captain, set the people in array by their kindreds, appointed them their standing places and weapons, and conveyed himself into some corner to breathe and refresh himself, he looked about him, and, behold, Sanballat, Tobias, and their fellows were at hand, appeared in sight, and marched forward in battle array toward the walls stoutly, to dash them out of countenance, if it had been possible. But then Nehemiah, though he was weary and sat down to rest himself, bestirred him, rose up quickly, forgat that he was weary, plucked up his spirits, and called the nobles, officers, and the people together: and because the time would not suffer him to use many words, the enemies drawing so near, he maketh a short but a pithy oration to them, and in effect so much as could have been spoken in a long time and at leisure; and all to this end, to embolden them to cast away the fear of man, and fear the mighty Lord of hosts, in whose hand it was to dispose as he thought good: and not only that, but the honesty of the cause was such, that they could not without great shame and reproach leave it undefended, so far as their power would stretch. They fought against infidels for the maintenance of God his true religion; they fought for their brethren, for their sons, their daughters, their wives, houses, life, lands and goods. They had of late been in captivity, they felt the smart, what it was to live under strange princes; God had mercifully restored them to their country again, and prospered well the beginning of their buildings; and should they now cowardly

fly away, lose all that they had gotten, fall into their own slavery, live among idolaters, their wives and children to be prisoners afore their face? He that had any blood in him, and either feared God or loved his country and people, would first step out in so good a cause, manfully defend it, spend his blood in it, would strive who should be the first and foremost to give the onset, not doubting but that mighty God, who had so prospered their doings hitherto, would with good success finish it to their great comfort and perpetual commendation. Joab useth the same reason to Abisai and his soldiers, to "fight for their people and country." God never faileth them that fail not themselves: do thou thy duty, and no doubt God will fill out the rest. 2 Sam. x.

What a courage had Nehemiah, that, being come thither but of late, durst speak so boldly to the noblemen and rulers with the people, which should have taken the matter in hand themselves, and encouraged others, rather than he! But in God's cause, when those that should be furtherers of it wax cold, and either will not or dare not, then those whom God doth thus earnestly move, may and ought, so much as in them is, encourage all sorts of men manfully to go forward in serving the Lord. And whereas fear is a great hinderer of all well doing, he beginneth to pluck away that block first, which being removed, boldness must needs follow and take place. Fear not, saith he, their brags, their stern countenance and proud looks, their glistering armour, their great bands of soldiers, their mighty captains, their long spears and sharp swords; they are cowards, their heart faileth them, they are like mules with golden trappers and costly foot-cloth, which outwardly shew bravely unto the eye, but underneath are slow asses and dull beasts. So these big boasting Thrasones and vaunting *milites gloriosi* make a shew of great matters, as though they would and could pull down all, destroy all afore them at their pleasure, where indeed they be fainthearted lubbers, and dare do nothing, as it appeareth hereafter. Our God is an almighty Lord, at whose look the earth quaketh and the devils tremble; and these wretches be vile worms' meat, mortal men, God's enemies, and children of darkness. Our God alone is strong enough for all the devils in hell, and out of hell, with all their members

and partakers. Why should ye be afraid to fight in his
[Psal. cxv.] quarrel? "He hath done what he will in heaven, earth, and
hell," as the psalm saith. All things bend when he doth
beck, and all be at his call and commandment. Shrink not
from this captain, and he will defend you: manfully fight
under his banner, and the victory shall be yours. The worst
that the wretches can do you is to hurt the body; but our
God teacheth us to "fear him that casteth both body and
soul into hell fire." Remember the old grand captain of our
fathers, Moses, when Pharao with a mighty power chased
them to the Red Sea, where the people were afraid, and
saw no remedy but either leap into the sea and be drowned,
or else tarry Pharao and be killed; call to remembrance, I
say, what Moses, in the like distress and jeopardy then that
Exod. xiv. ye be now in, said unto them in few words: "Stand still,"
saith Moses, behold, and mark the end; when ye are not
able, "the Lord himself will fight for you: these cruel enemies whom ye see this day, ye shall never see any more."
And so it came to pass: for by God's mighty hand the
Israelites passed through the sea safe, and Pharao with his
people were drowned.

Rev. xxi. The scripture teacheth that "the fearful, unfaithful, murderers, adulterers, enchanters, idolaters, and liars shall have
their parts in the burning lake of fire and brimstone." If
ye will not stick unto this God, and fear him as children
ought to love and reverence their father, yet fear him as
servants do their masters, and as ill men do, which are afraid
of punishment, and forbear ill doing for fear rather than for
love. The grievous punishment which is threatened to fearful men, is the second and everlasting death both of body
and soul: which whosoever hath any true fear of God in
him, will tremble and quake when he thinketh on it. Be
not therefore afraid of them, but pluck up your stomachs,
and boldly stand in the defence of that city, which the Lord
God hath given you to serve him in. To "fight for sons,
daughters, wives and houses," I think it were an easy matter
to persuade any man; for they be our flesh and bones, and
we be ready enough to such matters; and surely not without a cause, for both the law of God and the law of nature
bindeth us to defend them in their well doings. Moses in

his law saith, that "if thou travelling by the way do find [Exod. xxiii. 5.] thine enemy's ass fallen in the mire under his load, thou shalt not pass by, but help him up." Surely the meaning of this law was not for the ass; but as St Paul, alleging the like law, "Thou shalt not muzzle the mouth of the ox that 1 Cor. ix. treadeth out the corn," said, "Had God care for the ox? Nay, verily; but for you it is written," that ye should feed your painful teachers, which labour for you as the ox; so I say, this law was not made for the ass his sake, but even for thy enemy, who is overloaden as the ass was, and specially those to whom thou art bound by nature; for else thou art worse than an infidel.

But in this matter men are soon resolved what to do: there is a harder matter in men's minds, that is, *whether we should fight for religion as these men did, or no.* We see great troubles in many countries against their princes in our days for religion, and many doubt what they may do herein. Let the case stand as these men's did, and it is soon answered. These Samaritans, Sanballat and his fellows, were no princes, but subject to Artaxerxes, as the Jews were, nor had any authority over them; they were God's enemies, and did the Jews wrong, that would not suffer them to go forward with that building, which the king had given them licence and commission to do. Therefore they might justly defend themselves against such thieves.

Further, here is to be noted also, that they defend themselves only, and do not invade the other, offering any violence to them, but would quietly enjoy their own, if they might. And this is a great difference in the wars, whether a man stand to defence of himself and his people in any cause, or do invade others and offer them wrong. Defending a man's self is allowed by all laws in many causes, and yet in religion by flying, and not by drawing the sword against his prince; but to rebel and draw the sword against thy lawful prince for religion, I have not yet learned, nor cannot allow of it; nor I cannot see, how so many martyrs in all ages would have submitted themselves to death willingly, if they might have fought for it. "Peter drew his sword to cut off Malchus' ear," and would have fought for his master; but Christ Jesus bade him "put up his sword;" for if the matter stood by fighting, he "could ask his heavenly Father, and he would give many thousands of angels to fight for him." The prophet biddeth the Israelites in their captivity in Babylon "pray for the life of Nebuchadnezzar and Balthasar his son, and seek for the peace of the city in which they were prisoners," and not trouble them. St Paul biddeth "pray for all them that were in authority," and then was Nero emperor, a beast in condition rather than a man; yet he must be prayed for. David would never hurt king Saul, though he might, and had him in his danger sundry times, and might have killed him, if he would. Therefore, as Christ overcame his enemies by suffering, so they that be Christ's shall get the victory by patientness and bearing the cross, not by rebelling and drawing the sword.

<small>Jer. xxix.</small>

<small>1 Tim. ii.</small>

<small>1 Sam. xxiv. xxvi.</small>

As Nehemiah therefore here encourageth "the nobles, rulers, and people, manfully to stand in defence of their country, city, wives, children, brethren and houses against their enemies;" so in the spiritual kingdom of Christ must the preachers and pastors encourage all sorts from the highest to the lowest, manfully to stand to that wholesome doctrine of salvation, which they have been taught out of God's holy book, and not be afraid nor change with every blast of wind, and turn with the world, as all sorts in this land have done, to the offence of God's majesty, and their great reproach, and specially of those that were the heads and should have been stays to others. Religion is not a thing at the pleasure of princes, to change as they list, (though the outward circumstances in it may be changed by them;) but it is the unchangeable will and determinate pleasure of the almighty Lord of heaven and earth, decreed by high court of parliament in heaven, afore the world was made, and declared unto man by his prophets and apostles, in such times as his infinite wisdom thought meet, and cannot be altered by any man nor authority in any age. "I am God, and am not changed," saith the Lord; "my thoughts and my ways are not like your thoughts and ways," which are ever changeable and uncertain, but I am ever one and change not. Stick therefore fast unto that Lord, which shrinketh not away from his people, but manfully delivereth them, and by suffering we shall have the victory, as our captain Christ Jesus had; for "if we suffer with him," St Paul saith, "we shall reign with him." In bearing his cross and sufferance then standeth our conquest, not in rebelling; in dying to him, and not living to ourselves.

Mark now the mighty hand of God fighting for his people, and the cowardly hearts of these boasting braggers, how soon they come to nought: they but heard tell that the Jews understood their conspiracy, how they thought to have come suddenly and murdered them, and that they were ready in armour to withstand and defend themselves against them; their hearts fail them, they run away, lay down their weapons, and the Lord defeated their whole purpose and devices. Thus light heads they had, that when they heard tell that the Jews went forward with this building, they prepare themselves to fight with them; and when they heard tell that they were ready to defend themselves, they run away. Such rash heads have wicked men always, unconstant, and changing with every wind: but Nehemiah is ever one man, constant and bold in well-doing, and goeth forward in building God's city, notwithstanding all their brags.

Here appeareth how true it is that David said, "The Lord bringeth to nought the counsel of the heathen, and disappointeth the devices of the people; but the counsel of the Lord endureth for ever, and the thoughts of his heart throughout all ages." [Psal. xxxiii.] The scribes and Pharisees, and the high priest, gathered a council against the Lord Christ, thinking to have overthrown him and his doctrine, that it should never have been heard of more: but David said truly of them, "Why did the heathen fret, and the people imagine a vain thing? the kings of the earth stood up together, and the princes assembled against the Lord and against his Anointed:" [Psal. ii.] but all in vain, for the Lord raised up his Son Christ from death, and destroyed them. Judas with a band of soldiers thought he should have been able cunningly to have wrought his pleasure against his master, Christ Jesus. But as soon as Christ asked them that came to take him, "whom they sought, they all fell flat to the ground," [Joh. xviii.] and were not able to stand at the hearing of his word. Achithophel thought by his wicked counsel to have overthrown his lord and king David; but God overthrew his device, and he "went and hanged himself:" and so did Judas too, when he saw the matter fall out otherwise than he looked for.

These and such other terrible examples may teach men to be wise, and that they take nothing in hand against the Lord, though it be never so wisely devised; for it shall prove true that the prophet saith, "There is no wisdom, no foresight, no counsel against the Lord." All shall be overthrown, and the more cunning it is, the sooner it shall be cast down: none can stand against him; he only is wise; and all other, that have it not from him, be fools. Good men may also learn here not negligently to look to themselves, nor to go nakedly without weapon, to yield themselves into their enemies' hands: for so they may be guilty of their own death. "A weapon bodes peace," as the common saying is: for God hath made the weapon to defend the body, as he made the meat to feed the body; and these braggers, like thieves, will set on no man that they see weaponed, and will stand against them, but on those that be naked or faint-hearted they will be cruel. God requireth not such peakishness in a man, that he suffer himself to be wounded, that by the law of nature alloweth every man to defend himself with weapons against such thieves, if peace cannot otherways be had.

Now that their enemies were vanquished and fled away, they brag not of their strength and courage; they go not to the tavern to toss pots, and boast of their great victory; but in the fear of God return to the walls, and every man falleth to his work again. Thus we learn here, both in the spiritual battle against Satan and his members, to "put on the spiritual armour," that St Paul armeth the christian soldier withal, and they will fly away as these braggers did, if we stand boldly prepared to fight against them, as Nehemiah and his fellows did. It is true that the common verse teacheth,

<small>Eph. vi.</small>

> Hostis non lædit, nisi cum tentatus obedit:
> Est leo, si cedis; si stas, quasi musca recedit.[1]

<small>James iv.</small> St James agreeth to the same, saying, "Withstand the devil, and he will flee from you." And St Peter teacheth how to withstand him, saying, "Stand against him, being strong in faith, &c." And also we learn not to be idle, unprofitable, or unthankful after the victory and our deliverance; but to return to our work again, and sleep not, nor be negligent: for our

---

[1] The enemy hurteth not, except when the assailed person yields to him: he is a lion, if you submit; if you stand, he retires like a fly. Ed.]

mortal enemy never sleepeth; and if he prevail not one way, he attempteth another; he is not ashamed to take a foil, but he will assault us again some other way; he is not weary, for he hopeth to speed at length, and take thee napping.

All histories declare that the greatest kingdoms, which came to great power and authority by taking pains, by painful battles, by suffering hunger and cold, even the same, when they fell to idleness, wallowing in wealth and riotous feasting and daintiness, they lost their former glory faster than they won it. Such be those "time-servers" which the gospel speaketh of, that "for a time make a shew in serving the Lord, but in the time of trial they fall away:" their hollow hearts declare plainly, that they never feared the Lord uprightly. Thus must the men of God neither be rash in attempting things unadvisedly, nor negligent in providing things necessary for their defence, or desperately fear the brags and power of the enemy; but in the fear of God stand to their lawful defence, committing the success to the Almighty, whose wisdom ruleth all things at his pleasure, who defendeth his people, and no power can withstand him.

v. 16. *And it fell forth from that day forward, that the half part of the young men did work, and the other part of them held their spears, shields, bows, and breast-plates: and the rulers were behind the whole house of Juda.* The Text.

17. *They that builded the wall, and those that bare burdens, and those that laid on the burdens, with the one hand wrought their work, and with the other held their darts.*

18. *And every one of the builders girded their swords upon their loins, and so they built; but he that blew the trumpet was by me.*

19. *And I said to the nobles and to the rulers, and to the rest of the people, This work is great and large, and we are scattered on the walls far every one from other.*

20. *In what place soever ye shall hear the sound of the trumpet, thither come together to us: our God will fight for us.*

21. *And we will labour at the work. And the half of them held their spears from the day-spring until the stars did rise.*

22. *And at that time also I said unto the people, Let every one with his servant lodge in the midst of Jerusalem, that in the night we may have watch, and in the day labour.*
23. *As for me, my brethren, my servants, and the watchmen that followed me, we put not off our clothes, any of us, but only to wash them in water.*

Although Sanballat and his fellows were fled and retired back, yet Nehemiah, like a wise captain, fearing some new practice, and lest they might hide themselves for a time, and come again on the sudden and overthrow them, divideth all the young men into two parts, and the one half followeth their work, and the other standeth ready in armour to defend them, if any sudden assault should be made against them. So must good captains not be negligent nor careless, when the enemy is fled; for many times they will retire for a time, for policy's sake, to see whether the other part will be careless and negligent, and yet come again on a sudden; or else to draw them into the field from the defence of their town, and there join battle with them, and having some ambush of soldiers lying privily, who should invade the town, being left without sufficient defence, might sack and burn it at their pleasure, as we read the Israelites did against Gibea of Benjamin, in revenging that horrible abusing of the Levite's concubine. Such other policies ye shall read divers both in the scriptures and other histories. A good captain therefore, as he must not be a coward and fearful, so he must not be too careless and negligent, but still provide for the safety of his people; though he had good success of late, and seemed to have vanquished his enemies.

Judg. xx.

So must the preacher not be careless, when he seeth that God hath blessed his labour, moved the people's hearts to the receiving of his doctrine, and that a reforming of life and love to the truth doth appear; but he must water his gardens, pluck up the weeds, and labour continually: for Satan never ceaseth; and though he be once cast out, yet he "will return to his old house, and if he find it swept and made clean, he will come with seven other devils worse than himself, and then the end shall be worse than the beginning,"

Luke xi.

as the gospel teacheth. Christ our Saviour saith also, that when "tares and darnel appeared among the good corn, that it was done by the enemy, when men were on sleep." Watch therefore and pray continually, that we be not taken napping.

These young men stood not naked, but had armour of all sorts, both to defend themselves and to hurt the enemy; to shoot and smite far off, and keep them that they drew not near: so must every Christian in his spiritual battle against Satan and his members "put on the whole spiritual armour of God," which St Paul teacheth him, that he may " quench the fiery darts of Satan," and not stand naked of God's grace, trusting in his own strength. It is marvel to see how Nehemiah, being so long a courtier, is now become so cunning a soldier on the sudden, being not used to it afore: he setteth "the young men before" to bear the brunt of the battle, as most strong and able to bear it; and "the rulers come behind," as being wise men to direct and teach the younger sort what they should do, and how to behave themselves: young heads of themselves are unskilful, and therefore it is necessary they should be directed by others; so that, when youthful courage is governed by the sage counsel of the wise and ancient ruler, the battle will fall out well. Tully said well, *Parvi sunt arma foris nisi sit consilium domi:* and as it were determining whether strength or wisdom in the wars be more profitable, he saith, *Cedant arma togæ, concedat laurea linguæ*.[1] Courage and strength without wisdom is foolish rashness, and wisdom without courage and strength is fearful cowardliness: join them together, and they make a perfect soldier.

And here the wise ruler cometh behind in a place of more safety, and as it were a thing more necessary in the wars to save a wise captain and counsellor, than to save the strong and lusty soldier. The stronger that a man is, wanting wisdom, the sooner he overthroweth himself: as a tree that the wind hath shaken loose at the root, the higher and greater that it is, the sooner it is overthrown. In persecutions, therefore, every man must stand armed with these spiritual wea-

[[1] De Offic. I. 22. Arms abroad are of little use without counsel at home.—Let arms give place to the gown, and the laurel (of war) to eloquence. ED.]

pons, and the preachers would be preserved so much as may be, lest the people, being destitute of faithful guides and counsellors, cowardly fall away, or else overthrow themselves by rash dealing. When the emperor Julian took displeasure with Athanasius, and needs would have him banished, the people wept, and he comforted them, saying, "Be of good cheer; this is but a little cloud, it will pass away[1]."

<small>Niceph. x. cap. 19.</small>

17. *They that built.* Not only the young men were thus weaponed, set in order, and exercised to pains-taking, and taught to defend their fellows; but "the workmen" themselves, both that were master-masons, and cunning in their occupation, and also the common labourer, both they that laid on the burdens, and they that bare burdens of stones and mortar, had every one "his sword or his dart" by him while they wrought, that they might be ready to keep off the enemy, defend themselves, when need shall require. This kind of weapon was to pick, as a dart, and is light and easy to carry, and would not hinder their working much; and so "with the one hand they wrought, and with the other hand they held their weapon." O worthy workmen! O noble captain Nehemiah! what a godly sight was this, to see every one so full of courage that they feared not the enemy, and so willing to work that they would not be weary, but with the one hand work, and with the other hand hold their weapon!

Let christian men look into this notable example, and be ashamed of themselves, that are afraid of every blast of wind. And where these people, being under the dark shadows and heavy burden of Moses' law, would take these pains for building an earthly city to serve their God in, yet we that live under that blessed light of the gospel, so plenteously poured on us, lie loitering, and will not open our eyes to see the light, nor put forth our hand to receive that which is so freely offered to us, that it would fall into our mouths if we would gape. Let the fine courtier, that had rather be a dainty carpet gentleman, than a labourer at God's building, look at Nehemiah, and learn to be like him.

[1 Ἔνθεν τοι καὶ φεύγειν κατὰ τὸ τοῦ βασιλέως θέσπισμα βιαζόμενος, τοῖς περὶ αὐτὸν ἀσχάλλουσι καὶ ἐν δεινῷ ποιουμένοις τὴν φυγαδείαν ἀτενίσας εἶπε, Θαρρεῖτε, ὦ τέκνα· νεφύδριον γάρ ἐστι, καὶ ταχέως διαλυθήσεται. ED.]

18. *And every one.* The chief "workmen had their swords girded unto them" also: by the which we learn, that in the building of this spiritual Jerusalem, not only the people, princes and rulers must be armed, but the preacher, the minister, must stand in armour against God's enemies, and work and not forsake his flock, but comfortably assist them, and take such part as they do. Paulinus, bishop of Nola, when his flock were taken prisoners, and led forth of the country, he followed them, wrought for his living, preached unto them, and comforted them; and when for one widow's son, being a prisoner, he offered himself to lie in prison for him, so that he might be restored to his mother, it so moved the tyrant's heart, that he let them all go free.² Moses commanded that the priest should go to the field with the people, to comfort and teach them, because soldiers commonly fall to licentious living, if they may have their will, and be not called back: yet the pope will have his chaplains free from going, except they take some hedge priest to say them a mass; but they will not have a preacher in any case, no, not oft among the professors of religion, because they will not be told of their duty, but more licentiously live at their pleasure, follow the spoil, and get the gains; and this is a great occasion of much wickedness committed among soldiers, and oft causeth God to plague the whole host, and the enemy to prevail. How many lessons the best cap-

Gregor. Dialog.

[Deut. xx.]

[² The following extracts state the chief particulars: Vir Dei petenti feminæ respondit dicens, "Mulier, quod possim dare non habeo: sed memet ipsum tolle servum; me juris tui profitere; atque ut filium tuum recipias, me vice illius in servitium trade. * * * Suscepit itaque servum (vir barbarus), et roganti viduæ tradidit filium. Quo accepto vidua ab Africa regione discessit; Paulinus vero excolendi horti suscepit curam. * * * Cum instanter ille requireret ut non quis esset, sed quis in terra sua fuisset indicaret, atque hoc ab eo iteratione frequentis inquisitionis exigeret; vir Domini, constrictus magnis conjurationibus, jam non valens negare quod esset, episcopum se fuisse testatus est. Quod possessor ejus audiens valde pertimuit, atque humiliter obtulit, dicens, "Pete quod vis: quatenus ad terram tuam a me cum magno munere revertaris." Cui vir Domini Paulinus ait, "Unum est quod mihi impendere beneficium potes; ut omnes civitatis meæ captivos relaxes." Qui cuncti protinus in Africana regione requisiti cum onustis frumento navibus pro venerandi Paulini viri satisfactione in ejus comitatu laxati sunt. Gregorii Papæ Opera, Dialog. Lib. III. cap. i. Tom. I. p. 1380. Basil. 1564. ED.]

tains may learn of this worthy man Nehemiah, God grant they may well consider!

He keepeth "the trumpet by himself" at his elbow, to blow when and after what sort he would command: and good reason it should be so; for he that was appointed to be the chief builder by the king's commission, reason would that he should have the disposition of the chief things that belonged thereto, at his discretion. And every one would not be trusted with such a charge as the trumpet was; for some were hollow-hearted, bewrayed his secrets to Sanballat and his fellows, and received letters from them. Some gave ill counsel, and would have had him to have left off his work; as appeared by Judas afore in this chapter, and by Semaias, Noadia, &c. in the sixth chapter. The "trumpet" is a thing of such importance in the wars, that if it be not in the hand both of a skilful and trusty man, he may discomfit the whole host on a sudden. Therefore he trusteth himself best with that charge. Moses committed the blowing of the trumpet unto the sons of Aaron, as a thing of great trust and importance; and they were counted as men of better credit than other for their vocation sake: though now, I cannot tell how, every common man is put to that office, though his credit be not much. God in his law made such a count of the trumpet in the wars, that he appointed yearly a solemn feast and holy day of the trumpets, to put them in remembrance how oft he had given them the victory by sounding the trumpet; that they should not brag of their own strength and policy, as though they had conquered all by their own power, but praise the Lord of hosts who vanquished their enemies, and rejoice in him.

Yet now, I cannot tell how it falleth out, every thing being turned contrary ways, the trumpet is used at great feasts and solemnities to make us merry, rather than to stir us up to any praising of the Lord for his blessings bestowed upon us, or to put us in remembrance of the last trump, when "the dead shall arise out of their graves," and the Lord shall come in his majesty to judge the world. These were good lessons to think on at the sounding of the trump, and not only for mirth and solemnity, to strive who shall blow the loudest and be the merriest; though mirth is not ill.

19. *And I said to the nobles.* The more that a man looketh into Nehemiah's doings, the more godly wisdom, manly courage, earnest zeal, and painfulness that would not be weary, appeareth in him: so that he may be a pattern for all good captains and builders to follow; a mark to shoot at, but few or none will hit it. Now he turneth him to the nobles, rulers, and rest of the people that wrought not, but serve in other turns, in watching, warding, and preparing things necessary for the workmen, and maketh a short, but a wise and pithy oration unto them, as the time would serve. In wars, and specially in dangers, many words are not to be used; but briefly the captains and soldiers are to be warned of their duty, and encouraged to go forward boldly.

So Nehemiah telleth them here of their danger; for the compass of the walls was great, the labourers were not many, and yet those that were, were scattered on every corner of the walls, one far from another, so that when any assault was made, one should not nor could not be ready for to help another in any short time. The compass of the walls at this time is thought by good writers to be certain miles about, and yet was enlarged as much afterwards by Herod. Many thousands would not serve to man such a ground, to keep out the enemy; but while they defended one piece, another would be assaulted. Thus in peace he provideth against danger to come, as all wise men will; for else oft it will be too late, if such good foresight be not had. A wise man should not say, Had I wist this or that, I would have provided for this and that: provide for the worst, and the best will save itself; and if the worst fall not out, thou hast more to thank God of.

Possibly some man would think Nehemiah too bold, or rather saucy, that he, being a stranger and new come, would take in hand to teach the nobles and rulers, what they had to do: but surely he that with reason will consider all the circumstances, shall easily perceive that neither he passeth the bounds of modesty and duty, nor taketh more on him, than he had authority given him to do. The king by commission appointed him to be the chief doer at this building, as appeareth hereafter, and therefore he presumed no farther than he lawfully might: and in many of the rulers he perceived either a coldness or fearfulness to set forward this work; so that, if he had tarried on their leisure, little or nothing should have been done at all. So in God's cause a man must be bold and blush not; and if he see them slow that should be forward, he may and ought with modesty to put them in remembrance of their duty, as Nehemiah doeth here, neither chiding nor reviling them, but brotherly, godly, quietly, and modestly encourage them, telling them the danger that hangeth over them, if they do not wisely provide for it, and manfully withstand it. "A man forewarned is half armed," as the common saying is.

20. *In what place soever.* And because they were scattered so far asunder on the walls, working in every corner of them, he giveth them warning, that "wheresoever they heard the trumpet blow, thither they should all resort;" for there was then some danger toward: he himself would walk round about the walls continually, searching the watch, how diligently they kept their standings; he would spy if any enemies drew near, and then by the trumpet he would give them warning, whither they should resort unto him, to defend such or such a place: and if they would brotherly and manfully join together, no doubt "God would fight for them" and deliver them. This reason to hang upon God is sufficient for him that feareth the Lord, and knoweth that all victory cometh from him; and in that he will quiet himself, not doubting of his aid: but the worldly-wise man, that trusteth in his strength, policy, ordinance, friends, and soldiers will laugh such reasons to scorn, and the mighty Lord of hosts will make such proud braggers to become a laughing stock to the whole world in the end. Nehemiah knew well that David had written long afore, "Except the Lord defend the city, the watchmen watch in vain which defend it;" and he knew also that David had said, "Blessed be the Lord my God, which teacheth my hands to fight, and my fingers to the battle:" yet he ceaseth not to keep watch and ward night and day, to search the watch himself, to teach the soldiers how to use their weapon, to set them in array, to encourage them, to teach them to understand what the trumpet meaneth, and how in all things to obey their captains, and to be loving and true one to another.

Psal. cxxvii. cxliv.

And all this is to let us see, that although God do work all things himself, and as he hath appointed, so they fall out, yet he worketh them not without us: we must not be idle, we must shew our diligence and due obedience to our God, that hath made us, and commanded us to exercise ourselves in these things; and yet, when we have done all we can, all the praise must be given to him, and we must say, "We be unprofitable servants." We be as an axe in the carpenter's hand, where the axe may not claim the praise of well-doing from his master that worketh with it: and though the axe be a dead instrument without life or feeling, and man hath life, wit, and reason given him to do things withal; yet is man as unable to work his own salvation without the free mercy and special grace of God, as the axe is unable to build the house without the direction and ruling of the carpenter. *Crearis, sanaris, salvaris: quid horum tibi ex te, homo?*[1] saith Bernard. Let every man be diligent, and a painful labourer in his vocation, and work his own salvation as far as an instrument may, not loitering nor living unprofitably, thinking that God will bring such things to pass if we lie down and sleep; but the chief praise and effect must be given in all good things to God alone. The Lord hath promised nothing to idle bellies; and unto him that laboureth to serve his God faithfully, he hath promised his sure aid, and will surely perform it. Adam in paradise was not suffered to be idle, even in his innocency, afore he sinned; and shall we misers, that have so oft and grievously offended our merciful God, think to live as we list at our ease? Josue at his death putteth the people in remembrance, "how the Lord had fought for them, and driven out their enemies;" and to encourage them still to serve their God faithfully, and forsake strange gods, he promiseth them that, if they will so do, "the Lord will fight for them still;" and so did Moses afore him. Josh. xxiii.

Exod. xiv.

God's bare promise by his word is surer than any promise made by man, though you have never so many good sureties and bonds with forfeitures, and it be sealed and delivered, and devised as cunningly as law can think. God is truth

[1 "Thou art created, healed, and saved: what of all these hast thou of thyself, O man?" ED.]

itself, and therefore cannot lie; and whatsoever he promiseth he performeth: for else he should be untrue, like a miserable man, which cannot be. God grant us such captains as Moses, Josue, and Nehemiah were, that with like persuasions they may encourage their soldiers! For surely, if they went to the field with like mind, faith, reverence, and due obedience unto the Lord, that these godly men did, the same God liveth still, and would bless their enterprises, as he did the other; for he is not weary of well doing and relieving his people.

21. *And we will labour.* Among all these great troubles he forgat not his principal work in building of the walls, but went on forward still, like a faithful servant to his Lord and God. Such earnest zeal the Lord poureth into his servants, when he will declare his majesty and mercy to the world. For as the greedy merchant for love of himself runneth by sea and land, so far as sea or land will carry him, to increase his worldly goods; so he that is inflamed with this spirit of jealousy toward God's house, will go through thick and thin with wisdom, feareth no dangers, and will suffer neither open enemy to invade, nor flattering friend to deceive, the dear spouse of his Lord and Master, but manfully will stand in defence against all sorts, deal they never so cunningly.

I cannot tell whether is more diligent and praiseworthy, the soldiers or the workmen. They be both at their business "from the day spring unto the late in the evening, that the stars did rise." A rare example to be found at this day: for the labouring man will take his rest long in the morning; a good piece of the day is spent afore he come at his work; then must he have his breakfast, though he have not earned it, at his accustomed hour, or else there is grudging and murmuring: when the clock smiteth, he will cast down his burden in the midway, and whatsoever he is in hand with, he will leave it as it is, though many times it is marred afore he come again; he may not lose his meat, what danger soever the work is in. At noon he must have his sleeping time, then his bever in the afternoon, which spendeth a great part of the day; and when his hour cometh at night, at the first stroke of the clock he casteth down his tools, leaveth his work, in what need or case soever the work standeth. The common soldier thinketh long, while his course is to watch and ward; it is cold standing on the walls, he must to the alehouse, refresh himself with gaming, swearing, whoring, or else he thinketh himself nobody: he thinketh it shame to live honestly in order. Thus all sorts are out of order: and though abbeys be gone, yet the abbey-lubbers, which will work until they be cold, eat until their belly ache, and sleep until their bones ache, are too common in every house. A lither[1] day's work is thought with many no sin, but a pastime; and yet is it thievery to take the day's wages, and do not a good day's work for it. St Paul biddeth "servants obey their masters," not only when they stand by and look on, but in their absence, and where they see them not. What is more hard in these days than to find a faithful, true servant? Good masters complain, and find great lack, though many be better rewarded than they deserve. It is lamentable to see the stones in the wall many times bear witness of the murmuring of the one against the other. The servant, he will write on the wall, *Fidelis servus perpetuus asinus:*[2] the master will answer, Deserve, and then desire; and both misliking the one and the other, when the servant cannot have that he gapeth for, then he taketh bribes; and the master must wink at it, because he will not otherwise prefer him: so both being to blame, both procure God's anger towards them.

Eph. vi.

Beda, considering the great troubles that fell on the building of this second temple and walls, asketh why it should fall out so now, rather than in the building of the tabernacle by Moses, or the first temple by Salomon, which both were finished with great quietness: and when he hath mused on it long, he saith that "it fared with this outward temple as it doth with every particular man, that is the spiritual temple of the Lord." When God made man in his innocency, it had been easy for him to have stood, if he had would; but after that he fell, it was much harder to restore him again. It is harder to repair an old rotten house, than to build a new; and to make an old man strong, than a young. God made Adam with a word easily, and breathed life into him: but after that Adam fell, what trouble and misery fell afore

[1 Lither: lazy. ED.]
[2 A faithful servant is a thorough ass. ED.]

he could be restored? Christ Jesus must come down from heaven unto the earth, nay, into hell, to pull us out of hell: he must be accused, whipped, scourged, falsely condemned, thrust to the heart with a spear, die and be buried, ascend unto his Father again, open heaven gates, which afore our sins had locked up, and abide many more sorrows, afore we could be restored into God's favour again, and follow him where he sitteth on the right hand of his Father. So it is an easy matter to enter into God's church by baptism; but if thou fall after, how hard it is to rise again, daily experience teacheth. We must repent, fast, pray, give alms, forsake ourselves, condemn ourselves, with bitter tears and trembling work our salvation, stand in continual war against the devil, the world, and our own affection: which things to do, are more common in our mouths than in our lives, and more do talk of them than practise them. God for his mercy's sake forgive us and amend us all!

It fareth so likewise in the outward church of God in all ages. [Acts ii. iv.] In the beginning, Peter converted at one sermon three thousand, and at another two thousand: Paul filled all the countries "from Jerusalem to Illyricum with the gospel." [Rom. xv.] The apostles and their successors converted the whole world unto the Lord in few years; but how many of these countries, where their successors preached, have fallen back, and how little hope there is of their returning again unto the faith, the Jews, Turks, and Infidels declare, whom God hath given up to their own lusts; and though they inhabited the same countries where true Christians dwelt afore, yet they have hardened their hearts, that they will not understand, nor open their eyes to follow the footsteps of them that went afore, that they may see the light. How hard a thing it is at this day to turn a papist, and specially to see one that knew the truth once, if he fall to popery or other errors, to rise again and believe the gospel, we have too many examples to teach us. I fear the saying of the apostle may be verified on them: "It is impossible for them that were once enlightened and knew the truth, if they fall away, to be renewed by repentance." [Heb. vi. x.] The Lord in his mercy stay us that we fall not from him! for "it is horrible to fall into the hands of the living God" in his anger.

22. *And at that time also.* Now, when Nehemiah had thus persuaded "the nobles, the rulers, and the people" manfully to stand in defence of their city, and diligently to follow their work in building of the walls; had set both the soldiers and the workmen in order and array, like a good captain and master of the works, looked diligently to each of them all the day long, that they slipt not away from their charge, nor loitered at their work; kept the trumpet with himself, as a thing of great importance and trust, to give warning if the enemy did approach; lest there might some mischief fall out in the night, he appointeth "a watch for the night season" also, to prevent all practices that might be devised against them. A good captain will so provide both for day and night, in peace and war, that the enemy, who is ever to be feared, even when he pretendeth most quietness and friendship, and when he seemeth to flee, retireth oft on a sudden, to see whether there be any power remaining to hold him out; he will foresee, I say, that the enemy have no advantage against him, but every place be well manned and fenced to withstand him.

He willeth the people therefore, that every man shall "watch in the street afore his own door with his servants," that no mischief fell out within the city, where so many hypocrites and hollow-hearted people, and unwilling folk of all sorts to further this work, did dwell. The outward enemy might do much harm, but inward treason might overthrow all in a short time. For the utter enemy, the watch of the wall would be able to withstand him, and give warning to the rest for aid; and if any practice were within the city, the watch in the streets might suppress it for a time, until more aid came. He had good cause to provide for this; for experience taught him, as is written afore, that "the tribe of Juda was weary, and discouraged the people to work:" Semaia, and Noadia, as though they were prophets sent from God, counselled him to "take sanctuary and save himself, for they sought his life;" which was not for any good will, but to discourage him from his work: and "divers of the rulers were joined in friendship and marriage with Sanballat and Tobias, received messengers from them, and bewrayed his doings to them again," as appeareth hereafter; and therefore, not knowing whom he might well trust, he could do no less but keep watch and ward day and night, on the walls and in the streets, both against the outward and the inward enemy. O worthy, wise, and stout Nehemiah! where is one courtier that hath followed thy footsteps since thou wast born? God for his mercy raise up some, that though not with that fulness of spirit, yet with such courage and measure of grace as shall please him to give, some one may in jealousy of spirit take in hand the repairing of the old ruinous walls of God's church, house, and city; that both the outward and inward enemy, which have wrongfully possessed, invaded, and wasted the Lord's inheritance, may be vanquished and suppressed; and God's children may in quietness of mind worship and serve the Lord our God, as he hath taught us.

After all this watching and warding he is not weary; but, "We will to our work again," saith he, "as soon as the day peeps." Who could or would have taken these pains, but he? it would have discouraged any man but him. But Nehemiah knew well, that Satan never ceaseth to trouble the Lord's flock: and though slothful idleness be meetest for him to work by, yet he forsaketh not the painful labouring man, and will assault him likewise. Let every man therefore take heed how he standeth, and see that he fall not; for Satan refuseth no sort of men to overthrow them, no time nor place he disdaineth; but is glad if he can devour the poorest simple sheep of the Lord's, if he cannot meet with a better prey. The people are worthy no less praise than the rulers: for they are as ready to obey as the other to command; and so joining together in the fear of God, brotherly love and due obedience to their rulers, this work goeth forward, and God blesseth their labour.

23. *As for me and my brethren.* Now, lest Nehemiah should seem too busy and impious [imperious] to command all other, and to do nothing himself, which were a point of oppression or tyranny, as Pharao did to the Israelites in Egypt, he saith, both "he, his brethren and servants and watchmen," took as much pains as the worst of them, which is the property of a good captain to do: for they wrought and watched so diligently, that "they put not off their clothes to sleep or take rest, but only when they were foul and must needs be washed." O worthy example! God grant us many such rulers

Margin: Exod. iii.

and captains, both in God's church and commonwealth! When the people and soldiers shall see the rulers and captains take pains, as well as they do, it maketh them both ashamed if they draw back, and also encourageth them to be with the foremost. Julius Cæsar, to encourage his soldiers, would not take pains himself; but the rather to stir them more willingly to labour, he calleth them not "soldiers," nor commandeth like a captain, but gently speaketh unto them, and calleth them "fellow soldiers," as though he were no better than one of them. So in great works the chief master, when it cometh to a dead lift, or some danger like to follow, he will lay to his hand himself, he will climb, he will lift as busily as any of his servants, and say to them, 'Now, good fellows, spit on your hands, lift once again, and we have won it; now play the men, and we shall be past the worst straightway.'

Such examples of the better sort, with gentle persuasions in words, will make the common sort to refuse no pains, be the danger never so great. Abimelech, when he would smother the men that fled into the tower of Sichem, and could not get them out, he "gat first himself boughs of green trees," and bade every one of his soldiers "do as they saw him do." When every man had loaden himself with green boughs, Abimelech goeth first, and setteth his boughs on fire: the rest of the soldiers seeing him so bold and forward, they set their boughs on fire too, and so easily they killed them that were within with smoke. So much can the example of a captain or good master do. God grant many such foregoers in God's church, and then the people will follow fast enough. What maketh the people draw back so much at this day, but that gentlemen and priests go not afore? Want of good example and due correction maketh many to do ill without fear of God and man. David, when he would stir up the people earnestly to serve the Lord, and diligently to resort to the tabernacle of prayer, saith, "O come, let us sing unto the Lord, let us rejoice in the strength of our salvation." He biddeth them not go pray, and he will go play; but he will be foremost himself in praising the Lord, and call on them to follow.

When they were thus to watch and ward night and day, to forego their pleasures, and take infinite pains in building this earthly city and walls of Jerusalem; it teacheth us, how diligent we ought to be in building the spiritual Jerusalem, Christ his dear spouse and church, by prayer, preaching, watching, fasting, and all other godly exercises.

A PRAYER.

As thou, O Lord, of thy infinite and undeserved goodness, stirredst up thy faithful servant, Nehemiah, to pity the lamentable state of Jerusalem, and gavest him such favour in the sight of king Artaxerxes, procuredst licence and liberty, great rewards and liberality, to all them that would repair the broken walls of the city, movedst his heart to leave the wanton pleasures of the court, and madest him willing to toil at thy work, and not only prosperedst their doings, but defendedst them from their mortal enemies many and sundry times, being cruelly assaulted both by inward hypocrites and outward force; so, we beseech thee, most merciful Father, for thine own mercy's sake look pitifully at thy ragged and torn church, the contemned spouse of thy dearly beloved Son, Christ Jesus: raise up some faithful servants in every country, that may obtain such favour in the sight of christian princes, that with freedom of conscience and quietness of the country the kingdom of thy Son and our Saviour may be truly preached, obediently received, faithfully believed, and diligently followed, to the overthrow of antichrist and all his members, and the endless comfort of thy poor afflicted people. Confound, O gracious God, Sanballat, Tobias, and all their partakers, which laugh to scorn the simplicity of the gospel and builders of the church: make them to be scorned, that the world may see, what foolish wickedness it is to rebel against thy holy will, and how little all such shall prevail in the end. Turn away all open violence, that shall be devised against us outwardly; keep us from civil war and sedition inwardly; confound all wicked counsels and conspiracies of Ahitophel with his fellows, and overthrow the subtle practices of Judas and such hypocrites: encourage the people, that they fear not their brags nor big looks, but manfully may stand in defence of thy truth, and boldly confess thee in all dangers, knowing thee to be the only Lord and giver of all victory, and that none shall be ashamed nor left succourless, that fly unto thee in their great necessity. Give us grace to pray and put our trust in thee, as this people have done afore us; that we may find the like grace, favour and deliverance, that they did. Give us, we most humbly beseech thee, O gracious God, such guides and rulers in the commonwealth, as will work with the one hand, and fight with the other, keep watch and ward night and day, to drive away the outward enemy, and will defend thy poor sheep from the rebellious practices of Satan among ourselves. Thrust forth such faithful preachers for the advancement of thy glory only, which, without any worldly respect of profit or pleasure, may purely teach thy holy will declared in thy blessed word, root out all errors in doctrine and deformities of life, and may by the power of thy Holy Spirit bring home all those that be run astray, confirm and strengthen those that do stand, and raise up those that be fallen; that in unity of mind, brotherly love and christian faith, we may be lively stones in the spiritual building of thy house, may acknowledge thee our only God, and thou of thy accustomed goodness and free mercy mayest take us to thy children, and defend us as our Lord, teach us as a schoolmaster, feed us as a shepherd, make us partakers of thy glorious conquest of sin, death, hell, the world, and the flesh; that afterward we may reign with thee in thy blessed kingdom, which thou hast so dearly purchased for us by the death of thy Christ our Saviour, thy Son our Lord, to whom, with thee and the Holy Ghost, be all honour and glory for ever. Amen.

CHAPTER V.

The Text. v. 1. *And there was a great cry of the people made and their wives against their brethren the Jews.*

2. *And there were that said, Our sons and our daughters and we are many; therefore we must take corn, that we may eat and live.*

3. *And there were some that said, Our fields and our vineyards and our houses we have laid to pledge, that we might have corn in this hunger.*

4. *And there were some that said, We have borrowed money for the king's tribute upon our lands and vineyards.*

5. *And now, as the flesh of our brethren is, so is our flesh; and as their children be, so are our children; and mark, we bring into bondage our sons and our daughters as servants: and there be some of our daughters in bondage already: and there is no power in our hands: our lands and our vineyards are in other men's hands.*

WHILE that Nehemiah had travailed himself weary in keeping watch and ward, and setting the people to building the walls again, and thought all was quiet, both within the city, and safe against the utter enemy, behold, now bursteth out a new sore, worse than the former. "The people and their wives" come with open mouth, and make an outcry against the rich and rulers among them, which unmercifully had spoiled and oppressed them, insomuch as they were not able to live. Such is the state of God's people here in the earth, 1 John iii. that as our Master Christ saith, he came "to overthrow the works of the devil," so the devil ceaseth not by all means to overthrow, or at the least, so much as in him is, to hinder by his partakers the building of God's house and the setting forth of his glory. And to declare the vehemency of the cry, the Holy Ghost noteth it by such a word in the Hebrew,[1] as signifieth those uproars and outcries which are made in rebellious or seditious riots, or else of such as cry out for great grief and anguish of heart.

[[1] צעק. Compare 2 Kings vi. 26. Job xix. 7. ED.]

The parties that make their cry are the common people and women, of which it is hard to tell whether of them is often more importune in outcrying, and many times without just cause. The people, if they smart a little and have not their own wills fulfilled, are ready to exclaim; and women can weep and howl when they list, and the basest sort are the worst. The parties against whom they cry be "the Jews their countrymen," brethren in kindred, and professing one religion. If this oppression and cruel dealing had been by strangers, where no mercy is commonly shewed nor looked for, it would have been less marvelled at, and less it would have grieved them: but to be entreated cruelly by their countrymen, kinsmen, and those that served the same God, and professed the same religion that they did, and at whose hands they looked for aid and comfort, this was thought so strange, that it would make any astonied to hear tell of it. With these circumstances the Holy Ghost setteth out the greatness of the cry, to make it more horrible in men's sight, and so the more easily to bring them to repentance, and make them ashamed of their cruel dealings. When the devil prevailed not by Sanballat and his fellows to overthrow the building, he setteth now on the poor common sort and women to cry out against their rulers, thinking by this means to overthrow all, rather than to procure any remedy or relief for them: though God of his accustomed goodness (turning oft our wicked doings to the setting forth of his glory,) by this means wrought their deliverance and liberty. Such is the wisdom of our God, that by our foolishness he declareth his mighty power, wisdom and majesty; and our ill dealing sheweth forth his justice and mercy, and that against our will and meaning.

2. *And there were that said.* The cause of their cry is set forth in these four verses following; hunger, need, oppression, pinching poverty, and pining penury, made them so to cry out. And this is too common a fault in our days, in the preaching of the gospel. Some of the poorer sort, though they had not lands and goods, yet God, as he useth commonly, had blessed them more than the richer sort with children so many, that they could not tell how to get bread for them, except they should sell them as slaves; and where they were free born, they should now become bond and be used

as beasts. What a grief that is to a good father, that loveth his child dearly in the fear of God, to be driven by the unmerciful dealing of the rich, to sell his own children for bondmen, I leave it to the consideration of those that be natural and loving parents: for none can express the greatness of that grief, but he that hath been pinched with it and felt the smart of it. When Jacob should send little Benjamin into Egypt with his brethren for corn, it was long or he could be brought to it, and he almost had rather died for hunger than let him go from him. What a love had David toward his wicked son Absolon, even in the midst of his rebellion, and what charge gave he to his captains that they should not kill him! Such is the love of natural parents towards their children, that they will love them, and cannot cast them off, even in their ill doings, though many times the children be most unthankful. Liberty is a thing that every man naturally desireth, and by all means seeketh for; therefore bondage must needs be such a thing as every man doth abhor and fly from: yet hunger is such a thing, that it will break stony walls, and, rather than a man will bear it continually, he will sell lands, goods, wife, children, yea, himself, to be slaves for ever. Nay, hunger is so pinching a pain, that a woman will eat her own child, as in siege of Jerusalem, in Samaria, and Saguntine; yea, a man his own flesh, rather than he will die for hunger. Hunger of all things may not be abiden, what inconvenience soever fall out after.

Consider then, what miserable case these poor men were in, that had so many children, and could get no bread to put in their mouths; and wicked men, the richer sort, were they that had brought them to this poverty, and now would not relieve them in this their extremity. We read of a bishop of Mentz in Germany, called Hatto, who had great store of corn, and would not relieve the poor with it in time of great dearth, but let the rats eat it; in revenge of which God raised so many rats about him, that they drove him from house to house to save his life: and where he had a strong tower in the midst of the great river of Rhene, which yet standeth there to be seen in the midst of the river, he thought himself sure, if he could fly thither: notwithstanding the rats swam after him thither, and there devoured him,

2 Sam. xviii.

and it is called the rats' tower at this day.¹ Salomon saith, "He that hideth up his corn shall be cursed among the people, but blessing shall be on them that sell it." God grant the richer sort pitiful hearts to open their barns and purse to the relief of the poor, that they may escape God's plague and man's curse! Prov. xi.

3. *And there were some that said.* Thus far goeth the cry of the poorest sort: now followeth another company, that cry as fast, but they are not altogether so poor. They were pinched with hunger; but they had some "lands, vineyards and houses to lay to pledge, that they might have some corn" to fill their bellies withal. These men were hunger-bitten also; for though they had land, yet they were not able to store it, nor husband it as husbandry required; and therefore had no profit by it. And like enough they were such as Aggeus the prophet complained on, saying, that "every man buildeth for himself fair houses," and God's house lay unbuilt, and therefore God plagued them. They "had sown much, and reaped little, their corn wasted in their barns, and their grapes consumed away in the wine-press." These days were like the time of Micheas the prophet, who crieth out against the rulers for their oppressing of the poor so extremely, saying, "They pluck off their skins from them, and their flesh from their bones: and they eat also the flesh of my people, and flay off their skin from them, and they break their bones, and chop them in pieces, as for the pot, and as flesh within the caldron." Mic. iii.

4. *And there were some that said.* Yet cometh another sort; but they were in some better case, for they had some corn, and no money, and they cry out as fast as the rest. The king of Persia, although they had given the Jews licence to go home to build their temple and city, yet they laid a great task on them, which they should pay in token of their subjection, and recompence for their liberty's sake.

The rulers and chief of the Jews had engrossed up in their hands unmercifully all the corn and money that could be come by, so that little or nothing could be gotten to fill their bellies, and to pay the king's tribute withal; therefore these men must "pledge their lands and vineyards to get some money" for this purpose. O miserable wretches, that

[¹ See above, p. 30. ED.]

had thus miserably oppressed their poor brethren and countrymen, who had taken as much pains as they, or more, for the defence of their country, building of their temple and city; and now in their great need could find no comfort nor relief at their hands! But these be no new things in the world; for Amos the prophet complaineth likewise of the oppression that the richer sort used toward the poor in his time: "When will this moon pass away," say they, that hath so much plenty; "and the time come that we may make the measure less, and buy the poor for silver, and the needy for shoes, and sell the outcast of the wheat?"

Amos viii.

5. *And now as the flesh of our brethren is.* But now come they all howling and crying together, and say, What better case are we in, that be come home to our country, than our brethren which live in captivity under the Chaldees, Assyrians, Babylonians, Medes, and Persians, or any other country, wheresoever they be scattered on the face of the earth? They live in penury and hunger, and so do we. They be oppressed with their rulers, and so be we. Their flesh is parched with toiling in the heat, and frozen up with cold, and so is ours. Their bellies cleave to the very back for hunger, and so do ours. There is no strength nor courage left in them, no more is there in us. They be weary of their lives, and so be we. They have not wherewith to fill their belly, and cover their back, and no more have we. They pine away for sorrow, and so do we. They have nothing left but skin and bones, and those will scarce cleave together for sorrow; and in the same case be we. If they get a penny with great labour, one or other is ready to snatch it from them; and so it is with us. As their children live in as great slavery and misery as their fathers, so do our children live as miserably as we do. There is no respect of age nor youth, neither there nor here, but all kinds of sorrow are laid upon us without mercy: if this sorrow were laid on us alone, we could better bear it; but when we see our children, young infants that cannot help themselves, to be wrapt in the same misery that we be, and can help neither them nor ourselves, it doubleth and trebleth our sorrow, and yet both is remediless, endless, and comfortless.

These be strange things which were laid to their charge

for their ungentle dealing: but lo, mark and consider farther, and these dealings that follow are much worse; monsters in nature, and things intolerable, both afore God and man. This word, "Lo, mark or behold," *ecce*, ever betokeneth throughout the scripture some notable thing, either very good or very ill, that is spoken of immediately afterward, and such a one as commonly falleth not out among men. And the Holy Ghost of purpose useth to mark such notable things with this word, "lo," *ecce*, mark or behold, to put men in remembrance, and awake them to the consideration of the weighty matter that followeth, that they should not lightly pass over it, but deeply mark and consider it.

Mark the greatness of this oppression and unmerciful dealing of the richer sort toward us, their poor brethren and countrymen, of the same religion and serving the same God that they do, and have taken as much pains in building the temple, city, and defending our country as they have done, or more; and yet can find no mercy at their hands, but are made their slaves. For behold, in strange countries, where our brethren dwell, strangers take their sons and daughters by force, and make them bondmen and slaves; but we are brought into such misery, that we ourselves are driven by necessity, through the oppression of our rulers, against our will, and willingly, to bring and offer our sons and daughters to them to be their bond servants, slaves, and used as beasts at their commandment, that we and they may live, though it be in great misery, rather than perish for hunger or penury. And that ye may see the thing to be true, and not feigned, "some of our daughters are in bondage to them already." It is a great grief to parents to see their own children taken by strangers, and made slaves in their own sight; but it is a greater grief for fathers to be so cruelly dealt with in their own country, at their friends' hands and countrymen, that they shall be compelled willingly, though against their wills, to sell their children for slaves, or else die for hunger. At strangers' hands, and specially if they be of another religion, no man looketh for any favour; and if any do come, it is more than looked for, and so much the more welcome when it cometh: but at a friend and countryman's hand, where all courtesy is to be looked for, and to find none, but all extremity, is a grief above all griefs, and man's heart can never digest it. It is against God, against nature and common reason, which teacheth all gentleness to such: nay, it is worse than beastliness; for one beast will not deal so cruelly with another of his own kind, and one thief will not rob another; therefore to be spoiled and robbed by them of whom they should be defended and relieved, it is a grief that passeth all sorrows. But if these sorrows could have an end, or there were any hope to have release of them in time, we could take it the better, and have some comfort: but all hope is taken away, for we have no power left, we have nothing to help ourselves withal, we have wrestled as long as we might, and made shift as long as it would be; but now we are able to bear it no more, we have nothing left, all is spent and gone, and we cannot devise where to get any more; our houses, our lands, and vineyards other men have cruelly gotten from us, and unmercifully do keep them, and have no regard to help us in this our great and extreme necessity. We can do nothing but cry out on heaven and earth; but they hardened their hearts, and stopped their ears, that they will not hear nor pity us. Mercy is gone; cruelty, oppression and greediness carry them away, that both forget God and themselves.

This was the miserable state of that time: a man would have thought that the misery, slavery and bondage, that they themselves were in of late under heathen princes, in strange countries, and so late being restored through God's free and undeserved goodness to their own country, with liberty, great gifts, and liberality, to build their temple and city, should not have been so soon forgotten; but as they then would have been glad of some relief, succour and courtesy to be shewed unto them at strangers' hands, so they should now shew the like unto their brethren and countrymen. But such is the wickedness of man's heart, that the more mercies we receive at God's hand, the more unthankful we be: and such is the malice of Satan against God, his church and people, that when the Lord of his own free will and undeserved goodness bestoweth his mercy upon his servants, the devil, by his members and all devices possible, goeth about to overthrow and withdraw all sorts of men, so much as in him is, to a forgetfulness of such merciful goodness bestowed upon them, and maketh them unmerciful to their brethren, which have received so great mercy at the Lord's hand.

Religion is the chiefest help that God hath given us to know him by, to bridle our ill affections and desires withal, to make us love one another, and set forth his glory: and yet, if we look into ourselves in these days, we shall find that there was never greater cruelty, oppression of the poor, hypocrisy and dissembling in God's cause, and unmercifulness amongst men in this land, than hath been since the beginning of the reforming of religion amongst us; yea, and that is more wonderful, of such as would pretend to be favourers of religion. Hypocrites, as they use nothing well, so they misuse religion for a cloke to work their own will and pleasure by, to the defacing of all good religion. Things be fresh in memory, and cannot be forgotten of them that will not willingly be blind; but they that list to read may see in that worthy father, master Latimer's sermons, many such things opened, that then were preached; and would to God they were now reformed, or not fallen to worse and more shameful dealings, without hope of amendment! As for begging or buying good things at the king's hand, then selling the woods, surveying the land to the uttermost acre or roods of land, enhancing of rents to the highest, from twenty pounds to an hundred, racking the tenants by intolerable fines and incomes, *sine fine*, every five or seven year commonly, laying load on them to carry and recarry whatsoever is to be done, paying never a penny for their labour, ride and run when he is commanded, &c. then turn it into the prince's hand again, get as much, and use it as ill or worse; this practice hath been so common, and declared by divers, that few can be ignorant of it, and many cry out on it at this day, but remediless. Yet this is not the worst: if there be any broken title of the land that may make question in the law, or if there be any danger of waters or extraordinary charges, reparations, &c. then it is meet for the prince by exchange. When it is racked to the highest, and a good thing gotten instead of it, yet, that the prince shall not be thought to have an ill bargain, he will desire to be farmer of it himself after the same rate, to stop men's mouths for a time. As it is reason, honourable and godly, that the prince should liberally reward and encourage the good servitor; so is it reason again, that the prince's goodness nor the subject be misused. Master Latimer did freely speak of these things, not without blame, as peradventure this will be too; but would to God this had been used only in the prince's state! but he that will look abroad and see, shall find the like too common in mean men's doings.

As for pulling down of towns, turning tillage to pasture, and turning out the tenants, as Achab did to Naboth for his vineyard, that they may have elbow room, make them large domains, or set a shepherd and his dog where so many have dwelt, and that a poor man may not dwell so near a man of worship; these be so common among the meanest sort of purchasers, that men need not to study where to find them. Raising of rents, and taking unreasonable fines and gressans, is thought no fault, it is so common; but some are waxen so cunning, that it is strange to think of. A landlord is hungry, and needs must have fines, even of the poorest sort; and because he will be thought to deal mercifully, this way is devised. The poor man hath no money, and yet he must pay; his goods, and specially his sheep, though they be few, shall be praised, and according to the rate out of those goods the fine shall be raised. And that some pity shall be thought to be shewed, the poor man shall have his goods again by the price, to pay his fine withal, and for occupying of those his own goods he shall pay a yearly rent or interest, as it were an usury; and this dealing is thought great courtesy. Solon, when he was asked why, among the other good laws that he made, he made not one for him that killed his father, he answered, "because he would not put men in remembrance that there was any such a mischief, that could come into men's heads." So, I fear, the opening of these things shall give occasion to some ill men, but not to the good, to learn the like devices. So ready we be to learn that that is ill.

The law indeed openeth sin what it is, that a man should fly from it, and not be condemned for ignorance. St Paul saith, "I had not known lust and desire of ill things to be sin, except the law had said, Thou shalt not lust nor desire them."

Rom. vii. 7.

The law is not to blame in declaring what sin is, that by knowing of it we may fly from it, no more than the physician is to blame in opening the disease to his patient, and teaching him what things to avoid that he may recover health. But as an ill stomach, what good meat soever it eateth, turneth it into ill humours, and the spider gathereth poison on the same flowers that the bee gathereth honey; so on the holy word of God, and his blessed laws, which he made for our health and salvation, ill men gather death and damnation through their own wickedness, and no fault in the law nor law-maker. As the Israelites cried out in this time justly on their rulers for this great oppression, so it is to be feared that in our days there is no less cause to cry aloud, that God may hear when man will not.

There be four things that cry for vengeance out of heaven unto the Lord, and the scripture useth the same word of crying with them, which for memory's sake are contained in these two verses:

> Clamitat in cœlum vox sanguini', vox Sodomorum,
> Vox oppressorum, mercesque retenta laborum.

For murder and bloodshed God said to Cain, when he had killed his brother Abel, "The voice of thy brother's blood crieth out from the earth to me in heaven." For the filthy incest, fornication, pride, gluttony, wealth, and idleness of Sodom, the prophet Ezechiel and Genesis testify saying, "The cry of Sodom is come up to me." The Israelites oppressed in Egypt with making of brick, &c. God delivered them when they cried unto him, and drowned the oppressors. St James saith, "The wages withholden from those that reaped their fields cried out unto the Lord of hosts." These be good lessons for such as oppress the poor, or deal straitly with their tenants, thinking they may use them like slaves or beasts at their pleasure. Though they be servants here, yet they be children of the same God, and bought by the same price that their masters be; and therefore ought of duty to be used with christian and brotherly charity, as thou wouldst be if thou were so. *Gen. iv.* *Gen. xix. Ezek. xvi.* *Exod. ii. iii.* *James v.*

There be other sorts of cruel oppressors, but not so common as these: as cozening, by cunning dealing to creep into men's bosoms, to be feoffees of trust, executors of will, guardians of infants, and these play best be [by] trust; but they trust themselves best, and go away with all. Carriers of corn, victuals, and other commodities out of the realm, to make a dearth within the realm, yea, and oft to feed our enemies, and enrich themselves, by procuring licences to carry them out, are too well known how hurtful they be through all countries. As for engrossers, forestallers, regraters,[1] leasemongers, they are thought honest men. The lawyers of both sorts, by feeding their clients with fair words, and the questmongers with sluttish shifts, making them believe their matter to be good, and with long delays impoverish the suitors; and if he come to be judge in the same matter afterward, wherein he was a counsellor afore, he saith, 'I spake then as a counsellor, and now I must speak as a judge,' and thinketh that he hath spoken good reason; as though God had made it lawful at any time, or in any case, to bear false witness or speak untruths. The physician and the apothecary deal so cunningly that no man espieth them, and yet be as ill. The clergy that will take the profit and refuse the pains, lie at his ease from his charge, and let his sheep hunger, are not better than the rest. Pen-clerks, sheriffs, bailiffs, and summoners are not worthy to come to this company; for they can return, *non est inventus*, when they stand and talk with him, and make cunning delays, until they make men pay double fees for expedition. Worst of all cometh the common cut-purse, the usurer, and his broker: he standeth on his reputation, he sitteth highest on the bench, and looketh big; nay, it is crept into mean men's dealings; he speaketh courteously and dealeth cruelly; he defendeth his doings to be charitable, when he eateth up house, lands and goods, turneth infants a begging, and overthroweth the whole kindred. Captains convey as cunningly as jugglers with legerdemain. Merchants and artificers are so honest, that they may not be touched: they have so few faults, that they cannot be told; and yet there could never be laws enough made to bridle them, but they will creep out. When receivers are become deceivers, controllers be pollers, auditors searchers, and cus-

[1 Engrossing: buying *large* quantities of corn, &c. to sell again. Regrating: buying it to sell again in the same market. ED.]

tomers look through their fingers, and keep their old custom; and generally, "every man is a thief in his occupation," as the common proverb saith, "there is craft even in daubing;" it is to be feared that, as the course of a stream being stopped, it gathereth a great dam, and being let suddenly go, it overthroweth all in its way; so God's anger being staid a time, the windows in heaven being opened, it will pour down on our heads plentifully.

How should God's plague be far from us, when these cry vengeance daily? The thief by the highway is not so ill as any of those that deal not uprightly in their vocation. For against a thief a man may fight for his purse wittingly, and say, Master thief, gramercy! If a man consider in how little tents, shops, offices, and houses those men dwell, and how great gains they get, he shall easily see where the profitablest ground lieth in the realm. If this people had such cause to cry out then on their rulers, what cause have we now here among us, where not only the richer and mightier sort overload the poorer, but every one in his degree useth craft, subtlety, and deceit, to oppress, undermine, and scratch from other, without respect of friend or foe, what he can, not regarding how he cometh by it, by hook or by crook, by right or wrong, be it short or long!

Here is nothing spoken particularly against any man's vocation or occupation, nor any man that dealeth honestly in them; but generally to note the general faults of the offenders, that every man may look into his own bosom, consider his doings, and amend one. If every one would amend one, all should be well straight; but every one would amend another, see other men's faults, but not his own, and therefore all lie still as they did, nothing amended, and every one maketh courtesy who shall begin. Sophony the prophet complaineth of his time, and saith, "Thy rulers are roaring [Zeph. iii.] lions, thy judges are ravening wolves in the evening, and will not leave the bones until morning; thy prophets are lewd and unconstant, thy priests have defiled the holy place, and broken thy law." Micheas crieth out, and saith, "There is [Mic. vii.] not a good man left on the earth, and not a righteous man among men; all lie in wait for blood, every man hunteth his brother unto death, &c." God grant our times were not like!

Among us it is merrily said of some, that there be some courts where law is executed without conscience; another, where conscience is without law; the third, where neither law nor conscience; the fourth, where both law and conscience shall rule, I can rather pray for than look for, until the last day come, when the righteous Judge shall judge both with law and conscience. In the meantime we may mourn, and turn unto the Lord, that he may forgive us, and receive us in his many and great mercies; for we are full of many and great miseries. The pride of women is through the fault of men; therefore they be blameless: God amend us all!

Gen. xlvii.
It is written, that Joseph in Egypt used the people almost of like sort that they do here, and yet is he praised and these justly reproved; which possibly some marvel at, not understanding the diversity of their doings. Joseph laid up corn in the time of plenty, when every man had enough: these men did it at all times without respect, in plenty and scarcity. Joseph brought the money into the king's coffers to serve the commonwealth: these men laid it up in their own coffers to their own private use. Joseph "bought their cattle" for such price as they were worth: these men pay not the just price for any thing they take. Joseph "buyeth their land, and maketh the people bond unto the king," restoring them again the land, the king finding the seed to sow, the people only labouring to till the ground. And where we think we deal courteously if we let them sow to halves, the Egyptians have the fourth part for their labour, and pay the king the fifth part of the increase for the land and seed; but these men kept all in their own hands. Joseph "bought not the priests' lands," but gave them allowance of such things as they wanted out of the king's store; and these men, like unto our days, if they can scrape any thing from the church, that is a pastime among all other to laugh at, and thought best gotten. So much more is a minister of God's gospel thought meeter to be spoiled by these cut-purses, than Joseph thought meet to do to those idolatrous priests. Joseph opened his barns in time of dearth, and sold liberally to the needy; these men, the greater the need was, the faster they locked it up, until they had their desire of the poor. Joseph restored their land, and took but the fifth part

of the increase: these men restore nothing, and yet take interest.

As this cruel dealing toward their brethren and countrymen was thought strange to be found amongst this people, in the time that God had shewed to them such great mercies, in restoring them again to their country, giving them the liberty to build their temple and city, with great gifts, liberality, and favour of the kings, under whom they were bondmen and slaves; so it is much more marvel, that among Christians, in the time of the gospel, so mercifully restored unto us and so freely taught, greater cruelty should be found and exercised, than among the hard-hearted Jews or infidel pagans.

But this is the common practice of Satan, that in no age, people, nor country, he can be quiet to see God's kingdom set up and flourish, and his power fall; but he will rage, storm, bestir him, and by all devices that may be, and by all power that he can, overthrow it. And seeing this is no new thing, but hath fallen out divers times afore, let us not now be astonied nor dismayed at it, nor murmur and grudge against the doctrine of our salvation, so mercifully offered unto us, as though it were not the true word of God, because men live so far contrary to that which is taught, and they openly profess. The devil is content, when he cannot overthrow the truth of the doctrine, to deface it so much as he can with the ill life of those that profess it. But the gospel teacheth us what to do in this case, saying, "Do as they say, but do not as they do." The doctrine is good, though they be ill. The truth and worthiness of God's word hangeth not on our life and doings, but our life and doings should be reformed by God's word; for that "it is a lantern to our feet, and a light to our steps," that we may know when we be in the right way, and how to come into it. We must be judged by God's word, and not it by us: we must be ruled by it, and not overrule it according to our fantasies: we must hang on God's true saying, and not on man's evil living.

Matt. xxiii. 3.

Psal. cxix.

Because the Author, being prevented by death, could not finish the rest of this treatise, much less of this and the other chapters which remain untouched, I thought it good, for the better instruction of the reader, and instead of a supply for this point of oppression, which that godly and zealous father had begun, to annex and set down that which of late was published by ROBERT SOME, D. IN DIVINITY.

TO THE READER.

It hath pleased an English papist to give out in print, that the church of Rome doth both teach and require actual restitution, and that our church doth neither. His speech of us is very slanderous, and my treatise against oppression is argument enough to confute him. If they of Rome teach and require actual restitution, it is no work of supererogation: they do no more but their duties. If we should fail in this clear point, we deserve great condemnation at Almighty God's hands. I confess that a man is good, (and therefore justified in God's sight,) before he doth good works; but withal I set down this, that good works do follow him that is truly justified, and that such as have oppressed or injured any man, shall not be pardoned at God's hands, unless they make actual restitution, if they be able to do it. If any require proofs of this, I refer him to this treatise of mine against oppression.

A GODLY TREATISE

AGAINST

THE FOUL AND GROSS SIN OF OPPRESSION.

QUESTION.

What is oppression?

ANSWER.

It is unjust dealing, used of the mightier, either by violence, colour of law, or any other cunning dealing, against such as are not able to withstand them. The ground of this definition is contained in these places of Scripture. Micheas, chap. ii. verse 1, 2. 1 Thess. chap. iv. verse 6.

2. *It is not lawful for any man to oppress another.*

"Give us this day our daily bread." Every Christian desireth God Matt. vi. 11. to give daily bread, (that is, all things necessary for this life,) both to himself and to others: therefore no Christian is privileged to spoil another of his necessary food.

If one of us must pray for the good of another, one of us may not prey upon another. "He that taketh his neighbour's living is a murderer." Ecclus. xxxiv. 22.

"Thou shalt not desire thy neighbour's house, his field, &c." If we Deut. v. 21. may not desire his house or land, then we may not spoil him of his house or land, or inclose that ground, whereby the poor either by right are, or by right ought to be, relieved.

"If thou meet thine enemy's ox or his ass going astray, thou shalt Exod. xxiii. bring him to him again. If thou see thine enemy's ass lying under 4, 5. his burden, wilt thou cease to help him? thou shalt help him up with it again." Almighty God commandeth us to deal well with our enemy's ass: therefore we may not by undoing our neighbour, or spoiling him of any part of his land or goods, make him an ass, and send him a begging.

"He that oppresseth the poor, reproveth him that made him, &c." It Prov. xiv. is a gross sin to reprove the majesty of God; therefore it is a gross sin 31. to oppress the poor.

It was one of the sins of Sodom, "not to reach out the hand to the Ezek. xvi. poor." If it be a great sin not to relieve the poor, it is a very gross 49.

sin to spoil the poor. "The bread of the needful is the life of the poor; he that defraudeth him thereof is a murderer."

<small>Ecclus. xxxiv. 21.</small>

There is a writ in England which beareth this name, *ne injuste vexes*, that is to say, "vex not any man unjustly." This is a godly law, and is derived from the law of God, which forbiddeth and condemneth oppression.

There are certain beggars, which of purpose keep their legs sore, to get money by it. If they are justly misliked, which gain by their own sore legs, what deserve they to be thought of, which gain by other men's sore legs?

"When thou sellest ought to thy neighbour, or buyest at thy neighbour's hand, ye shall not oppress one another." "This is the will of God, that no man oppress or defraud his brother in any matter." Therefore men of trade may not gain by little measures, false weights, and false speeches and oaths; nor any mighty men may gain by cunning dealing, by colour of law, or by using any violence whatsoever.

<small>Levit. xxv. 14. 1 Thess. iv. 6.</small>

3. *They which have done wrong unto or oppressed any, must make actual restitution.*

God saith thus unto Moses: "Speak unto the children of Israel, When a man or woman shall commit any sin that men commit, and transgress against the Lord, when that person shall trespass, then they shall confess their sin which they have done, and shall restore the damage thereof with his principal, and put the fifth part of it more thereto, and shall give it unto him against whom he hath trespassed. But if the man have no kinsman, to whom he should restore the damage, the damage shall be restored to the Lord for the priests' use, &c." We are taught in this place, to whom this actual restitution must be made, even to him whom we have injured: if he be dead, we must restore it to his kinsman; if he have no kinsman alive, actual restitution must be made to Almighty God for the priests' use, and in our time for the poor's use.

<small>Num. v. 6, 7, 8.</small>

Michah robbed his mother of eleven hundred shekels of silver: his mother did not know that he had it; but he had remorse of that sin, and made actual restitution.

<small>Judg. xvii. 2, 3.</small>

Samuel saith thus of himself: "Whose ox have I taken? whose ass have I taken? or whom have I done wrong to? or whom have I hurt? or of whose hands have I received any bribe to blind my eyes therewith? and I will restore it you, &c." It is certain that Samuel did not deal either corruptly or unjustly in his office: if he had, he would have made actual restitution.

<small>1 Sam. xii.</small>

Zaccheus was sometimes very disordered in his life: it pleased our Saviour Christ to be a good God unto him, and to lodge in his house. Zaccheus, having feeling of his former wants, uttered these words, "If I have taken from any man by forged cavillation, I restore him fourfold." If Zaccheus of Jericho after his conversion was content to restore fourfold, it is a good consequent, that they have little sense of religion, which will not restore the principal.

Question.

If a man have deceived, robbed, or oppressed other men, shall he be pardoned at God's hand, if he make not actual restitution?

Answer.

God will not pardon him, unless he make actual restitution, if he be able to do it: my reasons are these.

"If the wicked restore the pledge, and give again that he had robbed, he shall surely live and not die, saith the Lord." Therefore it is a sure consequent, that he shall not live eternally, which, being in case to make actual restitution, doeth it not accordingly. Ezek. xxxiii. 15. xviii. 12, 13.

"Is not this the fasting that I have chosen, to loose the bands of wickedness, to take off the heavy burdens, and to let the oppressed go free, and that ye break every yoke, &c.? Then shalt thou call, and the Lord shall answer; thou shalt cry, and he shall say, Here I am, &c." If the oppressor must let the oppressed go free, he must make actual restitution. If Almighty God will not hear the prayer of the oppressor, until he let the oppressed go free, it is a necessary consequent, that God will not pardon him. Isai. lviii. 6, 9.

Augustine is very flat for this point: "If men be able to make actual restitution, and do it not, *pœnitentia non agitur, sed fingitur*[1]:" that is to say, "their repentance is no repentance," and their sin shall not be pardoned until actual restitution be made. Epist. 54.

Question.

If a man have secretly either robbed or deceived another, and is very willing to make restitution, but cannot do it without some worldly danger and disgrace to himself, what must he do in this case?

Answer.

Let him send that which he hath taken unjustly by some trusty messenger to him whom he hath wronged, and let his name be concealed.

Question.

If he that hath taken unjustly from others, hath wasted all, and is not able to make restitution, what shall he do?

Answer.

Such a one must desire pardon very humbly at God's hand, and water the earth with his tears.

4. *It is the duty of the magistrate to deliver the oppressed out of the hand of the oppressor.*

"Execute judgment in the morning, (that is, carefully and without delay,) and deliver the oppressed out of the hand of the oppressor, saith the Lord, &c." "Seek judgment, relieve the oppressed, judge the Jer. xxi. 12. Isai. i. 17.

[1 Si enim res aliena, propter quam peccatum est, cum reddi possit, non redditur, non agitur pœnitentia, sed fingitur. August. Epist. LIV. (CLIII.) Tom. ii. p. 794. Ed. Paris. 1836. ED.]

fatherless, and defend the widow." Almighty God commandeth the magistrates to execute judgment in the morning; therefore they must use no delays in doing justice. God commandeth the magistrates to seek judgment; therefore, in cases of oppression, they must not stay till they be called for. God commendeth unto the magistrates all that are oppressed, but specially the fatherless and widow, because they want the defence of their parents and husbands, and every man goeth over where the hedge is lowest.

Jer. xxii. "Josias executed judgment and justice: he judged the cause of the afflicted and poor," saith the Lord of Josias.

Job xxix. Job saith thus of himself: "I delivered the poor that cried, and the fatherless, and him that had none to help him, &c. I put on justice, and it covered me: my judgment was the eye to the blind, and I was a father unto the poor; and when I knew not the cause, I sought it out diligently. I brake also the chaws of the unrighteous man, and plucked the prey out of his teeth, &c." It appeareth by this, that Job was a worthy magistrate. God send us many such as Job was!

The Shunamite, whose son Eliseus raised to life, sojourned in the time of famine seven years in the land of the Philistines: in her absence her lands and goods were unjustly entered upon: at her return she complained of the injury to Jehoram the king of Israel; Jehoram without delay commanded an eunuch to restore her goods and lands 2 Kings viii. unto her: "Restore thou," saith Jehoram, "all that are hers, and all the fruits of her lands, since the day she left the land, even until this time."

The Jews in Nehemiah's time were greatly oppressed: Nehemiah was very angry with the princes and rulers which oppressed them, Neh. v. and said unto them, "You lay burdens every one upon his brethren, &c. Restore unto them this day their lands, their vineyards, their olives, and their houses."

If it be the magistrate's duty to deliver the oppressed, they must take great heed, that themselves be neither principals nor accessaries Amos v. 7. in the sin of oppression. If they be guilty, "judgment shall be turned & ii. 6. into wormwood, and the righteous shall be sold for silver, and the poor for shoes:" that is to say, filthy bribes shall be more accounted of than men's lives, which are most precious.

5. *The magistrate loseth nothing by delivering the oppressed.*

If he do it with a single heart, beside the testimony of a good conscience, (which is a continual feast,) he may assure himself of God's favour and blessing, and of the singular liking of all God's people.

Jer. xxii. "Josias did eat and drink and prosper, when he executed judgment and justice, when he judged the cause of the afflicted and the poor."

Job xxvi. Job "delivered the poor that cried, and the fatherless, and him that had none to help him; and the blessing of him that was ready to perish came upon him."

Our sovereign Lady Queen Elizabeth hath dealt graciously with many poor suitors at the court: she hath spoken comfortably to them, and procured restitution accordingly. If it be no disgrace to this noble lady, which sitteth under the cloth of estate, to deliver the oppressed, it is no blot to inferior magistrates if they do the like. If the prince pleaseth God highly, and winneth the hearts of her subjects soundly, for relieving the oppressed, it is very certain, that those cormorants, which grind the faces of the poor, are accursed of God, and lose the hearts of his people. If the prince sitteth fast in the seat of her kingdom for tendering the cause of the oppressed, can they assure themselves of sitting quietly under their vines and fig trees, which eat bread baked with the tears of men? It is certain they cannot; for (besides the manifold curses of God and his people,) their own consciences do mightily sting them, and are enemies enough to torment them.

6. *Oppressors shall be grievously punished.*

"Cursed be he that removeth his neighbour's mark; and all the people shall say, Amen." If they are accursed by God and his people, which remove the mark of the land, they are more accursed, which take away house and land. [Deut. xxii. 16, 17.]

"Oppression maketh a wise man mad." Madness is a grievous punishment. God punisheth oppression by madness, one gross sin by another. [Eccles. vii. 9.]

"Ye have builded houses of hewn stone, but ye shall not dwell in them; ye have planted pleasant vineyards, but ye shall not drink wine of them." The reason of this is set down by Almighty God in the same verse, in these words: "Your treadings are upon the poor, and you take from him burdens of wheat," (that is to say, the necessary relief of him and his family.) If the taking away of burdens of wheat from the poor was so great a sin, the taking away of arable ground, which by tillage and God's blessing bringeth relief to a man and his family, is no little sin. [Amos v.]

"They shall not mourn for him," saith God of Joachim, the king of Juda, (which was a great oppressor;) "he shall be buried as an ass is buried, and cast forth (as a carrion above the ground,) even without the gates of Jerusalem." Joachim had closed himself in cedar, but that was not able to keep God's judgments from him. [Jer. xxii.]

"The stone shall cry out of the wall, and the beam out of the timber shall answer it, &c." As if Almighty God should say, Rather than the vile dealings of oppressors should not come to light, the stone shall cry out of the wall, I am built of blood and iniquity; and the beam out of the timber shall answer, I am built likewise of blood and iniquity. If the stones and beams of oppressors' houses give in their evidence (like honest jurates,) against such houses, the oppressors must prepare themselves to hear this fearful sentence pronounced by the Lord chief justice of heaven and earth against them: "Woe [Hab. ii. 11.] [Hab. ii. 12.]

unto him that buildeth a town with blood, and erecteth a city by iniquity!"

They which oppress others, do more hurt themselves than those whom they oppress. "The smart of the oppressed hath an end, the smart of the oppressor is everlasting; for he heapeth unto himself wrath against the day of wrath, and of the declaration of the just judgment of God[1]."

<small>Aug. Epist. 211. Rom. ii.</small>

There were never any oppressors so many and mighty, but at the length they were met with. God's judgments have feet of wool, but they have arms of brass: it is long ere God begin; but when he striketh, he payeth home.

<small>Isai. xxx. 14, 17.</small>

"Woe unto them that imagine iniquity and work wickedness upon their beds! when the morning is light, they practise it, because their hand hath power, and they covet fields, and take them by violence, and houses, and take them away: so they oppress a man and his house, even a man and his heritage: therefore thus saith the Lord, Behold, against this family have I devised a plague, whereout ye shall not pluck your necks." God be merciful unto us, and make us afraid of his judgments!

<small>Jer. v.</small>

<small>Mic. ii. 1, 2, 3.</small>

7. *Oppressors have no religion in them.*

"God looked for judgment, but behold oppression; for righteousness, but behold a crying, &c." Judgment and righteousness are the true fruits of God's religion: therefore oppression is no branch of God's religion: and consequently the oppressor is void of all religion.

<small>Isai. v. 7.</small>

"Do not all the workers of iniquity know, that they eat up my people as they eat bread? they call not upon the Lord." Oppressors call not upon the Lord; therefore they are void of religion: for invocation is a principal and necessary fruit of religion. If the oppressors say, that they stretch out their hands and make many prayers, I grant they do so; but Almighty God giveth them this answer, "I will hide mine eyes from you, I will not hear; for your hands are full of blood."

<small>Psal. xiv. 4.</small>

<small>Isai. i. 15. Mic. iii. 4.</small>

"I will be a swift witness against those that wrongfully keep back the hireling's wages, and vex the widow and fatherless, and oppress the stranger, and fear not me, saith the Lord of hosts, &c." They which oppress others fear not God; therefore they are void of religion. If they say they fear God, they deserve no credit, because their doings confute their speech. "A good tree bringeth forth good fruits," and a justifying faith appeareth by good works.

<small>Mal. iii. 5.</small>

"The former governors did burden the people, but so did not I," saith Nehemiah, "because of the fear of God." If Nehemiah did neither oppress nor deal hardly, because he feared God, it is manifest that oppressors fear not God, and therefore are void of religion.

<small>Neh. v. 15.</small>

[¹ Utinam vel tantum tibi obesset iniquitas, quam miseris et pauperibus facis, quantum obest ipsis quibus eam facis! Illi enim ad tempus laborant; tu autem vide quid tibi thesaurizes in die iræ et revelationis justi judicii Dei, qui reddet unicuique secundum opera sua. August. Epist. ccxi. (ccxlvii.) Tom. ii. p. 794. Ed. Paris. 1836. Ed.]

"When he, (that is, Josias,) judged the cause of the afflicted and the poor, he prospered: was not this because he knew me? saith the Lord. But thine eyes and thine heart, (he speaketh to Joachim, the king of Juda,) are but only for thy covetousness, and for to shed innocent blood, and for oppression, &c." Josias was a singular defence to the oppressed, because he did know and fear God: Joachim was a notable oppressor, because he did neither know nor fear God, that is to say, because he was void of God's religion. Jer. xxii. 16, 17.

THIS which I have set down against oppression, may serve for oppressors to look upon, and to reform themselves by. If it work their good, it is happy for them; if it do not, let them remember that die they must, and that after death they shall have a fearful judgment. The best advice that I can give to them which are oppressed is, that
they desire the magistrate to be their defence. If by this
ordinary means they cannot compass their own, they
must patiently bear injuries, and commit their
cause to Almighty God, who hath their
flittings in his register, and their Psal. lvi. 8.
tears in his bottle, and will be
surely, but yet justly,
revenged of their
oppressors.

Veritas et dulcis est et amara. Quando dulcis est, parcit; quando amara, curat. Aug. Epist. ccxi[1]. *ad Romulum.*

[[1] CCXLVII. in the later editions. See the last note. ED.]

The text.

v. 6. *And I was very angry, when I heard their cry and these words.*

7. *And my heart within me advised me, and I chid the noblemen and the rulers, and I said unto them, Every one of you lay burdens on your brethren; and I assembled a great congregation against them.*

8. *And I said unto them, We have redeemed our brethren the Jews, which were sold to the Gentiles, as far as we were able; and will ye sell your brethren again, and shall they be sold to us? And they held their tongue, and found not a word to speak.*

9. *And I said, The thing that ye do is not good: ought ye not to walk in the fear of God, for avoiding the slander of the heathen which hate us?*

10. *Both I, my brethren, and my servants, lent them money and corn: I pray you, let us leave off these burdens.*

11. *I pray you, this day restore them their land, their vineyards, their olive gardens, and their houses, and the hundredth part of money, and of the corn, and of the wine, and of the oil, which ye do exact of them.*

12. *And they said, We will restore them again, and we will require nothing of them; we will do as thou hast said. And I called the priests, and did swear them to do according to these words.*

13. *And I also did shake my lap, and said, Let God thus shake every man which maintaineth not this word, out of his house and his labour; and after this manner let him be shaken out, and void. And all the multitude said Amen, and praised the Lord; and the people did according to this word.*

Here we shall learn well, both what the cry of the poor oppressed prevaileth in the ears of the godly, and what a good ruler ought to do in such a case. Magistrates are mortal gods, and God is an immortal magistrate: therefore as the merciful God heareth in his holy habitation in heaven the cry of the miserable oppressed people in earth, so should every godly ruler hear and relieve the pitiful cry of the oppressed, being his brethren, seeing he is God's lieutenant, and hath the sword and law in his hand to bridle such ill doers, and must not for favour, gifts, nor fear, suffer it unamended: else he doeth not his duty unto the mighty Lord, who set him in that place, gave him the authority, and will ask a strait account how he hath used it to the relief of the oppressed.

Nehemiah, hearing this open outcry of the people, and fearing the inconvenience that might follow of it, dealeth wisely. First, as justice requireth, he is very angry at it, and yet with wisdom bridleth his affection, that he doth not rashly punish them, but after due consultation within himself, and good advice taking, first with words sharply rebuketh them, and after by authority compelleth them, not only henceforth to leave their cruel dealing, but also to restore that which they had so wrongfully gotten.

Some be of opinion, that a magistrate should not be moved with anger in doing his office, but give every man fair words, pass over matters slowly, please all men, though he do them little good; but, the truth being well considered, it may be judged otherwise. Lactantius writeth a book *De Ira Dei*, wherein he proveth *that God himself is angry, and every anger is not sin.* If God then be angry against sin, why may not a good man in God's cause then do the same? Hate not the man, but his ill doing; be not angry without a just cause unadvisedly; keep not thy anger long, that it grow not into hatred; let it be no more nor no less than the fault deserveth, and let it be without raging, fuming, fretting, swelling, and raving and disquieting of body or mind; not for malice of revenging, but for pity or justice to correct and amend: and anger well qualified is not ill. Phinees, being angry with the filthy whoredom committed openly and unpunished by those that were in authority, took his sword, killed both the parties in his zealous anger, and for so doing the Lord blessed him, and "the plague ceased." Moses is called the "mildest man upon earth;" and yet in his anger he threw down the tables wherein God wrote the ten commandments, and brake them, when he saw they had made the golden calf. Jesus Christ our Lord was angry, when he "whipt the buyers and sellers out of the temple." St Mark saith, "he looked on them round about with anger." Every anger therefore is not ill.

Exod. xxxii.

This is not spoken to give liberty to anger, for we are too ready to it by nature; but rather to bridle it, seeing it standeth on so narrow a point to keep measure in. This qualifying of anger is declared in the scripture, as that it should not continue: St Paul saith, "Let not the sun set upon your anger;" and that it should not be rashly without cause, nor more than the cause requireth, the gospel teacheth, saying, "He that is angry with his brother without a just cause is guilty of judgment." This anger of Nehemiah was just in all circumstances, and kept the rule of St Paul, "Be angry and sin not;" which is a hard point to keep.

[Ephes. iv.]

Matt. v.

FINIS.

SOLI DEO SIT GLORIA.

THE BURNING OF ST PAUL'S CHURCH:

THE ADDITION

AND

CONFUTATION OF THE ADDITION.

The burnynge

of Paules church in London in the yeare of oure Lord 1561, and the iiii. day of June

by lyghtnynge, at three of the
clocke, at after noone, which
continued terrible and
helplesse vnto
nyght.
(*)

VVERE THESE GREATER SINners, than the rest? No: I saye vnto you except ye repent, ye shall all lykewyse* peryshe.
Luc. 13.
(*)

AN ADDICION, WITH AN AP-
POLOGIE TO THE CAUSES OF BRINNYNGE[1] OF PAULE'S CHURCH, THE WHICH CAUSES WERE UTTRED AT PAULE'S CROSSE BY THE REUEREND BYS-SHOP OF DURESME, THE 8TH OF JUNE, 1561.[2]

ALTHOUGH Almighty God be patient, merciful, and long-suffering, willing all sinners to repent their wickedness, to rise from sin, and come to his mercy; yet, if sinners will not amend after monition and warning had, at the last God strikes suddenly and sore, as appears in the scripture by Sodom and Gomorra, upon the which cities God rained fire and brimstone, wherewith the five cities were destroyed miserably. Also Pharao and the Egyptians, that would not be moved

[1 Brinning: burning, as *brent* is the old form of the participle *burnt*.—The occasion of this controversy is thus stated by Strype: "When by lightning, on the 4th day of June, this year, [1561] the steeple, the bells, and roof of St Paul's church were burnt, a papist, soon after this accident, spread certain papers about at West Chester concerning it. * * * And whereas, June 8, that is, the next Sunday after this fire, Pilkington, bishop of Durham, preached at Paul's Cross, and took notice in his sermon of the dreadful devastation of this church, exhorting the people to take it to be a warning of a greater plague to follow to the city of London, if amendment of life were not had in all estates: he did also recite certain abuses of the said church; as talking, buying and selling, fighting and brawling there: he shewed also, how the virtue of obedience to superiors was much decayed in those days: these causes assigned for this judgment were reflected upon in the said paper; making the chief causes rather to be, 'that the old fathers and the old ways were left, together with blaspheming God in lying sermons preached there, polluting the temple with schismatical service, and destroying and pulling down altars, set up by blessed men, and where the sacrifice of the mass was ministered.' This occasioned the writing of a tract in confutation of the paper aforesaid; printed by Will. Seres, ann. 1563." Strype, Annals, Vol. I. Part i. p. 390. ED.]

[2 It is to be regretted, that the sermon preached by the bishop on the occasion referred to is not now extant. It does not indeed clearly appear that it ever was printed, though it is so stated by Surtees, History of Durham, p. LXXVIII. and others; but Strype, whose authority is referred to, (see the last note,) makes no mention of its being printed. In his life of Grindal, p. 53—55, fol. Lond. 1710, he gives a full account of the circumstances of the fire, and of the bishop's sermon, which was "preached with great applause of the hearers," and appears to have embraced many points afterwards enlarged upon in the "Confutation." "All this," he adds, "and much more was written in Latin, and afterwards entered into Bishop Grindal's Register by his special command to Peter Johnson, his Registrary, for a perpetual memory of this fire and of so great a destruction."—We have therefore the "Addition" without that to which it was originally added. This "Addition" was put forth anonymously by John Moren, or Morwen, Bonner's chaplain, and replied to in the Bishop's "Confutation." ED.]

[PILKINGTON.]

by the words of Moses and Aaron, nor with the ten plagues, at last were suddenly drowned in the sea.

Also Chore, Dathan and Abiron, with a great number of people, that would not obey the ministration of Aaron and the priests appointed by God, but went from them, seeking a new way to serve God; part of them were suddenly swallowed up of the earth, and part brent suddenly with fire from heaven in the tabernacle. After, when the people of Jerusalem would not hear the true prophets of God, but would believe false lying prophets, and so declined from the steps of David, Ezechias, and Josias, which walked in the fear of God; because they forsook their fathers' steps, and fell to idolatry, the temple was brent, the city destroyed, and the people taken captives to Babylon. Also our Saviour Christ, for the tender love he had to mankind, came into this world; by his doctrine he gathered twelve apostles disciples, and a great multitude of people in one unity of faith, and sanctified them, his church, by his precious blood-shedding,

I. "committing the rule and government of his church to the bishops:" after his ascension he sent the Holy Ghost in Jerusalem, in likeness of fiery tongues, among the apostles, and straightway they preached as the Holy Ghost taught them: and there in Jerusalem St Peter converted a great multitude to the faith, which faith at Jerusalem was first taught and declared upon by a council of the apostles and seniors,

II. "there St James being bishop, and there said mass:" and afterward the same faith was taught in all lands, as the prophet David says, *In omnem terram exivit sonus eorum.* The faith of Christ's church hath been from time to time established by general councils: the which faith what country soever hath forsaken it, hath been miserably scourged and plagued; as about forty years after the ascension of our Saviour Christ, because the Jews would not abide in that religion that was decreed by the apostles, and walk in their steps, miserably Jerusalem was plagued with fire, pestilence, famine, battle, and murder. Also in all other countries, as well with the Greeks as other parts of the world, when the people have declined from the fear of God, forsaking the steps of blessed fathers, miserably they

III. have been plagued. And " in England, where the faith of Christ and " true religion was planted about the year of our Lord 182. by Eleu-" therius, pope, sending legates to Lucius then king of England, which " converted this realm to the faith, and established true religion in " England, which continued two hundred years;" but when the people did decline from the fear of God, and the steps of God and blessed fathers, they came to great calamity and misery by the scourge of God. Cadwallader, last king of the Britons, did confess by the hand of God with pestilence and famine they were driven out of this land.

IV. "After that again, this land being inhabited with Saxons, being Pai-" nims, St Gregory, pope of Rome, about the year of our Lord God, 595. " sent St Augustine and other monks with him into England, Ethel-" bert being king; and then St Augustine and his company by their " doctrine and virtuous living planted the faith, and so established a

"true religion in England: the which faith and religion ever when
"the people have declined from it, they have felt great calamities, as
"well by the hand of God, as by the conquest of the Danes, and
"after by the Normans; and sith the conquest from time to time" God
hath plagued this realm for sin and infidelity. And "now, whether V.
"the people of this realm be declined from the steps of St Augustine
"and other blessed fathers and saints, which had mass and seven sa-
"craments in the church; and God was honoured night and day in
"the church with divine service; I think there is no man so simple
"but he may easily perceive, except malice have blinded his heart.

"As in St Paul's church in London, by the decrees of blessed
"fathers, every night at midnight they had matins, all the forenoon
"masses in the church, with other divine service and continual prayer;
"and in the steeple anthems and prayers were had certain times:" but
consider, how far now contrary the church has been used; and it is
no marvel, if God have sent down fire to burn part of the church as
a sign of his wrath. And where a reverend bishop at Paul's cross
did exhort the people to take the burning of Paul's to be a warning
of a greater plague to follow to the city of London, if amendment of
life be not had in all estates, it was well said: but we must add,
accedentem ad Deum oportet credere; the scripture says, "He that will
come to God must first believe." St Paul says, "Without faith it is Heb. xi.
impossible to please God:" and the prophet Jeremy saith by the Jer. vi.
Spirit of God speaking, *State super vias, et interrogate de semitis
antiquis, quæ sit bona ; et ambulate in ea, et invenietis refrigerium ani-
mabus vestris:* that is, "Stand upon the ways of blessed fathers, and
consider and ask of the old paths and high-ways, which is the good
way; and walk therein, and ye shall find refreshing to your souls."

"First search, whether the faith and religion now used was taught VI.
"with the blessed fathers in Christ's church in times past: ye shall
"prove by no record of authority or chronicle, that this manner of
"service now used in the church was ever heard tell of afore Luther's
"time, which is not forty years old. Therefore it is to be rejected
"and put away, as a new-fangled doctrine and schismatical: there-
"fore come back again unto the old fathers' steps," as well in faith
and religion, as godly conversation and living; or a greater plague is
at hand.

"Also, where the said preacher did recite certain abuses of the VII.
"said church, as talking, buying and selling, fighting and brawling;
"although these be very evil and worthy much rebuke, yet there be
"worse abuses, as blaspheming God in lying sermons, polluting the
"temple with schismatical service, destroying and pulling down holy
"altars, that were set up by good blessed men, and there the sacrifice
"of the blessed mass ministered according to the order of Christ's
"catholic church. Yea, where the altar stood of the Holy Ghost, the
"new bishops have made a place to set their tails upon, and there
"sit in the judgment of such as be catholic and live in the fear of
"God. Some they deprive from their livings; some they commit to

"prison, except they will forsake the catholic faith, and embrace a faith
"and religion, that has no foundation laid by general council nor blessed
"fathers in times past, but invented by heretics that do not agree one
"with another nor themselves." Thus the bishops that now be have
abused the church, and polluted it, as the prophet Jeremy says, "They
have put offendicles in the house of God, and polluted it."

VIII.

Also the said preacher in his sermon at Paul's cross did declare the
virtue of obedience to be much decayed in these our days; but he leaves
out, who they be that cause disobedience. For "there is none more
" disobedient than the new bishops and preachers now a days, which
" disobey the universal church of Christ: the which church whosoever
Matt. xviii. " will not obey, our Saviour in the gospel commands us to take them
" as infidels. As, where the universal church of Christ commands mass
" and seven sacraments, as necessary for our salvation, they call it
" abomination with their blasphemous mouths: where the church
" commands to fast, they command to eat: where the church com-
" mands continual prayer of the clergy, they call it superstition and
" blind ignorance: where the church commands the clergy to live in
" chastity, they command and exhort the clergy to marriage: where
" the church and all laws, civil and canon, yea, the laws of this realm
" do prohibit marriage of priests, they allow marriage of priests, obeying
" no law, but follow their own carnal lust. Yea, where the Queen has
" given strait commandment to abstain from flesh in Lent and other
"days commanded by the church, these new preachers and protestants
"have eaten flesh openly, to the great slander of other:" so they obey
neither the Queen nor the church; so that Almighty God complains
Isai. lii. by his prophet Esay, *Tota die blasphematur nomen meum:* "With
these men God is continually blasphemed." "Woe be to you," says
Isai. v. Esay, "that call good evil, and evil good, putting darkness light, and
Ezek. xxxii. light darkness;" as by Ezechiel says Almighty God, "The priests have
contemned my law, and have polluted my sanctuary." Also Osee the
prophet does say, "The bread that they do offer is full of mourning,
and all that eat thereof shall be defiled."

IX.

We may see how they contemn all that blessed fathers, holy martyrs
and saints have decreed: they disobey all that have been virtuous and
good in Christ's catholic church. As now of late "they have invented a
" new way to make bishops and priests, and a manner of service and
" ministration, that St Augustine never knew, St Edmund, Lanfranc, St
" Anselm, nor never one bishop of Canterbury, saving only Cranmer,
" who forsook his profession as apostata: so that they must needs con-
" demn all the bishops in Canterbury, but Cranmer, and he that now is;
" all the bishops in York, saving Holgate, and he that now is: although
" St Wilfred, St William have been taken for saints, and were bishops
" in York. In Coventry and Lichfield St Chad was bishop, and many
" blessed bishops: and he that is bishop now can find not any one that
" was made as he is, nor of his religion. Therefore he must prove, all
" bishops of Lichfield were deceived, walked in blindness and igno-
" rance; or else he that now is must needs be deceived and be in blind-

" ness. In Duresme have been many good fathers; but he that is now
" bishop can not find any one predecessor in that see, that was of his
" religion, and made bishop after such sort as he was: so that he that
" now is must take in hand to condemn all the bishops afore him, that
" they were in ignorance and blindness, or else they will come to his
" condemnation at the day of judgment. And this in all bishopricks in
" England: some can find one, and some none, that ever was of their
" religion. What arrogancy may be thought in those men that will take
" in hand to condemn[1] so many blessed fathers all to be in blindness!"
But now they say, they have found a light, and reform religion according to the primitive church. Then "seeing they reform religion so   X.
" well (as they say), it were meet, as they forsake all the religion that
" their predecessors used, as mass, matins, ministration of sacraments,
" that they should also forsake houses, parks, lands and revenues, that
" their predecessors had, and go from place to place for God's sake
" and preach," and then were some likelihood of reformation: or else
it may be called rather a deformation than a reformation.

    " In Christ's church has ever been a succession of bishops from the   XI.
" apostles' time to this day, in every see. And Tertullian says: 'If in
" any see there be a bishop that walks not in his fathers' steps, he is
" to be counted a bastard, and no true inheritor in Christ's church.'
" Saint Cyprian does say: 'They that be made bishops out of the
" order of the church, and not by tradition and ordinance of the apos-
" tles, coming by succession from time to time, are not bishops by the
" will of God,' but thieves and murderers," coming to kill the flock of
Christ with heresy and lies. And " where the said preacher does af-   XII.
" firm greater matters than the burning of Paul's to have chanced in
" time of superstition and ignorance, (as the church of Paul's was
" burnt in the first year of Stephen, and the steeple of Paul's set on
" fire by lightning in the time of king Henry the VI.,) they that count
" that to be the time of superstition and ignorance, when God was
" served devoutly night and day, the people lived in the fear of God,
" every one in his vocation, without reasoning and contention of mat-
" ters of religion, but referred all such things to learned men in gene-
" ral councils and universities, there to be disputed: then was the
" commandments of God and virtue expressed in living; now all is
" in talk and nothing in living: then was prayer, now is prating: then
" was virtue, and now is vice: then was building up of churches, houses
" of religion and hospitals, where prayer was had night and day, hos-
" pitality kept and the poor relieved; now is pulling down and de-
" stroying such houses, where God should be served, hospitality kept,
" and the poor relieved; by means whereof God's glory is destroyed,
" and the commonwealth impoverished: then was plenty of all things,
" now is scarceness of all things: therefore *operibus credite;*" the fruit
will shew whether then was superstition and ignorance, or now in
these days.

    Further: where the true word of God is taught the Holy Ghost

[¹ Old edition, *contemn;* but it is afterwards quoted *condemn.* ED.]

does so work therewith, that virtue does increase: but as the prophet says, *sicut populus ita et sacerdos*, " as the people be, so God sends them priests." *Apprehenderunt mendacium et noluerunt reverti*, "the people have apprehended a lie and will not come back, but trust in lying sermons which will not profit them," as Almighty God says by his prophet Jeremy, thinking they have done well because they have done these abominations, says God by his prophet Jeremy. So as the priests be, so be the people: blinded in heresy, as God says by his prophet Esay, that their hearts do not understand, their eyes do not see, their ears be stopped for hearing the truth: so that this may well be called the time of superstition and ignorance, calling darkness light, and light darkness, that which is evil good, and good evil. And for the burning of Paul's church which he speaks of "was "in time of civil war, and not destroyed by the hands of God, as it was "at this time," whosoever reads the chronicles shall perceive that and this be not like. Therefore beware of false prophets and preachers, which come with fair words in their mouths of the gospel, but mark the fruits that come of their preaching; how they have set the people in such case, that no prayer is used, no fasting, little almsdeeds, "all liberty used;" what disobedience children be in against their parents, how untrusty servants be, what swearing and blaspheming of God is used of all people; what theft, whoredom, craft, subtlety and deceit: these be fruits that come of this new-fangled doctrine. Therefore return back again to the steps of good fathers afore us: be not carried away, as St Paul says, with a strange and diverse doctrine; "embrace the religion and faith taught in Christ's " church from time to time continually, and frame your living ac- " cordingly; or else God's vengeance hangs over your heads, ready " suddenly to fall upon you: so says the scripture, and let this token " of burning of Paul's be an example and token of a greater plague " to follow, except ye amend." (*₊*)

Marginalia: Hos. iv. / Jere. viii. / Jere. vii. / Isai. vi. / Isai. v. / XIII. / XIV.

A CONFUTACION OF AN AD-
DICION, WITH AN APPOLOGYE WRITTEN AND CAST
IN THE STRETES OF VVEST CHESTER, AGAYNST
THE CAUSES OF BURNYNG PAULE'S CHURCH
IN LONDON: WHYCH CAUSES, THE
REUEREND BYSHOP OF DU-
RESME DECLARED AT PAU-
LE'S CROSSE 8. JU-
NII. 1561.

OUR Saviour Christ, when the devil spake the truth plainly, did not confute or gainsay it: but when he did it frowardly, Christ rebuked him sharply. As when the devil said, "Jesus of Nazareth, what have we to do with thee? art Luke iv. thou come to destroy us? I know that thou art the Holy One of God;" he did not refuse nor deny that truth which he spake: but when the devil tempted him to throw himself down from the pinnacle of the temple, he rebuked him Matt. iv. quickly, because he alleged the true scripture maliciously. So it is not sufficient to do a good deed barely, or speak the Truth must truth only, except it be done rightly, and with such circum- uttered. stances as be necessarily required to make it good: as, that it be from the heart, and for God's cause willingly, &c. In like manner, where this scavenger, sweeping the streets with his books (as a fit broom and officer thereto), has spoken the truth, not truly, because it is for an evil purpose and frowardly, I shall pass over it with silence: but where he follows his master, the father of lies, in falsifying the truth, or racking the scripture subtilly, I shall by God's grace let the world see his juggling, and by truth truly uttered disclose his shameless lying.

The first examples that he brings, declaring how God does justly plague the obstinate sinners, that will not repent after many warnings given, are true all: but being alleged to bring us back to popery, and for another purpose than God our Lord has taught them, they be craftily misused, and ye see whose footsteps he followed. And as he uses them to persuade us to superstition, so they may and ought to be used specially, for maintaining true religion. The rhetoricians teach, that such kind of beginnings as may be applied to two contrary parts, are faulty. Therefore, seeing I may use the self-same reasons and words, that he has from the beginning hitherto, to train us to love and embrace our godly reformed religion, he cannot much crack of his wisely placed examples or reasons. But I will not stick with him in such small points as these, although they be false: but I will join with him in matters of weight, and those chief points of religion which he has touched, and we differ from him and his sort in them.

I. Committing the rule and government of his Church to the Bishops, &c.

THE first is concerning the authority and government given to bishops over God's church: wherein his words are not so untrue, as they contain a false doctrine and meaning in them. If ye think that I too boldly enter to judge his meaning, confer these words with such as follow in his own writing, wherein untruly he claims those privileges to his bishops, which neither he nor they are able to justify; and there at large ye shall easily perceive what he means by these few words here. But I will follow him where away he leads me; and because he does here but briefly touch it, I shall likewise shortly pass over it, and more throughly search it, where he does more at large press it.

In the beginning of their late revived tyranny, and afore they had obtained their long desired authority to reign over kings and princes, it was my chance to talk with one of their stoutest champions, and of those that he calls the godly bishops in prison. Among sundry things that were to be redressed in talk, as he thought, he took this self-same matter first, and said it was not fit for any temporal officer to sit as judge on any priest or spiritual man, specially in any spiritual matter. For the same cause began Thomas Becket to rebel against his prince, not suffering his priests to be punished for their murders and robberies; and now like good children they follow his steps. I asked, Why? for the laws were then

What authority bishops have over the church.

as they be now; and both very well, that justices in their sessions and assizes might and should inquire who then offended the civil laws and the order of religion established, whether he were priest or other. He answered, that in the 20th of the Acts of the Apostles it was plain that God had set the bishops to govern the church. I said, that was another kind of government that St Paul there grants to bishops, and differs from that which kings or princes claim and ought to have. "No," says he, "mark the words, and it is *ad regendum ecclesiam, et regere regum est:* therefore bishops have authority to rule as kings." "No," said I, "if ye will be judged by the word, the Greek word must be judge in this case; for in Greek it was first written and spoken: and there will appear another kind of government, far diverse from that which belongs to princes. The Greek word in that place is ποιμαίνειν, which signifies *to feed*, as the shepherd feeds his sheep; and yet not without all government or authority, but only such a simple kind of rule and authority as shepherds have over their flock. If ye will confer one place of the scripture with another, where this word is read or found, (which is the best kind of interpreting the scripture rightly, as St Austin teaches,) and see what kind of government it signifies there, then this place shall more easily be understand." "Feed the flock that is among you," says St Peter. "Feed my sheep," says our Saviour Christ to Peter. Where, and in other like places also, the same Greek word, that is commonly translated in the Acts, *regere, to rule*, is put, and signifies (as ye see) *to feed*. The same word is applied also to our Saviour Christ in the gospel, where is declared plainly, what kind of authority it signifies: "Thou, Bethleem, in the land of Juda, thou art not the least of the princes of Juda; for out of thee shall there come to me a prince, that shall rule, or feed, my people Israel." Also, "I am the good Shepherd," says Christ; where likewise is the same Greek word placed. Then, if Christ our Lord had any temporal jurisdiction, or these other places, using the same Greek word, contain any such thing, they might have some appearance to claim their usurped authority: else, it is not probable to give the same word in that place alone that meaning, contrary to so many other places having the self-same word.

1 Pet. v.

John xxi.

Matth. ii.

John x.

Nay, further to say: did not our Lord and Master Jesus Christ refuse this worldly authority himself, when it was offered unto him, and the one brother desired him to "divide the inheritance" betwixt him and his other brother? He would not, but said, "Who appointed me a divider betwixt you?"—as though he should say, It is not my calling, nor belongs to me. His kingdom was not of this world; but he came to teach his Father's will. Likewise he taught his apostles not to challenge this superiority, saying, "The princes of the people have rule over them, but it shall not be so among you; but he that would be the greatest, shall be the least;" that they might follow his steps truly.

But the manifest place, where the proper signification of this word appears, is in Paul, where he reckons what officers God has set in his church, and says, "First he set some apostles, other prophets, some evangelists, other shepherds and teachers." These shepherds, which are noted there by the same word that they claim their authority by, are placed by St Paul almost the lowest officers in God's church: then much more they cannot have the highest room in the commonwealth and church both.

I know, the Greek poets attribute this word to kings, but I trust they build not on heathen men's writings; and yet that name there is given them for their fatherly love towards their subjects, rather than their royal authority. But compare them with shepherds that keep our sheep in deed, of whom they have their name; and easily their nature, property, office, and authority shall be spied. God's people are called oft in the scripture sheep, (as, "We thy people and the sheep of thy pasture will praise thee;") and their teachers are called shepherds: because the one should in living follow the simplicity and obedience of sheep; and the other, the careful pains and diligence of shepherds, in feeding, healing, relieving, guiding, correcting, &c.

Look then, what temporal authority the shepherd has over his sheep; and the same spiritual power have the bishops over the church. The good shepherd will not let his sheep feed in hurtful and roating[1] pastures, but will remove them

---

[1 Rooty, rowty: coarse, or over-rank; said of grass or corn. Brockett's Glossary of north country words. ED.]

to good feeding grounds: no more will God's good shepherds let God's people and his brethren be poisoned with false doctrines, but by his authority root out and confute them. The true shepherd, if he see the wolf or fox come to devour the flock, he will watch and defend the fold: so should the good bishop by his office. The good shepherd will save the scabbed sheep, bring home the stray, and feed the weak and hungry: so will the good bishop, according to his duty. The good shepherd, if his sheep be unruly, will set his dog to pull him down and tame him: if any cannot be healed, he will cut it off, and kill it, for infecting the rest: so will God's good bishop with the threatenings of God's vengeance pull down the unbridled stomachs of the people, make them to tremble and quake at God's judgments; and if any cannot be reclaimed, he will cut him off by excommunication, separate him from the fellowship of God's people, not suffer him to communicate the Lord's supper, which is the band of brotherly love, and forbid all good folk his company, if through such shame he may be brought to knowledge his fault and amend, that he may joyfully be received as a brother in the company and fellowship of God's people again, and communicate with them in prayer, doctrine, discipline, and sacraments, as afore.

In these points the authority of bishops is so great, that it extends to prince, pope, and prelate, and none is exempt; but as they be subject to God's word, sacraments, and doctrine, so must they obey God's true minister and dicipline. As for example, the good bishop Ambrose did sharply correct and excommunicate the emperor Theodosius for a rash murder done by his commandment: and whether he is more praiseworthy that would or durst rebuke and excommunicate so mighty a prince, or the good emperor, that willingly submitted himself and obeyed his correction, it may be doubted.[2]

The power and authority then of bishops is spiritual, belonging to man's soul, as their office and ministery is; and it stands chiefly in these two points, in doctrine and discipline. As the temporal officer in the commonwealth has not the sword committed to him in vain, but to defend the good, and punish the evil; to smite the enemy and save the subject; to prison the froward, and loose the guiltless: so has God's minister in his

[[2] See above, p. 381. Ed.]

church full power and authority to teach sound doctrine and confute the false; to beat down haughty minds, and raise the weak; to bind and loose the conscience by virtue of God's word; to throw into hell the obstinate, or lift into heaven the penitent; to cast out of God's church, and receive again, such as he rightly judges by the scriptures meet for mercy or justice. And as St Peter calls Christ our Lord "the Shepherd and Bishop of our souls;" so those bishops that follow Christ will challenge no more authority to them, than their Master Christ had.

I am sure this pleases him well to hear, specially of my mouth, that such spiritual authority is given to spiritual ministers, to execute on all sorts of people: for as they belie us in other things, saying, we teach false doctrine, and move the people to sin; so they say, that in denying them their usurped authority, we take from them that which is due to them. Yet in granting thus much unto them I mean not, as they teach, that priests and bishops have this power of themselves, or when they be greased with the pope's oil, that they may execute it when and on whom it pleases them; but that God works it by them, as his wisdom thinks good, when they use them as he appointed them. For as the judge or pursuivant, that brings the king's pardon to save a thief on the gallows, is but the prince's servant, and not the chief saviour and deliverer of the condemned; so in this absolving and raising up the sinful clogged conscience, the chief praise and work is God's, and the bishop or minister is but God's servant, going his message by his word and commandment, to save and loose them whom it pleases God to offer this grace unto.

But methink I hear him say, If bishops in temporal causes have not this authority, why sit they so oft by commission now under the gospel in temporal matters? Indeed, forsomuch as they sit by commission, it proves that it belongs not to their office, as appointed by God, but in that they serve the prince, as they be bounden. Who wills and commands them by commission to serve in such place and time? The bishop's office is chiefly taught in the scripture by the Holy Ghost, and from him he receives his commission, and is not invented by pope or man. If ye compare together St Paul's bishop, described in Timothy and Titus, with such toys as the pope's prelates are ordained to play and feed the people withal, they are as like as black and white. St Paul's bishop is in the first place licensed to marry: the pope's are forbidden wives, and allowed whores for money. St Paul's bishop must preach: the pope's think it shame to stand in the pulpit. St Paul wills his bishop to "have his children obedient with all reverence:" the popish priest's children sit by other men's fires, and brought up most wantonly. The pope has commanded his bishops to christen bells and ships, to hallow mitres and staves, rings, church-yards, altars, superaltars, albs, vestments, chalices, corporas, palms, ashes, candles, water, fire, bread, oil, cream, flowers, strips, swords, crowns, fingers, &c. This is their whole life; and yet not one such word appointed them by God in scripture. What is this but to forsake God's ordinance, and follow their own devices, to prefer man and his doings to the wisdom of the Holy Ghost? When he has done all these things, he may say, he has served his master the pope, and done his commandment, but not one thing that God bids him.

Yet remains one doubt unanswered in these few words, when he says, that "the government of the church was committed to bishops," as though they had received a larger and higher commission from God of doctrine and discipline than other lower priests or ministers have, and thereby might challenge a greater prerogative. But this is to be understood, that the privileges and superiorities, which bishops have above other ministers, are rather granted by man for maintaining of better order and quietness in commonwealths, than commanded by God in his word. Ministers have better knowledge and utterance some than other, but their ministery is of equal dignity. God's commission and commandment is like and indifferent to all, priest, bishop, archbishop, prelate, by what name soever he be called, "Go and teach baptizing in the name of the Father, the Son, and the Holy Ghost:" and again, "Whose sins soever ye forgive, they are forgiven, and whatsoever ye loose in earth, it is loosed in heaven, &c." Likewise the Lord's supper, by whomsoever, being lawfully called, it be ministered, it is of like strength, power and holiness. St Paul calls the elders of Ephesus together, and says, "the Holy Ghost made them bishops to rule the church of God:" he writes also to the bishops of Philippos, meaning the ministers: for neither Ephesus nor Philippos were so great towns, but one little

Mark xvi.

John xx.

Acts xx.

bishoprick is a greater compass of ground; then they needed not many bishops. Therefore this diversity of absolving sins, invented by idle brains, that a simple priest may absolve some small ones, other greater belong to the bishop; the archbishop claims another higher sort; the rest and foulest sort pertain to popes and cardinals, as the fathers and maintainers of them; these, I say, are so foolish and childish to believe, that I think it not needful to speak of them: they are not grounded on God's word, and therefore must needs be untrue, and not to be credited, because our faith hangs only on the holy scripture. Greedy covetousness to enrich themselves has invented these, as also the rest of their superstition, which they term religion. St Jerome, in his commentary on the i. chapter *ad Tit.* says, that "a bishop and a priest is all one;" and in his epistle *ad Evagrium* he says, that "the bishop, wheresoever he be, he is of the same power and priesthood[1]." Rome makes him not better, nor England makes him worse.

<small>Ministers' authority is of like power, all.</small>

A bishop is a name of office, labour, and pains, rather than of dignity, ease, wealth, or idleness. The word *episcopus* is Greek, and signifies a scoutwatch, an overlooker, or spy; because he should ever be watching and warning, that the devil our enemy do not enter to spoil or destroy. And as in war the watchmen, scouts, or spies, if they fall on sleep or be negligent, they betray their fellows, and deserve death; so in God's church, if the bishops watch not diligently, and save their sheep, God has pronounced sentence of death against them by his prophet. "I made thee a watchman to the house of Israel, says the Lord: thou shall hear the word of my mouth, and declare it them from me. If I say to the wicked, Thou wicked, thou shalt die, and thou wilt not warn him to take heed to his way, he shall die in his wickedness, but his blood I will require of thee."

<small>Ezek. xxxiii.</small>

But I think the holy bishops he cracks so much of, have

---

[1] Qui, qualis presbyter debeat ordinari, in consequentibus disserens, hoc ait, Si quis est sine crimine, unius uxoris vir, et cetera, postea intulit, Oportet enim episcopum sine crimine esse, tanquam Dei dispensatorem. Idem est ergo presbyter qui episcopus. In Titum, c. i. v. 5. T. iv. p. 413. Paris. 1706.—Ubicunque fuerit episcopus, sive Romæ, sive Eugubii, sive Constantinopoli, sive Rhegii, sive Alexandriæ, sive Tanis, ejusdem meriti, ejusdem est et sacerdotii. Epist. ci. Ad Evangelum. ("Falsely inscribed," say the Benedictine editors, "in the old editions, *Ad Evagrium*.") T. iv. Pars ii. p. 803. Ed.]

their calling of the Dutch name, that signifies *bite sheep*, rather than of the Greek, that teaches to save sheep by his painful diligence. If they were not too much blinded in their own foolishness, they might see in the last subsidy granted in the time of their own reign[2], that they grant those to be their betters and above them, from whence they receive their authority. The parliament gives them and their collectors power to suspend, deprive, and interdite any priest that pays not the subsidy: in that doing they grant the parliament to be above them, and from it to receive their power; yea further, to let them see how they be contrary to themselves, they give a lay-man (as most part of their collectors were) power to interdite, suspend and absolve a priest: which both be contrary to their own doctrine.

I had not thought to have said so much on these his few words; and yet much more hangs on this their opinion of claiming their usurped power above princes and other ministers. For if this their opinion were true, that God gave them such authority over his church as they claim, it might be said on them, as the poet says, *Ovem lupo commisisti*,[3] that God had appointed wolves to keep his sheep.

II. There Saint James being Bishop, and there said Mass.

ALAS, poor mass! that has no better a ground-work to be built on than false lies, and so unlearned a proctor to speak for it. I pray you, who helped St James at mass? who hallowed his corporas, superaltar, chalice, vestments, &c.? who was deacon and sub-deacon to read the epistle and gospel? who rang to the sacring, and served the pax?[4] For I am as sure it was a solemn feast, and that these things were done, as he is that St James said mass. He that told you the one, could have told you the

[[2] Anno 1557. "The clergy gave her [queen Mary] an entire subsidy of eight shillings in the pound, 'now,' as the act ran, 'when the imminent necessity of the defence of the realm required present aid and remedy.' The parliament gave her one subsidy, one 15th and one 10th." Strype's Memorials, Vol. III. Part ii. p. 105. Oxford, 1822. ED.]

[[3] Terence, *Eunuch.* v. 1. You have committed the sheep to the care of the wolf. ED.]

[[4] Pax: A board, or plate of metal, on which there was a representation of the crucifixion, handed round to the people at mass for them to kiss instead of a mutual salutation—the kiss of peace. Fosbroke. ED.]

other as well as this, if he had lust; and ye say your mass cannot be said without these trinkets. I pray you, what mass was it? Began it with a great *R.* of *requiem*, or *scala cœli*, or *resurrexi*, for the plague, or murrain of beasts? part of a trental, or for all christian souls? If ye will have us to believe it, ye must tell us some more. I pray you also, which St James was it? for we read of divers of that name, both in the scripture and others histories, living at that time. It is not enough to say, so it is; but ye must prove it, if ye will be believed. I pray you, whose mass, as they term it, used he, and of whose making was it? Chrysostom's or Basil's, Gregory's or Ambrose', or that which bears his own name of St James? What language spake he? Hebrew, Greek, or Latin? These things must be proved, afore your Latin popish patched mass by so many popes in so many years, or it was brought to his perfection, can be proved. Do they think that, because my lord bishop, master doctor, or such scavengers and corner-creepers as this champion is, say it is so, and deceive the people with lies privily in corners, that none dare say against it openly, but all their sayings must be believed? I do not take them to be of that authority or credit.

But I will not stand with him in all these narrow points, although I could keep him much play in so doing. I agree that James, brother of our Lord, was bishop there at Jerusalem, as the ancient writers testify: but that he said or did any thing like the popish clouted Latin mass, that I utterly deny. For that the church, altar, superaltar, vestments, chalice, &c. should be hallowed, afore they could have mass said in them, on them, or with them, it is plain written in their own law, *de Consecra. distinct.* i.[1] When they have proved that St James had these hallowed, how and by whom they were hallowed, then I will believe he said their foolish mass, and not afore: for their mass cannot be done without them. Also, if they will be believed, they must declare what order of mass he used: was it Chrysostom's, Basil's, Justin's, Tertullian's,

---

[[1] *Sacrificia non nisi super altare et locis Deo consecratis offerantur.* Sicut non alii quam sacrati Deo sacerdotes debent missas celebrare, sic non in aliis quam in Domino consecratis locis, id est in tabernaculis divinis precibus a pontificibus delibutis missas cantare aut sacrificia offerre licet. Decret. Gratian. p. 1979. Antv. 1573. ED.]

Austin's, Dionysius', Isidorus', Gregory's, Rabanus', the Romans', or whose else? Surely all these were unborn many years after St James died, that it could not be theirs. Why, I am sure, some will say, Is there so many divers sorts of so many holy fathers to minister the Lord's supper, and our holy bishops of late have burned so many innocents, that would not use their only one disordered order of massing, as though all other were heretical and schismatical, (as they term it,) but that only one which they have devised, disguised and misused? Yea, surely these diversities all be printed and to be had with many more godly ones, and therefore they cannot deny it: and because they be printed, I will not stand to rehearse them wholly, for it were infinite. There is yet another liturgy in print, (which word they call and unlearnedly translate ever *a mass*,) bearing the name of St James: but even in their late raging time of madness, when they had gotten certain copies of these Greek liturgies, or ministering the Lord's supper, thinking to have printed them, and that it would have stablished their doings, when in trial and translating them they see it fall out otherways and to make against them, they let it alone, and suppressed it: like as the same holy father and cardinal[1] first printed his book, that he wrote against king Henry the eighth, to please the pope withal, and to stir the emperor to war against England for falling from popery; and after, his conscience accusing him to have done amiss, he burned all the books he could come by, and yet now they be commonly sold to his shame, as these liturgies be to theirs. All these orders of ministering the communion differ from their pope-holy relic, their Latin mass, in the chiefest points: that is, that the priest prays not alone, nor in a strange language, eats not, nor drinks up all alone, nor receives it for other; sells it not for money, nor sweeps the pope's scalding house, his purgatory, with it; but the people pray with him in their mother tongue, receive with him for the comfort of their own souls, and not for pocky pigs, scalled horse, nor scabbed sheep; neither making trentals or merchandise of it, but in remembrance of Christ's death, who died for them.

But that St James never said the popish mass, as they

[[1] Cardinal Pole. The book referred to is his work on the King's Supremacy, entitled *De Unitate Ecclesiæ*, anno 1535. Ed.]

would father it on him, the pope himself grants. Pope Gregory the first (called the great for his great holiness and learning, in comparison of the rest) says, that "the apostles consecrated the host only with the Lord's prayer," when they ministered[1]. Then St James, if he ministered any thing at all there, even by the pope's confession, never said their Latin mass, nor any thing like it. For that consecration in Latin of theirs has many long other prayers, crossings and blessings, and superstitious ceremonies, as all men see, beside the Lord's prayer. And in that same-self chapter of Gregory, ye shall see other diversities of ceremonies and prayers there rehearsed, wherein the Latin mass differs from the Greek and other. Wherefore it was not thought of old time to so many holy fathers a wicked thing to have divers orders in ministering the communion, though our bloody butchers will not swerve an inch from their father of lies, but burn all that gainsay them. How many toys, crossings, blessings, blowings, knockings, kneelings, bowings, liftings, sighings, houslings, turnings and half turnings, mockings, mowings, sleepings, and apish playings, soft whisperings, and loud speakings, have we to consecrate our own devices withal, or it can be getten done!

Moreover, if St James should have used our Latin canon and privity of the mass (as they term it) in his consecration, or any such like, he should have prayed to himself, and worshipped himself, being alive, which were a great absurdity to grant. For the Latin canon and privity of the mass is full of praying to saints, and names them particularly; among whom St James is one himself. Then St James using the Latin mass, as they say he did, he should have prayed to himself, and worshipped himself, being alive: which I think, when they advise themselves better, they will not grant to be true nor meet to be done; and with such wicked foolishness I trust they will not burden St James withal. Furthermore it skills much, what language St James used: for our holy bishops think it not meet that their holy relics should be uttered in our English tongue. St Paul says, he "had rather speak five words that he understands, and to teach other, than ten

[1 Orationem autem dominicam idcirco mox post precem dicimus, qui mos apostolorum fuit, ut ad ipsam solummodo orationis oblationis hostiam consecrarent. T. II. p. 960. Basil. 1564. ED.]

thousand in a strange tongue:" our prelates say, Nay. "None will prepare himself to war, except he understand what the trumpet blows:" no more can any learn his duty to God, if he understand not the thing that is taught, and the language. Our prelates say, that blind ignorance is the mother of devotion; but Christ says, "Ye err, because ye know not the scripture:" then ignorance is the cause of error. By like God either understands not English, or else he is partial, and loves not our English tongue so well as the Latin: and yet to speak or understand divers languages is the gift of the Holy Ghost. Surely, if the Holy Ghost give the grace to speak and understand divers languages, God cannot hate them that use any of them, nor disallow the gifts of the Holy Ghost in any man.

We read (for they be turned into Latin and printed), that other countries have used of old time, and yet do at this day, their own language in ministering the Lord's supper. Why then may not England do the same? What fault have we made, more than other? Chrysostom's order of the communion, Basil's, and that which bears the name of St James, were written in the Greek, which the people understood, and answered in the same language. The Syrians, Ethiopians, Armenians, Muscovites, and the dominion of prester John do at this day, and ever did, use their own language when they ministered, and out of them are turned into Latin, that easily it may be seen how we differ. The good christian emperor Justinian commands plainly in his civil laws, Novell. Constitut. 124 and 126, "That all things should be done in the churches in those languages which were known in the countries, and also that the words of baptism and the Lord's supper should be spoken in a loud voice, that thereby the devotion of the hearers might be stirred up[2]:" which all (although they were written a thousand

[[2] Ad hæc jubemus ut omnes episcopi pariter et presbyteri non tacito modo, sed clara voce, quæ a fideli populo exaudiatur, sacram oblationem et preces in sancto baptismo adhibitas celebrent; quo majore exinde devotione in depromendis Domini Dei laudibus audientium animi efferantur. Ita enim et divus apostolus docet, dicens in prima ad Corinthios epistola, Enimvero si solummodo benedicas spiritu, quomodo is, qui privati locum implet, dicet ad gratiarum actionem tuam Deo ipsum Amen, quando quidem quid dicas non videt? Novell. Constitut. cxxiii. *De Ecclesiasticis Diversis Capitulis*, p. 215. Paris. 1562. ED.]

years since) our holy papists deny, and say it was never done, nor ought to be done, nor that princes have any such authority to command or meddle in. Pope Pius the second bears witness, that the Sclavons, when they made suit to minister in their own tongue, and the pope made courtesy to grant it, "a voice was heard from heaven, that every spirit and language should praise God; and so it was granted them to use their own language[1]." The popish kind of marriage, although the rest was Latin, yet the best part was English: "I, N. take thee, N. to my wedded wife, &c. I, N. take thee, N. to my wedded husband, &c." If this was well, why not the rest also? If in making promises we use that language which we understand, why should we not do it to understand what God commands us? Is a promise to man more to be considered than that which is made to God? If these things should be denied, they be in print, that every man may read; and therefore I will not stand long in rehearsing of them. Are these tongues more holy than ours, that the holy mysteries may be used in them, and not in ours? I leave out the Bohemians and Waldenses, which have used to communicate in their own language many (though not all) these three hundred years. The Germans, the Italians, and the French I pass over, because it is not old.

Æneas Sylvius, Histor. Bohemica, cap. 13.

But these countries, they will say, are in the east part of the world, and parts of the Greek church, which never was subject to their holy father, the pope, and in these things they do err; but the west church, worshipping the pope, would never suffer any such thing. In thus saying they prove the pope to be worse than the Turk, prester John, the Sophi, or any heathen prince, that will not suffer God's people to worship their God in their own language, as they do. It is great marvel to me, why our holy prelates will not have the people to pray in English, seeing the common rude sort and altogether unlearned in all the far north parts of the realm, even the bor-

[1 Referunt Cyrillum, cum Romæ ageret, Romano pontifici supplicasse, ut Sclavorum lingua ejus gentis hominibus, quam baptizaverat, rem divinam faciens uti posset. De qua re dum in sacro senatu disceptaretur, essentque non pauci contradictores, auditam vocem tanquam de cœlo in hæc verba missam, "Omnis spiritus laudet Dominum, et omnis lingua confiteatur ei." Indeque datum Cyrillo indultum. Æn. Sylv. Historia Bohemica, cap. XIII. p. 91. Basil. 1571. ED.]

ders, have ever used the Lord's prayer, the articles of our faith, and ten commandments, and yet do, in English metre, differing nothing from the true sense of the scripture. They never learned them in Latin, and cannot nor will not learn that they understand not. Surely, God's wisdom in their rude simplicity does confound these proud prelates' wicked popery.

Yet is there remaining one of the foulest lies that is commonly read or written in the pope's testament, the decrees whereon they build their faith; which if this proctor and all his partakers can prove to be true, I will say with them. It is written *de Consecra. distinct.* i. cap. *Jacobus*, that "St James, the brother of our Lord, bishop of Jerusalem, and Eusebius, bishop of Cesarea, made their mass[2]." If this have any likeness of a truth in it, let the world judge. St James was bishop of Jerusalem, and there lived continually, not wandering into other countries, as other apostles did, but there suffered martyrdom, being thrown down from the pinnacle of the temple, where a fuller smote out his brains with a club. In Jerusalem then their natural speech was Hebrew, and the prayers that they used in the temple were only the scriptures, and in the Hebrew tongue, as the Jews do to this day in their synagogues: (wherein they prove themselves better than the papists, which in their churches have few prayers of the scripture, but many foolish ones devised of their own brain, and in a language that the people understand not.) Therefore, when they have proved that the Latin tongue was used in Jerusalem, or that St James prayed in Latin, (although I doubt not but he had the gift of tongues, as well as other apostles had,) I shall then believe them.

The order of the communion which is abroad in the name of St James, is in Greek; but that he wrote or spake Latin in Jerusalem, there is no probability in it. And if he made our Latin mass then, that should be used now throughout the world, why would he make another in Greek so far unlike to it? Both cannot be true, that he made one in Greek and

[[2] *A quibus fuerit tradita missarum celebratio.* Jacobus, frater Domini secundum carnem, cui primum credita est Hierosolymitana ecclesia, et Eusebius, Cæsariensis episcopus, cujus claritas per totum orbem refulsit in scripturis, addiderunt nobis missæ celebrationem. Dist. i. Gratian. Pars III. p. 1990. Antv. 1573. ED.]

another in Latin, so far unlike one to the other. Afterward the gloss upon this text of the pope's decree, afore rehearsed, *de Consecra. distinct.* i. says, that " St James made the canon of the mass, and Eusebius added other pieces to it afterward:" but beside that inconvenience which I spake of afore, that St James then should pray to himself, if that were true, a greater untruth would follow, that is, to pray to saints that were unborn, some one hundred, some two hundred, some three hundred year after, and more; as to Cyprian, Cornelius, Laurence, Chrysogonus, Damianus, which, and such-like women as Luce, Agnes, Cecily, &c. are put in their canon, or privity of their Latin mass. Is this like, that St James, a saint himself, would pray to a saint (if they were saints), that was yet unborn so many years after his death? But it may be thought that they knew these things to be so foolish, that if they were openly read and understand, they would be laughed at and despised, and therefore they enjoin their chaplains to speak softly when they say these things, that none should hear them what they say. If it were good, it were no danger in letting it be heard, for it would make them good that heard it (for faith comes by hearing), though their opinion is that it would be despised. But surely hearing is the way to make men good.

Yet follows a greater inconvenience, if this pope's decree were true. For as the gloss there says that St James made their canon, so it says that Eusebius, which lived (as he says) under the emperor Julianus Apostata, should make the rest. How can their great relic, the mass, then be one thousand five hundred years old, as they crack it to be? This council of the apostles, where St James said mass (as this proctor says), was about fifty years after Christ our Lord was born, and not full twenty years after he was crucified, as many histories do testify; but Eusebius lived under Julian the emperor three hundred and sixty year after the birth of our Saviour Christ: and now since Christ's birth it is one thousand five hundred and sixty-two. Then take three hundred and sixty out of one thousand five hundred and sixty-two, and so remains but one thousand two hundred and two. So by their own account they lie three hundred and sixty year in the anciety of their mass.

But yet a greater lie. Eusebius was a Grecian, and never wrote in Latin, that any history makes mention of: how then wrote he their Latin mass? Yea, where Gregory, bishop of Rome, in the epistle afore alleged says, that one Scholasticus[1] made the prayers of their canon, how can this be true that St James made it? Dare they deny that which the holiest of the popes, their fathers, says is so?

Epist. Lib. vii. cap. 63.

But because they charge us with contrarieties and diversities of opinions, and are most in that fault themselves, I will yet let them see more wherein they differ among themselves. *Isidorus*, lib. i. *de Origine Officiorum*, cap. v, as Faber alleges him[2], says that "St Peter ordained first the order of the mass or prayers, with which the consecration is made, and that the whole world followed the same order;" and this was done by Peter at Antioch, as the same Joan. Faber says. Then how is that true, that St James and Eusebius made it at Jerusalem? Nay, how can any of these sayings agree with Platina[3], one of the pope's sworn men, which affirms that pope Sixtus appointed the *Sanctus* to be sung; Gregory, the *Kyrie Eleeson*; Telesphorus, *Gloria in excelsis*; Jerome, the epistle and gospel; Leo, the censing; Innocentius I. the pax; Sergius, the Agnus, &c.; which all lived a great sort of years asunder; and from the first to the last, afore it could be

Joan. Fabe de Missa Evangel.

[1 Et valde mihi inconveniens visum est, ut precem quam Scholasticus composuerat, super oblationem diceremus; et ipsam traditionem, quam Redemptor noster composuit, super ejus corpus et sanguinem non diceremus. Gregor. Op. T. II. p. 960. Basil. 1564. ED.]

[2 Isidorus, qui ante nongentos floruit annos, lib. I. de Origine Officiorum, cap. 5. Ordo missæ vel orationum, quibus oblata Deo sacrificia consecrantur, primum a S. Petro est institutus: cujus celebrationem uno eodemque modo totus peregit orbis, &c. Lib. IV. cap. iii. p. 97. Petrus quidem missam celebravit Antiochiæ. Lib. I. cap. ii. p. 8. Paris. 1564. ED.]

[3 In celebratione vero mandavit (Sixtus I.), ut *Sanctus, sanctus, sanctus, Dominus Deus sabaoth* cantaretur. Nuda primo hæc erant, et omnia simpliciter tractabantur. Petrus enim ubi consecraverat, oratione *Pater noster* usus est: auxit hæc mysteria Jacobus episcopus Hierosolymitanus: auxit et Basilius; auxere et alii. Nam Celestinus missæ introitum dedit, Gregorius *Kyrie eleeson, Gloria in excelsis Deo* Telesphorus, collationes Gelasius primus, epistolam et evangelium Hieronymus, * * * thus Leo tertius, osculum pacis Innocentius primus; ut caneretur *Agnus Dei*, Sergius pontifex instituit. De vitis Pontificum, p. 16. Colon. 1540. ED.]

patched together, it was six hundred year? For Gregory was pope six hundred year after Christ was born. Other sorts of reckoning there be, which pope added which part to the mass, and they agree not on the names; but in the number of years there is no great difference: for it was seven hundred year after Christ afore they had perfectly patched it together, and brought it in estimation, as appears by these reckonings. Where is now their one thousand five hundred year they crack so much on? When they have learned to speak the truth, and agree among themselves, they may better blame other that do not. I will not lay all their lies and disagreeings to their charge, for it were too long; but when they have answered these, then they shall have more. In the mean time, these are sufficient to let them see that have eyes, and be not wilfully blind, how vain their bragging lies be, when they crack that their superstition, which they term their religion, is so old, and that the contrary was never heard of unto now a few years past.

There is another subtler sort of papist; and when they see these things to be so foolish, that they have no good groundwork, nor able to be defended, they say, that Christ himself said the first mass: and yet that is as untrue as the rest. For the reasons that I made against the canon of St James (as they call it), the same may more justly be applied for our Saviour Christ. I am sure they will not say that he ate all alone, nor prayed to any saints; nor what kind of mass it was, they are not able to shew, and prove it so to be. I grant, and most true it is, that our Saviour Christ instituted the holy Communion, or the Lord's Supper (as St Paul calls it); but for any thing done by him to prove their mass, I utterly deny. In his last supper he sacrificed not for the quick and the dead, as they do in their mass: but that sacrifice was offered by himself in his own body and blood shed on the cross, on Good Friday, the next day after that he instituted his holy Supper the night afore, and bid them do that in remembrance of him unto his coming again. This is that which we desire all to follow: this is that which condemns their mass: this is that which we would have, all to eat and drink of that bread and cup with the minister, as he did with his apostles, and as St Paul wills the Corinthians to do; and not one priest to stand lifting it over his head to be worshipped, and the people to stand gazing at it, and be content with looking at it: and when they receive, to take both the bread and the cup, and not to rob God's people of the one half of the supper, the blood of our Saviour Christ, which he shed for the lay-people, as well as for priests; and bad them drink it, as well as the priests: for he loved them, and died for them, as well as for the priests. And priests can no more save themselves than they can, but have the same Saviour that they have, and must go to heaven the same way that they do.

And because they crack so proudly of the ancienty of their mass[1], let me see in what ancient writer they read of it or find the word written. I know they would fain have the word to be Hebrew: but if it be so, it rather makes against them than with them. For if it be a sacrifice of the Jews, then it is taken away by our Saviour Christ, and fulfilled by him, as all other sacrifices of Moses be; or else, they be Jews, using those sacrifices which God forbad to use at these days after the coming of Christ. The apostle to the Hebrews says, that "if the priesthood be taken away and translate to another sort, then the law is taken away too:" but the priesthood of Aaron is taken away and all his sacrifices, (or else Christ is come in vain); why, then the law of sacrificing must be taken away too, as the apostle there says. If they consider the nature of the Hebrew word, they would not strive so much about it. They glory much that the name of their mass is *missah* in Hebrew, and should be written, Deut. xvi. and thereof should *missa* come in Latin, or else the Hebrew name to remain still. The word *missah* signifies *a freewill gift*, that a man offers willingly unto the Lord; and not only that which the priests offer of themselves, but also which any other man freely brings to be offered: therefore, if this word or place make for them, it proves that all manner of men may say mass; for every man may willingly bring what he lust to offer; and then priests have spun a fair thread in alleging this against themselves, and proving that every man may say their mass. But the word signifies also a

Mass.

Heb. vii.

[1 In the *Acts and Monuments* of John Foxe, a contemporary of bishop Pilkington, will be found an interesting and valuable treatise on the Origin and Canon of the Mass. See the beginning of Book x. Edit. 1583. and in Vol. III. Edit. 1684. ED.]

lifting up, as some do take it, and therefore they prove their elevation by it. Thus they be driven to hard shifts, that they cannot well tell what to make of it. They are well content with either signification, or both, if they might keep it; for the one bids men bring, and they would gladly take; the other to lift up as a sacrifice, and that maintains their state. Read the place, and then judge the meaning: "Thou shalt keep the holy day of weeks, says Moses (that is, Whit-sunday seven weeks after Easter), and thou shalt bring a gift of thine own free will according to thy power, as the Lord has blessed thee with much or little."

<small>Deut. xvi. [10.]</small>

This free gift is called *missah,* and the people must give it: then, if it make any thing for mass, it makes also that the people should say mass; for they bring every one this gift as they be able. The priests say not mass freely, but for money, and therefore it cannot be called a freewill gift on their part. But because they are delighted with gifts, and will not say mass freely, they rather ground themselves hereon, that they may not only sell, but raise the price of them, and lift it high over their heads. They may speak well of the gospel, if they would, or had any good natures in them. For their mass was never so honoured, nor at so great a price, as the gospellers have made it, at a hundred marks, where they will sell it for a groat; and God forbid that ever it be better cheap! Surely, if it be so good as they report it to be, it is too good cheap yet, and they with selling so good cheap have brought it out of estimation. A good thing cannot be too dear: and surely he that will lie broiling in purgatory for sparing one penny, a groat, or ten shillings for a trental, he has few friends; and if he be able to pay it and will not, I will never be sorry for him, though he lie there still.

There is another Hebrew word called *mass,* that signifies a tribute, which may well be applied to it, (because they be delighted with ancient names, I shall help them,) for it is the greatest tax that ever was laid on the world. All princes, heathen and christened laid together, never took such a tribute of the people, as the pope and his collectors do by mass. For mass princes have given whole countries, noblemen their land, and the people their goods; they have disherited their children, and impoverished themselves, to feed the pope's chaplains and buy masses. Alas, dear pennyworths for so vile a thing! The

Dutch word *messe* helps them well too, which signifies a free mart or fair for all people to resort to with all wares to buy and sell, and with such liberty, that those evil men, which dare not nor may not come near at other times without danger, then may freely go and come without harm after that the market bell be rung, as they use. So is their mass. What ware soever is brought for it, it is welcome, they refuse none: wool, bacon, cheese, freers never refused; and be he never so wicked, it is not denied him; it is a salve for all sores, and heals all wickedness and sorrows, that fall either on man or beast.

They would fain have it ancient, and therefore they seek the old authors, where the word *missa* may be found. They allege Ignatius, Clemens, Dionysius, Sozomenus, &c., where they would make men believe it were read. Indeed, in translating these out of Greek they use the same word; but he that has read his Greek grammar can soon understand, that there is no such word in Greek. Therefore, as the interpreter does foolishly use the word, so foolishly they follow and believe him. The word is Latin, and is used in no Latin writer commonly afore Gregory the first, who lived six hundred year after Christ, save twice or thrice only in Ambrose in his Epistle[1], and yet he lived four hundred year after Christ. Then they have not so great cause to crack of anciety of the thing, nor of the word, seeing neither Hebrew, Greek, nor Latin can be proved to have such a word in such a signification the space of four hundred year after Christ, no, nor then neither; for though Ambrose used the word, yet it signifies far otherways, as Ambrose's order of communion well declares. I will not stand to rehearse the manifold interpretation of the Latin word, and what the meaning of it is, lest ye would laugh: hereafter, if occasion be given by them, I shall more fully entreat of it.

<small>Lib. v. Epistola 33.</small>

One thing I would demand of master proctor; and if his answer be not ready, I am content he ask counsel, so that he answer substantially, that it may abide trial. Good Friday-mass, why does it differ from all the year beside? One of these three must needs follow, either that one mass only is good, and the rest naught; or the rest good, and that naught; or else (as I am sure he will say) both are good. If both be

<small>Good Friday's Mass.</small>

[1] Ego tamen mansi in munere; missam facere cœpi. Class. I. Epist. xx. § 4. ED.]

good, then there may be divers sorts of them: if there may be two divers sorts, and both good, why may there not be a third or a fourth as good? Why then may not the order now appointed in English be good too? On Good Friday there is neither epistle, nor gospel, *gloria in excelsis*, nor creed, *sanctus* nor *agnus*, canon nor privity, crossing, toying nor blowing, nor their words of consecration, pax, nor *Ite, missa est*, not so much as *Dominus vobiscum*, but straight after *confiteor* he leaps post haste over all to the *Paternoster*. Surely, if this be good one day, it may be used oftener: and this agrees best with that that Gregory says, "The apostles consecrated only with the Lord's prayer:" and therefore it seems, that if any of their masses should be good, that this goes next to the best and simplest sort, without all curiosity. If they may do all perfectly this day without their canon, then their canon and privity is not of so great force as they make it to be. For sure, if this be well on this day, it may be well on other days too; for God is no changeling, nor he commands not one sort of communicating his supper to-day and another to-morrow, but always such a one which agrees with his word. Their common answer and solution is known, but it will not serve: they must provide better stuff, or else their doings be foolish.

But to make an end of this great controversy for the ancienty of their mass, ye shall hear it determined by a miracle from heaven. When there were divers sorts of masses, as they be called, used in Latin in divers places, as at Milan, and every where almost generally, there was used St Ambrose's order of communion, which there continues to this day, and Gregory's order was used also in other places; the pope, to determine the matter, would try whether should be allowed through his dominion; for Gregory's was not used at all in France, and it was thought shame that Ambrose's order, being but a bishop, should be preferred to the pope's. Therefore he took either of their mass-books, as they term them, in an evening laid them on the altar, locked the church-doors, and desired God to declare by some miracle, whether book should be used generally of all sorts. In the morning Gregory's book-leaves were found scattered all the church over, and Ambrose's lay still; the doors being fast locked all night, as he says, but wise men may doubt. This miracle master pope, like a wise expounder of dreams, says, that as the leaves were torn and blown abroad all the church over, so should Gregory's book be used throughout the world. For this was done by God, as well as their great god Bel did eat up all the meat that was set afore him all night, as Daniel writes. But that a man may not be wiser than mounser pope, I would interpret this great miracle thus: That God was angry with Gregory's book, and therefore rent it in pieces, and scattered it abroad; and the other, as good, lay sound untouched, and at the least so to be preferred. This was done by pope Adrian the first, more than seven hundred and seventy-seven years after Christ; and thus long their holy mass was in controversy afore it was determined. Then it lacks much of one thousand five hundred, as they untruly and proudly crack. These things are not written by any new men, or heretics, as it pleases them to term them, but by their own catholic fathers, Durandus and Nauclerus[1]. Yea, Polychronicon, lib. vii. chap. 10, writes, that the white observant monks[2] use by their profession St Ambrose's order, and not Gregory's, even at these days: wherefore their mass is not general.

I would they did make an end of lying, that we might make an end of reproving them, and both join together in worshipping the living God only, and believing his holy word afore all other. St Austin, in a like controversy of religion

[1 Concilio igitur iterum congregato, omnium patrum fuit una sententia, quod missale Ambrosianum et Gregorianum super altare sancti Petri apostoli ponerentur, plurimorum episcoporum sigillis munita, et fores ecclesiæ clauderentur, et ipsi tota nocte orationi insisterent, ut Dominus per aliquod signum indicaret, quod horum magis ab ecclesia servari vellet; sicque per omnia factum est. Mane igitur ecclesiam intrantes, utrumque missale super altare apertum invenerunt; vel alii asserunt, Gregorianum penitus dissolutum et huc illucque dispersum invenerunt; Ambrosianum vero solummodo apertum super altare in eodem loco, ubi positum fuerat, invenerunt. Quo signo edocti sunt divinitus, Gregorianum officium per totum mundum dispergi, Ambrosianum vero tantum in sua ecclesia observari debere; et sic usque hodie servatur. Gul. Durandi Rationale Divinorum Officiorum, Lib. v. cap. ii. p. 139-40. Venet. 1609.—Nauclerus's account, after the introductory circumstances, proceeds: Mane facto invenerunt missale Ambrosianum in loco suo clausum, Gregorianum vero apertum et per quaternos dispersum: ex quo statuerunt, &c. Chronica, Generat. xxi. p. 628. Colon. 1579. Ed.]

[2 "That order is named order Cystersiensis in Latin. *** They use Ambrose's office, and have charge of sick men, &c." Polychron. vii. 10. Ed.]

Retract. I.
cap. xv. betwixt him and the Manichees, prays thus: "O great and Almighty God, and God of all goodness, whom we ought to think and believe that thou art inviolable, incorruptible, and immutable! O triple Unity, which all the church does worship, I, having experience of thy mercy toward me, pray thee humbly, that thou wilt not suffer them to differ from me in thy religion and worship of thee, with whom since I was a child I have had a most special agreement in fellowship of men. Amen[1]."
God grant us all this to pray, and diligently endeavour ourselves to seek this unity of religion, in worshipping the living God only as he has taught us in his holy word, and no otherways, for his Son's sake, our Lord and Christ! So be it.

> III. "In England, where the faith of Christ and true religion was planted about the year of our Lord 182, Eleutherius, pope, sending legates to Lucius, then king of England, which converted this realm to the faith, and established true religion in England, which continued 200 years."

As the rest of all their doctrine is founded on the pope, so is this. This is their subtlety, to make men believe that England has ever received the christian faith and religion from Rome; and therefore we must fetch it from thence still: which are both most untrue. If nothing else would, this one saying proves him to be unlearned, that thus says. Gildas[2], England received not the faith first from Rome, but in the Apostles' time. our countryman, in his history says, that Britain received the gospel in the time of Tiberius the emperor, under whom Christ suffered. Does not Tertullian, who lived at the same time of this pope, write in his book against the Jews thus? "The

[1 Deus magne, Deus omnipotens, Deus summæ bonitatis, quem inviolabilem et incorruptibilem credi atque intelligi fas est, Trina Unitas, quam catholica ecclesia colit, supplex oro, expertus in me misericordiam tuam, ne homines, cum quibus mihi a pueritia in omni convictu fuit summa consensio, in tuo cultu a me dissentire permittas. T. I. p. 59. ed. Paris. 1836. ED.]

[2 Interea glaciali frigore rigenti insulæ, et velut longiore terrarum secessu soli visibili non proximæ, verus ille non de firmamento solum temporali, sed de summa etiam cœlorum arce tempora cuncta excedenti, universo orbi præfulgidum sui coruscum ostendens tempore, ut scimus, summo Tiberii Cæsaris, quo absque ullo impedimento ejus propagabatur religio comminata senatu nolente a principe morte dilatoribus militum ejusdem, radios suos primum indulget, id est, sua præcepta, Christus. Rerum Britannicarum Scriptores, p. 116. Fol. Heidelb. 1587. ED].

apostles are declared in David's psalm to be the preachers of Christ. Their sound, he says, went out in all the earth, and their words unto the coasts of the earth. In whom else have all people believed but in Christ, which is now comen? Whom have other people believed? The Parthians, the Medes, the Persians, they that dwell in Mesopotamia, Jury, Cappadocia, Pontus, Asia, Phrygia, Pamphylia, Egypt, and the parts of Libya about Cyrene, the strangers of Rome, the Jews, proselytes, men of Crete and Arabia; and other people, as now the diverse sorts of the Getes, and many coasts of the Morians, all the borders of Spain, divers nations of France, and the places of the Britons, which the Romans could never attain to, now are subject to Christ, and the places of Sarmatia, of the Danes, the Germans, the Scythians, and of many other hid people and provinces, and many isles unknown to us, and which now we cannot reckon. In all which places reigns the name of Christ, which is now comen[3]."

Thus far Tertullian. Mark in how many countries, he says, the name of Christ reigned, it was so commonly and well believed; and how among them he reckons the wildest places of the Britons to be of the number: and these were christened in his time, who lived in the same pope Eleutherius' time. Then it was not pope Eleutherius, that first sent the christian faith hither, but they had received the gospel afore he was born. Does not some chronicles tell, that Joseph of Arimathea came hither and preached here? No doubt, either he or some apostle, or scholar of theirs, had preached Christ

[[3] Cujus et prædicatores apostoli in psalmis David ostenduntur: "In universa," inquit, "terra exiit sonus eorum, et usque ad terminos terræ verba eorum." In quem enim alium universæ gentes crediderunt, nisi in Christo, qui jam venit? Cui enim et aliæ gentes crediderunt? "Parthi, Medi, Elamitæ, et qui inhabitant Mesopotamiam, Armeniam, Phrygiam, Cappadociam, et incolentes Pontum et Asiam, Pamphyliam, immorantes Ægyptum, et regionem Africæ, quæ est trans Cyrenen, inhabitantes Romam et incolæ tunc, et in Hierusalem Judæi," et ceteræ gentes: etiam Getulorum varietates, et Maurorum multi fines, Hispaniarum omnes termini, et Galliarum diversæ nationes, et Britannorum inaccessa Romanis loca, Christo vero subdita, et Sarmatarum, et Dacorum, et Germanorum, et Scytharum et abditarum multarum gentium, et provinciarum et insularum multarum, nobis ignotarum; et quæ enumerare minus possumus: in quibus omnibus locis Christi nomen, qui jam venit, regnat. Adv. Judæos, cap. VII. ED.]

here, and he was received and believed afore this pope was born. Beda writes, that in his time and almost a thousand year after Christ, here in Britain, Easter was kept in the full moon, what day in the week soever it fell on[1], and not on the sunday after, as we do now. Wherefore it appears that these preachers came from the east part of the world, where it was so used, rather than from Rome, which condemned that use. Peradventure, Eleutherius helped to increase it, and send some preachers hither, but that he was the first it cannot be proved: yet would to God they would follow that gospel, religion, laws, and counsel, that Eleutherius gave king Lucius!

Polychronic. lib. v. cap. 17.

But let it be granted them, that Eleutherius established religion in England: will it make any thing for their purpose? Read the pope's epistle to the king, and then judge. There is great controversy what time this king lived, as appears in Fabian's table; and therefore a froward man might doubt, whether any such thing were or not: but I will not deal so precisely with him.

Eleutherius' epistle to king Lucius.

"In the year from Christ's passion one hundred and sixty-nine, the lord Eleutherius, pope, wrote thus to king Lucius, king of Britain, for the correction of the king and his nobles of the realm of Britain: Ye required of us the Roman laws and the emperor's to be sent over to you, the which ye would practise and put in ure within your realm. The Roman laws and the emperor's we may ever reprove, but the law of God we may not. Ye have received of late, through God's mercy, in the realm of Britain, the law and faith of Christ: ye have with you in the realm both the parts of the scriptures: out

[[1] Permansit autem hujusmodi observantia paschalis apud eos tempore non pauco, hoc est, usque ad annum dominicæ incarnationis 716. per annos 150. Bed. Lib. III. cap. IV.—That time was a great question made and moved of the Easter day, that was not that time holden lawfully of Scots and of Britons.***There in that one side came Colmannus the bishop and Hilda the abbess, and alleged for them that their predecessors were worthy men and holy, and held the Easter tide from the 14th day of the moon unto the 20th day of the moon; and specially St John the Evangelist held so the Easter tide in Asia. In the other side against them Egylbertus, &c. alleged, that the manner and the usage of all holy church of Greeks, of Italy, of Rome, of Gallia, and of France should be set tofore the manner, custom, and usage of a corner of the world, that knew not the decrees of synods. Polychron. v. 17. See Bed., Lib. III. cap. xxv. ED.]

of them by God's grace, with the counsel of your realm, take ye a law, and by that law, through God's sufferance, rule your kingdom of Britain. For ye be God's vicar in your kingdom, according to the saying of the psalm, &c. "O God, give thy judgment to the king, and thy righteousness to the king's son." He said not, the judgment and righteousness of the emperor, but thy judgment and justice, that is to say, of God. The king's sons be the christian people and folk of the realm, which be under your government, and live and continue in peace within your kingdom, as the gospel says, "Like as the hen gathers her chickens under her wings, so does the king his people." The people and folk of the realm of Britain be yours, whom, if they be divided, ye ought to gather to concord and peace, to call them to the faith and law of Christ, and to the holy church, to cherish and maintain them, to rule and govern them, and to defend them always from them that would do them wrong, from malicious men and enemies, &c. A king has his name of ruling, and not of having a realm. Thou shalt be a king while thou rulest well: but if thou do not, the name of a king shall not remain with thee, and thou shalt lose it, which God forbid! The Almighty God grant you so to rule the realm of Britain, that ye may reign with him for ever, whose vicar ye be in the realm[2]!"

Rex a regendo, non a regno.

[[2] This letter to king Lucius is quoted, as here translated, in Foxe's *Acts and Monuments*, Vol. I. p. 107. Ed. 1583. This letter is noticed by Usher, Spelman, Stillingfleet, and many others. Collier in his Eccles. Hist. of Great Britain has given a full account of the particulars stated by historians respecting king Lucius. Concerning this letter, of which he gives a translation from Lambert *de Priscis Anglorum Legibus*, he states various objections against its authenticity, concluding thus: "Sir H. Spelman observes, that this letter is not to be met with till a thousand years after Eleutherius' death, and where it was first found, is altogether uncertain. The author of "The customs of London" printed it in the 12th year of Henry VIII.: afterward Lambert inserted it among the laws of Edward the Confessor; but there it is printed in an italic letter, as a mark of its being spurious. Hoveden's manuscripts of about 400 years' standing take no notice of it; and, which is remarkable, his contemporary, Geoffrey of Monmouth, who did not use to suppress or overlook any British antiquities, says nothing about it. And as for the manuscript in Guildhall, London, it seems, at the most, to be no more than 200 years old." Collier's Eccles. Hist. 1708. Book I. Cent. 2. Mosheim observes, "These ancient accounts are exposed to much doubt, and are rejected by the best informed persons." Vol. I. Cent. 2. ED.]

[PILKINGTON.]

Thus far the epistle. Mark, I pray you, what this good pope grants, and whether he be of this peevish proctor's opinion, or of his holy bishops' that he cracks so much on. First, he wills him not to take the Romans' laws to rule his realm by, for they may ever be reproved; but to make laws according to the scripture, which never can justly be gainsaid, and by them to rule. Further, he calls the king "God's vicar" twice in this letter. Thirdly, he says the king ought to call the people to the faith of Christ. How can papists then be disobedient to kings, when they see the pope grant so much to kings? The pope calls the king God's vicar; and our papists deny it, and say the pope is God's vicar. The pope bids rule by the scripture, and refuses his own laws: but our holy bishops say scriptures make heretics, and will be subject to no laws but the Romans'. Lastly, he charges kings to bring the people to the faith: but our spirituality say, kings have nothing ado in ecclesiastical matters nor religion. They stick much on ancienty, and the pope's authority: and yet those godly things which godly ancient popes have said and decreed, they cannot abide, because it takes away their authority and pride.

Platina and Polychronicon[1] write, that this pope decreed that no man should refuse any meat that man eats. If this pope say true, why have we then commanded, upon pain of deadly sin, by papists so many superstitious kinds of fastings and forbearing meats at certain times? If they be not superstitious, because they would bind the conscience with them, and make it sin to break them, let them prove it by the scripture to be godly. If they be catholics that believe and follow the pope, why are we called heretics in believing and teaching that which the pope has written? If they will be called the pope's darlings, why do they deny the pope's writings? If true religion was stablished here by this pope, why then does this scavenger sweep the streets with contrary doctrine to this pope, and with false lies? If they would have us believe and honour the pope, they must first begin themselves. Who will think that he

[[1] Idem etiam statuit, ne quis ob superstitionem cibi genus ullum respueret, quo humana consuetudo vesceretur. Platina De Vitis Pontif. p. 21. After Soter Eleutherius was pope 15 years: he ordained that christian men should not forsake nor forbear no meat that is skilful and reasonable for mankind. Polychron. Lib. IV. ch. 16. ED.]

gives good counsel, and would have men to follow him, which will be the first that will do and teach contrary to his own sayings? These holy bishops of ours honour their pope in suffering for him, that never will thank them, and say, they would have all to do the same: yet they themselves are the first that teach and do contrary to this pope, and many other of the eldest sort, in all such things as please them; and so they will correct him rather than follow the ancientest and best of them.

IV. After that again, this land being inhabited with Saxons, being Painims, Saint Gregory, pope of Rome, about the year of our Lord God, 595, sent Saint Austin and his company, who by their doctrine and virtuous living planted the faith, and so established a true religion in England: the which faith and religion ever when the people have declined from it, they have felt great calamities as well by the hand of God, as by the conquest of the Danes, and after by the Normans; and sith the conquest from time to time.

As I noted afore, they derive all their religion from Rome, to make men believe that place (which is a sink of all sin, and esteemed of none but them that knows it not) to be the fountain of all godliness. But as I declared afore, that they forsake all the ancient goodness in Rome, so shall I by this pope's doings too let the world see, if they will, that in maintaining the pope in words by outward appearance, they utterly deny him in their deeds; and they only pick out of the filthiest of them that which may maintain their superstition, pride, and tyranny. That the Saxons invaded and obtained this realm for the sins of the country, it is too plain; but whether Austin planted true religion, the doctors may doubt, and his deeds will prove. It were too long to write all that Galfridus Britannicus in his history wrote, about the year of our Lord one thousand one hundred and fifty, in the latter end of his eighth book, cap. IV. how the holy learned bishops withstood the teaching of Austin at his coming into the realm, and the pope's authority that sent him; but these few words of his are sufficient to declare their mind. "In the mean while was Austin sent of Gregory," he says, "into Britain to preach the word of God to the Englishmen, which almost had driven out all christian religion of that part of the isle where they dwelt in Kent: but among some of the Britons the faith of Christ did yet flourish;

and there were seven bishops, and an archbishop, and many holy prelates and abbeys remaining, which taught their flock the right order. At Bangor in one church were two thousand one hundred monks, which get their living with their hands: their abbot was called Dinoth. When Austin required of the bishops subjection, Dinoth proved by divers arguments that they ought [owed] him none. Then Ethelbert, king of Kent, perceiving that the Britons disdained to submit themselves to Austin, he stirred up the other Saxons' kings to fight against Dinoth and his clerks. They gathered a great army, and came to West Chester, where Bremael was mayor. The monks and eremites met him there to pray for the safeguard of their people. Eldefridus, king of Northumberland, fought with Bremael, and slew one thousand two hundred monks, and had many of his own men slain. Then the dukes of Britain, hearing of his cruelty, Blederic duke of Cornwall, Margadud duke of South Wales, Caduane duke of North Wales, came and fought with him, and slew ten thousand of his men, and about sixty-six more; and Blederic, that was the grand captain, was slain there[1]." Thus far says he. First mark here, that the christened Britons would not submit themselves to Austin, the pope's legate, as they that had fallen from religion did. Secondly, that so many monks lived not idle, but wrought for their living. Thirdly, note the old practice of papists, to shed blood cruelly, if their superiority be denied them.

Margin note: The best withstood Austin, the pope's legate.

Polychronicon, lib. v. chap. 9, and Fabian, chap. 119, write all this same in effect, and also further, that Austin called a council for stablishing his religion; and when the bishops asked Dinoth whether they should go to it or no, he said they should go, and obey him if he behaved himself lowly, like a disciple of Christ. His lowliness they should try, if he would rise and reverence them when they come into the council. But when Austin gave no reverence to them at their coming, they were angry, and went their ways. Among other things mark also the pride of the Roman legates, that would not as much as make any kind of curtesy to so many bishops coming to the council.

[1 The passage is in Lib. xi. capp. xii. xiii. of Galfredus, p. 85. of Rerum Britannicarum Scriptores Vetustiores, Heidelberg. 1587. The mayor of Chester is there called *Brocinail,* instead of Bremael. Ed.]

Gildas, which writing laments this miserable destruction of Britain by bringing in the Saxons, and complains as much of the decay and neglecting of religion as of wicked living in all sorts of men, from the highest to the lowest, to be the cause of this plague of God, and overthrow of the realm; he sharply rebukes the kings, but priests and bishops rather more than any other sort of men: so that it seems to be a double plague, both in bringing strangers to rule, and strange religion to blind us withal. And because they crack so much of the religion that Austin brought in, ye shall see what he used. There be eleven questions written in the latter end of Gregory's works in Latin, which Austin, being in England, desired Gregory, pope of Rome, to write him his mind and opinion in them. The third question is this, which Polychronicon also touches, lib. v. ch. 9: "Why, seeing there is but one faith, there be divers customs of masses in the churches; and one custom is in France, and another in Rome?" To this Gregory answers, that Austin "should pick out of the Romish church, or the French church, or any other, the best, and use them in England[2]." Mark here, I pray you, the beginning and ancienty of their mass here in England, and the patching it together, and beggarly picking it out of all countries; and also, that the pope did not condemn those divers kinds of masses, as our butchers have, and burned them that gainsaid it; and then ask my masters, that so shamefully lie and proudly crack their mass to be one thousand five hundred year old, whether these sayings be truly alleged or no.

[2 To the second that is asked, "While the faith is all one, why be there so many divers usages in churches?"—hereto it is answered in this manner: "What thou knowest is most pleasing to God Almighty, gather thou together, and make that to be used in churches of England. Things be not loved for the place, but the places be loved for good things." Polychron. v. 9. Fo. CLXXXIV. col. 4.—The whole of Gregory's answer on this point is as follows: Novit fraternitas tua Romanæ ecclesiæ consuetudinem, in qua se meminit nutritam. Sed mihi placet, ut sive in Romana, sive in Gallicana, seu in qualibet ecclesia aliquid invenisti, quod plus omnipotenti Deo possit placere, sollicite eligas; et in Anglorum ecclesiam, quæ adhuc in fide nova est, institutione præcipua quæ de multis ecclesiis colligere potuisti, infundas. Non enim pro locis res, sed pro bonis rebus loca amanda sunt. Ex singulis ergo quibusque ecclesiis quæ pia, quæ religiosa, quæ recta sunt, elige; et hæc quasi in fasciculum collecta apud Anglorum mentes in consuetudinem depone. Gregor. Op. Tom. II. p. 1191. Basil. 1574. ED.]

But believe neither me nor them; look your book of Gregory, and judge yourself who lies.

<small>Austin's christening.</small> Fabian also writes, chap. 119 and 130, that this Austin christened the people in the river called Swale, in Swaldale, not far from York; and that Paulinus, instead of fonts, at the same time (who was one of those whom Gregory sent from Rome hither to preach here) baptized many also both in the same river and in another called Gweni, in Gwensedale, in Yorkshire too[1]. Was it lawful then to christen without hallowing of fonts, yea, without fonts, without crossing, blowing, censing, salting, spitting, oil and cream, &c., and now is not? Who has made it unlawful since? Are we heretics in doing it without conjured water, as Austin did, whom they so much commend? Nay, we do it not, nor wish it to be done, in the river, as they did, but in the church. Are they worthy to be called papists, and glory so much in it, which will not follow the pope's legate, nor allow his doings, and dispraise them that do as he did? I speak not this because I would be called a papist, or make the pope my schoolmaster; but that we would not untruly be called forsakers of true religion and ancient customs of the church, when we have the old popes and ancient Romish church to teach and allow that which we do.

And because this scavenger cracks so much of his holy bishops, that suffer so great pains for disobeying their prince, and cleaving to their holy father the pope, they that be not wilfully blind shall see here, that there is none more enemy to that usurped power of the pope, claiming to be above other bishops and princes, nor to that blasphemous name, to be called the universal bishop of the whole church, than this Gregory was, as fully appears in sundry places of his works. In his time began this ambitious desire to creep into the mind of John, archbishop of Constantinople, to be called the head bishop of the world, because Maurice, then emperor, and head above many princes, lay then at Constantinople, and not at Rome, as his ancestors

[1] When he had in one day christened ten thousand of Saxons or Angles in the west river, that is called Swale, before York, &c. Fabian, Chron. Cap. cxix. p. 115. Lond. 1559. From that time forward, by the term of six years, during the life of king Edwin, Paulinus christened continually in both provinces of Deyra and in Brennicia, in the rivers of Gweny and Swala, which he used for his fonts. Ib. Cap. cxxx. ED.]

did for the most part. While the emperor lay at Rome, the bishop there was more reverenced than other bishops were, as it is in all commonwealths, wheresoever the prince lies: therefore he thought that, like as when the emperor lay at Rome, the bishop was preferred above other (because commonly princes will have the learneder sort near them), so he thought that the emperor now lying at Constantinople, that that bishop should likewise be esteemed; and therefore he caused the emperor to write to Gregory, bishop of Rome, in this behalf, and that he should submit himself to the bishop of Constantinople. Gregory answers divers of the emperor's letters sharply, godlily, wisely, and learnedly, saying, that neither he at Rome, nor the other at Constantinople, nor no other in any place, should challenge to him that proud name nor authority above other. "None of my predecessors," says Gregory, "would use this cursed name (to be called the universal bishop of all); for if one patriarch should be called universal, then the name of patriarchs should be taken from other: but God keep this far from a christian mind, that any man should challenge that to himself, whereby he might any thing at all diminish the honour of his brether." Note, that he says none of his predecessors used this cursed name. Then in his time it began to be desired: then also they lie, saying that Christ gave this authority of being above other to Peter and his successors from time to time. He calls it also a wicked and cursed name, wherein they glory, and so much desire: wicked and cursed therefore is he that has it or desires it. He says further, they do their brother wrong in taking that honour from them that is due to them, which is, to be of like power and authority with them. If any man now a days should write thus, he would be called a railer, a fool, a prater, &c. but seeing this good pope says so to them, let them take it among them, and believe their pope; for it is true. Again he says: "I say boldly, that whosoever calls himself, or desires to be called, the universal priest, in his pride he runs afore antichrist; because in being proud he prefers himself above other[2]." This is their parts then that they play,

Neither pope nor other ought to be called the universal nor head bishop of all.
Lib. iv. Epis. 8.

Lib. vi. Epis. 30, cap. 194.

[2 Ego autem fidenter dico, quia quisquis se universalem sacerdotem vocat, vel vocari desiderat, in elatione sua antichristum præcurrit, quia superbiendo se ceteris præponit. Greg. Epist. Lib. vi. Epist. xxx. p. 888. Basil. 1564. ED.]

to be antichrist's forerunners, or rather to be antichrist himself. Much good do it them with their popes, that so reward their followers: and, seeing their master gives them that name, they may be glad of it, and neither refuse it, nor be angry with them that so call them.

It were an easy thing to take many such like sayings out of other doctors; but because he cries out so oft of this holy father's religion, I keep me within his compass, and allege his writings only. Gregory in his epistle to Maurice the emperor, among many other words, says thus: "Who is this that against the ordinance of the gospel, and against the decrees of the canons, presumes to take this new name? Let this blasphemous name be far from christian men's hearts, to be called the universal bishop, by which the honour of all priests is taken away, when it is foolishly claimed of one man. This name was offered in the synod of Chalcedon to the Romish bishop, but none of them did take this name of singularity, nor did agree to use it; lest, while any private thing should be given to one man, all priests should be robbed of their due honour. He is to be bridled, which does wrong to the universal church, which by this private name sets himself above the honour of your empire, &c.[1]"

Lib. iv. Epis. 76.

Thus much Gregory. I marvel that the later popes scraped not these sayings out of Gregory's works, or else condemned not his books for heresy, seeing he does so plainly condemn their proud prelacy. But surely, as God has preserved the true text of the bible by the Jews, that are his enemies, to the comfort of his people; so for the glory of his name he has saved the writings of good popes, to condemn the foolishness of the

[[1] Quis est iste qui contra statuta evangelica, contra canonum decreta, novum sibi usurpare nomen præsumit? * * * Sed absit a cordibus christianorum nomen istud blasphemiæ, in quo omnium sacerdotum honor adimitur, dum ab uno sibi dementer arrogatur. Certe pro beati Petri, apostolorum principis, honore per venerandam Chalcedonensem synodum Romano pontifici oblatum est. Sed nullus eorum unquam hoc singularitatis vocabulum assumpsit, nec uti consensit, ne dum privatum aliquid daretur uni, honore debito sacerdotes privarentur universi. * * * Ille coercendus est, qui sanctæ universali ecclesiæ injuriam facit, qui corde tumet, qui gaudere de nomine singularitatis appetit, qui honori quoque imperii vestri se per privatum vocabulum superponit. Ibid. Lib. iv. Epist. xxxii. Tom. ii. p. 793. Basil. 1564. Ed.]

late presumptuous tyranny of popes after their times. Remember that he calls it a blasphemous name, and that it is against the gospel and canons, that it was never used, and is a wrong to all the rest. Thus many years it was, six hundred and five, afore the pope had any supremacy granted him; but straight after his death, when Phocas had murdered the emperor Maurice his master, and made himself emperor, pope Boniface the third and fourth obtained at his hand, that Rome and the bishop there should be the head of other churches and bishops. A meet man to set up a bishop like himself! the one murdered his master, and the other kills souls. When they have answered this pope, that denies any of his predecessors to have had this name and authority, then they may crack that they have had it one thousand five hundred since St Peter's time.

And where he says in the latter end, that when the people fell from this religion that Gregory send and Austin brought in, they felt great calamities by the conquest of the Danes and the Normans; if he had advised himself well, he would not have said thus. But as Caiphas prophesied truly, saying, that "it was necessary that one man Christ should die for the people, and not all perish," not understanding what he said; so this unlearned proctor has spoken more truly than he wots of. For God indeed plagued this realm for falling from true religion taught in his holy word, rather than by Austin, and submitting themselves to the pope, who, as ye heard, refused that name and authority. The conquest of the Danes was not long nor great, but then followed the Normans, five hundred year since save five. And if ye mark, even about that time was Hildebrand, commonly called Gregory the seventh, pope, who with his fellows brought more wicked superstition into the church of God than ever was afore. Afore his time there was no swarm of idle monks and friars in England, nor in the world, but they wrought for their living; no such gadding of pilgrimages, selling of masses, &c. And therefore God justly plagued the world for falling from him, and defiling themselves so filthily with the dregs of popery. I speak not this because I think all was well afore, or that all the doings of Gregory and Austin were perfect, but to let you see that our papists leave the best, and pick out the worst to follow, as meetest for their purpose.

V. Now, whether the people of this realm be declined from the steps of St Austin, and other blessed fathers and saints, which had mass and seven sacraments in the church, and God was honoured night and day in the church with divine service, I think there is no man so simple but he may easily perceive, except malice have blinded his heart. As in St Paul's church in London, by the decrees of blessed fathers, every night at midnight they had matins, all the forenoon masses in the church, with other divine service and continual prayer, and in the steeple anthems and prayers were had certain times.

That the people of this realm be swerved from the steps of Austin, I will not greatly stick with him to grant: but how? Not in falling from any goodness that he used (for that they either keep still, or the better instead of it), but in refusing such abuses as he first began, and since his time the church of God has been overloaden by the pope's oppression withal. And because he says, that we swerve from Austin and other blessed fathers and saints, which had mass and seven sacraments; who those fathers and saints be, I would he had named them, that it might be seen how truly he says. I think he durst not, nor yet can, lest he be taken with a loud lie. I think he means that Austin which is called the apostle of England, and not that other Austin, which is taken for one of the four doctors of the church. There is great difference betwixt them two, both in anciety of time, in learning and godliness. The English Austin lived here six hundred year after Christ, the other in Afric four hundred: and that the elder Austin and blessed fathers afore him agree better with our reformed religion than with their popery, I boldly affirm; and if he or his partakers have or can say any thing to the contrary, they should prove it better than they have done hitherto, or else the world may judge, that they more proudly brag (as Golias did God's people) than can truly prove it. But as David with his sling and stone overcame that mighty giant, so I doubt not but they shall find many, that with the simplicity of God's truth shall be able to confound their wicked subtlety.

1 Sam. xvii.

I am sure, he means chiefly the doctrine of the sacrament of Christ's body and blood: but in that he is already overmatched. I remember, in the time of that blessed king, Edward the sixth, Doctor Ridley, late bishop of London, came in visitation to Cambridge; and because that doctrine of the sacrament seemed strange then to many, he propounded this proposition to the whole university to dispute on: That it could not be proved by any ancient writer, Greek or Latin, which lived a thousand year since, or within five hundred year after Christ, that the substance of the bread was changed in the sacrament to the substance of Christ's body[1]. There was the eldest and stoutest champions of the whole university, and the pertest lusty young princocks[2] also that could be picked out, to say what they could two or three days together: and one while they had liberty to speak what they could in defence of it, and another while to speak against them that withstood it with what reasons or authorities they could devise. But the pithy solutions of that godly learned bishop were so strong then, that, unto the world changed, his enemies praised him, and wondered at his learning, and liked the doctrine so well, that their lusty younker would have turned bishop Cranmer's book into Latin, yea, and married too (as was needful), if the good king had lived awhile longer. If this be true in the chiefest point of their religion (as it is most true indeed), that they have not one ancient writer without wresting to seem to make for them, it is much more true in the rest. There is another conference of late betwixt the reverend bishop of Sarum[3] and Doctor Cole, wherein that learned father lays to their charge, that for the rest of their trash (which they reverence as holy relics) they have neither scripture, ancient writer, doctor, nor general council, to defend their doings. The writings of good Cranmer and these learned bishops are in print, and yet unconfuted and in strength, although one attempted with small praise of late to defend Doctor Cole's part; but if they could have gainstand it, no man doubts of their good will. They need not to fear their recognizance, fire nor fagot, nor any punishment according as they deserve; their bloody laws are laid on sleep, though their hearts be bloody still.

And because he but only names particularly mass and

[[1] See Foxe, *Acts and Monuments*, Vol. II. p. 1378. ed. 1583. for a full account of this disputation. Ridley's Determinations are given p. 1387. See also Ridley's Works, Parker Society, p. 171. ED.]

[[2] Princocks: pert forward youths. Perhaps from the Latin *præcox*. ED.]

[[3] Bishop Jewell, whose challenge given in his sermon at Paul's Cross led to a correspondence with Dr Cole. These letters were printed A.D. 1560, and are reprinted in bishop Jewell's works. ED.]

seven sacraments, and proves it not to be so, I will not use many ways in disproving it; for he is not a man of that authority, learning, nor credit, that because he says it is so, therefore straight it must be so, and be believed: for I may say it is not so with as good reason as he, if saying without proof were sufficient. For their mass I said enough afore, and proved of what ancienty it was. I declared afore[1], how Gregory's mass-book was allowed seven hundred and seventy-seven years after Christ; and also how Austin, by Gregory's commandment, out of such diverse orders of massing as ye see in other countries, patched their order of mass together that they used here in England. Seeing then by their own doctors' confession it is manifest to be so many years after Christ, afore their mass took place here or elsewhere, I may boldly say, that never one holy father, afore Gregory, knew nor allowed any such kind of massing: for then was no such thing made nor used. These, unto they be answered, are sufficient.

For their seven sacraments I will not say much at this time, because he stands not any thing in the proof of them. The question is meeter for the learned sort than the people, to try out such narrow points. The controversy is more about the word and name, than the thing itself and use of it. We use six of them that he calls sacraments as well as they, though not without great reason we forbear to call them all sacraments; and differ much in the doctrine, the order and using of them, with other ceremonies and language than they do. Baptism, the Lord's supper, confirmation of children, marriage, ordering of ministers, we use them all as well as they, though not in the same sort that they, and teach the people to have them in reverence better than they. Confession is left free to all that feel themselves burdened in conscience, and want either counsel or comfort, and the weak and ignorant are moved to resort to a learned minister to receive the comfortable promises of absolution and forgiveness of sin by the lively word of God, applied to so troubled a mind as a sovereign salve for all such griefs.

The only controversy in number then betwixt us is for extreme unction, whether that be so necessary to be observed continually in the church. The chief reason whereon they ground it, is the saying of St James, "If any be sick, let him

James v.

[1 See pp. 508 and 517. ED.]

call the elders of the congregation, and let them pray for him, anointing him with oil in the name of the Lord, &c." The other place of St Mark, where the apostles used oil in healing the sick, though they allege it, it proves not their purpose, even as their own doctors teach. Then was a time of miracles, and God gave that power of healing diseases to confirm his gospel withal: now it is not lawful to look for such miracles. If they weigh the words of St James well, they will not so much glory in that their sacrament. St James bids them "anoint him with oil." I ask them, with what oil? I mean not, whether with oil-olive, or lamp-oil, or other kind of oil (although that question cannot be answered out of the text of the scripture, and yet, according to the general rule, I grant that where oil alone is named, there is meant oil-olive), but whether it be hallowed and consecrate oil, or common and unhallowed? I trust, they will not say unhallowed; for then their holy sacrament should stand on an unhallowed thing, which is a great inconvenience: then, if it must be consecrated, I ask with what words, and after what sort must it be done? There is no words of consecration for the oil in St James, nor in any place of the scripture. If there be, let them shew them: but their own doctors say that there is none. Then it must be hallowed with words of their own devising: why, then follows it consequently, that man is better than God; which is blasphemy to grant. It is a greater might and power to make a holy thing than to make the unholy and bare thing itself, as the baker makes the bread, but Christ's holy ordinance sanctifies the bread in his holy supper; but in this their sacrament, God should make the oil, and the bishop should make it holy. And because they stick so stiffly, that all consecrations stand in speaking certain words, I ask what those words be, where they be taught in the scriptures, and whether man have power of his own head to make a thing holier than God has done, and to devise the words himself also, wherewith it shall be consecrated and made so holy? The scripture has no such words; and that man should devise those holy words, is great absurdity. When these are answered, more may be replied against them.

Mark vi.

Whether extreme unction be a sacrament or no.

Again, I demand what scripture they have to prove that bishops only must hallow this oil; for those that be sacraments indeed, as baptism and the Lord's supper, every priest has authority to use, minister, and consecrate them according to their holy institution, and do all that belongs thereto, as well as the bishop. Is this their sacrament of an oiling more holy than the other, because bishops, as more holy men, are put to the doing and consecrating of the oil? Yet one doubt more. They have two sorts of oil to anoint withal, differing in holiness, consecration, and use of them, and yet both hallowed by the bishop. One is of oil and balsam blend together, which is called commonly oil and cream, wherewith bishops and priests in their consecrating, and children are anointed in christening: and that is more holy than this for sick persons is, for this is oil alone without other things blend thereto, as their master teaches[1]. What scripture is there for these toys, and the consecrating of them? St Paul says, that our meat "is sanctified by the word and prayer:" but I trust they will grant a better consecration than this, and more holiness in that oil than in our daily meat. But how will they prove it? Further, every sacrament has a promise annexed of God working some spiritual grace by them in the receiver: here is none such, but St James says, "the faithful prayer shall heal the sick man." The promise here named is corporal, bodily health, and is attributed to prayer, and not to their sacrament. Then, as the promise is corporal, so was this oil a corporal medicine and salve for diseased bodies; although I doubt not but then by such godly prayers and exhortations God wrought a spiritual grace inwardly.

Mag. sententiar. lib. 4. dist. 23.

Nothing was more commonly used for weak and weary bodies than oil in all those countries, and nothing does more ease the pains of the sick body than these suppling oils: therefore, partly for the custom of the country, partly for the wholesome strength and medicinable nature of oil, and partly for an outward sign of an inward grace wrought by God (while that gift of healing diseases did continue in Christ's church), St James bids them "call the elders, anoint him with oil in the name of the Lord, and the faithful prayer shall heal the sick person;" but what does that belong, or how is it to be applied, to our days, where no such gift is? I would fain make an end of

[1 Nec tamen omne oleum ad unctionem sanctificatum chrisma vocatur, sed illud solum quod miscetur cum balsamo, &c. Magister Sententiarum, Lib. IV. Dist. xxiii. cap. 1. ED.]

their foolishness, if it had any end. Their own doctors teach ^{Joan. Duns Scotus,} further, that this anointing takes not away mortal sin, but venial ^{Senten. iv. dist. 23.} only, and that it must not be used as long as there is hope of life in the sick person[2]: then by their own doctrine it is not so holy a sacrament, nor a sacrament at all. Their opinion holds, that sacraments do both give grace and forgive sin, and should be given only to them that have use of reason to repent for their sins, and call on God for his mercy, being not children, but come to full age. This does not so, nor is so used by their own doctrine; and therefore no sacrament. The pope's holy water is as good, or better, as this their sacrament, by this doctrine: for he says that his conjured water can forgive venial sin, and drive away devils too. Then, after their own teaching, this their sacrament is not so good as the pope's holy water; for it can drive away devils, beside forgiving venial sin, which this oiling cannot. But thus to teach is to blaspheme God, in making God's sacraments worse than the pope's dregs.

To conclude the authority and ancienty of this their sacrament, from whence it comes, and what it is, Polychronicon teaches, lib. v. chap. 5, that pope Felix IV. grandsire to pope Gregory's father, (mark, whether he was married or no,) ordained the sick to be anointed with oil[3]. If ye look for greater authors, Volaterran teaches the same[4]; but I had rather prove it by their own doctors, because they call other new fellows. Then Christ taught it not.

Further, where he charges us with declining from the steps of blessed fathers, which ordained in Paul's matins to be had at midnight, all forenoon masses, and in the steeple anthems; these things we do not only not deny, for we do not count such

[2 Non intelligit de mortalibus (Jac. v.) quia hæc non remittuntur nisi in baptismo vel pœnitentia: ergo de venialibus. Jo. Duns, Sent. IV. Dist. xxiii. Concl. i.—Ideo non debet conferri sano, nec qualitercunque exposito periculo mortis, * * nec qualitercunque infirmo, sed periculose, ita quod probabiliter immineat sibi exitus de statu viatoris ad terminum. Concl. ii. Tom. II. p. 114. Venet. 1598. ED.]

[3 After John the fourth, Felix was pope four years. He was St Gregory's father's grandsire. He ordained that sick men should be anointed with holy oil, or they passed out of this life: and cursed patriarch of Constantinople. ED.]

[4 Quodque morientes ungerentur instituit. Comm. Urban. Anthropolog. an. 533. Lib. xxII. p. 790. Ed. 1603. ED.]

superstitious idolaters to be our fathers in religion, but we rejoice and praise God for our deliverance from such superstition. They crack much of blessed fathers, and yet name not who they be; but much it shall not skill, for their deeds will prove their holiness. What great holiness was this, to have matins at midnight, when folk were on sleep in their beds? Is not common prayer to be had at such hours, when the people might resort commonly unto it conveniently? if midnight be such a time most convenient, let the world judge. I grant, in the primitive church God's people had their prayers early afore day, because at other times they were not suffered; but in those assemblies were not only monks or priests, but all sorts and degrees of men were gathered to pray, hear sermons, and receive the sacraments: for at other times of the day they durst not for the greatness of persecution. In Paul's and abbeys at their midnight prayers were none commonly, but a few bawling priests, young quiristers and novices, which understood not what they said; the elder sort kept their beds, or were worse occupied. A prayer not understand in the heart, but spoken with the lips, is rather to be counted prating and bawling, than praying with good devotion. The elder sort, both in cathedral churches and abbeys, almost never came at their midnight prayer: it was thought enough to knoll the bells, and make men believe that they rose to pray: therefore they have not so much to crack of this their doing. The papists have a rule of their own making, to say their matins in, which I think was a great cause of these early matins, and also of saying them over night: *Ante tempus meritum, in tempore debitum, post tempus peccatum.* "To say matins afore the time due is a merit, to say them in due time it is duty, but after the appointed time is sin." But as all their religion is of their own devising, so is their reward: God has made them no such promise, and therefore they can claim nothing at his hands.

For their continual massing afore noon, we praise God that has delivered us from it, as a thing contrary to his holy will and ordinance. St Paul says, that "when they came together to eat the Lord's supper, they should tarry one for another;" but these shorn, shaveling, shameless priests would neither receive together one of them with another, nor yet let the people have any part with them. Every one would creep into a corner to an altar alone, there lift up on high, eat and drink up all alone, sell good pennyworths, and bless them with the empty chalice. Then all was well, as they thought, and God well served; but to break God's commandment of receiving together, they passed not of it, so that they might follow their own device.

I know their shift in writhing this text to their purpose, and saying, that St Paul spake this of that feast which they used then to have, when they received the communion: but that wresting will not serve; for both for that feast, and all other kind of eating to fill their belly, St Paul gave that commandment that follows, "If any man be an hungered, let him eat at home: have ye not houses to eat and drink in? or do ye despise the congregation of God?" Seeing that Paul speaks there but of two sorts of eating, the one for hunger to fill their bellies, the other feeding the soul with the spiritual food of Christ's body and blood; for nourishing and feeding our weak bodies he bids us "eat at home," but for the lively food of our souls, in the sacrament of his body and blood, he bids us "tarry one for another;" for it is the seal and band of brotherly love, as well as the sacrament of Christ's body and blood. [1 Cor. xi.]

Every pillar in the church commonly had his altar, every altar his priest, and his god, to whom the altars were dedicate: thus, like men not regarding God's commandment, they followed their own devices; and yet having the truth revealed, they harden their hearts, and stop their ears, that they will not learn.

For climbing up to the top of the steeple to sing their anthems, I demand of them to shew a reason, if there be any, why it is done there, rather than on the ground? and why on such saint days rather than on other? and why that time of the year rather than other? When Baal's priests were assembled against the prophet Elias, to try whether of them served the living God, and Baal's priests began to pray, and call on their God, but he would not hear them, Elias said, "Cry louder: peradventure your god is busy, he is chasing his enemies, from home, or on sleep:" so, unto ye find a better answer, I am content freely to lend you this, without paying any penny for it, that ye may frankly say, ye go up to the top of the steeple to call on your god, that he may the more easily *[Anthems in the steeple.]*

[PILKINGTON.]

hear you, standing so high, rather than on the ground so far off, and at night when other suitors take their rest: for all the day long peradventure he has been otherways occupied; and now waxing old, his hearing decays so much, that if ye stand not near hand and cry loud, he cannot help you. These and such other are meet for them that serve strange gods: but he that calls on the living Lord knows him to be present in all places, and therefore makes no such difference of them. Again, if according to their own doctrine a prayer made in a hallowed place be better than that which is made in an unhallowed, then better it is to stand on the ground than to climb on height; for the top of the steeple was never hallowed, as the church was beneath. When such foolishness is wisely proved, we shall straightways believe it.

VI. First search, whether the faith and religion now used was taught with the blessed fathers in Christ's church in times past. Ye shall prove by no record of authority or chronicle, that this manner of service now used in the church was ever heard tell of afore Luther's time, which is not forty year ago: therefore it is to be rejected and put away, as a new-fangled doctrine and schismatical: therefore come back again into the old blessed fathers' steps.

In that he denies this faith and religion ever to be heard tell of unto within these forty years, and bids try the records whether it be true that he says, and seems to charge us with forsaking the old faith and fathers, alleging the epistle to the Hebrews, that "he that comes to God must believe," and that "without faith it is not possible to please God;" and Jeremy, that we should "search out the old way, and walk in it;" I am well content to stand with him in these points, and prove that this faith and religion was taught in Christ's church continually from the beginning, and that this service now used goes nearer the order appointed in the scripture, than any that ever they have received from the pope. If we had not this faith spoken of to the Hebrews, we durst not so boldly come to the throne of grace, without making any more mediators than one only, Jesus Christ: whereas they, in making so many means and intercessors for them, (as though God were a cruel judge, and not a merciful Father,) declare themselves to want this faith, in that they dare not so boldly come to the

Heb. xi.

Jer. vi.

throne of grace, without such spokesmen as we use none; for faith only makes us bold to come into God's presence, and beg of his grace. But according to their desire, let us "search out the old way" which is good, that we may walk in it.

The faith of a christian man is generally contained in the creed, and particularly declared in the scripture at large; and whether we keep that better than they, let wise men judge. We do esteem these articles of the christian faith so much, with the Lord's prayer, and the ten commandments of Almighty God, that by common order it is appointed, and good ministers practise it, that children shall learn them, not in a tongue that they understand not, as the pope would have them, but in their mother tongue, with such a short declaration on it by a catechism, that now a young child of a ten year old can tell more of his duty toward God and man, than an old man of their bringing up can do of sixty or eighty year old. All the canonical scriptures we do so reverently receive, and faithfully believe, that we stand in contention with the papists, that nothing is to be believed as necessary to salvation, but only the old testament and the new: where their faith is never certain; but when it pleases the pope or his council to make them a new article of their faith, or condemn or change any that they have, they receive it willingly, believe it faithfully, and follow it earnestly with fire and fagot. It is not long since that by common authority, where our creed has but twelve articles, they added six more articles, and with no less danger of withstanding them, than of life[1]. This six-stringed whip did vex God's people sore, unto God of his undeserved mercy provided a remedy.

And where they think no faith nor religion to be good, allowed or received, but that which is confirmed by general councils or written by the doctors; for that I say, their religious superstition cannot be proved by general council, nor doctor, as the reverend bishop of Sarum lays against doctor Cole: but so far as either general council or the doctors' writings do agree with the body of the holy scriptures, we do not only reverently and willingly receive them, but diligently, so far forth as we may, practise them. They crack much of the autho-

Councils.

[1 The bill of the six articles, passed in 1539, upholding by the penalty of death some of the most obnoxious dogmas of popery. ED.]

rity of a general council, and blear the people's eyes with so glorious a name, and also with the reverend name of the fathers, doctors, and ancienty, where indeed they make more for us than them.

If they considered what Gerson and Panormitanus[1] write, which were ancient fathers, and not new protestants, and were at the council of Basil, where it was disputed what authority a council has, they would not so stiffly stick to so weak a staff: "We must rather believe one simple layman," say they, "alleging the scripture, than the whole council to the contrary." *De Elect. ca. Significasti.* This thing was well proved true in the great Nicene council, where many would have forbidden priests' marriage, and only Paphnutius, being unmarried, and alleging the scriptures which allow marriage in all men, did stop it.[2] Gregory Nazianzene says, that he "never see good end of a council."[3]

[[1] The following appears to be the passage of Panormitanus: Nam in concernentibus fidem etiam dictum unius privati esset præferendum dicto papæ, si ille moveretur melioribus rationibus novi et veteris testamenti quam papa. Panormitan. Prima super primo Decretalium, T. I. p. 122. col. 1. 1534. The following is from Gerson, De Examinatione Doctrinarum, Pars I. Consideratio quinta: Jungatur huic considerationi cum sua declaratione duplex veritas. Prima, staret quod aliquis simplex non auctorisatus; esset tam excellenter in sacris litteris eruditus, quod plus esset credendum in casu doctrinali suæ assertioni quam papæ declarationi; constat enim plus esse credendum evangelio quam papæ: si doceat igitur talis eruditus veritatem aliquam in evangelio contineri, ubi et papa nesciret vel ultro erraret, patet cujus præferendum sit judicium. Altera veritas, talis eruditus deberet, in casu si et dum celebraretur generale concilium cui et ipse præsens esset, illi se opponere, si sentiret majorem partem ad oppositum evangelii malitia vel ignorantia declinare: exemplum beatissimus dedit Hilarius. Gersoni Opera, Tom. I. p. 11. Edit. Antverp. 1706. Ed.]

[[2] Ἐν δὲ τῷ περὶ τούτου βουλεύεσθαι, τοῖς μὲν ἄλλοις ἐδόκει νόμους ἐπεισάγειν, ἐπισκόπους καὶ πρεσβυτέρους διακόνους τε καὶ ὑποδιακόνους μὴ συγκαθεύδειν ταῖς γαμεταῖς, ἃς πρὶν ἱερᾶσθαι ἠγάγοντο. ἀναστὰς δὲ Παφνούτιος ὁ ὁμολογητὴς ἀντεῖπε· τίμιον δὲ τὸν γάμον ἀποκαλῶν, σωφροσύνην δὲ τὴν πρὸς τὰς ἰδίας γυναῖκας συνουσίαν, συνεβούλευσε τῇ συνόδῳ μὴ τοιοῦτον θέσθαι νόμον· χαλεπὸν γὰρ εἶναι τὸ πρᾶγμα φέρειν· ἴσως δὲ καὶ αὐτοῖς καὶ ταῖς τούτων γαμεταῖς τοῦ μὴ σωφρονεῖν αἰτία γενήσεται. * * * ἐπῄνεσε δὲ καὶ ἡ σύνοδος τὴν βουλήν, καὶ περὶ τούτου οὐδὲν ἐνομοθέτησεν. Sozomen. Eccles. Hist. Lib. I. cap. 23. Ed.]

[[3] Ἔχω μὲν οὕτως, εἰ δεῖ τἀληθὲς γράφειν, ὥστε πάντα σύλλογον

They allege much general councils, when indeed very few of them be general: if it be but a provincial council, they themselves grant that it may err. Now then look how many may be called, or are called, general in their own books, and ye shall find very few. Take heed therefore of these foxes, ye that will not be deceived, when they allege a council, and try even by their own book of councils, whether it be general or no. Ye shall find that every tenth that they allege is not general: then, being a particular and provincial, they give us leave to deny it; and so they condemn their own doing, when they allege nothing but provincial councils. There is no creed made at any general councils, nor Athanasius' creed, but we willingly embrace it, receive it, and believe it. Seeing then we openly profess and teach all things contained in the holy scriptures, and all the articles of any creed determined in general council, or written by Athanasius, or any catholic father, how can it be that we be out of the faith? and how can it be, but this slanderous proctor of the pope has blasphemed God, belied his ministers, God's people and his truth? Thus much I have spoken particularly to purge us from his lying lips, where he speaks generally, naming nothing, but meaning all, that we should forsake both faith and religion, and devise a new one of our own; where they themselves are guilty in this, as more plainly shall appear.

This shall be sufficient, I trust, to them that will be satisfied, to declare that we be not out of the faith, seeing we profess our faith. Now to try whether we be fallen from the old ways of holy fathers, and whether ancient records do testify this manner of church service to be godly, and have been heard tell of afore Luther's time, and whether it be elder than theirs, I am content to join with him in trial thereof. I trust they will be content to call Moses, David, and the prophets ancient fathers: why then, look what order of prayer was in the tabernacle of God, and Salomon's temple in their time, and see whether it go nearer our service, or the pope's portus? Read David's psalm, and mark how many of them have their title directed to the chanter, or chief singer and player on the instruments, to Asaph, Heman, Dithum, &c., to be sung in the temple, and *Our church service agrees with the ancient church.*

φεύγειν ἐπισκόπων, ὅτι μηδεμιᾶς συνόδου τέλος εἶδον χρηστὸν, μηδὲ λύσιν κακῶν μᾶλλον ἐσχηκυίας ἢ προσθήκην. Epist. LV. (XLII.) Tom. I. p. 814. Paris. 1630. Ed.]

ye shall find a great sort such. Read the twenty-fifth chapter of the first book of the Chronicles, and there it appears whom David appoints to be singers of the psalms in the temple with their posterity. Read the thirteenth chapter of the Acts of the Apostles, and there it appears that the law and the prophets were read in the temple every sabbath-day, for their service, with a sermon. "After the reading," says St Luke, "of the law and the prophets, the rulers of the synagogue sent to Paul and Barnabas, saying, Ye men and brether, if ye have any exhortation to the people, speak." Again, in the fifteenth chapter he says: "Moses has of old time them that preach him in every city in the synagogues, where he is read every sabbath-day." Mark what prayers or kind of service, as we term it, St Luke says here, was then used in the temple of Salomon: the law and the prophets, he says, were read. In the Hebrew bible appears the division in the books of Moses, how far was read weekly and monthly. So that, as they had then the law and the prophets read in their temple for their common prayer and service, so have we now the psalter of David monthly read over, and one chapter of the old testament and another of the new read daily, in our churches, in our own tongue, as they had then in theirs. The new testament was not then written, so that it could not be read: but as the new testament now does more plainly set out to us the office and mediation of our Saviour Christ, so did then the prophets more plainly speak of the coming of Christ, than the law of Moses did signify him; and therefore was orderly read with Moses the law, as a fuller declarer thereof: so that in effect our church service disagrees not from theirs, in this reading together of the old testament and the new in our common prayer, as they read the law and the prophets together.

This order is three thousand year old: when they have proved their popish portus to be much above three hundred year old, then they may begin to try ancienty. Their matins and evensong are appointed them out of their portus: and when any old record of authority teaches them, that so many false miracles, feigned lies and tales, as be there written, with serving such saints, as no scripture does allow, nor good history makes mention of, (but only the pope's calendar and his scholars,) were used in the church for common prayer and God's service, then let them crack of the blessed fathers' steps that they follow.

Let them try their ancient portus of Sarum, York's use, Bangor, or the great diversity of friars, monks, canons, nuns, which for every order of them had their divers sorts of matins and evensong; and if they be proved three hundred year old, they have much to rejoice in, and yet far short of three thousand.

But of all other blasphemies the psalter of Brigit, where every word and prayer that David names God in, is turned to our Lady, is most horrible, to pervert the scripture to man's fantasy. Pope Paul the third, but twenty year ago, was so ashamed of his portus, that he printed a new one, putting out many of the blasphemous lies that were in the old; yet this popish pricker thinks all in it to be so good, that it cannot nor should not be amended. The English priests' portus and order of service, that he cracks so much of for ancienty, is full of memories[1] daily, and service of Thomas Becket twice in the year: and yet it is not long since he was bishop of Canterbury; he lived under king Henry the Second, four hundred year since. The feast of Corpus Christi, and the service of that day, was invented by pope Urban the fourth, scarce three hundred year since. The feast of the visitation of our Lady, commonly called the new found Lady-day, and the service for that day, is not two hundred year old, and decreed by pope Urban the sixth. What ancienty then is their portus and mass-book of, which received these solemn feasts and their service of so late years? And yet he would make men believe that it has been from the beginning, and that old records make mention of them.

The portus' antiquity.

Many such other may be found in their popish service, whereby it may easily be seen how falsely he brags of their ancienty. The ancientest beginning of their portus of Sarum was under William Conqueror, not five hundred year since, by Osmundus, the second bishop of Sarum, as Polychronicon writes, Lib. VII. chap. 3[2]; but it has been increased

[1 Memories: commemorations, memorial services—a sense preserved in our communion service: "He did institute, and in his holy gospel command us to continue, a perpetual *memory* of that his precious death." ED.]

[2 After him the king's chancellor, Osmundus, was bishop twenty-four years. He builded there a new church. * * * Also, he made the ordinal of the service of holy church, and named it the *Consuetudinary*. Now well nigh all England, Wales, and Ireland used that ordinal. ED.]

since with many a loud lie, as though they should strive who should tell the greatest for the best game. Our service has nothing in it but it is written in God's book, the holy Bible (where no lie can be found), saving *Te Deum* and a few collects or prayers, which although they be not contained in the scripture, yet differing in words, they agree in sense and meaning with the articles of the faith and the whole body of the scripture. Their portus and missal has many untrue fables and feigned miracles for their lessons, written neither in the scripture, old history, nor ancient record of authority; many invocations of such as be no saints, and wickedly calling on saints of their own making, instead of the living God, as Thomas Becket, and many popes; some charms, as St Agatha's letters[1] for burning of houses; some witchcrafts, as holy water for casting out devils, holy bread instead of the communion, ringing the hallowed bell in great tempests or lightnings, and all in an unknown tongue, contrary to God's commandment, yet craftily devised to deceive the people, lest in hearing them in their own tongue, and proving them false, they would laugh them to scorn. Ansegisus,[2] Lib. i. cap. 20 and 76, writes that Charles the great emperor decreed, that nothing should be read in the churches, but only the scriptures, nor any thing taught, but out of the scriptures; but none is so ignorant, but he sees the popish service and doctrine to agree little with the scriptures, and ours to contain nothing else but the scriptures. Now compare these together, and judge whether that be the elder and more to be allowed, that has nothing in it but the scripture itself, and that which is drawn out of it, or that which is devised of man's

[1] See p. 177. The story is, that when the emperor, Frederic II. was about to destroy Agatha's native city, Catana, while engaged in prayer to the virgin Mary, the book he had opened exhibited these words in golden letters: Noli offendere patriam Agathæ, quia ultrix injuriarum est. This was done three times; and what result followed such a miracle, need not be told. ED.]

[2] Capit. xx. Item in eodem concilio, ut canonici libri tantum legantur in ecclesia. LXXVI. Ut presbyteri quos mittitis per parochias vestras ad regendum et prædicandum per ecclesias populum Deo servientem ut recte et honeste prædicent, et non sinatis nova vel non canonica aliquos ex suo sensu et non secundum scripturas sacras fingere et prædicare populo. Baluzii Capitularia Regum Francorum. T. I. pp. 707, 716. Paris. 1677. ED.]

brains alone, beside and contrary to God's word. Is that newfangled and schismatical, that contains nothing but the doctrine of the prophets and apostles; and is that ancient, that cannot be proved good at all?

This text of Jeremiah, that bids them "search out the old way, and walk in it," does not mean all old ways; but he says, "Search of the old ways which of them is good, and walk in it," as though he should say, all old ways are not good. If all old ways were good, he would not bid try which were good: therefore it is not enough to have it old, but to have it good also, and then to cleave to it. If bare words would serve, there is manifest sayings for the contrary. Ezechiel says, ch. xx. "Walk not in the commandments of your fathers, nor keep not their judgments." I might as well beat in this text as he the other, and of like strength: therefore it is not sufficient to say it is old, or to follow fathers; but to try that it be good, and that godly fathers used it, and then be bold to follow it. Evil has been from the beginning as well as good, and there have been in all ages evil fathers as well as good. Cyprian notes well therefore and goodly, saying that "Christ said not that he was ancient custom, but he was the truth itself."[3] To follow Christ then, and his doctrine, is to follow the true old way. For he is both the truth itself, and was from the beginning: and those fathers that follow not his steps, are not our mark to follow, though the world do never so much reverence them. St Paul says to the Corinthians, "Be ye followers of me, even as I follow Christ:" this is then the right way of following fathers, as they followed Christ our Lord, and no other way; for Christ is the way and truth itself. And because he charges us with schismatical doctrine and service, because we either differ from the pope's synagogue, or else we have not all one order in all points of our church service; to them that be offended with such divers orders of ceremonies of prayers or ministering the sacraments in the church, Anselm shall an-

[[3] Nam consuetudo sine veritate vetustas erroris est: propter quod relicto errore sequamur veritatem. * * * Quam veritatem nobis Christus ostendens in evangelio suo dicit, "Ego sum veritas." Propter quod si in Christo sumus, et Christum in nobis habemus; si manemus in veritate, et veritas in nobis manet; ea quæ sunt vera teneamus. Epist. LXXIV. ad Pompeium. p. 317. Ed. Fell. Oxon. 1700. ED.]

swer now, as he has done afore, in his Epistle III. ch. 27, to the same case:

"To the lord and his friend Waleram, by the grace of God the worshipful bishop of Nicenburge, Anselm the servant of Canterbury church, greeting, &c.

"Your worship complains of the sacraments of the church, that they are not ministered every where after one sort, but are handled in divers places after divers sorts. Truly, if they were ministered after one sort, and agreeingly through the whole church, it were good and laudable: notwithstanding, because there be many diversities which differ not in the sum of the sacrament, nor in the strength of it, or in the faith, nor all can be gathered into one custom, I think that they are rather to be borne with agreement in peace, than to be condemned with offence. For we have this from the holy fathers, that if the unity of charity be kept in the catholic faith, the diverse custom hurts nothing. If it be demanded, whereof these diversities of customs do spring, I perceive nothing else than the diversities of wits; which although they differ not in the strength and truth of the thing, yet they agree not in the fitness and comeliness of the ministering. For that which one judges to be meeter oftentimes other think it less meet. And not to agree in such diversities, I think it not to swerve from the truth of the thing."[1]

[1 Queritur vestra reverentia de sacramentis ecclesiæ, quoniam non uno modo fiunt ubique, sed diversis modis in diversis locis tractantur. Ubique si per universam ecclesiam uno modo et concorditer celebrarentur, bonum esset et laudabile: quoniam tamen multæ sunt diversitates, quæ non in summa sacramenti neque in virtute ejus aut fide discordant, neque omnes in unam consuetudinem colligi possunt; æstimo eas potius in pace concorditer tolerandas, quam discorditer cum scandalo damnandas. Habemus enim a sanctis patribus, quia si unitas servatur caritatis in fide catholica, nihil officit consuetudo diversa. Si autem quæritur, unde istæ natæ sunt consuetudinum varietates; nihil aliud intelligo, quam humanorum sensuum diversitates: qui quamvis in rei virtute et unitate non dissentiant, in aptitudine tamen et decentia administrationis non concordant. Quia [quod] enim unus aptius esse judicat, alius sæpe minus aptum; neque in hujusmodi varietatibus non consonare puto ab ipsius rei veritate exorbitare. Anselm. Epist. cxxxvi. Waleranno Numburg. Episc. Tom. IV. p. 157. Colon. 1612. ED.]

VII. Also, where the said preacher does recite certain abuses of the said church, as talking, buying and selling, fighting and brawling, (although these be very evil and worthy much rebuke,) yet there be worse abuses, as blaspheming God in lying sermons, polluting the temple with schismatical service, destroying and pulling down holy altars, that were set up by good blessed men, and there the sacrifice of the blessed mass ministered according to the order of Christ's catholic church. Yea, where the altar of the Holy Ghost stood, the new bishops have set their tails upon, and there sit in judgment of such as be catholic and live in the fear of God. Some they deprive from their livings, some they commit to prison, except they will forsake the catholic faith, and embrace a faith and religion that has no foundation laid by general council, nor blessed fathers in times past, but invented by heretics, that do not agree one with another nor themselves.

We both do agree the church of Paul's to be abused, and therefore justly plagued. God grant that henceforth it may be amended, that worse do not follow! When Josue had conquered Jericho so marvellously with carrying the ark of God about it, the priests blowing their trumpets and the people shouting, by the might of God rather than strength of man, he said, "Cursed be the man afore the Lord that builds up Jericho again: in his first-born son let him lay the foundation, and in his last child let him set up the gates of it." Which thing was truly verified many years after by Hiel of Bethel, as it is written. So God grant that the citizens of London may more warily build, and provision be made, that Paul's be not so misused again, as it has been, lest the like plague follow as did on Jericho, or worse. *Josh. vi.* *1 Kings xvi.*

Surely, if vain glory be the cause to build a more stately house than it was, and not to foresee that God's house be better used for a house of prayer, than aforetime it has been, a greater scourge must needs follow. Costly solemn buildings are not to be condemned altogether in commonwealths; but if the merchants of London say, as Nimrod said to his fellows, "Come, let us build ourselves a city and tower, whose top may reach to the heaven, and let us get ourselves a name afore we be scattered abroad," surely they will be overthrown in their own device, as Babel was. God, and not man, will be glorified in God's house: God's house must be a house of prayer, and not the proud tower of Babylon, nor the pope's market place, nor a stews for bawds and ruffians, nor a horse fair for brokers, *Gen. xi.* *Paul's.*

no, nor yet a bourse for merchants, nor a meeting-place for walking and talking. If a convenient place to meet for honest assemblies cannot be found nor had conveniently other where, a partition might be had to close up and shut the praters from prayers, the walkers and janglers from well disposed persons, that they should not trouble the devout hearers of God's word, so that the one should not hear nor see the other. God has once again with the trumpet of his word, and the glad receiving of the people, thrown down the walls of Jericho, and the pope's bulwark there, by his own might, without the power of man, if man would so consider it and fear the Lord. No place has been more abused than Paul's has been, nor more against the receiving of Christ's gospel: wherefore it is more marvel that God spared it so long, rather than that he overthrew it now.

From the top of the steeple down within the ground no place has been free. From the top of the spire at coronations, or other solemn triumphs, some for vain glory used to throw themselves down by a rope, and so killed themselves vainly to please other men's eyes. At the battlements of the steeple sundry times were used their popish anthems to call upon their gods with torch and taper in the evenings. In the top of one of the pinnacles is Lollards' tower,[1] where many an innocent soul has been by them cruelly tormented and murdered. In the midst alley was their long censer reaching from the roof to the ground, as though the Holy Ghost came in their censing down in likeness of a dove. On the arches,[2] though commonly men complain of wrong and delayed judgment in ecclesiastical causes, yet because I will not judge by hearsay, I pass over it, saving only for such as have been condemned there by Annas and Caiphas for Christ's cause, as innocently as any Christians could be. For their images hanged on every wall, pillar, and door, with their pilgrimages, and worshipping of them, I will not stand to rehearse them, because they cannot be unknown to all men that have seen London, or heard of them. Their massing and many altars, with the rest of their popish service, which he so much extols, I pass over, because I answered them afore.

[1 So named from the followers of the truth, called Lollards, confined there. ED.]

[2 The court of arches, the bishop's court, held in the cathedral. ED.]

The south alley for usury and popery, the north for simony, and the horse fair in the midst for all kind of bargains, meetings, brawlings, murders, conspiracies, and the font for ordinary payments of money, are so well known to all men as the beggar knows his dish. The popish clergy began and maintained these, and godless worldlings defend them; where the poor protestant laments and would amend them. Judas' chapel[3] under the ground, with the apostles' mass so early in the morning, was counted by report as fit a place to work a feat in as the stews or taverns. So that without and within, above the ground and under, over the roof and beneath, on the top of the steeple and spire down to the low floor, not one spot was free from wickedness, as the said bishop did then in his sermon declare; so that we should praise God for his mercy in sparing it so long, and now tremble at his fearful judgment in justly revenging such filthiness. God, for his mercy's sake, grant it may now be amended!

Secondly, where it pleases him to term this church service now used schismatical, it is as true as afore, when he said that no ancient record made mention of any such afore forty years past. Why do ye call it a schismatical? Because it differs from the pope's portus? That it differs we deny not, but rejoice and praise God for it: but if it agree with the holy scriptures and the ancient fathers, as I have proved afore, then be ye schismatics in swerving from them, and not we. *We follow the old fathers, and the papists be schismatics.*

In our morning and evening prayer we agree with the old prayers of Salomon's temple, as I proved afore. In baptism we follow Christ Jesus, his apostles, Austin and Pauline, whom pope Gregory sent into England, in the chief points; which all christened in unconjured water, without salt, spitting, oil, and chrism, &c. *Common Prayer. Baptism.*

In the Lord's supper we receive together, as St Paul commanded: and pope Gelasius teaches either to receive both parts, or to refrain from both; for it is sacrilege to divide them. *De Consecra. distinct.* ii.[4] We give the people the cup of Christ's *Communion.*

[3 "Misnamed on purpose for Jesus' Chapel." Strype, I. p. 392. ED.]
[4 Item Gelasius Papa Majorico et Joanni episcopis: Comperimus autem quod quidam, sumpta tantummodo corporis sacri portione, a calice sacrati cruoris abstineant. Qui proculdubio (quoniam nescio qua superstitione docentur astringi) aut integra sacramenta percipiant, aut ab

<small>Lib. i. Ep. 2.</small> blood, as well as to the priests, as Cyprian teaches, saying, "How do we teach or provoke them to shed their blood in confessing his name, if we deny them that shall be Christ's soldiers the blood of Christ? Or how do we make them meet to the cup of martyrdom, if we do not admit them to drink first in the church the cup of the Lord by the right use of communicating[1]?" Again, St Matthew says, "Drink ye all of this :" lest any should think himself exempt from drinking, he says, "Drink ye all." God is the God of the lay-people as well as of the priests, and offers his sacraments and salvation to them as well as to other. We move the people also often, and not once in the year, to receive the communion (as the papists do), following St <small>De ecclesiast. dogmat. cap. 53.</small> Austin, who says, "Every day to communicate, I neither praise nor dispraise it; but I counsel and move all men to receive it on the Sunday, if the mind be without desire to sin."[2] Chrysostom says, that when they ministered the communion in his church, <small>Ad Heb. Hom. 13.</small> "the deacon stood up, gave warning to the people, and said *sancta sanctis*, those holy mysteries were ready for them that were holy and had worthily prepared themselves:[3] they that would not <small>Ad Ephes. Hom. 3.</small> receive went their ways, would not stand gazing on them that received, but thought themselves unworthy to be partakers of the prayers, which would not communicate."[4] The pope's law

integris arceantur; quia divisio unius ejusdem mysterii sine grandi sacrilegio non potest pervenire. Decretum Gratiani, &c. Tertia Pars. De Consecra. Distinct. ii. fo. cccxcviii. Antv. 1573. Ed.]

[1 Nam quo modo docemus aut provocamus eos in confessione nominis sanguinem suum fundere, si eis militaturis Christi sanguinem denegamus? aut quo modo ad martyrii poculum idoneos facimus, si non eos prius ad bibendum in ecclesia poculum Domini jure communicationis admittimus? Epist. lvii. p. 253. Ed. Fell. 1700. Lib. i. Ep. ii. Erasm. Ed.]

[2 Quotidie eucharistiæ communionem percipere nec laudo nec vitupero: omnibus tamen dominicis diebus communicandum suadeo et hortor, si tamen mens in affectu peccandi non sit. De Eccles. Dogmatibus Liber Gennadio tributus. Tom. viii. August. p. 1698. Paris. 1837. Ed.]

[3 "Ὅταν γὰρ εἴπῃ, Τὰ ἅγια τοῖς ἁγίοις, τοῦτο λέγει, Εἴ τις οὐκ ἔστιν ἅγιος, μὴ προσίτω. Chrysost. in Hebr. Hom. xvii. Tom. xii. p. 245. Paris. 1838. Ed.]

[4 Οὕτω δὴ καὶ σὺ παραγέγονας· τὸν ὕμνον ᾖσας, μετὰ πάντων ὡμολόγησας εἶναι τῶν ἀξίων τῷ μὴ μετὰ τῶν ἀναξίων ἀνακεχωρηκέναι· πῶς ἔμεινας, καὶ οὐ μετέχεις τῆς τραπέζης; Ἀνάξιός εἰμι, φησίν. Οὐκοῦν καὶ τῆς κοινωνίας ἐκείνης τῆς ἐν ταῖς εὐχαῖς. In Ephes. Hom. iii. Tom. xi. p. 27. Ed.]

says, *de Consecra. distinct.* ii : " The temporal men, which will not communicate at Easter, Whitsunday, and Christmas, are not catholics."[5] Let papists then note, what their master says to them.

In burials we do not assemble a number of priests to sweep purgatory, or buy forgiveness of sins of them which have no authority to sell; but according to St Jerome's example we follow. "At the death of Fabiola," says he, "the people of Rome were gathered to the solemnity of the burial. Psalms were sung, and Alleluia sounding out on height did shake the gilded ceilings of the temple. Here was one company of young men, and there another, which did sing the praises and worthy deeds of the woman. And no marvel if men rejoice of her salvation, of whose conversion the angels in heaven be glad[6]." Thus Jerome used burials. Likewise Gregory Nazianzene has his funeral sermons and orations in the commendation of the party departed: so has Ambrose for Theodosius and Valentinian the emperors, for his brother Satyrus, &c. Their *dirige* groats,[7] masses, and trentals, tapers, and ringings, have no foundation on the scripture nor good ancienty to maintain them. Jerome says, that Alleluia was sung so loud, that it made the church roof to shake : and our papists will not sing Alleluia at all, neither at burial, in Lent, nor Advent, and say they follow ancienty. Alleluia is as much in English as, "praise ye the Lord;" as though they should say, Praise the Lord that has called his servant out of this misery to himself in hea-

Burials.

Epitaph. Fabiolæ.

[[5] Ex Concilio Agatheno: *Non habeantur catholici, qui his tribus temporibus communicare desinunt.* Seculares, qui in natali Domini, pascha, pentecoste non communicaverint, catholici non credantur, nec inter catholicos habeantur. Decret. Gratian. Tertia Pars. De Consecra. Dist. ii. Ed.]

[[6] See above, p. 320. Necdum spiritum exhalaverat, necdum debitam Christo reddiderat animam; *et jam fama volans tanti prænuncia luctus,* totius urbis populum ad exequias congregabat. Sonabant psalmi, et aurata templorum reboans in sublime quatiebat ALLELUIA. *Hic juvenum chorus, ille senum, qui carmine laudes femineas et facta ferant.* * * * Nec mirum si de ejus salute homines exultarent, de cujus conversione angeli lætabantur in cœlo. Hieronymi Op. Epist. LXXXIV. (XXX.) Tom. IV. Pars ii. p. 662. Paris. 1706. Ed.]

[[7] The groat was a common charge for a *dirige* or dirge for the dead. Selden, *Table Talk,* speaks of "twenty dirgies at fourpence a piece." Ed.]

ven: but the desperate papists say, Weep; rejoice not for the dead, but mistrust of their salvation; think that they be gone from one sorrow to another, and therefore buy masses apace; the pope's proctors for money enough will sell that which God cannot, or will not, give freely, as they think. God is weary, as they say, of well-doing, and turned over the matter to these the pope's proctors.

Eccles. xii. But Salomon teaches, that in death "the body turns to earth from whence it came, and the soul to him that gave it." Look how both body and soul is bestowed, whatsoever greedy gaping cormorants do say, to get money withal. "Blessed be the dead that die in the Lord," says St John; "for they rest from their labours:" the popes say, the dead be accursed, and go into purgatory, from sorrows here to greater there: choose whether ye believe.

Marriage. In marriage, as in other things beside, we are but too much like unto them: that is our fault generally, that we differ not more from them in all our ministery. We have all in English, where they have but "I, N., take thee, M., &c." And here I would ask master D. a reason, why this piece in marriage is used of them in English, and not more; or the like in other sacraments? Is marriage so holy a thing, that the parties must needs understand in English, what promise the one makes to the other; and other sacraments be not so to be regarded, what we promise unto God? Do we not in baptism and the Lord's supper make as solemn a vow to God, to serve him only and forsake all other, as in marriage the one party does to the other? Seeing then we differ not from the scripture nor ancient fathers, they do us much wrong to charge us with a schism, where they themselves are rather schismatics in swerving from the ancient fathers' steps, than we that would bring home again their old religion.

But as hitherto I have answered them out of their own doctors, so in this thing also I will be judged who be schismatics by their own books. Look all the histories and chronicles written within this thousand year, and in religion ye shall find almost none called schismatics, but papists. For when there were two or three popes at once, and some countries followed one pope claiming to be head, and some another, so they made schisms. Papists then are called schismatics commonly, and not protestants. *Fasciculus temporum*[1], a book made by one monk of their own sect, rehearses twenty-three schisms betwixt popes and their partakers: when they find the third part of so many among the protestants, then they may have some face of appearance to call us schismatics. At the council of Constance were three popes in three diverse countries, Italy, France, and Spain, all claiming to be chief, and some countries followed one, some another; but all were deposed, and a fourth chosen little more than a hundred and fifty year since[2].

It were too long to rehearse all the schisms spoken of: whoso lust, there may read. This schism that I named last, and the other, when there was one pope at Rome, and another at Avignon in France forty years together[3], are the notablest, and troubled the world most, in striving who should have the most followers and partakers: the other I pass over for shortness sake, unto these be considered better of them, how they may defend themselves, that they be not proved schismatics. If that be schismatical service, when one differs from another, then be all orders of friars, monks, canons, nuns, York's use, Sarum, Bangor, &c., schismatical; for they differ every one from other. *The communion table.* *Luke xxii.* *1 Cor. x.*

Now for pulling down altars, and ministering the communion on tables, a few words to try, whether we do this without reason or example. First, our Saviour Christ ministered it sitting at a table: then it is not wicked but best to follow his doings; for he did all things well. St Luke says, that "the hand of the traitor was with him at the table." St Paul, for the use of it in his time, says, "Ye cannot be partakers of the Lord's table, and the table of devils:" where it appears plain, that both idolaters at their sacrifices, and the Christians also in their holy mysteries, used tables. Theodoret writes, that after Ambrose had excommunicated the emperor Theodosius, and received him again to the church, "the em- *Lib. v. cap. 18.*

[1] The whole series is given in order, pp. XLV.—LXXXVIII. Paris. 1524. ED.]

[2] In the year 1410. The popes were Gregory XII. Benedict XIII. Alexander V. and John XXIII. upon whose deposition Martin V. succeeded. ED.]

[3] From about the year 1390 to 1447. ED.]

peror, lying flat on the ground, weeping and tearing the hair of his head for sorrow and shame of his offences, he rose up and offered at such time," says he, "as the gifts were offered at the holy table[1]." Sozomen writes, lib. VIII. cap. vii. how Eutropius fled to the church as a sanctuary for succour, because he had offended the emperor: and when John, bishop of Constantinople, "see him lie afore the holy communion table, he preached unto him, and rebuked him of his pride, when he was in authority[2]." The canon of the great Nicene council says thus: "In the godly table we must not lowly cleave to the bread and cup set afore us; but lifting up our mind on high by faith, we must consider the Lamb of God to be set afore us in that holy table[3]." Wherein I note that they all call it a table, and not an altar, where they ministered the communion. This was four hundred year after Christ, above a thousand year since: why then, altars were not continued from the beginning, as they say, and we are not the first that used tables, but we would gladly restore these old customs again. If Ambrose lawfully and well used tables at the communion at Milan, and the bishop at Constantinople in Greece, and elsewhere, I see no reason why we should be rebuked for following them, except they can prove that they did it against the scripture. I know that the scripture, and old writers also, make mention of altars: but that is because Moses in the law commanded them to offer their sacrifices upon altars, because the sacrifices then commonly used were heavy, as oxen, calves, sheep, &c., and tables were not able to stand and bear such weights continually.

These sacrifices were a figure and shadow of that only

[1] Ἐπειδὴ δὲ ὁ καιρὸς ἐκάλει τῇ ἱερᾷ τραπέζῃ τὰ δῶρα προσενεγκεῖν, ἀναστὰς μετὰ τῶν ἴσων δακρύων τῶν ἀνακτόρων ἐπέβη. Eccles. Hist. P. 343. Ed. 1544. ED.]

[2] Ἡνίκα δὴ λαμπρόν τινα κατ' αὐτοῦ, ὑπὸ τὴν ἱερὰν τράπεζαν κειμένου, κατέτεινε λόγον Ἰωάννης. Ibid. P. 108. Ed. 1544. ED.]

[3] Ἐπὶ τῆς θείας τραπέζης πάλιν κἀνταῦθα μὴ τῷ προκειμένῳ ἄρτῳ καὶ τῷ ποτηρίῳ ταπεινῶς προσέχωμεν, ἀλλ' ὑψώσαντες ἡμῶν τὴν διάνοιαν πίστει νοήσωμεν κεῖσθαι ἐπὶ τῆς ἱερᾶς ἐκείνης τὸν ἀμνὸν τοῦ Θεοῦ. Gelasius, Hist. Concil. Nicen. cap. xxx. ap. Labb. Tom. II. col. 233. Ed. 1671. ED.]

pure sacrifice, which Christ should offer on the cross for us all: for as those innocent beasts were killed for other men's faults, so Christ without sin should die for the sins of the world. For this cause the cross, whereon Christ our Lord died, is called an altar also; because the sacrifice for the sins of the whole world was thereon offered, as those were on an altar. Wheresoever, therefore, the new testament or old writers use this word *altar*, they allude to that sacrifice of Christ, figured by Moses, and use the word still that Moses used to signify the same sacrifice withal; and rather it is a figurative, than a proper kind of speech in all such places. And because altars were ever used for sacrifices, to signify that sacrifice which was to come, seeing our Saviour Christ is come already, has fulfilled and finished all sacrifices, we think it best to take away all occasions of that popish sacrificing mass (for maintaining whereof they have cruelly sacrificed many innocent souls) to minister on tables, according to these examples. Altars.

It grieves him that the bishops set their tails, (as it pleases him to speak,) when they sit in judgment, where the altars were: but if they were handled as Jehu did Baal's priests and his altars, God did them no wrong. It is a common true saying, "He that will do no ill, must do nothing that longs theretil[4]:" so surely, if we will warily avoid the wickedness of popery, we must flee from such things as maintain their doings. There is nothing more profitable unto them than massing sacrifices: therefore, because altars import and maintain their gainful sacrificing, it is necessary they be removed. 2 Kings x.

For their sacrifice of the mass, that he so much laments to be defaced, and all good consciences rejoice that God of his undeserved goodness has overthrown it, I refer all men to the fifth and last book that the blessed souls now living with God, bishops Cranmer and Ridley, wrote of the sacrament, whose bodies they cruelly tormented therefore. There whosoever lust, may read, and with indifferency weigh the reasons of both parties, and judge with the truth. Stout Stephen[5] would gladly have overthrown that book: but God

[4] Longs theretil: belongs thereto. ED.

[5] Stephen Gardiner, bishop of Winchester, who wrote several treatises on the subject of the sacrament against Cranmer and Ridley. ED.

confounded him, and their names live for ever. So long as that book stands unconfuted, they may bark against the truth, as the dog does against the moon, and not prevail.

And if ye will call but a little to your remembrance, how many divers sorts of masses there were used in divers countries, as appears in the words afore rehearsed, ye shall see how loud he lies, in saying here, that their mass was according to the order of Christ's catholic church. That is catholic, as the Greek word signifies, which is universal and general, both in time, person and place: therefore he must prove, if he will be believed, that this popish Latin patched masking mass has been used at all times, of all men, and in all countries. But I have declared afore both many sundry sorts of ministering the Lord's supper in several countries, and also how of late years this his order has been violently and by blind ignorance brought in: therefore it cannot be catholic.

Mass is not catholic.

None that be counted learned can be ignorant of the general points, wherein the Greek east church differs from the west Latin Romish church. The Grecians never received the pope for their head, nor the doctrine of purgatory; their priests were ever free to marry; they ministered the Lord's supper always in their own language, with leavened bread, in both kinds to the lay-people, both the bread and the cup severally; the priests never received alone without other to receive with him; they never made trentals of it, nor knew transubstantiation; they never used pardons, images, with many other more things, like as auricular shriving to a priest, &c.; which all the Latin Romish church defends, and does contrary, and their [these] religion stands in them. Therefore none of these opinions can be called catholic, because the Greek church, which is the greater part of the world, never received, believed, nor used them. Thus many lies then this master D. has made in one word, calling it catholic, as there be things wherein their Romish mass differs from the Greek liturgies and orders of ministering the Lord's supper; as I have declared most of them. If I should particularly and throughly handle all his foolish sayings, it would grow to too great a work: therefore briefly I touch the chiefest.

The difference betwixt the Greek church and the Latin.

He charges us with a faith and religion that has no foundation laid by general councils; which saying when he better considers, I trust he will be content to be reckoned in the same number with us. Was not the first general council, under Constantine the emperor, at Nice, above four hundred and thirty[1] years after Christ was born? Shall I say then, or is he so shameless to think, that there was no religion nor faith in the world so many years together after Christ, because there was not of so many years a general council to build upon? No; and because we say and prove our faith and religion to be the best and ancientest, we build not on councils, as they do, but on God's word, which is above the council, and rules all, being not ruled of any, has been from the beginning, and shall continue to the end: and we say with Paul, that we "be builded on the foundation of the apostles and prophets, Christ himself being the head corner stone." The prophets, whereon we build, lived many of them a thousand year afore any general council was heard of, and the apostles lived four hundred year afore them. Wherefore our foundation and religion is much elder than theirs. Councils are like to parliaments: that that pleases one pope in his council, pleases not another, as the books do easily declare; and that which one thinks good, and makes a law one year, another condemns and disannuls. What a vain thing is it then, to build on so uncertain a groundwork! Heaven and earth shall pass, change and decay; but the word of the Lord our God, from whence comes our religion, "remains for ever," as the prophet says. Therefore the wise builder will follow that which will not fade.

Our religion is elder than councils.

Eph. ii.

Lastly, where he charges us that we agree not one with another, nor with ourselves, I may say to him with the gospel, " Thou hypocrite, first pluck the mote out of thine own eye, and then thou shalt better see to take the beam out of thy brother's eye." There is no sort of people more guilty in this behalf than the papists be. The heathen philosophers had not so many sundry sects and opinions among themselves in their schools, as the papists have in their doings. D. Ponet, late bishop of Winton, in his answer to the book that bears Martin's name, for marriage of priests, proves well that popery is a monster patched of all kinds of heresy, and worse than they all. Where such things are fully taught and proved, I had rather

Luke vi.

[1 Old edition, IIII. c. xxx. The real date is 325. ED.]

refer you to the reading of them there, than to write one thing oft. I declared to you afore also, where ye shall find twenty-three schisms among the popes themselves. These holy bishops that he cracks so much on for their imprisonment, and other that in losing their livings live more wealthily and at ease than ever they did afore, or the protestants do in their liberty now, mark how like themselves they be, and agreeing with themselves. As long as king Henry lived, and all the time of blessed king Edward, they taught, they preached, they subscribed, they sware and believed all this that they now deny. As oft as they had any living in any college of the universities, as oft as they took degree in the schools, as oft as they took any benefice, and when they were made priests or bishops, so oft they sware and forsware all that now they deny. Perjury in other men is punished with bearing papers, loss of their ears, and other worldly shame: but these men, abusing the gentleness of the prince, being thus oft forsworn, are counted holy in the world.

The papists turn with the world, and differ one from another.

The papists in their religious monsters have more kind of monks, friars, canons, nuns, differing in their coats, than any people have; some be white, some black, some gray; differing in their shoes, some having whole, some half, some nothing but soles under the foot; differing in shaving their heads, some more, some less; differing in meats, some eating fish only, some flesh and fish at their days and times appointed; differing in places, for some never go abroad, but are kept still within compass of the house, some walk abroad at their pleasure, and some locked up in stone walls; differing in their service, for every order had his diverse order of mass and matins, in many points; differing in their saints, or rather their gods, whose names they bear, whom they worship, and striving which of them should be the holiest. Some hold of Francis[1], some of Benet, some of Dominic, some of Brigit, and others of other, as they lust to devise. In their schoolmen is found more diversity of opinions, than among any sort of philosophers. Some hold of Thomas, some of Duns, some of Albertus, some of other, as they like; for there be so many that almost they cannot be reckoned. Which things being all considered, and known of all men to be true, except they be wilfully blind, how

[1 See above, p. 80. ED.]

can they say that they agree in one unity of the truth? Pilate and Herod agreed to crucify Christ: so these in mischiefs agree to set up superstition, but in their private opinions none are more contrary and divers. In their pilgrimages, pardons, relics, fastings, what diversities and striving which should be the greatest! Among so many ladies and roods, what striving in every country which should be the holiest, and work most miracles! Among pardons, Boston bare the name, and yet other would compare: among relics, the blood of Hales passed other, unto their juggling was known. Fastings were more than I know: some used St Rinian's[2], some our lady's, some the golden Fridays, some every Wednesday, some half Lent, some whole; some with fish only, other as they lust. What reason is it, that they which fasted our lady's fast, some fasting to bread and water ended it in three years' space, other in eating fish had seven? and why should they follow the lady-day in Lent, more than other lady-days? And why yearly do they change their day, &c.? When these and such other their doings are proved to agree in one, and good reason shewed for their doings, they may better charge other men with disagreeing: but they may think it shame to burden other with that wherein they be most guilty themselves.

VIII. There is none more disobedient than the new bishops and preachers now a days, which disobey the universal church of Christ, the which church whosoever will not obey, our Saviour in the gospel commands us to take them as infidels. As, where the universal church of Christ commands mass and seven sacraments, as necessary for our salvation, they call it abomination with their blasphemous mouths: where the church commands to fast, they command to eat: where the church commands continual prayer of the clergy, they call it superstition and blind ignorance: where the church commands the clergy to live in chastity, they command and exhort the clergy to marriage: where the church, and all laws civil and canon, yea, the laws of the realm, do prohibit marriage of priests, they allow marriage of priests, obeying no law, but follow their own carnal lusts. Yea, where the queen has given strait commandment to abstain from flesh in Lent, and other days commanded

Matt. xviii.

[[2] St Rinian's, or Ronian's,—the same, no doubt, as is mentioned before, p. 80, where the author, or his printer, erroneously calls it St Tronion's. Ed.]

by the church, the new preachers and protestants have eaten flesh openly to the great slander of other.

O God, how many lies in so few lines! The universal church of Christ agrees in the necessary articles of our salvation; but in certain outward orders and ceremonies, every country differs from other, without any dishonour to God.

I declared afore, how we agree with the universal church, and confess the necessary christian articles of our faith, religion, and salvation, better than they; and also I touched some diversities of outward orders in the church, whereof many or all were tolerable: and now, by occasion of these matters ministered by him, I shall touch some more. He lays to our charge, that we disobey the universal church: if he mean, in those things which afterward follow, I am content to try with him. Where under the name of mass he understands the Romish Latin mass, it appears afore how many sundry good sorts of ministering the Lord's supper be in other countries at this day, and have been of old time: therefore he makes a loud lie in saying or thinking, that whosoever disagrees from their popish mass disobeys the universal church; for the most part of christendom neither does at this day, nor at any time has used it. In the substance and doctrine of the holy communion, we agree with the scripture and the catholic church, though we differ in some piece of the outward order of it from other countries: but we profess an open disagreeing from the Romish synagogue, both in the order and substance thereof.

The church of God, according to the scriptures, does profess and believe that all faithful Christians, worthily coming to the Lord's table, receive by faith in those holy mysteries the body and blood of Christ, which was given, broken and shed for the sins of the whole world. This we teach, believe and follow, and exhort all men often to prepare themselves worthily thus to receive. The popish synagogue, contrary to St Paul, teach, practise, believe, (and persecute with fire and fagot all gainsayers,) that in the sacrifice of their bread and wine the creatures be changed from their natural substance, and are made a god to be worshipped, when they lift it over their heads, hang it in a cord over the altar, or carry it about the fields; and if the people will buy trentals or masses of it at their

Mass.

hands, they can sweep purgatory clean, and make souls fly to heaven as thick as dust. These have no groundwork on God's word, and therefore we cannot believe them: for we read that Christ took the substance of his flesh of the virgin Mary, but never of bread. Only the Romish prelates have made this merchandise, put in that article, taught this doctrine, and believe this, contrary to the whole church of Christ beside themselves. Then it is they that disobey the church, and not we. I spake sufficiently for their mass and sacraments afore; yet for their sacraments now a little more.

He says here, that there be seven sacraments necessary to salvation; and yet within few words following, he denies marriage to priests; and that is as much to say, as either that marriage is no sacrament, or that priests shall not be saved. There is but one way of salvation for all men: then priests must either be saved that way, or else condemned. But it is too foolish to say that any man shall be condemned, except he be married. Shall none be saved but married folks? When he looks at himself, being unmarried, and yet not so chaste, he will say, Nay. Then seven sacraments are not necessary for salvation to every man; for many have been saved without many of them, as marriage, extreme unction, order of priesthood, shriving, bishoping[1], and the Lord's supper. Who is so ignorant but he knows, that many children never, yea, and old folk too never, received all those his sacraments? which God forbid should all be condemned! No learning can bear this saying to be true, that there be seven sacraments necessary to salvation: therefore by this judge the rest of his sayings.

And lest he should think the general order of the church to be thus, though many particulars never receive them, yet in searching he shall find that to be untrue too. Socrates, lib. v. cap. xix. and Sozomen, lib. vii. cap. xvi. in their ecclesiastical histories write and teach, that shriving to a priest was not com- *Confession.* manded by God, but invented by man; and therefore, when they see it abused, they took it away, and used it not any more. In the time of Theodosius the emperor, four hundred year after Christ, and Nectarius being bishop of Constantinople, as they write there[2], a deacon of the church get a gentlewoman with child

[¹ Bishoping: confirmation. ED.]

[² Ἐν τούτῳ δὲ τὸν ἐπὶ τῶν μετανοούντων τεταγμένον πρεσβύτε-

the appointed penance by her ghostly father. The whole church was so offended at it, that not only there, but many other bishops beside in their churches left off afterward that order of shriving, and left every man free to the examination of his own conscience for his sins. There has been nothing more profitable to the pope than this ear-shriving has, beside many such like filthiness done by it, as this deacon did; for no time was fitter to woo or work their feat in, without suspicion, than shriving time. No prince could enterprise or purpose any great thing, but his confessor would by some means learn it under confession, and declare it to the pope or his chaplains. Eliseus by the Spirit of God never told more secret things, what the king of Syria did in his privy chamber, than the pope could learn by these his confessors the secret purposes of all princes. Then, if confession might be taken away, as here appears it was, it is not so necessary to salvation: nor the universal church has used it ever, as he says; nor we disobey not the church in leaving it off, seeing so many holy men have done it afore us.

_{2 Kings vi.}

John Duns, writing on the fourth book of sentences, *distinct*. xvii. and searching out where this their sacrament should be builded, writes thus: "If we say it is grounded on the saying of St James, 'Confess you one to another,' many inconveniences will follow; for so every man might hear another's confession; and how should St James, bishop of Jerusalem, command Peter the highest and the Romish church? If it be grounded on St John's saying, 'Whose sins ye do forgive, they are forgiven;' yet there is no mention to do it in his ear. If that will not serve then, say that it comes from the apostles: if that serve

ρον οὐκέτι συνεχώρησεν εἶναι πρῶτος Νεκτάριος ὁ τὴν ἐκκλησίαν Κωνσταντινουπόλεως ἐπιτροπεύων. ἐπηκολούθησαν δὲ σχεδὸν οἱ πάντων ἐπίσκοποι. * * * ἐπεὶ γὰρ τὸ μὴ ἁμαρτεῖν παντελῶς θειοτέρας ἢ κατὰ ἄνθρωπον ἐδεῖτο φύσεως, μεταμελομένοις δὲ καὶ πολλάκις ἁμαρτάνουσι συγγνώμην νέμειν ὁ Θεὸς παρεκελεύσατο, ἐν τῷ παραιτεῖσθαι συνομολογεῖν τὴν ἁμαρτίαν χρεὼν φορτικόν, ὡς εἰκὸς, ἐξ ἀρχῆς τοῖς ἱερεῦσιν ἔδοξεν ὡς ἐν θεάτρῳ ὑπὸ μάρτυρι τῷ πλήθει τῆς ἐκκλησίας τὰς ἁμαρτίας ἐξαγγέλλειν· πρεσβύτερον δὲ τῶν ἄριστα πολιτευομένων, ἐχέμυθόν τε καὶ ἔμφρονα, ἐπὶ τοῦτο τετάχασιν, ᾧ δὴ προσιόντες οἱ ἡμαρτηκότες τὰ βεβιωμένα ὡμολόγουν. Sozom. Lib. VII. cap. xvi. p. 98. The incident that follows is narrated with some difference of circumstances by the two historians. Ed.]

in the church, that came to be shriven, while she was there doing not, because the Grecians use it not, then say it comes from Rome, as does the communion in unleavened bread[1]." Thus ye see, what hard shifts they are driven to, in trying out the authority and anciency of this their sacrament, and how small it is when it comes to proof.

But if ye will indifferently judge, whether the new bishops or the old obey their prince and God's church better, read the oath of them both, and then judge. The pope first devised an oath for his bishops to swear at their creation, and when that was not thought strait enough, he devised this afterward: "I, N., bishop of N., from this hour forward, shall be true to St Peter, and the holy Romish church, and to my lord pope N., and to his successors, entering canonically: I shall not be in counsel, consent, nor at deed, that he may lose his life, or that any member may be taken from him by deceit, or violent hands laid on him, or wrong done to him by any means. That counsel that shall be declared to me by himself, letters, or messengers, I shall not disclose to any man wittingly to his harm. I shall help to defend the popedom of the Romish church, and the rules of holy fathers, and the royalties of St Peter against all men, saving my order. I shall not be at any counsel or deed, where any evil is devised against the honour and power of them, but my power I shall stop it, and so shortly as I can signify it to our lord pope, or some other that will tell it his holiness. Heretics, schismatics, and rebels to our lord pope, to my power I shall pursue, &c." Look how well our holy prelates keep their oath to the pope, and deny it to their lawful prince. The oath of the new bishops is in print in English, and so known of all that lust to learn, that I need not to write it; and al- *The prelates' oath to the pope.*

[1] Dicitur quod sic de illo verbo Jacobi quinto, *Confitemini alterutrum peccata, &c.* Sed nec per hoc videtur mihi, quod Jacobus præceptum hoc dedit, nec præceptum a Christo promulgavit. Primum non. Unde enim sibi auctoritas obligandi totam ecclesiam? cum esset episcopus ecclesiæ Hierosolymitanæ: nisi dicas illam ecclesiam in principio fuisse principalem, et per consequens ejus episcopum principalem patriarcham; quod non concederent Romani, nec quod illa auctoritas proprie pro tempore illo erat sibi subtracta. Duns, Tom. II. p. 103. Venet. 1598.—After a long discussion the conclusion arrived at is, that it rests upon tradition orally handed down from the apostles! ED.]

though the popish prelates refuse to take that oath, because it makes the prince the chief governor over them, (which they cannot abide,) hereafter in his proper place, where he falls into that question, I shall entreat of it.

Fasting.

Secondly, where he charges us, that where the church commands to fast, we command to eat, and have eaten flesh in Lent and other forbidden days, we speak plain English, and say he lies. Under the name of the church he ever understands Rome, yea, and not when it continued in any pure religion, but even in these latter days, when it is overwhelmed with infinite superstitions. Fasting days be appointed commonly by every particular church and country, rather than by the universal church; but if any kind of fasting be general,

Ambrose.

I say they break that order rather than we. Ambrose writes on the 17th chapter of Luke, that "for the space of fifty days betwixt Easter and Whitsunday, the church knows no fasting day[1]". Mark, what the church used in his time, and what it is grown to since. How many fasting days in that space have popes brought in since? From whence came all the gang-days to be fasted in the cross-week[2]? Was it from the church or no? If the church did it, then the latter church and popes were contrary to the old church in Ambrose' time; or else the church is free in all ages to disannul that which was done afore them. If it be free, why then may not the church now disannul that which was done afore our time, as well as they break the custom of the church in Ambrose' time afore them? Has not the church like power in all ages to decree or disannul what they lust? Are we more bound that we shall not break old customs, than they were? What is the reason that we should be so, or where is it so written? If the church be ruled by general councils, where is that council that decreed so many fasting days to be betwixt Easter and Whitsunday? And Ambrose says none was afore his time. Is council so contrary to council, or does one council deface that which another determined? Then is that true, where I said afore

[1] Ergo per hos quinquaginta dies jejunium nescit ecclesia, sicut dominica qua Dominus resurrexit, et sunt omnes dies tanquam dominica. Ambros. in Luc. xvii. 4. § 25. ED.]

[2] Gang-days: procession-days. Cross-week: the week in which the feast of the *Invention of the Cross* (May 3) occurs. ED.]

that their councils were like our parliaments, and they are no longer to be observed than other councils following shall think meet. Which being true and granted, who will be so mad to build his faith upon councils, which have so often changed, and one sort believe contrary to another? And although Ambrose say, that the church knew no fasting day betwixt Easter and Whitsunday, yet beside these many fasts in the Rogation week, our wise popes of late years have devised a monstrous fast on St Mark's day. All other fasting days are on the holy-day even; only St Mark must have his day fasted. Tell us a reason why so, that will not be laughen at. We know well enough your reason of Thomas Becket, and think you are ashamed of it: tell us, where it was decreed by the church or general council. Tell us also, if ye can, why the one side of the street in Cheapside fasts that day, being in London diocese, and the other side being of Canterbury diocese fasts not? And so in other towns more. Could not Becket's holiness reach over the street, or would he not? If he could not, he is not so mighty a saint as ye make him: if he would not, he was malicious, that would not do so much for the city wherein he was born. This is his great ancient holy church that he cracks so much of. Becket was living since the conquest under king Henry the second, not four hundred years since: and yet all, as they think, that will not believe their trumpery to be fifteen hundred year old, and ought not to be broken, is an heretic, disobeys the universal church, and not meet to live.

Monica, St Austin's mother, seeing them fast at Rome on the Saturday, and coming to Milan see them not fast there, marvelled at it, and asked Austin, her son, the cause of such diversity of fasting, thinking that both did not well. Austin, being yet but a young scholar in Christ's school, asked Ambrose the cause: Ambrose said, "Fasting was free, and therefore, when he came to Rome, he fasted, and did as they done; when he was at Milan, he fasted not, but did as they did[3]." Afterward Austin, being better learned, gave this lesson

<small>August. Ep. 86.</small>

[[3] Quando hic sum (Mediolani), non jejuno sabbato; quando Romæ sum, jejuno sabbato: et ad quamcunque ecclesiam veneritis, inquit (Ambrosius), ejus morem servate, si pati scandalum non vultis aut facere. August. Epist. xxxvi. (al. lxxxvi.) Tom. ii. p. 120. Paris. 1836. Ed.]

in the same epistle, and said, that "he found written in the New Testament, that we ought to fast; but he never found it there written, what days we should fast." Therefore the time is free to all Christians by the scripture, to eat or not eat: but they must eat so soberly every day, as though they fasted, and see that they surfeit not. Montanus, an heretic, was the first that made laws for fasting; and they, like good children, make it heresy to break their days, or fast otherways than they appoint.

There be two sorts of fasting from meat, which we be bound unto: the one *voluntary*, when we feel ourselves by too much eating given to any kind of sin; then the flesh must be bridled by abstinence, that it rebel not against the spirit, but the mind may more freely serve the Lord: the other is *by commandment*, on such days as be appointed by common order of the country, wherein we must beware that we be not breakers of polities. These kinds of fasting stand in outward discipline, and are to be observed with freedom of conscience, so far as the health of the body may bear, and superstition be not maintained. There is a third sort which Esay speaks of, that stands not in forbearing meats only, but in exercising the works of mercy. "Is this the fast that I choose," says the Lord, "that a man should punish himself, pinch his belly, and pull down himself, so that for hunger and pain he cry out or fall into sickness, that he writhe and lap his head in hoods and kerchiefs? No," says the Lord; "but this is the fast that I have chosen; bring the poor and strangers to thy house, feed the hungry, clothe the naked, &c." God is not delighted with a hungry belly for meat, but with the soul that hungers for his righteousness. Furthermore, this general kind of fasting, which stands in forbearing flesh, and eating but one meal a day, to many it is no grief nor a bridling to the lust of the flesh. Some love fish so well, that they had rather feed of that than of other meat; and some have so weak stomachs, or live so idle lives, that they can scarce digest one meal a day. Again, other some have so costly and great dinners, that they eat more at that one dinner, than the poor man can get at three scamlings on a day[1]. Therefore I cannot say that he punishes his body by abstinence, that

[1 Scamlings or scamblings: meals obtained by shifting or scrambling. ED.]

eats fish which he loves; nor that for weakness of stomach cannot eat more, although his appetite desire it; nor he that gorges himself so full at one meal, that he cannot be hungry of a whole day after. Hard it is therefore to appoint to every particular man, what, when, or how seldom he shall eat when he fasts: but because generally every man loves flesh better than fish, and eats twice a day at the least, generally it was well appointed in fasting to forbear flesh, and eat but once a day, though it fail in many particulars.

Therefore, when any is to be charged with breaking his fast, the *person* is to be considered, whether he may do it with the health of his body; the *kind* of fasting, whether it be superstitious, to buy forgiveness of sins and righteousness; the *time*, that it be not with Jewish observation of days; and the *meat* itself, that it be not thought unclean by nature and unlawful; and the *cause*, that it be for taming the flesh, and not to compound with God or bargain, that for so many days' fasting God shall reward him with such worldly blessings as please him to appoint. In Flanders, every Saturday betwixt Christmas and Candlemas they eat flesh for joy, and have pardon for it, because our lady lay so long in child-bed, say they: we here may not eat so; the pope is not so good to us: yet surely, it were as good reason that we should eat flesh with them all that while that our lady lay in child-bed, as that we should bear our candle at her churching at candlemas with them, as they do. It is seldom seen that men offer candles at womens' churchings, saving at our lady's: but reason it is, that she have some preferment, if the pope would be so good master to us, as let us eat flesh with them. Every one, even by the pope's law, is not bound to fast, as children, old folks, women with child, pilgrims, poor prisoners, labouring or journeying men; and by the consent of the physician and ghostly father, even in the midst of blind popery, all sick persons might eat flesh at all times: and those that be bound to fast may be dispensed with for a little money. That is good holiness, that is bought for so little money. Our Saviour Christ, seeing the Pharisees offended with eating meat, said to them, "That which enters in at the mouth defiles not the man;" and when they would not be so satisfied, he said, "Let them alone, they be blind, and guides of the blind." So surely to such obstinate blind papists, as will not

Matt. xv.

learn the freedom of conscience taught in the scriptures, and serve the Lord in singleness of heart, but put their whole devotion in outward observation of man's traditions, it may well be said, "Let them alone, they be blind, and guides of the blind." It is the weak conscience that is to be borne with, as St Paul teaches, saying, "I had rather never eat flesh, than offend my brother;" and not the obstinate wilful blindness of the superstitious, that may learn and will not. When he has proved that the protestants upon their wilful lusts, and not for such necessary considerations as is here rehearsed, have contemptuously broken the fasting-days appointed by common order, he may well rebuke them: but there be too many witness, which have heard many of them, sundry times, out of the solemnest places and pulpits in the realm teach the contrary: therefore none can believe these his lying words to be true. Breaking thy fast stands not so much in eating any kind of meat, as in the quantity of it, or doing it with contempt of the higher powers and common order appointed; or else in offending the weak conscience, which has not learned his liberty given by God in his holy word.

Lent.

Where he casts in our teeth the breaking of Lent, as though that were commanded by God's own mouth, and should be observed without all excuse, they that lust shall see how great diversities of fasting Lent have been in old time before, and then judge, whether this their one kind of fasting Lent be so necessary. Socrat. lib. v. cap. xxii. of his ecclesiastical history[1] writes of the diversities of sundry things in the church, as keeping of Easter, baptizing, marriage, and the communion, &c.; among which he touches the diversity of Lent fast, and says, that "the Romans fasted three whole weeks afore Easter, except

[1 Ὅτι δὲ ἐξ ἔθους μᾶλλον ἢ ἀπὸ νόμου παρ' ἑκάστοις ἐξ ἀρχαίου τὴν παρατήρησιν ἔλαβεν, αὐτὰ τὰ πράγματα δεικνύει. * * * αὐτίκα τὰς πρὸ τοῦ πάσχα νηστείας ἄλλως παρ' ἄλλοις φυλαττομένας ἐστὶν εὑρεῖν. οἱ μὲν γὰρ ἐν Ῥώμῃ τρεῖς πρὸ τοῦ πάσχα ἑβδομάδας, πλὴν σαββάτου καὶ κυριακῆς, συνημμένας νηστεύουσιν· οἱ δὲ ἐν Ἰλλυρίοις, καὶ ὅλῃ τῇ Ἑλλάδι, κ. τ. λ. * * ἐστὶ δὲ εὑρεῖν οὐ μόνον περὶ τὸν ἀριθμὸν τῶν ἡμερῶν διαφωνοῦντας, ἀλλὰ καὶ τὴν ἀποχὴν τῶν ἐδεσμάτων οὐχ ὁμοίαν ποιουμένους· οἱ μὲν γὰρ πάντη ἐμψύχων ἀπέχονται, οἱ δὲ τῶν ἐμψύχων ἰχθῦς μόνους μεταλαμβάνουσι· τινὲς δὲ σὺν τοῖς ἰχθύσι, κ. τ. λ. p. 249. Ed. 1544. It is needless to quote more at length. Ed.]

Saturday and Sunday; some Grecians fast six weeks; some begin seven weeks afore, and fast but fifteen days in that space, and those not all together. They differed also in meats, for some would eat nothing that had life; some would eat no lively thing but fish; some would eat both fish and fowl; other forbare berries and eggs; other forbare all things save dry bread; and other would not eat that: some would not eat afore the ninth hour, but then would feed of divers meats; some at one hour of the day, some at another, &c." If all these christian men served God, and yet had such diversities of fasting their Lent, why should they be counted evil men, that do no worse than they did, or swerve but a little from this their used Lent fast? Is this so well, that nothing is well but this? And because they stick so much to the Romish church, note that he says the Romans fasted but three weeks; why should we then fast six? Or how has Rome changed this old custom? Or may it be changed? If it may not, why have they done it? and if it may, why blame they them that do it? Polychronicon, lib. v. cap. ix. writes, that pope Gregory the first ordained fasting of all Lent[2], who lived six hundred year after Christ: then it lacks much of their authority and ancienty, that they crack so much of.

We read that our Saviour Christ eat flesh at his last supper on maundy-thursday, which day of all in Lent is one of the holiest. If Christ then fasted Lent, I speak not this because I would have men to break the common appointed order of fasting without lawful cause; but that I would every man should know the liberty of conscience that Christ has given and taught us in his word. Let every man obey the ordinance of the rulers, which command not any thing contrary to God; and let them know also the freedom of conscience, that they be not boundmen to the creatures, which God of love has made to serve, and not to rule us. Surely these people were christened, and holy members of the church of Christ: and yet so shamelessly he cracks so much of the whole church to maintain their doings. Spiridion, bishop of a town in Cyprus, when his friend came to him on the fasting-day after dinner, bade his daughter Irene dress a piece of bacon, because he had no other meat in

Sozo. lib. i. cap. 11.

[2 Also in all the churches of Rome he ordained fasting every day in the Lent for forgiveness of sins. ED.]

the house: "Nay," says the man, "I am a christian man; I eat no flesh on the fasting-day." "Why," says Spiridion, "because thou art a christian man, thou should eat¹." O worthy lesson, teaching both the marriage of bishops, and also liberty of meats!

Prayer.

Thirdly, where he belies us, saying that we call prayer superstition, read the books of prayers which the protestants have made, the order that they teach to pray in; mark their prayers openly in their sermons, with what fervent zeal it is done; and judge then, how falsely he misreports them. But if he mean the prayers of monks, friars, nuns, &c. we will not greatly stick to grant them to be so indeed: and good reasons we have out of their own doctors, why to say so. St Thomas in his *secunda secundæ*, Quæst. xcii. writes, that "it is superstition when a man is too holy²." As when he is so pope-holy, that he believes things not to be believed, fears things not to be feared, worships things not to be worshipped, or does things as holy which be not holy indeed. Confer these sayings with monkish prayers, and such like, and see whether we say true. Things necessary to be believed are written only in the scriptures: so be things to be worshipped, to be feared as godly, or counted holy, are taught there only. Then

Superstition.

he that believes more than the holy bible teaches, or worships, fears other gods than the only living God, or does any thing for the service of God, or counts holy that which is not taught there generally, he is superstitious, and the use of the thing itself is superstition.

The English word is the harder, because we use the Latin word *superstition*, and makes it English: but the Greek word makes the nature of it, and the things afore rehearsed, plainer by much. There be two Greek words signifying this superstition;

Ethelothresceia.

Ethelothresceia [ἐθελοθρησκεια] and *deisidæmonia* [δεισιδαιμονία]. The further word signifies, as the interpretation of it

[¹ Ταύτῃ μᾶλλον, ἔφη, οὐ παραιτητέον· πάντα γὰρ καθαρὰ τοῖς καθαροῖς, ὁ θεῖος ἀπεφήνατο λόγος. Sozomen. Eccl. Hist. ii. 11. ED.]

[² Dicitur enim superstitio esse religio supra modum servata, ut patet in Gloss. ad Coloss. ii. super illud, *Quæ sunt rationem habentia sapientiæ in superstitione.* Quæst. xcii. Artic. i. p. 266.—Simulata religio ibi dicitur, quando traditioni humanæ nomen religionis applicatur, prout in Glossa sequitur. Ibid. Artic. ii. p. 267. Antverp. 1575. ED.]

declares, all such religious worshipping of God, as man devises on his own head, and is not taught in the holy scripture. So says the Gloss. Coloss. ii. "When man's tradition is taken for religion, then it is superstition[3]:" as, either to worship any other God than the only true living God, or to worship the only God otherways than he has appointed us in his word, as with lady psalters, trentals, pilgrimages, &c. And because the chief part of godly worship stands in praying to God, and calling on him in our necessities with a stedfast belief of his holy word and promise; he that calls on any creature but God alone for help, or believes other doctrine necessary to salvation than God's book alone, he is well called superstitious. The latter word signifies that godly fear in their opinion which is due to God alone; which whosoever gives to any other creature beside the true God, he is superstitious also: as they that to know things to come will counsel with spirits, or in their sickness or trouble seek help at their hands, hang upon the stars for lucky or unlucky days, or fear any creature more than the Lord and creator. All the pope's creatures therefore be superstitious, putting their holiness and religion in their cowls, cloisters, order invented of men, and fearing more to break the rule of Austin, Dominic, Benet, than of any apostle, evangelist, or Christ himself. They also be superstitious, that put holiness in meats, days, times, places, beads, holy water, palm, cross, pardons, St Agathe's letters for burning houses, thornbushes for lightnings, &c.

Superstitions.

Deisidæmonia.

Learn therefore to put difference betwixt religion and superstition, and then ye shall easily know how we disallow no prayer but the superstitious. The scribes and Pharisees prayed at every corner of the streets, and fasted oft: yet our Saviour Christ rebuked them, not condemning prayer, but their misusing of it. So we will every man to pray in every time and place; yet superstition we abhor in all sorts of men, prayer, time and place. What wicked blindness is this then, to think that bearing prayers written in rolls about with them, as St John's gospel, the length of our Lord, the measure of our lady, or other like, they shall die no sudden death, not be hanged, or if he be hanged, he shall not die! There is

Prayer.

[3 See the preceding note. ED.]

too many such, though ye laugh and believe it not, and not hard to shew them with a wet finger.

Prayer then is of two sorts, either in begging that that we want, or giving thanks for that which we have received: and it is the earnest lifting up of a man's mind to God, or a familiar and reverent talk and complaint to our heavenly Father of our miseries, with a craving of his mercies, and trusting to obtain of his mercy that which shall be necessary; or else an humble thanksgiving for his liberal benefits, so plenteously bestowed on us undeserved. These stand in deep sighs and groanings, with a full consideration of our miserable state and God's majesty; in the heart, and not in ink or paper; not in hanging written scrolls about the neck, but lamenting unfeignedly our sins from the heart, accusing and condemning ourselves, and begging pardon for them; not in speaking a number of words with the lips unconsiderately, be they never so holy, but with bitter tears weighing from the heart every syllable that he thinks or speaks. Thus prayed Anna to have a son, 1 Kings i. so sorrowfully pouring out her griefs afore God in her mind, that the priest, seeing her lips move and hearing not her words, thought she had been drunken. Thus earnestly called Moses on God in his sorrowful meditation, that the Lord said to him, "Why criest thou so to me?"—and yet we read not that he spake any word at all. The other is lip-labour in speaking much, or saying a great number of their own devised prayers, or else a charming; thinking that in certain words speaking they could make things come to pass as they lust. These, with such other as popery is full of, we say be superstitious. [1 Sam. i.]

Lastly, he burdens us with breaking all laws of the church, civil, canon, and the realm, in that we say, marriage of priests is lawful. This is that which may not be borne: this is thought so heinous, that christian men should not suffer it. If he were learned, he could never have heaped so many lies together. All writers confess, that the Greek church in the east part of the world (which is the greater part of christendom) never forbad their priests marriage, nor do at this day. For the west and Latin church now will I try a little, whether any such have been borne by law, or no. Hildebrand, commonly called Gregory VII. (who for his deeds might be turned and

Marriage of priests.

called a *hell-brand*) was the first that ever brought about (but with much ado,) that priests should not marry[1], and the married should lose either their wives or livings: but the priests of Spain withstood him by their bishop. Some afore attempted it, but never one could compass it. This pope lived about the conquest, five hundred year since; and since the beginning of the world unto his time it was not brought to pass. There is a great difference in continuance of time then, that marriage was allowed, and a small that they were forbidden. In Moses' law it was not forbidden, two thousand year afore Christ. Peter the apostle and Philip the evangelist were married, and had daughters. Gregory, bishop of Nazianzum, was bishop there, as his father was afore him[2]. Polycrates, bishop of Ephesus, says, that "seven of his cousins and ancestors had been bishops afore him[3]." When Phileas, bishop of Chinna, was led to martyrdom, the greatest reason they had to persuade him to recant, was that he would have pity on his wife[4]. Eustathius and his scholars are blamed because they despised married priests[5]. Polyd. lib. v. cap. 4. DeInventor.

Acts xxi.

Ruff. lib. ii. cap. 9.

Euseb. lib. v. cap. 25.

Sozo. lib. iii. cap. 14.

These among the Grecians, I trust, prove that the church

[1 Ita aliis denique super aliis promulgatis legibus, non ante pontificatum Gregorii septimi, qui anno salutis MLXXIV. est pontifex creatus, conjugium adimi occidentalibus sacerdotibus potuit.—The remark which the writer subjoins, shortly after, is too much to the purpose to be passed over: Illud tamen dixerim, tantum abfuisse ut ista coacta castitas illam conjugalem vicerit, ut etiam nullius delicti crimen majus ordini dedecus, plus mali religioni, plus doloris omnibus bonis impresserit, inusserit, attulerit, quam sacerdotum libidinis labes. Polyd. Vergil. Lib. v. cap. 4. pr. fin. p. 298. Argentor. 1606. ED.]

[2 Gregorius vero apud Nazianzon oppidum in locum patris episcopus subrogatus hæreticorum turbinem fideliter tulit. Auctores Hist. Eccles. Lib. xi. (Ruffini ii.) cap. ix. ED.]

[3 In his letter addressed to Victor, bishop of Rome: Ἑπτὰ μὲν ἦσαν συγγενεῖς μου ἐπίσκοποι, ἐγὼ δὲ ὄγδοος. Translated by Ruffinus, Septem namque ex parentibus meis per ordinem fuerunt episcopi. ED.]

[4 Πρὸς δὲ καὶ αὐτοῦ τοῦ δικαστοῦ παρακαλοῦντος, ὡς ἂν αὐτῶν οἶκτον λάβοιεν, φειδώ τε παίδων καὶ γυναικῶν ποιήσαιντο. Euseb. Eccl. Hist. Lib. viii. cap. ix., where it is told of Phileas, bishop of Thmuis, and his fellow-martyr, Philoromus. ED.]

[5 Ἐπαιτιῶνται δέ τινας τῶν αὐτοῦ μαθητῶν, ὡς γάμῳ καταμεμφομένους, καὶ ἐν οἴκοις γεγαμηκότων εὔχεσθαι παραιτουμένους, καὶ τοὺς γεγαμηκότας πρεσβυτέρους ὑπερφρονοῦντας. P. 42. Ed. 1544. ED.]

has had married priests of old time. The fiftieth canon of the apostles says: "If any bishop, priest, deacon, or any of the clergy, forbear marriage, flesh and wine, not for that his mind might be fitter to godliness, but for abomination, forgetting that all that God has made is good, and that he made both male and female; let him be correct or deposed[1]." The third council of Carthage says thus: "Let not priests' children make any plays and games." "If any," says the pope's canon law, "should teach that a priest for religion sake should despise his wife, accursed be he." *Distinct.* xxviii[3]. Again, the next chapter following: "If any make a difference of a married priest, as though he should not minister by occasion of his marriage, and therefore forbear from his ministration, accursed be he." When this foolish unlearned papist has scraped these and such like sayings out of the pope's testament, commonly called his decrees, then he may say the pope's law has utterly condemned marriage of priests in the Latin church.

St Paul.

But what needs these proofs, when St Paul says plain. "A bishop must be the husband of one wife?" And Ambrose, writing on the same place, says that "he is not forbidden to have a second[4]." Pope Pius II. writes, that "there were great causes why priests were forbidden wives, but there were greater causes why they should be restored.[5]" Jerome

Ambrose.
Platina.

Jerom.

[1] Si quis episcopus aut presbyter aut diaconus, aut quivis omnino de sacerdotali consortio, nuptiis et carnibus et vino abstinuerit, non propterea quo mens ad cultum pietatis reddatur exercitatior, sed propter abominationem, oblitus, quod omnia pulchra valde, et quod masculum et feminam Deus creavit hominem, sed diffamationibus lacessens creationem Dei vocat ad calumniam; aut corrigitor, aut deponitor, et ex ecclesia rejicitor. Consimiliter et laicus.—Canones sanctorum apostolorum per Clementem, a Petro Apostolo Romæ ordinatum episcopum, in unum congesti. Can. L. ED.]

[2] Held in the year 397. Cap. xi. Ut filii episcoporum vel clericorum spectacula secularia non exhibeant, sed nec spectent. Concil. Tom. III. p. 486. ED.]

[3] Si quis docuerit sacerdotem sub obtentu religionis propriam uxorem contemnere, anathema sit. Decret. Gratiani, Pars I. Distinct. xxviii. p. 148. Antverp. 1573. ED.]

[4] Sed conjugia non resolvuntur, si quis iteraverit. * * * Qui autem iteraverit conjugium, culpam quidem non habet coinquinati, sed prærogativa exuitur sacerdotis. Class. I. Epist. LXIII. (LXIV.) § 63. ED.]

[5] Sacerdotibus magna ratione sublatas nuptias, majori restituendas videri. Platina, De Vit. Pontif. fo. 157. Colon. 1540. ED.]

grants that in his time many priests were married, *contra Jovinian.*⁶ And on the sixth chapter of the epistle to the Ephesians he writes thus: "Let bishops and priests read these, which teach their children worldly learning, and make them to read comedies, and sing bawdy songs of minstrels, &c.⁷ Nauclerus, Part VII. Generat. XXXVII. writes thus: "Gregory VII. de- Gregory VII.
creed in the year one thousand and seventy-three, that from thenceforth priests should not have wives; and they that had, should leave them or be deposed. He wrote to the bishops of France and Germany, that they should procure it so to be with them. The whole clergy cried out against this decree, calling him heretic; who had forgotten the word of the Lord, who said, Matt. xix.
"All receive not this saying; and he that cannot refrain, let 1 Cor. vii. him marry; and it is better to marry than to burn." How violent a thing is this to compel, that men should live like angels! and when he denies the accustomed course of nature, he should give liberty to whoredom! If he continued to confirm this decree, they had rather leave their priesthood than marriage. Gregory, notwithstanding, was instant, and rebukes the bishops Gregory. of slothfulness, that these things were not done among them. The archbishop of Mentz, perceiving how hard a thing it was, to break so long a rooted custom, and to reform the world in his old age⁸, appointed his priests six months to do that in, which they must necessarily do: they purposed then to lay violent hands on the bishop, except he changed his purpose. The year following Gregory attempted that divorcing of them by his legate, which he could not bring to pass by the bishop. The priests were so moved against the legate,

[⁶ Eliguntur mariti in sacerdotium, non nego; quia non sunt tanti virgines, quanti necessarii sunt sacerdotes. Hieron. adversus Jovinianum, Lib. I. Tom. IV. Pars ii. p. 175. Paris. 1706. ED.]

[⁷ Legant episcopi atque presbyteri, qui filios suos secularibus literis erudiunt, et faciunt comedias legere, et mimorum turpia scripta cantare. In Ephes. vi. Tom. IV. p. 396. ED.]

[⁸ i.e. *its* old age, the world's. Ad rudimenta nascentis ecclesiæ senescentem jam mundum reformaret.—It is unnecessary to quote the original, of which, in substance, the text gives an accurate translation. The conclusion is as follows: Hanc disceptationem horrenda ecclesiæ occidentalis pestis secuta est; adeo ut et laici in hoc sacerdotum dissidio sacra tractarent, baptizarent, inungerent sordibus pro vero pietatis oleo, &c. Naucleri Chronica, Tom. II. Generat. xxxvi. p. 777—8. Colon. 1579. ED.]

that they had almost torn him in pieces, except he had gone away, and left the matter undone. A horrible plague," he says further, "did follow this contention of the west church, insomuch that laymen did christen and minister sacraments, because the priests had rather forsake their priesthood than their wives, and would not minister, &c." Thus far the history. Mark when this was done, the trouble in doing it, the plague that followed, and that marriage, as he says, was long used afore him.

<small>Note also this notable epistle concerning the same matter.</small>

"To the lord and father Nicholas, the diligent provider for the holy Romish church: Huldrich, bishop of Augsburgh in name only, wishes love as a son, and fear as a servant.

"Where I found, O father and Lord, your decrees for the continenty of clerks, which ye send me of late, to be without discretion, a certain fear and heaviness both troubled me: fear, because the judgment of the shepherd, whether it be right or wrong, is to be feared; for I was afraid lest the weak hearers of the scripture, which will scarce obey a righteous judgment, not regarding this of yours, as wrongful, should boldly break this so heavy a commandment of the shepherd, that it may not be borne: sorrow, or rather pity, troubled me, when I doubted by what means the members might escape, where their head was so sore sick. What can be more grievous, or more to be pitied of the whole church, than that you, the bishop of the chiefest see, should swerve but a little from a holy discretion? Thou swerved much from this, when thou would that clerks, (whom thou should warn for the continenty of marriage,) should be compelled to it by a certain imperious violence. Is not this worthily to be counted a violence, by the common judgment of all wise men, when any man is compelled to execute private decrees, contrary to the doctrine of the gospel and decree of the Holy Ghost?

"Therefore, where there be many examples of the old testament and new, teaching discretion, as ye know; I beseech your fatherhood, be content that some few among many may be put in this writing. Our Lord appointed marriage to priests in the old law, which is not read to be forbidden them afterward. But he says in the gospel, "There be eunuchs which have gelded themselves for the kingdom of heaven: but all men receive not this word; he that can take it, let him take it." Therefore the apostle says, "For virgins I have no commandment of the Lord, but I give counsel." Ye see that all men cannot take this counsel, according to the saying of the Lord. And ye see also many flatterers of the same counsel, willing to please men and not God, with this false shew of continenty, to do more heinous things; as to provoke their fathers' wives, not abhor to lie by beasts and men. But lest the state of the whole church should be decayed by the great mischiefs of this filthiness, he said, "For fornication let every man have his own wife." Yet these hypocrites falsely say, that this same belongs specially to laymen: which hypocrites, although they be in a most holy order, yet they doubt not to misuse other men's wives. These men understood not the scripture rightly; and because they wrung the pap too sore, they sucked blood instead of milk. For that saying of the apostle, "Let every man have his own wife," excepts no man indeed, but him that professes continenty, or him that determines to continue his virginity in the Lord, &c. And that ye may know that they which have not made this vow, ought not to be compelled, hear the apostle to Timothy, saying, "It becomes a bishop to be blameless, the husband of one wife:" and lest any man should turn this saying to the church only, he adds, "He that cannot rule his own house, how can he rule the church of God?" Likewise he says, "Deacons must be the husband of one wife, which can well rule their children and houses."

" I know that ye have taught by the decrees of holy Silvester, pope, that this wife must be blessed of the priest. The writer of the rule of clerks' lives, agreeing with these, and such sentences of the scripture, says, "A clerk must be chaste, or else bound with the band of one marriage." Of all which sayings he gathers truly, that a bishop and deacon are to be blamed, if they be divided into many women: but if either bishop or deacon forsake one woman for religion sake, the canonical sentence here condemns them without respect of their degrees, saying, "A bishop under pretence of religion must not put away his own wife: if he put her away, let him be excommunicate; but if he continue, let him be deposed, and *postea*. There be some which take St Gregory for a help of this opinion; whose foolishness I laugh at, and am sorry for their ignorance: they know not that the perilous decree of this heresy, made by St Gregory, was purged afterward of him by worthy fruit of repentance. For on a time when he send to his pond for fish, and see more than six thousand children's heads brought, he sighed, moved with inward sorrow, and confessing that decree, which he made for forbearing of marriage, to have been the cause of so great a slaughter, did purge it with worthy fruit of repentance; and condemning his own decree praised that counsel of the apostle, "It is better to marry than to burn;" adding for his part this, It is better to marry, than give occasion of murder[1]."

Thus much, among many other reasons concerning this matter, this bishop wrote a seven hundred year since. Friar Mantuan says that Hilary, the learned writer and bishop of Poitiers in France, was married. The council Grangrense, about a three hundred year after Christ, says: "If any man think that it is not lawful for a married priest to use his ministery, or abhor him for that cause, cursed be he[2]." The priests of Spain did earnestly defend their marriage against pope Syricius, being angry with them.

Thus far ye see of how late years, and how troublesome a beginning this forbidding of priests' marriage had in other countries: now let us see a little how and when it began here in England, that this proud pricker and unlearned papist may see his own foolishness. If I should begin at Wales, the relics of the old Britons, which have at all times suffered their priests to marry in all popery, peradventure some would call them concubines for a shift, rather than wives, as they be indeed; but surely, if papists will suffer fathers so to bestow their daughters, and their chaplains to keep unlawful women, rather than their lawful wives, (as Pighius, their great patron, says it is better for a priest to keep a whore than have a wife[3],) they declare

[1] For the original of this letter, with some further notice of it, see Note C in the Appendix. ED.]

[2] Quicunque discernit a presbytero qui uxorem habuit, quod non oporteat eo ministrante de oblatione percipere, anathema sit. Cap. IV. De oblatione Presbyteri conjugati. Concil. Tom. II. p. 501. Paris. 1644. ED.]

[3] Having explained just before the sense of *uri* ($\pi\upsilon\rho o\tilde{\upsilon}\sigma\theta\alpha\iota$, 1 Cor. vii. 9.), Non est *uri* tentari, ut adversarii falsissimo intelligunt et persuadent miseris, sed tentationi succumbere, Pighius discusses the question as follows: Sed esto, non faciunt obligati voto omnes, quod possunt et debent, ut habeant continentiæ gratiam, et proinde non solum tentantur,

whose children they be: marriage is of God, whoredom is of the devil. Therefore I come to more certain things. In the time of king Henry the first, Paschal being pope, and Anselm bishop of Canterbury, about four hundred years since, this divorcing of priests began chiefly here with us. The pope willed Anselm to do it: he attempted to do it, and the king withstood it, as appears by sundry epistles of Anselm concerning the same matter, Epistle 77, and 376.

"Anselm to his brether and sons, the lord prior Ernulph, and other serving God under him in Christ's church in Canterbury, greeting and his blessing. As concerning priests, of whom the king gave commandment that they should have both their churches and their wives, as they had in the time of his father, and of Lanfranc, late archbishop; yet both because the king has revested and reseised me of the whole archbishoprick, and also because so cursed a marriage was forbidden in a council in the time of his father and the same archbishop, boldly by that authority which I have by the archbishoprick, I command, not only within the archbishoprick, but also throughout England, that all priests which keep their wives, shall be deprived of their churches and ecclesiastical benefice."[4]

Mark the things contained in these few words: the king's commandment for priests to keep their benefices and wives both, contrary to pope Gregory's decree afore, and yet not contrary to the custom in his father's time and bishop Lanfranc. And

Ernulph.

sed etiam uruntur eorum plerique. Quid igitur? An nubere his minus malum erit? Nam melius hoc dicere non potes, quod apostolus damnationi imputat, si primam fidem irritam faciant. His, inquam, an saltem minus malum minusque damnabile erit nubere, quam uri? Tu vide, quis pejor servus est? * * * In quibus si quando remissiores ex infirmitate carnis ceciderimus, tolerabilius hoc peccatum est, quam si jugum in totum excutiamus, i. e. *by marriage*. Alberti Pighii Explicationes Catholicæ præcipuarum Controversiarum. p. 215. Paris. 1586. ED.]

[4 Anselmus Archiepiscopis, &c...... De presbyteris et quibus rex præcepit, ut et ecclesias et feminas habeant, sicut tempore patris sui et Lanfranci archiepiscopi habuerunt; et quia rex me resarsivit de toto archiepiscopatu, et quia tempore patris ejus et ejusdem archiepiscopi in concilio prohibitum est tam execrabile conjugium; fiducialiter ea, quam in archiepiscopatu habeo, auctoritate præcipio, non solum in archiepiscopatu, sed etiam per totam Angliam, ut omnes sacerdotes, qui feminas tenuerint ecclesiis et omni ecclesiastico beneficio priventur. Lib. III. Epist. cx. Tom. IV. p. 143. Colon. 1612. ED.]

Anselm. where Anselm demanded the pope's advice what was best to do, seeing it was so hard to divorce them, note the pope's answer, Epistle 331.

Paschal. "Paschal bishop, servant of God's servants, to his reverend brother Anselm, bishop of Canterbury, greeting and apostolical blessing. We believe your brotherhood is not ignorant, what is decreed in the Romish church concerning priests' children: but because there is so great a multitude of such within the realm of England, that almost the greater and better part of the clerks are reckoned to be on this side; we commit the order herein to your charge: for we grant those to be promoted to holy offices (by reason of the need at this time, and for the profit of the church) whom learning and life shall commend among you, and yet notwithstanding the prejudice of the ecclesiastical decree be taken heed to hereafter[1]."

Here I note the pope's confession, that almost the greater and better part of the clergy here in England were married then, and that he suffers them to be promoted to benefices, and afterward, as time would suffer, to execute the pope's divorcing decree. When the bishops could not well bring those divorces to pass, the pope send Joan, his cardinal, to do it: and he, as *Polychron.* Polychronicon writes, lib vii. cap. xvi. was taken the same night in bed with a whore, in the time of Henry the first.[2] O holy single life that the pope went about!

But not only this hardness was in beginning of this divorce, but after that they were separated, divers came together again, as appears in the epistle that Anselm wrote to William his archdeacon in this behalf. "Anselm, archbishop,

[1 In Lib. iii. Epist. xlv. of Anselm is pope Paschal's letter, giving a succinct account of the various points on which Anselm asked for counsel, with the respective answers. The answer to the second question is as follows: De sacerdotum filiis vel concubinarum quam vitam tenendam prædecessores nostri sedis apostolicæ pontifices instituerunt, nosse te credimus: nec nos ab illorum volumus aberrare vestigiis. Quod igitur tibi super his in barbaris regionibus sit disponendum, ex ipsius præcepti poteris collatione distinguere. Ed.]

[2 John, cardinal of Rome, came into England, and made a grievous process against priests' concubines, and said, that "it is a foul sin and a great to arise from a strumpet's side to sacre [consecrate] Christ's body:" but the same day, after that he had sung mass, he was taken with a strumpet at even. Thing that was openly known might not be forsake: it must needs be known. Ed.]

to the reverend Gundulph bishop, and to Ernulph prior, and to William, archdeacon of Canterbury, and to all in his diocese, greeting. Epistle 373. William our archdeacon has written to me, that some priests which be under his custody, taking again their wives that were forbidden them, have fallen into uncleanness, from which they were drawn by wholesome counsel and commandment. When the archdeacon would amend this thing, they utterly despised his warning and worthy commandment with a wicked pride. Then he, calling together many religious men, and obedient priests, excommunicated worthily the proud and disobedient, which beastly despised his curse, and defiled the holy ministery as much as in them lay, &c[3]."

Here appears, how hard it was to divorce the married priests, and how some would not obey, though they were excommunicate. I mark also, how the bishop calls these marriages "uncleanness," and says, they "defile the ministery:" but to an indifferent judge the priests have better reasons out of the scriptures for themselves, than the bishop had. Let all them therefore, that have the fear of God afore them, consider the great plagues that God laid on this realm at that time. The realm was conquered by strangers, William conqueror and his fellows, the pope's chaplains. Lanfranc, bishop of Canterbury under king William the second, brought in transubstantiation, and Anselm under Henry the first, next king following, brought in unmarried priests, and divorced the married. The doctrine of transubstantiation is so holy, that a married priest may not handle it : the one cannot stand without the other, and the one necessarily brings in the other. The late popes were better

[[3] Nuper relata est mihi Deo execrabilis et omnibus christianis odibilis superba quorundam, qui se sacerdotes nominant, præsumptio. Scripsit namque mihi archidiaconus noster Willelmus, quia nonnulli presbyteri, qui sub ejus sunt custodia, iterum repetentes prohibitas feminas, in immunditiam, a qua salubri consilio et jussione abstracti fuerunt, se revolverunt. Quod cum idem archidiaconus vellet corrigere, omnino ejus monitionem et susceptibilem jussionem nefanda superbia contempserunt. Qui, convocatis secum pluribus religiosis et obedientibus sacerdotibus, superbos et inobedientes gladio dignæ excommunicationis percussit: quam excommunicationem bestiali insania contemnentes, ministerium sanctum polluere, quantum in ipsis est, non formidant. Lib. III. Epist. cxii. Tom. IV. p. 144. Colon. 1612. ED.]

than they; for in the time of pope Paul the third, keeping his council at Trident a seventeen year since, came forth that worthy book *Interim,* wherein is entreated the marriages of priests, and concluded that those which be married should not be divorced; but whether any more should marry, it should be referred and deferred to a general council. These men were more reasonable, modest, and wise than our late brutish papists: for in the late days of their raging madness, contrary to this decree of the pope made not sixteen year afore, they divorced here with us all priests that afore were married.

But when these old popes see how hard it was to drive priests from their wives, that hell-brand Gregory VII. decreed that none should hear his mass, that was married: and by this polity he brought more to pass, than by excommunication or any other way. Such practices the pope's prelates are full of: for when the priests perceived their ministery was despised, it made them something to relent, and at length altogether to quail. At the same time, and straight after the conquest, were swarms of monks brought almost into all the cathedral churches of the realm. As at Duresme, in the year one thousand and eighty-three, the priests (which then were married) were brought from Duresme, and had the prebends of Aucland, Darnton, and Norton; and monks were placed in their steads at Duresme, in the eighteenth year of William the Conqueror: and these prebends were then first founded and appointed for these secular married priests. O gentle papists of old time, that would not displace married priests, but provide livings for them, where our Edomites persecute them without mercy! Marriage, God's holy ordinance in paradise, and blessed, is punished of popery in the world: such is their wickedness. In other places, as Winchester, Worcester, and elsewhere, this bringing in of monks and driving out married priests began a little afore the conquest under king Edgarus, but no great difference in the years. Dunstan and Oswalde, bishops of Worcester first, and after of Canterbury and York, were great helpers in this matter. Oswalde thrust all the clerks out of Worcester church, which would not be made monks. Ethelwoldus, bishop of Winchester, thrust out his married priests likewise, if they would not forsake their wives, and become monks, and placed monks in their stead: but they so hated the monkish life, that they were content to leave all rather than become monks, every one of them save three. But after the death of Edgarus, Aelfer, king of Mercia, (which was the middle and chief part of England,) and many other nobles of the realm, drove out the monks, and brought in the married priests again. These and such like are written in the records of these churches, and were done many of them about the year of our Lord nine hundred and sixty-three, and after. Polychronicon also, in his sixth book, touches many of these things.

These things I have spoken more largely, because he charges us with disobeying all laws, as though these were never done in England afore, and good men should not suffer them; and also, that the world may see how lewd, unlearned a proctor has taken their case in hand. If he were not too far past shame, he would not deny the laws of the realm to suffer priests' marriage, seeing the twenty-ninth Injunction, which the queen's highness set forth, entreats of their marriage only[1]. But this is their obedience that they shew to their princes, in denying their laws: and it is their old opinion, that injunctions be not laws, nor princes have that authority over them to make such laws. God give them better minds, or grant the prince better subjects!

It were too long to write all that may be said in this behalf, and it is not my meaning: only I would let them see which would learn, how wrongfully priests' marriage is accused. For the froward obstinate, that will not learn, but contemn and condemn all that gainsay it, afore they hear them speak, I say with our Saviour Christ in a like case, "Let them alone, they be blind, Matt. xv. and guides of the blind." They are not to be passed on: do as truth, God's word, and a good conscience teaches you, nothing regarding their railing blasphemies. Austin, in his book *De Bono Conjugali*, cap. 21, comparing the chastity of marriage and single life together, says thus: "The virtue of continency must be always in the power of the mind, but indeed it must be shewed as things and times change. For as there was not a diverse merit of suffering martyrdom in Peter that suffered cruel death, and in John that suffered not; so there is not a diverse merit of chastity in John which was not married, and

[1 Queen Elizabeth's Injunctions published in 1559. Injunction xxix. See Bp. Sparrow's Collection, p. 76. Lond. 1675. Ed.]

in Abraham which gat children. For both his single life and this man's marriage served Christ, as the time changed; but John had chastity both in power and deed, Abraham only in power[1]." Again, cap. 22, " Evil men say to him that is chaste, Art thou better than Abraham? But when he hears it, let him not be afraid; but say, I am not better, but the chastity of single men is better than the chastity of marriage[2]." Again, cap. 23, " If we compare the things themselves together, it is sure that the chastity of continenty is better than the chastity of marriage, and yet both good: but when we compare the men together, he is the better that has a greater goodness and virtue in him than the other has[3]." Thus far Austin. Mark the difference that he puts betwixt the goodness of things themselves, and the goodness of the men that have them.

I am sure many will judge, that I speak this to please my wife: but we read that Paphnutius unmarried, when some in the council would have determined that priests should leave their wives, persuaded the contrary[4]. Spiridion, being married, as he writes also[5], and having children, was never the worse, or hindered to minister the sacraments. Chrysostom, in his homily on the marriage in Cana of Galilee, writes thus: "Thou reprovest marriage, that they be a let to godliness: but wilt

Sozo. lib. i. cap. 23.

Ibid. cap. 11.

[1 Qui vident continentiæ virtutem in habitu animi semper esse debere, in opere autem pro rerum ac temporum opportunitate manifestari. * * Quocirca sicut non est impar meritum patientiæ in Petro qui passus est, et in Joanne qui passus non est; sic non est impar meritum continentiæ in Joanne qui nullas expertus est nuptias, et in Abraham qui filios generavit. Et illius enim cælibatus et illius connubium pro temporum distributione Christo militarunt: sed continentiam Joannes et in opere, Abraham vero in solo habitu habebat. Cap. xxvi. (21.) Tom. vi. p. 564. Paris. 1836. ED.]

[2 Ac per hoc ab eis, qui corrumpunt bonos mores colloquiis malis, inani et vana versutia dicitur homini christiano continenti et nuptias recusanti, Tu ergo melior quam Abraham? Quod ille cum audierit, non perturbetur; * * sed dicat, Ego quidem non sum melior quam Abraham; sed melior est castitas cælibum quam castitas nuptiarum. Ibid. xxvii. (22.) ED.]

[3 Res ergo ipsas si comparemus, nullo modo dubitandum est meliorem esse castitatem continentiæ quam castitatem nuptiarum, cum tamen utrumque sit bonum: homines vero cum comparamus, ille est melior qui bonum amplius quam alius habet. Ibid. xxviii. (23.) ED.]

[4 See above, p. 532. ED.]
[5 See above, p. 561. ED.]

thou know that it hurts not to have wife and children? Had not Moses wife and children? Was not Elias a virgin? Moses brought manna from heaven, and Elias fire: God spake to Moses, and was conversant with Elias. Did not Moses make quails to come? and Elias shut up heaven from rain with a word? Did not Moses divide the sea, and brought through the people? Was not Elias taken into heaven in a fiery chariot? Did virginity hurt the one, or was wife and children a hindrance to the other? Hast thou marked Elias in his chariot in the air, and Moses going on foot in the sea? Mark Peter also, a Matt. viii. pillar of the church, that he had a wife; for it is written, that Jesus went in to Peter's mother-in-law, being sick, touched her, and the fever left her. Where there is a mother-in-law, there must needs be a wife and daughter-in-law. Seest thou not then that Peter had a wife? Blame not marriage then, &c." Thus far Chrysostom⁶.

I could shew you like examples of married ministers at these days, which are not hindered in their duty doing thereby, nor in any part of godliness; but rather furthered, in that household cares be taken from them thereby, and in sickness they better cherished. These be enough for them that will be persuaded, or more will not serve. It is not hard to bring

[⁶ Σὺ ἐνυβρίζεις τὸν γάμον, καὶ λέγεις ὅτι ἐμπόδισμά ἐστιν ὁ γάμος; οὐδὲν ἐμπόδισμα πρὸς εὐσέβειαν. βούλει μαθεῖν ὅτι οὐδὲν παραβλάπτει ἔχειν γυναῖκα καὶ τέκνα; Μωϋσῆς οὐχὶ γυναῖκα καὶ τέκνα εἶχεν; Ἠλίας οὐχὶ παρθένος ἦν; οὐχὶ Μωϋσῆς μάννα κατήγαγεν ἐκ τοῦ οὐρανοῦ; οὐχὶ Ἠλίας πῦρ κατήγαγεν ἐκ τοῦ οὐρανοῦ; οὐχὶ Μωϋσῆς ὀρτυγομήτραν ἐξεπέτασεν; οὐχὶ Ἠλίας τῷ λόγῳ τὸν οὐρανὸν ἔκλεισεν; οὐχὶ Μωϋσῇ ὁ Θεὸς ὡμίλει; οὐχὶ καὶ Ἠλίᾳ Θεὸς ὡμίλει; οὐχὶ Μωϋσῆς θάλασσαν ἔσχισε, καὶ διήγαγε τὸν λαόν; οὐχὶ Ἠλίας ἐν ἅρματι πυρίνῳ ἀνελήφθη; μή τι παρέβλαψε τοῦτον ἡ παρθενία; μή τι παρενεπόδισε τοῦτον ἡ γυνὴ καὶ τὰ τέκνα; εἶδες Ἠλίαν τὸν τοῦ ἀέρος ἡνίοχον, εἶδες Μωϋσῆν τὸν τῆς θαλάσσης ὁδοιπόρον; βλέπε καὶ Πέτρον τὸν στῦλον τῆς ἐκκλησίας, ὅτι καὶ αὐτὸς γυναῖκα εἶχε· πόθεν οὖν δῆλον ὅτι γυναῖκα εἶχεν; ἐγὼ λέγω. Εἰσῆλθε, φησὶν, ὁ Ἰησοῦς πρὸς τὴν πενθερὰν Πέτρου· καὶ ἦν ἐκείνη ἀρρωστοῦσα, καὶ ἥψατο αὐτῆς, καὶ ἔφυγεν ὁ πυρετὸς αὐτῆς, καὶ διηκόνει. ὁρᾷς ὅτι καὶ Πέτρος γυναῖκα εἶχεν; ὅπου γὰρ πενθερὰ, εὔδηλον ὅτι καὶ γυνή. ὁρᾷς ὅτι καὶ Πέτρος γυναῖκα εἶχε; μή τι διαβάλλῃς τὸν γάμον. Homil. contra Judæos, Gentiles, et Hæreticos. Tom. I. p. 1009. Paris. 1839.—But the genuineness of this Homily is questioned. Ed.]

divers more authorities out of the pope's *distinct.* XXVIII. and XXXI.[1] to prove this withal: but he that is father of all filthiness, is not worthy to bear witness in so honest a matter. In Moses' law, where every one should marry within his own tribe, the priests had this privilege, that they might marry with the king's stock: but our men abhor priests' marriage, lest they should get gentlewomen, and so possibly might inherit their lands. God was not so wise to foresee these things as we be; and that which God's wisdom thought good and commendable, we with our polities think hurtful and unprofitable. God make us wise in him! For the foolish writhing and racking of the scriptures following, because they be so unaptly applied that a blind man may see them, I will not stand to set out his folly; for they contain no matter of weight against us.

IX. They have invented a new way to make bishops and priests, and a manner of service and ministration that St Austin never knew, St Edmond, Lanfranc, St Anselm, nor never one bishop of Canterbury, saving only Cranmer, who forsook his profession as apostata; so that they must needs condemn all the bishops in Canterbury but Cranmer, and he that now is; all the bishops of York, saving Holgate, and he that now is; although St Wilfride, St William have been taken for saints, and were bishops in York. In Coventry and Lichfield St Chad was bishop, and many blessed bishops; and he that now is bishop, can find not any one that ever was made as he is, nor of his religion. Therefore he must prove all bishops of Lichfield were deceived, walked in blindness, and ignorance; or else he that now is must needs be deceived and be in blindness. In Duresme have been many good fathers; but he that now is bishop cannot find any one predecessor in that see that was of his religion, and made bishop after such sort as he was: so that he that now is must take in hand to condemn all the bishops afore him, that they were in ignorance and blindness, or they will come to his condemnation at the day of judgment. And this in all bishopricks in England; some can find one, and some none, that ever was of their religion. What arrogancy may be thought in those men that will take in hand to condemn so many blessed fathers all to be in blindness!

Here this proud papist triumphs, as though nothing could be said to the contrary. For our church service I said enough afore: now mark what weight his raging railing words have.

[1 See p. 566. Ed.]

He says St Edmond, Lanfranc, Anselm never knew such an ordering of priests and bishops: how proves he that? I think they did: for they lived in that age when religion began to decay, blindness and superstition to creep into the world, and therefore could not be ignorant of such good order as had been afore them, although they themselves then began to change and bring in the contrary; whereof I declared part afore, as marriage of priests, church service, &c. To grant that so many bishops of Canterbury, York, Lichfield, and Duresme were in blindness, he thinks it such an inconvenience as no man will do it; and therefore these that now be bishops must needs be deceived. I am not of that opinion, to think it a shame to grant that bishops be deceived, either in that age or other: for there has been no man so holy (except Christ Jesus) but he has been deceived and ignorant in many things, even in religion. Did not Paul rebuke Peter for dissembling in meats with the Jews? Only Christ has the full truth. That is the proud principle of popery, to think that they cannot be deceived: yet in that saying they are most foully deceived. The scribes and Pharisees used the same reasons against Christ our Lord, and the false prophets against the true, saying that they kept the old true learning, and the other brought in a new, and deceived the people.

But in granting these old bishops to be made after another sort than these be now, what harm may follow? What ancienty be they of? All since the conquest, and not past five hundred year since. Then it is but new in comparison of one thousand five hundred and fifty. And if our order agree with Christ's doings and his apostles' writings better than theirs, are we to blame in forsaking them and following Christ and his apostles? or are we to be counted devisers of a new way, when we follow that which is a thousand year elder than theirs? Nay surely, their devices be new, and we restore the old religion again, practised and taught by Christ and his apostles, which they have defaced with their new devised superstition and popery. Whether is it more to contemn or correct these bishops of Canterbury, York, Lichfield, and Duresme, that he names, rather than Christ our Lord, Peter, Paul, Timothy, Titus, &c.? Whether is to be judged elder, wiser, and godlier, these bishops that he names, which are not five hundred year old, or Christ and his apostles, which be one thousand five hundred year old and more?

In the Acts of the Apostles, where Matthias was chosen instead of Judas the traitor, where the seven deacons were chosen, and when Paul and Barnabas were sent forth to preach, how few ceremonies were used in comparison of that multitude which the papists use now! And how much does it agree with our kind of ordering ministers better than with theirs! When Paul taught Timothy and Titus to appoint ministers and bishops in every town, how far differs it from the pope's oiled shavelings! Acts i. Peter calls the disciples together, preaches unto them; they fall to prayer, and chose Matthias instead of Judas. In the sixth of the Acts the apostles assemble the people, declare to them how they themselves should follow preaching, and wills them therefore to pick out men of honesty and godliness to serve the poor: they pray together, lay their hands on them, and made them deacons to provide for the poor. In sending forth Paul and Barnabas, when they were assembled, to their ministry, they fasted, prayed, laid their hands on them, and send them forth. In the fourteenth, Paul and Barnabas "ordained in every church ministers," requiring the consent of the people by holding up their hands, as the Greek word there signifies[1]. In the first epistle to Timothy, chap. v. he bids him, that he "lay not his hands rashly on any man," where afore he had taught him sufficiently what manner of men, and with what qualities he should call and think them meet for the ministery.

But because he finds not so great fault with the men that be called now a days, (although other do grudge at them,) as with the order and manner of their calling, I will only answer to that point which he touches. In these places of the scripture afore rehearsed, there be these things to be noted, in sending forth ministers. First, an assembly of the clergy and people, to bear testimony of their honesty and aptness that be called: for it must not be done in corners, lest such be admitted as be unworthy, and with whom some could or would have found fault, if it had been known and done openly. The ministery is so godly a vocation, that none ought to be admitted to it having any notable fault in them, or if they

[^{1} χειροτονήσαντες, v. 23. ED.]

may not abide the trial and judgment of the multitude, yea, though they be heathens. For St Paul says, they must have good testimony of their honesty, even " of them that be out of the church." Secondly, I note they used exhortations, with fasting, prayer, and laying on of hands. These ceremonies we be sure are good and godly, because the apostles used them so oft: and these, except some great cause to the contrary, are to be used of all in calling of the ministers.

All these things the order now appointed observes, and no more: all the popish ceremonies be cut off as vain and superfluous. The time of giving orders now is the holy day, when the people be assembled, that they may see who be called: and if they know any notable fault in any of them that are there to be appointed ministers or bishops, they may declare it, that they may be rejected as unworthy. The popish prelates give their orders on the Saturday, when the people is not present, and commonly at home in their chapels, where few resort to see. The bishops now use in giving their orders an exhortation, common prayer, the communion, and laying on of hands, which the apostles used. The pope and his prelates have devised of themselves clippings, shaving their crowns, an unlawful compelled vow to live unmarried, oil for anointing their fingers, and power to sacrifice for quick and dead, their double Latin matins and even song daily, with such a kind of apparel, that they be more like to Aaron and Moses, priests of the old law, than a simple preacher of Christ's gospel, or minister of his sacraments of the new testament.

When we do that which Christ and his apostles did and used, we may be sure it is good, lawful, and necessary: when we add any thing of our own, it may be doubted on; and if it be commanded as necessary, or as the true worship of God, it ought to be refused, changed, yea condemned. For Christ says, "They worship me in vain, teaching doctrines the commandments of men." Therefore, as he reasons here, that it should be too great an inconvenience to say, that these bishops which he names were blind and ignorant in their doings, and that they would come at the judgment to the condemnation of these new bishops which follow not their ways, I had rather turn his argument against himself on his own head, and say, that it is a greater inconvenience, yea blasphemy, to

Matt. xv.

say that Peter, Paul, Timothy, Titus, &c., were in blindness, and had not the right order of appointing their ministers, but that these latter popish prelates have invented of late years a perfecter way to do it than they knew or used. Let them prove that either the apostles themselves, or any of their scholars, used clipping, shaving their crowns, the vow of single life, sacrificing for the dead, oiling their fingers or crown, their Jewish apparel, their hallowings, crossings, blessings, or such trash as their order is full of, and then blame this new order: but because they cannot, the scripture teaching no such thing, I say they be hypocrites, laying heavy loads on men's backs and consciences, yea, greater than any may bear, not touching them with their finger to ease them, but rather to press them down lower, in preferring man's dreams before the simple truth of the gospel. Christ and his apostles, with their scholars, shall come in judgment to their condemnation, for that they have maintained their own devices afore the infallible truth of the scripture, the perfect rule and only example of all our doings and religion. Then, if our bishops now use all such order as the apostles themselves used (as in comparing them together it will easily appear), why should any proud papist be so bold to correct *magnificat*, to reprove them, and say that the pope has devised a better way than the apostles used? Or why should any weak conscience, hanging on man rather than on God, be offended to see such vain, superfluous, and wicked toys left off and not used? If they left out any thing that the apostles used, they might well be blamed: but seeing they had rather follow them as their schoolmasters, and not the pope, they were to be praised. Are popes wiser than the apostles? Or shall papists, for following their father of lies, be preferred to protestants, which have God's word and his truth, with the doings of the apostles, for their defence to allege for them? God forbid!

But I think, this good proctor of the pope is offended, because the new bishops run not to Rome themselves, or by their deputy to do their homage to their holy father, and swear an unlawful and traitorous oath against their lawful and natural prince, and bring home the holy relic, their pall, which many have bought so dear, that in gathering money for it they beggared their whole diocese. Yet, that the blind may see that these ragged popish clouts, which they think so holy relics and necessary, are not of such worthiness, nor to be regarded so highly, it is easy to see even in this realm and others, that both they have been not regarded of old time, and also that they had another fashion of making priests and bishops, than our papists of these days have, and more agreeing with the order that the new bishops use. Fabian writes, part III. cap. lx. that the bishop of St David's had no pall from Rome at all, from the time that Samson was bishop there, unto the time of king Henry the first, in which space were there twenty-one bishops[1]. Polychronicon writes, lib. v. cap. xii[2]. that Northumberland was without bishop thirty year; without pall one hundred and twenty-five year; nor had any altar at all unto the six hundred and twenty-third year of our Lord. Then these things are neither so ancient nor so necessary as papists would make men believe: seeing they had no altars, then they had no popish masses; for they may not be said but on a hallowed altar or superaltar. The pope decreed that all abbots and bishops, being chosen to their dignities, should come to Rome to be confirmed and blessed: by which means, he and the cardinals made them to pay such sums of money to be speedily dispatched (as our under officers do now for expedition), that they impoverished many realms by it, and enriched themselves; by reason whereof king Edward the first, perceiving the bishop of Ely and the abbot of St Edmond's Bury, being then chosen to their dignities, to have spent so much money, was ashamed of it, and forbad any more to go thither afterward themselves. For they beggared their churches, or they could pay their debts, as Matthew Parisiensis writes all this at large and more, speaking against this decree of the popes. The bishops of Colen and Mentz pay either to the pope for their pall

Pall.

[1 The said Sampson took with him the pall, and sailed into Amorica or Little Britain, and was there bishop of Dolence or Dolences. And from that time unto the first Henry's time, king of England, had sitten at Menevia, or St David's, one and twenty bishops, and all without pall. Chap. LX. col. 3.—The *pall* was a short cloak, or rather strip of woollen cloth, worn by an archbishop, who received it from the pope. ED.]

[2 And so the church of men of Northumberland was without bishoprick after Paulinus' death xxx. year; and was without the use of pall six score year and five. * * * To fore that time was no church that had an altar in Brenicia, till king Oswaldus had raised that cross at that battle. Lib. v. chap. xii. col. 5, 6. ED.]

twenty-four thousand ducats. The same man says also, that Thurstan, archbishop of York, going to a council, holden at Remis by pope Calixtus, was forbidden of the king to be consecrate of the pope, and sworn also: but he notwithstanding, as a wicked man, obtained of the wicked Romans by rewards to be consecrate there of the pope: which thing when the king heard tell of, he forbad him all places of his dominion. Thomas Hatfield, bishop of Duresme, chosen A. D. one thousand, three hundred and forty-five, and the nineteenth year of Edward the third, payed to pope Clement the sixth nine thousand florins of gold, for his common service, beside five accustomed services, which were forty-three florins yearly: which appears by the pope's acquittance made to him. The bishop of Lyons declared in the council of Basil, that the pope had nine millions of crowns yearly out of France of the bishops. A million contains ten hundred thousand. If these be not his griefs, peradventure because they have not the cruche [crook] and mitre, as the old bishops had, displeases them: surely such horned beasts be fitter for the pope than the gospel; for as the Latin proverb says of unruly beasts, that they were wont to be known by hanging hay on their horns, *fœnum habet in cornu*[1]; so these unruly popish cattle have their mark that they might be known by, their horned mitres; or else, because they were of the generation of the horned beast, that Daniel in the seventh chapter and St John writes of in his Revelation, thirteenth and seventeenth.

Read the latter end of Gildas[2], our countryman, in his chronicle and chiding exhortation to the priests; and ye shall find, that in his time, which is a thousand year since, there were divers other parts of the scriptures appointed to be read out of the Acts of the Apostles and Peter's epistle, when they were appointed ministers and made priests, which the popish prelates use not in ordering their chaplains now. Whereby it may be gathered, that the ceremonies differed also. But the barbarousness of the time has been such since, that scarce any perfect memorial of their doings remain. The rude Saxons

[1 Horat. Satir. I. iv. 34. ED.]
[2 In the *Rerum Britannicarum Scriptores Vetustiores*, referred to before, p. 515. Audistis etiam illo die, quo multo dignius multoque rectius erat, ut ad carcerem vel catastam pœnalem quam ad sacerdotium traheremini, &c. p. 145. ED.]

overran this realm, and destroyed all learning and religion, with help of the pope and his creatures, the monks and friars: so that unto now of late years very little good learning has been heard of. Dionysius Areopagus, as he is commonly called, and whom they say was Paul's scholar, and of whom St Luke writes, Acts xvii., says in his book, (if it be his book, as they say it is,) that "in making their priests and bishops in his time they used no more ceremonies, than to bring him that was to be called a bishop, to kneel afore the altar, to lay the bible on his head, and the bishop his hands also, with certain prayers and salutations."³ This simple fashion was used of old time, without any further ado. The priests and deacons had not all these ceremonies in their creating: and yet our bishops, which follow this ancient simplicity, are blamed that they have devised new fashions of their own, which never were heard of afore. But by these few things that I have recited it may well be seen, how malice has blinded their popish hearts, falsely to accuse the protestants of those things which are not true. And to put away all doubts, that may be moved for the ancienty and authority of their order and fashion of making priests and bishops, Polychronicon writes, lib. v. cap. 12, that pope Honorius sent to Honorius, bishop of Canterbury, the pall and the order how to make bishops: this was about the year of our Lord one thousand one hundred and twenty-seven⁴. Look how ancient it is; and they cry one thousand five hundred year old, where it is not past four hundred.

And as Dionyse in this ordering of priests declares, how

Ecclesiast. Hierarch.

[³ Ὁ μὲν ἱεράρχης ἐπὶ τὴν ἱεραρχικὴν τελείωσιν προσαγόμενος, ἄμφω τὼ πόδε κλίνας ἐπίπροσθεν τοῦ θυσιαστηρίου, ἐπὶ κεφαλῆς ἔχει τὰ θεοπαράδοτα λόγια καὶ τὴν ἱεραρχικὴν χεῖρα, καὶ τούτῳ τῷ τρόπῳ πρὸς τοῦ τελοῦντος αὐτὸν ἱεράρχου ταῖς παναγεστάταις ἐπικλήσεσιν ἀποτελειοῦται. Ὁ δὲ ἱερεὺς, ἄμφω τὼ πόδε κλίνας ἐπίπροσθεν τοῦ θείου θυσιαστηρίου, ἐπὶ κεφαλῆς ἔχει τὴν ἱεραρχικὴν δεξιὰν, καὶ τούτῳ τῷ τρόπῳ πρὸς τοῦ τελοῦντος αὐτὸν ἱεράρχου ταῖς ἱεροποιοῖς ἐπικλήσεσιν ἁγιάζεται. Dionys. Areop. De Ecclesiastica Hierarchia, Tom. I. cap. v. p. 363. Antverp. 1634.—Usher says, (*Answer to a Jesuit*, p. 507. 1836.) "The books that bear his (Dionysius') name seem to be written in the fourth or fifth age after Christ." ED.]

[⁴ That year the pope Honorius sent the pall to Honorius, archbishop of Canterbury, with letters that informed him of the manner of the ordaining of archbishops in Britain. Lib. v. chap. xii. col. 4. ED.]

far they differed in his time from all these popish toys, that this beast would burden the church and simple souls withal; so shall ye find in him also, how much they differed in his age, in ministering the communion, in burying the dead, and other such service and ceremonies, from the pope's synagogue in our days: in so much that it may be truly said of this our religion, that friar Mantuan said: *Hæc novitas non est novitas, sed vera vetustas.* The pope's superstition may well be called new, as I have proved by many particulars afore: but this of ours is both old and true, as it may be more fully proved than I have yet spoken. Therefore let them set better clerks to speak for them, and prove it by the scriptures, or else for shame hold their peace. But a scalled horse is good enough for a scabbed esquire; and for so false a doctrine, so foolish unlearned a drunken dotel is a meet schoolmaster. They know well enough, that they be not able to stand in defence of it, and therefore they set up such a dolt, that when he takes a foil, no man will marvel; and yet they shall think that the stout champions are behind, which can bind bears and confute all men. But surely this rude ass is the mouth of them all to utter what they think, and they have no better ware than he has uttered: let them put their helping hands to, and bring better stuff, if they have it; but if they run to the later constitutions of Gregory and Clemens, or such like, we know what ancienty and authority they be of, and our answer is ready: for they themselves keep them not.

What religion the old bishops have been of from the beginning in these sees which he names, or how they were made, I think no good record declares. The rudeness of the times have been such, and such destruction of old monuments, both by inward and outward war, that none or few remains. I will note only therefore such things as were done in our days, that every man knows, or else such as be in print. In Duresme I grant the bishop that now is and his predecessor were not of one religion in divers points, nor made bishops after one fashion. This has neither cruche nor mitre, never sware against his prince his allegiance to the pope: this has neither power to christen bells, nor hallow chalices and superaltars, &c. as the other had; and with gladness praises God, that keeps him from such filthiness: his predecessor wrote, preached, and sware against the pope, was justly deprived afterward for disobedience to his prince; and yet, being restored, submitted himself to the pope again. Stout Stephen and bloody Bonner, with other champions yet living, be in the like case. God defend all good people from such religion and bishops!

For these other holy bishops that he reckons and calls saints, if I should speak all that I know and they deserve, it were too long a book, and to wise men it would be thought a scorn, rather than a praise. There is no good ancient history that makes mention of them; for they themselves are not ancient, nor long it is since they lived here. There is no better history than the pope's portus and *Legenda Sanctorum*, with such like, that speaks of them; and to read those miracles would make a horse to laugh: yet something will I say. In the time of that famous prince, Henry VIII., when God's enemy and the overthrower of all princes, the pope, was banished this realm, it was decreed well, that all doctors, deans, and other head men of the clergy, should declare to the people in their sermons the usurped power of the pope divers times in the year. Among other, one D. Str. preaching at York, and inveighing against the abuses of popery, (although in many things a papist himself,) and namely against his canonizing and making of saints; among other, he fell in talk of St William of York, and said, that St William's horse was more worthy to be made a saint, than St William himself. The reason was this: St William on a time, when he was made new bishop, riding in his royalty over Ouse bridge within York, (as he was wont to do oft very gloriously, and as stoutly as Thomas Becket, in whose time he lived also,) the bridge brake, and many that followed were drowned. St William's horse, as full of courage as his master, with wrestling and spurring up, saved himself and his master from drowning. The horse did the notable deed, and deserved the praise: but the master won the reward, and was made a saint by the pope. This and such other is enough, with the pope, to make his servants saints: but this bishop's life and doings otherwise, afore God and godly men, are in wickedness as evil as Thomas Becket's. He was so unhappy a man, that when he was first chosen bishop of York, the pope Eugenius would not confirm him,

St William of York.

but made Henry Murdach bishop there in his stead. When both that pope and bishop were dead, then he was chosen again and made bishop of York, and coming so gloriously into the city as I spake of, the bridge brake for the weight of men that followed, as *Legenda Nova Sanctorum* says in his life. St Edmond was so holy, as the same worthy history says, that when divers women came to his chamber to him, he would not touch them. If ye believe him, he ever set great store by women, for honour of our lady, the same writer says also; and when one of his friends rebuked him because he talked so oft with a certain wife, he said, "Seest thou not how fair she is, and oft sat by me, and yet I was never tempted with her?" Polychronicon also tells the same tale, lib. vii[1]. Further, when one of his clerks, sitting at dinner, did eat nothing, because that day was ordinary to have his fit of a quartan, he asked why he did not eat: "because I look for my fit," says he. "I will make a cross on this lamprey in my dish," says Edmond, "and put in thy mouth in the name of the Trinity, and thou shalt be whole." But that such holy men may do what they lust, and have it for well, yet if poor souls should have done it, it would have been laughed at, and counted a charming; for lamprey is very evil for a quartan.

Lanfranc brought in the heresy of transubstantiation. Anselm divorced married priests, and says also further, that Linus was the first bishop of Rome, writing in the latter end of his commentaries on the second epistle to Timothy[2]. Let the papists look their books, and see whether I say true; and then judge how truly they crack, that Peter was the first pope at Rome, and that all the rest have their authority from him. If this fool had looked, he should find some bishops of Canterbury, even papists, as Austin and Anselm, to have been of our religion in some opinion of the greatest matters, more than Cranmer: whose writings and doings, because they be in print and so fresh memory, like a barking cur in the night at the moonshine, he may declare his own malice rather than deface the godly memory of that holy

[1 Chap. xxxv. col. 8. ED.]

[2 Romæ vero morantes *te salutant Eubulus, et Pudens, et Linus*, (iste Linus fuit primus Romanæ sedis episcopus,) *et Claudia.* Anselm. Tom. ii. p. 379. Colon. 1612. ED.]

martyr, and therefore I will not speak of him. But that the world may see how lewdly he lies, when he says that no bishops have been of our religion, the same *Legenda Sanctorum* tells that Anselm, bishop of Canterbury, came to king Henry the first, to desire licence to go to Rome to pope Urban to fetch his pall. The king said, he knew him not for pope, nor it was not lawful for any to name any pope without his licence. The prelates and noblemen were called together, and Anselm accused; and all the bishops there said, it was not lawful for him to take Urban for pope in his realm, and keep his oath that he made to the king: and so all the bishops (except Rochester) forsaked him, and would not obey him as their archbishop. Judge now, whether any bishops in this realm have refused the pope afore these our days.

And because I have entered to entreat of these holy fathers that he cracks so much on, I will shew you what is written in the life and history of Thomas Becket, bishop of Canterbury, their stinking martyr, and traitor to his prince. When the bishop was fled out of the realm, the king sent embassadors by the consent of the nobles and prelates to Rome after him, to declare the matter, and accuse him of disobeying the king, troubling the realm and the clergy, and of perjury in not keeping the laws which he sware to first. The embassadors were Roger, archbishop of York, Gilbert, bishop of London, Roger, bishop of Worcester, Hilary, bishop of Chichester, Bartholomew, bishop of Exeter, the Earl of Arundel, with many other noblemen and clerks. Their orations, wherein they accuse this holy traitor, be there in print severally, and somewhat long to recite; but judge indifferently, when so many bishops and the earl accuse Thomas Becket afore the pope so earnestly, whether we be to blame to accuse him now. The effect of the bishop of London's oration to the pope and cardinals was this; and the other bishops' orations are like: Fathers, the care of the church belongs to you, that they which be wise might be cherished by you, and they that be unwise might be corrected, that they might be wise: but he is not thought wise to your wisdoms, that trusts in his own wisdom, and goes about to trouble the peace of his brother and the king. Of late there fell a debate in England betwixt the king and the clergy, for a light cause, which might have been easily

Thomas Becket.

buried, if a gentle medicine had been ministered: but the bishop of Canterbury, using his own will, and not ours, was too earnest, not considering what harm might come by such headiness. And because he could not get our consent, he went about to cast the fault of his rashness on our lord the king, and the realm: and that he might deface our brotherly love, he flees away, no man compelling him, as it is written in the psalm, " The wicked flees when no man persecutes him." The other bishop and earl follow with like or more vehement words.

When king Egfride had married Etheldrede, and she had rather live a virgin than do the duty of a wife, the king desired St Wilfride to counsel his wife to do her duty: the bishop would not, but rather encouraged her, divorced her, made her a nun[1], and the king married another; which counsel of Wilfride was plain contrary to St Paul, saying, "The woman has not power of her own body, but the man; for she cannot depart from her husband without licence, and but for a time." God keep us from such holy bishops! Polychronicon, lib. v. cap. xxii. declares a knot of these his holy fathers. Adelme, first priest, then abbot, and lastly a bishop, when he was tempted in the flesh, took a fair wench into bed with him while he might say the psalter; and yet would not marry[2]. Lib. vii. cap. ii, Walter, bishop of Hertford, was slain by a woman, which gored him in the groin[3] with her shears, because he would have ravished her.

St Wilfride.

Legenda Nova Sanctorum, in his life.

[[1] Juncta est tum (Etheldreda) regi præfato lege conjugali, non conjunctioni carnali. Cujus rei gratia beatum Wilfridum tam per se quam per alios rex convenit, orans et obsecrans quatenus reginæ persuaderet, ut omisso virginitatis proposito regiæ voluntati assensum præberet. Ille tamen non consentiens vigilanti animo procurabat, nequa femineæ mentis inconstantia propositum virginitatis postponeret, et terrenis illecebris animum divicta supponeret. Sua enim erat industria ut virgo divortium quæreret, quatenus libertate potita seculum relinquere et regi eterna (*sic*) feliciter inhærere posset. Et factum est ita. Nam cum regi constaret nullo illam pacto a proposito posse mutari, licet invitus concessit, ut relicto seculo, sicut volebat, virginitatis velamen acciperet. Legenda Nova Angliæ, fo. cccii. col. 4. Lond. 1516. ED.]

[[2] He took upon him this martyrdom, that when he were tempted in his flesh, he would hold with him, &c. col. 2. ED.]

[[3] This expression is slightly altered from the original. The story is in Polychron. Lib. vii. chap. ii. col. 2. ED.]

Cap. xi, Walter, bishop of Durham, made women to serve him and the monks at the table, with their hair hanging down, where few scaped their hands[4]. Cap. xii, Giraldus, bishop of York, was, says he, "a lecherous man and a witch[5]." The same Polychronicon says also, lib. vii. cap. xxxi. that Fulco, a French priest, came to king Richard the first, and bad him marry his three daughters. The king said, he had none: "Yes," says he, "pride, covetousness[6], and lechery." Then the king said: "Pride I give to templers; covetousness to white monks; and lechery to prelates." This marriage was so knit then, that it could not be broken since; and this was the king's opinion of them.

O holy fathers! I trust, whosoever considers these things well, will judge the holiness of these good bishops, on whom he glories so much. The rest of the bishops which he names be such like; and because he speaks not much of them, I will let them pass, for they be no better: and out of the same worshipful history ye shall read of them, because no learned man has thought meet to lose his time in commending such. They lived all since the conquest, not five hundred year since: all made saints, and promoted by the pope, and he by them: therefore they must need maintain his doings, and he theirs.

I would not have blotted so much paper with so much wickedness, nor filled your ears and eyes with such filthiness, but that he provoked me to it, and calls that good, which is evil, and light, darkness: the rest be no better. In every bishoprick ye shall find some bishops, that were enemies to the pope and his doings in that blind age. In Lincoln, Robert Grosshead appealed from the pope to Jesus Christ, and wrote divers good books against many his doings. Ranold Pecocke of Chichester was condemned in the twenty-sixth year of Henry VI. for this new learning, and specially for saying

[4 Col. 2. But, continues Polychron. this is worthy to be greatly praised: for by his procuring, St Cuthbert's body was taken out of the grave, and clothed worshipfully in new clothing. ED.]

[5 And Gyralde was archbishop after him, a lecherous man, a witch, and an evil doer, as the fame telleth. Chap. xii. col. 2. ED.]

[6 In the old edition, *covetous*: in Polychron. *covetyse*. It occurs in the beginning of the chapter. ED.]

that a general council and the church may err in religion. In the late days of popery were burned five bishops, and five banished: let them shew so many bishops that suffered within this thousand year for their god, the pope, and they might have some shew of honesty for them. It is a rare thing to see a bishop die for religion, and specially a papist.

X. Seeing they reform religion so well, as they say, it were meet, as they forsake the religion that their predecessors used, as mass, matins, ministration of sacraments, that they should also forsake houses, parks, lands, and revenues, that their predecessors had, and go from place to place for God's sake and preach.

If nothing else, this one saying will prove him a dissembling lying hypocrite. All the world knows, that the greatest fault and readiest that they have to lay against the gospel-time, is, that church-lands and livings are taken from spiritual men, and bestowed on other; and of this thing he complains himself in manifest words hereafter. Therefore it is manifest, that he would not have the bishops to give away their lands, seeing he complains of the taking it away: but he would so fain find a fault in the new bishops, that rather than he find none, he will shew himself a fool in blaming them wherein they deserve it not, and which he thinks to be no fault indeed. Why they forsake their mass and matins, is sufficiently declared afore. For their houses, parks and lands, why some few that have any such do not forsake them that be left, there is good reason: but why other some have them not (that they might forsake them, if they should), I fear their popish predecessors have provided too well for them against reason. They keep house, and such lands as they can get, because they be not anabaptists, nor heretics, thinking it not to be lawful for them so to do, (for God's good creatures are ordained to serve God's good ministers;) and also, because they be not so superstitious as the observants friars, which thought themselves so holy that they might not handle money. They remember also, that God commands them to keep hospitality to their power: and because by this means it may the better be done, they do not refuse it, although greedily they do not desire it. The prince also and commonwealth desires a service of them, which they cannot so well perform without these;

Spiritual men's lands.

but chiefly for the maintenance of learning, which is so decayed almost remediless, and so little hope to recover it, if these helps be clean taken away, that extreme blind ignorance is like to follow this age.

Look into the universities, and spy what ancient learned men ye find there, either papist or protestant. I am ashamed to tell, and it is to be lamented to see that there is so few, and it is earnestly to be begged at God's hand that it may be amended: but I fear it is rather to be wished than hoped for. This plague is over our heads not regarded, and cannot be avoided, howsoever the world go. These few that now live, both papist and protestant, must needs die. Where is there then any learned number to supply their rooms? There be few schools abroad to bring up youth; but so many benefices so small, that no man will take them, and so the parishes be unserved, and the people wax without fear of God. The universities have many goodly fresh wits in them, but so young, and without a sufficient number of ancient guides to teach and rule them, that many men's days shall be spent afore any number come to ripeness, although for their young years many can do well. But fathers and mothers must answer this question; and they, if they be asked why they keep not their children at school, will say, there is more profit to be had in making his son a lawyer, a physician, or any thing except a minister: for when they have bestowed all they can get on one child in the university, he shall not be able to live himself, nor help any friend he has; where the lawyer will become a gentleman, a purchaser, within few years. They will do any thing with him, rather than make him a priest.

St Paul bids, "He that is taught, let him give part of all his goods to him that teaches him:" and the next words following be, "God is not mocked;" as though he should say, If ye deal not liberally with your teachers, and think nothing so precious, but they should have their part of it in their need, ye but mock God in so mocking his ministers; but "he that dwells in heaven will mock you again," says David. Let them weigh these words well, which in paying their tithes, if they find one sheaf, lamb, or fleece, worse than another, cast it out in scorn, and say it is good enough for a priest, or with worse words, as they be full of such. "If they sow spiritual things, is it

Gal. vi.

Psal. ii.

1 Cor. ix.

much if they reap your carnal things?" No, sure: ye have nothing good enough to recompense their labour withal. In the primitive church it was not unlawful to have lands, though many sold their lands for to relieve the poor Christians withal. It is no more unlawful to keep lands, than to keep the money for which he sold the lands; and Peter said to Ananias that sold his land, "Did it not remain to thee, and when thou had sold it, was it not in thine own power to do with it what thou would?" So Peter grants that it was lawful for him both to keep the lands, and to keep the money too, that he received when he had sold it: and yet I doubt not but the new bishops, if case so should require, could be content to forego all, and live as God would, as their deeds of late well declared, so that they might serve God or his people the better, and rather than they defile themselves with popery. We read that divers of the holy fathers and bishops had lands with their churches: but it is folly to answer so curious a fool in a matter of no doubt, but invented of an idle scoffing brain. If ye demand, why some bishops have so little lands, few houses and parks, the reasons also be sundry: but surely, few or none have so much as to keep them out of debt, or to maintain that hospitality which is looked for at their hands. Some of their lands and parks against their wills be exchanged by order of law: but the most part, the malicious popish prelates, that were their predecessors, seeing their kingdom decay, and that professors of God's gospel should follow in their places, would rather give it women, children, horsekeepers, (I say no worse,) by lease, patents, annuities, than any that loves God should enjoy it. This is the greatest reason why they have not lands, and that cannot be avoided; more is the pity. How many bishopricks in the realm have they impoverished by these means! So that they which now succeed, are not able to relieve themselves nor the poor as they would and should.

Acts v.

The multitude cry out on the protestants, that they keep not houses, like the papists, nor such a number of idle servants: they consider not how barely they came to their livings, what pensions they pay, and annuities, which their predecessors granted; how all commodities be leased away from them; what charges they bear for first-fruits, subsidies and tenths; how they lack all household stuff and furniture at their entering; so that for three years' space they be not able to live out of debt, and get them necessaries. The popish prelates, afore they were bishops, had divers fat benefices and prebends, which they kept still for a commendam: they were stored of all necessaries of household afore they entered; they paid no first fruits; so that they may do on the first day more than the other can do in seven year. "If ye were of the world," says our Lord, "the world would love you; but because ye be not of the world, therefore the world hates you." The world loves the papists; therefore they be worldlings, and not of God: the poor protestant, because he will not lie, not flatter, is despised of the world. The world gives to the papist honour, castles, towers, and all that it has: to the protestant if he give any thing, it is thought too much; and of those things that it gives, it gives the worst that can be picked out, and yet thinks it too good. Therefore, surely the one has his reward in this world: the other must look for it at God's hand. For the proud papist there is nothing good enough: for the poor protestant every thing is too good. What can the professors of God's truth therefore look to have here, but to follow the example of the apostles whose doctrine they teach, to suffer wrongs, slanders, contempt, to be counted as outcasts, and sheep appointed to the slaughter? When the pope's butchers are aloft, they broil and brenne, they prison, hang and torment the sely gospeller at their pleasure: when the protestant is at the best, and the world seems to laugh on him, he is scarce able to live, runs in contempt and slander of the world; and the lurking papist, looking for his day when he may run loose again, gapes to satisfy his bloody heart and hands, which never will be satisfied with blood. [John xv.]

Divers of these holy prelates, that he cracks so much of, had so leased out their houses, lands and parks, that some of the new bishops had scarce a corner of a house to lie in, and divers not so much ground as to grese [graze] a goose or sheep; so that some were compelled to tether their horse in their orchard: and yet have these holy fathers provided, that if they be restored (as they look for, as many think,) that they shall have all their commodities again. O notable charity, and meet for the children of such a father! The Lord God for his mercy amend this at his good will and pleasure! The people are so blind, that they rather believe him that fills their belly, than him that teaches them Christ; so rude, that they care more for the body than for the soul: even as Christ, when he filled five thousand with five loaves, they would have made him a king; but within few days after they would have stoned him. Paul wrought for his own living, and would not be a burden to any congregation: yet he says, that it was lawful for him to take all his necessaries of them whom he taught. Chrysostom in the eighty-sixth homily on Matthew, writing, entreats the like question, and tells causes why he and others had lands belonging to their churches. He says, " The unthankfulness of the people was such, that if they had not such provision, they should go a begging[1]." So surely I think now, if the bishops and ministers had not that provision, they might starve for hunger. Love and duty to God, his word, and ministers, is so decayed, that to get away from them is thought godliness, pastime and profit. Surely God will not have his servants so mocked: God turn from us for Christ's sake that which we deserve and provoke him to in these our doings! Julianus apostata, the emperor that forsaked his faith, hearing that the gospel taught the Christians to live in poverty and suffer persecution, took their goods from them, and punished them, saying, he would help them to heaven, because their gospel taught them to live poor and suffer:[2] so our papists, hearing the protestants preach poverty, and condemn their proud prelaty, have leased, granted, and given away their livings, that now the poor gospeller has scarce whereon to live, through their malice.

margin: 2 Thess. iii.

XI. In Christ's church has ever been a succession of bishops from the apostles' time to this day, in every see. Tertullian says: " If in any see there be a bishop that walks not in his father's steps, he is

[1] Καὶ γὰρ μεθ' ὑμῶν ἡμᾶς καταγελάστους ἡ ἀπανθρωπία αὕτη ποιεῖ, ὅτι τὰς εὐχὰς ἀφέντες καὶ τὴν διδασκαλίαν καὶ τὴν ἄλλην ἁγιωσύνην, οἱ μὲν οἰνοπώλαις, κ. τ. ἑ.—The passage in the text is rather an allusion to the whole passage, than a direct quotation. In Matth. Homil. LXXXV. (al. LXXXVI.) Tom. VII. p. 915. Paris. 1836. ED.]

[2] Quod Imperator audiens, Christianis videlicet adeuntibus eum, defendere contemnebat, dicens, "Vestrum est ut patientes mala sustineatis; hoc enim est præceptum vestri Dei." Hist. Tripart. Lib. VI. Cap. 39. p. 436. in Auctores Historiæ Ecclesiast. Basil. 1535. ED.]

to be counted a bastard, and no true inheritor in Christ's church[3]." St Cyprian does say: "They that be made bishops out of the order of the church, and not by tradition and ordinance of the apostles, coming by succession from time to time, are not bishops by the will of God," but thieves and murderers[4].

A succession of bishops or ministers, we grant, has been in the world, rather than in any one see or country, since Christ: which succession we say we have and follow better than they, but not after such sort as he says and means. God is never without his church in the world, although some countries fall; and his church never wants his ministers and true teachers, at the least privily, although in some ages it has them more plenteously than in other some, and sometimes the outward face of the church wants not his errors and blots. But where he says, there has been bishops in every see since the apostles' time, it must needs be false: for here with us unto the time of king Lucius, almost two hundred year after Christ, there were no bishops in this realm at all, but flamines, as Fabian[5] and Polychronicon[6] say,

[3] Quos apostoli (*al.* ab apostolis) in episcopatum constitutos, apostolici seminis traduces habeant, &c. See the whole passage. De Præscript. Hæreticorum, cap. xxxii. Tom. II. p. 31. Magd. 1828. But in this and other instances the author cited is so overlaid by the mass of papistical comment, that it is not easy to identify the passage intended. See what Pilkington says on this practice at the end of his answer to the first question of the papist. ED.]

[4] Plane episcopi non de voluntate Dei fiunt, qui extra ecclesiam fiunt; sed contra dispositionem et traditionem evangelii fiunt. Epist. LIX. (LV.) p. 261. ed. Fell. Oxon. 1700. ED.]

[5] The which Lucie, after the faith thus by him received, * * instituted and ordained, that all or the more part of arch-flamines and flamines, which is to mean archbishops and bishops of the pagan law, which at that day were in number, as witnesseth Gaufryde and other, three of the arch-flamines and twenty-eight of the flamines, were made and ordained archbishops and bishops of the church of Christ. Fabian, Part III. chap. lix. fin. ED.]

[6] In his time (Lucius') were three archbishops' sees in Britain. * * * To these archbishops' sees were subject eighteen bishops, and were called flamines. Polychron. Lib. I. chap. lii. init. Here XVIII. is apparently a mere error for XXVIII. the number twice given by Fabian, who cites Polychron. as his authority.

The Polychronicon, so frequently cited by this author, was originally compiled in Latin by Ranulph, monk of Chester, translated into English by

and heathen priests; and sundry times since divers sees in this realm many years together had no bishops at all, when the unchristened Saxons were here; and divers bishopricks here are not half so old as the apostles' time. Yet in all these ages were some that both knew, taught privately, and followed the truth, though they were not horned and mitred bishops, nor oiled and sworn shavelings to the pope. Such popish bishops I am sure no man is able to prove to have been in every see of this realm continually, since the apostles' time, nor elsewhere: when he has proved it, I will say as he does. Does the see make the bishop and his doctrine good or bad? Does the place make him good or bad? If his saying be true, that they have such a succession, the man must needs be good because he is bishop of such a place or such, (for he means to have a continual succession of good bishops everywhere without interruption:) but whether they succeed in agreement of one true doctrine, as they do of one see or place, he cares not. If succeeding in place be sufficient to prove them good bishops, then the Jews and Turks have their good bishops and religion still at Jerusalem, Constantinople, and elsewhere; for there they dwell where the apostles did, and have their synagogues, Levites, priests and bishops after their sort.

We do esteem and reverence the continual succession of good bishops in any place, if they can be found: if they cannot, we run not from God, but rather stick fast to his word. I think there is no place, where evil bishops have not been. If Corinth, Galatia, Ephesus, Philippos, Colossa, Thessalonica, Macedonia, where Paul preached, and to whom he wrote his several epistles, might fall and have Turkish prelates; why may not Rome fall too? The same may be said of Jerusalem, where St James was, and of Africk, where Cyprian and Austin were, and of other places where the apostles preached,

by "one Trevisa, then vicar of the parish of Barkley," and afterwards continued by William Caxton, "a simple person," as he calls himself, from the year 1357 to the year 1460, in which he complains that he has not "ne can gete no bokes of auctoryte treatynge of such cronycles, except a lytel boke named *Fasciculus temporum*, and another called *Aureus de Universo*." ED.]

[¹ This is a general reference to the state of things under the Saxons, not to any particular passage. ED.]

and now be fallen away. Succession of good bishops is a great blessing of God: but because God and his truth hangs not on man nor place, we rather hang on the undeceivable truth of God's word in all doubts, than on any bishops, place, or man: for "all men are liars," and may be deceived; only God and his word is true, and neither deceives, nor is deceived. In the ten tribes of Israel, where Jeroboam made him priests against God's law, and the greater part of their religion was defaced with idolatry, yet were there ever some good prophets among, that taught God's people their duty, though not of the higher sort of priests and in authority, as there be some few among the Turks at this day also. Elias complains that he was left alone: of all the true followers of God's law, he knew none that feared God beside himself: but God said, he had "reserved seven thousand that never bend their knee to Baal." So, surely, though the great number of priests and bishops, having authority, have been these many years the pope's darlings, rather serving Baal than God; yet our good God, pitying his people, has in all ages reserved some few that taught the truth and feared him.

God has not promised that every bishoprick, no, nor any one bishoprick, should have always good bishops one after another, no more than one good father should have always good children born of him, nor a good king should have good princes to reign after him. After wise Salomon reigned foolish Roboam: after godly Ezechias reigned wicked Manasses; and after Jesus, the son of Josedec, followed not long after Annas and Caiphas, and many wicked ones afore them. Contrariwise, of sinful ancestors came the innocent Lamb of God, Christ Jesus, and after the traitor Judas followed the good apostle Matthias. So that, both in kingdoms and priesthood, the good has followed the bad, and the bad the good. The gospel says, that "in Moses' chair the scribes and Pharisees sit:" if after Moses followed the wicked scribes and Pharisees, what privilege have our bishops or popes more than Moses, that their successors should continue in pureness of religion, and not fall away as the Pharisees did? Are they better than Moses? Or where is this their promise written in God's book? The glorying of this succession is like the proud brags of the Jews for their

Matt. xxiii.

genealogies and pedigrees, saying, "We have Abraham for our father;" but our Saviour Christ said, "Ye are of the devil, your father, and his works will ye do." So it may be said to these which crack that they have the apostles for their fathers, that they have the pope their father; for his works and doctrine they follow, and not the apostles'. As Christ our Lord therefore proved the Jews to be of the devil, because they filled his desires, and therefore not the children of Abraham; so it is easy to see whose children these be, when they follow the pope and not the apostles. Succession in doctrine makes them the sons of the prophets and apostles, and not sitting in the same seat, nor being bishop of the same place.

<small>John viii.</small>

There is one of his holy bishops that he cracks so much of, a little wiser and subtler than he in words, although in sense they agree. He says, that in every see there has been a succession; but for example he takes Canterbury, and says in a little scroll that he wrote for the authority of the church, and sent it privily to his friends, to comfort and confirm them with that they should stick fast, thus: "We can reckon all the bishops there since St Austin, that was the first, and from him go to Gregory, bishop of Rome, who sent Austin hither, and from Gregory up to Peter, and so prove that all our religion came from Rome by succession; and therefore we must hang on Rome still." He says, the like may be done in every see: and when it is proved, I will believe it. But I am content to stand with him in trial of this. If Austin was the first, as he says, then Canterbury has not had a continual succession since the apostles' time. It is since Austin lived a seven hundred and sixty year, but since the apostles it is one thousand five hundred and sixty. How is there then a continual succession in Canterbury since the apostles' time, if they wanted bishops the space of eight hundred year? The same reason is against other bishopricks too; and there cannot be proved a succession of their bishops in any one place of this realm since the apostles.

And for a succession of agreement in one doctrine, religion, and other their doings, they cannot find it in Rome, neither afore Gregory nor after. Clemens, in the book that goes in his name, says, that wives ought to be common, which God forbids: and hereof, I think, the papists are so bold with other men's wives,

<small>Clemens.</small>

and will none of their own. Alexander made holy water[1], as *Alexander.* they say, to drive away devils and heal diseases, as though it were more holy than Christ himself: for the devil tempted him, and yet runs away from their conjured water, as they would make fools to believe. But what papist was ever so mad to forsake the physician's help in his sickness, and say he was healed by the pope's holy water? If that were true, physicians might put up their pipes. Pope Pius bad keep Easter *Pius.* in the full moon, what day in the week so ever it light on; and not always to keep it on the Sunday, as we do now[2]. Mar- *Marcellinus.* cellinus, in persecution, sacrificed [to] idols[3]. Liberius[4], Fe- *Liberius, Felix,* lix[5], and Anastasius[6], popes, were Arians and great heretics, *Anastasius.* denying Christ to be God equal with his Father. Pope Leo *Leo.* cut off his hand, because a woman kissed it, and he felt himself something tempted[7]. John the first was sent to the emperor as *John.*

[1 Instituit item ut aqua, quam sanctam appellamus, sale admixta, interpositis sacris orationibus, et in templis et in cubiculis ad fugiendos dæmones retineretur. Platina, De Vitis Pontificum, fo. 9. Venet. 1511. ED.]

[2 Hoc tempore Pius pontifex consuetudinem, et quidem magnam, cum Hermete habuit, qui librum scripsit titulo *Pastoris* insignitum; quo quidem in libro angelus pastoris personam induens ei mandat, ut omnibus persuadeat pascha die dominico celebrari: quod etiam fecit. Ibid. fo. 11. ED.]

[3 At Marcellinus pontifex, ad sacrificia gentium ductus, cum nimis instarent carnifices ut thura diis exhiberet, metu perterritus deos alienos adoravit. Ibid. fo. 19. ED.]

[4 Qui, imperatoris beneficio motus, cum hæreticis in rebus omnibus, ut quidem volunt, sentiens, illud tamen cum catholicis tenebat, hæreticos ad fidem redeuntes non esse rebaptizandos. Ibid. fo. 25. ED.]

[5 Hic vero (Achatius) tantæ auctoritatis apud Constantium fuit, quemadmodum Hieronymus dicit, (quod ego certe miror,) ut Romæ in Liberii locum Felicem Arianum episcopum constitueret; quem profecto catholicum fuisse constat, ut scripsimus, et Arianos semper damnasse. Ibid. fo. 26. ED.]

[6 Anastasius (Secundus) Anastasium imperatorem excommunicavit, quod Acatio faveret: tametsi postea ipse ab Acatio seductus, dum eum revocare clanculum tentat, clerum a se graviter alienavit; qui se a communione pontificis tum maxime subtraxit, quod etiam sine catholicorum consensu Photino Thessalonicensi diacono communicasset, qui tum Acatii errorem imitabatur. Ibid. fo. 34. ED.]

[7 This circumstance, and some others referred to in the following passage, are not mentioned in Platina, who is the only authority named by the author. ED.]

embassador from the king of Goths, to counsel him to restore
the churches to the Arians, heretics[1]. Sergius, pope, set forth
yearly a piece of a cross (which he said was Christ's) to be
worshipped and kissed. Gregory the third granted licence to
marry his uncle's wife, plain against the scripture. Zachary
the first, pope, absolved the Frenchmen from obeying their
king, deposed him, and confirmed Pipin for their king[2]; and so
did pope Stephen too[3]. Leo the third allowed the blood of
Christ at Mantua[4], such a one as was the sweet blood of Halis
here. John the eighth, a harlot wearing man's apparel, was
made pope, and got with child, and delivered as she went in
procession solemnly[5]. Nicholas the first was so proud, that
he said "it was not lawful to reprove the pope's judgments[6]."
Silvester the second[7] and Benet the ninth[8] gave themselves to

[1 Quam quidem rem Theodoricus ægre ferens, Joannem pontificem, Theodorum, duosque Agapitos oratores ad Justinum mittit, qui cum adhortarentur, ut Arianos restitueret. * * Ad lacrymas versi, ac suppliciter petentes ut perituræ Italiæ una cum catholicis omnibus subveniret, eo tandem pium hominem pepulere, ut Arianos restitueret. Ibid. fo. 35. Ed.]

[2 At Pipinus, regnandi cupidus, legatos suos ad pontificem mittit, eumque rogat ut regnum Franciæ sibi auctoritate sua confirmet. Annuit pontifex ejus postulatis, accepti beneficii et veteris benevolentiæ memor, quæ inter pontifices et principes hujus familiæ intercesserat: atque ita ejus auctoritate regnum Franciæ Pipino adjudicatur, anno Domini 753. Ibid. fo. 53. Ed.]

[3 After Zacharias Stephen was pope five year. This anointed Pipinus' two sons. Polychron. Lib. v. chap. xxv.—Platina, without expressly mentioning the fact, assumes it, fo. 54. Ed.]

[4 At Leo, cum seditionibus semper vexaretur, ab urbe discedens Mantuam proficiscitur ad visendum Christi sanguinem, qui tum miraculis magno in pretio erat. Platina, fo. 59. Ed.]

[5 Postea a servo compressa, * * inter theatrum, quod Colosseum vocant a Neronis colosso, et sanctum Clementem doloribus circumventa peperit, eoque loci mortua, pontificatus sui anno ii. Ibid. fo. 64.—The disgusting story is told also in Polychronicon, Lib. v. chap. xxxii. The papists in general deny the truth of it: several works have been written on the controversy. Ed.]

[6 Is Nicholas I. the person here intended? It is of Paul II. that the memorable expressions are recorded, Nos ad judices revocas? ac si nescires omnia jura in scrinio pectoris nostri collocata esse, &c. Platina, fo. 158. See above, p. 99. Ed.]

[7 Pontificatum postremo majore conatu, adjuvante diabolo, consecutus est; hac tamen lege, ut post mortem totus illius esset, cujus fraudibus tantam dignitatem adeptus erat. Ibid. fo. 75. Ed.]

the devil, and offered sacrifice to him, that he would make them popes, and promised after their death wholly to be his: they enticed women to naughtiness with them by witchcraft. Innocent the third dispensed with the emperor Otho to marry his niece, plain contrary to God's word. John the twenty-third denied the souls to live after this life, the cardinals finding no fault with him: but the French king compelled him to recant. *Innocent III.* *John XXIII.*

This is the goodly succession, that he would have us to follow, of doctrine in Romish popes, written by Platina and such like, no protestants: these be the successors and fathers, whom he would have us to be like unto. God defend all good folk from all such doings, sayings, believing, living, loving, or following! Except God dwell and be tied in chairs, seats, and places, he cannot dwell in such wicked men as these popes be. God " dwells not in houses made with man's hands," nor in the mighty prelates of the world: but he dwells in the pure minds and consciences of his elect people, of what estate or degree soever they be. Compare the doings, preachings, and troublesome life of Peter the apostle, from time to time, with the wicked blasphemies of these Romish prelates, and with their lordly idleness; and mark in what thing he is like to them, or they to him. They are no more like than an apple and oyster: then cannot he be their predecessor, nor they his successors. If they claim to be Judas' successors, I will not stick with them.

In temporal inheritance an evil man may succeed as right heir to a good; but in matters of pure religion a heretic, or he that differs from the truth, cannot be a lawful follower in God's church, and defender of the same religion and truth from which he is fallen, and become an enemy. Therefore, as the succession of good kings stands not only in enjoying the lands, goods, possessions and pleasures of the realm, but in the painful ministering of justice, defending his subjects from strangers, maintaining the good, and punishing the evil, by wholesome

[8 Constat enim simulacrum ejus admodum monstruosum post mortem cuidam apparuisse; interrogatumque, quid illa horrida imago præ se ferret, cum antea pontifex fuisset, "Quia," inquit, "in vita sine lege et ratione vixi, ideo, volente Deo et Petro, cujus sedem omnibus probris fœdavi, simulacrum meum plus feritatis quam humanitatis in se habet." Ibid. fo. 77. ED.]

and godly laws: so stands the succession of the church not in mitres, palaces, lands, or lordships, but in teaching true doctrine, and rooting out the contrary; by sharp discipline to correct the offenders, and godly exhortation to stir up the slothful, and encourage the good, to raise them that be fallen by comfortable promises, to strengthen them that stand, and bring home them that run astray. He that does these is the true successor of the prophets and apostles, though he live in wilderness, as Elias did, or be tied in chains, as Peter and Paul: he that does not, is not their successor indeed, but in name only, though he have the pope's blessing, cruche and mitre, lands and palaces, hallowings and blessings, or all that the pope has devised for his prelates.

To be a bishop is to be an officer, a ruler, a guide, a teacher of God's flock in God's church; and to be a true successor in a bishoprick, is to succeed in like pains, care, and diligent regard of God's people. Is he an officer that does not his office? Nay, surely, but only in name; for he is a thief in his office, and an usurer, that takes the profit and not the pain. An office stands properly in doing the duty of it, and not in talking of it, setting in deputies, bearing a shew, brag and face of a bishop. When they can bring the apostles' doctrine or life for example to be like their life and teaching, they may say they follow the apostles: but because they seek to be lords over [1 Pet. v.] the flock, contrary to Peter's doctrine, and be enemies to the gospel, and murderers of the professors of it, they be traitors to their Lord God.

What does Tertullian make for his purpose? "If he walk not in his father's steps," says he, "he is a bastard." Content: who be the fathers? Surely, the apostles; for in his time the pope had no such authority, nor there were any such horned cattle of the pope's made bishops. Prove then, that the pope walks in the apostles' steps, and we will reverence him. Surely he is like no apostle, except Judas; and these popish prelates, so as the father is, such is the son. Judas sold and betrayed his master for thirty pieces of silver; and our papists sell their purgatory for thirty groats, the price of a trental. Or else, for their pleasure, I will grant them something. The pope may be Matt. xvi. like to Peter in such case as Christ our Lord said to him, "Go after me, Satan, for thou understandest not the things of God."

Peter was ambitious, and therefore our Lord called him devil, and bad him go back: so the pope, desiring to be above all, follows the devil his father; and therefore we may justly say to them with Christ, "Come after me, thou devil."

But I put case a man should grant, that the fathers which Tertullian speaks of, be the popes indeed of Rome: what then? what makes it for this man's purpose? Tertullian lived within one hundred and seventy-seven years after Christ's death: why then, prove that any of these popes, and their trash which he esteems so highly, to be of that authority and anciety, that he would, and then let him begin to crack something. He is not able to do it. Thirty of the first popes, which lived almost three hundred years after Christ, were persecuted, suffered death for their religion, lived in caves, and had none of the royalty of the world, but were subjects to princes according to their duty: then these latter proud popes, that would rule both God and the world, by Tertullian's saying, be bastards, and follow not their ancient fathers, the first popes. And thus he has brought a good reason against himself.

Does Cyprian make any more for his purpose? Mark his words, and judge. "They that be made bishops" (says he) "out of the order of the church, and not by tradition of the apostles by succession, are not bishops, but thieves, &c." I am content to be judged by these words. I proved afore by Paul and Timothy, by Dionysius, &c. that the order, by which our bishops and priests are made now, is more agreeing to the order of the church in Cyprian's time, and tradition of the apostles, than that misorder whereby the popish prelates order their clergy. Let them prove by good writers, that their oiling, shaving, vowing, sacrificing, apparel, &c. was used in the church in Cyprian's time, and I submit myself. Cyprian was living more than two hundred and fifty year after Christ, in which time was no such proud pope nor popish order used in the church as he requires of us, but only such a simplicity as I spake of afore. Thus, like a foolish boy, he has gotten a rod to beat himself withal: God send him more wit!

XII. Where the said preacher does affirm greater matters than the burning of Paul's to have chanced in the time of superstition and ignorance, as the church of Paul's was brent in the first year of Stephen, and the steeple of Paul's set on fire by lightning in the time of king Henry the sixth; they that count that to be the time of superstition and ignorance, when God was served devoutly night and day, the people lived in the fear of God, every one in his own vocation, without reasoning and contention of matters of religion, but referred all such things to learned men in general councils and universities, there to be disputed: then was the commandments of God and virtue expressed in living; now all is in talk, and nothing in living: then was prayer, now is prating; then was virtue, now is vice: then was building up of churches, houses of religion and hospitals, where prayer was had night and day, hospitality kept, and the poor relieved; now is pulling down, and destroying such houses, where God should be served, hospitality kept, and the poor relieved: by means whereof God's glory is destroyed, and the commonwealth impoverished: then was plenty of all things, now is scarceness. Therefore *operibus credite*.

If I should fall into a comparison of the plagues in the time of popery and the gospel, although both were great, yet in superstitious times were the greater. Many did not believe that these other brennings of Paul's were true, which the bishop declared, when he spake it openly there: but it was either for ignorance or malice, or both; for all these were true, as appears in records, and many more. In the year of our Lord one thousand and eighty-seven, and the seventh day of July, the church of Paul's and all that was in it, with a great part of the city, were burned, Maurice then being bishop of London, and the twenty-first year of William conqueror. In the year one thousand one hundred and thirty-two, the most part of the city of London was burned by the fire of Gilbert Becket, and in the thirty-second year of king Henry the first. Of this kindred came that goodly imp, Thomas Becket. In the year one thousand one hundred and thirty-seven, and the first year of king Stephen, began a fire at London bridge, and burned all the city and church of Paul's, unto ye come out at Temple-bar, to St Clement's church, which was then called the Danes' church.

More and greater plagues in popery than the gospel.

In the year one thousand three hundred and eighty-two, and the twenty-first day of May, with a great earthquake through the realm, the cross in Paul's churchyard was overthrown, in the sixth year of Richard the second. To the building of that cross again William, then bishop of Canterbury, gathered great sums of money, and enriched himself. And because men should be more willing and liberal to give, he and the rest of such holy bishops granted many days of pardon to them that would freely give money to the building of that cross again. Canterbury granted forty days; London, Ely, Bath, Chichester, Carlisle, Llandaff, Bangor, every one forty days: the sum in all three hundred and twenty days of pardon; but not one dodkin[1] of money came out of their purse. All which things, and more, the dean of Paul's declared well at the cross out of the records of their church and city. Three year afore Lanfranc was made bishop of Canterbury, as *Legenda Sanctorum* writes, the whole city of Canterbury almost, and Christ's church there, was burned up with fire, in the beginning of William conqueror's days. Polychronicon tells, lib. VII. cap. 4, that "a great piece of London, and Paul's church, with the principal cities of England were burned." Cap. 7, he says, "a whirlwind threw down a hundred houses in London[2], and many churches also." Lib. VIII. cap. 1, Basil, a great city with many towers fell with earthquake in Edward the third's days; and in Naples forty thousand were killed, cap. 28. On Candlemas even, in midwinter, Paul's steeple was burned with lightning in the time of Henry the sixth, cap. 22. The church of Durham likewise, about forty year since; with many other like.

But why should I stand to prove that which every man knows to be true, if he be of any learning and knowledge, as though it were a doubt or strange thing? What great town or church can ye reckon within the realm, or without almost, that has not suffered the like? Why should we then marvel of this? Call to remembrance the late days of popery here with us, not seven year since; and see what horrible storms, thunders, and lightnings, was here by Nottingham, where houses, churches, bells, woods, and loaden carts were overthrown and carried away. But, he says, these chanced some in time of civil war, and not all with fire from heaven. What then? What helps that his case? All were in the time of popery, and many more like. And though all these were not with fire from heaven, yet it is as great a token of God's anger as well as the other, or more. Says not David, "Fire, Psal. cxlviii.

[1 Dodkin: little doit. A Dutch *duyt* is the eighth part of a penny. ED.]

[2 Also, at London a whirlwind threw down six hundred houses or more, and many churches thereto.—The other facts stated in this passage are accurately quoted. ED.]

hail, snow, ice, and windy storms do his commandment?" If they do his commandment, then the one is his doing as well as the other. Does not God rule the earth as well as the heaven? These fires from heaven chance more seldom than the other, and therefore more fearful when they come: yet these on earth obey his word as well as the other, and are not done without him. And not without a cause it may be a token of God's greater anger to punish us rather with those things that be daily among us, and were ordained to serve us for our health, than to correct us with those that fall so seldom, and are made to fear us, and declare God's great fearful majesty.

But this grieves him, to call that the time of superstition and ignorance, when God was served night and day so devoutly, as he thinks, and every one lived quietly without reasoning of the scripture, and believed whatsoever the pope sent them, and served God after their own device, and not as God himself taught them; and, so that the belly were full, all was well, though they maintained idle lubbers, which was no more alms afore God than their prating was praying. For their monkish night-prayer, how vain lip-labour it was, and mumbled up of an unlearned sort, I said enough afore, and declared how far it differed from true prayer: but this is that may not be borne, when the people have the scripture in their own tongue; for then they are able to tell the priests their duty, and correct their superstitious idolatry. It skills not much, though the papists would have the people to live in blindness still: for in that the pope and the Turk *The people should learn the scriptures.* agrees well, that their people shall be unlearned, and understand nothing but whatsoever it pleases the priests to teach them, which is neither much nor good: but God in his word, and the ancient fathers in their writings, do teach christian Psal. lxxviii. people otherways. David says, "The father should declare Deut. xxxii. his truth to their children." Moses says, "Ask thy father, and he will tell thee; demand of the elders, and they will declare unto thee." Paul says, "Wives, if they would know any thing, let them ask their husbands at home." If fathers must teach their children, and children learn of their fathers, and wives of their husbands; how should either party be ig-Psal.cxxxiii. norant? Jerome says, "Men are wont, women are wont, and monks are wont, to strive among themselves, who should learn most scriptures, and thinks them best that learns most; but he learned most, that does most[1]." Chrysostom, in his thirty-first homily on St John, rebukes the people "that were so unwilling to learn the scriptures, seeing the woman of Samaria, of whom there he writes, was so desirous; and that at home in their houses they had tables and chesses, rather than books; and if they had any books, they were not occupied, &c."[2] In his second homily on Matthew, in declaring how "the scriptures refresh the mind, as a wholesome air does the body," he moves them to the reading of it, and rebukes them that say it "belongs to monks and priests to read it and study it, and not to the people[3]." Thus in corners these enemies of God and his word would draw the people from their salvation, and would make them believe that it were not their duty to learn. What blindness is this, to think ignorance better than learning, and blindness than sight? St Paul says, "the gospel of God is the power of God, to save them that believe." St James says, "the word of God is able to save our souls." Then surely, those thieves that would rob God's people of God's word, would rob them of their salvation by Christ, and sell them such filthy salves as the pope would heal his scabbed sheep withal, which stinks in God's sight. Christ

Rom. i.
James i.

[1 Solent et viri, solent et monachi, solent et mulierculæ, hoc inter se habere certamen, ut plures ediscant scripturas; et in eo se putant esse meliores, si plures edidicerint: ille plus edidicit, qui plus facit. Hieron. Opera, Tom. II. Pars ii. p. 474. Paris. 1699. ED.]

[2 Ἡμεῖς δὲ οὐ μόνον περὶ δογμάτων οὐ ζητοῦμεν, ἀλλὰ καὶ περὶ πάντων ἁπλῶς καὶ ὡς ἔτυχε διακείμεθα. διὰ τοῦτο τὰ πάντα ἠμέληται. τίς γὰρ ὑμῶν, εἰπέ μοι, ἐν οἰκίᾳ γενόμενος, πυκτίον ἔλαβε χριστιανικὸν μετὰ χεῖρας, καὶ τὰ ἐγκείμενα ἐπῆλθε, καὶ ἠρεύνησε τὴν γραφήν; οὐδεὶς ἂν ἔχοι ταῦτα εἰπεῖν· ἀλλὰ πέττους μὲν καὶ κύβους παρὰ τοῖς πλείοσιν εὑρήσομεν ὄντας, βιβλία δὲ οὐδαμοῦ, ἀλλὰ καὶ παρ' ὀλίγοις. Hom. in Joann. XXXII. (al. XXXI.) Tom. VIII. p. 216. Paris. 1836. ED.]

[3 Ὥσπερ γὰρ σῶμα ἀέρος ἀπολαῦον καθαροῦ ὑγιεινότερον ἔσται, οὕτω καὶ ψυχὴ φιλοσοφωτέρα τοιαύταις ἐντρεφομένη μελέταις. * * * ἀλλὰ τίς ἡ ἀπολογία ἐγκλημάτων τούτων; οὐκ εἰμί, φησί, τῶν μοναχῶν, ἀλλὰ καὶ γυναῖκα ἔχω καὶ παιδία, καὶ οἰκίας ἐπιμελοῦμαι. τοῦτο γάρ ἐστιν ὃ πάντα ἐλυμήνατο, ὅτι ἐκείνοις μόνοις νομίζετε προσήκειν τὴν ἀνάγνωσιν τῶν θείων γραφῶν, πολλῷ πλέον ἐκείνων ὑμεῖς δεόμενοι. Hom. II. in Matth. Tom. VII. pp. 32, 34. ED.]

[PILKINGTON.]

Matt. xv.   our Lord says, "If the blind lead the blind, both fall into the ditch." Then it is not enough to say, Sir John our priest taught me thus: for surely, if he be as bold as blind Bayerd[1] to lead thee wrong, and thou be so mad to follow him, thou shalt be condemned as well as he. If he alone might fall in the ditch, thou might more boldly follow him: but now thou art warned, learn and take heed; for ignorance will not excuse thee.

Hospitality.   The hospitality and alms of abbeys is not altogether to be either allowed or dispraised. The most of that which they did bestow was on the rich, and not the poor indeed, as halt, lame, blind, sick, or impotent, but lither lubbers, that might work and would not: insomuch that it came into a common proverb to call him an abbey lubber, that was idle, well fed, a long lewd lither loiterer, that might work and would not. On these and the richer sort was the most part of their liberality bestowed, that I need not to speak of any worse: the smallest portion was on them that needed most, not according to their foundation. Polychronicon says, lib. v. cap. xxxii, that abbeys "wasted their goods in gluttony and outrage[2];" lib. vii. cap. vi, that "monks used hawking, hunting, dicing, drinking;" and therefore under king Richard I. monks were put from Coventry and clerks brought in, lib. vii. cap. xxv. and Baldwin a monk, and bishop of Canterbury, did the like with his monks the same time, cap. xxviii. But whether the new monks with their short coats, and almost without all religion, keeping a shepherd and a dog, where all this good cheer was afore, be worse than the monkish idolatrous popish creatures, which devised a religion of their own, shewing their holiness in their long coats, I leave it to the disputation of the learned. Look into London, and see what hospitals be there founded in the gospel time, and the poor indeed relieved, youth godly brought up, and the idle set to work. Popery would sometime feed the hungry, but seldom correct the unprofitable drones that sucked

[1 *Bayard,* a name commonly applied to a horse. The proverb here used is frequent in Chaucer and the old writers. Ed.]

[2 But in our time covetyse (covetousness) and pride hath so changed all things in England, that things that were given to abbeys in old time be now more wasted in gluttony and outrage of owners than in sustenance and help of needy men and guests. Chap. xxxii. fin. Ed.]

the honey from the labouring bees, nor bring up children in the fear of God: but to fill the belly, and not to teach virtue, is to increase vice. Well worth Bridewell[3] therefore, for it is a good school.

The rest of his railing is not worthy answering, for there is as much and more virtue and keeping God's commandments used now as was then, and more; though both sorts be bad enough, and the best may be amended. Ask an old papist of the common sort, how many commandments of God, and what they be, and he cannot tell. Ask a protestant's child of seven year old that has learned his catechism, and he can tell his duty to God and man, how to live and die, what to love, and what to flee, better than all their popish priests. Is it like that he keeps God's commandments, which knows not what they be? How many of the people were taught then, would learn, or were moved to learn, their commandments? No: few such at these days are willing to hear them, or learn them; how much less to practise them! What a wicked opinion is this, to think that ignorance is better than learning, or that a man shall better serve God without knowledge of God, his duty and his word, rather than by knowing, feeling, and understanding God's goodness and man's frailness, God's mercy and man's misery, our wretched worldly state and God's everlasting blessed felicity! God give us grace to think and thank!

The last reason that he lays for maintaining his superstition, declares what religion and opinion he is of. "Then was plenty," he says, "and now is scarceness of all things:" which how true it is, let the world judge." Look at the late days of popery, and see what dearth, death, and scarceness was then; and compare it with these days, and the plenty of God's undeserved blessing poured on so unthankful a people. Then acorns were good to make bread of, and under Henry the Sixth they made bread of fern roots, as Polychronicon says, lib. VIII. cap. 21: now commonly the poorer sort almost have disdained with brown bread. Then scholars of the universities brake up their houses, went and lived abroad with their friends, being not able to continue at their study: then was such dearth and scarcity, as the

Dearth.

[[3] Bridewell was one of the hospitals founded by king Edward VI. whose reign is meant by "the gospel time." It was especially designed for the employment of the idle. ED.]

like has not oft been read of: then a bishop of Mentz was so pursued with rats in a time of dearth, that he was compelled to flee to his tower standing in the midst of the river Rhine, a mile from any land; yet the rats followed him and devoured him there, for his unmercifulness, and therefore is called the rats' tower to this day[1]. This bishop was no protestant. Whether the like be now, the blind may see. Who feels it? God gives his blessing plentifully, if man could consider it thankfully, and use it liberally. Who has cause to complain, or where is it seen? I think, England had not the like plenteous time so commonly these many years, although this year corn be dear, and somewhat scarce[2].

But I put the case, that there were scarceness and dearth of all things, plagues and war, &c. Were this a sufficient cause to condemn our religion? No, sure: no worldly thing, good or evil, will move God's people to judge God's truth by any other thing than by God's holy book. Should we condemn St Austin, because the city where he was bishop was besieged and won by God's enemies, Austin himself being within it, and died a little before the winning of it? Should Elias and Eliseus have forsaken God's law, because there was so great dearth and scarceness in their times? Should Daniel for the lions' den, or Paul for his chains, have forsaken their God? In the days of Elias it rained not the space of three year and a half: under Eliseus, in the siege of Samaria, women eat their children, and dove's-dung was good meat. Only the worldlings judge by their belly their religion. The godless people said to Jeremiah, "We will not hear the word of God of thee: for while we worshipped the moon and stars, we had plenty of all things; but since we heard the word of God of thee, we have had scarceness of all things." This is the reason that led the Jews, and by the same is this Jewish papist moved to judge of God's truth. Therefore I cannot judge him to be of another religion than those, whose belly is their God.

Jer. xliv.

Let us praise God for our health, wealth, and liberty, that he bestows on us undeserved so plenteously, lest in not thankfully

[1 Bishop Hatto. See p. 30. ED.]

[2 In the year 1561-2 wheat and rye were 8s. the quarter; in 1562-3 rye was 12s. 4d.—Fleetwood, *Chron. Prec.* ED.]

receiving his word, and murmuring against his blessings, we provoke him to plague us worse than afore. If wealth may move, consider what great things the Lord has wrought by the queen's majesty, and then judge. When the realm was in danger to be given into strangers' hands, and none could tell how to deliver themselves, God of his undeserved goodness set up the queen our mistress, who quietly, contrary to all men's expectation, avoided them all. What danger was Scotland in! Yet so God blessed the queen's majesty, that she not only delivered us, but them from their enemies' hands. What release in France the poor oppressed have had at her highness' hands, the blind see, all her loving subjects rejoice, though the envious papists murmur and grudge. God grant her highness grace to be thankful to God's majesty, who does so past all man's expectation prosper her doings, that he only may have the praise! What cause we have to praise God for restoring religion through the queen's travail, all men of God do see and praise him for it, though blind papists be sorry therefore. What cost her highness has sustained in restoring us a fine coin from so base, wise men rejoice, though this malicious fool say we be in great poverty. Look how few taxes she has taken to do this withal, and how many and how great were levied afore. How was this realm pestered with strange rulers, strange gods, strange languages, strange religion, strange coins; and how is it now peaceably rid of them all, to the great glory of God, that has wrought so many wonderful, strange, great things in so short a time in a weak vessel, which he never did by any her noble progenitors, which have been so many and so worthy! Could any be so blind, but that malice has bewitched, to not see, or not praise God for these worthy deeds? I would have wanted the suspicion of flattery in rehearsing these things, but that I would the unthankful world should see the disdainful blind malice of popery, which cannot say well by God's good blessings.

The foolish linking and clouting of the scriptures together which follows, declares what wit he has: they may be applied all against himself, and such as he is, rather than against the professors of God's truth. What blasphemy is it to lay all kind of wickedness on God's word! What evil soever reigns in the world, it is to be imputed to man, and not to God; to man's frailness, and not to God's truth and goodness. God and his holy word punish and condemn all false doctrine and filthiness: therefore God will confound all such filthy mouths, as blaspheme him or his holy word, to be the cause of any kind of naughtiness.

XIII. "All liberty is now used," he says:

<small>Justice.</small>

where indeed justice was not better ministered these many years, even as the wiser and indifferenter sort of papists do grant. Call to remembrance how sharply unnatural lust[1], conjuring, witchcrafts, sorcery, &c. were punished with death by law in the gospel time of blessed King Edward. When were these laws repealed, but in the late days of popery? Then judge, whether there was greater liberty to sin under the christian king, or under superstitious popery. But the sodomitical papists think these to be no sins, and therefore beastly do misuse themselves, defiling themselves both with spiritual and sodomitical uncleanness. Whether is there more liberty given to sin, when such sins be made death by order of law, or when the laws appoint no punishment for them? Surely the gospel is unjustly blamed in giving carnal liberty, and popery rightfully condemned in taking away the pain, and opening a door to all mischiefs. Who lives more licentiously than the pope himself, without all fear of God, good order, and God's law, doing what he will? So be all his scholars, following their own father's steps.

In these my sayings I go not about to prove us angels, yet surely not such devils as he would make us, but in comparison of them we be saints. Therefore let us both amend, that God may be merciful to both, and glorified in both. And as the examples in his beginning were good, if they had been well applied, so is his conclusion.

[[1] This expression is altered from the original.—"This offence, being in the times of popery only subject to ecclesiastical censures, was made felony without benefit of clergy by statute 25 Henr. VIII. c. 6. revived and confirmed by 5 Eliz. c. 17." Blackstone's Commentaries, Book IV. chap. 15. Vol. IV. p. 216. Lond. 1791.—It was made felony, punishable with death, loss of lands, &c. by the statute of Henry, which was *so far* repealed by 2 and 3 Edw. VI. as to remit the forfeiture of lands, &c. and wholly repealed, with several other penal statutes, by 1 Mar. c. 1. ED.]

XIV. I will conclude with him therefore, in the right sense and meaning of it saying with him: "Return to the steps of the good fathers, the prophets and apostles, framing yourselves to follow their doctrine: be not carried away with strange and diverse doctrine of popes, contrary to God's holy word, and invented of late by men. Embrace the religion and faith taught from the beginning, in Christ's church, from time to time continually." Flee this new-fangled popish superstition, which has crept into the church of late years, and believe that only which Christ has taught, and his apostles and martys have confirmed, "and frame your lives accordingly; or else God's vengeance hangs over your heads, ready suddenly to fall upon you: and let this token of brenning of Paul's be an example and token of a greater plague to follow, except ye amend;" which God grant us all to do! Amen.

A PRAYER.

MOST righteous and wise Judge, eternal God and merciful Father, which of thy secret judgment hast suffered false prophets in all ages to rise for the trial of thine elect, that the world might know who would stedfastly stick unto thy undoubted and infallible truth, and who would be carried away with every vain doctrine; and yet by the might of thy Holy Spirit hast confounded them all, to thy great glory, and comfort of thy people: have mercy upon us, we beseech thee, and strengthen our weakness against all assaults of our enemies: confound all popery, as thou did the doctrine of the Pharisees; strengthen the lovers of thy truth, to the confusion of all superstition and hypocrisy: give us due love and reverence of thy holy word; defend us from man's traditions: increase our faith; grant us grace never to fall from thee, but uprightly to walk according as thou hast taught us, swerving neither to the right hand nor the left, neither adding nor

taking any thing away from thy written word; but submitting
ourselves wholly to thy good will and pleasure, may so
pass this transitory life, that through thy goodness
we may live everlastingly with thee in thy
glory, through Christ our Lord, who with
thee and the Holy Ghost lives and
reigns one God and our
Saviour, for ever
and ever.
(*)

Have not I hated them, O Lord, that hate thee, and even pined away because of thine enemies? Psal. cxxxix.

I will give you a mouth and wisdom, which all your enemies cannot gainsay and withstand. Luke xxi.

FINIS.

HERE FOLOWE

ALSO CERTAINE QUESTIONS PROPOUNDED BY HIM, WHICHE ARE FULLYE ALTHOUGHE SHORTLY AUNSWERED.

I. Which is the catholic church?

St Augustine and St Jerome do say: "The church is a visible company of people gathered of Christ our Lord and the apostles, and continued unto this day by a perpetual succession, living in one faith apostolical, under Christ the head, and his vicar in earth, being the pastor and high bishop. Out of this catholic and apostolical church is no trust of salvation[1]." August. cap. 4. Epist. Fund. Hiero. contra Lucifer.

St Augustine says: "Whosoever shall be out of this church, although his life be esteemed to be very good and laudable, by this only fault, that he is disjoined and separated from the unity of Christ and his church, he can have no life, but the wrath of God hangs over him[2]." August. Epist. 1512.

St Cyprian says: "He separates himself from Christ, that does against the consent of the bishop and clergy[3]." Cyprianus de Simplici.

St Jerome does say: "We must remain in that church which is Hiero. contra Lucifer.

[1 In catholica ecclesia * * tenet me consensio populorum atque gentium: tenet auctoritas miraculis inchoata, spe nutrita, caritate aucta, vetustate firmata: tenet ab ipsa sede Petri apostoli, cui pascendas oves suas post resurrectionem Dominus commendavit, usque ad præsentem episcopatum successio sacerdotum. Augustin. contra Epist. Manich. cap. 5. (IV.) Tom. VIII. p. 269. ed. Paris. 1837.

Super illam petram ædificatam ecclesiam scio. Quicunque extra hanc domum agnum comederit, profanus est: si quis in arca Noe non fuerit, peribit regnante diluvio. Hieron. Epist. XIV. ad Damasum. Tom. IV. Pars i. p. 19. ed. Paris. 1706. If the reference in the margin to the treatise "contra Lucifer." be correct, the passage intended must be that quoted below in note 1. p. 618. ED.]

[2 Ab ea vero separati, quamdiu contra illam sentiunt, boni esse non possunt: quia etsi aliquos eorum bonos videtur ostendere quasi laudabilis conversatio, malos eos facit ipsa divisio. August. Epist. CCVIII. (al. CCIX.) Tom. II. p. 1177. ED.]

[3 An esse sibi cum Christo videtur, qui adversus sacerdotes Christi facit; qui se a cleri ejus et plebis societate secernit? De Unitate Ecclesiæ: (*vulgo* De Simplicitate Prælatorum:) p. 83. Ed. Fell. Oxon. 1700. ED.]

founded of the apostles, and does endure unto this day by a succession of bishops, to whom the Holy Ghost has appointed the rule and government of this church, sanctified by Christ's blood-shedding. Nor let heretics take any comfort to themselves, if they can frame out of the chapters of the scripture for their purpose that which they say, seeing the devil has alleged some things of scripture: for the scriptures consist not in reading, but true understanding."[1] If we will be members of Christ's church, we must continue firmly in that faith and religion, that was sent from the apostolical see of Rome, by St Gregory, into England: which faith and religion was planted and stablished by St Augustine in this realm." St Augustine stablished mass and seven sacraments to be used in the Latin tongue, as Gildas does witness, and such manner of divine service as is now used.

The Answer to the First Question.

St Austin, in the first place alleged, has no such definition, although the most part of the words which he puts there are true: and would to God he considered how much he speaks against himself herein! This is that which we defend, that the church is gathered by Christ and the apostles first, and continues, not in the papistical but in the apostolical faith, under Christ our head, who rules his church still by his Holy Spirit and word, and has not put it into the hands of any one only general vicar in the earth, as he untruly says: whereas their church is builded not on Christ, but on the pope's decrees, which the apostles never knew, and were unwritten many years after the death of the apostles, and are always uncertain, changing ever, as it pleases the pope for his time to determine: and their church has had at one time three or four popes for their heads, like a monster with many heads; some country following one pope, some another, as their head. We say also, that the papists have divided themselves from this church of Christ, making themselves synagogues and chapels, gods, and religion of their own devising, as Micha did, contrary to God's word: and therefore the wrath of God hangs over them, except they return, how holy soever they pretend to be.

Judg. xvii.

[[1] In illa esse ecclesia permanendum, quæ ab apostolis fundata usque ad diem hanc durat. * * Nec sibi blandiantur, si de scripturarum capitulis videntur sibi affirmare quod dicunt, quum et diabolus de scripturis aliqua sit locutus, et scripturæ non in legendo consistant, sed in intelligendo. Adv. Luciferianos. Tom. IV. Pars ii. p. 306. Paris. 1699. ED.]

Cyprian's words are not altogether so plain as he sets them; but if they were, he means another sort of priests and clergy than the pope's: for neither they did take then to them, nor he knew no such authority in them, as they now usurp unto themselves; for he writes as sharply and homely unto Cornelius, then bishop of Rome, as he does to any other his fellow bishops. Surely, whosoever divides himself from Christ's ministers and people, refusing their doctrine and discipline, separates himself from Christ: even as he that flees from the filthy dregs of popery, and his chaplains, is cut off from the pope, the father of such wickedness.

In Jerome's words we most rejoice, teaching us to continue in that church, which is founded by the apostles, and not popes, and endures to this day. The words of "succession," &c. following, are his own, and not Jerome's. By this doctrine of Jerome we flee to the apostolical, and flee from the papistical church, which was never known of many years after the apostles. And we grant that the devil, papists, and heretics can allege some words of the scriptures; and therefore we say that the papists be devilish heretics, because they rack and writhe the scriptures to a contrary meaning, to their own damnation, as the devil did. For succession and government of bishops, for Austin's religion, massing and seven sacraments, I said enough afore: but where he alleges Gildas as father of his lies, he does him much wrong; for he has never such a word in all his writings. If he have, let him shew it. This is ever the fashion of lying papists, to have the names of doctors and ancient writers in their mouths, as though they were of the same opinion that they be, where indeed they be nothing less: and if they get a word or two that seems to make for them, they will add a whole tale of their own making, as though it were a piece of the same ancient man's saying; and by this means they deceive the simple, which have no learning to judge, or have not the books to try their sayings by; as this miser goes about in these places afore.

II. Who is an heretic?

He that teaches, defends, or maintains any erroneous opinion against the decrees, judgment, or determination of Christ's catholic church, is an heretic.

III. Who is a schismatic?

He that is divided or separate from the unity of the catholic church in ministration or receiving the sacraments or divine service, is a schismatic and in state of perdition.

The Answer to the Second and Third Questions.

He would gladly appear to be well seen in logic, if he had any. If all be heretics that defend an erroneous opinion, then many disputations shall be condemned.

In disputing, it is oft seen that of ignorance, or for his learning sake, many defend an untruth: yet God forbid that they should all be heretics! Austin says well, "I may err, but I will not be an heretic." Then he is an heretic properly, that defends an error obstinately, and will not be corrected. So teaches St Paul, "Flee from an heretic after one or two warnings:" he says not, for once teaching or defending of it. Also he is not a schismatic, that differs in small points or circumstances of ministering the sacraments from other; for then should all the Greek church be in a schism, because they differ in some ceremonies from the Latin church, and also one from another, as I declared afore in the ministration of Basil, Chrysostom, St James, &c.: the same may be said of the Latin church too, as for Ambrose' order, Gregory's, &c. And because ever under the catholic church he signifies Rome, we say that no country, which uses other ceremonies than they do, is in this case a schismatic; for that their Romish orders and ceremonies be of their own devising for the most part, and not commanded by God, nor never were used generally in the universal catholic church, as I proved afore, and therefore they be free to use or not use, as shall be thought meet. To differ in the substance and doctrine of sacraments may make a schism or heresy: but such ceremonies are free to all countries, which may edify, as appeared in Anselm's epistle afore.[1] These few words are sufficient to let him see his own foolishness: more might be said, but I will not be so curious nor tedious to note all. St Paul calls the Corinthians schismatics in hanging on men's sleeves for opinions in religion, and for misusing the communion; and not for every diversity of trifling ceremonies, as he defines it here.

[[1] See p. 538. Ed.]

IV. Whether be priests in schism that have subscribed to the religion now used in England?

In subscribing to this religion now used in England, they have both refused the power and authority which was given to them by the bishop, when they were made priests, (that is to say, power and authority to consecrate and offer, and to celebrate mass for the quick and the dead;) and also they have refused their canonical obedience solemnly promised to the bishops with a kiss. And where the bishops of this realm with the clergy assembled at time of parliament would agree to no part of this religion, (in witness whereof the bishops be in prison, and put from all their livings, and a great number of the clergy have lost all their livings, some be in prison, some banished from their friends; both the bishops and all the clergy that has lost their livings, are all ready to suffer death afore they will consent to any part of this religion; but all they which have subscribed, have forsaken the bishops, their true pastors and captains, obeying and following wolves and apostates; in witness whereof they have subscribed their names;) so separating themselves from the bishops and clergy, they must needs be in schism.

The Fourth Answer.

Where he lays to the priests' charge, that in subscribing to this religion they have refused both the power that was given to them to offer sacrifice and celebrate mass for the quick and dead, and also their canonical obedience promised to the bishops by a Judas kiss, because the old bishops in parliament did not agree to it; he does the priests more honour than he knows of, or thinks well bestowed. If he would call to remembrance the answer that the pillar of their church, stout Stephen, makes in his book *De Vera Obedientia* to the like reason, where he was charged with falling from the pope, and breaking that oath and vow of subjection which he made unto him, when he was first made bishop; he might better defend the priests of our time than accuse them. In our baptism we all make a solemn vow to God our Lord, that him only we will serve, and believe his word: all vows following, which are contrary to that, not only may and ought to be broken, but it is wicked to keep them; for we must serve God only, as he has taught us in his holy word. But the scripture condemns all such sacrificing now for sin, save only that sacrifice which Jesus Christ offered once for the sins of the whole world, and bids us also obey our king as chief and highest governor: therefore the priests, forsaking these later wicked vows and powers, which are contrary to God's word and their solemn profession made in baptism, (as Stephen did well then, though he flattered afterward, and turned to his old vomit,) are more worthy to be praised than these obstinate prelates, which now, misusing the gentleness of the prince, deny with mouth that which they know in conscience to be true, and yet charge the priests with it, although they subscribed to the same things themselves under that good king Edward, because both they knew it to be true, and see the rod then more sharply shaken than it is now.

And though he crack in their name, that they will rather die than agree to any part of this religion, which they themselves used, ministered, taught, and received afore; I doubt not but, if they were opposed as they opposed other, they would as soon eat the fagot, as feel it burn them. The apostle says, "By one offering he has made perfect all them that be sanctified." If one offering once made have made all perfect, then cursed be they that will correct or amend Christ's death, as though it were not perfect to save all without their often sacrificing. "We must obey God rather than man," as St Luke teaches: therefore that unlawful obedience promised to the pope and his prelates, contrary to their due allegiance to their prince commanded in the scripture, not only may, but ought with safe conscience to be broken. At the preaching of Christ our Lord and his apostles, many forsaked the traditions of the elders and Pharisees, receiving and believing the gospel of Christ Jesus, and forsaking the Jewish ceremonies, and were not counted forsakers of God and his word: no more are they surely to be reckoned apostates, that forsake the pope's draff, the clog of all good consciences, and cleave to the simplicity of God's truth, taught in the scripture.

And where he cracks much, that they have lost their livings, and be in prison, or banished, let the world judge whether they ever lived more merrily, quietly, fared better, lay easilier, had more plenty of all things, than they have now. They are far short from such handling as they dealt with other. Some they hungered to death, some they beat in prison, some they cast on dunghills, being so murdered at their hands, some they burned, after they had been long buried: but every one was so miserably handled, that christian ears and hearts abhor to think or hear of it; and yet, like shameless beasts, they blush not nor repent, but wish and look to be murdering again. They are as pale in prison as a butcher's boll: they are as lean as a fat hog; they lie at ease unto their bones ache with rising early; they fare of the best; they take no thought, but look for a day, and think long unto they may imbrue their hands in blood again, and make all officers to be their hangmen, and the stoutest to be afraid of a priest's cap, as they did afore. They provided so well for themselves in their summer, that they need not to starve in this gentle winter: the world is so much their friend, that they can lack nothing: they would fain be counted to suffer for religion, if any man would believe it[1]. The poor protestant, which has his liberty, lives in more misery, need, debt, reproach and contempt, than these the pope's prisoners, who, he says, have lost all. It is better in the world to be the pope's prisoner than Christ's preacher. God amend all!

V. Whether be priests in schism that minister the communion and other sacraments according to the book of common prayer now set forth?

This manner of ministration of sacraments, set forth in the book of common prayers, was never allowed nor agreed upon by the universal church of Christ in any general council or sacred synod; no, not by the clergy of England at the last parliament: but only it was agreed upon by the laity, which have nothing ado with spiritual matters or causes of religion, but ought to stand to the decrees, judgment and determination of the clergy in causes of faith and religion. For so it was used in the apostles' time, as appears in the Acts of the Apostles: As when the apos- Acts vi. tles took then order to make seven deacons, and when they put away Acts xv. the ceremonies of the old law. Such decrees as the apostles and clergy made at Jerusalem, without any council of the laity, St Paul and other

[1 The papists had much liberty in the early part of queen Elizabeth's reign, till the bull of Pius V. in 1570 required them to rebel against their sovereign. Even of Bonner, who was committed to the Marshalsea in 1560, Strype says: "He grew old in prison, and died a natural death in the year 1569, not suffering any want, or hunger, or cold. For he lived daintily, had the use of the garden and orchards, when he was minded to walk abroad and take the air; suffering nothing like imprisonment, unless that he was circumscribed within certain bounds. Nay, he had his liberty to go abroad, but dared not venture: for the people retained in their hearts his late bloody actions. Strype, Annals, I. chap. xi. p. 214. Oxford, 1824. Ed.]

of the apostles taught all countries and nations to obey and observe: and sith the apostles' time the clergy has ever decreed matters of religion and faith. Nor it cannot be proved, that ever the laity in any country or nation, afore the last parliament, did presume to set forth a religion against the whole consent of the clergy. Therefore this manner of ministration of sacraments now used, being against the consent and determination of Christ's church, which ought to be ruled and governed by bishops, it must needs be schismatical, and they that use this manner of ministration must needs be in schism. The blessed martyr, St Cyprian, does declare what danger they do stand in, that do use this manner of ministration against the order of Christ's church, saying these words: "They be enemies of the altar, and rebels against the sacrifice of Christ, contemning the bishops and forsaking the priests of God: they are bold to set up another altar with unlawful voices, to make another manner of prayer, to profane with false sacrifices the verity of the blessed sacrament of the altar: nor they will not know them that fare about to do against the ordinance of God, for their bold rashness, by the punishment of God they shall be punished; as he punished Chore, Dathan, and Abiron, which would offer up sacrifice against the consent of Moses and Aaron: some were swallowed up of the earth, and the rest brent with fire, to the terrible example of all others."[1] Hitherto be St Cyprian's words.

_{Acts xx.}

_{Mal. i.}

Also Almighty God, by his holy prophet Malachi, does cry out upon such priests as minister against the ordinance of Christ's church, saying, "they despise his name in offering up polluted bread."

_{Hosea ix.}

The prophet Osee does call the sacrifice of such priests "bread of mourning, and all that eat thereof shall be defiled," says the prophet.

_{Ezek. xxii.}

Almighty God does complain by his prophet Ezechiel, saying: "The priests have condemned my law, and have polluted my sanctuary." "Woe be unto you, that go from the truth," says our Lord by Esay. Our Lord

_{Mal. ii.}

says by his prophet, "except such priests will amend quickly and give glory to his name, they shall be brought into great necessity and poverty, and he will curse their blessings; and because they have made void the pact of Levi, they shall be in contempt in all people."

[[1] Hostis altaris, adversus sacrificium Christi rebellis, pro fide perfidus, pro religione sacrilegus, inobsequens servus, filius impius, frater inimicus, contemtis episcopis et Dei sacerdotibus derelictis, constituere audet aliud altare, precem alteram illicitis vocibus facere, Dominicæ hostiæ veritatem per falsa sacrificia profanare; nec dignatur scire, quoniam qui contra ordinationem Dei nititur, ob temeritatis audaciam divina animadversione punitur. Sic Chore et Dathan et Abiron, qui sibi contra Moysen et Aaron sacerdotem sacrificandi licentiam vindicare conati sunt, pœnas statim pro suis conatibus pependerunt. Terra compagibus ruptis in profundum sinum patuit, stantes atque viventes recedentis soli hiatus absorbuit. The *fire* and *example of others* are afterwards mentioned. Cypr. De Unitate Ecclesiæ, p. 83. ed. Fell. Oxon. 1700. ED.]

The Fifth Answer.

What if this order of ministering and common prayer was not agreed on by the universal church in general council? Is it not good therefore? Then is neither their Latin portus, nor missal and mass-book good; for the general church never allowed them, as I declared afore. It is free for all countries to differ in outward order of prayer and ceremonies, so that they agree in substance of doctrine with the scripture. But the laity, he says, has nothing ado with spiritual matters and religion, and alleges the Acts of the Apostles: how will he prove that none of the elders there were of the laity, nor none of the multitude in the choosing of the deacons? Unto it be well proved, it may well be doubted on. As in other things, so in this, he shews himself, how learned he is. When the law of God was neglected in the days of Saul, David coming to be king, and moved with love of religion, calls all the nobility and worship of the realm together, thirty thousand, and also the Levites and priests, to know their minds, whether they would bring home the ark of God, and restore the religion decayed, or no? And they answered all, "Yea." What a great parliament was this, and full of the laity, to determine for receiving of religion! Josaphat, Ezechias, and Josias, good kings, sent their visiters abroad through the realm, joining in commission from the king noblemen of the laity, to go in visitation with the Levites. *Legenda Sanctorum*[2] tells, how king Oswi called a synod at Whitby, for taking away that diversity of keeping Easter which was here in the realm, when some kept it in the full moon, what day of the week soever it fell on, other only on the Sunday following: wherein appears the authority that the king justly claims to himself in religion, even in that blind age, when he calls the learned men together to dispute on it, hears what they can say, and concludes so the matter himself that all other did follow his sentence.

Marginal notes: Acts xv. 1 Chron. xiii. 2 Sam. vi. 2 Chron. xxx. xxxiv. xvii. In Wilfrido.

[2 Facta est itaque synodus in monasterio Hildæ abbatissæ apud *Streneshalch*, quod modo *Whiteby* vocatur, ubi quæstio ventilari deberet et terminari; ubi convenerunt reges Oswi et filius ejus Alfredus, Ailbertus episcopus cum beato Wilfrido. * * Habito autem silentio rex Oswi tali modo loquutus est: "Hactenus, patres venerandi, scisma, &c. * * Ea re in hanc me sententiam ipsa rationis necessitas potissimum duxit, quatenus utriusque partis defensores una venire jussio nostra constringeret, &c." Nova Legenda Angliæ. fo. ccc. ccci. Lond. 1516. ED.]

John Gerson and Panormitanus, as I alleged afore[1], no new protestants, but ancient catholics, and both being present in the last councils at Constance and Basil, said they would rather believe a poor simple learned layman that brings and alleges the holy scripture, than all the whole council having no scripture for them. God's truth is not bound to mitres, bishops and priests alone; but laymen may have, and oft have, better the true understanding of it, than those that look highest in the clergy: and therefore they are to be believed and heard, as well as the priests. Did not king David, no priest, set in order the Levites, how they should resort in course to serve in the tabernacle, made the psalms, appointed them, how, where and when they should be sung? Ezechias and Josias pulled down the brazen serpent and other images. Did not Priscilla and Aquila teach Apollo the mysteries of the scripture? By these, I trust, it appears that laymen may do something in religion. If these may not serve, look the statutes of Queen Mary, how she takes away one religion, and brings in another: and there is no more done now. How blind be they in their own causes, and partial to themselves!

But it was never heard of, he says, that the laity in any country presumed to set forth a religion against the whole consent of the clergy, afore the last parliament. O proud brag! Was all the clergy of the realm contained in a few horned popish bishops? Was there no clergy in the university[2], nor other parts of the realm, beside those few bishops? Did not many in the university and abroad in the realm use this service openly and commonly in their churches, afore it was received or enacted by parliament? Because the rulers, the scribes, and all the priests, Acts iv. forbad the apostles in their parliament and council, that they should not preach Christ any more, were not the apostles therefore of the clergy, or was not their doctrine good, because it was condemned in that wicked council? Was there not a disputation for religion appointed by the queen's majesty, wherein your clergy was afraid to utter their foolishness in defending their superstition, lest they had taken more shame in answering

[1 See p. 532. ED.]

[2 Both here and in the next line Strype, (who quotes this passage, *Annals,* Vol. I. p. 202. Oxford, 1824.) reads *universities.* The old edition of Pilkington has *universitie.* ED.]

than they did in holding their peace, which well they could not?[3] I think the universities, with so many places of the realm receiving religion, and these other disputing for it, may be counted to be some part of the clergy of the realm; and so it was not received without consent of the clergy. But these were not of the parliament: what then? Is religion to be determined no where but in parliament? He is wont to say, and did afore, in universities and councils. To make a religion, as he terms it, no man has authority, (for that belongs to God alone;) but to restore pure religion, which has been defaced by superstition, princes in their countries ought to do, though their prelates be against it. Did not king Joas command the priests to restore the temple, and first ordained the poor man's chest in the church? Did not Nabuchodonozor and Darius make proclamation through all their countries, without and against the consent of their priests, that all people should worship Daniel's God? Though there was not a perfect order then set forth by them to do it in, yet it was much for heathen princes to do so, and it teaches christian princes how to do in the like case. But as Joas, Josaphat, Ezechias and Josias did not make a new religion, but restore that which afore was defaced and had long lien buried; so our parliament did not set forth a new religion, but restore that which was godly, begun under good king Edward, confirmed by the parliament and the clergy then, but suddenly by violence trodden under feet by bloody papists a little after.

Yet all this satisfies not them; for nothing can be concluded as a law by parliament, say they, without consent of the clergy there present; but this, having not their consent, cannot be counted a law, as they think. I had rather leave this to be answered by the lawyers than otherwise, because it is a mere temporal case to dispute on, and concerns their profession: yet that the world may see that something may be said in it, we grant him not this to be true, that no law at all can be made without consent of the bishops. Look your old statutes of parliament, when bishops were highest, afore Edward III. and ye shall read that they passed by the consent of the lords temporal and commons, without any mention of the lords

[[3] For an account of this disputation, see Strype, *Annals*, Vol. I. chap. iv. p. 128, &c. Ed.]

spiritual; which statutes many of them stand in strength at this day. Then it may well be gathered, that the consent of the clergy was not always so necessary as they think it.

If it be so strong a reason, as he thinks it to be, to have consent of the bishops, I will prove by the same reason, that it is as necessary to have abbots of the parliament: for they were present of old time, and their consent was required as well as the bishops', and but of late years they were put off the parliament, and it is not long since the convocation house was separate from the parliament too. The lawyers, judges and justices, put in practice and execute these laws: therefore their doings may be a sufficient reason to lead the unlearned, what opinion they have of these statutes for religion, except justice Rascal, first executing them and after running away, may condemn the rest, which I trust he may not. I think they would not execute them, except they had the strength and nature of laws: if they do contrary to their knowledge and opinion, they cannot be able to answer their doings. But I think no wise men are of this opinion; only these corner-creepers that dare not shew their face, and would deceive the people, go about thus to deface all good and godly order that displeases them. In the days of blessed king Edward, they had the like fond opinion, that a king could not make laws in his minority until he come to full age: but this and that was only to hinder religion, and to make the people disobey their prince: yet God has, and I trust will confound all such wicked devices.

Cyprian's words are not truly alleged; and if they were, what do they make against us? How could Cyprian write against our order, which he never knew, being found of so late years as they say? And he does not mean them that differed in outward order of prayer, but that swerved from the substance and verity taught in the scriptures. In ceremonies he himself differed from other countries, and every country almost from others, as I declared afore: and the bishops which he speaks of, are as like our popish prelates as William Fletcher and the sweet rode. The prophet's words may all be turned against him and his, so wisely he applies them.

 VI. Whether they be in schism that minister no sacrament, but only instead of divine service read chapters and psalms, &c. afore the people?

To read afore the people, instead of divine service, psalms and chapters, or other such like, being not appointed by the universal consent of the church of God, but against the decrees of the church, must needs be schismatical, and they in schism that do it. For as the two sons of Aaron Lev. x. were stricken with sudden death, because they offered up strange fire, which was not appointed to them by Moses and Aaron; even so do they offend that will, instead of matins and evensong and other divine service appointed by the church, read psalms and chapters and such like, not appointed by the catholic bishops lawfully consecrated. For our Saviour says in the gospel: "He that will not hear and obey the church," Matt. xviii. that is to say, the bishops, "take him as an infidel." And St Clement does say in an epistle that he writes to St James: "By the judgment of God they shall suffer everlasting torment in the fire of hell, that neglect the decrees of the church[1]." Therefore the holy martyr, St Cyprian, does say: "He that has not defiled his hands with these wicked sacraments, and has polluted his conscience otherwise, let him not comfort himself that he needs to do no penance: for he has broken his profession and canonical obedience, that he made to the bishops when he was made priest[2]." Also, this decree was made in the canons of the apostles: *Si quis clericus aut laicus synagogam Judæorum aut conventiculum hæreticorum ingressus fuerit, ut preces cum illis conjungat, deponatur*[3]*:* that is, "If any of the clergy or laity shall enter into the synagogue of the Jews, or the company of the heretics, to say prayers with him [them,] let him be deposed."

The Sixth Answer.

The cuckoo has but one song, and that is unpleasant: no more has this cokewold maker but one foolish false principle to ground his sayings on; that is, the Romish church. I said afore, (and no man is able to improve[4] it,) that the universal church never made any one order of service to be used through the whole world, but every country has and may have divers without

[[1] Hæc ergo præcepta nemo credat absque sui periculo negligere vel dissimulare, quia in judicio Dei ignis æterni tormenta sustinebit, qui ecclesiastica decreta neglexerit. Clemens Rom. Epist. ad Jacob. Concil. Tom. I. p. 104. Paris. 1644. But the epistle is considered spurious. ED.]

[[2] Nec sibi, quo minus agant pœnitentiam, blandiantur, qui etsi nefandis sacrificiis manus non contaminaverunt, libellis tamen conscientiam polluerunt. * * * Minus plane peccaverit non videndo idola, nec sub oculis circumstantis atque insultantis populi sanctitatem fidei profanando, non polluendo manus suas funestis sacrificiis, nec sceleratis cibis ora maculando: hoc eo proficit, ut sit minor culpa, non ut innocens conscientia. Cyprian. De Lapsis, p. 95, 96. Oxon. 1700. ED.]

[[3] Concil. Tom. I. p. 22. Canon 63. ED.]

[[4] Improve: disprove. ED.]

offending, so they agree in one substance of true doctrine. He knows no church but Rome, and yet Rome never decreed any one general order for the whole world; nor the whole world never obeyed nor received any. The pope's portus and missal has been oft changed, as I proved afore, and every country has their divers order of service. Aaron's sons did plainly against God's express commandment, and therefore were justly plagued: ours do not so, and therefore they be not in like case, but undeservedly blamed. Clement's words and Cyprian's, when they are proved to be truly alleged, touch not us, but such as he is; for they knew no such priests nor church as he means, nor any such were many years after. The papists differ very little from Jews; for both of them set their whole religion in ceremonies and old customs. We stick stiffly to the word of God only, and build not on such vain foundations. Therefore he brings that canon against himself and his sort, being as superstitious as the Jews, and blinded obstinately in errors as heretics.

VII. *Whether is it lawful for priests that say the communion also to celebrate mass?*

Cyprianus de Laps.

The holy martyr, St Cyprian, says: "It is not leaful by and bye afore penance done, to consecrate or touch with his wicked hands the body of our Lord, and with his polluted mouth to receive the blood of our Lord; but first let him do penance[1]." "Does thou think," says St Cyprian, "that our Lord will be so suddenly mitigated, whom thou has refused, and has more esteemed thy worldly living than him?[2]" St Cyprian says: "The blind love of their patrimony and worldly goods has deceived many, and bound them as it were in stocks and fetters, that they cannot follow Christ[3]." "A great number, for fear of words of such as be not

[1 A diaboli aris revertentes, ad sanctum Domini sordidis et infectis nidore manibus accedunt. Mortiferos idolorum cibos adhuc pene ructantes, exhalantibus etiam nunc scelus suum faucibus, et contagia funesta redolentibus, Domini corpus invadunt. * * Ante expiata delicta, ante exomologesin factam criminis, ante purgatam conscientiam sacrificio et manu sacerdotis, ante offensam placatam indignantis Domini et minantis, pacem putant esse, quam quidam verbis fallacibus venditant. De Lapsis, p. 92. ED.]

[2 Putasne tu Dominum cito posse placari, quem verbis perfidis abnuisti, cui patrimonium præponere maluisti? Ibid. p. 98. ED.]

[3 Decepit multos patrimonii sui amor cæcus; nec ad recedendum parati aut expediti esse potuerunt, quos facultates suæ velut compedes ligaverunt. Ibid. p. 90. ED.]

good, have refused their faith, not cast down by any violence of persecution, but by a voluntary lapse have cast down their selves[4];" although they have perceived the bishops and a great number of the clergy not to be afraid to lose all their livings, not fearing loss of goods, or imprisonment, or banishment from their friends; yea, all ready to suffer death in this case. Our Saviour in the gospel says, "No man can serve two masters:" that is, to say the communion decreed and appointed by the laity parliament against the consent of the clergy in Christ's church, and also celebrate mass, decreed and appointed by the clergy in sacred synods, representing the whole estate of Christ's church. St Paul says: "Ye cannot be partakers both of the table of our Lord, and the table of the devils." St Cyprian says: "It is an horrible abomination to fare about to serve both Baal and Christ: it is contumely and not religion, it is injury and not devotion, if thou communicate of the cup of Christ with the devils[5]." Hitherto be St Cyprian's words. St Paul says: "We have an altar, whereof they may not eat that serve the tabernacle." By these examples it is evident, that the priests may not minister the communion to one sort, and mass to another sort. In *Tripartita Historia* it appears, the catholics and the Arians did not communicate one with another[6]. Cyprianus de Cœn. Dom.

VIII. Whether it be lawful for priests to say mass which say no communion, but only read psalms and chapters to the people instead of service?

St Cyprian says: "The verity is not to be dissembled[7]." It is naught to halt upon both the parts: "if God be the Lord, follow him; if Baal, follow him." Even so, if matins and evensong be the ordinances of Christ's church, use them: if the psalms and chapters, use them. It is no less offence to allow a schism with assent, than to offer to idols. St Austin Cyprianus de Laps.

[4 Ad prima statim verba minantis inimici maximus fratrum numerus fidem suam prodidit; nec prostratus est persecutionis impetu, sed voluntario lapsu se ipse prostravit. Ibid. p. 89. ED.]

[5 Tu si templum Spiritus sancti violas, si intra te sacrarium Dei deturpas et fœdas, si cum calice Christi de calice dæmoniorum communicas, contumelia est, non religio; injuria, non devotio. Idolorum servitus et horrenda abominatio, velle simul Baal famulari et Christo. De Cœna Domini.—This treatise is not Cyprian's, but Arnold's, abbot of Bonavalla. It is printed with his other works in the appendix to Cyprian, and the passage here cited will be found in p. 77. of Fell's edition, Oxon. 1700. ED.]

[6 Sunt aliqui in Alexandria populis tuam declinantes communionem, are the words of Constantius to Athanasius in Trip. Hist. Lib. IV. cap. 31. p. 359. And see the passage quoted below, p. 633. from Lib. V. cap. 31. of the same work. ED.]

[7 Dissimulanda, fratres, veritas non est, nec vulneris nostri materia et causa reticenda. De Laps. p. 90. ED.]

August. de CivitateDei, lib. xxi. cap. 25.

says: "Such as be in schism, that is to say, in sacraments or divine service separated from the unity of Christ's mystical body, and not in joining together of christian members, not in the band of peace, which is expressed in the sacrament of the altar, they may consecrate and receive this sacrament; but it is not profitable to them, but very hurtful, whereby they shall be judged more grievously of Almighty God[1]." St Paul says:

[Rom. ii.]

"Not only they that do evil be worthy death, but also they that consent to the doers." The Holy Ghost does cry by his prophet Esay, saying, "Get you hence, go forth, beware that you touch no unclean thing." The scripture says: "Thou shalt love the Lord God with all thy heart, with all thy strength, &c." God loves no half service. As

[2 Sam. x.]

for example, it is written in the book of Kings, that king David sent his servants to comfort Anon for the death of his father: albeit king Anon took them as espies, and caused the half of their beards to be shaven, and cut their clothes by their buttocks, and so sent them back again to king David. But when king David heard of this, he would not suffer them to come in his sight at Jerusalem, but commanded them to tarry at Jericho until their beards were grown out again. Even so such priests as has gone out of Christ's church, and entangled themselves with any part of this religion against the decrees of the church, are not worthy in ministration of sacraments to come in the presence of the faithful, that continue still in Christ's church, until they be reconciled, and have done penance for their lapse into schism.

IX. Whether is this to be called a wicked time, that such heresy and schism does reign?

Cyprian. de Laps.

No, rather it is a blessed time: for now "God tries his family," as St Cyprian says; "for the long rest and peace, which has been in Christ's church aforetime, caused the clergy to be almost on sleep; by reason whereof devout religion was not in a great number of priests, in works was small mercy, no discipline in manners[2]." St Paul says, "It is meet that there be heresy, that the good may be tried;" so that such as have grace to stand this troublous time, and be not spotted with schism, shall

[1 Qui ergo est in ejus corporis unitate, id est, in Christianorum compage membrorum, cujus corporis sacramentum fideles communicantes de altari sumere consueverunt, ipse vere dicendus est manducare corpus Christi, et bibere sanguinem Christi. Ac per hoc hæretici et schismatici, ab hujus unitate corporis separati, possunt idem percipere sacramentum, sed non sibi utile, imo vero etiam noxium, quo judicentur gravius, quam vel tardius liberentur. Non sunt quippe in eo vinculo pacis, quod illo exprimitur sacramento. Tom. VII. Pars i. p. 1033. Paris. 1838. ED.]

[2 Dominus probari familiam suam voluit; et quia traditam nobis divinitus disciplinam pax longa corruperat, jacentem fidem et pene dixerim dormientem censura cœlestis erexit. * * * Non in sacerdotibus religio devota, non in ministris fides integra, non in operibus misericordia, non in moribus disciplina. Cyprian. de Laps. p. 88. ED.]

be kindled more fervent in the love and fear of God; and such as be fallen in lapse, if they will seek to come back again to our mother holy church with penance, that is, with prayer, satisfaction and tears, she shuts her bosom from none that will so come; for God is near at hand to all that call on him in virtue, and will rejoice more in them, than in other. But " some are not to be gathered out of schism," says Cyprian, " so that such as be whole and stedfast be thereby wounded; nor he is not a profitable and wise pastor, that gathereth the sheep that be diseased, scabbed, or sick unto the whole flock, afore they be whole, lest they infect all the flock[3]. Nor the bishop must not have a respect to the greatness of the number: for better it is to have one good priest that feareth God, than a thousand that be evil." This says St Cyprian.

Answer to the Seventh, Eighth, and Ninth Questions.

What a fool is he that goes about to prove by so many bald reasons, (clouting such patched pieces together,) that which is already granted him! We confess that no man ought to say mass at all, much less they that say the communion should become mass-mongers: his authorities are fondly brought to prove his purpose, and may be turned against himself all; for there is no sort of men that use double dissembling so much as the pope's do. Other things that I proved afore I will not repeat again now; but I wish of God that, as David would not suffer his men that were shaven so to come in his sight, so all christian princes would banish the pope's shavelings: for so the reason holds in like of both. The time for trial of God's people we do not greatly mislike: only this grieves us, that so many withstand the manifest truth, which their conscience acknowledges to be true, and yet for fear of a change or flattery of the world they be cold, and will not or dare not openly profess it; and also that another sort of turn-tippets, for lack of discipline, occupy the place of pastors, serving rather to fill their belly, than for love, conscience, or duty; where good order would that either such should be displaced, or else do great and worthy open penance solemnly, afore they ministered. The alleging of these sundry authorities are untrue and foolish.

[[3] Quibusdam enim ita aut crimina sua obsistunt, aut fratres obstinate et firmiter renituntur, ut recipi omnino non possint, cum scandalo et periculo plurimorum. Neque enim sic putamina quædam colligenda sunt, ut quæ integra et sana sunt, vulnerentur: nec utilis aut consultus est pastor, qui ita morbidas et contractas oves gregi admiscet, ut gregem totum mali cohærentis afflictatione contaminet. Epist. LIX. (al. LV.) Cornelio Fratri. p. 267. ED.]

X. Whether it is lawful for the laity to receive the communion as is now used?

In receiving the communion as now used, you break your profession made in baptism, and fall into schism, separating yourselves from God and his church, refusing the bishops, your true pastors; so entering into the malignant church of Satan. St Paul does command us to obey the bishops, for they watch as to give an account for our souls. The bishops be in prison ready to suffer death, afore they will either minister or receive the communion, like true pastors: they put themselves walls and a sure defence for the people. The catholic church, which we professed at our baptism to believe and obey, teacheth us to receive Christ's body consecrate at mass with prayers, invocations and benediction, with the sign of the holy cross, and not bare bread and wine without consecration and benediction, as is used in this communion, being against the decrees and ordinance of Christ's catholic church. Almighty God does command us to separate ourselves from such as take in hand a ministration of sacraments against the ordinance of Christ's church, and that ye touch nothing pertaining to them, lest ye be lapped in their sin. The prophet Osee does say, that "all that receive that bread of mourning," over the which words of blasphemy be spoken at the table, "shall be defiled." Therefore St Cyprian says: "Forasmuch as we can exhort you by our letters, that you come not to the cursed communion with priests that be maculate; for they be not worthy death that do evil, but all that consent to the doing of evil. Nor let not the people persuade with themselves, that they can be free without spot of sin, communicating with a priest in sin[1]." No man can be well excused by ignorance: be he never so gross of wit, he may perceive it is not that which we have professed to believe, but against it; and if it were for a worldly gain, every one would learn a longer matter, and keep it in memory.

[Heb. xiii.]

Num. xvi.

Cyprian. Epist.

The Tenth Answer.

In receiving the communion now used the laity keep their profession made in baptism, where they promised, like good sheep, to believe the catholic church, which hears the voice of

[1 Et quantum possumus, adhortamur literis nostris, ne vos cum profanis et maculatis sacerdotibus communicatione sacrilega misceatis. * * Quoniam qui talia, inquit, agunt, morte sunt digni, manifestat et comprobat morte dignos esse, et ad pœnam venire non tantum illos qui mala faciunt, sed etiam eos qui talia agentibus consentiunt. * * * Nec sibi plebs blandiatur, quasi immunis esse a contagio delicti possit, cum sacerdote peccatore communicans, et ad injustum atque illicitum præpositi sui episcopatum consensum suum commodans; quando per Osee prophetam comminetur et dicat censura divina, Sacrificia eorum tanquam panis luctus: omnes qui manducant ea, contaminabuntur. Epist. LXVII. (al. LXVIII.) Cyprianus, &c. Felici Presbytero, &c. p. 291, 288. ED.]

their shepherd only, and flees from strangers: the popish church and prelates have devised a fashion of the communion, contrary to Christ's and his apostles' doings; and therefore they be worthily abhorred. Ye lie in saying, that the catholic church teaches to receive Christ's body consecrate at mass with the sign of the holy cross, or that we give nothing but bare bread and wine now. Prove where the church teaches so. I proved afore, how many diverse sorts of ministering there was of old time, and all good: therefore this your one only popish way is not decreed by the universal church, nor never was generally received throughout all the world. With what face can they say, we have no consecration, and give nothing but bare bread and wine? If they have any in their mass, if the evangelists have any consecration, or Paul, or if the apostles, we have it also. For if consecration stand in words, we have all the words that their mass, the gospel, St Paul, or the apostles had. Read Matthew, Mark, Luke, and the eleventh to the Corinthians, what is written of the Lord's supper; and see whether our communion want any one word that is in any of them. Then if we have all (as we have indeed), why is there no consecration with us? Gregory says, the apostles consecrated only with the Lord's prayer[2]; and that we use as well as they. John Duns says, the words of consecrating the bread be these, "This is my body:" and those words we have too. Further he says: "Neither Christ nor the church has defined which be the words of consecrating the cup;" and therefore he will not determine them[3]. What are we now worse than their own doctors, and why do ye lie in saying the church has defined it? Duns knew it not in his time, nor the church. Where is one

Lib. vii. epis. lxiii.

Lib. iv. sentent. distinc. 8.

[2 See before, p. 498. ED.]

[3 *De secundo* dico, quia verba consecrationis corporis sunt quatuor, scilicet illud pronomen *hoc*, et verbum *est*, et in apposito *corpus meum*. p. 36, G. Venet. 1598.

De verbis autem consecrationis sanguinis est dubium magis, quia quantum ad duo. Primum est, quia formam, qua utimur, nullus evangelistarum recitat; ideo non videtur ex evangelio certa. Græci etiam alia forma utuntur, dicentes, *Hic est sanguis, &c.* Et per consequens forma nostra non est præcisa. * * * * De isto secundo articulo dico breviter, quod non est nobis traditum omnino certitudinaliter, an ad formam consecrationis sanguinis pertineant aliqua verba post illud *sanguinis mei*, vel an aliquod illorum sequentium usque illic, *Hoc facite, &c.* Imo periculosum est hoc asserere, de quo sufficiens auctoritas non habetur. Ibid. p. 36, F. 37, A. ED.]

so mad, except priests, to say that consecration stands in crossing, or that *benedicite* is to make a cross? Prove it, if ye can; or else hold your tongue for shame. Deceive not the people. "All ye works of the Lord, praise ye the Lord," says the psalm. Is *blessing* there to make a cross, or in any other place ye can find? I have seen and heard many foolish unlearned papists, but a more ass than this I have not. He says, the people which communicate with a priest that is in sin, cannot be free from sin. If the priest be a drunkard, art thou a drunkard too in communicating with him? If he be a whore-hunter, art thou one too? I trust ye can judge, how false and foolish this is. St Paul says, "He that eats and drinks unworthily, eats and drinks his own damnation:" he says not, "thy damnation, or any other man's," but "his own." Chrysostom notes well, that he says, *sibi ipsi, non tibi:* "He eats it and drinks it damnation to himself, and not to thee[1]." God forbid the evilness of the priest should defile them that receive with him! for what priest is so clean that he has no sin in him? If the sin of the priest should defile the receiver, who would ever receive at any priest's hands, seeing all be sinners? It is a general rule and true in their own books: the unworthiness of the priest hurts not the goodness of the sacrament. God forbid that the evilness of man should hurt or defile God's holy ordinance, or that the wickedness of the priests should be imputed to them that receive the sacrament at their hand! "The father shall not bear the sin of the son, nor the son of the father, but the soul that sins shall die itself," as the prophet says. Much less shall the sin of the priest condemn the people, but every one shall answer for himself.

[Ezek. xviii.]

XI. Whether the people, compelled with fear for loss of worldly goods or temporal punishment, may receive the communion as bread and wine, not consenting to it in the heart?

Rom. x.
Matt. x.

St Paul says, it is requisite to our salvation with our mouths to confess the truth: also our Saviour Christ says, "he that denies him afore men, he will deny him afore his Father in heaven." And to kneel down to receive that cursed and polluted bread, ye commit idolatry: nor it is

[¹ Καὶ οὐχ ἕτερον ἑτέρῳ κελεύει δοκιμάσαι, ἀλλ' αὐτὸν ἑαυτόν· ὁ γὰρ ἐσθίων καὶ πίνων ἀναξίως κρίμα ἑαυτῷ ἐσθίει καὶ πίνει. In 1 Corinth. Homil. xxviii. Tom. x. p. 293. Paris. 1837. ED.]

not lawful to dissemble herein; as we have example Eleazarus, which [2 Macc. vi.] rather than he would dissemble to eat swine's flesh, forbidden by the law, he was content to suffer a very cruel death. Also it is read in *Tripartita Historia* of a good woman, one Olympias, that rather than she would receive the communion, was content to have her paps writhen off, or any other punishment, saying, "Lay upon me more punishment; for it is not lawful for me to do that which the good priests refuse to do[2]." Even so at this time the bishops and good priests refuse to meddle with the communion: therefore it is evident, it is not lawful for any of the laity to receive it for any cause. Also, when Constantius the emperor persecuted the church of God, such as would not receive the communion with the Arians, the bishop Macedonius put them in prison, and caused the communion to be brought unto them in prison, and opened their mouths with sticks and hot irons[3]. Yet for no punishment the good catholic people would in any wise receive with the Arians: much less ought we to receive the communion now used, for any punishment. For if we receive it against our conscience, we be traitors to God, and dissemblers with the queen, as Ustazadis did say to the king of Persis, lamenting that he did live; for he confessed (after the archbishop Simeon had rebuked him) that he was worthy to have a double death, for he was a traitor to God in forsaking his profession in religion, and a dissembler with the king; for to please the king, and to avoid punishment, he had done against his conscience; but utterly he did protest that he would never dissemble again, offering his whole body to make amends: and in conclusion had his head stricken off[4]. Would to God all, that by dissimulation be traitors and dissemblers with the queen against their conscience, would follow the example of Ustazadis in earnest repentance! Our Saviour commands us "not to fear them that can but only kill the [Matt. x.] body, but fear him that can kill the body, and after cast the soul into the fire of hell."

XII. How should the people do, that cannot have the sacrament ministered to them according to the ordinance of Christ's church?

[2 Olympias autem, injustum credens malitiæ satisfacere, dixit, "Adjice mihi calumniatores, et violentiam majorem impone: mihi vero fas non est communicare, et ea facere quæ piis non licet perpetrare." Quam cum nequisset flectere præfectus, ut communicaret Arsatio, tum dimissam, et paulo post tentam, multo nudavit auro, hoc modo credens ipsius frangi constantiam. Hist. Eccles. Tripart. Lib. x. cap. 21.—The original is in Sozomen, Lib. VIII. cap. 24. ED.]

[3 Plurimi vero insignes viri detenti, nolentesque ei communicare, puniti sunt: qui post tormenta violenter communionem ore suo suscipere et tenere compellebantur. Ligno namque ora hominum aperientes, eis sacramenta inserebant. Histor. Eccles. Tripart. Lib. v. cap. 31. p. 388. See Socrat. Eccl. Hist. Lib. II. cap. 38. ED.]

[4 The story is in the Historia Tripartita, Lib. III. cap ii. p. 325-6. of *Auctores Historiæ Ecclesiasticæ*. Basil. 1535. ED.]

In no wise they ought to receive the communion, but to commend their minds and good wills to God with devout prayer, firmly continuing in that faith that they were christened in; which sith the apostles' time has ever been taught by blessed fathers in Christ's catholic church. And so being in will to receive the blessed sacrament, if he were in place where it is ministered according to the ordinance of Christ's church, God will accept your will and good intent, as if you did receive it corporally: and by that will and intent ye be partakers of the sacraments and prayers of the universal church of Christ in all christian countries and nations, as well as if you were present bodily. But if you receive this communion, ye separate and divide yourselves from the sacraments and prayers of all the universal church of Christ, and so wander in the way of perdition.

The Answer to the Eleventh and Twelfth Questions.

To receive the communion dissemblingly, we grant to be damnable, as well as he: and therefore we exhort all men with an earnest faith and pure love, sorrowful repentance, and full purpose of a new life, to resort unto the Lord's table devoutly, without all hypocritical dissimulation. God will confound such blasphemers, as open their filthy mouths to rail against his holy sacraments, as this wicked Morian does here, calling it "cursed bread." Eleazarus did well in obeying God's law; and papists be God's enemies in their doings contrary to God's law. The Arians were heretics and enemies to the truth, denying Christ our Lord to be God equal with his Father, and saying he was but a weak simple man as we be. So the papists be, saying Christ's death is not a sufficient sacrifice for the whole world, except their sacrifice be joined to. They do both err in the chief article of our faith and salvation; and surely to communicate with such is to deny our faith and salvation: therefore Olympias and other well abhorred them. He that has not a right faith of Jesus Christ that instituted the sacrament, he cannot have the true use of the sacraments which Christ ordained. It is well that he wishes all dissembling papists, which have turned with every world, to repent as Ustazadis did; and God grant that they may! if they will not, if their reward were like his, they had no wrong. And thus, as all dissembling papists, receiving the communion against their consciences, are worthily condemned; so surely are all dissembling protestants, resorting to mass for fear of worldly losses. God grant us all uprightly to walk, not feigning a conscience to ourselves of man's device, but following the rule of scripture without halting, whatsoever the world say of us!

If this counsel that he gives for not receiving the communion now used were turned and applied against their mass, it were well and truly applied. We were never christened in any faith of the mass, but in the name of the Father, and the Son, and the Holy Ghost, who in the holy scriptures condemn all sacrificing massers: and surely to communicate with mass-mongers is to forsake God's institution, and follow the pope; to forsake Christ, the head of his church, and join himself to papists, and become a member of his synagogue, robbing Christ of his glory, and preferring man's dreams and doctrine, devised of late years by popes, as was proved afore, afore the infallible truth of the gospel, which Jesus Christ himself brought from heaven, preached it, and commanded us all diligently to follow it. To be partaker of prayers made in other countries is true that we may, and to be wished of God that it were diligently used: but unto he have proved that we be partakers of sacraments, wise men will not believe it. No man is christened one for another, nor receives the communion one for another. This doctrine comes from the pope, and fed his chaplains fat, when they taught, that it was sufficient to come and see the priests lift up their sacrament, offer it for the dead and quick, and eat all up when they have done.

XIII. Whether is not every one, as well the priests as laity, bound to obey the queen and her laws?

Both priests and the laity be bound to obey the queen and her laws, as far as God's law will permit: but no man ought to obey the queen and her laws against God and his laws. For lands, goods, and body, every one is bound to obey the queen and her laws, and no man ought to disobey or resist her or her laws: for God in the scripture commands. But for matters of faith and religion, pertaining to our soul health, she hath nothing ado to meddle: for Christ himself hath dearly bought our souls with his precious blood-shedding, and committed them to the rule and government of the bishops, which watch as to give an account for our souls. Therefore the scripture commands us to obey the bishops in matters of faith and religion pertaining to our souls' health, and the queen in temporal causes concerning lands, and goods, and body.

The Thirteenth Answer.

For obeying the queen's majesty and her laws, or for disobeying, we do not greatly differ from him: but where he says, she has nothing ado with matters of faith and religion, we utterly deny it. For that is as much to say, as that she were not a christian prince, no, nor a prince at all; for princes are charged by God to maintain true religion, and suppress superstition and idolatry. This is the mark that they shoot at, to be exempt from all correction of princes, that they might do what they lust, bring in superstition instead of religion, and nourish the people in blood devotion, rule all other, and be ruled of none, no, not of God himself. So much obedience the Turk's subjects owe him, and yet deny him not authority in their religion. But this matter was more fully handled in the fifth answer. King Richard the second proves well in his epistle to pope Boniface the ninth[1], that temporal rulers have often from the beginning bridled and ruled the spirituality, even the popes. Salomon, says he, put down the priest Abiathar, and set up Zadoc. Otho the emperor deposed pope John the twelfth. Henry the emperor put down Gratianus. Otho deposed pope Benet the first. The controversy betwixt Symmachus and Laurence, who should be pope, was ended afore Theodosius, king of Italy. Henry the emperor deposed two, striving who should be pope, and set up a third, called Clement the second. Frederick the emperor corrected four popes. By these and many such like he proves, that princes have corrected and brought in order so many popes: therefore they have lawful power so to do.

And shall not our queen have power to see whether the clergy here within her realm do their duty, in teaching true doctrine, pure ministering of the sacraments, and an upright godly life? Indeed, this was the beginning of the controversy betwixt Thomas Becket and king Henry the second; and these, like good scholars of the same school, follow the same way. Certain priests were complained on for their lewd living, whom the king would have punished: but Becket withstood him, saying it belonged not to the king to handle such holy anointed spiritual men. Austin in his book *contr. Liter. Petiliani*, 11.

[[1] The whole letter is in Foxe, *Acts and Monuments*, Vol. i. p. 509. ed. 1583. Ed.]

in the sixth and other sundry chapters, proves that it belongs to kings to have care and charge for religion, both in maintaining the good and pulling down the evil. He alleges this of the second psalm, " Serve the Lord in fear, &c." " How should kings," says he, " serve the Lord in fear, but in forbidding and punishing those things that are done against the Lord's commandment? He serves in one sort, inasmuch as he is a man; and in another, insomuch as he is a king: he serves him as a man in living truly, but as a king in making laws, which command just things and forbid the contrary. So served king Ezechias in descrying the groves and temples of idols: so served Josias, so the king of Nineve in compelling the whole city to pacify the Lord. Thus served Nabuchodonozor, in forbidding by a fearful law that they should not blaspheme God. Kings serve the Lord in this point, when they do those things to serve him, which none can do but kings, &c.[2]" Thus far Austin. Constantine also, the good emperor, commands the Donatists to come to Rome to hear the bishops' judgment; but afterward, when he had heard the matter debated, he judged the cause himself, and made a law against them, as Austin writes, Epist. LXVIII.[3]

Thus princes then, calling their clergy together, because few of them have sufficient learning of themselves, and hearing the matters of religion debated, and the truth tried, may and

[[2] Mirantesque fortasse quærunt, propter id quod in consequentibus audiunt, *Servite Domino in timore,* in quo illi servire possint in quantum reges sunt. Omnes enim homines servire Deo debent: aliter communi conditione, qua homines sunt; aliter diversis donis, quod ille aliud agit in rebus humanis, ille aliud. Non enim auferenda idola de terra, quod tanto ante futurum prædictum est, posset quisquam jubere privatus. Habent ergo reges, excepta generis humani societate, eo ipso quo reges sunt, unde sic Domino serviant, quomodo non possunt qui reges non sunt. Contra Lit. Petiliani, Lib. II. cap. 210. Tom. ix. p. 449. Paris. 1837.— Compare also the following: Quomodo ergo reges Domino serviunt in timore, nisi ea, quæ contra jussa Domini fiunt, religiosa severitate prohibendo atque plectendo? Aliter enim servit, quia homo est; aliter quia etiam rex est. Epist. CLXXXV. Tom. II. p. 977. ED.]

[[3] Post hanc relationem ad se missam jussit Imperator venire partes ad episcopale judicium in urbe Roma faciendum. * * * Postea et ipse coactus episcopalem causam inter partes cognitam terminavit, et primus contra vestram partem legem constituit. Epist. LXXXVIII. (al. LXVIII.) Tom. II. p. 321. ED.]

<small>Isai. xlix.</small> ought by their law and royal power defend that truth, and punish the disobedient, whosoever they be. The prophet says, that God made kings and queens to be nurses to his church. The nurse's duty is to feed, guide, and cherish the child; yea, to correct, instruct, and reform him when he does a fault. She must not be a dry nurse, but with the two paps of the new testament and old feed her children: she must teach him to go; when he is fallen, take him up again; and give him such wholesome meat, that she may and dare taste and try it herself. God grant princes thus to be nurses, and not stepmothers, that God's children may serve their Lord God, Master and Father, quietly under their wings!

THE CONCLUSION.

OUR Saviour Christ, when they called him Samaritan, a friend of publicans and sinners, a drunkard, &c., held his tongue, and made no answer: but when they said he had a devil, he said, "I have no devil." It is written also *in vitis patrum* of Agathon, whom certain would try whether he could patiently bear slanders, and called him proud, advoterer [adulterer], a thief and heretic: all other he let pass, and said, "I am a sinner, but I am not an heretic." They asked him, why he answered to that rather than to the other: he said, he learned of Christ his master to suffer lies, but not his doctrine to be touched; for heresy separates a man from God[1]. So among all slanderous tongues, that go about to deface God's truth by railing on the ministers of it, many are borne of many with grief of mind: but to be charged with false doctrine, no honest mind

---

[[1] Illa prima mihi ascribo, utilitas enim animæ meæ est: quod autem dixistis hæreticum me esse, ideo non acquievi, quia separatio est a Deo, et non opto separari a Deo. Vitæ Patrum, Lib. v. Libell. x. cap. 10. p. 597. Antverp. 1615. ED.]

can bear, nor good man should suffer. For as he teaches the good and wholesome doctrine, so he should confound the contrary to his power. And this was among other a great cause, why I (though not hurt by this his foolish railing) took in hand to answer this blind papist; and because those learned fathers, whom he would seem to touch, thought it unworthy any answer. When I see this copy cast abroad by a malicious member of antichrist, to withdraw God's people from his truth, my spirit was stirred to the answering of the same: but many, when they see how foolish it was, laughed at it, and thought it to be passed away with silence, for that foolishness of itself would confound itself to them that had wit or learning. Yet that the simple ones, for whose cause chiefly this labour is taken, should not be deceived and overcome with fond fantasies of idle brains, and lest God's enemies should crack, that none could or durst answer it; I thought good, because other that can do better would not, thus shortly to answer the chief points of popery, touched in this his unlearned apology.

This is the polity of papists, to set out a broker to utter their ware, and catch the unlearned, but the subtler sort hold their tongue, stand aloof to see how this forerunner will take place, and are thought by their silence to be able to say much more; when as they fear indeed, lest in being answered they should take the foil, to the clean overthrowing of their cause. This proud Golias has cracked and provoked all God's people, as though none durst meddle with him: but I trust poor David has wiped his nose, and given him a fall with his poor sling and few stones. But I fear I lose my labour: for as the prophet says, "Can the black man of Ind change his colour?" Jer. xiii. No more can this Morian learn to say well. If the miserable state of the people had not moved me, I would have holden my tongue, and laugh at it, as wise men do; but that with the poor simple ones, whom they deceive in corners with such lies as these, such common bald reasons as he has brought should not prevail, I thought good for pity sake to say thus much, to stay them whose eyes God shall open to see.

My reasons and authorities of purpose are commonly taken out of their own doctors and writers, and such books as are not counted protestants, nor made by any of this new learning.

For the nonest[1], I forbare to allege the learneder sort, lest the unlearned should say, they could no skill on such books, nor knew not whether they were truly brought in: and seeing their own doctors and schoolmasters have given us this vantage against them, I fear not to try with them in writers of greater authority and ancienty.

Thus much I have spoken for my part: let the rest, whom God has given greater knowledge and utterance unto, help thus to stop the mouths of God's enemies; and I trust, by the power of his Holy Spirit, antichrist with his members shall daily decay, and God's glorious truth shall shine to the comfort of all his elect; though their eyes be not yet fully opened to see,
nor their hearts lightened to understand it. God the Father
grant for his Son's sake, Jesus Christ crucified, that
we all may be partakers of his Spirit of truth, and
his wilful obstinate enemies confounded,
his poor lambs delivered from the
wolves, and strengthened against
the assaults of Satan; that
at the length we may
be glorified with
him for ever
and ever.
Amen.
(*)

Behold, says the Lord of Hosts to thee, I will lay thy skirts on thy face, and open thy filthiness to the people, and thy shame to kingdoms; and I will cast thy abominations upon thee, and I will revile thee, and make thee like dung: and it shall come to pass, that every one that sees thee shall fall from thee. Nah. iii.

Have mercy on us, O Lord, have mercy on us, for we are utterly despised. Our soul is filled with the mocking of the rich, and despite of the proud. Psalm cxxiii.

[[1] The nonest: the nonce. For the purpose. ED.]

COMMON PLACES ENTREATED.

The authority of bishops 488
St James's mass and others' 495
England received not the faith from Rome 510
None is universal bishop over all 518
Extreme unction is no sacrament 524
Our church service 533
Communion. Burials. Communion-table 541
Altars 547
Confession 553
Fasting 556
Lent 560
Marriage of priests 564
Ordering of ministers 580
Succession 597
The people learn the scriptures 608
The prince's authority in religion 625

[¹ Though the Sermon of bishop Pilkington, which gave rise to the preceding controversy, is not extant, and probably never was printed, (see note, p. 481.) yet we have a very minute abstract of its contents, published by Seres himself only on the *Tuesday following* the sermon. This abstract is preserved in a Tract printed and published on that day by Seres, and reprinted in the Archæologia, Vol. xi. p. 74, London, 1794, and from thence in the new edition of Dugdale's History of St Paul's. The title-page of this Tract is:

"The true Report
of the burnyng of the Steple
and Churche of Poules,
in London.
Jeremy, xviii.
I will speake suddenlye agaynst a nation, or agaynste a kyngdome, to plucke
it up; and to roote it out, and destroye
it. But yf that nation, agaynste
whom I have pronounced, turne
from their wickedness, I wyll repent of the plage that I thought
to brynge uppon
them.
Imprynted at London, at the
West ende of Paules Church
at the Sygne of the Hedghogge,
by Wylliam
Seres.
Cum privilegio ad imprimendum
solum.
Anno 1561. The x of June."

The Rev. S. Denne, in communicating this tract to the Archæologia, says: "The passage from Jeremiah printed in the title-page was, it may be presumed, the text to bishop Pilkington's sermon, the substance of which so speedily issued from the press of Master Seres."

The former part of the tract gives an interesting narrative of the fire, and then concludes with the following abstract of the bishop's Sermon:

On Sunday folowing, beynge the viii day of June, the reverend in God, the Bishop of Duresme, at Paules Crosse, made a learned and fruit-ful sermon, exhorting the auditory to a general repentance, and namely to humble obediĕce of the lawes and superior powers, which vertue is much decayed in these our daies. Seeming to have intellygĕce from the Queenes highnes, that her Majestie intendeth that more severitie of lawes shall be executed against persons disobedyent, as well in causes of religion as civil, to the great rejoysing of his auditours. He exhorted also hys audiēce to take this as a general warninge to the whole realme, and namelye to the citie of London, of some greater plage to folow, if amendemente of lyfe in all states did not ensue: He muche reproved those persons whiche would assigne the cause of this wrathe of God to any particular state of mē, or that were diligent to loke into other men's lyves, and could see no faultes in themselfes; but wished that every man wold descend into himselfe, and say with David, *Ego sum qui peccavi:* I am he that hath sinned; and so furth, to that effect very godlye. He also not onely reproved the prophanatyon of the said churche of Paules, of long time heretofore abused by walking, jangling, brawling, fighting, bargaining, &c., namely in sermons and service time; but also aūswered by the way to the objections of such evil-tunged persōs, which do impute this token of God's deserved ire, to alteratiō or rather reformatiō of religiō, declaring out of aūcient records and histories, ye like, yea and greater matters, had befallen in the time of superstitiō and ignorance. For in the first year of King Stephē, not only the said churche of Paules was brent, but also a great part of the city, that is to say frō Londō Bridge unto St Clemēts without Tēple bar, was by fier cōsumed. And in ye daies of King Hēry VI. ye Steple of Paules was also fired by lightning, although it was then staide by diligēce of ye citizens, ye fier being thē by likelyhode not so fierce. Many other suche like cōmon calamities he rehersed, which had happened in other coūtreis, both nigh to this realm, and far of, where the church of Rome hath most authority, and therefore concluded the surest way to be, y^t every man should judge, examin, and amēd himselfe, and embrace, beleve, and truely folow ye word of God, and earnestly to pray to God to turn away frō us his deserved wrath and indignation, whereof this his terrible work is a most certein warning, if we repent not unfeinedly. The whiche God grāt may come to passe in all estates and degrees, to ye glory of his name, and to our endlesse comforte, in Christ our Saviour, Amen.

God Save the Queene.

So ends the Tract published by W. Seres, probably from his own notes of the Sermon, only two days after it was preached. And this is perhaps all the *printing* of the sermon which Strype refers to, Life of Parker, Book II. ch. 5. where he states that "Pilkinton, bishop of Durham, a great preacher, made a sermon at Paul's Cross on this occasion, which was afterwards printed and entitled, &c."

After all that has been written on the subject of this fire, it is stated by Baker, (MS. History of St John's College, Cambridge, of which the original is in the British Museum,) that it arose from an accident through the carelessness of a plumber: he remarks, "Had he (Pilkington) outlived the plumber that burnt that church by his carelessness, he would have known the true cause by the poor man's own confession." But whatever may be the case as to the fact here mentioned, the conclusion intended to be drawn does not follow: the pious bishop would still have dealt with circumstance as a judgment and warning. See his remarks in p. 608—9. ED.]

MISCELLANEOUS PIECES.

SERMON

AT THE RESTITUTION OF

MARTIN BUCER AND PAULUS PHAGIUS.

(From Foxe's *Acts and Monuments*, p. 1966—8, edit. 1583.)

[The Commissioners appointed by the queen to make a reformation of religion in the University of Cambridge and other parts of the realm, having addressed their letters to the Vice-Chancellor of the University touching the restitution of Bucer and Phagius to the degrees and titles of honour which had been taken from them after their death, and the repealing of all acts done against them and their doctrine; these demands were openly consented unto by all the graduates of the University: and a congregation being called in St Mary's Church on the 30th of July, 1560, an oration was made on the occasion by Master Acworth, the common orator of the University.]

WHEN Acworth had made an end of his oration, Master James Pilkington, the queen's reader of the divinity lecture, going up into the pulpit, made a sermon upon the 112th psalm, the beginning whereof is: "Blessed is the man that feareth the Lord."

Where, intending to prove that the remembrance of the just man shall not perish, and that Bucer is blessed, and that the ungodly shall fret at the sight thereof, but yet that all their attempts shall be to no purpose, to the intent this saying may be verified, "I will curse your blessings, and bless your cursings;" he took his beginning of his own person, that albeit he were both ready and willing to take that matter in hand, partly for the worthiness of the matter itself, and in especial for certain singular virtues of those persons for whom that congregation was called, yet notwithstanding, he said, he was nothing meet to take that charge upon him. For it were more reason, that he which before had done Bucer wrong, should now make him amends for the displeasure. As for his own part, he was so far from working any evil against Bucer, either in word or deed, that for their singular knowledge almost in all kind of learning he embraced both him and Phagius with all his

The sermon of Doctor James Pilkington.

[Mal. ii. Psal. cix.]

heart: but yet he somewhat more favoured Bucer, as with whom he had more familiarity and acquaintance. In consideration whereof, although that it was scarce convenient that he at that time should speak, yet notwithstanding he was contented, for friendship and courtesy sake, not to fail them in this their business.

Having made this preface, he entered into the pith of the matter; wherein he blamed greatly the barbarous cruelty of the court of Rome, so fiercely extended against the dead. He said, it was a more heinous matter than was to be borne with, to have shewed such extreme cruelness to them that were alive; but for any man to misbehave himself in such wise toward the dead, was such a thing as had not lightly been heard of: saving that he affirmed this custom of excommunicating and cursing of dead folk to have come first from Rome. For Evagrius reporteth in his writings, that Eutychius was of the same opinion, induced by the example of Josias, who slew the priests of Baal, and burnt up the bones of them that were dead, even upon the altars. Whereas, before the time of Eutychius this kind of punishment was well near unknown, neither afterward usurped of any man, that ever he heard of, until a nine hundred years after Christ. In the latter times, (the which how much the further they were from that golden age of the apostles, so much the more they were corrupted,) this kind of cruelness began to creep further. For it is manifestly known, that Stephen the sixth, pope of Rome, digged up Formosus, his last predecessor in that see; and spoiling him of his pope's apparel, buried him again in layman's apparel, (as they call it,) having first cut off and thrown into Tiber his two fingers, with which, according to their accustomed manner, he was wont to bless and consecrate. The which his unspeakable tyranny used against Formosus, within six years after, Sergius the third increased also against the same Formosus. For taking up his dead body, and setting it in a pope's chair, he caused his head to be smitten off, and his other three fingers to be cut from his hand, and his body to be cast into the river of Tiber, abrogating and disannulling all his decrees; which thing was never done by any man before that day. The cause why so great cruelty was exercised (by the report of Nauclerus) was this: because that Formosus had been an adversary to Stephen and Sergius, when they sued to be made bishops.

This kind of cruelty, unheard of before, the popes awhile exercised one against another. But now, or ever they had sufficiently felt the smart thereof themselves, they had turned the same upon our necks. Wherefore it was to be wished that, seeing it began among them, it might have remained still with the authors thereof, and not have been spread over thence unto us. But such was the nature of all evil, that it quickly passeth into example, for others to do the like. For about the year of our Lord 1400 [1428], John Wickliffe was in like manner digged up, and burnt into ashes, and thrown into a brook that runneth by the town where he was buried. Of the which self-same sauce tasted also William Tracy of Gloucester, a man of a worshipful house, because he had written in his last will that he should be saved only by faith in Jesus Christ, and that there needed not the help of any man thereto, whether he were in heaven or in earth; and therefore bequeathed no legacy to that purpose, as all other men were accustomed to do. This deed was done sithens we may remember, about the twenty-second year of the reign of king Henry the eighth, in the year of our Lord 1530.

Now, seeing they extended such cruelty to the dead, he said, it was an easy matter to conjecture what they would do to the living. Whereof we had sufficient trial by the examples of our own men, these few years past. And if we would take the pains to peruse things done somewhat longer ago, we might find notable matters out of our own chronicles. Howbeit it was sufficient, for the manifest demonstration of that matter, to declare the beastly butchery of the French king, executed upon the Waldenses at Cabrier and the places near thereabout, by his captain Miner, about the year of our Lord 1545; than the which there was never thing read of more cruelty done, no, not even of the barbarous pagans. And yet for all that, when divers had shewed their uttermost cruelty both against these and many others, they were so far from their purpose in extinguishing the light of the gospel, which they endeavoured to suppress, that it increased daily more and more. The which thing Charles the fifth, (than whom all christendom had not a more prudent prince, nor the church of Christ almost a sorer enemy,) easily perceived; and therefore, when he had in his hand Luther dead, and Melancthon and Pomeran with certain other preachers of the gospel alive, he not only determined not any thing extremely against them, nor violated their graves, but also entreating them gently sent them away, not so much as once forbidding them to publish openly the doctrine that they professed. For it is the nature of Christ's church, that the more that tyrants spurn against it, the more it increaseth and flourisheth.

A notable proof assuredly of the providence and pleasure of God in sowing the gospel, was that coming of the Bohemians unto us, to the intent to hear Wickliffe, of whom we spake before, who at that time read openly at Oxford; and also the going of our men to the said Bohemians, when persecution was raised against us. But much more notable was it, that we had seen come to pass in these our days; that the Spaniards, sent for into this realm of purpose to suppress the gospel, as soon as they were returned home, replenished many parts of their country with the same truth of religion, to the which before they were utter enemies. By the which examples it might evidently be perceived, that the princes of this world labour in vain to overthrow it, considering how the mercy of God hath sown it abroad, not only in those countries that we spake of, but also in France, Pole, Scotland, and almost all the rest of Europe. For it is said, that some parts of Italy, (although it be under the pope's nose,) yet do they of late incline to the knowledge of the heavenly truth. Wherefore sufficient argument and proof might be taken by the success and increasement thereof, to make us believe that this doctrine is sent us from heaven, unless we will wilfully be blinded. And if there were any that desired to be persuaded more at large in the matter, he might advisedly consider the voyage that the emperor and the pope with both their powers together made jointly against the Bohemians; in the which the emperor took such an unworthy repulse of so small a handful of his enemies, that he never almost in all his life took the like dishonour in any place. Hereof also might be an especial example that death of Henry, king of France, who the same day that he had purposed to persecute the church of Christ, and to have burned certain of his guard, whom he had in prison for religion, at whose execution he had promised to have been himself in proper person, in the midst of his triumph, at a tourney, was wounded so sore in the head with a spear by one of his own subjects, that ere it was long after he died. In the which behalf the dreadful judgments of God were no less approved in our own countrymen. For one that was a notable slaughterman of Christ's saints, rotted alive; and ere ever he died, such a rank savour steamed from all his body, that none of his friends were able to come at him, but that they were ready to vomit. Another, being in utter despair well nigh of all health, howled out miserably. The third ran out of his wits. And divers other, that were enemies to the church, perished miserably in the end. All the which things were most certain tokens of the favour and defence of the divine majesty towards his church, and of his wrath and vengeance towards the tyrants. _{Stephen Gardiner of Winchester.}

And forasmuch as he had made mention of the Bohemians, he said, it was a most apt example that was reported of their captain Zisca: who, when he should die, willed his body to be slain, and of his skin to make a parchment to cover the head of a drum: for it should come to pass, that when his enemies heard the sound of it, they should not be able to stand against them. The like counsel, he said, he himself now gave them as concerning Bucer; that like as the Bohemians did with the skin of Zisca, the same should they do with the arguments and doctrine of Bucer: for as soon as the papists should hear the noise of him, their gewgaws would forthwith decay. For saving that they used violence to such as withstood them, their doctrine contained nothing that might seem to any man, having but mean understanding in holy scripture, to be grounded upon any reason. As for those things that were done by them against such as could not play the madmen as well as they, some of them savoured of open force, and some of ridiculous foolishness. For what was this first of all? was it not frivolous, that by the space of three years together mass should be sung in those places where Bucer and Phagius rested in the Lord, without any offence at all; and as soon as they took it to be an offence, straightway to be an offence if any were heard there? or that it should not be as good then as it was before?—as if that then upon the sudden it had been a heinous matter to celebrate it in that place, and that the fault that was past should be counted the grievouser, because it was done of longer time before.

Moreover, this was a matter of none effect, that Bucer and Phagius only should be digged up, as who should say, that he alone had embraced the religion which they call heresy. It was well known, how one of the burgesses of the town had been minded toward the popish religion: who, when he should die, willed neither ringing of bells, diriges, nor any other such kind of trifles to be done for him in his anniversary, as they term it; but rather, that they should go with instruments of music before the mayor and council of the city, to celebrate his memorial, and also that yearly a sermon should be made to the people, bequeathing a piece of money to the preacher for his labour. Neither might he omit in that place to speak of Ward, the painter; who, albeit he were a man of no reputation, yet was he not to be despised for the religion sake which he diligently followed. Neither were divers other more to be passed over with silence, who were known of a certainty to have continued in the same sect, and to rest in other churchyards in Cambridge, and rather through the whole realm, and yet defiled not their masses at all. All the which persons, (forasmuch as they were all of one opinion,) ought all to have been taken up, or else all to have been let lie with the same religion: unless a man would grant, that it lieth in their power to make what they list lawful and unlawful at their own pleasure.

In the condemnation of Bucer and Phagius, to say the truth, they used too much cruelty and too much violence. For howsoever it went with the doctrine of Bucer, certainly they could find nothing whereof to accuse Phagius, inasmuch as he wrote nothing that came abroad, saving a few things that he had translated out of the Hebrew and Chaldee tongues into Latin: after his coming into the realm he never read, he never disputed, he never preached, he never taught; for he deceased so soon after, that he could in that time give no occasion for his adversaries to take hold on, whereby to accuse him, whom they never heard speak. In that they hated Bucer so deadly for the allowable marriage of the clergy, it was their own malice conceived against him, and a very slander raised by themselves. For he had for his defence in that matter, over and besides other helps, the testimony of the pope Pius the second, who in a certain place saith, that upon weighty considerations priests' wives were taken from them, but for more weighty causes were

Faude, sometime mayor of the town.

to be restored again; and also the statute of the emperor, (they call it the *Interim*,) by the which it is enacted, that such of the clergy as were married should not be divorced from their wives.

Thus turning his style from this matter to the university, he reproved in few words their unfaithfulness towards these men. For if the Lord suffered not the bones of the king of Edom, being a wicked man, to be taken up and burnt without revengement (as saith Amos), let us assure ourselves, he will not suffer so notable a wrong done to his godly preachers, unrevenged. [Amos ii. 1.] Afterward, when he came to the condemnation (which we told you in the former action was pronounced by Perne, the vice-chancellor, in the name of them all), being somewhat more moved at the matter, he admonished them, how much it stood them in hand to use great circumspectness, what they decreed upon any man by their voices, in admitting or rejecting any man to the promotions and degrees of the university. For that which should take his authority from them, should be a great prejudice to all the other multitude, which (for the opinion that it had of their doctrine, judgment, allowance, and knowledge) did think nothing but well of them. For it would come to pass, that if they would bestow their promotions upon none but meet persons, and let the unmeet go as they come, both the common-wealth should receive much commodity and profit by them, and besides that they should highly please God. But if they persisted to be negligent in doing thereof, they should grievously endamage the common weal, and worthily work their own shame and reproach. Over and besides that, they should greatly offend the majesty of God, whose commandment, not to bear false witness, they should in so doing break and violate.

In the mean while that he was speaking these and many other things before his audience, many of the university, to set out and defend Bucer withal, beset the walls of the church and church-porch on both sides with verses, some in Latin, some in Greek, and some in English, in the which they made a manifest declaration how they were minded both toward Bucer and Phagius. Finally, when his sermon was ended, they made common supplication and prayers. After thanks rendered to God for many other things, but in especially for restoring of the true and sincere religion, every man departed his way.

[PILKINGTON.]

LETTER

TO

THE EARL OF LEICESTER,

IN BEHALF OF THE

REFUSERS OF THE HABITS.[1]

(From Strype's Life of Archbishop Parker, Appendix xxv. Vol. III. p. 69. Oxford, 1821.)

RIGHT honourable, my duty considered, and under correction:

I understand by common report, and I fear too true, that there is great offence taken with some of the ministery for not

[1 In Tanner's account of Bishop Pilkington there is mention made of an "Epistola Consolatoria (contra usum vestium pontif. in sacris)" as existing in the MSS. of the Bodleian. This appears to be a mistake. There are two MS. letters of Pilkington's in that collection, viz. this to "the Right Hon. Lord Rob. Dudley, Earl of Leicester," and the Latin letter to his brother-in-law, Andrew Kingsmill, inserted in the Appendix to this volume. The "comfortable letter" is found in a *printed* volume in the same library, and is only another form of the present letter. The author appears to have made a double use of this letter, addressing it as a letter of comfort to the refusers of the habits, and as a letter of intercession to the earl of Leicester on their behalf: or more probably, the former use was not made of it by himself, but by some one else after his death. There is no reason to think that in either form he wrote it in Latin. There are some unimportant variations between the letter as printed by Strype from a manuscript in his possession, and that in the volume above mentioned; chiefly to change the form of the letter from that of an address to an influential individual to that of a consolatory epistle to "the refusers of the habits": but these, as already noticed, do not appear to have been made by Bishop Pilkington himself, but at a later date.—
The beginning and ending are here subjoined, as they stand in the printed book; which is that "very rare" volume entitled, *A parte of a Register*, printed 1593, at Edinburgh, an account of which, and the circumstances attending its suppression, is given by Herbert in his *Typographical Antiquities*, Vol. III. p. 1414. See also Archbishop Bancroft's *Dangerous Positions*, as there quoted.

"Grace and peace, with all manner spiritual feeling and living worthy of the kindness of Christ, be with all that thirst after the will of God.—
To my faithful and dear brethren in Christ Jesu: As in common dangers

using such apparel as the rest do. Therefore, as in great common dangers of fire or such like, they that be far off come to succour those that have need; so I, being out of that jeopardy and far off, cannot but of duty wish well to those that be touched in this case. In this liberty of God's truth, which is taught plainly without offence in the greatest mysteries of our religion and salvation, I marvel much that this small controversy for apparel should be so heavily taken. But this is the malice of Satan, that where he cannot overthrow the greatest matters, he will raise great troubles in trifles. Peter and Paul agreed in the chiefest articles of our salvation; and yet they differed so about meats, that Paul withstood and rebuked him openly. Paul and Barnabas fell at such bitter contention, whether Mark should go with them or no, so that they parted companies, and went either sundry ways. God defend us from the like! Paul circumcided Timothy, when there was hope to win the Jews; but when they would have it of necessity, he would not circumcide Titus. Therefore compelling would not be used in things of liberty. In this rude superstitious people, on the borders, priests go with sword, dagger, and such coarse apparel as they can get, not being curious or scrupulous what colour or fashion it be, and none is offended at them. But such grief to be taken at a cap among them that are civil and full of knowledge, is lamentable. Consider, I beseech your honour, how that all countries, which have reformed religion, have cast away the popish apparel with the pope; and yet we, that would be taken for the best, contend to keep it as a holy relic. Mark also, how many ministers there be here in all countries, that be so zealous, not only to forsake that wicked doctrine of popery, but ready to leave the ministry and their livings, rather than to be like the popish teachers of such superstitions, either in apparel or behaviour. This realm has such scarcity of teachers, that if so many worthy men should be cast out of the ministry for such small matters, many places should be destitute of preachers.

of fire or such like, well beloved, they that be far off come to succour those that have need; so I, being out of jeopardy, &c."

"God grant that we may give all honour to whom all honour is due, both inwardly and outwardly, to serve him unfeignedly all the days of our life. Farewell, dear brethren in the Lord Jesus, who ever keep us in his faith, fear, and love for ever. Amen." ED.]

And it would give an incurable offence to all the favourers of God's truth in other countries. Shall we make so precious that, that other reformed places esteem as vile? God forbid. St Paul bids women use such apparel as becomes them that profess true godliness. Which rule is much more to be observed of men, and specially preachers. But if we forsake popery as wicked, how shall we say their apparel becomes saints and professors of true holiness? St Paul bids us refrain from all outward shew of evil: but surely, in keeping this popish apparel, we forbear not an outward shew of much evil, if popery be judged evil. As we would have a divers shew of apparel to be known from the common people, so it is necessary in apparel to have a shew, how a protestant is to be known from a papist.

It has pleased God to call your lordship to honour worthily, (God be praised for it!) and the same God will preserve and increase it, if ye diligently endeavour yourself to set forth his glory again. For so he has promised, " Honorantes me glorificabo; qui vero contemnunt me, contemnentur." When Hester made courtesy to speak for God's people, being in danger, Mardocheus said to her: " Si nunc tacueris, alia ratione liberabuntur, et tu et domus patris tui peribitis." Wherein it easily appears by these threatenings, how great a fault it is, not to help God's people in their need, or not to further religion when they may. But of your good lordship's inclination to further God's cause no man doubts; and seeing many good men have felt and rejoiced of it, I am bolder to crave it. When Terentius,[1] a good christian captain, returned with great triumph and victory, the emperor Valens bad him ask what he would, and he should have it, for his good service: he, having God afore his eyes, desired neither riches nor honour, but that those which had aventured their lives for true religion, might have a church allowed them to serve their God purely in, and several from the Arians. The emperor, being angry with his request, pulls his supplication in pieces, and bade him ask some other things. But he gathered up the pieces of his paper, and said, " I have received my reward, I will ask nothing else." God increase about princes the small number of such zealous suitors and promoters of religion; and then, no doubt, God's glory shall flourish, when we seek his due honour, and not our own profit.

[1 See p. 324. Ed.]

Your honourable gentleness toward all has encouraged me thus boldly to speak for this case; and I doubt not, but your accustomed goodness has sundry times spoken in it; and though ye speed not at the first, yet importunity procures many things in time. Austin in mine opinion gives a good rule, how a man should behave himself in contentions of religion, to avoid both schisms and breaking the quietness and peace of christian men; which God grant might take place in this case! "Quisquis quod potest arguendo corrigit, vel quod corrigere non potest, salvo pacis vinculo excludit, vel quod salva pace excludere non potest tolerat, æquitate improbat: hic est pacificus, et a maledicto alienus." Contra Epist. Par.[2]

But how this christian peace should be kept in this church, when so many, for so small things, shall be thrust from their ministry and livings, it passes my simple wit to conceive. St Paul's rule in such things is, "Omnia mihi licent, sed non omnia expediunt: omnia mihi licent, sed omnia non ædificant." Therefore in this case we must not so subtilly dispute, what christian liberty would suffer us to do, but what is meetest and most edifying for christian charity and promoting pure religion. But surely, how popish apparel should edify, or set forward the gospel of Christ Jesus, cannot be seen of the multitude. Nay, it is so much felt, how much it rejoices the adversary, when they see what we borrow of them, and contend for therein, as things necessary. The bishops' wearing of their white rochets began first of Sisinius, an heretic bishop of the Novatians: and these other have the like foundation. But they have so long continued and pleased popery, which is beggarly patched up of all sorts of ceremonies, that they could never be rooted out since, even from many professors of the truth.

Thus, setting shame aside in God's cause, and forgetting my duty in troubling your honour so much, I most humbly beseech your honour to defend this cause, though it be with some displeasure. God will reward it.

But while I defend others, it may be said, "Medice, cura teipsum:" and let your doings and sayings agree in yourself. Surely, my good lord, though I in this case follow St Austin's rule afore rehearsed, yet should not any man's doings be a

[[2] Con. Epist. Parmen. Lib. II. cap. 3. Tom. ix. p. 82, Paris. 1837. Ed.]

prejudice to others that would come to a better perfection. Though things may be borne with for christian liberty sake for a time, in hope to win the weak; yet, when liberty is turned to necessity, it is evil, and no longer liberty: and that that was for winning the weak suffered for a time, is becomen the confirming of the froward in their obstinateness. Paul used circumcision for a time, as of liberty; but when it was urged of necessity, he would not bend unto it. Bucer, when he was asked why he did not wear "quadrato pileo," made answer, "Quia caput non est quadratum." Wherein surely he noted well the comeliness of apparel to be, when it was fashioned like the body, and great folly, when a square cap was set on a round head. God be merciful to us, and grant us uprightly to seek his honour with all earnestness and simplicity! The Lord long preserve your lordship to the comfort of his afflicted church, and grant, that in this old age of the world we may serve the Lord of hosts in singleness of heart, and root out all stumbling blocks in religion; that Christ's glory may nakedly shine of its self, without all man's traditions or inventions, as in the beginning, when it was purest, and all such devices unknown, but invented of late to blear the eyes of the ignorant with an outward shew of holiness. So craving pardon for my boldness in so long a tale, I humbly take my leave, and commend your honour to him that gives all honour, and to whom all honour is due.

    Your honour's to command,

            J. A. DURESME.

From my house at Awcland the
 25th of October, 1564.

EXTRACTS

FROM

THE STATUTES OF RIVINGTON SCHOOL,

IN THE COUNTY OF LANCASTER,

FOUNDED BY BISHOP PILKINGTON.

From the "Statutes and Charter of Rivington School, &c. By the Rev. J. Whitaker, M.A." 8vo. London. 1837.)

I. *Meetings of the Governours.*

BUT before they begin to talk, they shall call on God by prayer severally, every one by himself, desiring God so to rule their minds, that they may do those things that be for his glory, and profit to his people; and if they meet for the choosing of a governour, or schoolmaster, they shall procure also an exhortation to be made by the schoolmaster, or some other learned man, to move them to consider deeply their duty and weighty cause that they have to do, declaring to them what good may follow in choosing a good man, and what harm, if they do not.

Chap. II. p. 147-8.

II. *Character of the Governours.*

The schoolmaster, usher, or curate, shall not be chosen a governour; but it shall be well to use the assistance and advice of them, and other honest neighbours, as occasion shall serve: none shall be chosen a governour also, but he that is sober, wise, discreet, a favourer of God's word, and professor of pure religion, and is a hater of all false doctrine, popish superstition and idolatry: further, he that is chosen a governour, must be of honest name and behaviour, no adulterer nor fornicator, no drunkard nor gamester, no waster of his own goods, but able to live of himself.

Chap. III. p. 150-1.

III. *An oath to be taken of every one that is appointed and chosen Governour.*

I, A. B., chosen governour of this school of Rivington, do swear and promise here afore God and the world, that I shall be true and diligent in this office of governing this school, scholars, and goods thereto belonging, to the uttermost of my power and knowledge; I shall suffer no popery, superstition, nor false doctrine, to be taught nor used in this school, but only that which is contained in the Holy Bible and agreeing therewith. These statutes of governing, nurture, learning, and teaching, which James Pilkington, bishop of Durham, hath allowed and appointed for this school, I shall see diligently practised and put in use. The goods and lands belonging now to this school, or that hereafter shall belong, I shall not consent at any time to turn them or any of them to any other use, but on the school, schoolmaster, usher, and scholars only; such lands or rents as be given or shall be given to this school hereafter, or bought, I shall never consent to sell, change, give, or put away, all or any part of them, except it be for procuring as good or better, and of the same yearly value at the least, and to be bestowed on this school as the other was; and that I shall see done afore any bargain and putting away of any lands, rents, or goods be made, stated, and delivered: what office or charge soever shall be put to me by the governours of this school, I shall willingly take it, and faithfully to my wit, power, and knowledge discharge it, so help me God, and as I hope to be saved by Jesus Christ.

p. 154-6.

IV. *Devotions of the Scholars.*

In the morning, afore they come out of their chamber, every scholar shall pray kneeling, as followeth:

In the name of the Father, and of the Son, and of the Holy Ghost, Amen. Most merciful God and loving Father, I give thee most hearty thanks for that it hath pleased thy godly Majesty to save, defend, and keep me thy unworthy servant all this night, and hath safely brought me to the beginning of this day, and for all other thy benefits and blessings, which of thine only goodness and not for our deserving thou hast bestowed, not only on me, most vile, wretched, and miserable sinner, but also on all other thy people and servants most plenteously. I beseech thy fatherly goodness for Jesus Christ's sake not to deal with us as we have deserved, but forgive us our manifold wickedness, whereby we have provoked thine anger and heavy displeasure to be poured upon us; and grant me and all thy people, quietly, without all dangers and assaults of our enemies, to pass this day, and all the rest of our lives, in thy holy service; that as the darkness of this night is past, and my weak body refreshed with sleep through thy goodness, so thy heavenly grace may lighten my heart, and stir up this sinful flesh and sluggish body, willingly to walk in thy commandments and obedience of thy word; that I may worthily praise thy holy name in this life, and after be partaker of that glory which thou hast prepared for them that love thee; through the bloodshed of thy dear Son Jesus Christ, our God and only Saviour. Amen.

After this he shall say the 25th Psalm, "I lift up my soul unto the Lord," &c. then desiring God to increase his faith, he shall rehearse the articles of his belief, "I believe in God the Father Almighty," &c., and last of all, the Lord's prayer, "Our Father, which art in heaven," &c.

Every time afore they begin to eat breakfast, dinner, or supper, they shall begin with prayer openly, that all in the house may pray with them, as this:—"The eyes of all things look up and trust in thee, O Lord," &c.; and so after meat likewise they shall give God thanks for the repast which they have received, as thus, viz. "Most mighty Lord and merciful Father, we give thee hearty thanks for our bodily sustenance," &c. Which graces and divers others more, because they be printed in the catechism and other places, I will not rehearse here, but will that the schoolmaster and usher see diligently, that every one of the scholars can say perfectly by heart divers sorts of them, and use them reverently, or else be duly corrected therefore.

Pietas Meridiana.

And because the number of God's mercies and blessings are infinite, and plenteously poured every minute of an hour upon us, and the forgetfulness of our dull and unthankful minds hath no measure, ever after dinner especially, and at other times also, in his chamber or elsewhere, every one shall by himself say, and consider with himself, the 103rd Psalm, "My soul, praise thou the Lord," &c. and then, as David doth here reckon the great number of blessings that God hath plenteously poured upon him, so every one shall enter an account with himself, what mercies and special blessings God hath poured upon him from his childhood, and give God hearty thanks for every one of them, as the prophet in the psalm doth: for this thankful kind of receiving goods is a provoking God, of his fatherly kindness, continually to pour more of them on us plenteously, as the unthankful taking and using of them is likewise a cause of the loosing and taking away of those mercies which he hath already given, or would most lovingly give us: that done, he shall pray as followeth: "Eternal God and loving Father, who lovedst us when we hated thee, and pourest thy blessings plenteously on us when we are unthankful unto thee; give us, we beseech thee now, hearts to love thee, that we may think upon thy manifold mercies, and thank thee for the same; root out of us this unthankful forgetfulness of thee, and of thy name and great mercies; make us often worthily to consider this thy fatherly dealing with us, that from henceforth we may become new men, and may worship, love, and obey thee as becometh good children, through Christ our Lord. Amen."

Pietas Vespertina.

Likewise at night, afore they go to bed, they shall, on their knees, first say the Ten Commandments; and afterwards examine themselves diligently, how they have lived according unto them, and spent that whole day; what company they have been in, what evil or bawdy talk, vain oaths, chiding, or slandering they have used; then, what shrewd turns they have done, how slow they have been to do good, and how much delighted in filthy thoughts and naughty deeds: which being done, they shall with sorrowful hearts and tears ask God forgiveness for that they have so lewdly misbehaved themselves, in breaking his holy laws, provoking him to anger, and deserving so grievous punishment for the same; and then say the fifty-first psalm, "Have mercy, Lord, on me, according to thy great mercy," &c., diligently considering every word and verse in it. Then shall follow this prayer:

"All praise and thanks be to thee, O Lord, for that thou hast vouchsafed to look down out of thy holy heavens in this vale of misery, on us thy miserable creatures, and hast saved us this day from all dangers and assaults of our enemies: Forgive us, most gracious God, where we have offended thy divine majesty in word, thought, or deed, and strengthen us by thy Holy Spirit, that we never fall more from thee: and as thou hast ordained the day for man to travel and labour in, and the night to rest and refresh our feeble bodies; so we beseech thy fatherly goodness, that thou wilt defend and keep us from all perils of this night, that, our bodies taking rest and sleep, which is the image of death, our minds may think on thee which only giveth life, and not be overcome with any temptations of the devil; that we may afterwards cheerfully rise, and painfully labour in our vocations to the praise of thy holy name, and the profit of thy people; and that lastly, both in body and soul, we may be partakers of that kingdom, which Christ thy dearly beloved Son, our Lord and Redeemer, hath wrought for us with the shedding of his precious blood: to whom, with thee and the Holy Ghost, be praise in all congregations for ever. Amen."

Then he shall say the Lord's prayer, "Our Father, which art in heaven," &c. And so commending himself and all christian people to God's goodness and merciful keeping, he may lie down and take his rest. But it is not sufficient only to use these prayers evening and morning, but every one shall learn more such out of the psalms and other godly prayer books, being not popish.

Chap. v. p. 165-71.

V. *The Oath of the Schoolmaster and Usher.*

I, A. B., appointed to be schoolmaster (or usher) of this grammar school in Rivington, do swear and promise here afore God and the world, that I will unfeignedly, unto the uttermost of my power, teach all such sorts of those that I have to do withal, the true fear of God, as it is written in his holy word, and shall set forward no other religion nor worship of God, but that which shall be contained in the Holy Bible, and agreeing therewith; all Romish superstition, doctrine, and idolatry, I shall not only in conscience abhor, and in deed flee from, but also shall diligently exhort, persuade, and teach my hearers to do the same.

I shall also teach my scholars, and bring them up in learning and good nurture, according to these orders and statutes, which the governours of this school, with the assent of James Pilkington, bishop of Durham, have appointed us for that purpose, and so diligently as they may in short time proceed to higher kinds of learning.

The goods belonging at any time to this school, I shall not only save as they were my own, and suffer none other to spoil or waste them to my power; but I shall counsel and persuade others to give more thereto; and if any waste be made of them, I shall declare it to the governours of the school, so soon as I know it and conveniently may, and help that it may be restored or recompensed with speed. All which things aforesaid I shall keep to my power, as I shall answer God at the dreadful day of judgment, and hope to be saved by the death of Jesus Christ, or look for the comfort of the Holy Ghost in this life.

Chap. vii. p. 193-4.

VI. *Morning and Evening Prayers in the School.*

As soon as the scholars be assembled in the school in the morning, at the master's or usher's appointment they shall all fall on their knees to common prayer openly, and begin first with some general confession, as that which is set forth in the common book, and appointed to be said before the receipt of the communion, "Almighty God, Father of our Lord Jesus Christ, Maker of all things, Judge of all men," &c. or this confession that followeth, or other such like, not being superstitious:

"Most terrible and merciful God, we do acknowledge before thy divine majesty, that we are miserable sinners, not only conceived and born in sin and blindness, but are daily heaping great wickedness in thy sight. We cannot for shame lift up our eyes and minds to thee, whom we have so often and so grievously offended; yet thy infinite goodness and mercy, shewed in all ages to them that repent, embolden and encourage us to present ourselves before thy goodness, to beg and crave some drops of thy manifold gifts and graces. Let not our miseries overcome thy mercies, nor our blind ignorance deface the brightness of thy gifts in us. We are unapt unto all goodness, until thou hast fashioned us anew by thy Holy Spirit, to understand some part of our duty to thee. We forget our bounden duties to thee and to thy people, until it please thy fatherly mercy to enlighten our minds with thy heavenly grace: frame us anew, most merciful Lord, from henceforth to serve and fear thee; stir up our dull and sluggish nature to the obedience of thy holy word; enlighten our blind and ignorant minds, that we may learn such things as may help us more plainly to behold the treasures thou hast laid up for us in Christ, thy dearly beloved Son; to whom, with the Father and the Holy Ghost, be praise for ever, in all congregations. Amen."

Then shall be sung or said a psalm or two in prose, if they be not long, at the discretion of the master or usher, in English, in order as they stand in the psalter, and then begin again continually; and when the psalm is ended, with the Lord's prayer, the schoolmaster or usher shall say the collect appointed in the morning prayer, " O Lord, our heavenly Father, almighty and everlasting God, who hast safely brought us to the beginning of this day," &c. and then this prayer following:

" Most loving God and merciful Father, which of thine own free good will hast stirred up the minds of some of thy well beloved servants to have a care and respect to thy church and people after them, and hast moved them to provide some places where youth may be brought up in learning and virtue; we give thee most hearty thanks for all such, but especially for this school, which of thy goodness thou hast provided for us. Make us, we beseech thee, profitable members of thy church and people, and as thou hast given us wit and aptness to take learning, so make us to take pleasure and to prosper in the same. Enlighten our ignorant minds, and stir up our dull and sluggish natures, to the learning and understanding of such things as may please thee, and serve to the setting forth of thy glory and the edifying of thy people. Bless and increase, we pray thee, the ministers of thy church; grant that their labours be not in vain. Send forth many diligent workmen into thy harvest, and of thy goodness accept our bounden duty and service, and frame us to serve thee; that we may apply our whole study and labour, so that out of this school may proceed a number of faithful and true ministers, that by their labours and study thy holy name may be better had in reverence among all people; and that learning and virtue may so appear in us, that we may serve thee as our Master, fear thee as our God, and love thee as our Father; to whom, with Jesus Christ thy Son our only Saviour, and the Holy Ghost the Comforter, be praise for ever. Amen."

Then shall they go to their lectures, and so continue till eleven o'clock, at which time, after the rehearsal of the ten commmandents, by a scholar appointed thereto in order through them all, they shall sing a psalm in English metre, in order through them as they stand, or part of one, if it be too long; and so every one go to dinner, after the master or usher hath read openly in English a common prayer drawn out of the psalms, gathered into the form of prayers by Peter Martyr, or some such like; that so the scholars may learn to gather the effect of the psalms into prayers, and use them to their comfort.

Likewise in the evening, before they depart from the school, they shall sing or say a psalm or two in English prose all together, if they be not too long, at the discretion of the master or usher; which being done, with the Lord's prayer and the articles of our faith said openly, the master or usher shall pray openly as followeth:

" O Lord, our God and only Saviour, which hast ordained all creatures to serve and obey us for our health and comfort, grant us, we pray thee, such plenty of thy grace, that we may never abuse them, nor be found unthankful unto thee: turn and subdue our stubborn and froward minds to the obedience of thy holy will. Save and defend, we humbly beseech thee, our realm and commonwealth; relieve the oppressed and comfort the heavy hearted. Protect our king and the honourable council; grant unto him and them, and all that be in authority under them, such godly wisdom, fear, love, and reverence of thy godly majesty, that they may maintain peace with justice, and punish sin. Set forward and advance pure religion; suppress idolatry and superstition; and of thy goodness make us, O Lord, thy poor servants, profitable members of this commonwealth. Bless our studies so in learning and good nurture, that we may be profitable to many others; and that by our travail and labour thy glory may shine and appear to the comfort of thy chosen people, through Christ our Lord, thy Son; to whom, with thee and the Holy Ghost, three Persons and one God, be praise and thanksgiving throughout all ages. Amen."

Chap. VIII. p. 199-204.

VII. *Catechising.*

On Saturdays and holyday eves the usher shall exercise his younger sort in learning their short catechism in English, in the common book; and the same days to all sorts the master shall read Mr Nowell's[1] or Calvin's Catechism, taught in Calvin's Institutions, willing the elder sort both to learn it by heart, and examine them briefly the next day after, when they come to school again, before they go to other things, how they can say it, and shall commend them that have done well, and encourage others to do the like.

Chap. x. p. 215-6.

VIII. *Nature and end of their Studies.*

But above all things both the master and the usher shall continually move their scholars to godliness, both in manners and conditions; and prosper their studies, that they may serve God and the commonwealth diligently, as becometh Christians and faithful members of his church; teaching and noting unto them such wise and godly sentences out of the scriptures, and other authors, as may stir them up more earnestly thereto, and will them to learn them by heart, and oft to think upon them.

p. 218-9.

IX. *Commemoration of the Founder.*

Every year once, on that day in which it shall please God to take James Pilkington, now bishop of Durham, out of this wretched life to a better with himself, the scholars shall have liberty to play, so that they exercise themselves in making verses, orations, or declamations severally in praising God, that moved him and others to prepare this school for the bringing up of youth, and profit of his church.

Likewise the schoolmaster shall yearly, on the same day openly in the school, or rather the next holiday in the church,

[1] See Nowell. Catechismus, p. xxix. Oxon. 1835. ED.

whethersoever the governours shall appoint him, make some exhortation to praise God for his fatherly care and providence towards his people, which stirred some to provide some means for posterity to be brought up in learning and the fear of God: and shall further declare the comfortable hope of the last resurrection both of body and soul to everlasting life, and of the blessed state in the mean time of those that die in the Lord and the faith of Jesus Christ; that so the hearers may learn both how to live, and bestow their goods on like godly uses, and not be afraid to die, nor of the pope's purgatory, when God calleth them; but desire with St Paul to be delivered out of this mortal, sinful, and most wretched body, and to reign with Christ and his holy angels for ever, at the right hand of God the Father, through the merits and bloodshed of Jesus Christ our Lord and only Saviour: to whom, with the Father and the Holy Ghost, be praise both now and ever. Amen.

p. 220-2.

TRACTATUS JACOBI PILKINGTON,

DUM ERAT STUDENS CANTABRIGIÆ.

(From the Parker MSS. of Corpus Christi College, Cambridge, Vol. cv. 15.)

Deus cujus vult miseretur, quem vult indurat.

HUMANA temeritas cum audit Deum ipsam esse caritatem et bonitatem, si quicquam de illius secretis judiciis in reprobos perceperit dictum, veluti quod indurat, excæcat, rejicit, indignum esse clamitat de tanta majestate talia cogitare: sic tamen hac cæcitate nobis placemus, ut ab ea divelli nequeamus, et nihil de Deo pronunciari velimus, quod non cum ratione justitiæ nostræ et humano judicio per omnia conveniat. Apud homines condemnare quenquam indicta causa et nullo commisso flagitio iniquum esse fateor: sed apud Deum, cujus voluntas est æquissima regula, et qui nihil quicquam cuiquam debet, sed pro arbitrio suo justissime quod vult facit, hæc juste fieri ante facta secula ratione summa contendo.

Sumus apud illum tanquam lutum in manu figuli: at nunquam dicit figmentum figulo, Cur me finxisti sic? cum aliud vas in honorem et aliud in contumeliam effinxerit. Sic tu, cum non potes capere cur ille reprobos nonnullos vult esse, noli quod ita fiat calumniari, sed illum qui id fecit venerare: noli figulum in operibus suis culpare, sed justam illius voluntatem in secreto suo consilio[1] cole, admirare, obstupesce. Audi apostolum intonantem, et nullam aliam causam reddentem nisi quia voluerit: *Cujus vult miseretur*, inquit, *quem vult indurat*. Ecce eandem causam utriusque, nempe misericordiæ et indurationis, nempe Dei voluntatem: hic conquiesce; hoc uno perturbatam conscientiam pacare potes.

Ne audias furores eorum qui dicant, Tyrannicum hoc est, quando quod libet licet, et quibus stat pro ratione libido: Deus est enim, cujus voluntas aberrare non potest. Nec illis credas, qui ob prævisa merita tua hæc fieri contendant. Hæc namque

[1 MS. *concilio*. ED.]

omnia ab humano nascuntur judicio, et iis qui nihil credant quod ratione humana non percipiunt. Crede apostolo cum dicit, *Numquid injustitia apud Deum? voluntati ejus quis resistit? Et, Annon habet figulus potestatem ex eadem massa facere aliud vas in honorem, et aliud in contumeliam?* Noli quærere causam antecedentem aliquam, quæ voluntatem Dei ad quicquam faciendum commoveat; sed illam intellige et crede priorem esse omnibus, et quæ ceteras omnes ad agendum concitet.

Audi Augustinum contra Manichæos disputantem, qui causam aliquam ponebant priorem voluntate divina, et quæ illam ad[1] agendum impelleret, his verbis: " Causas voluntatis Dei," inquit, " quærunt, cum voluntas ejus causa sit omnium quæ sunt: si namque causam aliquam habet voluntas Dei, est aliquid quod præcedat voluntatem Dei; quod dicere nefas est. Compescat se ergo humana temeritas, et id quod non est non quærat, ne id quod est non[2] inveniat. Voluntas Dei causa est cœli et terræ, et ideo major est voluntas Dei quam cœlum et terra[3]." Hæc Augustinus. Si ergo nulla causa, tum propter opera prævisa nec miseretur nec indurat, sed solum quia vult, attestante apostolo: *Non ex operibus, sed ex vocante, dictum est, Major serviet minori: et priusquam nati essent, et boni aut etiam mali quicquam fecissent, dixit, Jacob dilexi et Esau odio habui.* Hic conquiescendum; hic non disputandum, sed clamandum, *O altitudo divitiarum, &c.* Hæc de voluntate.

Misertus est nostri Deus ante jacta fundamenta mundi, eripiens nos e massa perditionis in qua jacebamus submersi, et adoptavit nos in filios per Christum suum, in quo et nos elegit ante tempora, ut essemus sancti et irreprehensibiles coram eo: miseretur etiam et quotidie tanquam pater dispensans nobis sua dona pro sua prudentia, prout novit ea nobis fore usui. Nihil novum tamen donat; sed quod pro beneplacito suo nobis daturum se decrevit in Filio ante secula, id nobis distribuit per Spiritum in tempora. Novit infirmitatem nostram et temeritatem, quam inepti sumus ad dispensandum illius dona et conservandum: reservat ergo sibi thesauros suos; et cum ad petendum accedimus, effundit in nos quam opulente.

[1 *Ad illam ad* MS. ED.]   [2 Deest *non* in MS. ED.]
[3 De Genesi contra Manich. Lib. I. c. 4. Tom. I. p. 1049. Paris. 1836. ED.]

Hæc certitudo prædestinationis nostræ per Christum, et fixa sententia Domini, quia decrevit apud se quod nobis impertiret boni, aut a Christo alienatis nobis eveniret mali, (et sic quidem ut nulla de causa commutari queat quin quod[4] statuit fuit, et quod non sit statutum non fuit,) alienum videtur nonnullis a recepta doctrina et orthodoxorum scriptis, ut ferri non queat. Verum qui præjudicatam non asserunt sententiam, longe aliud percipient ex iis quæ dixero, non tam quidem e cerebro meo, quam ex sacratissimis scripturarum penetralibus et patrum voluminibus.

A patribus, quod illorum auctoritas plus apud nonnullos poterit quam Spiritus Sancti majestas in scripturis suis: Gregorius, immensa bona illa descripturus, quæ nobis Pater per Filium communicavit, et non pœnitendo consilio suo et immutabili sententia prædestinavit, in hæc verba prorumpit: "Nulla quæ in hoc mundo fiunt, absque omnipotentis Dei consilio veniunt: nam cuncta Deus sequutura præsciens ante secula decrevit, qualiter per secula disponantur. Statutum quippe jam est homini, vel quantum hunc mundi prosperitas sequatur, vel quantum adversitas feriat; ne electos ejus aut immoderata prosperitas elevet aut nimia adversitas gravet. Statutum quoque est, quantum in ipsa vita mortali temporaliter vivat: nam etsi annos quindecim Ezechiæ regi ad vitam addidit omnipotens Deus, cum eum mori permisit, tunc eum præscivit esse moriturum. * * * Per prophetam Dominus dixit, quo tempore mori merebatur: per misericordiam vero illo eum tempore ad mortem distulit, quod ante secula ipse præscivit. Nec propheta ergo fallax, quia tempus innotuit quo mori merebatur; nec divina statuta convulsa sunt, quia ut ex largitate Dei anni vitæ crescerent, hoc quoque ante secula præfixum fuit, atque spatium vitæ, quod inopinate foris est additum, sine augmento in præscientia fuit intus statutum. * * Potest hoc quoque juxta spiritum intelligi; quia nonnunquam in virtutibus proficere conamur, et quædam dona percipimus, a quibusdam vero repulsi in imis jacemus. Nullus enim est, qui tantum virtutis apprehendat, quantum desiderat, quia omnipotens Deus, interiora discernens, ipsis spiritualibus profectibus modum ponit, ut ex hoc quod homo apprehendere conatur et

[[4] Deest *quod* in MS. ED.]

non valet, in illis se non elevet quæ valet. Unde Paulus, in tertium cœlum raptus, post revelationem non valebat esse tranquillus et intentatus[1]," ne extolleretur. Rursus de eo disputans, quod nullus possit mori nisi eo ipso momento quo moritur, plura asserit in eandem sententiam, quæ et utilia et jucunda sunt lectu, ego tamen tempori consulens singula prætereo. Alibi sic quoque generaliter: " Quicquid foris futurum est in opere, intus jam factum est in prædestinatione[2]."

Advertite per Deum quod dicit, hæc sic statuta esse ante secula, quæ nobis distribuit per tempora; tum quid boni et mali sequeretur singulos, tum etiam quamdiu in hoc ergastulo corporis viveretur, et postremo quantos progressus in virtutibus faceremus, quia hæc dividit singulis Spiritus prout vult. Et talia non[3] sunt dona Dei et vocatio, ut eum dedisse aut non dedisse pœniteat: sed sic omnia moderatur pro prudentia sua tam bene, ut melius quicquam excogitari non queat, nec aliter fieri quam sit hodie debebat. Eadem sunt quæ docet Evangelista, quamvis non eisdem verbis: *Passer non cadit in terram, &c. Capilli capitis vestri numerati. Conjicite curam vestram in illum, quoniam est illi cura de vobis.* Hæc de misericordia.

Quæ de induratione dici debeant aut possint, eo videntur esse duriora, quia non credimus ea quæ de voluntate Dei diximus esse vera. Putamus hoc esse tyrannicum, si Deus quæ velit faciat: si non omnibus æqualiter dona sua dispartiat, acceptorem personarum fore clamamus: si non futura merita vel bona vel mala respiciat, et ideo vel misereatur vel induret, injustum esse pronunciamus. Si quempiam rejiciat qui nihil mali sit commeritus, statim culpam omnem in Deum rejicimus, et auctorem flagitiorum nostrorum contendimus; et quia quod Dominus decrevit facimus, placemus nobis in nostris vitiis, et peccata recte facta dici volumus. Potius de tanta majestate sic cogitare fas est. Deus est: quicquid cogitat bonum est; quod facit justum est: sapientiæ ejus non est numerus: nihil ergo cogitari melius poterat. Nos tanquam lutum sumus in illius manu: injustus esse non potest, si te matulam et vas in con-

[1 Gregor. Op. Exposit. in Job. Cap. xiv. Tom. ii. p. 313. Antverp. 1615. ubi quædam aliter leguntur. Ed.]

[2 Ibid. p. 716. in Job. xxxviii. 4, &c. Ed.]

[3 Deest *non* in MS. Ed.]

tumeliam fecerit, quia figulus est. Causam ne quæras cur sic te fecerit, sed admirare tantam prudentiam, cujus consilii rationem in faciendis rebus perspicere non potes. Potius deplora cæcitatem tuam, quod in tantis tenebris versaris, quam illius justitiam culpes, cujus splendorem intueri non potes. Desine humano judicio divina consilia metiri: potius te intra tuos limites contine, et ne causam perquiras quod ita te fecerit, sed illum cole qui te ita fecerit. Nihil tibi debet: age perinde gratias, si quid dederit; et ne obmurmures, si non tantum quantum alii acceperis: respondet enim tibi, *Amice, non facio tibi injuriam;* nihil tibi debui, ne succenseas ergo quod plus aliis quam tibi dederim. *Estne oculus tuus malus, quod ego bonus sum? et annon licebit mihi facere de meis quod voluero*, et quibus libuerit impartire, et quibus visum fuerit subtrahere? *Tu, homo, quis es qui respondeas Deo?* Disce loqui de Deo et sentire, quemadmodum ipse in scripturis suis per Spiritum suum loquitur: ne time; si sic loquaris, non errabis, nisi novos loquendi modos tibi fingas. Sic dicit Dominus de seipso: quod tradit in reprobum sensum; excæcat cor populi ne intelligant, et aures aggravat ne audiant; inducit in tentationes; indurat Pharaonem; odit Esau prius quam natus, et boni quicquam aut mali fecisset; facit vasa quædam in contumeliam; præcepit Semei maledictis proscindere et lapidibus impetere David; seducit prophetas, errare facit, indurat cor nostrum, ne timeamus illum; immittit spiritum malum in Saul; abstulit omnia bona Job; voluit occidere filios Heli; projicit a facie sua, et Spiritum Sanctum aufert, obliviscitur nostri; non est malum in civitate quod non facit; immittit spiritum mendacem in prophetas Achab; præparat vasa iræ, scindit regnum Israel, et dat Jeroboam impio: mors et vita, bona et mala a Domino; mittit operationem erroris, ut credant mendacio.

Hæc et multa similia eisdem verbis de seipso pronunciat Dominus. Cur ergo timebimus sic de illo loqui, quemadmodum ipse nos docuit et loqui voluit? Stulta est prudentia, qua Domino placere studemus, cum tristitiam istarum rerum sæpe lenitate verbi mitigare velimus. Non opus habet prudentia nostra ad tollenda quæ nobis videntur esse injusta. Injustus es, si illud ei surripis quod ille sibi vindicat: non est tam otiosus aut invidus, ut velit uspiam deesse suis et gubernationem suarum rerum aliis concredere. Ne nega hæc esse vera, quia ratione non potes capere cur sint[1] vera: satis tibi sit quod hæc dixerit, et sua dici voluit. Nimis negligens suarum rerum esset, si hæc in suo regno sine se fieri permitteret: omnia non poterat, si hæc depellere non poterat et voluerit: imbecillis esset, si hæc invito illo fierent: sapientissimus non haberetur, si hæc futura ignoraret, sed fortuito aut in ignominiam Creatoris cederent. Sed qui excitavit Pharaonem ut in eo ostenderet potentiam suam, et potest et vult ex summis flagitiis nostris summam sibi comparare gloriam: et quæ a te percipi non possunt, cur fierent, ab illo cur fiant pervidentur clarissime.

Proinde cum nullus voluntati ejus resistere queat, quæcunque fiunt, eo volente fiant est necesse: et cum omnia quæ vivunt, moventur, et sunt, ab eo vivunt, moventur, et sunt, et in eo, ab ulla actione ille abesse non potest, sed omnibus agendi vires subministrat.

Plura possem et vellem, sed plura non vellet tempus.

[[1] MS. *sit*. ED.]

EPISTOLA AD ANDREAM KINGSMILL.

(MS. Bodl. Mus. 55. olim 9.)

GRATIA et pax. Gratulatorias tuas literas cum primas tum postremas grato quo decuit animo accepi, et magnas ob illas ago gratias. Perge porro in bonis literis, et cursum quem cepisti perfice. Dominus novit, qui has tibi dedit, in quem usum tibi subserviet. Otium tibi suppetit, ut Latine et Græce ad me scribas. Negotia mea non sæpe, in initiis terminorum (quos vocant jurisconsulti) præsertim, vix amicos salutare, aut de rebus gravioribus pro dignitate cogitare sinunt. Da igitur veniam, si non quæ velles aut ego exoptem scribam: nam defatigatus ad hæc pauca accedo.

Quod Cicero[1] de Hercule Prodico scribit, hoc tibi jam ego sic venire ex literis sororis tuæ intelligo. Ille cum in viam voluptatis amœnam et virtutis asperam incidisset, qua potissimum ingrederetur, dubitavit: tu num in contemptæ theologiæ an in splendidæ jurisconsultorum scientiæ scholam te tradas, ignoras. At bono sis animo: fidelem habes ducem et consultorem, qui ad exoptatum suum propositum te deducet. *Si cui vestrum desit sapientia,* inquit Jacobus, *petat ab eo qui dat, et dabitur.* In veteri lege de rebus dubiis consulebant Dominum per sacerdotem: is indutus Urim et Thummim, (gemmis in veste sacerdotali,) si resplenduerint, aggrediendum confidenter responsa ferebat. Sic tu, Andrea, ἄνδριζε· prostratus coram Domino, pete ἀρχιερέα Χριστὸν ἡμέτερον· pulsa, quære; benignus est Dominus, dabit, aperiet, invenies. In qua parte splendescentem Christum et mentem tuam magis illustratam videris, in illam inclina; si perturbatam et dejectam senseris, devita: nam pacis et consolationis Deus noster auctor est.

At me vis aliquid dicere? Vis enim certe, et in talibus non libenter respondere soleo. Non is sum e cujus consilio pendeas, neque per quem in aliquid certum vitæ genus te con-

[1 De Officiis, I. 32. ED.]

jicias: sed quum dicendum est, ingenue quid sentio dicam. "Dat Galenus opes, dat Justinianus honores;" quod vel pueri norunt: quid Christus? crucem et carceres. Elige jam: quid tibi videtur? Potes cum psalmista dicere, *Elegi abjectus esse in domo Dei magis quam habitare in tabernaculis peccatorum?* Si potes, sequere: sin minus, ora ut possis; est enim Dominus exercituum et potens; non sinet suos milites labescere. Proponunt leges nostræ præmia quidem, at peritura; sed Christus coronam, non lauream nec auream, sed æternam. Consiliis principum intersunt jurisperiti; at theologi Dei patris mandata deferunt: imo non solum secreta illius intelligunt, sed et interpretes illius sunt, ac cum eo regnabunt, regesque ipsi erunt, modo prius fideliter serviant.

Difficillima est hæc deliberatio, fateor, de deligendo certo vitæ genere; sed hæc non e re ipsa nascitur dubitatio, sed ex teipso, vel iis quæ in vita contingunt: nam si hæc inter se conferas, iniqua est comparatio; et tantum hoc illi præponderat, quantum cœlum terræ, si dignitatem rei subjectæ spectes. Divina oracula e cœlo sunt delapsa, auctorem habent Deum ipsum: majestas eorum tanta, ut vel Satanam ipsum comprimant; veritas ac certitudo talis, ut nec fallere nec falli queant; usus tam necessarius in omnem eventum vitæ, ut sine his beate vivi non possit. Mentem in cœlum sublevant: doctorem et interpretem habent Spiritum veritatis: in adversis sunt solatio, in prosperis ornamento. Hæc sola mentem perturbatam pacare possunt, mores formare, et inexhaustos fontes misericordiæ miseris aperire[1]: hæc ignaros docent, lapsos erigunt, robustos confirmant: ex his solum salus petenda, Deus invocandus; promissorum certitudo firmissima ad incitandum, minæque gravissimæ ad deterrendum proponuntur. Jura humana humi repunt, ab hominibus inventa: pro varietate loci varia, incerta, contentionum fomes: mentem perturbant, animum abducunt a meditatione rerum cœlestium et saluti propinquiorum. Quid Cyprianus de sui temporis legislatoribus scripsit? pete ex epistola 2. l. II[2]. Confer cum nostris hac tempestate, et num illos superant, adverte. Non hæc dico quod leges condemnem aut earum studium, sed ut quantum inter has intersit appareat. Sunt quidem leges et earum interpretes in republica bene in-

[1 MS. *reperire*. ED.]
[2 Ad Donatum, de Gratia Dei. p. 5. ed. Fell. Oxon. 1700. ED.]

stituta adeo necessariæ, ut sine his constare nequeat neque pax publica conservari. Non ergo de dignitate rerum est aliqua dubitatio.

De teipso dubitas: non satis instructus tibi videris; non bene jacta fundamenta, manus illotæ, lingua balbutiens, eloquentiæ carentia, animi juveniles, mysteria profunda; in reprehendendis principibus pericula, paupertas, exilium, ignes, equuleus, et malorum omnium tolerantia: hæc quidem sunt quæ plurimos deterrent, hæc causari solent. His moti Moses, Jeremias, Jonas legationem Domini detractabant; at vide quid Dominus responderit: *Qui finxit os, et illud aperiet.* Si gloriam illius, non tuam quæras, dabit os et sapientiam, cui contradici nequit. Etiam nostra præmeditatio luculentum cœnum humanæ eloquentiæ majus non mundat, sed coinquinat. In Hebraicis tantos progressus si feceris, quantos in Græcis et Latinis, multis non opus erit interpretibus. Timotheus in ipsa adolescentia fit episcopus; et quantumcunque sunt ardua mysteria, Spiritus veritatis omnem dabit intelligentiam. De ferenda cruce si dubites, *non est servus supra Dominum:* communis est hæc fors et omnium conditio, ut persecutionem patiantur qui pie volunt vivere. Quamprimum apostolos emisit, præmonuit, *Mitto vos sicut oves in medio luporum. Ora Dominum, ut extrudat in messem;* nam volens vix quisquam exit.

Non te pigeat laboris in legibus perdiscendis impensi; nam vellem et ego magna pecunia vel minimam partem cognitionis tuæ redimere. Magnam conciliat concionatori benevolentiam, si possit de jure respondere aut oppressis consilio adesse. Dominus concessit apostolis vim miraculorum edendorum, ut indocta plebs avidius eos audiret, et evangelium libentius in eorum animos influeret. Sic enim sunt affecti maxima ex parte omnes, ut facilius credant, faveant, ament, a quo beneficium expectant, vel quos sibi consilio aut auxilio profuturos sperant. Sic ergo tu pro sapientia tua hæc utraque conjunge, ut hæc præsit, illa prosit; hæc sit velut domina, et illa ancilla: furtivis quibusdam horis sic stude, ut et illud quod hactenus imbibisti de legibus, retineas, adaugeas, et in usum pauperum qui consilio carent convertas; et maximum quod datur temporis in sacras literas impende. Quod si Dominus ut publice profitearis leges te vocat ad annum unum aut alterum, ne contemnas: potes enim interim in Hebraicis sic proficere, ut paratior et instructior ad theologiam accedas; et annorum accessio auctoritatem secum adferet. Etsi Dominus sæpe "Væ" intonat legis peritis, Paulus tamen, ne vocatio rejicienda putaretur, virum Zenam bonum jurisperitum reperit quem commendet.

Quæris adhuc, quos auctores et historiographos tibi legendos censeam. E veteribus maxime popularis S. Chrysostomus, et formando concionatori accommodatissimus. Contentiones illius ætatis acutissime tractavit Augustinus, e cujus epistolis velut compendium totius illius doctrinæ hauries. E recentioribus duo sunt clarissima lumina Calvinus et Martyr: sed ille exlex est et devius, attentum petens lectorem; hic facilitate sua fluit, et tamen pondus rerum subtiliter satis inquirit. Historiæ seriem ab Adam ad Christum et Jerusalem subversam deducit Josephus; post Christum ad papas[1] Eusebius; post Gregorium Magnum paparum tyrannidem succincte et satis luculenter descripsit dominus Barnes noster et Bate. Chronographorum infinitus est numerus; sed illis per otium poteris uti; et interim contextum scripturæ potissimum, qua lingua conscribebatur, familiarem tibi facito: sic enim per omnes scriptores inoffenso pede pervagaberis; et quis dexterrime sit interpretatus, sine errore judicabis.

Vides quomodo, quicquid in buccam venerit, calamus errando obliteravit: sed mallem apud te loquendo peccare, quam tacendo ingratus haberi. Saluta fratres tuos meosque adeo quam potes officiosissime: quod tibi in hac re dictum sit, et illis dictum esse puta: et quum tres unus sitis, his unis, qui et unus esse vobiscum velim, vos omnes compellari existimo. Commendatissimum me habe domino D. Humfrey et domino Sampsono, Bernardo, et omnibus qui Christo bene volunt.

James Pilkinton the bishop of Duresmes
lettre to his brother in law Andrew
Kingsmill, fellow of Allsoules
College, in Oxon. 1564.

[[1] MS. *ad papas post Gregorium Magnum Eusebius; paparum.* ED.]

NOTES.

Note A. Page 141.

On the passage of Tertullian cited in the note a recent Editor remarks: Totum hoc descripsit Eusebius, et hist. suæ eccles. II. 2. inseruit. Narrat idem Severus et Ælius Lampridius: Tanaq. Faber tomo II. Epist. 12. multis evincere conatur, deceptum esse Tertullianum, veritatemque hujus rei elevat. Argumentis quatuor utitur: Quod historia ex libro supposito sit hausta, Actis Pilati scilicet. Quod religionis curam nullam gesserit Tiberius, unde Suetonio dicitur *circa deos ac religiones negligentior*. Quod senatus Romanus sub Tiberio ad vilissimam adulationem prolapsus, ne hiscere quidem contra principem ausus fuisset. Quod ex chronologia pateat, christianum nomen eo tempore vix notum Romæ fuisse. Quibus adde infensum potius Tiberium, ut Judæo, ita et christiano, nomini fuisse, ut clare patet ex Sueton. cap. xxxvi. ubi per *similia sectantes* nulli nisi christiani intelligi possunt.—See Tertullian. Semler. Tom. vi. Ind. v. *Tiberius*, Halæ Magd. 1825.

The passage of Eusebius is as follows:

Καὶ δὴ τῆς παραδόξου τοῦ Σωτῆρος ἡμῶν ἀναστάσεώς τε καὶ εἰς οὐρανοὺς ἀναλήψεως τοῖς πλείστοις ἤδη περιβοήτου καθεστώσης, παλαιοῦ κεκρατηκότος ἔθους τοῖς τῶν ἐθνῶν ἄρχουσι τὰ παρὰ σφίσι καινοτομούμενα τῷ τὴν βασίλειον ἀρχὴν ἐπικρατοῦντι σημαίνειν, ὡς ἂν μηδὲν αὐτὸν διαδιδράσκοι τῶν γινομένων, τὰ περὶ τῆς ἐκ νεκρῶν ἀναστάσεως τοῦ Σωτῆρος ἡμῶν Ἰησοῦ, εἰς πάντας ἤδη καθ' ὅλης Παλαιστίνης βεβοημένα, Πιλάτος Τιβερίῳ βασιλεῖ κοινοῦται· ὡς τάς τε ἄλλας αὐτοῦ πυθόμενος τερατείας, καὶ ὡς ὅτι μετὰ θάνατον ἐκ νεκρῶν ἀναστὰς, ἤδη θεὸς εἶναι παρὰ τοῖς πολλοῖς ἐπεπίστευτο. τὸν δὲ Τιβέριον ἀνενεγκεῖν μὲν τῇ συγκλήτῳ, ἐκείνην τ' ἀπώσασθαί φασι τὸν λόγον, τῷ μὲν δοκεῖν, ὅτι μὴ πρότερον αὕτη τοῦτο δοκιμάσασα ἦν, παλαιοῦ νόμου κεκρατηκότος, μὴ ἄλλως τινὰ παρὰ Ῥωμαίοις θεοποιεῖσθαι, μὴ οὐχὶ ψήφῳ καὶ δόγματι συγκλήτου, τῇ δ' ἀληθείᾳ, ὅτι μηδὲ τῆς ἐξ ἀνθρώπων ἐπικρίσεώς τε καὶ συστάσεως ἡ σωτήριος τοῦ θείου κηρύγματος ἐδεῖτο διδασκαλία. ταύτης δ' οὖν ἀπωσαμένης τὸν προσαγγελθέντα περὶ τοῦ Σωτῆρος ἡμῶν λόγον τῆς Ῥωμαίων βουλῆς, τὸν Τιβέριον, ἣν καὶ πρότερον εἶχε γνώμην τηρήσαντα, μηδὲν ἄτοπον κατὰ τῆς τοῦ Χριστοῦ διδασκαλίας ἐπινοῆσαι. ταῦτα Τερτυλλιανὸς, τοὺς Ῥωμαίων νόμους ἠκριβωκὼς ἀνήρ, τά τε ἄλλα ἔνδοξος, καὶ τῶν μάλιστα ἐπὶ Ῥώμης λαμπρῶν, κ. τ. λ.

He then proceeds to quote the passage of Tertullian cited in the note.

A modern writer, Mosheim, states the position of the question in the following terms:

Ex imperatoribus Tiberius Christum inter populi Romani deos co-optare voluisse, at senatu resistente haud potuisse, fertur. Quod licet multis hodie parum videatur probabile, sunt tamen egregii viri, qui, magnis ducti rationibus, licere sibi his accedere negant. Institutionum Historiæ Eccles. Sec. i. cap. iv.

Note B. Page 142.

A full account of this circumstance is given by Hottinger:

Constantiæ vero documenta dedit [Zuinglius] luculentissima, quando nullis vel pontificum promissis, vel pontificiorum minis aut insidiis a proposito terreri potuit. Promissiones Pontificis liberalissimas fuisse, vel spem saltem non obscuram lautioris conditionis factam, probat Adriani VI. Breve, quod vocant, an. Chr. 1523. d. 23 Januarii ad Zuinglium scriptum. Archetypon in bibliotheca adhuc publica asservatur; ectypum ita sonat: "Dilecte fili, salutem et apostolicam benedictionem: Remittimus venerabilem fratrem, Ennium, episcopum Verulanum, Prælatum, domesticum nostrum et apostolicæ sedis nuntium, hominem prudentia et fide præstantem, ad istam invictam, nobisque et huic sanctæ sedi conjunctissimam nationem, ut de maximis rebus nos, eandem sedem, totamque christianam rempublicam concernentibus, cum illa[1] agat. Licet autem ei dederimus in mandatis, ut ea communiter cum omnibus et publice tractet; tamen cum de tua egregia virtute specialiter nobis sit cognitum, nosque devotionem tuam arctius amemus ac diligamus, ac peculiarem quandam in te fidem habeamus, mandavimus eidem episcopo, nuncio nostro, ut tibi separatim nostras literas redderet, nostramque erga te optimam voluntatem declararet. Hortamur itaque devotionem tuam in Domino, ut et illi omnem fidem habeas[2]; et quo nos animo ad honores tuos et commoda tendimus, eodem tu in nostris et dictæ sedis apostolicæ rebus procedas, de quo gratiam apud nos invenies non mediocrem. Datum Romæ, &c." Eadem epistola inserta est προσωπογραφία Zuinglianæ, a Myconio editæ, et Epist. Zuing. et Œcolamp. præfixæ; cui editor subjungit: "Has literas propterea nolui nescires, ut constaret, si gratiam hominum quam gratiam Dei maluisset Zuinglius, quantusnam esse potuisset. Non enim ad hunc solum Papa scripserat, verum etiam ad eximium D. Franciscum Ziggium, ut sibi et sedi apostolicæ virum lucrifaceret. Dumque rogitarem a Francisco, quid pro illo pollicitus esset Papa, serio respondit, 'Omnia certe præter sedem papalem'." Ipse etiam Zuinglius an. Chr. 1523. præceptori suo, Thomæ Witenbachio, postquam dolorem suum expectorasset, quod præteritis ætatibus tempus suum non melioribus impendissent studiis, pauloque fusius suam de cœna Domini mentem aperuisset; indicavit, "Pontificem conatum esse se a proposito avocare, magnis oblatis pollicitationibus; se

[1 Hottinger *concernentem cum illo*, Myconius *concernentem cum illa*. Ed.]
[2 Hottinger *habeatis*, Myconius *habeait*. Ed.]

interea constanter docuisse Papam esse Antichristum." J. H. Hottinger. Histor. Eccles. Nov. Test. Sec. xvi. Pars ii. p. 233, &c. Tiguri, 1665.

The passage cited from Myconius will be found in his Letter De Vita et Obitu H. Zuinglii, prefixed to the Epistolæ Doctorum Virorum, quibuscum Eucharistiæ, &c. fo. η. 4. Basil. 1548.

Note C. Page 570.

Hæc est rescriptio sancti Hulderici episcopi, in qua Nicolao papæ, de continentia clericorum non juste, sed impie, non canonice, sed indiscrete tractanti, ita respondit:

Nicolao Domino et patri pervigili, sanctæ Romanæ ecclesiæ provisori, Huldericus solo nomine episcopus amorem ut filius, timorem ut servus.

Cum tua, O pater et domine, decreta super clericorum continentiam nuper mihi transmissa a discretione invenirem aliena; timor quidam turbavit me cum tristitia: timor quidem propter hoc, quod dicitur pastoris sententia, sive justa sive injusta, timenda esse; timebam enim infirmis scripturæ auditoribus, qui vel justæ vix obediunt sententiæ, ut injustam conculcantes libere, onerosa, imo importabili pastoris prævaricatione præcepti se obligarent: tristitia vero vel compassio, dum dubitabam qua ratione membra cavere possent, capite suo tam gravi morbo laborante. Quid enim gravius, quid totius ecclesiæ compassione dignius, quam te, summæ sedis pontificem, ad quem totius ecclesiæ spectat examen, a sancta discretione vel minimum exorbitare? Non parum quippe ab hac deviasti, dum clericos, quos ad continentiam conjugii monere debebas, ad hanc imperiosa quadam violentia cogi volebas. Numquid enim merito communi omnium sapientum judicio hæc est violentia, cum contra evangelicam institutionem ac Sancti Spiritus dictationem ad privata aliquis decreta cogitur exequenda?

Cum igitur plurima veteris ac novi testamenti suppetant exempla, sanctam, ut nosti, discretionem docentia, tuæ rogo ne grave sit paternitati, vel pauca ex pluribus huic paginæ interseri. Dominus quidem in veteri lege sacerdoti conjugium constituit, quod illi postmodum interdixisse non legitur. Sed in evangelio loquitur: *Sunt eunuchi, qui se castraverunt propter regnum cœlorum; sed non omnes hoc verbum capiunt: qui potest capere, capiat.* Quapropter apostolus ait: *De virginibus præceptum Domini non habeo, consilium autem do.* Quod etiam juxta prædictum Domini non omnes hoc consilium capere posse consideras; sed multos ejusdem consilii assentatores, hominibus, non Deo, pro falsa specie continentiæ placere volentes, graviora vides committere, patrum scilicet uxores subagitare, masculorum ac pecudum amplexus non abhorrere: ne morbi hujus aspersione ad usque pestilentiam convalescente, nimirum status labefactetur ecclesiæ totius, *propter fornicationem,* dixit, *unusquisque suam uxorem habeat.* Quod specialiter ad laicos pertinere iidem mentiuntur hypocritæ: qui, licet in quovis sanctissimo ordine constituti, alienis revera uxoribus non dubitant abuti. Et quod flendo cernimus, omnes in supradictis sæviunt sceleribus. Hi nimirum non scripturam recte intellexerunt, cujus mamillam quia durius pressere, sanguinem pro lacte biberunt. Nam illud apostolicum, *Unusquisque suam habeat uxorem,* nullum excipit vere nisi professorem continentiæ, vel eum qui de continuanda in Domino virginitate præfixit. Quod nihilominus tuam, pater venerande, condecet strenuitatem, ut omnem qui tibi manu vel ore votum faciens continentiæ postea voluerit apostatare, aut ad votum exequendum ex debito constringas, aut ab omni ordine canonica auctoritate deponas: et hoc ut viriliter implere sufficias, me omnesque mei ordinis viros adjutores habebis non pigros. Verum ut hujus voti nescios omnino scias non esse cogendos, audi Apostolum dicentem ad Timotheum: *Oportet, inquam, episcopum irreprehensibilem esse, unius uxoris virum.* Quam ne quis sententiam ad solam ecclesiam verteret, subjunxit: *Qui autem domui suæ præesse nescit, quomodo ecclesiæ Dei diligentiam habebit? Similiter,* inquit, *diaconi sint unius uxoris viri, qui filiis suis bene præsint et suis domibus.*

Hanc autem uxorem a sacerdote benedicendam esse, sancti Sylvestri papæ decretis scio te sufficienter docuisse. His et hujusmodi sanctis scripturæ sententiis regulæ clericorum scriptor non immerito concordans, ait: "Clericus sit pudicus, aut certe unius matrimonii vinculo fœderatus." Ex quibus omnibus veraciter colligit, quod episcopus et diaconus reprehensibiles notantur, si in mulieribus multis dividuntur: si vero unam sub obtentu religionis abjiciunt, utrumque, scilicet episcopum et diaconum, sine graduum differentia, hic canonica damnat sententia: "Episcopus aut presbyter uxorem propriam nequaquam sub obtentu religionis abjiciat: si vero rejecerit, excommunicetur; et si perseveraverit, dejiciatur." * * * *

Sunt vero aliqui, qui sanctum Gregorium suæ sectæ sumunt adjutorium: quorum quidem temeritatem rideo, ignorantiam doleo. Ignorant enim quod periculosum hujus hæresis decretum, a S. Gregorio factum, condigno pœnitentiæ fructu postmodum ab eodem sit purgatum: quippe cum die quadam in vivarium suum propter pisces misisset, et allata inde plus quam sex millia infantum capita videret, intima mox ductus pœnitentia ingemuit, et factum a se de abstinentia decretum tantæ cædis causam confessus, condigno illud, ut dixi, pœnitentiæ fructu purgavit; suoque decreto prorsus damnato, apostolicum illud laudavit consilium, *Melius est nubere quam uri:* addens ex sua parte, "Melius est nubere quam mortis occasionem præbere."

The whole of the letter, of which the above (being the original of the bishop's citation in p. 568-70.) forms about one half, is contained in a little volume published at Basil, anno 1555, consisting of various treatises against the papacy, and entitled *Antilogia Papæ: hoc est, De corrupto Ecclesiæ statu, et totius Cleri Papistici perversitate, Scripta aliquot veterum authorum, ante annos plus minus ccc. et interea: nunc primum in lucem eruta, et ab interitu vindicata.* At the end of the letter is subjoined the following note: "Inventa est hæc epistola in quadam bibliotheca oppidi Veteris Aquæ, Germanice *Altuuatter*, in Hollandia, inferioris Germaniæ provincia." Its heading is as follows:

"Epistola Divi Hulderichi, Augustensis episcopi, adversus constitutionem de cleri cælibatu, plane referens apostolicum spiritum: quam cum

Æneas Sylvius, tituli sanctæ Sabinæ presbyter cardinalis, ac Senensis episcopus, in sua Germania, cum Augustæ Vindelicæ mentionem facit, incessat, libuit hic subjicere: judicium esto apud lectorem, veri et publicæ utilitatis amantem. 'Transimus,' inquit, 'Campidonam et Memmingam, illustria oppida: Augustam Vindelicam (sanctus Udalricus huic præsidet, qui papam arguit de concubinis) ad Lycum fluvium jacentem:' qui vixit anno nongentesimo, ætatis suæ LXXXIII."

The passage of Æneas Sylvius is in his *Descriptio de Ritu, Situ, Moribus et Conditione Germaniæ*, and will be found in p. 1053 of his works, Fol. Basil. 1571. where however the concluding words of the above, *qui vixit*, &c. are not found. But Chemnitius, quoted by Bishop Hall, states, that "Æneas Sylvius writes him to have *died* anno 900, and in the year of his age 83." (It cannot be doubted that *vixit* is an error.) See Bishop Hall's *Honour of the Married Clergy*, Book III. Sect. ii. In that and the following section the bishop vindicates the genuineness of the letter against the cavils of his popish adversary, summing up the argument for it in the following particulars: "Whereas their own cardinal, Æneas Sylvius, almost two hundred years ago, mentions it, and reports the argument of it; whereas it is yet extant, as Illyricus, in the libraries of Germany; whereas Hedio found an ancient copy of it in Holland; and our John Bale, Archbishop Parker, Bishop Jewell, John Fox, had a copy of it, remarkable for reverend antiquity, in aged parchment, here in England, which I hope to have the means to produce; whereas, lastly, the very style importeth age."—While thus vindicating the letter itself, the bishop further remarks on one particular in it which has been made a ground of objection: "As for the number of children's heads, I can say no more for it than he can against it. This history shall be more worth to us than his denial. But this I dare say, that I know persons both of credit and honour, that saw betwixt fifty and threescore cast up out of the little mote of an abbey where I now live. Let who list cast up the proportion." Ib. Sect. iii.—Errors in numbers are of such obvious occurrence, that they can seldom seriously affect the credit of an ancient document.

ADDENDUM.

P. 26. Pambo. The circumstance here recorded of him will be found in Socrates, Eccles. Hist. Lib. iv. c. 23. Παμβῶ δὲ ἀγράμματος ὢν προσῆλθέ τινι ἐπὶ τῷ διδαχθῆναι ψαλμόν. ἀκούσας δὲ τὸν πρῶτον στίχον τοῦ λή ψαλμοῦ, τοῦ λέγοντος, Εἶπα, φυλάξω τὰς ὁδούς μου, τοῦ μὴ ἁμαρτάνειν με ἐν γλώσσῃ μου· δευτέρου ἀκοῦσαι μὴ ἀνεχόμενος ἀνεχώρησεν, ἀρκεῖσθαι φήσας τούτῳ τῷ ἑνὶ στίχῳ, ἐὰν δυνηθῶ ἔργῳ αὐτὸν ἐκμαθεῖν. ἐγκαλέσαντος δὲ τοῦ παραδεδωκότος τὸν στίχον, διατί ἐξαμηνιαίου παραδραμόντος τοῦ χρόνου μὴ ἑωράκει αὐτὸν, ἀπεκρίνατο ὅτι τοῦ ψαλμοῦ τὸν στίχον οὔπω τῷ ἔργῳ ἐξέμαθον. μετὰ ταῦτα δὲ πολλοὺς ἐπιβιοὺς χρόνους, πρός τινα τῶν γνωρίμων ἐρωτήσαντα εἰ τὸν στίχον ἐξέμαθεν, Ἐν ὅλοις, ἔφη, ἐννεακαίδεκα ἔτεσι μόλις αὐτὸν πράττειν ἐξέμαθον.

ERRATUM.

In p. 486, the figures in the margin are misplaced. The XIII. should be where the XIV. now stands, opposite " all liberty used," and the XIV. should be removed five lines lower. These figures and the accompanying marks of quotation are to indicate the corresponding sections of the bishop's Confutation.

INDEX.

A.

ABBEYS, hospitality of, 610; gluttony, &c., ib.
Abdia, meaning of, 216; some think him the same as Ahab's steward, 217.
Abel, a chosen vessel, 168.
Abimelech, 451.
Abraham's faith, 352.
Absalom, 289, 309.
Absolution, general and particular, 131.
Acta Conciliorum, 19, 22, 629.
Actius Sincerus, 336.
Adam, meaning of, 94, 95, 219; supposed to be buried in Jerusalem, 373; his fall, 447.
Adelme, bishop, 590.
Adonibezec, 257.
Adrian, the emperor, built Ælia, 372, 375.
Adrian IV. pope, his arrogance, 22.
—— VI. his offers to Zuingle, 142, 684.
Ælia, the city built by Adrian in place of Jerusalem, 372.
Æneas Sylvius (see Pius II. pope.) 687.
Affections in religion, divers good, 127; of the mind shewn in the face, 292, 312; must be kept under, 313.
Aga, St, (Agatha's) letters, 177, 536, 563.
Agathon, 642.
Agesilaus, 429.
Agrippa, troubled at Paul's preaching, 141.
Ahasuerus, king, husband to Esther, 14; raised up to punish the Jews, 37.
Ahithophel, 242.
Alexander, his visit to Jerusalem, 69, 148; appealed from, 98; his answer to Darius, 187; punishment of Bessus, 188.
Alexander, pope, 601.
Alleluia, not used by papists at funerals, 320; anciently used, 321, 543.

Altar of the Holy Ghost, 483, 539; altars, use and meaning of, 547.
Ambrose, 156, 381, 409, 491, 507, 543, 546, 556, 566.
Ammonites, 409.
Analogy between David and Christ, 371-2; Adam and Christ, 374; the earthly and heavenly Jerusalem, 375.
Anastasius, pope, 601.
Angels, 134; happiness of, 61. Angel, a piece of money, 429.
Anger, when good, 391, 477; a kind of madness, 408; sin of, 478.
Ansegisus, ap. Baluz. Capit. 536.
Anselm's letter to Waleram, 538, 620; forbids priests' marriages, 571, 588; pope Paschal's letter to him, 572; his letter to his archdeacon, 573; accused for acknowledging pope Urban, 589.
Anthems in St Paul's, 483; why in the steeple, 529.
Antilogia Papæ, 686.
Antiochus Epiphanes, 4, 88.
Antiquity to be followed, that of Christ and his apostles, 579.
Antony, the monk, 146.
Apostles, their faith, 352; the true fathers, to whose steps we should return, 615.
Apostolical Canons, 566, 629.
Apparel, costly, 55, 56; love of, reproved, 386–7.
Appose, pose or question, 160.
Arches, court of, 540.
Arius, his death, 29.
Artaxerxes, name of Persian kings, 14, 307.
Ascham's *Toxophilus*, 429.
Astronomers censured, 17, 18.
Athanasius, 440.
Augustine, 130, 144, 158, 208, 269, 286, 320, 471, 474, 475, 542, 557, 575, 612, 617, 620, 632, 641, 661, 674.
Augustine, missionary to England, 482, 483, 515; his reception, 516;

44

[PILKINGTON.]

his letter to Gregory, 517; his christening, 518; England declined from his steps, 522; established mass and seven sacraments, 618.
Aurelius, Marcus, 286.
Authority, how it began, 125.

B.

Babel, tower of, 30, 231.
Babylon, greatness of, 231; country of, &c. 281, &c.
Babylonian captivity, Romish slavery compared to, 4, 277; Babylonians' cruelty to the Edomites, 235, &c.
Badge, pricked on the sleeve, 356.
Bale, ii.
Baptism, of faithful ministers to be preferred to that of papists, 171; sin after, 448; our vows in, 621.
Baronius, 76.
Basil, fell by an earthquake, 607.
Bayard, a horse, 610.
Beasts, their disobedience reminds us of our sin, 91.
Becket, Thomas, canonized, 19; his service, 535, 536, 557; accused before the pope, 589; quarrel with Henry II., 640.
Bede, 447, 512.
"Behold," its use, 72, 225, 459.
Benedict IX. pope, 602.
Bene't, St, 80, 550.
Bernard, 158, 445.
Billingsgate, 345.
Bishop's office laborious, 36, 494, 604; blessings, 64; popish, 82, 197, 603; church committed to government of, 482, 488; succession of, 485; their authority, what, 488; spiritual, in doctrine and discipline, 491; how to be executed, 492; their temporal authority derived from the prince, ib.; grounds of their superiority, 493; Universal, a cursed name, 519; popish, their oath to the pope, 555; protestant, impoverished by their predecessors, 592, 594–5; by tradition of the apostles, 605.
Bishoping, confirmation, 553.
Blasphemy, law of, 361.
Body and blood of Christ, how received in the Lord's supper, 552.

Bohemians, came to England to hear Wickliffe, 654.
Boniface, made pope by Phocas, 76, 521.
——— VIII. pope, 18.
Bonner, called a butcher, 361, 400, 587, 623.
Boulogne won, 70, 86.
Bow, great importance of, in war, 428.
Brast, brust, burst, 264.
Brent, brinning, burnt, burning, 481.
Brether, brethern, brethren, 233.
Brother, how used in scripture, 187, 288.
Bucer, dug up from his grave, 65; his disinterment and restitution, 651; his learning, ib.; his doctrine, 655.
Builders of God's house must seek his glory, 363; must not fear mockers, 365; blessedness of being one, 366; will have no fellowship with hypocrites, 367.
Burials, out of the church or church yard, 64; place of, 316; three rules for burials, 317–8; comely order in, 318; in the English service, 543.
Burning of St Paul's cathedral, circumstances of, 481; a warning, 483, 648; whether by lightning or by accident, ib.
Buskle, prepare, 353.

C.

Cæsar, Julius, 286, 451.
Calais lost, 70, 86.
Calendar, of the Roman church, 15, 19.
Canaanites, what, 268.
Canterbury burnt, 607.
Canute, 51.
Capitolina, built by Adrian, 372.
Captain, benefit of a stout one, 377; especially Christ, 383; good, duties of, 449.
Captivity in Babylon, length of, 127.
Carthage, third council of, 566.
Casleu, Jewish month, 287.
Catholic church, agrees in the substance of doctrine, differs in ceremonies, 552; what? 617; papists divided from, 618; never had one order of service, 629.

Cedron, brook, 345.
Celibacy of clergy, 527; difficulty of enforcing it, 567.
Ceremonies, of the old law, 129; popish, 130.
Chabrias, a saying of his, 377.
Chance, things do not turn out by, but by providence, 308.
Charlemagne's decree for reading scripture in churches, 536.
Charles V., opposer of the gospel, 265, 653.
Charms, popish, 177, 536, 563.
Children, said to have that which their fathers had, 135.
Choreb, chereb, explained, 87.
Christ, his zeal for God's house, 5; the only schoolmaster, 81; salvation only by, 81; before his incarnation present with the fathers, 134; promise of, 138; connected with trouble, 139; trouble at his birth, 140, 335; the desire of all people, 147-8; glory of in his church, 148; his kingdom shadowed forth by temporal conquests, 261; the Holy One, 262; in Sion, 264; difference of his kingdom from an earthly one, 269; all night in prayer, 340; his voluntary humiliation, 341; zeal for the house of God, 344; signified by different gates of Jerusalem, 378-9; his body and blood, how received in the Lord's supper, 552; his one sacrifice for sin, 621.
Christians serving heathen, lawfulness of, 311; accused of troubling the state, 359.
Chrysostom, 23, 45, 58, 542, 576, 596, 609, 636, 682.
Church, use of, 64; to be built for God's glory, 539.
Church goods, not to be taken away, 61.
Cicero, 317, 408, 439, 679.
Clemens, held wives should be common, 600.
Clemens Romanus, 629.
Comfort, most to greatest offenders, 131.
Communion service of the English Church not contrary to our vows in baptism, 634, 639.
Communion table instead of altars, 545.

Confession, 553; on what grounded, 554.
Conjuring among the Jews, 385.
Consecration of the elements by the apostles, 498, 508, 635.
Constantine the Great, 8, 413, 641.
Constantius, the emperor, 637.
Contentment with God's will, 153.
Corah, &c., their punishment, 28, 624.
Corporas, 46.
Councils, popery not proved by general, 531; Gregory's (of Nazianzum) opinion of, 532; but few general, 533; our religion older than, 549.
Courtiers, Nehemiah an example to, 288; their character, 289, 309; examples of good, 294.
Cranmer, his reformation, 37; his disputation at Oxford, 400; book on the sacrament, 523, 547.
Crantz, or Krantz, Albert, 247.
Creatures, the, obey God, 59, 90; refuse to serve man through man's sin, 91; not to be considered in themselves, 230.
Cross, must be borne strongly, though it seem long, 127; the livery of Christ, 191; cross-week, 556.
Cruche, crook, 584, 586.
Cyprian, 144, 245, 537, 542, 597, 605, 617, 619, 624, 628, 629, 630, 631, 632, 633, 634, 680.
Cyrus, raised up to deliver God's people, 4, 11, 12; restores the vessels of the temple, 8.

D.

Dalida, Delilah, 169.
Daniel, his diet in Babylon, 52; his visions, 186.
Darius, how far removed from Cyrus, 13; son of Esther, 14; same with Artaxerxes, ib.; his embassy to Alexander, 187.
David, his zeal for God, 7; for the ark, 340; collects for building the temple, 8; reproved by Nathan, 12, 112, 161; kills Goliath, 30, 120, 360, 415; analogy between him and Christ, 371-2; tomb of, 389.
Days of the week, how named, 16; cer-

tain days improperly called unfortunate, 17, 18.
Dearths in England, 289; in the time of popery, 611.
Demaratus, 424.
Δεσμὸς, excommunication, 381.
Devil, the, works with God and man in one deed, 178; incarnate, worse than in his own nature, 363; constantly hindering the building of God's house, 454–5; tries to deface the gospel, 467.
Diogenes, 314, 317.
Dionysius Areopagus, 585.
Discipline, want of deplored, 5, 6, 211, 382; must be impartial, 67; necessary in a church, 129, 176; controversy about, 379; insufficiency of that proposed, 381.
Disobedience, to God, defiles all our doings, 172; to the church, protestants charged with, 484.
Disputation on religion in Elizabeth's time, 626.
Dodkin, little doit, 607.
Doors, locks, &c. the emblems explained, 382-3.
Duddles, 212.
Dung-gate, its use, 387.
Duns Scotus, 80, 527, 550, 554, 635.
Durandus, 509.
Durham, the church burnt, 607.

E.

Edmond, St, 588.
Edom, Esau, 219; several prophesied against, 222.
Edomites, who, 219; cruelty to Israel, 223, 251, 252; deceived by their prosperity, 232; their utter destruction, 235; beginning of their enmity to Jacob, 248.
Egfrid and Ethelreda, 590.
Egypt, plagues of, 28, 29, 75; no refuge to the Jews, 240.
Elder brother, privileges of, 223; refused by God, 224.
Eleutherius, pope, 482, 510, 512; his letter to Lucius, 512-3; his ordinance about meats, 514.
Eli, his neglect to punish his sons, 35.

Elijah, 54, 358, 599, 612; his zeal for God, 7, 98.
Elizabeth, queen, compared to Esther, 4; the gospel restored by her, 13; her injunctions, 575; prosperity in her reign, 613.
Enemies, how to pray in regard to, 404-5; kindness to, 433; outward and inward, 449.
England, conduct of in time of persecution reproved, 24; long neglect of building God's house, 25, 37; plagued for neglecting, 58; oppressed by Romans, Saxons, &c., 73; called to repentance, 82; warned, 89, 188; English apparel, 56; Englishmen, nothing to boast of in their origin, 125; planting of christianity in England, 481; received not the faith from Rome, 510; conquered by Danes and Normans, 521.
English Service, its antiquity, 530; based entirely on scripture, 531; agrees with the ancient church, 533; common prayer, 541, 562; baptism, ib.; communion, 541-2; burials, 543; marriage, 544; confession, 553.
Engrossing, 460.
Enk, ink, 211.
Envy, its nature illustrated, 335–6; of the wicked against the good, 398.
Esther, 310, 660.
Eunuch of queen Candace, 149.
Eusebius, Eccles. Hist. 333, 365, 413, 565, 682, 683.
Eustathius despised married priests, 565.
Evil company to be avoided, 169; minister, does not hinder the sacrament or word, 170, 636; evil-gotten goods never thrive, 57, 58; evil to be imputed to man only, 613.
Example, want of good, 451.
Excommunication, 381, 388.
Excuses of negligence vain, 32, 41, 43, 172.
Exemptions, claim to, reproved, 390.
Exhumation of the dead, 217.
Ezra, would not ask for a guard, 327; Pilkington's exposition on, 308, 367.

F.

Faber, Joan., 503.

INDEX.   693

Fabian, 512, 516, 518, 583, 597.
Fagius, associated with Bucer, 651, 655-6, 657.
Faith, how gotten and increased, 112; the same in different effects, 132; sight by faith surer than the eye, 215; necessary in prayer, 295.
Faithful, the, cannot want, 154.
Fasciculus Temporum, 80, 545, 598.
Fasts, different among papists, 80; fasting regulated by particular churches, 556; none between Easter and Whitsunday, ib.; laws for, first made by Montanus, 558; two sorts of, voluntary and by commandment, ib.; several things to be considered in, 559.
Fathers, different children from the same, 219; of the church, their authority, 484; called to return to their steps, 486; followed by the English church, 541.
Faude, mayor of Cambridge, 656.
Fear goes before love, 104; two sorts of, ib.
Fearfulness condemned, 378, 432.
Felix, 184.
―――― pope, 601.
Feries, 17.
Fire, used for the influence of the Holy Ghost, 266; wind, &c., God's instruments, 608.
Florence, council of, 145-6.
Fonts, baptism without, 518.
Food, moderation in, 52; miracle by which it nourishes, 53.
Forgiveness, hope of, as long as God speaks to us, 25.
Formosus, pope, disinterred, 652.
Foxe, John, 505, 523, 640.
France, bloody marriages in, 420.
Fratricelli, 18.
Frederick, king, story of his physicians, 336.
Frederick Barbarossa, letter to Pope Adrian, 22.
Freres, friars, 205; and monks, their privileges, 380.
Friar Mantuan, 586.
Friday, named from Fria, 16; golden, 80.

G.

Galfridus Britannicus, 515.

Gangrense, council, 570.
Gardiner, bishop, his threat, 197, 254; his works on the sacrament, 547; his changing, 587, 622; his book *De vera obedientia*, 621; his death, 655.
Gates of cities, how named, 345; ministers compared to, 348.
Gelasius, pope, 541, 546.
Genesius, a jester, 401.
Gentleness better than sharpness, 183.
Gerson, 532, 626.
Gibeonites, 246; burying Saul, 318; commended, 392.
Gideon, 29, 47, 109.
Gildas, 510, 517, 584, 618, 619.
Giraldus, bishop of York, 591.
Gluttony, 52; of abbeys, 610.
God, his house, building of, 3; to be built before our own, 39; building of hindered by sin, 40; God delights in, 68; his long suffering, 11, 119, 179; God to be obeyed rather than man, 24, 41; his blessing prospers labour, 50; makes food serviceable, 53; his delight in his people, 71; giver of all good things, 85; his providence, 93; his presence with his people, 108; not a partial God, 133; effect of his blessing, ib.; wise in disposing of his goods, 153; his doings to be marked, 173, 175; punishes by his creatures, 177, 220; as a token of love, 181; his punishments at first gentle, 178; for our good, 179; turns to us when we turn to him, 182; his love to his people, 189; saves them in all dangers, 191, 196; his will the first cause of good, 195; tries his people, 207; punishes us by the offending parts, 226; to be looked to in all things, good or evil, 227; his deed, that which his servants do, 234; slow in punishing, but sure, 248, 258; his righteous retribution, 257; jealous for his religion, 258; his relations to his people, 259; majesty, 296-7; specially the God of his people, 331, 351; righteousness of his judgments, 346; his goodness not to be mistrusted, 353; watchfulness over his people, 422; an almighty helper, 431.
"God, little" of the papists, 129, 156.
Godly, patience of, 248; punished for a time, 250.

Godly-wise, 245.
Goliath, 30, 120, 246, 360, 416.
Good, the, persecuted by the wicked, 204; and evil mixed in the church, 388; dwell among the wicked, why, 424; forgive injuries, ib.; judge others to be like themselves, 425.
Good returned for evil, nature of God and his people, 261.
Gospel, enemies of, 44; follows the law, 96, 108; its use, 97, 107; gives life, 111; its general reception, 145; preaching of makes a church pleasant to God, 156; spread by persecution, 264.
Grace, necessary for worthily considering God's plagues, 174; freeness of, 194.
Gratian, Decretal. 496, 501, 543, 566.
Grave called *coimeterion*, *Beth-haiaim*, 319.
Greediness, insatiable, 51.
Greek names, Aggeus, &c. 11; histories, whether agreeing with the scriptures, 13; church, not agreeing with Rome, 145, 205, 500; and Latin churches, difference between, 548.
Gregory Nazianzene, 312, 532, 543, 565.
Gregory, the first pope, 76, 344, 441, 482, 498, 503, 508, 515, 517, 518, 519, 520, 635, 675; his letter to Austin, 517, 524; his opposition to John of Constantinople, 519; his mass-book, 508, 524; ordained fasting of all Lent, 561.
————— III. pope, 602.
————— VII. (Hildebrand) 521, 564, 567, 574.
Groat, price of a *dirige* or mass, 543.
Grosshead, or Groseteste, bishop of Lincoln, 591.

H.

Habits, the, regarded by some as relics of popery, 659.
Haggai, intent of his prophecy, 3; a poor Levite, 19, 99.
Hales, blood of, 551, 602.
Half-service not accepted, 632.
Hall, bishop, 687.
Hallelujah. See Alleluia.

Hallowing, popish, vanity of, 163, 316, 496.
Haman, 242, 290.
Hand, use of the term in Hebrew, 21; good hand of God upon us, 331.
Hannah, her prayer, 322, 564.
Harrow, destroy, 171.
Hatto, bishop of Mentz, his death, 30, 456, 612.
Hearing, benefit of, 291.
Heathen called into the church, 61.
Helen's day, 15.
Henry, king of France, his death, 654.
Heretics, not generally unlearned, 120; learned, refuted by an unlearned man, 267.
Hermanius or Hermannus, a reputed heretic, 18.
Herod, troubled at Christ's birth, 140, 335, 359, 423; Agrippa, his death, 29, 233; troubled at the gospel, 141; his pride, 233.
Herodotus, 424.
Hezekiah commended, 360.
Hickscorners, 357.
Hilary, of Poitiers, married, 570.
Hildebrand, 521; *hell-brand*, 565, 574.
Historia Tripartita, 596, 631, 637.
Holiness only in and from Christ, 164; of temple, &c. what, 165; popish, vain, 262.
Holy flesh, what, 162; how the unfaithful part made holy by the faithful, 164.
Holy Ghost, his influence compared to fire, 266, 342; the schoolmaster of all truth, 329.
Homo, meaning of, 94.
Horace, 584.
Hospitals, founded in the time of the gospel, 610.
Hosts, the Lord's, what, 27, &c., 59, 132, 138.
Hottinger, 142, 684.
House of God, general and particular, 65; spiritual, 66; building of, 3; Christ's zeal in, 5; what it consists in, 7, 62, 73; promoted by David, Cyrus, Darius, Artaxerxes, Constantine, &c., 8; negligence in, 11, 13, 90; vain excuses for, 32, 42; all required to build it, 66, 94, 378; men build their own rather, 83; all that build it not sleep in sin, 116; builders of, need

not fear want, 150, 154-5; blessed of God, 184.
Houses, of princes, &c. according to their degree, 42; of priests, 391.
Huldrich, his letter to pope Nicholas, 568-70, 685-7.
Humility, examples of, 47.
Hunger, force of, 456, 458.

I.

Idleness, the evil effects of, 437; of labouring men, 446; of servants, 447.
Ignorance, none excused by, 146; comparative, of popish and protestant times, 611.
Images, 540.
Improve, disprove, 629.
Innocent III. pope, 602.
Interim, the, 574, 657.
I. P. L. C. D. These initials explained, 10, 273.
Isaiah, his death, 361.
Isch, 94, 187, 245.
Ishmael, an archer, 428.
Isidore, 503.

J.

Jabesh Gilead, neutrality of, 344.
Jacob, banished by Esau, 256.
James, St, bishop of Jerusalem, 482; his mass, 497; in Greek, 499; never used the popish mass, 498.
Jealousy for God's glory, 351.
Jebusites, account of, 371.
Jehovah, 27.
Jehu, his zeal against Baal, 7.
Jephthah, 360.
Jeremiah, his prophecy of the captivity, 12.
Jericho, taking of, 29.
Jerome, 294, 320, 494, 543, 566, 609, 617, 619.
Jerusalem, its temple, 13, 14, 68, 69, 70, 88; hills and walls of, 87-8, 372-3; destroyed by Titus, 88, 89, 346, 372; by Nebuchadnezzar, 89, 346; the holy city, 315, 372; its lamentable state, 345; the new building of, what it teaches, 370, 452; called Salem, Solyma, Jebus, 370-1; won by David from the Jebusites, 371; Adam supposed to be buried in, 373; compass of its walls, 443.
Jewel, bishop, conference or correspondence with Dr Cole, 523.
Jews, their mode of reckoning years and months, 15; government of their commonwealth, 23; their backwardness in building the temple, 37; their present dispersion, 74; their usury, heathen marriages, &c. reproved, 162; their miserable state after their captivity, 291.
Job, his country, 244.
John, archbishop of Constantinople, 76, 518.
——— prester, 205, 499, 500.
——— the pope's legate, sent to enforce divorces of the clergy, 572; his infamous conduct, ib.
John I. pope, 601.
——— VIII. pope, 602.
——— XII. pope, vii.
——— XXIII. pope, 603.
Jonathan, slaughtering the Philistines, 29.
Joseph, his conduct as governor of Egypt, 466; of Arimathea, preached in England, 511.
Josephus, 69, 682.
Joshua destroys the Amorites, 28.
Judah, good kings of, prosperous, 75; tribe of, grow faint-hearted, 415-6.
Judas' chapel, 541.
Judges, of Israel, 23. Judges on the hill Esau, 270.
Judgment, human and divine, 97.
Judith, kills Holofernes, 29, 360.
Julian, 312, 440, 596.
Justice better ministered under Edward VI. than Mary, 614.
Justification, by faith or works, 167.
Justinian, *Novell. Constitut.*, 499.

K.

King, the, God's vicar, 512, 514.

L.

Labour, vain without God's blessing, 50.

Labouring men, idleness of, 446.
Lacklatin, Sir John, a nickname for an ignorant popish priest, 20, 160, 271.
Lactantius, 477.
Laity, may interfere in religion, by the example of David and others, 625.
Lanfranc, archbishop of Canterbury, brought in transubstantiation, 573, 588.
Latimer, his preaching, 427, 461.
Laurence, St, martyr, 144, 157.
Law, use of, 104; kills, 111; necessary to be taught, 354; law and gospel, their order and use, 96, 97, 108, 111; different effects, 354; courts of law, 466.
Laws repealed under Mary, 614.
Layman a, alleging Scripture, to be believed against a whole council, 532.
Laymen's books, 146.
Lazarus, 52.
Legenda aurea, 18; Nova Sanctorum, 587, 588, 589, 590, 607, 625.
Lent, flesh eaten in, 484; diversities of fasting in, 560.
Leo, pope, 601.
—— III. pope, 602.
—— X. confounded with Adrian VI., 142.
Liberius, pope, 601.
Liberty, love of, 455.
Linus, first bishop of Rome, 588.
Lither, lazy, 447.
Lollards' tower, 540.
Lord of hosts, 48, 59; a name rarely used in the New Testament, 27; why God calls himself, 132, 138.
Lord's day, 17.
Love, faithful, seeks no delays, 119; true, only among the godly, 240; draws to earnestness in religion, 354; of parents, 456.
Lucian, 312.
Lucius, king of England, 482, 510, 597.
Ludgate, 345.
Lukewarmness reproved, 342.
Luther, his preaching, 265.

M.

Maccabees, 23, 68, 181, 207.
Macedonius, bishop, 637.
Magister Sententiarum, 526.

Magistrates, the walls of a city, 348; their duty to defend religion, 360; to care for the church, 429; to deliver the oppressed, 471-2, 476.
Mahomet, God's plague, 75; his rise, 77.
Malice, blinds men, 407.
Man, different names of, 94; God and the devil, work together in one deed, 178.
Marcellinus, pope, 601.
Marriage, in the English church, 544; accounted a sacrament, yet denied to priests, 553; of priests condemned by papists, allowed in the Greek church, 564.
Martyrs, their blood the seed of the church, 144.
Mary, the Virgin, her humility, 47.
Mass, &c., differences in, 81, 496, 497; at Jerusalem, 482, 495; Latin, full of prayers to saints, 498, 592; by whom made, 501-2; language used in, 499; its antiquity denied, 502; determined by a miracle, 508; its different parts, by whom appointed, 503; the first, said by Christ, 504; origin of the name, 505; price of a mass, 506; the word in Ambrose, 507; Good-Friday mass, 507-8; mass, not catholic, 548; forbidden to married priests, 574.
Masses, popish, we must not communicate at, 171, 633; forenoon, 483, 528.
Matins, midnight, 483, 528; papists' rule about matins, 528.
Means to be used, not trusted in, 194.
Measure, second, what, 391.
Meats, popish differences in, 46.
Melchisedec, 370.
Memories, memorials, 535.
Mentz, Hatto, bishop of, 30, 456, 612.
Mercy, ready to all repentant, 101; former, a pledge of future, 136.
Messages of God, how sent, 222.
Micher, pilferer, 290.
Minds, month-minds, &c., 318.
Ministers, not to thrust themselves into office, 102; must not forsake their flocks, 441.
Ministry, zeal for maintaining and the contrary, 9; unprofitable, in a worldly view, 105, 593; in all, of equal dignity, 493.

INDEX.   697

Miriam (Mary), 361.
Missah, 506.
Moabites, build with the Jews, 384.
Mocking, sin of, 357, 401; Ishmael's, 358.
Momus in Lucian, 312.
Monks brought into the cathedral churches, 574.
Months, names and reckoning of, 15; how reckoned in scripture, 287, 307.
Month-minds, 318.
Mordecai, (Mardocheus), 384, 423, 660.
Moren, or Morwen, Bonner's chaplain, 481.
Moriah, Isaac offered up on, 374.
Moses, making the tabernacle, 8, 78; jealous for God's word, 24; inculcates the teaching of it, 26; and Aaron associated as rulers, 35; forsaking Pharaoh's court, 341, 425.
Mosheim, 19, 513, 684.
Mourning for the dead, to be bridled, 319.
Mumble-matins, a nick-name of popish priests, 26.

N.

Namely, 34, 40.
Names, in scripture not given in vain, 216.
Nauclerus, 509, 567, 652.
Nebridius, a courtier, 294.
Nebuchadnezzar, 8, 12, 29, 75, 238, 361; offended God, though he was his instrument, 221; his pride and punishment, 231, 233.
Nectarius, bishop of Constantinople, 553.
Negligence in building God's house, 11, 13, 90; in captains and preachers deprecated, 438.
Nehemiah, meaning of his name, 285; his example recommended, 286, 443; to courtiers, 440; his prayer paraphrased, 296-305; his promotion in the Persian court, 310, 325; his modest boldness, 314, 327; his love to his country, 315; his prayer for divine guidance, 322; difference between him and Ezra in going to Jerusalem, 327; his zeal in leaving the court, 332; his conduct on arriving at Jerusalem, 337-8; his secrecy, 341, 349; his zeal inspired by God, 342; boldness in withstanding their enemies, 360, 362; seeks comfort in prayer, 403; his laboriousness, 425, 450; a wise captain, 426; his address to the nobles, 430, 443; diligence and trust, 444.
Nero, 254, 314.
Nethinims commended, 391.
Neuters, uterques, omnia, 344.
Nicene council, 532, 546, 549.
Nicephorus, 312, 364, 375, 376, 381, 440.
Nicholas I. pope, 602.
Night, prayer by, 339.
Noah's flood, 28.
Nonest, nonce, purpose, 644.
Noting of time and circumstances an evidence of truth, 11.
Nowls, heads, 292.
Numbers, errors in, 687.

O.

Oil, used in popish hallowing, 163; hallowed for extreme unction, 525; two kinds of, 526; how used in eastern countries, ib.
Olympias, 637, 638.
Opposers of God's truth always overthrown, 206.
Oppression, complaint of, 454, 457, 458; by their own countrymen, 459; various kinds of, 461-2; general practice of, 465; what it is, 469; its unlawfulness, ib.; restitution required of oppressors, 470-1; they shall be punished, 473; have no religion in them, 474.
Or, ere, 86.
Ordering of ministers, the English service censured by papists, 484, 578; the scripture method, 580; our order agrees to this, the popish differs, 581; the ancient method, 584-5.
Oswi, king, called a synod, 625.
Ox, an emblem of a good builder, 380.

P.

Pall, brought from Rome, 582; several sees a long time without it, 583;

Edward I. forbid bishops to go to Rome for it, ib.; Rome enriched by it, 584.
Palladius, 26.
Pambo, a monk, 26, 688.
Panormitanus, 532, 626.
Paphnutius vindicates the marriage of the clergy, 532, 576.
Papists, their zeal and success, 6; their priests sell heaven, &c., 20; withhold God's word from the people, 25, 120; differences among, 80, 81, 549; change with the world, 100, 197, 550; despise preaching, 112; their dissimulation, 117; their worship, 129; fear the gospel, 142; in effect deny Christ to be God, ib.; their baptism not so evil as their mass, 171; their arrogant pretensions, 208; compared to Edomites, 211, 238, 255, 256; more cruel than they, 218, 253; their exhumation of the dead, 217; make the pope their god, 233, 420; their breed, 335; hard to be converted, 448; their marriage service, 500; their bloody practices, 516; are schismatics, 541, 544; suffered much less from the protestants, than the latter from them, 622; differ little from Jews, 630; their cruelty against the dead, 217, 652.
Parse, pierce, 273.
Paschal, pope, his letter to Anselm, 572.
Pastors, their office, 490.
Patience of the godly, 248; under scoffing, 402.
Patrons of benefices, their duties, 36.
Paul, St, exercises discipline, 7; jealous for God's word, 24; at Philippi, 145, 263; how he uses means, 328; delivered from the Jews, 423; wished himself " accursed from Christ," 424; his rule for eating the Lord's supper, 529.
Paul's, St, church, burning of, 481; abuses of, 483, 539, 540; several times burnt, 485, 606.
Paul II. pope, 99, 602.
Paulinus, of Nola, 441.
Pax, 495.
Peace, promised in Christ, 157; worldly, grievous, 158.
Pecocke, Ranold, condemned in Henry the sixth's days, 591.

Perne, vice-chancellor of Cambridge, 657.
Pernel, 56.
Persecutions, papal, 142, 205; remonstrance against, 212; effect of, 143; Christians supported in, 158, 197; place of worship provided in, 263; spreads the gospel, 264.
Persians, destruction of their kingdom, 185; their manner of deliberating, 325; their archery, 428.
Persius, 156.
Persuasions, of two kinds, 349-50; more effectual than threatenings, 354.
Peter, the apostle, the pope unlike him, 271; except in his faults, 604; cutting off Malchus' ear, 433.
Phagius, see Fagius.
Pharisees, troubled at Christ's preaching, 140.
Phileas, bishop of Chinna, 565.
Phinehas, zealous for God, 7, 343, 477.
Phocas, 76, 521.
Pighius, 570; (comp. 255.)
Pilate, troubled about Christ, 141; and Herod agree against Christ, 410, 551.
Pilkington, Bp., his birth, i; his college, ib. *note*; expositions at Basil, ii; whether printed, ib. *note*; signs the " peaceable letter" at Frankfort, iii; a commissioner for revising the Prayer Book, ib.; Master of St John's College and Divinity professor, ib.; his exposition of Haggai and Obadiah, iv; bishop of Durham, v; his Sermon at Paul's cross, ib.; Confutation of an Addition, &c. vi; his letter to archbishop Parker, vii; to the Earl of Leicester and the *Epistola Consolatoria*, viii; to Sir William Cecil, ix; another on the conclusions in the university of Louvain, x; foundation of Rivington School, xi; death and will, ib.; epitaphs on, xii, xiii; Commentary on Nehemiah, xiii; character, ib.; list of his works, xiv—xvi; Lancastriensis, Cantabrigiensis, Dunelmensis, 10; writes for the unlearned, 307, 376, 643; his exposition on Ezra xvi., 308, 367; commemoration of, at Rivington school, 671.

Pilkington, Leonard, John, and Laurence, v.
Pius, pope, 601.
—— II. pope, 500; in favour of priests' marriages, 566.
Pix, the box for the consecrated wafer, 129.
Places, supposed holiness of, 63, 64.
Placilla, wife of Theodosius, 386.
Plagues, God's, the cause of, 73; cause of to be searched, 50, 189; not to be resisted, 72, 77; difference of, under popery and the gospel, 85; of one a warning to others, 175; if despised, bring greater, 176; come from God, but man sins as the instrument, 220; greater in popery than in the gospel, 606.
Platina, 99, 503, 514, 566, 601-3.
Plautus, 215.
Pliny, 231, 333, 428.
Pluralities, 255.
Plutarch, 377.
Ποιμαίνειν, 489.
Pole, Cardinal, his commissioners, 65; his book *De Unitate Ecclesiæ*, 497.
Policy joined with prayer, 413, 415.
Polycarp, his martyrdom, 364.
Polychronicon, 509, 512, 514, 516, 517, 527, 535, 561, 572, 575, 583, 585, 588, 590, &c., 597, 598, 607, 610, 611.
Polycrates, bishop of Ephesus, 565.
Polydore Vergil, 565.
Ponet, bishop of Winchester, answer to Martin, 549.
Poor, as well as rich, builders in God's house, 33, 46; wants of their children, 455-6.
Pope's testament does not teach Christ, 20; pope, his seat shaken, 30, 421; when he began to flourish, 75; his power declining, 77; thinks his laws better than Christ's, 80; pride of, 99, 206; liable to err, 115; his church and Christ's, diversity of, 129; popes poison one another, 247; pope most unlike St Peter, 271; compared to Tobias, 410; several popes at once, 545, 618; pope's creatures all superstitious, 563; a woman, pope, 602; popes corrected or deposed by emperors, 640.
Popery, 6, 9; opposed to the grace of the gospel, 20; dregs of, 121; plagues in, greater than under the gospel, 606.
Popish questions, see Questions.
Popish rubbish left in the church, complaint of, 417-8.
Porters of the church, 383.
Portus, 17, 630; its antiquity, 534-5; of Sarum, 535.
Prayer, common places of, 63; fervency of, and the contrary, 292; outward forms and inward dispositions of, 295; in all places, 323; a sovereign salve for all sores, 405, 411; feeling of helplessness necessary for, 411; must be joined with means, 412; of Constantine's soldiers, 413; two sorts of, 564.
Preachers, the Lord's servants, 21; how called and sent, 22, 38; what to preach, 59, 218; not to be disdained for their simplicity, 99, 100; their office worshipful, 106; their high titles, 106, 107; sent to the builders of God's house, 184; gentle kind of, win most to God, 354.
Preaching, not to be despised, 12, 114; necessary, 112; its effect, to make us new men, 117; moves more than plagues, 183; conquers more than fighting, 265.
Preter tense used of things future, 226, 241.
Pride, the beginning of sin, 227; arises of good things, 228; of beauty, strength, &c., 229, 230; God throws down the proud, 233.
Priests, unable, their unprofitableness, 36; popish, wickedness of their trentals, &c., 126, 161; should be learned in scripture, 160; admonished by Nehemiah, 378; extent of their houses, 391; should go with the army to war, 414.
Princes, stand not by their own power, 188; not to be trusted in, 231; suits to, commended by prayer to God, 308; to be prayed for, 434; are to maintain true religion, 640, 642.
Princocks, 523.
Promises, effect of God's, 109; satisfy the conscience in all doubts, 186; Christ's, to be with his church, 110; given to rulers pertain to their successors, 185; those to fathers belong to

their children, 190; pleaded in prayer, 301; certainty of, 445.
Prophets, why called *seers*, and prophecies *visions*, 214; speak of the future as past, 226, 241.
Prosperity, not always to the wicked, 224.
Protestants, faint-hearted, 416-7; their religion older than councils, 549.
Purgatory, deliverance from for money, 21, 77; fear of, at death, 321.

Q.

Questions, popish, answered: which is the catholic church? 617; who is a heretic? 619; who is a schismatic? 620; whether protestant priests be in schism, 621; whether ministering the communion according to the book of common prayer be schism, 623; whether reading chapters and psalms, &c. instead of "divine service" be schism, 628; whether priests that say the communion may also celebrate mass, 630; whether priests who say no communion, but only read psalms and chapters, may celebrate mass, 631; whether it be a wicked time, in which such heresy and schism reign, 632; whether the laity may receive the protestant communion, 634; whether through fear they may receive it dissemblingly, 636; what they must do, who cannot have the mass, 637; whether all are bound to obey the queen and her laws, 639.

R.

"Rat's tower," 30, 457, 612.
Reformation, its slow progress complained of, 37; was not received without consent of the clergy, 627.
Reformers, their weapons, 265.
Register of the builders' names, 393.
Regrating, 464.
Religion, makes nearest friends extreme foes, 223; where it differs, no true love, 224; the true, restoration of, 3; false, how maintained, 78; brings evils, 73; withholds blessings, 85; whether we should fight for religion, 433; princes not to change it at their pleasure, 434; worldlings judge it by their belly, 612; no man has authority to make a religion, 627.
Remembrance of sin good, 181.
Repeating of instruction profitable, 84.
Rich, not allowed to misuse their goods, &c. 41.
Richard I., story of, 591.
——— II., epistle to pope Boniface, 640.
Riches, all belong to the Lord, 150; not to be wrongfully gotten nor wastefully used, 150-1; contentment with regard to, 152.
Ridley, Dr, his visitation of Cambridge, 522; on the sacrament, 547.
Rivington school, foundation of, xi; statutes of, 663.
Rochets, origin of, 661.
Ronian's, St, (or Tronian's) fast, 80, 551.
Rooty, coarse, 490.
Rout, stir, 356.
Ruffinus, 267, 333, 409, 414, 565.
Rulers, blamed if the people offend through their negligence, 34; temporal above spiritual, 22, 116, 124; have chief power 'in all commonwealths, 23; their ordinances in the church not articles of faith, 25.

S.

Sacraments, few in number, 130; God's seals, 192; seven, asserted by papists, 484, 522, 524, 553; ministration of, according to the book of common prayer, not schismatic, 623, &c.
Sacrifices, a figure of Christ's, 546; offered on altars, 547; sacrificing for sin now, condemned, 621.
Sad, solid, 418.
Saints, the right way of remembering them, 18; not to be looked to for protection, 92.
Sallustius, a Roman prefect, 333.
Salvation, one doctrine of, for all, 124; means of, given to all alike, ib.
Samaria, siege and famine, 28.
Sanballat, his name and country, 334; his violent rage, 397.

INDEX. 701

Satan's practices to hinder the building of God's house, 356, 418; his malice exhibited in Nehemiah's enemies, 419; in the papists, 420.
Saul, case of, 25.
Saviours promised, 269, 271.
Scamblings, 558.
Schisms, twenty three among papists, 545.
Schismatic, who? 620; papists are, 541, 544; differing in substance, not in ceremonies, makes one, 620.
Schoolmaster, a wise, 355.
Sclavons, their ministering the Lord's supper, 500.
Scots defeated, 86, 251.
Scriptures, necessary for all, 120, 608; God's indenture, 192; his letter, 286; nothing superstitious or unprofitable in, 370; antiquity of, 428, 531.
Seals, the sacraments and the Holy Ghost, 193.
Sely, simple, 209.
Sennacherib, overthrown, 28.
Sepharad, what, 268.
Sergius, pope, 602, 652.
Sermon on the burning of St Paul's, whether printed, 481; abstract of, 647.
Servant of God, a glorious name, 364.
Shadrach, &c. 384.
Shalmaneser, places strangers in Judea, 12.
Similitudes, a good kind of teaching, 161.
Sin, sleep in, 6, 12; insensibility produced by, 49; hinders every thing from doing good, 54; must be rebuked in all, 98; the sleep and death of the soul, 111; defiles even what God commands, 162; defiles every thing in the sinner, 165, 166; condemns, 169; sins of the mind, 231; sin crucified Christ, 347.
Sion, mount, holiness in, 261, 264; what, 262.
Six Articles, the bill of, 531.
Sixtus, see Xistus.
Slander, a kind of persecution, 210; worse than the fire, 361.
Socrates, 317.
Socrates, Eccles. Hist. 29, 146, 553, 560, 688.
Sodom and Gomorrah, their punishment, 28.

Soldiers, admonition to, 414; of one kindred should be joined together, 426.
Sozomen, Eccles. Hist. 532, 546, 553, 561, 565, 576, 637.
Spaniards, brought into England to maintain popery, 242.
Spiridion, a bishop of Cyprus, 561, 576.
Spirit, Holy, promise of, 136; efficiency of, 137.
Spiritual persons, their neglects reproved, 35; their lands, 592.
Stairs, the emblem explained, 389.
Stephen, pope, 602, 652.
Strabo, 281-3, 288, 325.
Strype:
  Annals, ii—vi, xiv, xvi, 481, 541, 623, 626, 627.
  Memorials, 254, 495.
  Life of Grindal, 481.
  Life of Parker, viii, 648, 658.
Subsidy granted by the clergy to queen Mary, 495.
Succession of bishops, 485, 597, 598; in succession, the good follow the bad, and the contrary, 599; that of doctrine, the true, 600; the claim of the papists, of a line of bishops from the apostles, denied, ib.; no succession of doctrine in the Roman church, 601; instanced in particulars, 601-3.
Suffering, victory by, 197.
Superstition, to be too holy, 562; two kinds of, 563.
Surtees, history of Durham, 481.
Swash-buckler, 151.
Sylvester II. pope, 602.

T.

Tax, paid by the Jews to the king of Persia, 457.
Temple, 46 years in building, how calculated, 13; under what kings built, 14; God's delight in it, 68; how honoured, 69, 70; defiled by Antiochus, 88; the first and second, 126, 128; comparative glory of, 155; desolation and restoration of, an emblem of the state of the christian church, 278.
Terence, 349, 400, 495.
Terentius, a Roman captain, 324, 660.

Tertullian, 144, 485, 510, 597, 604, 683.
Thacker, thatcher, 381.
Thecoites, 381.
Thecua, or Tekoah, widow of, 161, 309.
Theman, 244.
Theodoret, 165, 324, 386, 409, 546.
Theodorus, a confessor, 333.
Theodosius, favours the church, 8; excommunicated by Ambrose, 381, 491, 546; his law about punishment, 408; his prayer, 413.
Therfe, unleavened, 54.
Thomas Aquinas, 80, 550, 562.
Thraso, 400, 431.
Threatenings move the evil, 71; repeated, 84; God's, conditional, 89; benefit of, 96.
"Thunder, sons of," 265.
Tiberius, troubled at the preaching of Christ, wished him to be worshipped as a God, 141, 683-4.
Tobias, 57, 58.
Tooley, John, burned for a heretic after death, 217.
Tracy, William, dug up from his grave, 653.
Trajan, 333.
Traitors, punishment of, 188.
Transubstantiation and constrained celibacy must go together, 573.
Trees, simile of, 67, 68.
Trentals, 20.
Tronion's, St (Ronian) fast, 80, 551.
Troubles to be expected in building God's house, 396-7, 399.
Trumpet, its use and importance, 442.
Trust, not to be placed in physic, horses, &c. 230.
Truth, must be truly uttered, 487.

U.

Unction, extreme, no sacrament, 524, &c.
Universities, state of learning in, 593.
Unthankfulness, grievous to be charged with, 30, 31; great wickedness of, 460.
Unto, until, 205.

Urban, pope, set on foot the crusades, 372.
Ustazadis, 637, 638.
Usury reproved, 39, 162, 464.
Uterques, 344.

V.

Valentinianus, refused to be sprinkled with holy water, 165.
Vengeance, belongs to God, 249; the day of, not far off, 258; sins cry for, 465.
Vitæ patrum, 184, 642.
Volaterran, 401, 527.

W.

Waldenses, 264, 653.
Walter, bishop of Durham, 591.
—— bishop of Hertford, how killed, 590.
Water, conjured, 63, 64, 518.
Weak, how to be borne with, 45.
Weapons in war, simplicity of, 427.
Wednesday, named from Woden, 16.
Wicked, the, plague one another, 246; cruelty of, 248; punished for ever, 250; soon dismayed, 435-6.
Wickliffe, the persecution that followed after his death, 264; dug up from his grave, 653.
Wilfride, St, 590.
William, St, and his horse, 587.
Wisdom, worldly, is foolishness, 242, 245; in God's matters, 243; better than arms, 439.
Wolfius, Jo., 30, 376.
Women, offered for the tabernacle, 386.
Wood, mad, 160.
Woods, policy of preserving, 330.
Word of God, its effect either salvation or condemnation, 3, 266; only to be taught, 19, 24; profit of hearing, 103.
Work, required of us, the profit of it with God, 133; good for the man's sake, 167.
Worldliness decays the ministry, 105.

Worship, simplicity of protestant, 129.
Worthiness and unworthiness, 47.

X.

Xistus, or Sixtus, martyr, 144.

Y.

Years diversely reckoned, 15, 160.

Z.

Zarphat, what, 268.
Zeal for God's glory commended, 5, 8.
Zion, see Sion.
Zisca, 655.
Zuingle, the pope's offers to him, 142, 684; his preaching, 265.

www.ingramcontent.com/pod-product-compliance
Lightning Source LLC
Chambersburg PA
CBHW052108010526
44111CB00036B/1550